THE WAR IN BOSNIA-HERZEGOVINA
Ethnic Conflict and International Intervention

Steven L. Burg and Paul S. Shoup

"At last we have a book that makes sense of the savage Bosnian conflict. Burg and Shoup's study is thorough, balanced, and convincing. Using sources rarely consulted, they give a full picture of the political, military, diplomatic, and media aspects of the 1992-95 war in Bosnia—why it started; how it was fought; and what ended it. American actions are fully and fairly delineated. The maps, tables, and statistical data are invaluable and well presented. The book can be highly recommended to foreign policy specialists and the common reader alike for its scholarship, policy analysis, and common sense. It is likely to be the definitive study of the war in Bosnia for some time to come."

— Ambassador Herbert S. Okun

"There is no better book on the war in Bosnia-Herzegovina. . . . It is both a highly readable chronicle and a painstaking analysis of the many efforts by foreign powers, West and East, to intervene in the conflict, some for their own purposes, others for the most selfless humanitarian motivations. . . . Burg and Shoup have illustrated their account with 33 specially drawn maps that clearly reveal the course and dimensions of the Bosnian tragedy. In this and in many other ways, theirs is a major accomplishment."

— Richard H. Ullman, Princeton University

"The most lucid, comprehensive and balanced account yet written of the trials of Bosnia and the American role in them."

— Michael Mandelbaum, The Johns Hopkins University

THE WAR IN BOSNIA-HERZEGOVINA

Ethnic
Conflict
and
International
Intervention

Steven L. Burg & Paul S. Shoup

M.E. Sharpe
Armonk, New York
London, England

Library of Congress Cataloging-in-Publication Data

Burg, Steven L., 1950–
The war in Bosnia-Herzegovina : ethnic conflict and
international intervention / by Steven L. Burg and Paul S. Shoup.
p. cm.
Includes bibliographical references and index.
ISBN 1-56324-308-3 (c : alk. paper)
ISBN 1-56324-309-1 (pbk : alk. paper)

1. Yugoslav War, 1991–1995—Peace. 2. Yugoslav War,
1991–1995—Bosnia and Hercegovina. 3. Yugoslav War,
1991–1995—Diplomatic history. 4. Pacific settlement
of international disputes. 5. Bosnia and Hercegovina—
History—1992– 6. Bosnia and Hercegovina—Ethnic
relations. I. Shoup, Paul. II. Title.
DR1313.7.P43B87 1998
949.703—dc21   98-28005
CIP

Printed in the United States of America

BM (c)   10   9   8   7   6   5   4
BM (p)   10   9   8   7   6   5   4   3

To
Marija Shoup and Judith Burg

BOSNIA AND HERZEGOVINA

············· International boundary
─·─·─·─ Republic boundary
─── Provincial boundary
⊛ National capital
○ Town, village
✦ Major airport
╋ Railroad
─── Main road
─── Secondary road

BOSNIA AND
HERZEGOVINA

The boundaries and names shown on this map
do not imply official endorsement or acceptance
by the United Nations.

0 10 20 30 40 50 60 70 80 km
0   10   20   30   40   50 mi

Contents

List of Maps   xi

List of Tables   xiii

List of Abbreviations   xv

Note on Translations, Place-names, and Diacritical Markings   xvii

Chapter 1. Introduction: Bosnia, Ethnic Conflict, and International Intervention   3

Understanding Ethnic Conflict in Bosnia   4

Ethnic Conflict and International Intervention   9

Ethnic Conflict and the Moral Question in Bosnia   11

Sources   14

Chapter 2. Conflict and Accommodation in Bosnian Political History   16

Ethnicity in Bosnia-Herzegovina   18

Bosnia Before World War II   34

World War II and Its Aftermath   37

The National Question in Bosnia in the Titoist Period   40

Competitive Elections and Ethnic Polarization   46

The Choice Between Accommodation and Conflict   56

Chapter 3. The Descent into War   62

The Nationalist Revolution   63

The Dissolution of Yugoslavia . . . and of Bosnia   69

The Role of the International Community 79
The War in Croatia and the Greater Serbia Project 81
International Recognition and the Bosnian Question 92
Serbia, Croatia, and the Bosnian Question 102
Independence 105
The Parliamentary Showdown 105
The Cutileiro Negotiations 108
Referendum and War 117
Could Bosnia Have Been Saved? 120

Chapter 4. The War on the Ground, 1992–94 128

The Onset of Fighting 129
The Shelling of Sarajevo and the Opening of Sarajevo Airport 131
The War Outside Sarajevo 133
The Major Crises, 1993–94 140
Srebrenica, April 1993 140
The Strangulation of Sarajevo, July–August 1993 142
The Markala Marketplace Shelling, February 1994 145
Goražde, March–April 1994 146
Bihać, November–December 1994 154
The UN Mission Under Attack 159
Media, Public Opinion, and Western Policy 162
The Three Massacres 164
Ethnic Cleansing and Genocide 169
War Casualties 169
Ethnic Cleansing 171
Genocide 181
Conclusion 185

**Chapter 5. The International Community and the War:
The Vance-Owen Plan** 189

The Political Context 190
The Bosnian Serbs 191
The Muslims 194
The Bosnian Croats 197
Serbs, Croats, and Muslims: The Triangular Relationship 198
The International Community 198
The International Community Is Drawn In 203
The ICFY 211

The Vance-Owen Plan   214

The Death of the Vance-Owen Plan and the U.S. Proposal for
   "Lift and Strike"   250

Vance-Owen: An Assessment   255

Chapter 6. The International Community and the War:
Negotiating Partition, 1993–94   263

The *Status Quo* Prevails   264

Negotiating Partition   268

   The Owen-Stoltenberg Proposal   271

   The Invincible *Proposal*   280

The EU Action Plan and the Demise of the ICFY   281

Toward Reluctant U.S. Leadership   286

Croat-Muslim Relations and the Establishment of
   the Bosnian Federation   292

Formation of the Contact Group   298

Toward Coercive Diplomacy   307

Conclusion   314

Chapter 7. Imposing the Dayton Agreement   317

The Political Dimension of Western Policy   319

   Revising the Contact Group Plan   321

   The U.S. Decision to Use Force   322

   Coercive Diplomacy   328

The Military Dimension of Western Policy   337

The Military and Political Dimensions Are Integrated   348

The Dayton Agreement   360

   The Map   362

   The Constitution   367

   The Bosnian (Muslim-Croat) Federation After Dayton   373

   The Military   377

Conclusion   381

Chapter 8. Dilemmas of Intervention   388

Was Preventive Action Possible?   389

   Preventive Engagement: A Missed Opportunity?   390

The Difficulties of Early Intervention   393

Crisis Intervention 398
  Humanitarian Intervention 398
  The Use of Force 400
  Diplomacy 404
The Road to Dayton 407
  Cultivating Ripeness 408
  The Ripening of U.S. Policy 410
  Imposing Agreement 412
Beyond Dayton: Cease-Fire, Peace, or Partition? 415

Notes 419
Bibliography of Works Cited 469
Index 483

List of Maps

	Bosnia and Herzegovina	vi
2.1	The 1939 Serb-Croat Partition of Bosnia	22
2.2	Main Regions of Bosnia-Herzegovina	23
2.3	Names of *Opštine* (Counties)	24
2.4	Ethnic Majorities in Bosnia-Herzegovina by *Opština* (County), 1991	28
2.5	Electoral Districts, Chamber of Citizens, 1990	50
3.1	Territories of Bosnia-Herzegovina Claimed by Serb and Croat Nationalists	75
3.2	The Cutileiro Map, March 1992	111
3.3	The SDA Map, March 1992	113
3.4	The HDZ Map, March 1992	114
3.5	The SDS Map, March 1992	115
4.1	Areas of Control, May–June 1993	136
4.2	Areas of Control, September 1993	144
5.1	The Graz Map, May 1992	192
5.2	The Croat Map, December 1992	220
5.3	The Bosnian Government Map, December 1992	221
5.4	The Serb Map, December 1992	222
5.5	The Initial Vance-Owen Map, January 1993	223
5.6	Bosnian Government–Proposed Changes to Vance-Owen Map, January 1993	226
5.7	Revised Vance-Owen Map, February 1993	235
5.8	Second Revised Vance-Owen Map, March 1993	238

5.9   Bosnian Serb–Proposed Revisions (Eastern Bosnia),
      February 1993   239
6.1   Bosnian Presidency Proposal for Partition, June 1993   272
6.2   Serbian-Croatian Proposal for Partition, June 1993   273
6.3   Owen-Stoltenberg Proposal for Partition, August 1993   275
6.4   Map Negotiated Aboard HMS *Invincible,* September 1993   281
6.5   Bosnian Serb Proposal for Partition, January 1994   285
6.6   Bosnian Federation (Without Serb-held Territory)   296
6.7   Bosnian Federation (Proposed Serb Canton)   297
6.8   Contact Group Map, July 1994   304
7.1   Areas of Control, May 1995   332
7.2   Changes in Control, May–October 1995   333
7.3   November 1995 Areas of Control and Dayton Inter-Entity
      Boundary Line   365
7.4   The Bosnian (Muslim-Croat) Federation, May 1996   376

List of Tables

2.1 Population of Bosnia-Herzegovina by Religion and/or Nationality, 1851–1991 (in percent)   27

2.2 Population of the Regions of Bosnia-Herzegovina by Major Ethnic Groups, 1991 (by *opština,* in percent)   30

2.3 Distribution of Votes for Major Parties, Chamber of Citizens, 1990 (in percent of valid votes, first results)   52

2.4 Distribution of Seats by Electoral Region, Chamber of Citizens, 1990   53

2.5 Final Distribution of Seats, Chamber of Citizens and Chamber of Municipalities, 1990   54

2.6 Proportion of Seats in Local Assemblies Secured by Major Parties, 1990   54

2.7 Presidential Vote, 1990 (top three candidates only)   55

5.1 Approximate Ethnic Composition of Provinces, Initial Vance-Owen Proposal, January 1993 (based on 1991 census)   224

5.2 Vance-Owen Formulas for Ethnic Representation in Interim Provincial Governments   229

List of Abbreviations

BSA	Bosnian Serb army (in UN parlance)
CSCE	Conference on Security and Cooperation in Europe
EC	European Community
EPC	European Political Cooperation mechanism
EU	European Union
HDZ	Croatian Democratic Union
HNZ	Croatian National Union
HOS	Croatian defense forces
HVO	Croat Defense Council (Bosnian Croat army)
ICFY	International Conference on the Former Yugoslavia
ICRC	International Committee of the Red Cross
IFOR	Implementation Force
JMO	Yugoslav Muslim Organization
JNA	Yugoslav People's Army
LCY	League of Communists of Yugoslavia
MBO	Muslim Bosniak Organization
MPRI	Military Professional Resources, Inc.
NDH	Independent State of Croatia
RSK	Republic of Serb Krajina
SAM	Surface-to-air missile
SAO	Serb autonomous oblast
SDA	Party of Democratic Action
SDS	Serb Democratic Party
SFOR	Stabilization Force
SRBH	Socialist Republic of Bosnia-Herzegovina

SK-SDP	League of Communists–Social Democratic Party
SRSJ	Alliance of Reform Forces of Yugoslavia
UNPA	United Nations Protected Area
UNPROFOR	United Nations Protection Force
UNHCR	United Nations High Commissioner for Refugees
WEU	Western European Union

Note on Translations, Place-names, and Diacritical Markings

This study makes extensive use of source materials from the former Yugoslavia written in what used to be known commonly as Serbo-Croatian, but now is known as either Serbian, Croatian, or Bosnian. Unless otherwise noted, all translations are the authors' own. When citing these sources in the notes and bibliography, we have retained diacritical markings as they appear in the original. The attentive reader will note that some names, such as that of the *Vreme* journalist Miloš Vasić, appear both with diacriticals (when we cite sources in the original language or when we refer to him in the text itself) and without (when we are citing work published in a source that does not use diacriticals, such as *War Report*). Some place-names, such as Goražde, also appear both with and without diacritical markings, depending on the sources cited. We also follow original sources with respect to such issues as capitalization—even when the original appears to violate standard rules of Serbo-Croatian capitalization. This sometimes results in capitalization patterns that native English-speakers may find jarring. But this is no more of a problem than the variations in capitalization patterns among titles of English-language sources. We violate such rules, however, when it comes to place-names that appear in the narrative. In order to avoid complicating the task of the reader, we have chosen to capitalize all proper place-names; hence, for example, we refer to Gornji Vakuf rather than Gornji vakuf.

We have chosen to transliterate/translate *Hercegovina* as Herzegovina, and *Bosna-Hercegovina* as Bosnia-Herzegovina rather than Bosnia and Herzegovina (unless required to do so by the source involved). Often, we follow the increasingly common practice of referring simply to Bosnia instead of Bosnia-Herzegovina. References to Herzegovina, however, refer only to that particular region, as will always be clear from the context.

We avoid the common mistake of substituting the term "Serbian" for "Serb." The terms "Serb," "Croat," and "Muslim" are in this study used as ethnic, or national, labels. "Serbian," in contrast, refers to the place called Serbia. Hence, "Serbian irregulars" are irregular military formations from Serbia. "Serb irregulars" may be either from Serbia or elsewhere. In order to be as clear as possible, we refer to Bosnian Serbs whenever appropriate. The distinction between Serbs as a whole, Serbia, and the Bosnian Serbs is one that is crucial to the analysis that follows. Serbian leaders are the leaders of Serbia, while Bosnian Serb leaders are the leaders of the Serbs of Bosnia. We maintain a similar distinction between Croats and Croatia, and Bosnian Croats and Croatian leaders. Thus, it will be clear to the reader that when we refer to Croatian military units, or Serbian military units, we are referring to units from Croatia or Serbia, respectively. When we refer to Bosnian Serb military units and Bosnian Croat military units, we are referring to the military formations of the Bosnian Serbs and Bosnian Croats, respectively. Unfortunately, these distinctions are sometimes ignored in other texts, which we cite as originally given.

The terms "Muslim" and "Bosnian" also require elaboration. The distinctions between these two concepts of identity are treated in chapter 2. Here, we wish only to make the reader aware that we use the term Muslim in the ethnic, or national sense, to refer to Bosnian Muslims. When we refer to Bosnians as a group, we are referring to Bosnian Muslims—unless indicated otherwise.

We have followed the above conventions rigorously throughout the study, in an effort to be as precise in our narrative and analysis as possible.

THE WAR IN BOSNIA-HERZEGOVINA

CHAPTER 1

Introduction

Bosnia, Ethnic Conflict, and International Intervention

In this volume, we examine the dynamics of ethnic conflict in Bosnia-Herzegovina, and the dilemmas surrounding international involvement in it. We analyze the causes and conduct of the war; why, for more than three years, international efforts to resolve the conflict in Bosnia failed; and why they finally succeeded in late 1995. We review the Dayton accord produced in 1995 and ask whether, after two years of experience with its implementation, we can expect it to lead to long-term peace in Bosnia. Our analyses are intended to help citizens interested in understanding and learning from the events in Bosnia-Herzegovina; scholars attempting to understand the dynamics of ethnic conflict and develop strategies for managing it; and policymakers intent on preventing ethnic conflicts from undermining international peace.

We focus on the actions of the major participants in the crisis, including actors in the former Yugoslavia and the international community. The first half of the study is devoted to an examination of Bosnia-Herzegovina before the war broke out (chapter 2); the origins of the conflict, including events in Croatia (chapter 3); and the major developments in the war between 1992 and 1994, including the role of the media, ethnic cleansing, and the question of genocide (chapter 4). The second half of the volume is devoted to a detailed description and analysis of the efforts of the international community to resolve the conflict (chapters 5, 6, and 7). The accounts of the war provided in chapter 4 provide essential background for these analyses. Our conclusions concerning the war, Western responses to it, and the lessons to be learned from it are presented in chapter 8.

Each of the authors has long experience in Yugoslavia, and is intimately acquainted with the history of ethnic conflict and controversy over the national question that marked the life of the country and finally led to its demise. We view the conflict in Bosnia in the same light. Having adopted this approach, however, we are sensitive to its dangers. To embrace a narrowly ethnic definition of the conflict in Bosnia-Herzegovina, or in the former Yugoslavia more broadly, is to be tempted to exclude economic, political, and especially moral issues from the analysis. We try not to succumb to this mistake. We attempt to keep the larger issues before the reader when appropriate, even as we explore the details of the conflict in Bosnia.

Understanding Ethnic Conflict in Bosnia

The essence of ethnic conflict is the struggle between mobilized identity groups for greater power—whether it be for equality within an existing state, or the establishment of a fully independent national state. The collapse of communism, and with it the collapse of the remaining multinational states of Europe, was not followed by the victory of liberal democracy and the legitimation of new civil states. Instead, older, historical identities—religion, ethnicity, national identity, and even region—reemerged as bases of political mobilization and claims to statehood, and clashed with the state in almost all those areas where the existing or emerging state did not correspond to the identities of mobilizing groups. This produced a conflict between international norms of state sovereignty and territorial integrity on the one hand, and the power and violence of appeals to ethnicity as a basis of state formation on the other. Much of the story of Bosnia is the story of how the international community attempted, but failed, to reconcile the conflict between these mutually exclusive principles of state formation.

Several factors seem to contribute to the emergence of ethnic conflict. These include a history of intergroup antagonism; a pattern of ethnic domination and/or inequality; the perception of contemporary intergroup competition as a zero-sum game; an electoral triumph or other change that brings nationalist forces to power, and the inadequacy of existing political arrangements for moderating or constraining their behaviors; the existence of competing, exclusivist claims to authority over territory; a pattern of settlement that lends itself only too easily to secession or partition; and the existence of outside sponsorship or support for extremist politics. Differing subsets of these factors may explain the dynamic of differing cases. But there is widespread agreement in the literature on the importance of each of them.[1]

The literature on ethnic conflict distinguishes, sometimes explicitly but most times implicitly, between conflicts occurring in the context of democratic states and those taking place in nondemocratic states. In democratic states the level of violence associated with secessionist/separatist conflicts tends to remain low. The institutionalized protection of civil liberties and respect for human rights characteristic of democracies permits ethnic, linguistic, or other identity groups to translate their demands into electoral power. But, at the same time, it constrains the ability of any ethnically defined government to oppress its ethnic opposition. The means for resolving conflicts peacefully are institutionalized, and enjoy widespread popular legitimacy. Thus, electoral accountability constrains elite behavior.[2]

Even in democratic states, however, conflicts over demands for self-determination and secession arouse passions. In Quebec, the failure of the most recent referendum on independence by a narrow margin led the secessionist party leader to lash out publicly against ethnic minorities in the province.[3] In Switzerland, the 1975 vote on partition in Bern canton was accompanied by rioting and acts of intimidation that left one key town "intensely polarized."[4] Yet, analysts do not attempt to explain these cases (or the many other instances of ethnoregional autonomist or secessionist movements in democratic Europe) in terms of "age-old hatreds" or the nature of the cultures involved. They look instead to issues of power and interest, and to questions of institutions and decisionmaking processes to explain these conflicts and to find their solutions. We believe that to understand and explain the conflict in Bosnia-Herzegovina—despite the catastrophic violence it brought forth—requires a similar approach.

There were at least three major issues being contested in Bosnia as the nationalist leaderships mobilized their communities and the republic descended into war. The most basic contest was over defining the nature of rights in Bosnia; were they to be seen as residing in individuals, or in the ethnic communities as collective entities? Neither the distant Bosnian past, nor the immediate communist-era past, provided any clear answer to this question. The second major contest unleashed in Bosnia by the disintegration of Yugoslavia was over the "national question." This term, as commonly used throughout Eastern Europe, applied to all aspects of interethnic relations. But its most important element concerned defining the right to claim titular, or state-constituting status (usually reserved for the majority ethnic group), and defining the rights that accrued to "others" (minority ethnic groups). To achieve state-constituting status conferred superior cultural and political rights on a group, including control over the state itself. The struggle over rights and the struggle over the national question were thus intertwined, in Bosnia as elsewhere throughout Eastern Europe. But they were of fateful significance for Bosnia: a multiethnic (or multinational) state in which no one group could claim titular status on the basis of numbers alone, and all three major groups thus vied for the status of a state-constituting nation.

Because Bosnia was surrounded by the more powerful national states of two of the groups contesting these issues—the Croats and the Serbs—the contests over rights and the national question inside Bosnia could not be resolved without the participation of Croatia and Serbia. With the disintegration of Yugoslavia and the emergence of nationalist states in Croatia and Serbia, the struggles in Bosnia-Herzegovina took on international dimensions, and raised a third contentious issue: how the international community should respond to the collapse of a multinational state and the onset of conflict among its peoples. Each of these three contested issues was viewed differently by the parties to the conflict. Each raised fundamental issues for the international community as it attempted to mediate the conflict. The contests in Bosnia over individual versus collective rights and over the competing claims of the Muslims, Serbs, and Croats as state-constituting nations were manifest first in a political struggle over the definition of decisionmaking principles and institutions. This quickly escalated to a contest over a constitutional definition of the state itself and, ultimately, to a war over whether that state should exist at all.

The academic approach to these issues is dominated by two competing formulas: the pluralist, or integrationist approach, and the power-sharing approach.[5] The power-sharing approach can be boiled down to a few simple ideas: First, ethnic conflict is understood as originating in contact between groups holding incompatible, culturally rooted values. Hence, the power-sharing approach calls for the isolation of groups from one another at the mass level through entirely separate networks of social and political organizations. Second, in the apparent conviction that culturally distinct groups cannot reach compromise, each of the cultural segments or communities is to be granted a high degree of autonomy over its own affairs. Third, with respect to decisionmaking on issues of common interest to all groups, the power-sharing model calls for proportional systems of representation that ensure the participation of representatives of all such groups in the decisions that affect them. Fourth, each of the groups represented in authoritative decisionmaking processes is to be granted veto power when its "vital interests" are at stake. Because intergroup contact is restricted to elites, decisionmaking on issues of common interest, and the exercise of group vetoes on issues concerning "vital interests," are to be exercised by the leaderships of each group. Indeed, elites exercise a monopoly even over the definition of what constitute common interests, and what constitute the distinct "vital interests" of each group. Hence, the power-sharing approach lends itself to collectivist definitions of rights and group claims to state-constituting status. The obvious vulnerability of such a system to intransigent elite behavior is avoided by goodwill between elite representatives of the ethnic segments—a condition seen as essential for success.

The pluralist approach is based on a radically different understanding of the effects of intergroup contact. Stated most concisely, pluralists argue that, under critically important conditions of open communications and equality, contact between groups generates mutual understanding and cooperation, not conflict. While the advocates of power-sharing view institutions primarily as instruments of ethnic segmentation, pluralists view institutions as a means to *transform* intergroup relations. Contact in shared institutions is not seen as necessarily an agent of cultural assimilation. But sustained contact under conditions of open communications and equality is viewed as contributing to the emergence of a shared culture of interaction and cooperation, or what in the West has come to be called a "civic culture." The pluralist approach is thus premised on a commitment to individual rights.

The pluralist approach calls for avoiding definition of the state or state institutions in ethnic terms. It thus leaves little room to recognize the claims of ethnic groups to state-constituting status. From a pluralist perspective, behaviors based on ethnic identities should be required to compete with behaviors based on nonethnic identities and interests on an equal, rather than a privileged basis. Where the politicization of ethnicity dominates other bases of political behavior, as in Bosnia, the challenge in pursuing a pluralist approach to the resolution of contests over rights and status consists of establishing a balance between the ethnic and the nonethnic in participation, representation, and decisionmaking. But, to pursue a power-sharing strategy under such circumstances institutionalizes ethnic cleavages, excludes other interests, and creates the structural foundations for intransigent use of the veto and, ultimately, secessionism.

In Bosnia, the international community was faced with the challenge of reconciling pluralist and power-sharing arguments, advanced by opposing nationalist leaders. The Bosnian government argued that its refusal to accept autonomy for the Croats and Serbs was based on its adherence to the pluralist principles of individual rights. Serb and Croat nationalists argued that their claims to autonomy, an ethnic veto, and ultimately, the right to form separate states of their own were based on their claim to status as state-constituting nations in Bosnia, and on the collective right of nations to self-determination. In the end, as our account will show, the international community tried to combine these two approaches, but this did nothing to end the controversy between the pluralist and collectivist approaches, which continued to divide analysts and experts involved in finding ways to facilitate implementation of the Dayton accords.

The third major issue in Bosnia, the appropriate international response to the collapse of the multinational Yugoslav state and the conflicting claims of successor states and ethnic groups, was contested by the Bosnian Muslims, Serbs, and Croats; by Croatia and Serbia; and by the outside actors and organizations that were drawn into the conflict. They were deeply divided over this issue. Historically in Eastern Europe, the disintegration of multinational states or empires was followed by the formation of national states. The process began in the early nineteenth century, and was not over until the breakup of Czechoslovakia and Yugoslavia, following the collapse of communism in 1989–90. The Bosnian conflict of 1992–95 raised nineteenth-century and Versailles-era questions about state formation and the definition of borders in the Balkans all over again. Notwithstanding all that had happened in the interim, it is possible to draw parallels between the efforts of the European powers to resolve the Bosnian question at the Congress of Berlin in 1878, and the negotiations over the future of Bosnia carried out at Dayton. In both cases the international community was attempting to maintain the fiction of a preexisting status quo while acknowledging the emergence of new political realities. In both cases Bosnia ended up in limbo; in 1878 the international community maintained the fiction that Bosnia remained within the Ottoman empire while allowing Austria to occupy it; in 1995 the international community preserved a largely fictional Bosnian state while allowing Serbia and Croatia to partition it.

The conflicts that follow disintegration of multinational states are driven by a mixture of ethnic, territorial, and of course, power-political motivations. In the absence of a prior agreement on how to go about dissolving the old state and constituting new ones, these conflicts can escalate rapidly, exacerbated on all sides by extremist elements pursuing maximalist agendas. Realist theorists of international conflict suggest that such conflicts can be averted by ensuring a balance of military capabilities among the successor states,[6] ignoring the fact that the emotions aroused by ethnonational conflict may lead each side to use newly acquired capabilities in pursuit of maximalist agendas, rather than considering them instruments of deterrence.

For much of the literature on ethnic conflict, the path to peace lies through the electoral process. Proportionality systems recommended by the proponents of power-sharing ensure the representation of all groups, but also encourage ethnic bloc voting. Where ethnicity has been politicized, the result of proportionality rules is the conversion of electoral competition into an ethnic census. Donald Horowitz has argued that alternative rules may be devised that foster cooperation between groups in the electoral process, and produce representatives more inclined to intergroup cooperation than confrontation.[7] Such prescriptions, however, imply a fairly strong commitment to democratic elections and to the continued existence of the common state. In Bosnia, the continued existence of the common state was the object of contention.

Partition is rarely acknowledged in the literature on ethnic conflict as a viable solution, given the near impossibility of creating ethnically homogeneous successor states. For most states, it is nearly impossible to draw clean dividing lines between ethnic groups. The partition of multinational states into ethnically defined successor states therefore tends to produce internal conflict between the "state-forming nation" in each successor state and its minorities; as well as between successor states over territories inhabited by their respective nations, but assigned to the "wrong" side of the border. Such irredenta may be eliminated through the transfer or expulsion of ethnic populations. But even then disputes over the rights of minorities, or even conflicts over borders, may continue indefinitely.

Ethnic Conflict and International Intervention

What distinguishes conflicts surrounding the disintegration of multinational states is not the overlap between ethnic violence and state-directed violence—that is, the employment of regular armies, police, or militia of the disintegrating state against civilians. It is the uncertain international response to state-directed violence. The use of violence against traditional secessionist movements arising in otherwise stable states—rebellions—tends to be accepted by the international community. In these cases, the use of force is largely shielded by principles of sovereignty and territorial integrity. In cases of disintegration, in contrast, the status of the state itself is in dispute. State-directed violence may be commanded by leaders whose loyalties are divided between the existing order and an emerging successor state, or wholly devoted to an emerging state. Some international actors may be sympathetic to the claims of the secessionist state(s) to the right of self-determination, and may therefore be reluctant to endorse the right of the disintegrating state to use force in defense of its territorial integrity. A disintegrating multinational state and the entities in the process of emerging from it are even more likely to be perceived differently by different elements of the international community. Indeed, distinguishing ethnic conflict or ethnoregional secessionism from the disintegration of a multinational state is itself a task fraught with objective and subjective difficulties, as the controversies surrounding the European Community (EC) response to conflict in the former Yugoslavia make clear. These differences and difficulties further complicate claims to self-determination, sovereignty, and the use of force on the part of the states involved in the conflict, as well as the calculations of outside actors contemplating intervention.

If the literature on ethnic conflict tells us that such conflicts are difficult to resolve—"nasty, brutish and long," in the words of two British analysts[8]—it also tells us that almost all such conflicts have been contained within existing state boundaries. External intervention in such conflicts has been motivated by direct security concerns on the part of neighboring states, or the geostrategic concerns of states or alliances. Rarely has intervention been motivated by concern to uphold abstract principles such as human rights or minority rights. Fundamental principles of the postwar international system—most notably the right of states to defend their sovereignty and territorial integrity and to conduct their internal affairs free from external interference—mitigated against intervention on any basis other than that recognized in the United Nations Charter: to preserve international peace.

Until the collapse of Yugoslavia, straightforward cases of successful ethnic secession from an internationally recognized state were more the exception than the rule. Central governments enjoyed considerable advantages over secessionist movements not only in their ability to mobilize superior force, but in their ability to command the support of other states seeking to protect their own claims to sovereign control over their own territories. Until the disintegration of Yugoslavia, secessionist movements could expect a long and bitter struggle with uncertain results, and little sympathy from the international community. Indeed, the recognition of a secessionist entity before its conflict with the existing state had been settled was considered unlawful.[9] Violence and atrocities committed against secessionists would, as a rule, be overlooked as an internal matter of the existing state. By the late 1980s, however, these norms were beginning to change.

Individual states and international organizations have been severely criticized for their failure to prevent the conflict in Bosnia-Herzegovina, or to end it sooner. But the international community faced difficult questions of both principle and policy in dealing with the Bosnian crisis, as it unfolded against a background of shifting, and even conflicting principles, rights, and obligations that made the resolution of conflict more difficult. But, while international actors could not easily resolve the Bosnian conflict, they could not remain entirely aloof from it. Policymakers came under immense pressure to "do something." In the end, however, U.S. and other Western policymakers did only what was consistent with their own interests. Although we view the war in Bosnia as the tragic result of a series of failures on the part of local leaders rather than the failure of the West, it is our belief that opportunities to avert war in Bosnia were overlooked during the earliest stages of Western involvement.

The tensions between the international community and the actors in the Bosnian drama evident in the chapters to follow are, then, a reflection of the clash between two conflicting realities: that of the international actors, committed to the notion of the rule of law and the protection of human rights, and attempting to mediate among the rival ethnic communities by seeking out compromises based on some form of power sharing and respect for the rule of law; and those of the competing sets of nationalists and ethnic patriots seeking to impose on Bosnia their own, mutually exclusive views of the future, regardless of the cost. The result was a gap in perceptions between the international community and the nationalists concerning where the solution to the crisis lay; a gap in perceptions which runs like a thread through our entire account, and to which we shall return in the conclusions. This is what we call, in the pages to follow, the "reality gap."

Ethnic Conflict and the Moral Question in Bosnia

In addition to the complex political and constitutional issues surrounding Bosnia-Herzegovina's status as a successor state, moral issues constantly intrude into our narrative of events. Both authors believe that moral principles must be rooted in notions of individual, not collective, responsibility; and that nationalism, by denying this, sets the stage for ethnic conflict and the excesses that follow. On the other hand, we are aware that an abstract devotion to liberal principles is one thing, and the condemnation of societies or states simply because they are nationalist is another. To take such a position would be an arrogant presumption of the superiority of the West, and a poor starting point for understanding the conflicts in the Balkans.

But the issue remains whether all the nationalist leaderships were equally responsible for the Bosnian war and the suffering the war brought to the civilian population. The issue is difficult because it lends itself to ideological and political manipulation. Any responsible examination of the moral issues posed by the excesses of the war must nevertheless focus on the actions of each of the parties, and especially their leaders. All our sympathies are directed toward those who did not want to see Bosnia divided, who hoped to preserve the existing multicultural way of life, and who saw in that way of life the beginnings of a civil society constructed along West European lines. In our view, the extremists on all three sides were deficient, and those who advocated and practiced ethnic cleansing are more culpable for the Bosnian tragedy than those who did not. But we are convinced that a multicultural civil state could not have been achieved in Bosnia without some form of power-sharing which allowed for the fact that the Croat and Serb ethnic communities had strong political, cultural, and religious ties to countries and churches outside Bosnia.

Only a minority of the politically significant actors in Bosnia were committed to striking the kind of balance between civil society and nationalism that we are suggesting here was necessary for Bosnia to survive. None of the three nationalist parties in Bosnia was committed to the notion of a civil society (although the Muslim Party of Democratic Action [SDA] did support the idea of a civil society in its party program in December 1992). Each of the nationalist parties pursued goals that clashed with those of the other parties (although the Serb Democratic Party [SDS] and the Croatian Democratic Union [HDZ] did both favor the dismemberment of Bosnia).

Of the three nationalist forces, however, the Serbs have come in for special opprobrium. But the focus on Serb behavior that dominates most Western discussion of the war is not, as some believe, the result only of better propaganda by the Muslims. It arises out of the fact that the Bosnian Serbs engaged in ethnic cleansing on a greater scale than the rest (although, as our account will show, Serbs in Bosnia were also the victims of ethnic cleansing); that the mass killings of the war were largely, although not exclusively, the work of the Serbs (hundreds, if not thousands, of Serbs may have been killed by paramilitary Muslim forces in Sarajevo at the outset of the war, as we shall see in chapter 4); and that the Serb nationalist leaders, along with the Croat extremists, were bent on destroying the multiethnic society which, in the last analysis, was the greatest accomplishment of Bosnian history. Yet, these facts have led some to adopt overly simplistic views of the nature of the war, and to neglect the suffering of Serbs at the hands of Croats and Muslims. In the view of one of the authors there was, in fact, a "demonization" of the Serbs in the West. There was a rush to judgment about the war, which intensified the polarization of views which the war provoked. We strive not to make such mistakes in this study.

One can restate the case by comparing the attitude of the Bosnian government on the one hand, and the Serb and Croat extremists on the other, toward preservation of the Bosnian state. In the Bosnian case, the Muslim-dominated government was committed, at least in principle, to defend the traditions of multiculturalism in Bosnia. For some Muslim leaders that commitment may have derived from a cynical calculation of group interest rooted in nationalist conceit about their power to dominate. For others, that commitment was weakened by their interest in securing a dominant role for Islam in Bosnia. As the war continued, the Muslim leadership's ability and, perhaps, willingness to follow up on its commitment to multiculturalism eroded. Nonetheless, at the outset of the war Bosnian Muslim advocates of what we shall characterize in chapter 2 as "the multicultural ideal" stood in sharp contrast to Bosnian Serb and Bosnian Croat (as well as Serbian and Croatian) nationalist leaders. From the beginning of the conflict, none of the latter showed any willingness to consider the civic or the multicultural alternative to the nationalist concept of the state. Because of these facts, and because the Bosnian Muslims were on the defensive during most of the war and feared their own extinction, the most respected intellectuals in Sarajevo, notable among them Zdravko Grebo, criticized what they called "equivalence"; that is, the idea that all sides bore equal responsibility for the conflict.

These differences among the conflicting parties did not, however, translate mechanically into a desire for peace on the one side, and for war on the other. Nor do they excuse indifference to crimes committed by Croats and Muslims against each other, and against Serbs. Our analysis of the politics among Muslim leaders in Bosnia-Herzegovina and the negotiating positions taken by the Muslim-dominated government, for example, makes clear the conflicting motivations, interests, and preferences at play among Muslim leaders. At the same time, the image of the Muslim government as the more restrained and civilized party has been tarnished by recent revelations of systematic murders of Serbs in Sarajevo (by criminal gangs, to be sure, but without any effort by the Bosnian government to expose or stop the practice), by evidence that the Muslims were not beyond deliberately inflicting casualties on their own civilian population in order to gain the sympathy of the international community, and by evidence of ethnic cleansing conducted by the Muslims during the 1993 war with the Croats. In our view, only the antinationalist parties and leaders—those who unequivocally opposed nationalism from the start—could be said to enjoy the status of morally exemplary leaders; persons who, if given political power commensurate with their moral stature, could have provided leadership for a postcommunist Bosnian society modeled after the civic societies of the West. The point is central to our political analysis of the Bosnian crisis; for in our view, it was only an alliance between the antinationalist opposition and moderates in the nationalist parties that could have saved Bosnia. But, none of the leaders of the three nationalist parties was willing to attempt such an alliance.

Yet, much as we may not like it, it was the nationalists who were elected by their peoples to lead the country in 1990. The nationalist leaders retained the loyalties of their respective groups throughout the conflict. Indeed, they continue to command such loyalty even today. It was the nationalists with whom international negotiators had to deal; at least until Croatia and Serbia were ready to cooperate with the West—and the West was ready to cooperate with them—in imposing a solution on the warring parties in Bosnia. This is critical for understanding the harsh choices the war posed for Western leaders seeking to end it.

It is with these facts in mind and from this perspective that we approach the question of genocide, and the charges and countercharges that have swirled around the International Criminal Tribunal at the Hague; both for failing to apprehend Serb war criminals, and for indicting mostly Serbs and charging only Serb leaders with genocidal intent. The issue of genocide is discussed in chapter 4. In our view, the proper place for the issue to be resolved is the International Criminal Tribunal at the Hague. It should be added that the two authors are not completely of the same mind on the issue of genocide in the Bosnian war. For one of us, it is a central issue; for the other, a charge that is highly politicized and must therefore be made cautiously, if at all. We are both firm supporters of prosecuting war crimes, but may differ somewhat on the value of the court for providing catharsis for the people of Bosnia. If Bosnians seek only revenge, then the court can never live up to expectations as a vehicle for reconciliation. If the court's work is part of a larger effort at healing, then its work may serve to lessen national antagonisms. We both agree that the war criminals in this tragic conflict should not go unpunished, and that if they do avoid capture they should be forced to remain fugitives until such time as they are apprehended. Both of us feel it is extremely important, in this context, that the court remain in operation, and that it strive to become a model for other such tribunals as may follow.

Sources

We have utilized as wide a variety of sources as possible in collecting our data and determining historical events, not only in English, but in Serbo-Croatian, German, and French. We use materials from Belgrade, Sarajevo, and Zagreb. The European edition of the Sarajevo daily *Oslobodjenje* is cited extensively. We would be remiss if we did not point out the immense utility of the translations issued by the BBC, Agence France Presse, and the Foreign Broadcast Information Service, all now easily accessed electronically. The use of these data bases for carrying out research on the war in Bosnia is a sign of how research techniques have been influenced by the electronic age. At the same time, we wish to assure the reader that the sources in Serbo-Croatian, and most of the secondary material cited in this work, were accessed by old-fashioned, nonelectronic, means. When we do cite materials directly off the Internet, this is indicated in the relevant footnote.

We have also examined carefully the memoirs of statesmen and UN military personnel involved in attempting to resolve the conflict in Bosnia, as well as memoirs of local participants. We are aware that memoirs are being prepared by several actors in these events that should shed new light on the issues addressed in this volume, and that valuable information on the conflict has been appearing in the Sarajevo press since the war ended, not all of which has been available to us. Some key materials have not been made available to scholars. As a consequence, some of the most controversial aspects of the war remain unresolved, a challenge to future historians and political scientists. When possible, we have interviewed participants in the events described in this volume and, when able to corroborate and confirm their testimonies or assertions, have used these interviews to help shape our understanding of the events.

Much of the international diplomacy surrounding the war in Bosnia focused on maps. We have provided more than thirty maps relating to the distribution of the ethnic communities, proposals for creating ethnic or other divisions within Bosnia, the front lines, the Bosnian Federation, and related issues. The reader should pay close attention to the origin of these maps. Some are based on original, primary sources such as UN documents, while others originate in secondary sources such as Yugoslav newspapers. While we feel the secondary source maps used as sources for this volume are accurate, their origins must be kept in mind. In any event, our maps are intended solely to help the reader better understand the narrative and analysis.

Readers sensitive to symbols and their connotations will notice that Muslim areas are in most maps rendered in white; that is, they are left blank. This was not done to imply that Muslim areas were some kind of "residual" in Bosnia, but for quite the opposite reason. We chose this approach to indicate as clearly as possible how the Muslims were squeezed by the Serbs and the Croats in respect to plans for a settlement of the war; the distribution of forces during the conflict; and the administrative boundaries of the Bosnian Federation. The fear of being reduced to an "enclave" drove the Muslims to resist most plans for a settlement during the course of the war, and drives them still. The maps, we think, illustrate that their fears were not unfounded.

Finally, it should be borne in mind that the events we describe are still undergoing scrutiny. There is hardly an event in the pages to follow that does not cry out for further study and evaluation. As a result, we feel it is essential that we and other scholars and analysts of the Bosnian war be prepared to reassess our positions, not only on questions of fact, but also on the broader and more highly charged moral issues surrounding the war. Only through a complete and honest exchange of views can we ever hope to arrive at the truth about the war in Bosnia and, by learning the truth, achieve reconciliation among the peoples of Bosnia.

CHAPTER 2

Conflict and Accommodation in Bosnian Political History

The war in Bosnia-Herzegovina reflected the contradictory traditions of conflict and accommodation that have characterized intergroup relations in the republic for centuries. For most of its history, Bosnian society had been deeply segmented, with Muslims, Serbs, and Croats organized into distinct communities. The balance between conflict and cooperation depended heavily on external factors. When they created a stable political environment, cooperation—or, at least, coexistence—predominated. When external factors contributed to the destabilization of Bosnia-Herzegovina, intergroup conflict prevailed, sometimes with brutal consequences. Elements of a shared political culture that might have moderated conflict even in the face of external threat emerged only recently, with the onset of modernization and urbanization, and among only a limited segment of society. The habits of conflict avoidance and cooperation that have featured so prominently in explanations of political stability in other deeply divided societies had little time to spread in Bosnia-Herzegovina.

Unlike Serbia or Croatia, whose dominant ethnic groups and leaderships considered themselves as nations with natural borders embracing areas outside their existing frontiers, Bosnia-Herzegovina was first and foremost an administrative unit whose boundaries, because they persisted over time, came to gain a certain political weight. Increasing administrative autonomy and the natural processes of even limited social interaction, as well as conscious local and external leadership, encouraged the development of common cultural attributes and a shared economic life among Bosnia's three ethnic communities, at least in the major urban areas.

But the status of the territory as a whole was in dispute for much of the nineteenth and twentieth centuries. Bosnia-Herzegovina was at the center of a diplomatic crisis that ended in disaster in 1914. It was a major pawn in the "Eastern Question" that preoccupied Europe for most of the nineteenth century. Turkish rule, which ended only in 1878, left a legacy of deep social cleavages along ethnoreligious lines, as well as a society steeped in military traditions and values. The ethnic communities in Bosnia approached the national question from the "outside in." They developed external loyalties and orientations, rather than cultivating a distinct multinational tradition. As a result, cultural and religious differences that were tolerated in everyday life became markers for clashing political agendas and the emergence of distinct national ideologies.

Bosnia was not, however, a society in which ethnic conflict was the norm. Bosnians shared a common language, ethnic origin, and lifestyles. In urban areas after World War II, they intermarried. The horror of 1992–95 lay in the manner in which this functioning society was deliberately destroyed and a war of each against all, along ethnic lines, was introduced in its place. The ease with which this was accomplished was not the product of a single, deliberate act—whether it be called aggression or nationalism. It can be explained only in terms of the interaction between external forces; Bosnian society itself, with its deep ethnic, regional, and class cleavages; and Bosnian history. The violent history of Bosnia must be taken into account if one is to understand the war and the course it took.

But it was the breakup of Yugoslavia that opened the door to war by forcing the question of the self-determination of Bosnia-Herzegovina and its respective nationalities. Bosnia's violent past did heighten fears and produced the mentalities that placed communal solidarity over mutual reconciliation. But, if Yugoslavia had survived, and the issue of self-determination had not arisen—or if the dissolution of Yugoslavia had been managed by international and domestic actors in a manner that resolved the conflicts between republics and nations peacefully—the ethnic communities of Bosnia would in all likelihood have continued to live in peace. Tragically, however, domestic and international actors quickly proved themselves unable or unwilling to resolve the conflicts arising out of the disintegration of Yugoslavia, or to prevent them from turning violent. Nationalist leaders faced few obstacles to their efforts to play upon fear, to mobilize ethnic solidarity, and thereby to orchestrate the descent into violence that produced catastrophe for their peoples.

Ethnicity in Bosnia-Herzegovina

Bosnia-Herzegovina's difficult history was rooted in the most fundamental characteristics of Bosnian geography and the distribution of ethnic communities in the republic, in the character and ambitions of Serbian and Croatian nationalisms, and in the policies and actions of outside actors. Bosnia-Herzegovina could be seen as the archetypal Balkan state. Ethnically diverse, until recently economically passive and lacking in internal communications, it bred a culture and society of "mountain men." But it also lay across important lines of communication from the interior of Europe to the coast of the Adriatic, and occupied a strategic location that attracted the attention and ambitions of outside military powers from the time of the Turks to World War II.

Bosnia's most unique feature was its arrested national development. The process of nation-state consolidation that took place throughout Europe in the nineteenth and early twentieth centuries—and which frequently involved population transfers, major boundary shifts, and the assertion by "titular" nationalities of a right to rule—bypassed Bosnia-Herzegovina. The region passed from the control of one multinational empire to another during the nineteenth century, retaining many social and economic traces of its Ottoman origins until the Communists eliminated entirely the old social order after 1945. During all this time, Bosnia-Herzegovina was never an independent state. The closest Bosnia came to acting as an independent state was when a national council, meeting in Sarajevo in 1918, declared the adherence of Bosnia-Herzegovina to Yugoslavia. Yet, Bosnia retained its identity and boundaries through modern times. This was above all because the area posed such a problem for any power that wished to assimilate it. It was relatively vast, largely inaccessible, and ethnically indigestible.[1] Equally, if not more important, the existence of Bosnia in the nineteenth century served as a counterweight to the disruption of the European balance of power in the Balkans that might have resulted from the annexation of Bosnia by Serbia, and the resultant emergence of a greater Serbia. Bosnia did, therefore, endure. Its periodic descents into ethnic violence, especially during World War II, seemed to underscore the practical necessity of preserving the Bosnian state, geopolitical considerations and the rights of its peoples to self-determination quite aside.

Very few exogenous ethnic elements were introduced into Bosnia by the Turks, the apparent exception being in the northern portion of the Cazinska Krajina region (to be described below) where Muslims forced out of Hungary and Croatia by the Austrians were brought in to serve on the military frontier.[2] Population movements within Bosnia-Herzegovina were rare after the fourteenth and fifteenth centuries, when Serbs were brought into western Bosnia to replace Croats as part of the military frontier. Distinctions among the indigenous Slav population developed along religious lines, as a portion of the Slav population, most probably out of economic reasons, converted to Islam. Under the Millet system instituted by the Porte, the Orthodox and Catholic populations became the wards of their respective churches. Language, historical experiences, economic conditions, and other elements of culture were nonetheless shared, if not always experienced in identical ways, by the three religious communities.

At the same time, the peoples of Bosnia-Herzegovina never were viewed collectively as a "nation in the process of becoming." Bosnian Muslim historians have suggested that, over the centuries, a distinct "oriental-Islamic cultural heritage" developed in the territories under Ottoman rule. This heritage was shared even by the Christian population, and was "reflected in the adoption of Turkishisms and Arabisms in the Serbo-Croatian language, the style of dress in the region, its art and architecture, and even in the vocabulary and practice of the Christian churches."[3] The common cultural development of the Muslim and non-Muslim populations, they argued, arose out of their shared, pre-Ottoman historical memories, customs, and beliefs; their common Slavic origins and language; and their extensive "geographic interpenetration." They noted that the latter gave rise to "a cult of good neighborliness."[4] But they conceded that, despite these commonalities, the peoples of Bosnia-Herzegovina developed "only a common feeling of homeland, which . . . never developed into the idea of a Bosnian nation."[5]

Under Ottoman rule, the Slavic Muslim population called themselves *Turci* ("Turks"), a term which they understood to mean "adherents to Islam." For "Turks" in an ethnic sense, they used the term *Turkuši* ("Turkics") or *Osmanlija*.[6] This close identification with the Ottomans placed the Muslim community in a politically vulnerable position when the region fell under the control of the Austrians. Under Austrian rule, to identify oneself as a "Turk" was perceived as an indication of opposition.[7] Thus, the Muslim intellectual and cultural elite began to describe themselves and their fellow Muslims as *Muslimani;* that is, quite literally, as Muslims. A small number of Muslim elites began to identify themselves as "Serbs of the Muslim faith" or "Muslim Serbs." But this was primarily a reflection of their political attraction to the independent, vigorously nationalistic, and expansionist Serbian state as a potential counterweight to Austrian power. Other Muslims adopted a "Croatian orientation" during this period, largely as the result of the increasing education of Muslim children in Serbo-Croatian schools administered by Croats from Croatia and by Zagreb-educated Bosnian Muslims. The declaration of Croatian identity by Bosnian Muslims, therefore, represented a primarily cultural definition.[8] Both these tendencies remained limited, however. More important, the period of Austrian rule saw a dramatic expansion of separate Muslim religious, cultural, educational, economic, and political organizations.[9] Bosnia thus became a "segmented society," in which Serbs, Croats, and Muslims each could live their lives wholly within the framework of their own Serb, Croat, or Muslim institutions. This hastened the transformation of the meaning of "Muslim" identity from the narrowly religious to the broadly ethnic, or even national, as a means of distinction from both the Croats and the Serbs.[10]

While Bosnia-Herzegovina was not looked upon as an emerging nation, it was considered as the potential spoils of war or diplomatic intrigue. When Austria occupied Bosnia-Herzegovina in 1878, it did so more to prevent the expansion of Serbia than to enlarge the empire. Yugoslavia's acquisition of the province in 1918 was inevitable, once Slovenia and Croatia decided to form a union with Serbia and Montenegro. In 1941, the Independent State of Croatia (*Nezavisna Država Hrvatska,* or NDH) annexed Bosnia-Herzegovina, proclaiming the Muslims the "purest Croats." The fate of Bosnia-Herzegovina at the end of World War II, as we shall see below, was decided by a small group around Tito, whose primary concern was to preserve the unity of the Communist Party of Yugoslavia by taking the Bosnian issue off the agenda of the two most concerned republics, Croatia and Serbia. At no stage in this process of changing regimes were the peoples of Bosnia-Herzegovina free to choose their own destiny. It is, perhaps, only for this reason that Bosnia-Herzegovina endured intact.

Although the borders of Bosnia-Herzegovina remained largely unchanged for centuries, its boundaries while part of Yugoslavia were far from sacrosanct. Indeed, the region became the object of conflict and negotiation between Croatian and Serbian nationalisms, over the heads of the local Muslim elites. In 1921, the Yugoslav Muslim Organization (*Jugoslavenska Muslimanska Organizacija*—JMO) extracted a promise from Belgrade that the administrative boundaries of the new state would preserve the historical boundaries of Bosnia-Herzegovina. Following the imposition of a dictatorship in 1929, however, King Alexander attempted to ameliorate the growing conflict between Croats and Serbs by eliminating the nationally defined regions of the country and replacing them with nine administrative regions, or *banovine,* each named after the major river that defined the region. These cut across all preexisting historical provincial boundaries, including those of Bosnia-Herzegovina. Only two of the nine had their provincial seats in the former province: *Vrbas,* with its capital in Banja Luka; and *Drina,* with its capital in Sarajevo. In August 1939, this attempt at nonnational or cross-national division was abandoned and replaced by a straightforward Croat-Serb nationalist partition negotiated between Croatia and the Yugoslav government. Yugoslavia was reduced, in effect, to a greater Serbia. This agreement (*Sporazum*) created a large Croatian state-within-a-state. As can be seen in Map 2.1, shown below, Croatia incorporated a large portion of Bosnia-Herzegovina, including the areas of Posavina, Western Herzegovina, and much of central Bosnia. The remainder, including Cazinska Krajina, the Banja Luka region, Sarajevo, and eastern Bosnia was allocated to Yugoslavia (Serbia).[11] As Ivo Banac points out, the partition was agreed to without regard for Muslim interests.[12] While there was discontent with the result on both sides, the 1939 Sporazum marked the end of Bosnia-Herzegovina, and the fragile beginnings of a dualist Yugoslavia. If World War II had not intervened, that state would almost certainly have become a tripartite regime with the elevation of the third national entity, Slovenia, to equal status.

The reemergence of Bosnia-Herzegovina as a separate entity remained at risk during World War II. The Communists, before and during the initial stages of the war, favored autonomy for the province—a vague appeal that could be counted on not to alienate the Muslims, and interpreted to the Serbs and Croats as circumstances warranted.[13] It has been suggested that Tito considered partitioning Bosnia-Herzegovina, but that the task proved too divisive and was abandoned. In November 1943, at a meeting of the top leadership to decide the region's status, the Serb delegation favored autonomy (possibly under the federal government); the Muslim delegation favored republic status. Tito decided in favor of the Muslims, and Bosnia-Herzegovina was elevated to the status of a republic, equal to the five other Yugoslav republics.[14]

The grant of republic status formally rendered the boundaries of Bosnia-Herzegovina constitutionally inviolable. The Bosnian constitution of 1946, for example, provided that the boundaries of the republic could not be changed without its consent. In practice, however, the attitude of the Communists toward boundaries was decidedly cavalier. At the end of the war, and in secrecy, Bosnia-Herzegovina's only usable outlet to the sea—on the Bay of Boka Kotorska at Herceg-Novi—was transferred to Montenegro.[15] It is one of the oddities of the dispute over boundaries during the war of 1992–95 that none of the parties to the conflict renewed this claim.

For the 75 years during which Bosnia-Herzegovina was part of Yugoslavia, the boundaries of Bosnia-Herzegovina were for most purposes considered as administrative in nature, as were all other internal boundaries in Yugoslavia. The practical import of this can be seen in the manner in which the Belgrade–Bar railway line dips into Bosnia in the Rudo district on its way from Užica in Serbia to Prijepolje in Montenegro. (The importance of this became clear during the war when a group of Yugoslav Muslims were

Map 2.1 **The 1939 Serb-Croat Partition of Bosnia**

kidnapped from a train when it was passing through the Bosnian section of the Belgrade–Bar line.) On the Una river, the railway from Bihać in Bosnia to Knin in Croatia crosses and recrosses the Bosnian-Croat border. A vast underground military facility built in the Titoist period stretched from Bihać across the Bosnian border into Croatia. For at least the first 20 years of communist rule, republic borders were part of an essentially symbolic system for acknowledging and legitimating identities. It was only with the rise of regional power in the 1970s and, especially, 1980s, that borders took on political and economic significance. Thus, the status of borders was an essentially derivative rather than causative factor in Yugoslav politics; their

Map 2.2 **Main Regions of Bosnia-Herzegovina**

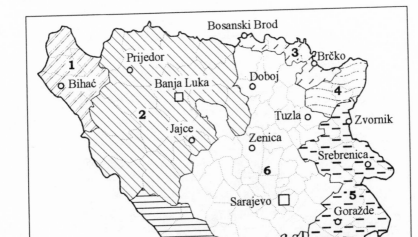

Bosanski Brod
Brčko
Prijedor
Bihać
Doboj
Banja Luka
1
2
Jajce
Tuzla
Zvornik
Zenica
Srebrenica
6
Sarajevo
Goražde
Foča
8
Mostar
7
Trebinje

1 - Cazinska krajina
2 - Bosanska krajina
3 - Bosanska Posavina
4 - Semberija
5 - Eastern Bosnia (Podrinje)
6 - Central Bosnia
7 - Eastern Herzegovina
8 - Western Herzegovina

importance was a product rather than a cause of interrepublic conflict.

The main regions of Bosnia-Herzegovina are shown in Map 2.2. While not everyone would agree with the number or distribution of these regions, and their borders are not easy to define precisely, we can say that Bosnia-Herzegovina was divided into eight regions by a combination of ethnic, histori-cal, political-administrative, and natural features. These regions differ from those drawn on the basis of either ethnic or geographic features alone.[16] They are: Cazinska Krajina (or the Bihać pocket, as it came to be referred to in the press), an overwhelmingly Muslim-populated region; Bosanska Krajina, largely Serb but with a significant Muslim population; Bosanska Posavina, largely Croat, except for Brčko; Semberija, largely Serb, except for Bijeljina, where a sizable number of Muslims were to be found; eastern Bosnia, with a mixed Serb-Muslim population, and a strong concentration of Muslims in the cities along the Drina River; eastern Herzegovina, largely Serb, with Croat and Muslim inhabitants in its western reaches; western Herzegovina, overwhelmingly Croat; central

Map 2.3 **Names of** *Opštine* **(Counties)**

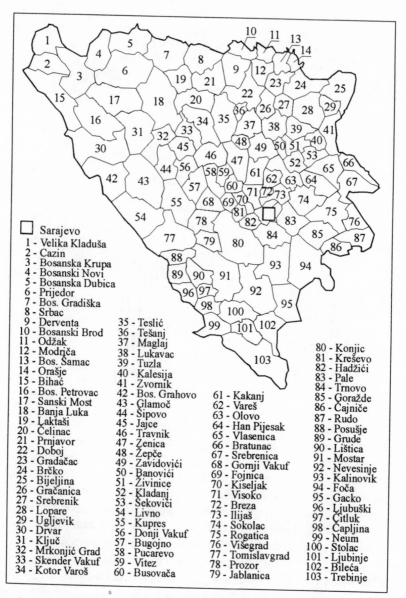

Sarajevo
1 - Velika Kladuša
2 - Cazin
3 - Bosanska Krupa
4 - Bosanski Novi
5 - Bosanska Dubica
6 - Prijedor
7 - Bos. Gradiška
8 - Srbac
9 - Derventa
10 - Bosanski Brod
11 - Odžak
12 - Modriča
13 - Bos. Šamac
14 - Orašje
15 - Bihać
16 - Bos. Petrovac
17 - Sanski Most
18 - Banja Luka
19 - Laktaši
20 - Čelinac
21 - Prnjavor
22 - Doboj
23 - Gradačac
24 - Brčko
25 - Bijeljina
26 - Gračanica
27 - Srebrenik
28 - Lopare
29 - Ugljevik
30 - Drvar
31 - Ključ
32 - Mrkonjić Grad
33 - Skender Vakuf
34 - Kotor Varoš

35 - Teslić
36 - Tešanj
37 - Maglaj
38 - Lukavac
39 - Tuzla
40 - Kalesija
41 - Zvornik
42 - Bos. Grahovo
43 - Glamoč
44 - Šipovo
45 - Jajce
46 - Travnik
47 - Zenica
48 - Žepče
49 - Zavidovići
50 - Banovići
51 - Živinice
52 - Kladanj
53 - Šekovići
54 - Livno
55 - Kupres
56 - Donji Vakuf
57 - Bugojno
58 - Pucarevo
59 - Vitez
60 - Busovača

61 - Kakanj
62 - Vareš
63 - Olovo
64 - Han Pijesak
65 - Vlasenica
66 - Bratunac
67 - Srebrenica
68 - Gornji Vakuf
69 - Fojnica
70 - Kiseljak
71 - Visoko
72 - Breza
73 - Ilijaš
74 - Sokolac
75 - Rogatica
76 - Višegrad
77 - Tomislavgrad
78 - Prozor
79 - Jablanica

80 - Konjic
81 - Kreševo
82 - Hadžići
83 - Pale
84 - Trnovo
85 - Goražde
86 - Čajniče
87 - Rudo
88 - Posušje
89 - Grude
90 - Lištica
91 - Mostar
92 - Nevesinje
93 - Kalinovik
94 - Foča
95 - Gacko
96 - Ljubuški
97 - Čitluk
98 - Čapljina
99 - Neum
100 - Stolac
101 - Ljubinje
102 - Bileća
103 - Trebinje

Bosnia, with a mixed Muslim-Croat population, and Muslim strongholds in Zenica and Tuzla in the north, and Konjic, Jablanica and Prozor in the south; and the Sarajevo district, of mixed population. The names of the individual *opštine* (counties) in Bosnia-Herzegovina are shown in Map 2.3.

Western Herzegovina was a breeding ground of Croat nationalism. Its population provided critical support to Croatia, in the form of recruits, financial aid, and leadership, in the war with Serbia in 1991. Cazinska Krajina, an island of Muslims detached from the Muslim centers of population in central Bosnia, attempted to stand aside in both World War II and the present conflict. In World War II, the local leadership eventually joined the communist partisans.[17] All three ethnic groups in Cazinska Krajina resisted communist efforts to impose collectivization in Bosnia in 1950.[18] According to Misha Glenny, relations among Serbs, Croats, and Muslims were exceptionally good in the region prior to 1992.[19] In 1993 Fikret Abdić, the local Muslim leader of Cazinska Krajina, sought to strike his own deal with the Serbs and the Croats, over the opposition of Sarajevo (this will be described in more detail in chapter 4).

Eastern Bosnia has without doubt been the most bitterly contested area in Bosnia-Herzegovina. It was the scene of a Serb peasant revolt protesting Austrian conscription in 1881–82, and of punitive forays by the Serbs against Muslim villages and by the Austrians against Serb villages during World War I. Thousands were deported by the Austrians in an effort to pacify the region.[20] Eastern Bosnia was the scene of vicious fighting during World War II, in which atrocities were committed on all sides; and again in 1992–95. As we shall see in chapter 7, the execution of thousands of Muslims in Srebrenica in eastern Bosnia in July 1995 by the Serbs helped push the United States toward military intervention in the Bosnian conflict. The region's tumultuous history has time and again invited intervention by the Serbs and Montenegrins from across the Drina. No picture of Bosnia is complete without an understanding of the troubled history of this region.

Central Bosnia, by way of contrast, was before the war one of the strongholds of multiculturalism, both in the urban working class cities (Sarajevo, Zenica, Tuzla) and in those districts where the Catholic Church had traditionally played a moderating role—so-called "Franciscan Bosnia." This should not, however, be confused with the Franciscan Bosnia of western Herzegovina, where the Catholic Church was a mainstay of Croat nationalism. It took a full year after the outbreak of the present conflict, and a fallout between the Croat and Muslim leaderships, before fighting broke out in the mixed Muslim-Croat areas of central Bosnia west of Sarajevo.

Within and among these regions, the three ethnic communities of Bosnia-Herzegovina were, before the 1992 conflict broke out, distributed in a pattern of disconnected ethnic majority areas that varied in character from nearly homogeneous to nearly evenly divided. The ethnic communities were interspersed, resulting in what Cyrus Vance called "leopard spots." The near impossibility of separating and consolidating these communities territorially argued for retaining the boundaries of Bosnia and seeking cultural, not territorial, autonomy for the three ethnic communities. Yet this very fact—that ethnic settlement patterns had changed little over time—suggested that ethnic relations in Bosnia were rooted in the past, and that ethnic leaderships were not yet ready to accept the de-territorialization of the ethnic question that cultural rather than territorial autonomy would necessitate.[21]

At the same time, on the eve of the 1992–95 war, Bosnia-Herzegovina faced the explosive issue of whether any ethnic community could claim the privileges associated with the status of a majority. Insofar as Bosnia-Herzegovina survived the collapse of Yugoslavia intact, the debate over which nationality—if any—could claim the right of the "titular" nationality was sure to arouse national passions. The sensitivity of the issue was all the greater because the total number of Serbs, Muslims, and Croats had not remained constant over time. Changes reflected the fortunes of war, out-migrations of one or another ethnic community, and of course, excesses committed against one or another of the three groups during periods of violence. In the sixteenth and seventeenth centuries, the Muslims were a majority.[22] By the middle of the nineteenth century—thanks to famines and wars (which affected the Muslim population, subject to military duty and living in urban areas, the most)—the Muslims lost ground to the Serbs. In 1851, in the closing decades of Turkish rule, out of a total population of 1,898,000 recorded by the Turkish authorities, 44.4 percent were Serbs (that is, persons of Orthodox faith), 37.3 percent were Muslims (of Islamic faith), and 18.5 percent were Croats (Catholic). Following the occupation of Bosnia-Herzegovina by Austria in 1878, an exodus of Muslims decreased their numbers relative to the Serbs and Croats. From that point to the mid-1950s, the proportion of the population belonging to the three groups did not change greatly. Then, thanks to changes in census procedures, outmigration of Serbs and Croats, and demographic growth patterns favoring the Muslims, the number of Muslims came to exceed the number of Serbs. By 1991, 43.7 percent of the population was Muslim, 31.4 percent was Serb, and 17.3 percent was Croat (the data are presented in Table 2.1).

The distribution of ethnic communities in 1991 can be seen in Map 2.4, which indicates the ethnic community that constituted an absolute majority in each of the 100-odd *opštine* (counties) of Bosnia-Herzegovina. *Opštine* in which there was no such majority are left blank (even though in some of these one group may have constituted a substantial plurality). The data shown in Table 2.2 (page 30) were used repeatedly to claim the "right" of one or another ethnic group to a given district. The same data guided the efforts of the international community in trying to draw lines among the warring parties, notably in the case of the Vance-Owen plan. The data are, however,

Table 2.1

Population of Bosnia-Herzegovina by Religion and/or Nationality, 1851–1991 (in percent)

Year	Muslims Religion	Muslims Nation	Serbs Religion	Serbs Nation	Croats Religion	Croats Nation
1851	37.3		44.0		18.5	
1879	38.7		42.9		18.1	
1885	36.9	42.8	42.8		19.9	
1910	32.3		43.5		19.9	
1921	31.3		43.9		23.5	
1931	30.8		40.5		22.2	
1948	30.7	34.5[a]	44.3	41.5	23.9	23.0
1953	31.3	31.3[b]	44.4	44.4	23.0	23.0
1961		34.1[c]		42.9		21.7
1971		39.6[d]		37.2		20.6
1981		39.5		32.0		18.4
1991	43.7	43.7	17.5	31.4		17.3

Sources: Shoup, The East European and Soviet Data Handbook, Table C-10, p. 156; Bogosavljević, "Bosna i Hercegovina u ogledelu statistike," pp. 34 and 37; Atif Purivatra, Jugoslavenska Muslimanska Organizacija, p. 515; and Savezni Zavod za Statistiku (SZS), "Nacionalni sastav stanovništva opštinama," Statstički Bilten broj 1934 (Belgrade: SZS, 1992), p. 9.

Notes: Data for 1931 estimate adjusted for historical boundaries. Source is Bogosavljević. Purivatra gives following figures for 1931: Muslims: 30.9 percent, Serbs 44.2 percent, Croats 23.6 percent.

[a] Includes "ethnic Muslims" (3.8 percent) and "Muslims-Other" (30.7 percent).

[b] "Yugoslavs, Undeclared."

[c] "Muslims in the ethnic sense" (25.7 percent) and "Yugoslavs, nationally undeclared."

[d] "Muslims in the national sense."

misleading. They give only an approximate notion of how the ethnic communities in Bosnia were distributed. Most obviously, the size and topography of these units vary, distorting the meaning of these ethnic maps. In addition, ethnic communities in Bosnia-Herzegovina tended to be found in clusters which had little to do with administrative lines. As we shall have reason to note, Serbs tended to inhabit rural areas, Muslims the cities (although the overall division of the two groups between rural and urban categories of the 1981 census does not differ greatly from the ethnic percentages for the population as a whole).[23] Thus, in a given district, a Muslim-majority urban center, containing the majority of the total population in the district, could be surrounded by a Serb- or Croat-populated countryside.

Map 2.4 **Ethnic Majorities in Bosnia-Herzegovina by** *Opština* **(County), 1991**

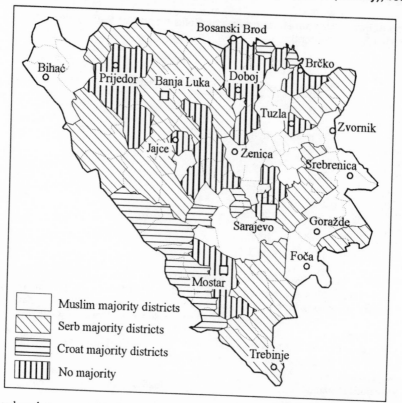

Based on data presented in Savezni Zavod za Statistiku, "Nacionalni sastav stanovništva po opštinama," *Statistički Bilten* no. 1934 (Belgrade: Savezni Zavod za Statistiku, 1992), pp. 9–12.

The smaller the units of measurement, the greater the proportion of land in the republic inhabited by Serbs, since sparsely populated rural areas were often Serb. If the cadastral *opština* was used as the unit to measure population distribution, about 56 percent of the area of Bosnia-Herzegovina could be said to have been inhabited by Serbs before the conflict began—a figure that should not be confused with the claim of the Bosnian Serbs that they "owned" 64 percent of the land. (This claim, even if true, can only refer to privately owned land.)

How different bases of mapping ethnic distribution could produce different results can be illustrated by the three districts of Prijedor, Sanski Most, and Ključ in western Bosnia, which were claimed by both the Muslims and the Serbs, ethnically cleansed by the Serbs in 1992, and partitioned between the two ethnic communities in 1995. In 1981, the number of Serbs slightly exceeded the number of Muslims in the Prijedor and Ključ *opštine,* while the Muslims outnumbered the Serbs in Sanski Most by a narrow margin. In 1991, the Muslims outnumbered the Serbs in all three districts, giving support to the claims of the Bosnian government that this territory should fall to the Bosnian republic. Data on the urban-rural distribution of the population by ethnic community did not reveal any marked difference between the percentage of the two ethnic communities living in rural and urban areas, and in the districts in their entirety. Yet the distribution of the population within each district when measured by the smaller cadastral *opština* revealed that the Muslim population was distributed largely along the Sana river and surrounding hills, while the Serbs appear to be in the majority elsewhere. It would be difficult to draw a boundary that separated the two ethnic communities in this region. Such difficulties were reproduced in many parts of the republic. As the data shown in Table 2.2 make clear, of the approximately 100 *opštine* that made up Bosnia-Herzegovina on the eve of the war,[24] in about one-third of them no ethnic community had a strong majority or could claim a clear-cut numerical advantage.

One can quickly discern from the data displayed in Table 2.2 how closely the conflict that began in 1992 focused on areas of mixed ethnicity: first, between Muslims and Serbs in eastern Bosnia and western Bosanska Krajina (Prijedor, Sanski Most, and Ključ); and second, between Croats and Muslims in central Bosnia and Mostar. It is also clear that very few districts pitted Serbs against Croats. This facilitated their cooperation in the first two years of the war, once the battles for Bosanski Brod (on the Sava) and Kupres (on the border of Bosanska Krajina and western Herzegovina) were over, and the Serbs had given up their claim to the eastern part of the city of Mostar, where the Serbs were less numerous than the Croats or Muslims.

In the republic's largest cities, a significant proportion of the population consisted of "Yugoslavs." In 1981, between one-fifth and one-quarter of the population in the five largest cities in Bosnia chose to declare themselves as Yugoslav instead of an ethnic identity, in response to the census question on nationality.[25] "Yugoslav" is best understood as a civil identity, and the large numbers of Yugoslavs in the largest cities reflected the integrative effects of interethnic contact in a multiethnic setting, and the impact of socioeconomic modernization on traditional identities—two processes that were far less advanced in the smaller cities and towns, and practically absent in the rural areas of the republic.[26] The increasing number of such "Yugoslavs" before 1991, together with the many Muslims, Serbs, Croats, and others who supported the idea of a common state, represented the emergence of precisely the kind of civic culture that would be required for a stable

Table 2.2

Population of the Regions of Bosnia-Herzegovina by Major Ethnic Groups, 1991 (by opština, in percent)

Region	Croats	Muslims	Serbs	"Yugoslavs"
Opština				
Cazinska Krajina				
Bihac	7.7	66.6	17.8	6.0
Bos. Krupa	0.2	74.5	23.6	1.2
Cazin	0.2	97.6	1.2	0.6
Vel. Kladuša	1.3	91.8	4.3	1.7
Bosanska Krajina				
Banja Luka	14.9	14.6	54.8	12.0
Bos. Dubica	1.5	20.5	69.1	5.8
Bos. Gradiška	5.7	26.5	59.9	5.4
Bos. Novi	1.0	33.9	60.4	3.7
Bos. Petrovac	0.3	21.1	75.2	2.3
Bos. Grahovo	2.6	0.1	95.5	1.5
Čelinac	0.4	7.7	88.9	1.9
Drvar	0.2	0.2	97.3	2.1
Glamoč	1.5	18.1	79.3	0.9
Jajce	35.1	38.8	19.3	5.5
Ključ	0.9	47.6	49.5	1.5
Laktaši	8.6	1.7	81.7	5.0
Mrkonjić Grad	7.8	12.0	77.3	2.1
Prijedor	5.6	44.0	42.5	5.7
Prnjavor	3.7	15.3	71.6	3.7
Sanski Most	7.1	47.0	42.2	2.0
Šipovo	0.2	19.3	79.2	1.0
Skender Vakuf	24.8	5.6	68.4	0.8
Srbac	0.7	4.3	89.1	3.5
Teslić	16.0	21.5	55.1	5.7
Bosanska Posavina				
Bos. Brod	41.0	12.2	33.8	10.6
Bos. Šamac	44.7	6.8	41.5	5.2
Brćko	25.4	44.4	20.8	6.4
Odžak	54.2	20.3	19.8	3.7
Orašje	75.3	6.7	15.0	2.1
Semberija				
Bijeljina	0.5	31.3	59.4	4.4
Lopare	3.9	37.7	55.5	1.7
Ugljevik	0.3	40.6	56.2	1.1
Eastern Bosnia				
Bratunac	0.1	64.2	34.2	0.7
Čajniče	0.1	44.9	52.7	0.9
Foča	0.3	51.6	45.3	1.1
Goražde	0.2	70.2	26.2	2.1
Han Pijesak	0.1	40.1	58.3	1.1

Kalesija	0.1	79.5	18.3	0.6
Kladanj	0.2	73.3	23.9	1.7
Rogatica	0.1	60.4	38.4	0.8
Rudo	—	27.2	70.8	0.8
Šekovići	0.1	3.4	94.3	1.2
Srebrenica	0.1	72.9	25.2	1.0
Višegrad	0.2	62.8	32.8	1.5
Vlasenica	0.1	55.3	42.5	1.0
Zvornik	0.1	59.4	38.0	1.5

Eastern Herzegovina

Bileća	0.3	14.7	80.3	1.7
Gacko	0.3	35.3	62.4	0.8
Kalinovik	0.4	37.1	60.6	1.0
Ljubinje	1.1	7.9	89.9	0.5
Nevesinje	1.3	23.0	74.5	0.9
Trebinje	4.0	17.9	69.3	5.3

Western Herzegovina

Čapljina	53.9	27.7	13.5	3.7
Čitluk	98.9	0.7	0.1	0.1
Grude	99.8	—	0.1	—
Lištica	99.2	—	0.6	0.1
Livno	72.0	15.0	9.6	2.8
Ljubuški	92.6	5.8	0.2	0.8
Mostar	33.8	34.8	19.0	10.0
Neum	87.6	4.6	4.9	2.2
Posušje	99.5	—	0.1	0.2
Stolac	32.4	44.5	20.8	1.7
Tomislavgrad	86.6	10.8	1.9	0.4

Central Bosnia

Banovići	2.1	72.4	16.8	7.3
Breza	5.0	75.6	12.3	5.8
Bugojno	34.1	42.1	18.9	3.3
Busovača	48.1	44.9	3.4	2.7
Doboj	13.0	40.2	39.0	5.5
Donji Vakuf	2.8	55.3	38.7	2.6
Drventa	39.0	12.6	40.8	5.9
Fojnica	40.9	49.4	0.9	2.4
Gor. Vakuf	42.6	56.1	0.4	0.6
Gračanica	0.2	72.2	23.0	2.5
Gradačac	15.1	60.2	19.8	2.5
Jablanica	17.8	72.1	4.0	4.5
Kakanj	29.8	54.5	8.8	4.5
Kiseljak	51.7	40.9	3.1	2.5
Konjic	26.0	54.5	15.2	3.2
Kotor Varoš	29.0	30.4	38.1	1.9
Kreševo	70.7	22.8	0.5	3.7
Kupres	39.6	8.4	50.7	0.7
Lukavac	3.8	66.7	21.6	6.0
Maglaj	19.3	45.4	30.7	3.4
Modriča	27.3	29.5	35.5	5.1
Olovo	3.9	75.0	18.9	1.7

(continued)

Table 2.2 *(continued)*

Prozor	62.3	36.6	0.2	0.5
Pucarevo	39.6	38.0	13.3	6.9
Sarajevo				
Centar	6.8	50.2	21.1	16.4
Hadžići	3.1	63.6	26.4	3.4
Ilidža	10.3	43.0	37.2	7.6
Ilijaš	6.8	42.2	45.1	4.6
Novi Grad	6.5	50.8	27.7	11.4
Novo Sarajevo	9.2	35.7	34.7	15.8
Pale	0.8	26.7	69.1	2.4
Stari Grad	2.4	78.0	10.2	6.4
Trnovo	0.2	68.9	29.5	1.0
Vogošća	4.3	50.8	35.8	7.0
Sokolac	0.1	30.2	68.6	0.6
Srebrenik	6.8	75.0	13.1	2.8
Tešanj	18.5	72.2	6.4	2.1
Travnik	36.9	45.3	11.0	5.2
Tuzla	15.6	47.6	15.5	16.6
Vareš	40.6	30.4	16.4	9.3
Visoko	4.3	74.5	16.0	3.2
Vitez	45.7	41.4	5.4	4.9
Zavidovići	13.2	60.1	20.4	4.7
Zenica	15.6	55.2	15.5	10.8
Žepče	39.8	47.2	10.0	2.3
Živinice	7.3	80.6	6.4	3.9

Source: Savezni Zavod za Statistiku, "Nacionalni sastav stanovništva po opštinama," *Statistički Bilten* no. 1934 (Belgrade: SZS, 1992), pp. 9–12.

Bosnia-Herzegovina. But the total number of "Yugoslavs" was relatively small. They constituted only about 8 percent of the population in 1981 (and decreased to 5.5 percent in 1991). They were limited to the cities, and they represented only one of the competing traditions in the republic.

The data for the population as a whole did not show a dramatic difference between the percentages of Serbs and Muslims in rural areas and in urban areas.[27] There were, however, cities where the proportion of Muslims was extraordinarily high compared to the surrounding rural areas. This was especially true of the cities in Bosanska Posavina, in the north and along the Sava river, where the cities were typically 40–50 percent Muslim and the rural areas predominantly Serb. These were regions where ethnic cleansing was carried out by the Serbs in spring 1992. In eastern Bosnia, on the other hand, Serbs and Muslims could be found in roughly equal proportions in both the urban areas and the countryside. This may have contributed to the drawn-out and savage fighting in the region, since each side had its own ethnic pockets, protected by the rough terrain, while the urban population of each group, where it was a minority, was at risk. The siege of Sarajevo by the Serbs was meant to achieve strategic Serb objectives, yet in practical terms it reflected the presence of Serb villages surrounding the city, except to the southwest where the Muslims were in the majority, a fact that was to have great significance for the survival of Sarajevo during the three-year siege. (The distribution of ethnic groups around Sarajevo is shown to dramatic effect in the outstanding maps produced by Michel Foucher.)[28]

To a large degree, the conflict in Bosnia can be explained in terms of the contrast between the secessionist peripheral regions and the nationalist cultures that dominated them on the one hand, and the central multiethnic core and the civic culture just emerging in its cities on the other. As Enver Redžić has noted, it was the border areas of Bosnia that were subject to massacres and ethnic cleansing during World War II.[29] Yet this was certainly not the whole story. Chetnik villages—that is, villages that served as recruiting grounds for Serb nationalists—were to be found on Mt. Romanija, north of Sarajevo, and in central Bosnia. Konjic, on the periphery of central Bosnia, was a stronghold of Muslim extremists. Kiseljak, in central Bosnia, became a Croatian nationalist outpost. Even within a single urban area one could find concentrated populations with differing attitudes. For example, in Sarajevo it is necessary to distinguish between the old quarters and the areas where the "people from Sandžak" (Sandžaklija) were settled, as the latter were notably hostile to the Serbs. The killing of Serb civilians in the Pofalići quarter of Sarajevo in May 1992 may have resulted from the proximity of a Sandžak settlement. With the breakdown of civil order, these complex patterns played themselves out in Bosnia, destroying the fabric of civility that was still in its infancy after forty-five years of communist rule.

Nevertheless, once the nationalists were in the ascendancy, it was the conflict between the periphery and the center that posed the greatest dilemma for the Bosnian government. Even before fighting broke out in earnest in April 1992, the secessionist and violence-prone peripheries of the republic had largely broken off relations with the central government in Sarajevo. Regaining control of these regions—of western and eastern Herzegovina, of Bosanska Krajina, and even Cazinska Krajina—was not immediately possible for the Bosnian government. Yet it could not afford to recognize the independence or autonomy of these areas lest it forfeit its most precious asset—international recognition of the borders it had inherited from the communist era. At best, recognizing such areas as autonomous ran the risk of delineating boundaries that would have institutionalized the independence of dissident Muslim-, Serb-, and Croat-controlled regions; at worst, it ran the risk that such boundaries would become *de facto* borders and candidates for international recognition in much the same way that the borders of Bosnia itself had been recognized.

Bosnia Before World War II

It was against the backdrop of this ethnic mosaic that the turbulent history of Bosnia-Herzegovina unfolded in the nineteenth and twentieth centuries. This was, in brief, a history of peasant uprisings, wars, and foreign occupations, interspersed between periods of civil order.[30] During a period of roughly 75 years, from 1878 to 1941, Bosnia-Herzegovina experienced five different regimes. In the course of this relatively short period, the republic's quasi-feudal way of life was undermined and partially replaced by the two great forces shaping European society: nineteenth-century nationalism, and twentieth-century modernization. Three fundamentally conflicting political currents came to dominate politics in the province: the efforts of the Serbs to create a greater Serbia, the efforts by Croats to create a greater Croatia, and the efforts of local Muslim leaders to secure cultural and political autonomy for their people and preserve the territorial integrity of Bosnia-Herzegovina. The policies of the great powers toward the Bosnian question in the nineteenth century were guided by concerns for the balance of power in Europe rather than by any interest in resolving the conflict among these local interests. The "Eastern Question" in its entirety, from the time of the first uprising of the Greeks in the 1820s to the outbreak of World War I, posed many of the same dilemmas that challenged the international community following the collapse of modern Yugoslavia. Then, as now, Europe intervened reluctantly in the Balkans, driven by emotion and public reaction to atrocities committed by combatants, as well as by larger policy considerations. Then, as now, intervention revealed the differing sympathies of the European powers toward the combatants. Finally, the central question of Balkan politics, then as now, was whether to permit one or more of the Balkan nations to assert itself as the hegemonic power in the area by redrawing existing boundaries in response to ethnic claims, real or inflated.

The driving force behind local uprisings in the latter half of the nineteenth century was peasant rebellions. Largely Serb affairs, these uprisings were born of the desperate social conditions of the time and intertwined with the desires of the Serbs of Bosnia-Herzegovina to be united with Serbia. The peasant rebellion of 1875 led Serbia and Montenegro to declare war on Turkey in 1876, and Bulgarians to rise up against the Ottomans, which resulted in the Russo-Turkish war of 1877–78. The rebellion prompted the Bosnian Serbs to proclaim their union with Serbia, only to be disowned by the Serbian government after Serbia's defeat at the hands of the Turks. (Not to be deterred, the Serbs of Bosnia formed their own government with a Russian at its head.)[31] Earlier, in 1827 and again in 1832, the Bosnian Muslim ruling elites—the Janičari and Kapitani—had themselves revolted unsuccessfully against the Porte. In 1878, the Bosnian Muslims put up a strong resistance to the occupation of Bosnia-Herzegovina by the Austrians. In the course of an eighty-day campaign, Austria was compelled to increase its forces from 82,000 to 300,000, in order to oppose some 93,000, largely Muslim, volunteers. The war cost an estimated 150,000 lives, according to a Bosnian historian.[32] The Serb peasants staged a brief rebellion in 1881–82 against Austrian authorities in response to the introduction of conscription, joined by at least some of the Muslim peasants of eastern Bosnia. The most recent, and least known, uprising of the peasants of Bosnia took place in Cazinska Krajina in 1950 against communist efforts to impose collectivization. All three national groups participated; the incident, taking place in an area that had been a communist stronghold during World War II, may have played a role in the decision of the Tito regime to abandon forced collectivization in Yugoslavia.[33]

Beginning with the Austrian appointment of Benjamin Kalaj as head of a common Finance Ministry to administer Bosnia-Herzegovina in 1882, the almost medieval conditions of the peasants in Bosnia-Herzegovina slowly improved, and political events militated against Serb demands for union with Serbia. But the pattern of peasant uprisings, which was rooted in the traditions of the region as a military frontier, became deeply ingrained—and pitted the ethnic communities against one another. The Serbs came to associate the Bosnian Muslims with the "Turks"—a synonym for exploiters. Brigandage was not ended by the Austrians in the more remote regions of Herzegovina until the 1890s. Rebecca West, upon visiting Sarajevo in 1937, remarked upon Serb peasants who had descended to market: "They seem to clang with belligerence as if they wore armor. In every way, I hear, they are a formidable lot."[34] The uprisings of the peasants against the occupying powers during World War II, which once again united at least some elements of the Serb and Muslim populations against an external enemy, represented the climax of this tradition of peasant revolts and gave the Partisan forces of Tito their start.

The nationalist fervor of the nineteenth century also pitted Serbs against Croats. The 1890s were a period of pronounced rivalry between the Serbs and Croats over the fate of Bosnia-Herzegovina.[35] Croat nationalists entertained ambitions for the incorporation of all of Bosnia-Herzegovina into Croatia. Even for more moderate Croats, the future of Croatia and Bosnia-Herzegovina appeared to be linked with hopes for a tripartite Austrian–Hungarian–Croatian state. In Bosnia-Herzegovina itself, the *Franjevci*

(Franciscans) supported the Croatian National Union (*Hrvatska Narodna Zajednica*—HNZ). The HNZ welcomed Catholic Austria's annexation of Bosnia-Herzegovina in 1908, and adhered to the position that Bosnian Muslims were Croats.[36] While Muslim, Croat, and Serb nationalist movements fought for influence, the administration of Bosnia-Herzegovina remained firmly in the hands of Austrians and Croats. The scale of the Croat presence in the provincial capital, Sarajevo, is attested to by the results of the Austrian censuses, which categorized population by religion: between 1879 and 1910, Catholics increased from 3.3 percent to 34.52 percent of the population of the city.[37]

To counter these nationalist currents, the Austrians began in the 1890s to favor the idea of a territorially defined Bosnian nationalism, complete with its own flag and coat of arms. But the notion of "Bosnianism" (*Bošnjaštvo*) found only a limited reception. The Muslims, the group most amenable to the idea of a Bosnian nation, turned instead toward more active pursuit of religious, educational, and cultural autonomy for the Muslim community, and toward self-identification as *Muslimani*.[38] They remained for the most part wedded to the idea of retaining or reestablishing their ties with Turkey, provided Bosnia could enjoy autonomy. The annexation of Bosnia-Herzegovina by Austria in 1908, followed shortly thereafter by the Balkan wars and the expulsion of Turkey from the Balkans, dashed these hopes. It forced the Muslims to focus on gaining their religious, cultural, and educational autonomy within Austrian-ruled Bosnia-Herzegovina. This goal was largely achieved the following year, thanks to concessions by the Austrians.[39] During World War I, the Muslim attachment to Austria was cemented when Turkey entered the war on the side of the Central Powers. The belief was widespread among the Muslims at the time that Franz Joseph had struck a deal with the Turks, and that in the event of victory, Bosnia-Herzegovina would be returned to Turkey.[40] In actual fact, Austria and Hungary were engaged in discussions over partitioning Bosnia at the war's end.[41]

With the formation of Yugoslavia in 1918, the national issue in Bosnia-Herzegovina was overshadowed by the struggle between Croatian and Serbian conceptions of the Yugoslav state. The former, inspired by the dualist traditions of the Austrian empire, sought autonomy for Croatia. The latter, faithful to the traditions of nineteenth-century Serbia, championed the cause of a unitary state. For the first twenty years after 1918, Bosnia-Herzegovina remained under the administrative control of Belgrade. But the Muslims— with the exception of the period 1929–35—enjoyed *de facto* autonomy with respect to religious matters and education.[42] The administrative boundaries of historic Bosnia-Herzegovina were retained, in the "Turkish" clause of the Vidovdan constitution of 1921.[43] The Muslims of Bosnia-Herzegovina remained sentimentally tied to the Islamic world, but threw their political support behind the idea of Yugoslavia. Because the new South Slav state included virtually all Serbs, Croats, and Muslim Slavs within its borders, the preservation of that state and of harmonious relations among its nationalities became the *sine qua non* of Bosnian Muslim policy. This remained true through all the changes in regime that followed, until the collapse of Yugoslavia in 1991.

The Sporazum of 1939 placed Muslim politicians on notice that Serb-Croat agreement on a common state could only be achieved by the partition of Bosnia-Herzegovina. In this situation, Muslim demands for the autonomy of Bosnia-Herzegovina within Yugoslavia appeared futile. As a consequence, some Muslim political leaders were drawn toward abandoning the idea of Yugoslavia and aligning themselves with either the supporters of a "greater Serbia" or those of "greater Croatia" as a means of keeping Bosnia-Herzegovina intact, if not independent. According to Wayne Vucinich, Mehmed Spaho, leader of the Yugoslav Muslim Organization (JMO), urged that if Bosnia-Herzegovina could not gain autonomy, the Bosnian Muslims should support the inclusion of all Bosnia-Herzegovina in Serbia.[44] Spaho and his brothers epitomized the complex interplay of ethnic and religious identities among the Muslims: While Mehmed Spaho refused to declare an ethnic or national identity, one of his brothers (Fehim) declared Croat identity, yet went on to become *reis-ul-ulema,* or Islamic religious leader, while another (Mustafa) declared himself a Serb.[45] Džafer Kulenović, Spaho's successor as head of the JMO, supported the notion of a Croatian-sponsored "greater Bosnia" that would include the Sandžak. It was the pro-Croat faction within the JMO that finally carried the day following the collapse of the first Yugoslavia in 1941.

World War II and Its Aftermath

The outbreak of the war in Yugoslavia in April 1941 found the Muslim elites sharply divided in their loyalties. Some joined the communist Partisans. Others among the urban intelligentsia protested the Croatian Ustashe massacres of the Serbs.[46] But the most visible elements of the JMO, including Džafer Kulenović, joined the Ustashe government in Zagreb.[47] A number of Muslim peasants were conscripted into the Croatian military, or homeguard (*Domobrani*), and into local Croatian police and militia units.[48] In certain places, notably Mostar, the Muslim intelligentsia were well represented in the communist party, and helped organize the Partisan resistance movement, although under Serb names.[49] Very few Muslims served in the ranks of the Partisans until the closing days of the war.[50]

The excesses committed in Bosnia during World War II by the occupying powers and by the ethnic communities against one another left deep scars on the region. The massacres of Serbs in Bosnia-Herzegovina, in which hundreds of thousands perished,[51] were largely the work of the Croatian Ustashe. But it appears that Muslims also participated in the Ustashe atrocities, notably in eastern Herzegovina, where the Croats depended on locally recruited Muslims to carry out their work. The historian Kržišnik-Bukić suggests that Croats masqueraded as Muslims in similar actions in Cazinska Krajina.[52] In any event, the anger of the Serbs appeared to be directed as much toward the Muslims as the Croats. The town of Kulen-Vakuf was the scene of a massacre of over 1,000 Muslims by the Serbs in September 1941 after Ustashe excesses the previous summer against the Serbs in eastern Herzegovina.[53] Serb Chetniks massacred Muslim peasants in eastern Bosnia, in Foča, and in Goražde in December and January 1941–42 and February 1943.[54] In Cazinska Krajina the Muslim followers of Huska Miljković organized the "Green Cadre" (*Zeleni kadar*), following Miljković's death. The group joined the Ustashe in carrying out atrocities against the Serbs, and continued terrorist actions in the region for several years after the war was over.[55] Muslim units engaged in atrocities as part of the German-trained, largely Muslim Thirteenth SS Handžar division which saw action in Bosnia at the end of the war.[56] The division committed atrocities against Serbs in northwest and eastern Bosnia, notably in the area of Vlasenica, the site of extensive ethnic cleansing of the Muslims by the Serbs in 1992. A Muslim unit, the Legija Kempler, operated in the Sandžak region (in Serbia). Thus, the defeat of Yugoslavia at the outset of World War II and the occupation of Bosnia-Herzegovina by the Axis powers took on the dimensions of a violent civil conflict in which the three ethnic communities fought a war not only against the occupation forces, but against one another, as well.

Casualties in the civil war in Bosnia during World War II were immense. While the question of war losses in Bosnia, as in the rest of Yugoslavia, remains a matter of dispute, the data assembled by Bogoljub Kočović appear to be as accurate as any.[57] According to his estimates, 16.7 percent of the 1941 Serb population of Bosnia-Herzegovina, 12.8 percent of the Croat population, and 8.6 percent of the Muslim population were victims of the fighting. Kočović estimated total population losses at 668,000, or 23.7 percent of the total estimated population in 1941. Of these, approximately half were killed and half had fled the region.

The chaos of the civil war ultimately forced the Germans and Italians to make concessions to the Serb majority in Bosnia-Herzegovina. In spring 1942 the Germans persuaded the Croats to adopt a more lenient attitude toward the Serbs. Military pressure from the communist Partisan resistance led the Serbian Chetniks and Croatian Ustashe to conclude a series of agreements staking out their respective spheres of influence in eastern Bosnia.[58] At approximately the same time, the Nedić government in Belgrade approached the Germans with a proposal that eastern Bosnia be placed under its control.[59] Muslim leaders, in a panic at the prospect of a Serb-Croat agreement that might receive German endorsement, petitioned the German high command to separate Bosnia-Herzegovina from the Independent State of Croatia (NDH) and declare it a German protectorate.

Comparisons between the conflict in Bosnia during World War II and the war of 1992–95 must be made with caution. The conditions under which the two conflicts were fought were not the same. Between 1992 and 1995, the mountain fastnesses of Bosnia-Herzegovina were more accessible than during World War II. The weapons employed, especially heavy artillery and mines, changed the tactics of the warring parties. But at bottom, the similarities between the two conflicts were greater than the differences. None of the nationalist forces in either war was able to consolidate its hold over Bosnia. "Ethnic cleansing" proceeded in much the same way in 1992– 95 as in World War II, although it was not the practice during the war of 1992–95 to massacre noncombatant women and children *en masse.* Lucien Karchmar describes how in 1941 the first to be targeted were the local intelligentsia (in this case, during the massacres of Serbs carried out by the Ustashe in eastern Herzegovina):

> The system, which was also applied in other parts of NDH, was fairly simple. First the Serbs were ordered, under pain of death, to surrender all arms. Next, prominent local Serbs, such as politicians, officials, teachers, priests, and village merchants, were ordered to report to the police stations, and were then arrested and quietly liquidated; this had the effect of decapitating the Serbian community. Finally, the Ustasi [sic] proceeded to the massacre of entire villages, which were tackled one by one.[60]

We shall see in chapter 4 that this time around it was the Bosnian Serbs who committed such atrocities.

Despite the ethnic violence of World War II, the Yugoslav idea remained intact, thanks to the prospect of an Allied victory. The Partisans were able to convince many of the Serb peasants, and a certain number of Muslims, to rally behind their slogan of "brotherhood and unity" in the struggle against the occupier, and in support of a federal Yugoslavia. The Serbs in Bosanska Krajina, who had championed the Yugoslav idea and had been supporters of King Alexander's dictatorship and his party of Yugoslav unity, were a fertile recruiting ground for the Partisans.[61] The success of the Partisans showed that under certain conditions—above all, strict discipline and an internationalist-minded leadership—ethnic divisions among the peasants could be overcome. Some of these traditions of cooperation were to linger on when the conflict broke out in Bosnia in 1992, although they proved less strong than many analysts would have hoped or expected.

In the last analysis, the military victory of the Partisans in World War II could be attributed to the defeat of the Axis powers and the desire of the Allies to see Yugoslavia reconstituted after the war. The ability of the Communists to transform Bosnia-Herzegovina into a model of multiethnic, multicultural coexistence after the war was more surprising. The reasons must be sought above all in the authoritarian nature of the communist regime, which exercised absolute control over the ethnic communities in Bosnia. The communist regime was able to reassure all three groups that their security was not endangered in the new Yugoslavia. With the recognition of Bosnia-Herzegovina as a republic within Yugoslavia, the Communists were able to attract a broad range of support in Bosnia from both Muslims and Serbs. The greater Serbian and greater Croatian ideas, in turn, were discredited. The remarkable success of the Communists in consolidating power in Bosnia must therefore be attributed both to their draconian methods in eliminating the nationalists after the war, and the compatibility of their political message with the underlying pro-Yugoslav orientation of significant segments of the Bosnian population. By the same token, it was the disintegration of Yugoslavia in 1990 and 1991 that undercut the powerful Communist and Partisan traditions in Bosnia, especially among the Serbs. No better example could be given than the Serbs of Bosanska Krajina, whose Partisan heroism and defense of "brotherhood and unity" during World War II disappeared overnight with the breakup of Yugoslavia.

The National Question in Bosnia in the Titoist Period

The communist regime in Yugoslavia was at first highly centralized, but over the years evolved into a loose federal system, albeit one based on an authoritarian one-party system. Bosnia-Herzegovina was incorporated into the federal system created during World War II as a republic, equal in all respects to the other republics of Yugoslavia. Initially, the Muslims were looked upon with distrust and the Serbs dominated the leadership in Bosnia-Herzegovina. With the passage of time, however, it became evident that for the Muslim population of Bosnia-Herzegovina, communist Yugoslavia offered an opportunity for economic and social advancement as well as national equality. By the 1970s, a Muslim political elite had arisen—built on several closely knit political families—which rivaled and perhaps exceeded the power of the Bosnian Serbs. Recognition of the Muslims as a distinct group was initiated with the 1961 census of Yugoslavia, for which the answer "Muslim" was accepted as an ethnic but not a national category. Over 840,000 individuals in Bosnia declared Muslim identity in 1961. Official recognition of the Muslims as a nation, equal in status to the other nations of Yugoslavia, came with the adoption of a new constitution for the republic in 1963. Clearly, such a change could not have taken place without the approval of the communist party in Bosnia, and of the Yugoslav communist leadership in Belgrade. The reluctance of the Bosnian party to recognize Muslim claims as a nation was evident. Throughout the 1950s, the Bosnian party required Muslims in the party to declare another nationality,[62] and did not support national status for the Muslims until 1968.[63]

By 1968 recognition of Muslim nationality offered important political benefits to the Bosnian political leadership as a whole. The conflict between Serb and Croat nationalisms had broken out once again in Yugoslav politics, and was of increasing concern to the Bosnian leadership. While the threat of dismemberment of the republic remained distant, Croat and Serb nationalists were already active in the republic. Recognition of the Muslims as a distinct nationality with its own political status could therefore be seen as part of an attempt to avoid the historical competition between Serbs and Croats for the loyalties of Muslim cultural, intellectual, religious and, especially, political leaders. Distinct national status for the Muslims meant, in the context of a political system that was moving rapidly toward full political equality among its constituent republics and nations, access to an equal share of positions in the state and party bureaucracies of both the republic of Bosnia-Herzegovina and the Yugoslav federation. This fact was not lost on Muslim political leaders.[64]

Recognition of Muslim nationality was also facilitated by the emergence of an active Muslim intellectual elite, supportive of and loyal to the existing political order. These intellectuals advanced a secular national identity that was built upon the party's own ideology of interethnic equality. This identity was not an artificial construction of the communist regime, but an authentic one that reflected sentiments among the Muslim masses and was endorsed by the official religious hierarchy. The concept of Muslim nationhood developed by these intellectuals was at the same time carefully circumscribed: it included only Serbo-Croatian-speaking, Slavic Muslims, primarily those in Bosnia-Herzegovina and the neighboring former Turkish *sandžak* of Novi Pazar that had been part of the Bosnian *sandžak* before 1878 and was now divided between Serbia and Montenegro.

Muslim scholars did not, of course, all agree on a single definition of the Muslim nation or its origins. One of the most prominent Muslim scholars, however, summarized the national feeling of the Muslims as one that "is of a different quality from the feeling of solidarity with [other] Muslims in the world or even with [other] Yugoslav Muslims for whom Serbo-Croatian is not [their] mother tongue. . . ."[65] It "has shown stronger cohesive force" than identification with either the Serb or Croat nation, and "has been manifest in institutionalized forms . . . analogous to the situation among Serbs and Croats."[66] One of these forms is Islam, and the Islamic religious hierarchy, which plays a role analogous to Catholicism and the Catholic Church among the Croats, and Orthodoxy and the Orthodox Church among the Serbs. Thus, according to this scholar, while "it is necessary to distinguish the feeling of membership in the community of Bosnian Muslims from the feeling of Islamic membership," it is also "necessary to keep in mind that in practice one and the other feeling are often intertwined."[67] Muslims were recognized as a fully equal nation in the 1971 census, and each succeeding Yugoslav census.

From the late 1960s on, Bosnia-Herzegovina witnessed a remarkable social and cultural renaissance, focused on Sarajevo. Social and ethnic barriers began to break down in the urban areas as the number of mixed marriages and the number of those who chose to identify as Yugoslavs increased. By the 1981 census, those who for census purposes called themselves Yugoslavs constituted 7.9 percent of the population, three-quarters of whom were to be found in the largest cities. Mixed marriages accounted for 15.3 percent of the total number of marriages in the republic in 1981. However, 95.3 percent of Muslim women and 92.9 percent of Muslim men entered into homogeneous marriages. Intermarriage rates were higher among Serbs, and still higher among Croats. Most of the intermarriage in the republic was thus taking place among non-Muslims.[68] At the same time, Srdjan Bogosavljević has calculated that, if children of mixed marriages were included, over half the population of Bosnia had a close relative of a different nationality.[69]

Public manifestations of national intolerance were ruthlessly suppressed by the communist regime. No effort was spared to assure, at least in theory, that the three national groups had equal access to education, jobs, and positions of responsibility in the government and the party. As fear and mistrust began to subside, the new intelligentsia in Bosnia found inspiration in the intertwined cultural values of urban Bosnia, and fused them with what might be called the modern outlook of civil society. This produced in Bosnia the same mix of secularism, dissent, and pro-Europeanism that dominated the intellectual scene elsewhere in Yugoslavia and across most of Eastern Europe in the 1970s and the 1980s. The 1984 winter Olympics in Sarajevo mirrored these developments, and established Sarajevo as a symbol of the new tolerance among nations that Europe had embraced.

The republic also made rapid economic progress, thanks in a large part to the federal leadership's decision to locate a large proportion of its defense industries in the more easily defended mountainous territory of the republic. Economic development was reflected in the rate of urbanization. The urban population accounted for 36.2 percent of the population in 1981, up from 19.5 percent in 1971.[70] But the republic remained less developed in comparison to other republics. GNP per capita was 35 percent below the Yugoslav average in 1981. The lower level of development of the republic contributed to a substantial net out-migration from the republic. Out-migration consisted very largely of Serbs migrating to Serbia and Croats migrating to Croatia. Migration of Muslims into and out of the republic was approximately in balance. Social development in the republic also presented a mixed picture. Illiteracy remained high among the female population (23.3 percent in 1981), but was lower among men (5.5 percent). The proportion of the population age 15 or older with completed secondary education in 1981 was 21.7 percent (up from about 4 percent of the population age 10 or older in 1953), but that with post-secondary education only 4.3 percent (up from 0.3 percent).[71] The level of development of the republic varied among its regions and, especially, between urban and rural areas.

Political development did not keep pace with economic and cultural development, however, and this proved to be a fatal weakness. As Yugoslavia evolved into a complex, and initially successful, model of authoritarian consociationalism, the political elite in Bosnia-Herzegovina remained highly orthodox, with a reputation for repression of political dissent. Politics remained cadre-driven, and the monopoly of a narrow circle of politicians. Responsibility for resolving ethnic disputes rested with this small group of Communists, for whom national feelings appeared secondary to considerations of power and control. Bosnia-Herzegovina was thus rigidly governed, and its broader social elites were without any experience in genuine power-sharing when the collapse of Yugoslavia left them on their own.

The political bottleneck in Bosnia-Herzegovina was intensified by the uncertain status of the Muslims as a political force, and the ambiguity of their relationship to the republic. At the level of the federation, the loyalty of the Muslim political elite and the new Muslim intelligentsia to Yugoslavia was unquestioned. Indeed, Bosnia was the source for much of the dwindling intellectual support for "Yugoslavism" in the 1970s and '80s. Yet this political loyalty did not translate into political influence in the federation, where the determination of federal policies remained concentrated in the hands of the Serbs, Croats, and Slovenes. In Bosnia-Herzegovina itself, recognition of the Muslims as a nationality, and the growing share of the Muslims in the republic population, raised the possibility that they would lay claim to the role of the "constitutive" or titular nationality, arousing unease among the Serbs.[72] This unease was reinforced by the growth in Islamic consciousness and organizational activity evident in Bosnia-Herzegovina in the 1970s.[73] Serb disquiet was not allayed by efforts on the part of some Muslim intellectuals to revive the notion of "Bosnianism" in place of "Muslimness" as a basis for defining the Muslims' claim to power in the republic.[74]

The Muslims' struggle for political and social equality was jeopardized by a campaign against Islamic fundamentalism, launched by Belgrade, which culminated in the trial of a number of Muslim intellectuals (including Alija Izetbegović) in 1983.[75] The pressure on the new Muslim elites spread to the political realm in the 1980s. The Agrokomerc affair of 1987 focused on the financial fraud perpetrated by Fikret Abdić, centered in Cazinska Krajina and the agro-industrial enterprise "Agrokomerc." But it also had a political objective: the discrediting of the old-guard Muslim political elites. The affair was followed by revelations of the high lifestyle and corruption of Bosnian communist leaders, which left the political leadership in Bosnia-Herzegovina in disarray. The political stock of the republic was also undermined by the poor performance of Bosnian Croat leader Branko Mikulić as prime minister of Yugoslavia. Until his removal in 1990, Mikulić resisted economic and political reform, thereby contributing to the systemic crisis in Yugoslavia and assuring his own political demise.

The political disarray in Bosnia-Herzegovina in the late 1980s was the first of many setbacks to befall the republic, for it opened the way for the sweeping victory of the nationalist parties in 1990. One wonders why the Communists, who enjoyed a great deal of grass-roots support in the republic, could not have developed a more capable and respected group of politicians. The source of the leadership problem appears to have been the oligarchic power of old-guard family cliques, the sweeping purge of the younger generation of leaders that followed the Agrokomerc affair mentioned above, and the inability of Bosnian intellectuals to formulate a new political doctrine suitable to an open, politically multinational society and attractive to Bosnian Serbs and Croats. At the same time, the conservatism and repressiveness of Bosnian politics prevented the emergence of alternative, democratically inclined leaders who might have bridged the growing divide between the Muslims and the Serbs.

At this critical juncture—the end of the 1980s—Slobodan Milošević seized control of Serbian political structures and assumed the leadership of a growing Serb nationalist movement that cut across republic boundaries, including those of Bosnia-Herzegovina. Mass meetings aimed at ousting the entrenched communist elites in Kosovo, Montenegro, and Vojvodina left the League of Communists of Yugoslavia (LCY) in total disarray. The period 1987–91 saw a profound change in Yugoslav society, marked by the end of one-party rule, the polarization of public opinion along national lines, and growing demands for secession by Slovenia and Croatia.

These developments affected Bosnia-Herzegovina in fundamental ways. Although the communist political elite was under attack from within and without, it was united in opposing the Serb nationalist campaign. Serb nationalism threatened to undo the Bosnian social compact, built on loyalty to Titoism, and to polarize Bosnian society along ethnic lines..The Bosnian party could not just simply "change its spots" as the communist party of Serbia did under Milošević. Its membership was multiethnic. Although Serbs constituted the largest single group in the party (42.8 percent in 1982), Muslims and Croats together outnumbered them (35.0 and 11.9 percent, respectively). And, in a reflection of both demographic and political realities, the Muslim share of the party was increasing over time. Those declaring Yugoslav identity also represented, at least in 1982, an important party constituency, comprising 8.4 percent of the membership.[76] None of these non-Serb constituencies would accept a Serb nationalist orientation. Moreover, the communist elite was itself nominally tri-ethnic and, as later events would show, genuinely opposed to nationalism.

The rank-and-file Serb party members in Bosnia behaved quite differently. They defected in large numbers to the nationalist Serb Democratic Party (SDS). Milošević formed an alliance with the SDS. The familiar dynamic by which increasing Serb and Croat nationalisms engendered rising Muslim consciousness took hold once again. The Muslims confronted two choices: either union with Serbia or Croatia as the means by which to preserve the territorial integrity of Bosnia-Herzegovina, or partition between its two more powerful neighbors. Unlike the past, however, a third choice now also seemed possible: following the lead of Slovenia and Croatia and opting for outright independence.

Had Milošević subverted Bosnia-Herzegovina politically, or had communist leaders persuaded the Serbs in Bosnia to remain faithful to the Bosnian communist party at the time of the elections in December 1990, it is at least within the realm of speculation that events might have taken a different course. Either development might have resulted in the republic's falling into the Serbian sphere of influence and becoming part of rump Yugoslavia (along with Montenegro and Serbia). But the latter outcome might also have made it possible for Bosnia-Herzegovina to succeed in establishing a genuinely multi-ethnic, independent republic.

Competitive Elections and Ethnic Polarization

From the end of 1988, however, and especially in the months preceding the elections of 1990, the polarization of Bosnian society along national lines gained momentum. Mass rallies of Serbs in support of Milošević, and among the Croats in support of Croat independence, took place during summer and fall 1989. In early February 1989 *Borba* published an article reporting that the process of internal homogenization and mutual differentiation of the ethnic communities was already under way.[77] Following the fragmenting of the Yugoslav communist party into separate republic organizations pursuing separate—and conflicting—agendas in January 1990, the Bosnian party leadership, like other republic leaderships, accepted the establishment of opposition parties. But they did so on condition that such parties not be established along national lines. They also pushed for early elections, to be held in spring 1990, before nationalist forces had had time to organize. The leadership relented only when it became clear that there would be no organized parties to contest the elections, thereby endangering their legitimacy.[78]

In preparation for the upcoming elections, the Bosnian parliament adopted an electoral law in March 1990 that banned political organization on the basis of nationality (ethnicity). The Constitutional Court, headed at the time by Dr. Kasim Trnka—who would later become an active member of the SDA leadership—declared this provision unconstitutional and removed it from the law under which the 1990 elections were later conducted. This accelerated the organization of opposition parties along national lines.[79] More than forty political organizations were established in the republic in the course of 1990. Most of these were exceedingly small. They either formed coalitions, or were of no consequence in the politics of the republic. Electoral competition was dominated by three explicitly ethnic, and *de facto* nationalist, parties created in 1990. Two nonethnic, antinationalist parties consisting of former Communists and communist-era elites also played an important role in the elections.

The Party of Democratic Action (*Stranka Demokratske Akcije*—SDA) was created in March 1990 and led by Alija Izetbegović.[80] Izetbegović had been an active proponent of expanding the role of Islam in public life and politics. Although he carefully avoided specifically advocating the establishment of an "Islamic state" in Bosnia, the call for a greater role for Islam contained in his *Islamic Declaration* of 1970 was widely interpreted as referring to Bosnia. It was for these views that he had twice been imprisoned under the Communists. He represented a faction of the SDA inclined toward an identity defined largely in terms of Islam, and intent on securing a dominant role for the Muslims in Bosnia-Herzegovina. While the party formally affirmed support for the continuation of a Yugoslav state, it defined that state as "a community of sovereign nations and republics, within current federal borders."[81] Thus, the SDA appeared sympathetic to the emerging Slovenian-Croatian tendency advocating the confederalization of Yugoslavia, if not outright secession. Izetbegović made it clear during the election campaign that if these republics did secede, then he would not keep Bosnia-Herzegovina "in a mangled Yugoslavia, in other words, in a greater Serbia."[82] In a speech to an election rally in Velika Kladuša in September, Izetbegović declared

> . . . there are three options for Bosnia: Bosnia in a federal Yugoslavia—an acceptable option; Bosnia in a confederal Yugoslavia—also an acceptable option; and finally an independent and free Bosnia. I must say here openly that if the threat that Croatia and Slovenia leave Yugoslavia is carried out, Bosnia will not remain in a truncated Yugoslavia. In other words, Bosnia will not tolerate staying in a greater Serbia and being part of it. If it comes to that, we will declare independence, the absolute independence of Bosnia and we will decide then in what new constellation Bosnia will find itself, as a sovereign republic that will use its sovereignty.[83]

The overtly Islamic and Muslim nationalist orientation of the SDA leadership around Izetbegović led to a split with the more secular Muslims within the party led by Adil Zulfikarpašić, who formed his own Muslim party, the Muslim Bosniak Organization, or MBO, in October 1990.[84] This party held little appeal outside of liberal Muslim circles.

The Serb Democratic Party (*Srpska Demokratska Stranka Bosne i Hercegovine*—SDS) was established in July 1990. Led by Radovan Karadžić, the SDS functioned as the nationalist leadership of the Serbs in Bosnia, opposed to any form of Bosnian independence from Yugoslavia, or to any changes in Bosnia itself that might subject the Serb minority to rule by an ethnically alien majority.[85] At the October founding of the Serb national council in Banja Luka, the leadership formally declared that they would not accept any changes adopted by representative institutions "instead of the people," and would recognize only those decisions taken "on the basis of a referendum of the Serb people."[86] Despite the dominant role of the SDS among the Bosnian Serbs in the 1990 elections and their aftermath, the Serbs were in fact internally politically fragmented. Suad Arnautović, for example, cites the existence of about twenty "particularly active" examples of local Serb political parties that participated in the 1990 elections. He calls these organizations "satellite" parties of the SDS in an effort to discount their significance.[87] But their activity reflected the real political significance of localism among the Bosnian Serbs. The Muslims, in contrast, were more cohesive politically and, according to Arnautović, "had no need to form their own satellite parties."[88]

The Croatian Democratic Union of Bosnia-Herzegovina (*Hrvatska Demokratska Zajednica Bosne i Hercegovine*—HDZ) was established in August 1990 as a branch of the ruling HDZ party in Croatia. The positions of the party reflected precisely those of the leadership in Croatia. It called for the independence of the republic. But, at the same time, the party declared it would support "realization of the right of the Croat people to self-determination including secession."[89] It was soon torn by rivalry between moderates who supported the integrity of Bosnia-Herzegovina, and extreme nationalists seeking to partition the republic and join Croat-populated areas to Croatia.

While the three nationalist party leaderships mobilized and politicized ethnic identities, two other major parties adopted non-nationalist positions and attempted to appeal across ethnic boundaries on the basis of liberal ideals. Both linked their appeals to support for the preservation of the Yugoslav federation, a preference supported by over 69 percent of the respondents in a public opinion survey conducted in the republic in June 1990.[90] The Bosnian communist party, formally the League of Communists of Bosnia-Herzegovina, transformed itself into a party supporting pluralistic political democracy and a market-based economy. It supported continuation of the Yugoslav federation, but called for maximum autonomy for the constituent republics. It tried to appeal to voters in nonethnic terms, affirming the full equality of all citizens. It adopted the name League of Communists–Social Democratic Party (*Savez Komunista–Socijalistička Demokratska Partija*, SK–SDP), and was led by Nijaz Duraković, an ethnic Muslim Communist. Despite polls suggesting that they would secure more support than any other party in the republic, the reformed communists of Bosnia-Herzegovina turned out to be politically the weakest of all the former communist regional party organizations. They secured the smallest proportion of the popular vote and the smallest parliamentary representation of any of the former ruling parties in the Yugoslav republics.

The failure of the SK-SDP reflected, in part, the fact that the nationalist parties—or, at least, the HDZ and the SDA—appear to have captured the anticommunist vote as well as the nationalist vote in Bosnia-Herzegovina. No clearly reformist, noncommunist, and non-nationalist party competed for power in the elections.[91] The Alliance of Reform Forces of Yugoslavia (*Savez Reformskih Snaga Jugoslavije*—SRSJ) was the closest thing to such a party. It was formed in August 1990 to support federal Prime Minister Ante Marković in his efforts to preserve a reformed, democratized Yugoslav federation, and to continue the program of economic reforms initiated with great success by his government. The Bosnian branch was headed by Nenad Kecmanović, rector of Sarajevo University and a prominent Serb exponent of liberal political views on both Bosnian and Yugoslav politics. The SRSJ functioned as an umbrella organization for many smaller, local groups with liberal-democratic and reformist views.[92] But it did not appeal to voters who supported Bosnian independence from Yugoslavia. Arnautović concludes, on the basis of pre-election survey data and voting patterns, that

> The political consciousness of voters in Bosnia-Herzegovina in the '90 elections was obviously determined by national identity in its most abstract form, which at that time did not have any greater political definition than Serb, Croat, or Muslim (conservative, liberal, social democratic, etc.). By such voting, the electorate of Bosnia-Herzegovina showed that it was not interested in the civil option for the organization of political life in Bosnia-Herzegovina, and especially not for the continuation of communist rule (not even if reformed).[93]

The elections to fill both chambers of parliament and to determine the members of the collective state presidency were held in November 1990. The elections combined proportionality rules of representation for the Chamber of Citizens, and majoritarian rules for the Chamber of Municipalities (opštine) and for the presidency. The ethnic composition of the parliament that resulted from these elections was required to conform—within a 15-percent deviation—to the ethnic composition of the population recorded in the 1991 census. Arnautović observes that "the electoral law and other accompanying electoral regulations promoted a completely new (old) political profile, and that was ethnic identity as the basis of political representation or political legitimacy."[94] Elections to the Chamber of Citizens were conducted on the basis of seven large, multi-member districts (shown in Map 2.5), within which seats were distributed proportionally on the basis of the total number of valid votes cast.[95] Preliminary data reported in Oslobodjenje suggests a very high proportion of the votes cast were declared invalid in each of the districts (see Table 2.3). It is impossible to determine the significance of this, except to note that about a quarter of the electorate was in this way excluded from determining the composition of the parliament. There were a total of 130 seats in the chamber. The Chamber of Municipalities consisted of 110 single-member districts, which corresponded to existing opštine, or counties (usually translated in official materials as "municipalities," a translation that tends to obscure the fact that these units ranged in character from sparsely populated rural areas to densely populated urban centers). Elections in these districts were based on

Map 2.5 **Electoral Districts, Chamber of Citizens, 1990**

1 - Bihać: 9 delegates
2 - Banja Luka: 25 delegates
3 - Doboj: 14 delegates
4 - Tuzla: 28 delegates
5 - Zenica: 15 delegates
6 - Sarajevo: 25 delegates
7 - Mostar: 15 delegates

Adapted from Suad Arnautović, *Izbori u Bosni i Hercegovini '90* (Sarajevo: Promocult, 1996), p. 136.

a majoritarian principle. If no candidate achieved a majority in the first round of voting, the two candidates who achieved the highest number of votes competed in a second round, or runoff election.

The results of the elections are shown in Tables 2.3–2.6 (pages 52–54). Although the three nationalist parties dominated the voting, almost one-quarter of the seats in the Chamber of Citizens were won by non-nationalist parties—most of them by the SK-SDP and SRSJ (see Tables 2.3 and 2.4). The majoritarian-based elections to the Chamber of Municipalities, however, effectively excluded the non-nationalist parties from power. Based on available data,[96] the SK-SDP and SRSJ, for example, appear to have shown far greater electoral strength in the *opštine* than is indicated by the small number of seats they were able to secure. The former communists won 20–24 percent of the vote in the first round in 15 districts they failed to win, and 25 percent or more in an additional 8 districts they failed to win. The SRSJ secured 20–24 percent of the vote in 7 districts they did not win, and more than 25 percent in another district. The combined vote for these parties exceeded 30 percent in over 20 districts in which neither party won. These included districts in such major cities as Jajce, Sarajevo (four districts), Travnik, and even Zenica, a city now seen as a bastion of extreme Islamic nationalism. In most of these districts, however, these results failed to produce even a run-off. In several districts, one or the other non-nationalist party lost the run-off to one of the nationalist parties. These distortions were compounded by the population differentials between electoral units. In several instances, the non-nationalist parties secured more votes in a losing effort than nationalist candidates did in winning efforts in less-populous districts. Turnout for second-round elections was in almost every instance substantially below the 80 percent recorded in the first round, further favoring the most highly mobilized, or nationalist electorates. The final distribution of seats, which differs slightly from the results shown in Table 2.4, is presented in Table 2.5.

Perhaps the most accurate reflection of the real strength of the non-nationalist parties is to be found in the results of elections to the local, or county (opština), assemblies. The accumulated results of these elections for the republic as a whole are presented in Table 2.6. Results for the individual assemblies reveal that the non-nationalist parties secured 25 percent or more of the seats in 31 out of 109 assemblies.[97] These results, together with available data for the elections to the Chamber of Municipalities of the republic parliament, suggest that, had a proportionality rule been adopted for the republic-level elections, the non-nationalist parties would have secured a significantly greater voice in Bosnian politics in 1990.

The elections to the collective state presidency, held coterminously with those to parliament, required the voter to choose seven members, two from each of the three major ethnic communities, and one "Other," that is, a "Yugoslav." The results of the balloting are shown in Table 2.7. The result was a victory for the nationalists. Fikret Abdić, victim of the Agrokomerc scandal and immensely popular among the Muslims, won the greatest number of votes, entitling him to claim the post of president of the collective presidency. Nonetheless, the post went to the leader of the SDA and second-largest vote-getter, Alija Izetbegović. Nijaz Duraković, the Muslim head of the SK-SDP, secured 23.85 percent of the vote, but failed to qualify for either of the two seats reserved for Muslims. Similarly, Nenad Kecmanović, leader of the SRSJ, won 21.40 percent of the vote, but was outpolled for the two Serb seats by the candidates of the SDS—Biljana Plavšić, an outspoken nationalist, and Nikola Koljević. Stjepan Kljujić and

Table 2.3

Distribution of Votes for Major Parties, Chamber of Citizens, 1990
(in percent of valid votes, first results)

Major Parties

Regions	SDA	SDS	HDZ	SK-SDP	SRSJ	DSS	MBO	Invalid votes*
Banja Luka	21.83	40.85	11.24	10.50	7.32	3.14	—	23.4
Doboj	19.41	23.11	23.05	12.57	12.21	1.30	2.38	27.5
Mostar	7.04	14.35	71.59	2.27	1.95	0.31	0.18	11.8
Sarajevo	32.63	22.97	7.97	13.38	11.27	1.48	1.85	24.9
Zenica	41.17	8.81	26.29	13.66	3.52	1.76		21.0
Tuzla	36.04	27.15	8.38	13.78	6.14	—	1.54	27.5
Bihać	63.20	21.56	0.44	5.97	3.29	6.50	0.91	25.4

Key:
SDA: Party of Democratic Action
SDS: Serb Democratic Party
HDZ: Croatian Democratic Union
SK-SDP: League of Communists–Social Democratic Party
SRSJ: Alliance of Reform Forces of Yugoslavia
DSS: Democratic Socialist Alliance
MBO: Muslim Bosniak Organization

Source: Oslobodjenje, November 20, 1990, p. 3.
*Percent of all votes cast declared invalid.

Franjo Boras, candidates of the HDZ, qualified for the two seats reserved for Croats with fewer votes than were secured by Kecmanović. The third-largest number of votes went to one of the candidates for the position reserved for "Yugoslavs." But this result was not a reflection of the strength of the nonethnic, multiethnic, or pro-Yugoslavia sentiment in the republic. The vote was secured by Ejup Ganić, a candidate of the SDA and a member of the hardline nationalist faction of the Muslim leadership. His candidacy for the "Yugoslav" seat reflected the cynicism and even contempt with which the emerging nationalist leaders viewed the concept of power-sharing.

The elections delivered substantial political power to the Muslims, but not enough for them to rule without support from another party, or parties. In the flush of victory, the nationalist parties pledged to cooperate with one another. But no consideration was given to extending cooperation to the non-nationalist parties in an effort to establish a "grand coalition." Instead, an uneasy "partnership" was established among the nationalists. It was reported that the parties had adopted a consensus rule,[98] and a division of the three most prominent positions in the state leadership was achieved after only moderately difficult negotiations.[99] Izetbegović assumed the most visi-

Table 2.4

Distribution of Seats by Electoral Region, Chamber of Citizens, 1990

	Total	Parties							
		SDA	SDS	HDZ	SK-SDP	SRSJ	DSS	MBO	SSO–DS/EKO
Regions									
Banja Luka	25	5	12	3	2	2	1	—	—
Doboj	14	3	4	3	2	2	—	—	—
Mostar	15	3	2	8	1	1	—	—	—
Sàrajevo	24	9	6	1	3	3	—	1	1
Zenica[a]	15	6	2	4	2	1[c]	—	—	—
Tuzla	28	11	6	2	4[b]	3	—	1	1
Bihać	9	6	2	—	1	—	—	—	—
Total	130	43	34	21	15	12	1	2	2

Key:
SSO-DS/EKO: Alliance of Socialist Youth–Democratic Party/Ecology Movement (Greens)
All other labels as in Table 2.3.

Source: Suad Arnautović, Izbori u Bosnia i Hercegovini '90. (Sarajevo: Promocult, 1996), pp. 109–110, and Oslobodjenje, November 24, 1990, p. 3.
[a]Arnautović reports only 3 HDZ delegates. Oslobodjenje (November 24, 1990) reports 4. The latter count is consistent with the overall count of HDZ delegates in the Chamber.
[b]Elected on a coalition platform (SK-SDP/DSS).
[c]Elected on a coalition platform (SRSJ/DP-Mostar).

ble office, president of the state presidency, as representative of the SDA; Jure Pelivan, a Croat and representative of the HDZ, was chosen as prime minister, and Momčilo Krajišnik, a Serb of the SDS, was made president of the National Assembly.

The lack of goodwill and argumentativeness of the three nationalist parties produced a dispute over appointments on the very first day of parliamentary work. Members from the SDS objected to nomination of an SDA candidate for general secretary of the parliament. Significantly, they claimed that the SDA failed to consult with the other parties over this position, a charge that was not denied by the SDA. Debate over the proposed text for the ceremonial oath of office produced further acrimony. Disputes broke out over the definition of "Yugoslavia" allegedly implied by the text. One Serb SDS member demanded that the oath be printed in the Cyrillic as well as the Latin alphabet. Croat members demanded that it be "translated" into Croatian (the only issue in this case, it appears, was one letter: the perceived difference between demokratija and demokracija). The

Table 2.5

Final Distribution of Seats, Chamber of Citizens and Chamber of Municipalities, 1990

Party	Chamber of citizens		Chamber of municipalities	
	Seats	Percent	Seats	Percent
PDA	43	33.00	43	39.09
SDS	34	26.15	38	34.64
HDZ	21	16.15	23	20.93
SK-SDP	11	8.50	3	2.72
SRSJ	11	8.50	1	0.90
SK-SDP/DSS	4	3.00	1	0.90
DSS	1	0.75		
MBO	2	1.50		
SRS/DP-Mostar	1	0.75		
SSO-DS/EKO	2	1.50		
SPO			1	0.90
Total	130	100.00	110	100.00

Key:
SRS/DP-Mostar: Serbian Radical Party/Democratic Party (Mostar)
SSO-DS/EKO: Alliance of Socialist Youth–Democratic Party/Ecology Movement
        (Greens)
SPO: Serb Party of Renewal
All other labels as in Table 2.3.
   Source: Arnautović, *Izbori u Bosni i Hercegovini*, p. 108.

Table 2.6

Proportion of Seats in Local Assemblies Secured by Major Parties, 1990

Parties	Number of seats	Percent of seats
SDA	1,888	29.97
SDS	1,801	28.59
HDZ	1,085	17.22
SK-SDP	571	9.06
SRSJ	414	6.57
SK-SDP/DSS	148	2.34
DSS	104	1.65
SSO-DS	70	1.10
Left Bloc	57	0.90
MBO	45	0.71
SPO	20	0.31
Other	95	1.50

   Source: Arnautović, *Izbori u Bosni i Hercegovini*, p. 118.

Table 2.7

Presidential Vote, 1990 (top three candidates only)

Name	Number of votes	Percent of votes
Muslim Candidates		
Fikret Abdić–SDA*	1,045,539	44.68
Alija Izetbegović–SDA*	879,266	37.57
Nijaz Duraković–SK-SDP	558,263	23.85
Serb Candidates		
Biljana Plavšić–SDS*	573,812	24.52
Nikola Koljević–SDS*	556,218	23.77
Nenad Kecmanović–SRSJ	500,783	21.40
Croat Candidates		
Stjepan Kljujić–HDZ*	473,002	20.21
Franjo Boras–HDZ*	416,629	17.80
Ivo Komšić-SK–SDP	353,707	15.11
Other Nations and Nationalities		
Ejup Ganić–SDA*	709,891	30.33
Ivan Čerešnješ–SDS	362,681	15.50
Josip Pejaković–SRSJ	317,978	13.58

Total votes cast = 2,339,958 (74.42 percent of registered voters).

Source: Arnautović, *Izbori u Bosni i Hercegovini*, p. 104.
*Denotes elected candidates.

latter demand was opposed by an SDS member who suggested sarcastically that the oath might also then be translated into "Muslim."[100] The deterioration in relations among the self-proclaimed partners in government was reflected during the debate over appointment of the secretary-general when the vice president of the SDA, Muhamed Čengić, referred in his remarks to the SDS as the opposition, and disputed its right to participate in negotiations over the division of government positions.[101]

Things were no better at the local (*opština*) level. The parties contested bitterly the division of government power in several mixed areas. In Bijeljina, for example, the SDA refused to participate in local parliamentary sessions in which the SDS, using its parliamentary majority, elected its own members to both of the two leading government positions, instead of splitting them with the SDA.[102] Similar disputes were unfolding in Banja Luka,

Goražde, and other communities and were to carry on into the war period, as we shall see subsequently.[103]

The initial mood of euphoria occasioned by the ouster of the Communists rapidly gave way to a fear of impending conflict. The Serbs, claiming that they were facing a coalition of Croats and Muslims that was disregarding Serb interests, declined to participate in the activity of the parliament. In fall 1991, the Serbs began to form Serb Autonomous Oblasts (SAOs), which took over power, in practice, from the central governmental authorities. The stage was set for a confrontation over the fate of Bosnia.

The Choice Between Accommodation and Conflict

Among the myriad causes of the war that followed—about which we shall have more to say in the chapter to follow—the outcome of the elections of 1990 was certainly crucial. It was a tragedy of the first order that the first truly free elections in Bosnia-Herzegovina should have delivered power to three nationalist parties claiming to represent the three ethnic communities, rather than to either of the non-nationalist forces, democratic or former communist. Two questions thus come to mind: Could this outcome have been avoided? And, if not, was Bosnia-Herzegovina inevitably headed toward civil war and partition?

The victory of the nationalist parties in the elections of 1990 was in some sense fraudulent, based on fear rather than on popular support for the views of the nationalists themselves. The timing of elections in Bosnia-Herzegovina contributed to increasing the dominance of ethnic identities in defining the pattern of voting, and to pushing the three nationalist parties toward conflict. By November 1990, the Yugoslav crisis had entered its final, dramatic stage. The Bosnian elections were held months after elections in Slovenia and Croatia had installed independence-minded governments in those two republics. They also came months after the outbreak of conflict between the nationalist government in Zagreb and the Serb minority in Croatian Krajina, mobilized by Serb nationalists with ties to Belgrade. That conflict intensified the politicization of the Serb and Croat communities in Bosnia-Herzegovina—a process stoked by exhumations of the mass graves of the victims of genocide in World War II.[104] The rise of extreme Serb nationalism in Serbia, and especially the repression of the Albanian minority in Kosovo, had made the prospect of remaining part of a Yugoslav state that did not contain Slovenia and Croatia, and thereby constituted little more than a greater Serbia, intolerable for the Muslim nationalist leadership. Moreover, the example of Serb efforts to dismember the Croatian republic hardened non-Serb leaders in Bosnia against compromise. On the eve of the Bosnian elections, the Slovenian and Croatian leaderships proposed their program for confederalization of the Yugoslav state, increasing the probability that the federation would not survive. Thus, the elections in Bosnia-Herzegovina unfolded in a context that called into question the republic's continued survival.

Everywhere, a feeling of fear drove persons to vote for the nationalist parties, even when they did not necessarily support these parties' aims. Arnautović presents a wealth of pre-election survey data demonstrating that, among Serbs and Muslims, support for the main nationalist party (the SDS and SDA, respectively) was exceeded by support for the main non-nationalist parties (SRSJ and SK-SDP), although support for the nationalist parties gradually increased over time while support for the main non-nationalist parties eroded.[105] Ljiljana Smajlović suggests that Serbs "simply acted out of fear that even if they withheld their vote from a Karadžić, their Muslim neighbor would still give his vote to an Izetbegović. In the end, they were afraid of weakening their own nation in an hour presaging the ultimate confrontation."[106] Arnautović suggests that "the elections in Bosnia-Herzegovina were characterized by the phenomenon of 'negative voting,' in which a significant number of citizens voted for one party only in order to prevent the victory of some other, and not because of the quality of the program or candidate of that party."[107]

In the second round of voting, for 54 seats in the Chamber of Municipalities, the non-nationalist parties lost a dozen contests to the SDA. The argument is often made that the nationalist parties traded votes in this round to ensure such outcomes. But the data reported in the Bosnian press suggest that these outcomes may have been the result of the unwillingness of losing nationalist voters to cross over to the non-nationalists, and the failure of non-nationalist voters to turn out a second time after having seen that the Muslim SDA secured the largest share of the vote on the first round.

There were some exceptions to these patterns in the voting; notably in Tuzla, a working-class city of mixed ethnic composition, where a coalition of the SK-SDP and the SRSJ was victorious. These parties secured the largest share of even the first-round vote, and all three nationalist parties fared poorly. With the outbreak of the war, the three ethnic groups cooperated in the defense of Tuzla, and largely avoided ethnic discord for the first month of the conflict. We have already noted that the two main non-nationalist parties secured 30 percent or more of the vote in over 20 districts, including several other major urban centers. Later, when we deal with the outbreak of the war, we shall see that there were a significant number of municipalities where efforts were made to ease the tensions that had been created by the nationalist parties, and thus to avoid interethnic violence.

It must remain a matter of speculation whether different election procedures might have influenced the outcome of the voting in 1990, or whether earlier elections would have produced a different outcome. Even under the most favorable rules of proportionality, the non-nationalists would not have secured a parliamentary majority. For them to have had a moderating effect on Bosnian politics would have required cooperation on the part of one or more of the nationalist parties. As we have seen, there appears to have been no inclination among the nationalists to cooperate with former communists.

Thus, Bosnia-Herzegovina, like most of the republics of the former Yugoslavia, was ill-prepared to assume the responsibilities of independence. By the 1990s, Western social scientists were converging around some basic principles for managing intergroup conflict in multinational societies. The dominant view was that power-sharing arrangements and proportional representation of some kind were effective institutional arrangements for managing conflict. The success of such arrangements, however, depends in large part on the behavior of elites.[108] It is clear that, in the case of Bosnia, power-sharing was never fully implemented, and elite behaviors never were fully consistent with the cooperative approach necessary to make such arrangements work. We shall see in chapter 3 how the opportunity to institute power-sharing was lost with the declaration of Bosnia's independence.

The victory of the nationalist parties in Bosnia-Herzegovina was part of the process of polarization of Yugoslav society generally. It was, in fact, unrealistic to expect the Bosnians to resist on their own the whirlwind of nationalist emotions that was sweeping over the entire country. The ability of the West to help the Bosnians during the collapse of communism was probably limited. But it was not negligible. The writing of election laws and parliamentary rules, the organization of political parties, and the conduct of campaigns, for example, were all areas in which Western involvement might have had a positive impact. This is not to mention the potential deterrent effect of the even simpler act of linking support and, later, diplomatic recognition openly and clearly—so that both elites and mass electorates could have no doubt—to the establishment of a tolerant, democratic political order, rather than a state dominated by nationalist parties. Efforts could have been undertaken to prevent non-nationalists from being excluded from parliament, from government, and, as we shall see, from the international politics surrounding Bosnia-Herzegovina. All these efforts would have stood a far better chance of success, of course, if they had been undertaken with respect to the whole of Yugoslavia as it began to disintegrate.

It remains open to debate as to what was the best course for Bosnia-Herzegovina: to adapt to the new situation by facilitating the regionalization of the republic into ethnic units—possibly even bowing to the necessity of

the partial breakup of the republic, if not its partition—or to fight to preserve Bosnia-Herzegovina. By examining its history, social conditions, and
ethnic makeup, one could argue that it would be (as indeed events proved) a
disaster to allow the process of disintegration to go forward unchecked. In
an article published after the war had started, Kemal Kurspahić, editor-in-
chief of *Oslobodjenje* during 1992–94, stated the case succinctly: Bosnia-
Herzegovina was ethnically a "leopard's skin." Trying to delineate
"cantons" or national areas would inevitably lead to ethnic cleansing; not
only of Muslims from Serb and Croat areas, but of Serbs and Croats from
Muslim areas. The division of Bosnia-Herzegovina by force would mean
decades of fighting and instability; a Palestine-like struggle spearheaded on
each side of the multiple ethnic divides by those seeking to regain the
territory from which they were expelled. Kurspahić concluded, therefore,
that peace could be preserved only by upholding the rights of individual
citizens, as opposed to the collective rights of the three ethnic communities.[109] A related position was that Bosnia should not be divided along
ethnic lines, but that the ethnic communities within Bosnia should be represented in a second chamber in the national assembly. Zdravko Grebo, an
influential member of the Muslim democratic intelligentsia in Sarajevo,
suggested such a plan.[110] Nikola Koljević, the moderate SDS leader, also
raised the possibility that the ethnic communities could exercise their political rights without regard to the territorial divisions of the republic.

There were two alternative views, both Serb. The first was that of Radovan Karadžić and members of the SDS. In this view, the Serbs, following
the collapse of Yugoslavia, had the right to self-determination. It was precisely in denying them this right that the danger lay of provoking a bloody
civil war. Karadžić's position reflected the changed situation that emerged
after the elections when all Bosnia-Herzegovina was being organized along
national lines, from politics to state employment to the mass media. The
second, more moderate Serb position, taken by a number of Bosnian Serbs
in the non-nationalist opposition, was that Bosnia-Herzegovina was a multinational state and society, and that this must be taken into account if civil
war was to be avoided. Nenad Kecmanović argued that historically, economically, and politically Bosnia-Herzegovina was not ready for civil society. Cantonization was unavoidable, with the devolution of considerable
autonomy to the country's regions (Bosanska Krajina, western Herzegovina, central Bosnia, and so forth). It was necessary to introduce strict
consensus into decision-making, create a chamber of nationalities in the
parliament, and undertake other constitutional changes to reflect Bosnian
realities.[111] Such an approach, of course, amounted to the "Yugoslavization" of the republic.

The international community, as our account will show, chose to emphasize both the integrity of the republic and the need for its regionalization. On balance, the international community was more sympathetic to Kurspahić's argument about the dangers of giving priority to collective rights over individual rights. Yet, if only for political reasons, the need to offer some form of territorial autonomy to placate the secessionist-minded Serbs and Croats was inevitable. Indeed, autonomy and power-sharing represented the core of each international peace plan, from Lisbon to Dayton.

We cannot hope to put this argument to rest. But it is clear that there were several Bosnia-Herzegovinas, which coexisted and were in tension with one another. On the one hand, there were areas of the republic where ethnic intolerance—indeed, hatred and suspicion—were deeply rooted. Some of these Serb and Croat regions were more or less homogeneous, and had a past record of peasant rebellions, mutual slaughter, and secessionist longings. Even after 45 years of communist rule, these ethnic communities did not share one another's political points of view. Each could easily feel that its survival was placed in danger by the political aspirations of the other. This sense of acute political difference would increase exponentially when war broke out in Croatia. On the other hand, there was the Bosnia-Herzegovina characterized by the successful integration of the three ethnic communities into a complex and unique social fabric. This Bosnia had real social, cultural, and political achievements to its credit that could not be lightly discarded by those who were part of it—especially not when the only apparent alternative was that offered by the nationalists.

In the last analysis, too much weight should not be placed on what Bosnia-Herzegovina was "really" like. It was a republic that was on the cutting edge of multiculturalism, with a strong indigenous culture and an outward-looking desire to join the new civic society of Europe. But it was also a society steeped in ethnic traditions and, unfortunately, ethnic feuds. Its "leopard spot" ethnic mix promoted accommodation among some local ethnic communities (notably in central Bosnia), local and regional tendencies toward secession, and an urge on the part of those most committed to maintaining Bosnia's integrity to do so by establishing a highly centralized central government—a view which owed more to Austrian tradition than to the practices of modern multinational federations in Europe such as Switzerland or Belgium. For all the historical reasons outlined above, the Muslims were the strongest proponents—but not the only ones—of this centralist view.

At the time the elections took place, there was hope that the accommodationist strain in Bosnian culture and politics would predominate, and the three political parties would cooperate. There was, in fact, an all-too-brief moment of such cooperation arising out of the euphoria surrounding the ouster of the communists. Kecmanović, in his account of the politics of the post-election period, speaks of how Izetbegović, Karadžić, and leaders of the opposition and of the three religions could all be found chatting at the Evropa Hotel in downtown Sarajevo, projecting an almost "Andrić-like appearance." The three parties, according to Kecmanović, began to celebrate each other's holidays "with brotherly enthusiasm":

> So much eating, so much drinking, celebrating, and with such brotherly love greetings were exchanged on all three sides—as if before the day of judgment, which did soon arrive.[112]

CHAPTER 3

The Descent into War

Between December 1990 and April 1992 the fate of Bosnia-Herzegovina hung in the balance. The first democratic elections in the history of the republic produced a deeply divided political system. As the republic became politically polarized from within, the external environment became chaotic. When war broke out in Croatia in summer 1991, Croats and Serbs from Bosnia joined in the fray. The Croats began training Muslims for war in Bosnia. The Yugoslav People's Army (JNA) trained and armed Serb reservists throughout Bosnia. In the fall, the JNA sent reservists from Montenegro rampaging across Herzegovina. Elsewhere, Bosnia was a zone of relative quiet, surrounded on three sides by violence, ethnic cleansing, and destruction. The Bosnian media propagated the notion that Bosnia's traditions of national tolerance would help it avoid war. President Izetbegović contributed to this "suspension of disbelief" by insisting that he knew—how, he did not explain—that war would not come to Bosnia. On the eve of the outbreak of the war, he insisted that the conflicts in Bosnia were being fabricated and would end after recognition.[1]

Yet the ability of Bosnia to avoid violence was rapidly diminishing as a result of two developments. The first was the onset within Bosnia of a veritable revolution from above. The three national parties began a purge of state administration, replacing those cadres still loyal to the Titoist system with persons loyal to the national parties. The nationalists thus destroyed the intricate system of interethnic checks and balances that had been at the heart of the Titoist system.[2] The second development took place outside Bosnia. We have argued in chapter 2 that Bosnia-Herzegovina had survived, despite its history of ethnic violence and social conflict, because it had been a ward of other multinational states from the middle of the fifteenth century onward. Periods of ethnic strife in Bosnia had been closely associated with the decline or military defeat of these states. The period from 1990 onward, when Yugoslavia collapsed, proved no exception. The breakup of Yugoslavia, the only authentic multinational state in the Balkans, generated deep fissures within an already politically divided Bosnia. Both these developments are examined here.

The Nationalist Revolution

The national parties in Bosnia sought to consolidate their newly won power through cadre changes designed to favor their respective ethnic communities. The process of inclusion and exclusion based on ethnic criteria, in both the public and private sectors, went forward by fits and starts after December 1990. But with time—and especially following the outbreak of hostilities in Bosnia in spring 1992—the process produced deep cleavages at all levels of Bosnian society. Thanks to these changes, and with the encouragement of all three national parties, multiculturalism was dealt its first blow in Bosnia. How these changes took place is evident only in scattered examples of the process, which continued up to the moment that war broke out—and beyond.

The first step was to remove communists from positions of responsibility at higher levels of state administration and replace them with representatives of the three nationalist parties. In a bow to the "key" (or quota system) employed under the old regime, the nationalists made an effort to assure that the ministers and deputy ministers in each ministry were not from the same party. In the highly polarized circumstances, this arrangement produced deadlock rather than cooperation. Each of the three national parties was deeply suspicious of the remaining two, and prone to use its blocking power to prevent the ministries from carrying out their normal functions.[3] In the paralysis that resulted, and thanks to the attrition of non-Muslim cadres in the ministries, the government in Sarajevo came to be largely under SDA control.[4] Since Bosnia-Herzegovina was a highly centralized state the danger was real that the SDA and the Muslim ethnic community would effectively shut out the other ethnic communities from power, at least at the level of the central government.

Outside Sarajevo, the Serb SDS consolidated its power where the Serbs were a majority. On the eve of the war in spring 1992, there were reports that the SDS had purged local governments in Serb-majority areas and was insisting that the tangible assets of the community be divided among the ethnic communities.[5] In Goražde, the Muslim SDA began a process of weeding out Serbs from responsible positions. According to Serb accounts, the Muslim mayor of Goražde set to work polarizing relations between the ethnic communities. His efforts were opposed by an ethnically mixed committee of intellectuals who tried to contain ethnic tensions in the town. Nonetheless, by the third week of March Goražde was a divided city, crisscrossed by barricades.[6] In Olovo, where the Muslims were the ethnic majority, both the SDA and SDS were responsible for dividing up positions and assets.[7] With the onset of the war, the Croat HDZ in Mostar began to purge the city administration of Muslims, even though the Croats were at war with the Serbs, and the Muslims in the city were supporting the Croats.[8] In the most extreme cases, two parallel societies emerged: one privileged, in power, and controlling the assets of the community; the other, made up essentially of second-class citizens. Usually this was a prelude to the expulsion of the ethnic community relegated to second-class status.

The efforts of the nationalists met with resistance from a combination of intellectuals who were committed to democratic values, and communists loyal to the Titoist creed of brotherhood and unity. The nationalists, for their part, were not terribly efficient in their purging, and each was reluctant to challenge the power base of the other ethnic communities. Thus, the process of breaking society down along ethnic lines proceeded unevenly. When fighting broke out in March–April 1992, a number of cities and towns were still able operate along multiethnic lines, and to protect themselves from the excesses committed by the armed extremists, at least for a time. We shall return briefly to the story of these towns in chapter 4.

The Ministry of the Interior in Sarajevo continued to resist nationalist pressures up to the outbreak of the war. In October 1991, the interior ministry launched a desperate appeal to the Yugoslav Army for assistance in disarming the paramilitary organizations of the three nationalist parties.[9] In March 1992 it was active in trying to ease tensions in Bosanski Brod and Mostar.[10] At a protest meeting at the beginning of April 1992, some 5,000 militia members, including Serbs, rallied in protest against the ethnic division of the ministry.[11] Even after the bulk of the Serbs had left and the ministry had come under the control of the Bosnian government, it continued to employ Serbs. Serbs remained in leading positions in other bodies, as well. Biljana Plavšić, for example, was president of the Council for the Protection of the Constitutional Order until the outbreak of the war. Nikola Koljević and Plavšić, the two Serbs in the state presidency, did not formally resign their positions until April 4.

Polarization in the work place and in government was accompanied by polarization of the media. All three national parties were guilty of attacks on the independent media. It became virtually impossible for the media to stand above the national question. Nenad Pejić, director of Sarajevo TV, was forced to resign, in part because he insisted on broadcasting daily newscasts from Zagreb and Belgrade, as well as Sarajevo.[12] All three national parties demanded that Radio-Television Sarajevo stop transmitting meetings of the All-National Parliament, which met the first week in April 1992 to protest the ethnic polarization of Sarajevo.[13] In the battle over control of television, TV relay towers became much-sought-after prizes. Serb seizure of several key TV relay installations meant that Sarajevo TV could reach only a relatively small part of Bosnia by spring 1992. Yutel stopped broadcasting in mid-May when its transmissions were limited to the city of Sarajevo.[14] *Oslobodjenje,* the newspaper whose staff included Serbs as well as Muslims, threw in its lot with the beleaguered Bosnian government after the war broke out.[15]

At the apex of the emergent power structures stood the newly anointed nationalist leaders. Radovan Karadžić, the president of the SDS, and Alija Izetbegović, president of the SDA, were closely associated with the formation of their respective parties and therefore wielded immense symbolic power as spokesmen for their respective national movements. Karadžić had been a sports psychologist, a familiar and well-liked figure in Sarajevo before the war.[16] In the crucial six months preceding the outbreak of fighting, Karadžić made inflammatory statements suggesting that the Muslims would be exterminated if war broke out in Bosnia. He provided the ideological justification for ethnic cleansing, insisting that Muslims and Serbs could not live together. He and the narrow circle of leaders in the SDS planned and oversaw the destruction of Muslim cultural monuments. Karadžić bore political responsibility, as president of the Bosnian Serb republic (*Republika Srpska*), for crimes committed by Serb forces during the conflict, leading to his indictment as a war criminal by the War Crimes Tribunal at the Hague. Corruption was endemic in the leadership circles of the SDS, suggesting that Karadžić had close ties with criminal elements in the Bosnian Serb republic. Karadžić was painted as an extreme nationalist and even fascist, "worse than Himmler," in the words of the U.S. ambassador, Warren Zimmerman. But Karadžić could not be dismissed simply as a national extremist. Within the SDS, Karadžić occupied a centrist position. His metamorphosis from a benevolent psychiatrist and environmentalist to an extreme nationalist reflected the larger forces at work in Bosnia at the time. Karadžić was at first blindly loyal to Milošević, only to break with Belgrade when it became evident that Milošević was prepared to sell the Bosnian Serbs short in order to end the war in Bosnia.

The Croat political scene, in contrast, was marked by an absence of strong leadership. The HDZ was split into two factions. The first and most powerful faction had its power base in western Herzegovina, and was anti-Bosnian. The second, which supported the integrity of Bosnia, had its roots in central Bosnia and especially Sarajevo. The Herzegovina faction was led by Mate Boban, who became president of the Bosnian Croat republic (*Herceg-Bosna*) after the region declared its independence in July 1992.[17] The Herzegovina Croats had strong ties to the HDZ leadership in Croatia and to President Franjo Tudjman. Tudjman's own political fortunes were, in turn, tied to the Herzegovinians and to Croatian emigres in the West, many of whom had emigrated from Herzegovina. Suspicion of the urban Croatian intellectuals in Sarajevo ran deep among the Herzegovinians. In Grude, the only Croatian majority district of Bosnia-Herzegovina to vote against the referendum in February 1992, local Croat leaders considered the Sarajevo intellectuals "Red Croats."[18]

The HDZ was under the control of first one faction, then the other, depending on Zagreb's policy toward Bosnia. Davor Peronić, who later became the head of the Bosnian branch of the extreme right-wing Croatian Party of Rights, was forced by Zagreb to relinquish the leadership of the Bosnian HDZ before the war broke out. He was replaced by Stjepan Kljujić, an urban Croatian intellectual and former sports writer from Sarajevo. Kljujić proved to be a relative moderate. He was compelled to step aside in spring 1992. Mate Boban then became acting president of the HDZ, to be replaced by Milenko Brkić in August 1992. Brkić, who was a professor in Sarajevo, was point man in the HDZ campaign to discredit the EC proposals for a solution to the Bosnian crisis in March 1992. He was replaced by Mate Boban in July 1993. In July 1994 Dario Kordić, a hard-liner who was charged with war crimes in fall 1995, took over from Boban as president of the Bosnian HDZ.[19]

Moderate Croat leaders in central and northern Bosnia found themselves in an extremely difficult position, torn between a sense of loyalty to the Bosnian government and their ethnic and political ties to the radical faction of the HDZ in western Herzegovina. On occasion, the moderate Croats opposed the policies of the Muslim-dominated government in Sarajevo, notably over the issue of whether Izetbegović should be permitted to serve successive terms as president. But because the Herzegovina lobby was strongly represented in Zagreb, the moderate Bosnian Croats were largely powerless to influence Croatian policy toward Bosnia. This became painfully evident after the establishment of the Muslim-Croat (Bosnian) federation in 1994, when the moderate Croats were unable to overcome the intransigent opposition to the federation on the part of the Croats in Herzegovina.

The SDA was founded by Izetbegović in March 1990,[20] and remained under his leadership throughout the period covered by our account. As a student during World War II, Izetbegović was a member of the Young Muslims, an organization of elitist Muslim youth with ties to the Ustashe youth movement. He was arrested in 1946 for membership in the Young Muslims and served a three-year sentence. Most of his later career was spent as a lawyer in Sarajevo. Izetbegović was a committed anticommunist, a deeply religious Muslim, and an ardent advocate of the regeneration of the Muslim world through what he called (in his work the *Islamic Declaration*) "the creation of a united Islamic Community from Morocco to Indonesia."[21] He was arrested in 1983 for the distribution of the *Islamic Declaration* some 13 years earlier and sentenced to 14 years in jail, to be released two years later. For the Serbs, the *Islamic Declaration* confirmed their suspicions that Izetbegović wished to transform Bosnia-Herzegovina into an Islamic state. Izetbegović insisted that he was committed to preserving Bosnia as a multicultural, secular society, and that the Muslims could not lay claim to the role of the titular nationality in Bosnia—at least not until they were 70 percent of the population.[22] He was quoted in a biographical sketch in the Western media as saying: "Our home is in Europe, and not in a fundamentalist state. My aim is to have an independent, democratic republic which conforms to European standards."[23] But Izetbegović was at heart not only a religious Muslim, but a Muslim in the national sense. When addressing Muslim audiences abroad, he spoke with great feeling about the need of the Muslim nation in Bosnia to have its own state, as we shall note in more detail in chapter 5.[24] Whether this was the result of the war, or a reflection of long-held convictions, we are not in a position to say.

Izetbegović's most intriguing feature was his apparent ability to combine the conflicting values of Islamic religiosity, Bosnian tolerance, and Western secularism. This seeming symbiosis of contrasting and even incompatible cultural traits made Izetbegović the most elusive of the nationalist leaders, but also the most authentically Bosnian. He was notoriously indecisive and prone to change his mind when dealing with international negotiators. (His inability to agree to closure at the Dayton peace talks drove the American negotiators to distraction.) He was modest, and appeared genuinely committed to peace, although not at any price, as our account will show. His public utterances were couched in the language of moderation and tolerance. The liberal Zagreb journal *Danas* remarked that he would have made a good *Reis-ul-ulema*.[25] He strongly opposed any devolution of power to ethnic regions in Bosnia. In this respect he had the near unanimous support of the Muslim, and a number of Croat and Serb, intellectuals.[26] But Izetbegović was accused by the democratic opposition of having an autocratic personality.[27] Izetbegović allowed corruption and crime to flourish in Sarajevo during the first year and a half of the war. While in jail, Izetbegović had become friends with the criminal Mušan Topalović-Caco and he came to rely on Caco to organize the defense of Sarajevo in the early months of the fighting. Izetbegović appears to have done little to stop the abuses committed against the Serbs in Sarajevo, or even the excesses perpetrated by Muslim forces against Croats, about which we shall have more to say in chapter 4.

The clash of values evident in Izetbegović's personality was mirrored within the SDA. It was divided into conservative and liberal wings, which Izetbegović tried unsuccessfully to span.[28] The conservative wing was willing to entertain thoughts of a partitioned Bosnia. But this did not exclude the reconquest of all or part of Serb-occupied Bosnia at some future date. Their notion of a Bosnian state was bound up with, and indistinguishable from, the affirmation of the Muslims as a nation. This faction of the SDA was itself sharply divided into subgroups, most notably the Islamic clergy and the nationalist intellectuals; the hawks within the ranks of the military; and the radical nationalists from the Sandžak, notable for their antipathy toward the Serbs. The second and smaller wing of the SDA, the secularists, viewed the state of Bosnia-Herzegovina as a means by which the multicultural traditions of Bosnia could be preserved, and a modern, Western democracy constructed. Those who espoused this view opposed the creation of ethnic cantons, or other schemes that would devolve power to the ethnic communities, fearing that this would lead to the breakup of Bosnia. Their secularism was therefore infused with centralism. It rejected ideas of consociational federalism and sympathized with the unitary principles espoused by the nationalists of all three ethnic communities in Bosnia.

Some Bosnian Muslims within and outside the SDA were willing to explore the possibility of tilting Bosnia toward Serbia and away from Croatia. Fikret Abdić belonged to this group, as did Adil Zulfikarpašić and Alija Delimustafić, a Sarajevo businessman who served as minister of the interior at the outset of the conflict and was later purported to have participated in an attempted coup aimed at removing Izetbegović and keeping Bosnia in rump Yugoslavia (see chapter 4).[29] All these individuals eventually were forced out of, or broke with the SDA. Zulfikarpašić formed the Muslim Bosniak Organization (MBO), a small party of liberal Bosnian Muslim businessmen and intellectuals. But Zulfikarpašić's interest in the Serbia option was, as we shall see, conditioned by a strong attachment to Croatia.

The nationalist party leaders were, however, only the most visible and influential of the new power holders thrown up by the victory of nationalism over the old order in Bosnia. Local politicians, criminal elements, military officers, and even some clergy were found among the new ruling elites in each ethnic community. There were few constraints on their exercise of local power. Over and over, the plans of the international community for reconciliation among the ethnic communities were thwarted by this new class of nationalists who profited from war and ignored the legal limits on their power in which the international community put such store.

The emergence of these new elites was dividing Bosnia even more deeply along national lines. But the nationalists had not completely achieved their goal when the war broke out. We know, from public opinion polls taken in fall 1991, that many if not most Bosnians outside the break-away peripheral areas such as western Herzegovina were not convinced nationalists. We shall see in chapter 4 that villagers in Bosnia turned against their neighbors only after nationalists employed various stratagems to set one ethnic community against another. Yet the polarization that was taking place was part of the pernicious dynamic of ethnic competition, jealousy, and mistrust characteristic of ethnic conflicts everywhere. What was missing in Bosnia was a tradition of political accommodation independent of the authoritarian, paternalistic context of Bosnia's past.

Simple electoral democracy was not the answer. As we have seen in chapter 2, the nationalist parties enjoyed enough support to exclude others from power, but could not devise formulas for sharing power among themselves. If the nonethnic or multiethnic parties had been able to escape their communist past and appeal to enough voters so that ethnic elites stood to lose critical electoral support if they became too extreme, then perhaps the incentives to find a successful formula for sharing power might have outweighed the incentives to extremism. But the structure of the electoral system itself, and the absence of cross-cutting, or moderating, interests in society, reinforced intransigence and extremism.

The Dissolution of Yugoslavia ... and of Bosnia

The polarization of Bosnian politics and society along ethnic lines after 1990 was accelerated by, and a reflection of, the disintegration of Yugoslavia. The demise of Yugoslavia is now a familiar tale. It is enough to remind the reader that following the electoral victories of nationalist parties in most of the republics in 1990, Yugoslavia found itself in a state of permanent crisis, culminating in the secession of Slovenia and Croatia in June 1991. Here, we shall focus on the impact of these events on Bosnia.

The future of the Yugoslav federation had become the subject of intense debate after Tito's death in 1980. Serbia sought constitutional changes that would have placed more power in the hands of the federal government.

Initially, Slovenia and Croatia argued for the *status quo*. But, by 1986 the force of regional ethnic, economic, and political interests led the Slovenian and Croatian leaderships to the idea of a loose confederation among the six republics.[30] Following the defeat of the communists in the elections in Slovenia and Croatia in spring 1990, the new leaderships in these republics opted for a confederal Yugoslavia of sovereign republics—in effect, for independence.

The debate over the future of the Yugoslav federation was a matter of life and death to Bosnia. Prior to the outbreak of the war in Croatia, all Bosnian parties with the exception of the radical wing of the HDZ opposed the breakup of Yugoslavia. At the same time, the SDA and the communists opposed the Serbian campaign for a stronger Yugoslav federation. In October 1990, while the communists were still in power, the Bosnian parliament adopted a resolution suggesting that Yugoslavia adopt a "Charter of the Community" that would have transformed Yugoslavia into a loose confederation of sovereign republics. If Yugoslavia could not be structured along democratic lines, the resolution continued, then Bosnia-Herzegovina should organize itself as an "autonomous sovereign and independent state, although this is not in the historical interest of its citizens and peoples, or of other republics."[31] As we noted in chapter 2, Izetbegović made it clear at about this time (September 1990) that he opposed Bosnia-Herzegovina remaining in a rump Yugoslavia, taking the position that if Croatia and Slovenia were to leave Yugoslavia, then Bosnia-Herzegovina should immediately declare its independence.[32] After he was chosen president, Izetbegović continued to hold to this position.

Izetbegović argued that Bosnia-Herzegovina would be forced to declare its independence should Croatia and Slovenia (but especially the former) leave the federation. On the other hand, he sought to facilitate an agreement among the quarreling republics that would allow Yugoslavia to survive.[33] With the support of Macedonia, Izetbegović argued for a "Yugoslav state community" that would acknowledge the sovereignty of the republics while retaining Yugoslavia's international legal status.[34] At one point in spring 1991 he even appeared open to the idea of an "asymmetric federation"; that is, one in which Bosnia-Herzegovina would have closer ties to the federal government than Croatia and Slovenia. Public opinion in Bosnia was against such a relationship with Belgrade, however, and Izetbegović was compelled to drop the idea.[35]

Karadžić and the SDS also supported a variant of this "asymmetric" approach. The SDS proposed that Bosnia-Herzegovina would be "an integral and equal republic of sovereign citizens and nations, organized under a regional system."[36] The "regional" dimension was not clearly spelled out, however. Nor was it clear whether Bosnia would be at the "tight" or "loose" end of the asymmetric scale.

Behind these debates over the future of Bosnia-Herzegovina lay fundamentally different views concerning the nature of the Bosnian state and its relationship to the external environment. Karadžić and the Serbs argued that Bosnia-Herzegovina was Yugoslavia in miniature, an artificial creation whose people could not, and should not, be forced to live in one state. Izetbegović and the non-nationalist opposition parties took the position that Bosnia-Herzegovina was a state in its own right, with its unique traditions, history, and stable borders that predated those of Yugoslavia. Paradoxically, the SDS resisted confederal solutions for Yugoslavia but advocated them for Bosnia-Herzegovina, while Izetbegović and the SDA opposed a unitary solution to the Yugoslav constitutional crisis, but favored such a solution for Bosnia-Herzegovina.

In February and then again in May 1991 the SDA attempted to push a declaration of sovereignty through the Bosnian assembly.[37] Both resolutions failed. Apparently, neither the Serbs nor the Muslims were yet ready for a showdown. The search for a way out of the impasse in Bosnia was renewed in summer 1991, sparked by the outbreak of the war in Croatia. The Serbian government participated in the effort to solve the Bosnian dilemma by organizing the so-called "Belgrade initiative," a meeting of delegates from Serbia, Montenegro, Macedonia, and Bosnia-Herzegovina on August 12, at which the idea of a new federation without Slovenia and Croatia was presented to the public. The gathering suggested the possibility that Bosnia-Herzegovina might become part of a new Yugoslavia made up of the non-Catholic republics.[38] But the effort was political theater. The Bosnian representative was a loyal SDS member, Momčilo Krajišnik, president of the National Assembly and a close associate of Karadžić. The key ingredient for the success of such a solution—the support of the Bosnian Muslims—was absent.

The August initiative nevertheless highlighted the risk that Izetbegović was taking by turning his back on Belgrade. The key to Izetbegović's stand was his insistence that Bosnia-Herzegovina could not be part of any federation that excluded Croatia. This ruled out Bosnia-Herzegovina joining a rump Yugoslavia. Of course, even if Izetbegović had opted for the path of Muslim collaboration with Belgrade, Bosnia would not have escaped without the loss of territory. Such a move would, at a minimum, have sparked the secession of western Herzegovina and its Croat population.

Nevertheless, there were a number of reasons why linking up with Yugoslavia might have looked attractive to the Bosnian Muslims. First, it would have brought the Yugoslav army into the Muslim camp and avoided civil war between the Muslims and the Serbs. Second, while it might initially have involved political costs, since the new federation would be dominated by the Serbs and Milošević, it would have united all the Muslims of former Yugoslavia in one state (that is, Muslims from Kosovo, Sandžak, and Bosnia-Herzegovina). Eventually, one can surmise, the Muslims would have become a political force to be reckoned with in the new Yugoslavia. Finally, Bosnia-Herzegovina probably would have been able, with the support of Montenegro, to retain its status as a republic and many of the powers it had enjoyed in the old Yugoslav federation.[39] As we shall see in chapter 4, a coup was apparently in the works in the state presidency in early May 1992 to replace Izetbegović with a leadership that would have kept Bosnia in rump Yugoslavia.

The opportunity to strike such a deal had offered itself in July and August 1991, at the time of the "August initiative" described above. In July, talks were held in Sarajevo between the president of the MBO, Adil Zulfikarpašić, and the SDS leadership. According to Zulfikarpašić, the outline of an agreement was reached which was then presented to Izetbegović, who agreed that he would support it upon his return from the United States. Koljević, who was considered the most moderate of the Serb leaders, announced on television that the Bosnian Muslims and the Serbs had reached an agreement on the future of Bosnia and that "we are no longer in danger of fighting with our neighbors."[40] But the nature of the final agreement between the SDS leaders and Zulfikarpašić remains unclear. In his collection of articles and speeches, Zulfikarpašić has reproduced two versions of an agreement drawn up during the discussion between the SDS and the MBO in the third week of July. Much of the language of the two drafts was identical. Both supported the continued existence of a Yugoslavia within which Bosnia-Herzegovina would retain its present boundaries. However, the MBO draft referred to "completely equal relationships [of Bosnia-Herzegovina] with Croatia and Serbia in a future Yugoslavia." It described Bosnia-Herzegovina not only as a republic but as a "state," with a unitary government without regionalization or cantonization. All three provisions were absent from the Serb draft. The most intriguing provision of the MBO draft called for autonomy of the Krajina Serbs within Croatia. But it asserted that if the Krajina Serbs should declare their independence, they should be made part of Bosnia-Herzegovina. In this case, Bosnia's borders should be redrawn to include the Sandžak. In effect, what began in 1991 as an effort to create a Greater Serbia by the Serbs in Croatia would then, in this MBO scenario, be transformed into a greater Bosnia-Herzegovina.[41] It is difficult to accept the assertion that the Bosnian Serbs agreed to such a draft.

During the course of these talks on July 17, Adil Zulfikarpašić met with Milošević in Belgrade. According to Zulfikarpašić's account, Milošević threw his support behind the agreement.[42] Upon his return to Sarajevo from the United States, Izetbegović also visited Belgrade and conferred with Milošević.[43] Leaks of the conversation between Zulfikarpašić and Milošević set public opinion in Bosnia against the projected union, and the prelude to the "Belgrade initiative" came to naught.

Without more information, it is difficult to know what to make of these discussions. From Zulfikarpašić's account it is not clear whether the MBO and the SDS finally produced a common version of their July agreement or not. According to the *Borba* account cited above, Izetbegović met with the Serb leaders on July 23. The meeting was marked by high tensions, with the Serbs insisting that the agreement include a statement that Bosnia could not be an Islamic state. It was a sign of the uncertainties of the time that Izetbegović would consider dealing with Milošević at all, in view of Izetbegović's deep aversion to the communist regime in Serbia. How the Bosnian Croats would react to an agreement between Sarajevo and Belgrade was made clear by Stjepan Kljujić, who declared that "to the extent that a four-member federation is formed by force, although we are for a confederation of Bosnia with Croatians, we would consider this an occupation and organize an uprising." The only terms under which the Bosnian Croats could accept the "asymmetric" solution acceptable to the Serbs was the annexation of western Herzegovina by Croatia. Such a step was acceptable to the SDS leadership, but rejected by Zulfikarpašić.[44] Yet, while the path to an agreed common state for the Serbs, Croats, and Muslims appeared extremely difficult, the path down which Bosnia was headed promised catastrophe. As Emir Hubul suggested several months later in a perceptive commentary for *Oslobodjenje,* the moment that the SDA made it clear that it would not remain in a Yugoslavia without Croatia, war was inevitable in Bosnia-Herzegovina.[45]

By fall 1991, as the war gained in intensity in Croatia, Bosnia-Herzegovina appeared to be on the verge of disintegration. Serb autonomous oblasts—SAOs—were formed in Serb areas throughout Bosnia. The SAO of Eastern and Old Herzegovina was established on September 12, the SAO of Bosanska Krajina on September 16, Romanija on September 18, and Northeast Bosnia on September 20.[46] This continued the process of wresting control away from Sarajevo started by the Serbs in October 1990, when they established a Serb National Council over the strong protests of the communist government.[47] The Croats followed by setting up two autonomous oblasts of their own—one for the Sava Valley, the other Herzeg-Bosna—in the second and third weeks of November 1991.[48] In the third week of October the Serbs created an Assembly of the Serb Nation of Bosnia-Herzegovina. In early November 1991 the Bosnian Serbs organized a referendum that asked Serb voters whether they wished to remain in a Yugoslavia that would include Krajina, eastern Slavonija, Baranja, and Srem—in effect, a Greater Serbia. There were two versions of the referendum. The first, for Serbs, asked, "Do you agree with the decision of the Assembly of the Serbian people in Bosnia and Herzegovina of October 24, 1991, that the Serbian people should remain in a common Yugoslav state with Serbia, Montenegro, the SAO Krajina, SAO Slavonija, Baranja, and Western Srem, and with others who have come out for remaining [in Yugoslavia]?" The second version, for non-Serbs, asked "Are you agreed that Bosnia and Herzegovina, as an equal republic, should remain in a common state of Yugoslavia with all others who take this position?"[49] The referendum received near unanimous backing from the Serbs. The leadership of the SDS argued that the vote dispelled any doubt that the Serbs wished to remain part of Yugoslavia, rather than accept the status of a minority in an independent Bosnia-Herzegovina.[50]

As Map 3.1 suggests, by March 1992 perhaps three-quarters of Bosnia-Herzegovina was claimed by either the Serb or Croat nationalists. As we noted earlier, Herzegovina experienced an incursion of Serbian and Montenegrin reservists in September 1991, an apparent prelude to the JNA attack on Dubrovnik in early October 1991. Tensions between the government and the Yugoslav army mounted over the government's refusal to cooperate in conscripting Bosnian youths to fight the war in Croatia. The Serbs of Bosanska Krajina were increasingly drawn into the war in Croatia, especially following the defeat of the Serbs in western Slavonija in late October and early November.[51] The Bosnian Serb and Muslim leaderships were deeply suspicious of one another, while the Croats of western Herzegovina had, to all intents and purposes, opted out of the task of governing the republic, choosing instead to create a *de facto* autonomous state tightly integrated with neighboring Croatia.

All the while, arms were pouring into Bosnia. The JNA began a transfer of arms to the Bosnian Serbs.[52] The Croatian paramilitary group—the Croatian Defense Force—was actively arming its members in Herzegovina.[53] The Bosnian Muslim Green Berets were organized in fall 1991. According to Izetbegović they numbered between 35,000 and 40,000 when the conflict began. The more inclusive Patriotic League was formed at the same time and, in February 1992, drew up a plan for the defense of Bosnia. According to Šefer Halilović, the League numbered 120,000 members by spring 1992.[54] Croat units from western Herzegovina returned home following the end of the fighting in Croatia, anticipating that war would soon break

Map 3.1 **Territories of Bosnia-Herzegovina Claimed by Serb and Croat Nationalists**

Based on unclassified CIA maps 724663 (R00389) 3–92 and 724510 (R00398) 3–92.

out in Bosnia. Serbs who were mustered out of the JNA units in Croatia returned to the Prijedor area from Croatia, bringing their weapons with them despite the objections of the Muslim-controlled city assembly.[55] According to Bosnian accounts, the JNA struck a deal with Karadžić in February 1992 to create a joint Bosnian Serb–JNA command and coordinate military actions in Bosnia.[56] Vitomir Zepenić, deputy minister of the interior in the Bosnian government, estimated that 250,00–300,000 persons were armed, and that some 10,000 Bosnians were engaged in the fighting in Croatia.[57] Journalists traveling through Bosnia described evenings filled with the sound of small-arms fire from villagers firing off their newly acquired weapons.[58]

There was still one last glimmer of hope for Bosnia if the three nationalist parties could agree on mechanisms of government that would protect the basic interests of each ethnic community while keeping Bosnia intact. A constitutional commission was formed in early 1991, but no agreement was reached on the nature of the Bosnian state—as a republic of citizens or nations—nor the manner in which power was to be exercised by the central and provincial governments.[59] A debate on the constitutional issues was forced upon the parliament in October 1991. Once again, the SDA brought the issue of sovereignty before the parliament on October 8, following the formal declaration of independence by Slovenia and Croatia and the formation in Belgrade of a rump Yugoslav presidency that excluded Slovenia and Croatia.

The vote on sovereignty confronted the Bosnian Assembly with the problem of how constitutional issues were to be resolved—consensually or by majority vote. The 1974 Bosnian constitution had, in Article 3, guaranteed proportional representation to the three "nations" (Muslims, Serbs, and Croats) in sociopolitical bodies of Bosnia, but no provision was made for super-majorities in decisions affecting the vital interests of the ethnic communities.[60] In a series of constitutional amendments adopted in July 1990, proportional representation of the nations in sociopolitical bodies was retained.[61] Amendment 70 provided for the formation of a "Council for Questions of the Establishment of Equality of the Nations and Nationalities of Bosnia and Herzegovina," what we shall refer to as the "Council for National Equality." The body was to have an equal number of Muslims, Serbs, and Croats. It was to consider any act of the Assembly that twenty or more deputies considered as undermining the equality of the nations of Bosnia. Decisions of the Council were to be taken by consensus. No other consensual mechanisms—neither a second house representing the ethnic communities, nor a collective presidency, nor voting by super-majorities in parliament—were included in the amendments. The powers and responsibilities of the Council for National Equality were vague. The Council could propose to the Assembly that a law touching on the question of the equality of the nations be adopted by a two-thirds majority.[62] But it appeared that the Council could act only with the approval of all three of the nations represented in it. If so, its decisions could have been blocked by any one of the groups. In any event, the status of the Council was a moot point—it never went into operation.

It was against this backdrop that the Bosnian assembly undertook to debate the Muslim call for sovereignty. The assembly considered a resolution entitled "Memorandum (Letter of Intent)," and a second resolution that elaborated on the Memorandum, the "Platform on the Position of Bosnia and Herzegovina and the Future Organization of the Yugoslav Community."[63] The debate began behind closed doors on October 14, 1991, and continued through the next day. The resolutions proclaimed the sovereignty of Bosnia-Herzegovina. They provided that Bosnia would not send representatives to the parliament or other organs of federal Yugoslavia if all the remaining republics were not also present. This effectively removed Bosnia from the federation, since Slovenia and Croatia had already seceded. The two resolutions expressed their backing for the formation of a Yugoslav "community"—the loose association of republics discussed above—but only if Serbia and Croatia were both members. The SDS presented its own competing resolution. It provided that Bosnia-Herzegovina would continue to participate in the institutions of the federal government. If Croatia were to secede from Yugoslavia and gain international recognition, a mechanism would be set in motion "for the realization of the right of self-determination, including secession of the constituent nations of Bosnia and Herzegovina."[64]

The outcome of the debate was a disaster. Karadžić first gave the impression of wishing to be conciliatory, speaking of the need for an institutional solution to the divide between the two camps.[65] Izetbegović offered the choice between a referendum on sovereignty and new elections. His words were unyielding:

> The debates between us and the SDS, and the problem has completely come to a head [*izoštren*] on the question of sovereignty—yes or no? We have no way out. Now we cannot put it off, for October 1991 has come, when it must be resolved. This way or that way. We must come to terms with this, to say, will we accept peace at any price in Bosnia, bend our heads once and for all [*definitivno*], because of peace accept an inferior position for the next fifteen years, or shall we say, we want sovereignty, risking a conflict. That is not a situation we created. That is a situation created by the disintegration of Yugoslavia. No matter who was in charge he would find himself in completely the same situation. . . .[66]

The Muslim-Croat majority refused a Serb demand to refer the Memorandum to the Council for National Equality on the grounds that that body was not yet in existence. Karadžić warned the assembled deputies that Bosnia was on the verge of civil war and that the Muslims risked annihilation:

> I am asking you once again. I am not threatening, but asking you, to take seriously the interpretation of the political will of the Serbian people who are represented here by the SDP [sic] and the Serbian Renewal Movement and a couple of Serbs from other parties. I ask you to take seriously the fact that what you are doing is not good. Is this the road onto which you want to direct Bosnia-Herzegovina, the same highway to hell and suffering that Slovenia and Croatia are traveling?

Do not think that you will not lead Bosnia-Herzegovina to hell, and do not think that you will not perhaps lead the Muslim people into annihilation, because the Muslim people cannot defend themselves if there is war.... How will you prevent everyone from being killed in Bosnia-Herzegovina?[67]

Izetbegović's rejoinder sought to downplay the spectre of war:

His manner and his messages perhaps explain why others also refuse to stay in such a Yugoslavia. Nobody else wants the kind of Yugoslavia that Mr. Karadžić wants any more, no one except perhaps the Serbian people. Such a Yugoslavia and such a manner of Karadžić are simply hated by the people of Yugoslavia.... And I then say to the people of Bosnia-Herzegovina that there will not be war, that is my prediction based on the facts, on some confirmed facts. Therefore sleep peacefully, there is no need to fear, because it takes two to tango.[68]

Following a walkout by the Serbs, the Muslims and Croats then convened a rump session of the parliament and adopted the memorandum and the platform by a majority vote.

The Memorandum justified the actions of the parliament as a matter of constitutional principle. It asserted that the positions in the Memorandum "express the will of the majority of the Assembly, and, as such, the political will of the citizens of Bosnia and Herzegovina; consequently, they constitute an obligatory basis for the conduct of the state and political bodies of the republic." This seemed to contradict the next point in the memorandum, that "the Assembly recognizes, simultaneously, the right of the parliamentary minority to claim and realize every one of its legitimate interests—ethnic, cultural, economic and social—provided this is achieved without the use of force and in a legal and democratic manner."[69] The rights of the minority thus depended entirely on how "legitimate interests" were defined.

The Platform provided some balance to the Memorandum by proclaiming the goal of creating a "civil republic" in Bosnia, in which the human rights and freedoms of all citizens would be guaranteed. Outvoting on all crucial issues "concerning the equal rights of all nations and nationalities" would be precluded "through an appropriate structure of the Assembly." But the document also closed the door against Serbian demands for secession. Changes in the borders of Bosnia, the platform stated, could only be approved by a two-thirds vote in a popular referendum.[70]

Much has been made of Karadžić's threatening statement in the Bosnian Assembly, including its use as evidence of a Serb intent to commit genocide against the Muslims. Izetbegović's response makes it clear that, at the very least—contrary to Karadžić's own intentions—the outburst hardened Muslim resistance to either continuing the *status quo* in Yugoslavia or allowing Bosnia-Herzegovina to become part of a Serbian-dominated rump state. On the other hand, the efforts of the majority to reaffirm the existing constitutional order while pushing for the adoption of a declaration of independence were also questionable. One cannot help but be struck by the hurried and crude documents produced in the course of the debate, documents that addressed the most delicate of all questions in Bosnian politics in a highly provocative language. While "constitutional" in nature, the Memorandum and the Platform hardly reflected the kind of consensus necessary to make a constitution meaningful. Instead they appeared to reflect the efforts of one or two groups to impose their will on the third. In this respect, the Bosnian Muslim leadership was simply following the practice that had taken hold in Yugoslavia since 1988: majorities using constitutional reform as a weapon to impose their own political agendas on minorities. During the earlier communist era, constitutional reforms had been the product of long, drawn-out negotiations designed to find common ground among competing views. Such negotiations, of course, contributed to the inability of the Yugoslav elite to move questions of reform on the agenda in the mid-1980s in the direction of genuine democratization.

The debate on sovereignty in October 1991 reinforced the determination of the SDA to break away from what remained of Yugoslavia. On October 16, the SDA held a press conference in Sarajevo. According to *Borba,* the spokesman for the Muslim party announced that with the adoption of the memorandum "we have cut out any possibility that Bosnia and Herzegovina, in some secret fashion, unconstitutionally, silently, will find itself in rump [*krnjoj*] Yugoslavia, with Serbia and Montenegro."[71] But the constitutional debate was not yet over, as our account will show. The outcome of that debate would be shaped by events outside Bosnia. Among the most important of these was the way in which the international community responded to the breakup of Yugoslavia and the onset of war in Croatia.

The Role of the International Community

It is not our task to follow, in precise detail, the actions of the international community in Yugoslavia prior to the time that the conflict in Bosnia broke out. But there is a close connection between the events in Croatia and those in Bosnia. To see why this is so, it is necessary to turn to the involvement of the European Community (EC)—after January 1993, the European Union (EU)—in the Yugoslav crisis. The United States played only a limited role in the initial stages of the Yugoslav and Bosnian crises. But, as we shall see, the U.S. role became more and more critical as the crises continued and the focus shifted to Bosnia.

The involvement of the EC in Yugoslavia came suddenly. Europe's priorities lay outside the Balkans, and its knowledge of the politics of Yugoslavia was superficial. There were no readily available guidelines by which the European powers could assess the Yugoslav crisis. Europe was committed only to general principles: first, that the territorial *status quo* should not be altered; second, that the use of armed force to resolve conflicts over borders in Europe was inadmissible; and third, support for self-determination, provided it was the expression of a democratic process and did not seek to alter existing borders by violence.

In practice it proved difficult to determine whether the resort to force in Yugoslavia was motivated by self-preservation or by aggression, or possibly both. Nor was it clear what constituted the *status quo* in a multiethnic state undergoing dissolution. The first effort of the EC in Yugoslavia came in March 1991, when EC leaders visiting Belgrade expressed their support for the current internal and external borders of the country.[72] This extended the application of Helsinki principles from internationally recognized borders to internal borders. At the same time, Washington expressed support for "democracy, dialogue, human rights, market reform and unity" in Yugoslavia, defining unity as "the territorial integrity of Yugoslavia within its present borders." The U.S. statement went on to suggest that dismemberment would worsen ethnic tensions and that unity must be democratic and based on mutual agreement. "The United States will not encourage or reward secession," and if borders were to be changed, they would have to be changed by "peaceful consensual means."[73] The U.S. statement did not completely rule out the possibility of redrawing internal borders as part of the dissolution process. At a press conference in early June the U.S. ambassador to Yugoslavia appeared to point to the need for internal negotiations to settle the issues in dispute.[74] But the United States offered no public support for border changes, even if such changes might have facilitated a peaceful solution to the looming civil war.

Thus, there was no public reaction on the U.S. side to an agreement between Serbia and Slovenia that seemed to embrace such a solution. The occasion was a meeting between Milošević and President Milan Kučan of Slovenia, which took place in January 1991. Kučan and Milošević appeared to have worked out an agreement permitting the secession of Slovenia within its existing borders in exchange for Slovenian acquiescence in Serbian efforts to redraw other borders. In a joint statement, Serbia acknowledged Slovenia's right to determine for itself the form of its ties with other Yugoslav nations, and Slovenia "acknowledged the interest of the Serbian nation to live in one state and that the future Yugoslav accord should respect this interest."[75] The statement suggested that Slovenia would stand to one side while Serbia made claims to Croatian territory, an understanding that meant little if the Croatians were not partner to the agreement. Kučan was compelled to retract the statement under public pressure in Slovenia, and to reassert his commitment to existing borders in Yugoslavia.[76] In talks with Izetbegović, Kučan defended the right of the Serbian people to live together, but agreed that the right to self-determination could not be exercised at the expense of other nations; that is, republics.[77] Nonetheless, the statement should have put Western policymakers on notice that the issue of borders would be on the agenda as Yugoslavia dissolved. In fact, the Milošević–Kučan exchange had raised precisely such concerns among mid-level U.S. analysts, but senior U.S. officials remained deaf to efforts to bring these concerns to their attention.

The first stage of the conflict in Yugoslavia began in Slovenia in June 1991, and was quickly ended following an agreement, signed by Yugoslavia, Slovenia, and Croatia on the island of Brioni on July 8, under the auspices of the EC.[78] The Brioni accords were hailed as the first success of Europe's new independent foreign policy. In fact, as Silber and Little show in their engrossing account of the Slovenian war, the Europeans had been in the dark the entire time, unaware that the concessions they extracted from Milošević and the JNA had already been agreed to by the Yugoslavs themselves.[79]

The War in Croatia and the Greater Serbia Project

Croatia was another matter altogether.[80] The elections of 1990 brought the Croatian Democratic Union (*Hrvatska Demokratska Zajednica,* or HDZ) to power in Croatia, setting the stage for a confrontation between the Serb minority located in Krajina and Slavonija, and President Tudjman's government in Zagreb. During the war in Croatia, the Serbs seized territory stretching from eastern Dalmatia to Baranja on the Hungarian border, a region roughly corresponding to the old Austrian military frontier. Properly speaking, only the eastern Dalmatian districts of Lika, Slunj, Banija, and Kordun should be considered as "Krajina." Slavonija (western and eastern) should be distinguished from Baranja, which borders on Hungary. The leadership of the self-declared Republic of Serb Krajina (*Republika Srpske Krajine,* or RSK), however, laid claim to all these regions and they are therefore often referred to collectively as "Krajina."[81] In summer 1990 the Serb Democratic Party of Croatia organized a referendum in these areas calling for autonomy.[82] Over the course of the next year, the Serbs expelled the local Croatian police and civil administration from parts of Krajina proper and eastern Slavonija. The first stage of this undeclared conflict ended with the ambush of Croatian police by Serbian irregulars in Borovo

Selo in May 1991. At first the JNA tried to remain impartial. But it was drawn into the conflict on the Serb side. By summer 1991, when the fighting in Croatia escalated sharply, the JNA was siding openly with local Serb forces, armed by Belgrade and under the direction of Milan Martić, a Knin police inspector who was to become minister of interior in the Krajina government.[83]

The outbreak of fighting between Serbia and Croatia did not bode well for Bosnia. We have seen that the confrontation between Croatia and Serbia in the interwar period was resolved, in 1939, by an agreement (the *Sporazum*) that gave Croatia autonomy within Yugoslavia and approximately one-third of Bosnian territory. With the breakup of Yugoslavia, Croatia and Serbia once more considered partitioning Bosnia. In March 1991, Milošević and Tudjman met at Karadjordjevo in an attempt to resolve their differences. Bosnia was discussed, as well as the fate of the Serbs in the border regions of Croatia. Silber and Little tell of Tudjman returning to Zagreb, confident that he had reached a deal with Milošević that would have allowed Croatia to deal with its Serb minority as it saw fit.[84] Boris Raseta claims that the two presidents agreed that the Serbs would get Posavina and eastern Slavonija while western Slavonija and Krajina would fall to the Croats.[85] Stipe Mesić, who helped organize the meeting, testified at the War Crimes Tribunal that Tudjman returned highly satisfied from Karadjordjevo, having received assurances from General Kadijević that the Yugoslav army would not attack Croatia.[86] Mesić himself received assurances in February from Borisav Jović that Belgrade was not interested in the Serbs in Croatia, but did want two-thirds of Bosnia.[87] Despite the apparent complementarity of interests between Serbia and Croatia in the dismemberment of Bosnia-Herzegovina, this first attempt at rapprochement failed, almost certainly over the issue of the Serbs in Krajina and Slavonija.[88]

On September 25, 1991, Milošević and Tudjman met again in eastern Slavonija. General Kadijević was in attendance. The meeting took place at a time of rising tensions in Bosnia and growing misunderstandings between the JNA and Croatia over how to end the siege of JNA barracks in Croatia. According to a *New York Times* account of the meeting, the three parties to the talks agreed to a cease-fire, as well as further talks to achieve a political settlement of the war.[89] It is possible that the cease-fire was meant to be a prelude to more substantive discussions between the two sides that would have dealt with the fate of the Serb minority in Croatia and the division of Bosnia. In the event, the encounter did nothing to move the peace process forward.

In early October the war in Croatia escalated in intensity. The JNA launched a new offensive against Vukovar. In Bosnia, the JNA provoked a confrontation with the Sarajevo government when General Nikola Uzelac, commander of the Banja Luka corps, ordered the general mobilization of the population of northwest Bosnia, presumably for action in Croatia. On October 1, Dubrovnik was attacked by the JNA. By the end of the first week in October, Serbian irregulars and JNA units were only fifteen miles from Zagreb. But the army was distracted by the barracks wars, abandoned by non-Serb officers, and suffering from disorganization and a lack of manpower as a result of desertions by Serbs and non-Serbs alike. It was unable to score a decisive victory over the vastly inferior Croatian forces. When Generals Panić and Adžić inspected the Vukovar front, they were appalled by the absence of a chain of command and by disorganization, desertion from the ranks, and "chaos."[90]

The final phase of the war in Croatia began in early November. The shock of the "Arrangements for a General Settlement" first issued by the EC Conference on Yugoslavia on October 18, revised several times thereafter, and finally rejected by the Serbian and Montenegrin governments on November 5 set the stage for a last effort by the JNA to regain the initiative and free army personnel still trapped in barracks in Croatia. General Kadijević called the EC proposal of October 18 the end of Yugoslavia as well as the JNA.[91] A general mobilization was declared in Serbia, Montenegro, and the Bosnian Serb SAOs. On November 5, the JNA began an all-out offensive against Vukovar. The city finally fell on November 18, after a savage artillery bombardment—a portent of what was to come in Bosnia.

The victory at Vukovar marked the high-tide of the Serbian campaign in Croatia. General Života Panić, who commanded the JNA forces in eastern Slavonija, was convinced that Croatia had lost the war, and that nothing could prevent the JNA from capturing Zagreb.[92] Developments on the diplomatic front in November and December—above all, Germany's campaign to gain recognition for Croatia and Slovenia—seemed to be shaped by the perception that Croatia was on the verge of collapsing in front of the JNA onslaught. Nevertheless, Panić was ordered by Milošević to restrict JNA operations to Serb-inhabited areas.[93] Panić's claim that Croatia had lost the war was in any case wide of the mark. Silber and Little conclude that "Milošević called a halt to the war when the Serbs, backed by the JNA, had won all they were capable of winning without an endlessly bloody and costly conflict."[94]

In late October, the JNA had attempted to consolidate Serb gains in western Slavonija north of Pakrac. General Kadijević, in his memoirs, reported that the JNA had hoped to muster five brigades for the campaign, but was able to raise only one and a half.[95] Despite the support of the local Serbs, the campaign was a disastrous failure. The JNA was forced to beat a retreat. The JNA pullback may have been the result of orders from Belgrade, based on the notion that Western Slavonija was outside the "Sava–Vinkovci–Osijek line" that defined the limits of the Serbian leadership's territorial ambitions at the time, and which is discussed further below. But the failed campaign was important as the first indication of the difficulty Serbia and the JNA would have in defending Serb-inhabited areas in Croatia.

The inability of the JNA to mobilize, train, and motivate Serb recruits from Serbia proper to fight in Croatia was critical.[96] The notion of a greater Serbia was fatally flawed if Serbs would not fight for one another. General Kadijević in his memoirs identified the failure of the Serbs to fight in Croatia as a major factor contributing to the poor performance of the JNA.[97] We know that thousands deserted. The Belgrade opposition weekly *Vreme* reported in late September that the Serbian parliament had been informed in a closed meeting that only 50 percent of the reservists in Serbia and only 15 percent in Belgrade had obeyed orders to report for duty.[98] Protest rallies demanding a return of recruits to Serbia were organized in Belgrade, Kraljevo, and Kragujevac the first week in December.[99] By way of contrast, General Kadijević noted the success of the JNA in recruiting from among the Bosnian Serbs, which, he added, helped make up for the failure in mobilizing Serbs elsewhere for the conflict in Croatia.[100] The fact that Serbs from Serbia proper were unwilling to fight outside their own republic became a major factor shaping Belgrade's strategy and goals in the war in Croatia and, later, in Bosnia.

The European approach to the Yugoslav crisis was another factor shaping Serbian strategy. The EC call on August 28, 1991 for convocation of a peace conference on Yugoslavia was accepted with great reluctance by the Serbs. The Europeans had already rejected in July a proposal by the Netherlands to consider redrawing borders as a means of achieving a comprehensive settlement of the crisis before it escalated any further.[101] The EC approach involved instead negotiations among representatives of the federal and regional leaderships and the leaders of the EC, based on the principles of "no unilateral change of borders by force, protection for the rights of all in Yugoslavia and full account to be taken of all legitimate concerns and legitimate aspirations." It also called for the establishment of an arbitration procedure to decide issues submitted by the parties to the conference.[102] The EC peace conference was initially linked to the establishment of a cease-fire. But heavy fighting continued even as EC military observers arrived in Croatia. As a result, this linkage was quickly abandoned.

The EC considered sending in its own military force to put an end to the fighting. In early August 1991, the Dutch government, then occupying the

EC presidency, proposed sending an "interposition force" to Yugoslavia. Despite support from Germany and France, the proposal failed.[103] On September 19, the French proposed the formation of an intervention force to accompany the arms embargo as a means to impose a cease-fire.[104] Germany supported this proposal as well, but appeared actually to be counting on the British to veto it, thus avoiding any responsibility for implementation.[105] The Netherlands then proposed sending 30,000 European troops to Croatia.[106] Since the EC has no military capacity of its own, the proposal was directed to the Western European Union (WEU). The WEU was asked to develop four options: (1) to provide armed escorts for European observers; (2) to escort and protect; (3) to provide 5,000–6,000 lightly armed peacekeepers; and (4) to send 25,000–30,000 troops. Salmon reports that the British opposed all four options.[107] All agreed, however, that any action would require the consent of all warring parties as well as all EC/WEU members, and that the force would have to be of sufficient size and strength to defend itself if necessary. These conditions ensured that no proposal would ever be approved. A secret seminar of senior officers of the Western European Union was held in Metz to consider options for Croatia. According to General Philippe Morillon, the two-week session produced a proposal for a rapid reaction force, equipped with helicopters and tanks, and mandated to "assert authority" and hold the ravage in check by military force. In the words of General Morillon, it was "discarded and buried."[108]

The scope and intensity of conflict in Yugoslavia accelerated while the Europeans debated their next steps. Croatian forces seized several military garrisons, gaining control of large numbers of heavy weapons, including tanks and advanced anti-tank weapons. These were deployed immediately to reinforce a counteroffensive against advancing JNA troops.[109] In an effort to limit the conflict, the Committee of Senior Officials of the Conference on Security and Cooperation in Europe (CSCE) agreed to the imposition of an arms embargo on Yugoslavia. The United Nations Security Council unanimously adopted the embargo on September 25, 1991 (Resolution 713). While this would have little effect on the ability of the Serbian/JNA forces to wage war, the fact that it applied to all of Yugoslavia—including Bosnia—would be of great importance for the war in Bosnia-Herzegovina.

Despite an EC statement of October 6 recognizing that "the right to self-determination of all the peoples of Yugoslavia cannot be exercised in isolation from the interests and rights of ethnic minorities within the individual republics,"[110] the EC conference remained unable to address Serbian concerns. The EC foreign ministers, at their October 6 meeting at Haarzuilen, agreed that the negotiations at the Hague should be followed by recognition of the former republics that supported the EC-proposed solution.[111] On October 18, the EC put forth its proposals for a settlement, prompting a fierce reaction from the JNA, as we have seen.

The draft settlement of October 18 attempted to reconcile the demands of the conflicting parties with the principles of human rights and the peaceful settlement of disputes embodied in the resolutions of the CSCE and the UN, and in treaties among the EC members. The successor states to Yugoslavia were to form a loose confederation of south Slav states consisting of the former republics within their existing boundaries. Republic boundaries were declared inviolable, although open to change through peaceful negotiation. The new states would be obliged to protect human rights at a European level, including the collective rights of minorities. At some future point, the successor states would become eligible for membership in the EC. In brief, the EC saw the solution to the crisis in Yugoslavia in the "Europeanization" of the republics. Recognition was tied to compliance with European norms of behavior, which implied that each republic would be considered for recognition on its own merits.[112]

On October 18, Momir Bulatović, the president of Montenegro, signaled his willingness to adopt the EC draft convention. The Montenegrin parliament gave its approval to the plan a week later. Consecutive drafts of the EC proposals then underwent modifications aimed at making the treaty conventions more palatable to the Serbs.[113] Provision was made for the formation of a federal Yugoslavia among those republics that so wished— a concession to the desire of Serbia and Montenegro to remain in a rump Yugoslavia. Serbia insisted that self-determination could only be exercised by those recognized as nations or peoples (*narodi*) in the former Yugoslavia, and not by nationalities or minorities. This formula deprived the Albanian and Hungarian minorities in Serbia of any such right. The Serbs argued further that the right to self-determination worked in both directions: allowing both secession from Yugoslavia, and the right to remain in the federation. Under this formula, the Serbs in Croatia and Bosnia-Herzegovina could not be considered a minority without first having had the opportunity to decide if they wished to remain in Yugoslavia. In a meeting of the rump Yugoslav presidency on October 22, Serbia demanded that a referendum be held in all of Yugoslavia before any fundamental change in the constitutional order was instituted.[114] Furthermore, the presidency defended the legal continuity of Yugoslavia in the face of the finding of the Badinter Commission that Yugoslavia was "in a state of dissolution," and called for a new Yugoslavia including Serbia, Montenegro, *and autonomous regions*. The latter could only have referred to the Serb-occupied portions of Croatia and the SAOs in Bosnia. The October 22 statement thus reflected continuing support for the Serbian claim to a single state encompassing most—although not all—of the Serbs in Croatia and Bosnia-Herzegovina.

The EC conference released a revised version of a peace settlement on October 23. A meeting of the EC foreign ministers on October 28 decided to give Serbia until November 5 to accept the EC plan. The October 28 ultimatum, which threatened rump Yugoslavia with sanctions, was the signal for both the EC and Belgrade to make a final effort to reconcile their differences. The November 1 version of the EC plan provided for "special status" for minorities in districts where they were a majority. It required that the republics (in this case Serbia) restore the constitutional rights enjoyed by the autonomous provinces before 1990.[115] In the final draft of November 4, however, the latter provision was deleted, presumably relieving Serbia of concerns that it would have to grant special status or restore pre-1990 rights to Kosovo. Finally, the clause permitting republics that so wished to remain in a federal Yugoslavia was added to the preamble.[116] While they showed some flexibility, noted below, the Serbs nevertheless turned down this draft as well. They continued to insist on the right of Serbs outside Serbia and Montenegro to self-determination. The Serbs' rejection of the draft proposal led the EC to turn to sanctions against Serbia and Montenegro. In a statement issued on October 27 in response to the JNA shelling of Dubrovnik, the EC also "forcefully remind[ed] the leadership of the Yugoslav Peoples Army and all those exercising control over it of their personal responsibility under international law for their actions, including those in contravention of relevant norms of international humanitarian law." This echoed an earlier statement by the CSCE that had also threatened to hold Serbian military and political leaders to account for accusations of war crimes. The next day, the EC called for stronger UN action and agreed to ask the UN secretary-general to use the coercive powers granted by Chapter VII of the UN Charter to bring peace to the region.[117]

One could argue, therefore, that the principal consequence of the EC Conference on Yugoslavia was to set the stage for isolating Serbia (and Montenegro) and recognizing the remaining former republics. However, the EC remained deeply divided over whether to focus solely on Serbia as the aggressor, or to try to some degree to stand above the conflict. It was the same division that was to become apparent during the course of the Bosnian conflict.

The Serbs themselves appear to have been no less divided over their own goals. As we reported earlier, Milošević was prepared as early as January 1991 to see Slovenia secede. On June 30, however, the JNA proposed that the Yugoslav Council for the Defense of the Constitution—the national security organ of the Yugoslav collective presidency—authorize an all-out attack to prevent Slovenia from seceding. Borisav Jović, Milošević's ally on the presidency, reports in his memoir that he not only turned this proposal down, but recommended that Slovenia be expelled from the federation. His recommendation was rejected.[118] While Jović reports that he and Milošević urged the JNA to deal forcefully with Slovenia, they were not seeking to prevent the Slovene secession, but rather to punish the Slovenians—perhaps as a deterrent to other regional leaderships. The proposal to expel Slovenia raised the option of establishing a smaller Yugoslavia. Whether this would include Croatia or some part(s) of Croatia, or exclude Croatia, was also in dispute.

While the secession of Slovenia did not threaten the fragmentation of Serb-populated territories, the secession of Croatia did. In light of the resurgent nationalism among the Serbs and the conflict already brewing in Bosnia, Milošević could not allow this to happen. However, to create a lesser Yugoslavia by allowing only Slovenia to secede would have required an all-out war against Croatia. Gen. Kadijević reports in his memoirs that the JNA had prepared precisely such a plan.[119] According to Jović, however, he and Milošević had already decided in May not to let all of Croatia secede—that is, to pursue a strategy that called for the *de facto* partition of Croatia. They appear to have pursued this policy in fall 1992. The October 22 statement of the rump presidency called for a new Yugoslavia consisting of Serbia, Montenegro, and two Serb regions of Croatia. The implications of this strategy for Bosnia had been made clear by Jović as early as February 1991. He had recommended to Milošević that Yugoslavia incorporate two-thirds of Bosnia-Herzegovina (everything except the mostly Croat region of western Herzegovina and the mixed Croat-Muslim region of central Bosnia). This would have brought all the Bosnian Serbs and almost the entire Bosnian Muslim population into the new Yugoslavia. The October 22 statement called for the inclusion of four Bosnian Serb autonomous oblasts, as well as the two Serb regions in Croatia.

The JNA leadership, heretofore committed to war against Croatia if not to the defense of all of Yugoslavia, appears to have fallen into line with Milošević's strategy by October 22. Kadijević reports that he proposed a similar plan to the rump presidency in October—what he calls in his memoir "Plan B."[120] It is not unreasonable to assume that the unexpected internal problems of the army noted earlier, and the poor performance of the JNA in Croatia in September 1991, contributed to this change.

Just how far Milošević was willing to go to meet EC demands for a settlement remains unclear. Srdjan Radulović, in his book on Krajina, states that Milošević accepted the EC plan for special status for the thirteen *opštine* in Croatia where the Serbs were a majority.[121] There were also reports in the German media that Belgrade had accepted this provision.[122]

According to a Sarajevo source, a secret meeting between Croatian Serbs and Milošević took place over the weekend of November 2–3, 1991, at which Milošević tried to persuade them to support the new Belgrade line, but failed.[123] By accepting the notion of "special status" but insisting on the right of the Krajina Serbs to self-determination, Milošević was rejecting Croatian claims to these areas, but not asserting Serbian claims, either. Such ambiguity was consistent with Belgrade's reluctance to acknowledge the existence of a Krajina state after it was formed on December 19, 1991. It was hardly surprising that the Krajina Serbs refused to accept the notion that they had a "special status." To them, this implied that Krajina was part of Croatia.

By November 1, the pursuit of a greater Serbia by force appears to have been replaced by a more nuanced strategy. The rump Yugoslav presidency, meeting on November 1, issued a statement in response to the October 23 version of the EC plan and the October 28 EC ultimatum.[124] The rump presidency suggested that the proposal for a special status for the Serbs in Croatia was basically acceptable. The presidency articulated several conditions for accepting the plan, however. The first was an amendment providing that those republics that wished to do so could remain in a common state community (that is, a Yugoslav federation). More important still—since the EC was willing to concede the preceding point—the amendment provided that this right accrued to both republics and peoples. The second condition set by the rump presidency concerned implementation of the EC plan: it would have to be internationalized. In a clear attempt to insulate the Kosovo question from international involvement, the rump presidency asserted that no state could be expected to adopt criteria for minority rights that exceeded those in effect in other European countries. As we noted earlier, the Yugoslav delegation to the Hague continued to insist that the Serbs, because they were a "nation," had the right to self-determination. Milošević, in a statement at the plenary session of the EC conference in the Hague on November 5, insisted that no decision on the future of Bosnia-Herzegovina could be made without the consent of all three of its constituent peoples.[125]

It would seem that Milošević had given away little, and that his refusal to agree to the EC declaration of October 28 indicated that he was still bent on creating a greater Serbia. Yet in fact, as we shall argue below, the message to the Krajina Serbs behind this policy was (as it would be to the Bosnian Serbs several years hence) "you are on your own." Undoubtedly, some very harsh lessons drawn from the military failures of the JNA were part of this reappraisal.

It was in this context that a bitter dispute broke out between Milošević and Milan Babić, leader of the Krajina Serbs. Under the Vance plan for Croatia (described below), UN troops were to replace the JNA in the UN Protected Areas. The withdrawal of the JNA was strongly opposed by Babić. His opposition delayed implementation of the Vance plan by at least a month, from February to March 1992. The details of the Babić-Milošević dispute do not concern us.[126] But the nature of the debate provides a clue to Milošević's thinking. Milošević justified his stand in favor of a UN presence in Croatia by admonishing Babić that not all Serbs can live in one state, and that the Serbs in the homeland (*matica*) cannot be held hostage to those living outside Serbia.[127] In order to gain Babić's cooperation, both Belgrade and the Bosnian Serb leadership went out of their way to pledge their support for the Serbs of Krajina.[128] But an analysis of the dispute published in the independent Croatian newspaper *Nedeljna Dalmacija* in mid-January suggested that Babić had good reason to be concerned. It concluded that the Serbs in Croatia had been abandoned by Milošević and would be left to wither on the vine.[129] It was a prescient observation.

The above analysis suggests that at the outset the Serbian leadership used the EC efforts to mediate a settlement among the former Yugoslav republics to nullify more forceful diplomacy by the international community, and in the process encouraged the JNA and Serbian nationalists to pursue their policy of creating a Greater Serbia based on military conquest. But, when the EC took more forceful action, by imposing sanctions on Yugoslavia and calling on the UN Security Council to use its coercive powers to bring peace to the region, the Serbian effort was redirected toward greater cooperation with the international community. Yet, Western policymakers failed to respond to changes in the Serbian position as they developed, and the opportunities to exploit the nuances evident in Serb positions by early November 1991. As we shall see in detail in chapter 5, the fighting in Yugoslavia was not perceived as threatening to Western—and especially not to U.S.—security interests. Policymakers therefore were disinclined to intervene directly in the conflict, and unwilling to make empty threats to do so.

This change in Serbia's policy from claiming part of Croatia for a new Yugoslavia to one of putative disengagement from the fate of the Serbs in Krajina and Slavonija would in all likelihood not have occurred without the emergence of the UN as a major player in efforts to solve the crisis in Yugoslavia. The United Nations had been reluctant to become involved in Yugoslavia. In its initial stages the dispute could be viewed as an internal conflict beyond the organization's competence. As we already noted, however, on September 25, 1991, the Security Council adopted Resolution 713, calling for a cease-fire, supporting the EC conference, and imposing an arms embargo on all of former Yugoslavia. On October 9, former U.S.

secretary of state Cyrus Vance was appointed Special Envoy of the Secretary-General to deal with the Yugoslav crisis. But there the matter rested. Little more could be done as long as Serbia opposed the presence of foreign troops in the combat zone. The Serbs insisted that UN forces patrol a line of demarcation between the combatants. Croatia feared that UN forces, if they were interposed between the Serbian and Croatian units, would legitimize Serbian military gains. (This was the same objection the Bosnian government was to have to UN proposals for a cease-fire in the Bosnian conflict.) Croatia therefore demanded that UN units be stationed on Croatia's borders with Serbia, a demand that Serbia rejected.[130]

The prospects for a UN peacekeeping mission in Yugoslavia changed dramatically when the rump Yugoslav presidency, in a letter to the Security Council on November 9, indicated its support for a UN peacekeeping force in Croatia.[131] Vance secured agreement to a cease-fire on November 23 in Geneva, and later negotiated agreement on the deployment of a UN peacekeeping mission to Yugoslavia.[132] Serbia's willingness to accept a UN peacekeeping role, in contrast to its resistance to EC involvement, can be explained in terms of the different conditions under which such intervention would occur. Under existing principles of UN involvement, UN peacekeeping troops could only "freeze" the situation in Croatia, and thereby allow local Serbian forces to consolidate their control over UN-protected areas. For Croatia, however, a UN cease-fire halted the fighting, prevented Serbia from annexing Croatian territory outright, and preserved the possibility that that territory might be regained.

The presence of UN forces in Croatia left open the question of the ultimate fate of the Serb minority regions. While the JNA withdrew from the United Nations Protected Areas (UNPAs), administrative control remained with the Serbs. Provisions of the plan that called for local police in proportion to the ethnic composition of the region before the conflict began were never honored by the Serbs. UN Secretary-General Boutros Boutros-Ghali, in his report of February 15, 1992, indicated that Croatia would not have responsibility for law and order in the region, and suggested that the UN forces would stay in the UNPAs even if the Croats asked for their withdrawal.[133] The consequences of the UN initiative in Croatia were complex and long-lasting. In retrospect, the presence of the United Nations Protection Force (UNPROFOR) provided Croatia with time to rearm. The war in Bosnia then isolated the Serb-held areas in Croatia from Serbia proper, and sanctions against Serbia undermined the economic and military strength of the Serb-held areas, rendering them vulnerable to Croatian attack in summer 1995. Thus, the UN presence in Croatia ultimately contributed to the restoration of Croatian rule over all of Croatia. Viewed in its own terms, however, the Vance plan was a failure. The provisions of the plan calling for the return of refugees and the establishment of an ethnically mixed constabulary were never implemented, imparting an element of dishonesty and cynicism to the peacekeeping operation. Deploying peacekeepers before a political solution to the Croatian war had been arrived at was in principle unsound, and turned out to be so in practice.[134]

With implementation of the Vance plan in March and April 1992, meaningful negotiations between Croatia and Serbia over the future of the Serb-occupied minority regions in Croatia came to a halt. A number of efforts to restart negotiations were made, but Croatia, following recognition by the international community in January 1992, had little interest in negotiations that might compromise its internationally recognized claim to sovereignty over these areas. At the same time, the presence of UNPROFOR reduced the incentives for the Krajina Serbs to negotiate by giving them a false sense of security and a feeling of relative power vis-à-vis Croatia. The situation in Croatia quickly turned into a stalemate and, eventually, simply an interlude before the Croatians tried to regain the Serb-occupied areas by force.

The commitment of peacekeepers to Croatia had major political consequences for the war in Bosnia. The UN presence allowed Serbia to retain control over territory it might have been hard put to keep if the fighting had continued, and which it appeared by early November ready to abandon in the face of international sanctions. This created a precedent that the Bosnian Serbs could seek to adopt for themselves; namely, to seize territory by force and then push for a cease-fire and a UN presence along the confrontation line in order to freeze their gains. At the same time, the unwillingness of UN forces to restore Croatian control over the UNPAs provided an object lesson for the Bosnian Muslims as to why they should opt for outright military action to reverse what they perceived as aggression, rather than negotiate a compromise that would require them to sacrifice territory. Finally, the Vance plan for Croatia required that JNA forces and irregulars withdraw from Croatia; many in fact crossed the border into Bosnia in March 1992, hastening the destabilization already well under way there.

International Recognition and the Bosnian Question

The debate within the EC over recognition of Croatia and Slovenia had immense importance for Bosnia. German pressure for recognition of Croatia and Slovenia, spearheaded by German foreign minister Hans-Dietrich Genscher, began in July 1991.[135] On August 24, Genscher informed the Yugoslav ambassador that Germany would recognize Slovenia and Croatia unless the JNA ceased intervening in the conflict in Croatia.[136]

From the outset, the German government was under intense domestic political pressure to recognize Croatia and Slovenia.[137] Nonetheless, German diplomatic pressure for recognition remained within the limits of the EC policy that recognition should come only after a political settlement of the Yugoslav crisis, and not as a unilateral German action. The difficulties of negotiating a settlement encountered during October 1991 seemed to bring the EC closer to the German position by raising the possibility that recognition would be withheld from Serbia, but granted to the remaining republics. Nonetheless, at an Extraordinary EPC (European Political Cooperation mechanism) Ministerial meeting in Rome on November 8, the EC reaffirmed its position that

> the prospect of recognition of the independence of those Republics wishing it, can only be envisaged in the framework of an overall settlement, that includes adequate guarantees for the protection of human rights and rights of national or ethnic groups.[138]

The breakup of the EC conference and the escalation of fighting in November then provided an incentive for Germany to act on its own. On December 8 Chancellor Kohl announced that Germany would recognize Slovenia and Croatia by Christmas. There followed a period of intense discussion within the EC over the wisdom of this action.

Meanwhile, the arbitration commission under French jurist Robert Badinter, established as part of the EC conference, issued a decision on November 29 that defined Yugoslavia as a country "in dissolution," rather than a country from which regions had seceded.[139] Although presented as if it were a finding based on international law, one analyst has suggested that the decision appears to have been based on "geopolitical concerns and imaginary principles of international law."[140] In its opinion granting international status to republic borders, for example, the commission appears to have misapplied the principle *uti possidetis juris*. In its response to the query whether the Serbs of Bosnia-Herzegovina had a right to self-determination, the commission offered unclear, even evasive responses. The decision made recognition of the former republics inevitable, and pushed Bosnia-Herzegovina closer to war.

In a contentious meeting of EC foreign ministers on December 15–16, it was agreed that the former Yugoslav republics would be recognized in mid-January, provided they met certain conditions. Without waiting for the Badinter commission to determine which republics met the criteria, Germany recognized Slovenia and Croatia on December 23. Germany's decision was made in the face of intense opposition from Britain, the United Nations, the United States, and—according to John Newhouse[141]—Balkan experts in Germany's own diplomatic corps. Great Britain's Lord Peter Carrington, chairman of the EC Conference on Yugoslavia, argued that withholding recognition was the only way to compel the former republics to reach a solution. Recognition of Croatia and Slovenia, in his view, would necessitate the recognition of Bosnia-Herzegovina and this could spark a civil war.[142] There was concern that recognition of Croatia might prompt the JNA to take more territory before Croatia began to receive military aid from the West—and even that the JNA might invade Bosnia.[143]

Carrington's views were paralleled by those of Cyrus Vance.[144] Both their views were incorporated in a letter sent by then UN secretary-general Xavier Perez de Cuellar to Van den Broek on December 10, 1991. The secretary-general's letter was leaked to the press, and occasioned a response from Genscher, the real object of Perez de Cuellar's warning. The secretary-general then responded directly to Genscher. The three letters dramatically reveal the issues and conflicting perspectives involved in the debate over recognition. Perez de Cuellar's letter of December 10 noted

> . . . the possibility of premature recognition of the independence of some of the Yugoslav republics and the effect such a move might have on the remaining republics. Leaders of Bosnia-Herzegovina and Macedonia were among the many political and military figures who last week underscored to Mr. Vance their own strong fears in this regard. More than one of his high-level interlocutors described the possibly explosive consequences of such a development as being a "potential time bomb."
>
> Given these anxieties, I believe that the Twelve were correct when they reiterated, at their special EPC Ministerial Meeting held in Rome on 8 November, that the prospect of recognition of the independence of those republics wishing it "can only be envisaged in the framework of an overall settlement. . . ." As we know, that overall settlement is being pursued by the Conference on Yugoslavia under the Chairmanship of Lord Carrington.
>
> Let me be clear: I am not in any way calling into question the principle of self-determination which is enshrined in the Charter of the United Nations. However, I am deeply worried that any early, selective recognition could widen the present conflict and fuel an explosive situation especially in Bosnia-Hercegovina and also Macedonia; indeed, serious consequences could ensue for the entire Balkan region. I believe, therefore, that uncoordinated actions should be avoided.[145]

Genscher's rejoinder came in a letter to the secretary-general dated December 13:

> The denial of recognition of any Republic, which wishes its independence, can only lead to a further escalation of force by the [Yugoslav] Peoples Army, for they would see that as a justification for their policy of conquest. I

may note that for Europe, after the Final Act of Helsinki and the Charter of Paris, the borders are inviolable and cannot be changed by force. The EC has therefore demanded respect for the inner and external boundaries of Yugoslavia.[146]

Perez de Cuellar then answered Genscher directly:

> Let me recall that at no point did my letter state that the recognition of the independence of particular Yugoslav Republics [sic] should be denied, or withheld indefinitely. Rather, I observe that the principle of self-determination is enshrined in the United Nations Charter itself. The concern that I continue to have relates to the prospect of early, selective and uncoordinated recognition. In this connection, I cannot but note the omission from your letter of any reference to the common position adopted by you and your colleagues of the Twelve at the Special Ministerial EPC Meeting held at Rome on 8 November 1991. You will recall that the Declaration issued by the Twelve on that occasion stated that "the prospect of recognition of the independence of those Republics wishing it, can only be envisaged in the framework of an overall settlement."[147]

Under classical international law doctrine, the recognition of a secessionist state before its conflict with the existing state had been substantially won constituted a form of intervention antagonistic to the existing state. In the view of Lori Fisler Damrosch,

> Neither the multilateralization of Germany's initiative within the framework of the EC, nor the fact that the EC acted after following what was purported to be a juridical procedure, should suffice to resolve doubts about the legitimacy of premature recognition—at least not against the urgent plea of the Secretary-General for all states to refrain from selective recognition outside the framework of an overall political settlement.... The Security Council had explicitly approved the Secretary-General's report, which embodied the plea to refrain from premature recognition. The EC's disregard of his appeal should therefore be considered legally suspect, as a derogation from the authority of UN organs in the sphere of international peace and security.[148]

But the debate, as the participants saw it, was not over the legal implications of recognition of the former republics. It was over timing and the political and military consequences of the decision.

On the matter of standards for recognition, the Europeans were in agreement. The EC decision of December 16 required Yugoslav republics to meet a broad range of political criteria in order to be recognized. These included internal democracy; a good faith commitment to the peaceful negotiation of their disputes; respect for the UN Charter, Helsinki Final Act, the rule of law, human rights, and the rights of ethnic and national minorities as called for by the draft plan prepared by the conference on Yugoslavia; and, respect for the inviolability of borders and the principle that they might be changed only by peaceful means. The EC also stipulated that states applying for recognition would have to accept the peace process embodied in the EC conference.[149] Bosnia-Herzegovina, Croatia, Slovenia, and Macedonia all submitted applications for recognition by the European Community. The EC refused to accept applications submitted by the Serbs of Krajina (Croatia) and the Albanians of Kosovo. The EC thus continued to support the existing borders of the republics and to insist on the solution of outstanding ethnic conflicts within the framework of those borders.

In a series of decisions handed down in January 1992, the Badinter commission provided belated legal justification for recognizing republic borders as international borders.[150] It ruled that Macedonia and Slovenia satisfied the criteria for recognition. It also ruled that Croatia should be recognized, but that it should comply with provisions of the draft treaty convention granting a special status to minority territories. In the case of Bosnia-Herzegovina, the Badinter commission noted that the government's efforts to declare an independent state within the existing republic borders were contradicted by the declarations of Bosnian Serbs in favor of continued membership in a Yugoslav state. It therefore ruled that "the will of the peoples of Bosnia Hercegovina to constitute the S[ocialist] R[epublic] of B[osnia] H[erzegovina] as a sovereign and independent state cannot be held to have been fully established." It suggested "a referendum of all the citizens of the SRBH without distinction" as a possible means by which the popular will might be determined.

The push by the EC for recognition of the former Yugoslav republics put Bosnia in a delicate and precarious position. Izetbegović was fully aware of the dangers such a step held for Bosnia. With the support of President Gligorov of Macedonia, he had argued against premature recognition of the former republics. It was clearly in the interest of the Bosnian government that the EC conference should be given a chance to craft an agreement by which Serbian designs on Bosnia could be contained. Early recognition worked against this goal. But it also became clear after the collapse of the talks in the first week of November that the chances of a comprehensive agreement that included and constrained Serbia were slight.

Following the Serbian refusal to accept the EC plan and the decision of the Badinter commission that Yugoslavia was in dissolution, it was of the greatest urgency to the Bosnian government that Bosnia-Herzegovina gain international recognition, lest Bosnia itself face dissolution. The Bosnian government was well aware of the danger to which it would be exposed if Germany recognized only Croatia and Slovenia, while holding off recognition of Bosnia. At a press conference on November 12, Izetbegović noted that "selective recognition of Slovenia and Croatia would cause great problems for Bosnia and Herzegovina."[151] A congress of the SDA, meeting in late November and early December, called for independence for all six of the Yugoslav republics.[152]

This was the situation when Izetbegović met with Genscher on November 22 in Bonn. Izetbegović was coached by the German ambassador in Belgrade to warn Genscher of the danger of unilateral recognition of Croatia and Slovenia. But, according to several different accounts, Izetbegović failed to do so.[153] The incident remains a puzzle. Izetbegović would certainly have warned against limiting recognition to Croatia and Slovenia, especially if Germany took this step without the agreement of the remaining members of the EC. Secretary-General Perez de Cuellar's letter revealed that Izetbegović was warning Vance in early December of the danger of recognizing "some" of the republics. Yet we have it on the testimony of a participant in the November 22 meeting—Michael Libal of the German Foreign Office—that Izetbegović did not warn Genscher of the danger recognition would pose for Bosnia. One suspects that by this time Izetbegović did not wish to do anything to deter the Germans from their decision to push ahead with recognition. For Bosnia, the critical moment had passed when the EC failed to persuade Serbia to recognize Bosnia as part of the EC peace settlement. At the same time, Izetbegović continued to push for the reconvening of the Hague conference, in the hope that a comprehensive solution to the Yugoslav crisis could be reached and the threat to Bosnia from Serbia removed. Izetbegović also pleaded, to no avail, for a UN presence in Bosnia and urged "parallel" recognition of all six former republics. But by the third week in November, it seems safe to assume, Izetbegović and the Bosnian government were likely to have been more concerned that Germany and the EC not fail to recognize Bosnia-Herzegovina at the same time that they recognized Slovenia and Croatia than with reconvening the Hague conference and the search for a comprehensive solution.

In Bosnia, the repercussions of the EC decision on December 16 to recognize the former Yugoslav republics were not long in coming. On December 18 the Serbian autonomous region of Bosanska Krajina declared that it was part of Yugoslavia, not Bosnia-Herzegovina, and that the EC decision to recognize Bosnia did not apply to its territory.[154] On December 21 the Bosnian Serb Assembly announced the formation of the Serb Republic of Bosnia and Herzegovina, and on January 9, 1992, declared its independence. (The Serb republic was recognized by the Republic of Serb Krajina within days of its formation.)[155] The Badinter commission's call for a referendum on independence for Bosnia-Herzegovina further complicated the internal political situation in Bosnia. The outcome of the referendum—as we shall see below—remained in doubt until the position of the Bosnian Croats, who were the swing vote, was clarified.

The decision to recognize Slovenia and Croatia, and the prospect that Bosnia might be recognized as well, seemed to intensify the Serbian threat to Bosnia. The war in Croatia broke out once more in December, as the cease-fire of November 23 was broken. The last week in December 1991 was notable for a number of threatening statements by JNA generals and Serbian hard-liners. On December 22 General Kadijević gave a speech suggesting that the army still had not fully given up the option of seizing territories outside Serbia by force.[156] According to a Croatian account, on December 27 Branko Kostić argued that the new federation must include Serbia, Montenegro, and the SAOs (presumably in both Croatia and Bosnia).[157] But Serbian accounts of the speech contain no such reference. Reflecting the pessimistic mood of that moment, Ambassador Zimmerman cabled Washington on December 20 suggesting war in Bosnia seemed certain following the decision to recognize Croatia and Slovenia.[158] Ian Traynor summed up this sense of anxiety in a dispatch to the *Guardian* on December 31, in which he noted that the major issues concerning borders had yet to be resolved, that the Croatian position had hardened after recognition, and that a Serbian offensive to fix the borders of a Greater Serbia might come before the EC recognized the former republics on January 15.[159]

Nevertheless, Serbia did not attempt to broaden the conflict to Bosnia. In late December 1991 a "Convention for a New Yugoslavia" met in Belgrade. It brought together Serbs from Serbia, Montenegro, and Bosnia. The meeting gave its support to the idea of a new Yugoslavia made up of Serbia and Montenegro within their existing borders. The possibility was left open for other Serbian regions in Yugoslavia to join the federation. But it was left unclear when and how this might be accomplished. By the end of January, despite various obstacles to implementation of the UN peacekeeping operation, tensions between Croatia and Serbia had eased. There was increasing agreement within the EC that recognition of Croatia had been the right decision,[160] and that the Bosnian government should press ahead with a referendum on independence. Even Lord Carrington admitted that the EC initiative "had pressed intransigents to negotiate rather than fight."[161]

The feeling that peace in Croatia was reducing the risks of recognizing Bosnia was reinforced by the conciliatory tone of the Serbian government during January and February 1992. In early January Milošević made a point of holding out the olive branch to the Bosnian Muslims, suggesting that "a common and equitable life of the Serbs and Muslims in Bosnia . . . is in the interest of both peoples." At the same time, however, he reiterated the contention that "borders will be decided by those peoples that wish to stay in Yugoslavia and those that do not."[162] On January 21, the Serbian government issued an appeal to Macedonia and Bosnia-Herzegovina to stay in the federation.[163] This was followed by a proposal for talks with the other republics over ways to restore ties among them. According to the Croatian newsweekly *Danas,* there were "completely reliable reports that President Slobodan Milošević has sent a letter, not only to Milan Babić, but also to Radovan Karadžić, in which he tried to explain to [them] why he had accepted Cyrus Vance's plan, and in which he tried to dissuade [them] from [their] pro-war policy."[164] On February 27, Milošević delivered a speech supporting a peaceful resolution of the Yugoslav crisis.[165] Shortly thereafter, Viktor Meier of the *Frankfurter Allgemeine Zeitung* noted a "Milošević boom" among diplomats in Belgrade, based on the belief that Milošević had decided to limit Serbia's claims to territory outside her existing borders.[166] On March 7 the usually astute *Economist* suggested that neither the Serbian government nor the federal army was in the mood for a new war, despite rising tensions in Bosnia.[167] The easing of tensions in Croatia and Milošević's conciliatory tone contributed to a sense of false optimism in Europe.

The Bosnian government contributed to this head-in-the-sand mood. Izetbegović, wary of frightening the international community before Bosnia was finally recognized, suggested in an interview with *Der Spiegel* that Serbia was exhausted after the conflict in Croatia, and that there was no danger that the JNA would intervene in Bosnia.[168] Izetbegović gained French support for holding a referendum on independence for Bosnia following a visit to Paris on January 15.[169] On January 23, the president of the EC Council of Ministers, João de Deus Pinheiro, announced that the EC was willing to recognize Bosnia-Herzegovina if the referendum on independence was adopted.[170] On January 24, the *Guardian* reported that the EC now accepted the fact that the recognition of Croatia had improved the prospects for peace, omitting any reference to the looming crisis in Bosnia.[171]

The European perception that recognition had not unleashed a new crisis was combined with a belief that the steps taken in November to ostracize Serbia should be reconsidered. The Yugoslav opposition press reported that Chancellor Kohl had made overtures to Serbia, indicating that Bonn was willing to consider lifting the trade restrictions on Serbia.[172] At this point the United States became actively involved in efforts to shore up Bosnia. On January 10 the United States sent a note to Belgrade warning Serbia against taking action that would threaten the territorial integrity of Bosnia-Herzegovina. On the occasion of Borisav Jović's visit to Washington on

January 27, U.S. Deputy Secretary of State Lawrence Eagleburger made it clear to him—according to Jović's own memoir—that "the division of Bosnia and Herzegovina is absolutely and totally unacceptable to the USA." Jović reports he told Eagleburger that Serbia was against the breakup of Bosnia-Herzegovina and that it was a "pure lie" that negotiations had taken place between Serbia and Croatia over the partitioning of Bosnia. Jović reports that he "emphasized that any effort at dividing Bosnia and Herzegovina would lead to war, as would its separation from Yugoslavia without the agreement of its three constituent peoples."[173] U.S. warnings to Serbia were matched by overtures to the Bosnian government. Izetbegović visited Washington on February 19 and was received by Eagleburger, who used the occasion to provide strong backing for the territorial integrity of Bosnia.

In the last week of February 1992 the Bush administration decided to push for recognition of Bosnia. The move coincided with the EC-sponsored conference on Bosnia in Lisbon and the referendum on independence for Bosnia (both of which are discussed below). As we shall see in detail below, Karadžić and Izetbegović appeared to have agreed at the Lisbon meeting that Bosnia-Herzegovina should retain its identity and existing borders, but be reorganized along cantonal lines. But the U.S. move was not designed specifically to bolster the European mediation effort. Ambassador Warren Zimmerman, in urging recognition, argued that Bosnia was threatened with isolation in a Milošević-dominated "Serbo-Slavia," and that EC negotiations to find a peaceful solution in Bosnia held little hope.[174] In Zimmerman's words:

> I believed that early Western recognition, right after the expected referendum majority for independence, might present Milošević and Karadžić with a *fait accompli* difficult for them to overturn. Milošević wanted to avoid economic sanctions and to win recognition for Serbia and Montenegro as successors to Yugoslavia; we could offer him that recognition in exchange for the recognition of the territorial integrity of the four other republics, including Bosnia.[175]

Zimmerman conceded that there was the possibility of violence if Bosnia won recognition, but added that "there is a much greater chance of violence if the Serbian game plan proceeds unimpeded."[176]

In line with this view, the United States urged the Bosnian government to carry out the referendum on independence called for by the Badinter commission. When the referendum provoked a confrontation between the Bosnian government and Serb extremists (described below), the United States pushed still harder for recognition. In a letter dated March 4, Secretary of State James Baker urged the EC to recognize Bosnia. There was widespread concern in the media that failing to recognize Bosnia at this point would send the wrong signal and encourage Serb radicals in their demands. Still, the Europeans hesitated. After Baker met with EC foreign ministers in Brussels, a compromise was announced on March 10. In a joint declaration, the United States and the EC agreed that the United States would recognize Slovenia and Croatia, and that the EC and the United States would coordinate their policies toward Serbia and Montenegro, emphasizing respect for the territorial integrity of other republics and the rights of ethnic minorities as well as the need to negotiate state succession issues. They also agreed that Bosnia-Herzegovina and Macedonia should be recognized, on condition that the parties in Bosnia-Herzegovina "adopt, without delay, constitutional arrangements that will provide for a peaceful and harmonious development of this republic within its existing borders."[177] According to media reports, they also agreed to delay recognition of Bosnia until April 6 in order to allow the parties to resolve their differences.[178]

Milošević, meanwhile, had already come to the conclusion that the recognition of Croatia and Slovenia would be followed by the recognition of Bosnia. According to Jović's memoirs, on December 5, 1991 Milošević suggested to Jović that it was time to redeploy the JNA in Bosnia in order to prepare for recognition. Milošević was convinced that following recognition the JNA would be seen as a foreign force in Bosnia. To counter this perception, non-Bosnians were to be withdrawn from Bosnia, while Bosnian Serbs serving in the JNA were to be organized as the nucleus of a Bosnian Serb army. The proposal was not received with enthusiasm by the JNA.[179] But by the end of December General Kadijević had informed Jović that 90 percent of the army in Bosnia had been redeployed in accord with the December 5 plan, and that only 10–15 percent of JNA forces in Bosnia were not from the republic.[180] Silber and Little note that in January 1992 Milošević issued a secret order transferring all JNA officers born in Bosnia back to that republic.[181]

The Jović revelations suggest that Serbian planning for an attack on Bosnia had begun well in advance of April 1992. Serbia had consistently opposed the recognition of Bosnia-Herzegovina under a Muslim-dominated government, and made no bones about the consequences of such a move. Although Milošević appears already to have been contemplating the day when he would be compelled to abandon Krajina to the Croatians, it seems likely that Bosnia was viewed in a different light. First, Serbia felt it had a proprietary interest in Bosnia. Geostrategic interest and greater Serbian nationalism combined with a genuine concern for the fate of the Bosnian Serbs under a Muslim government. Second, Milošević had every reason to believe that the war in Bosnia could be won without having to mobilize the

Serbs of Serbia proper. The officer corps of the JNA had substantial numbers of Bosnian Serbs. The portions of Bosnia of strategic interest to Serbia bordered directly on Serbia, allowing Belgrade to provide logistical and other means of support to the Bosnian Serb army. But the success of Milošević's Bosnian strategy, as we have presented it here, hinged upon the ability of the Bosnian Serbs to win the war on their own. Although some Serbian units from Serbia proper were to fight in the Bosnian war, and the Bosnian Serb army would receive logistical support, money, and supplies from Serbia, Milošević would not repeat the mistake of Vukovar, when he had relied on untrained and unmotivated reservists from Serbia proper to fight outside their own republic.

Serbia, Croatia, and the Bosnian Question

Belgrade's position toward Bosnia thus depended on the course of events inside Bosnia. An article in the Serbian Socialist journal *Epoha* in fall 1991 laid out two alternatives:[182] The first consisted of a voluntary union, if the Muslims could be persuaded to join in a new Yugoslavia. In this case, western Herzegovina and parts of Posavina would be ceded to Croatia. What remained of Bosnia would be divided into regions. This scenario enjoyed a brief period of popularity in Belgrade when Milošević engaged in his peace offensive in spring 1992. While it might seem far-fetched that the Muslims would join a new Yugoslavia, the outcome of the referendum on Bosnian independence was at this point still uncertain. Belgrade might have speculated that the defeat of the referendum would lead to a new political situation in Bosnia that would bolster the pro-Yugoslav camp within the SDA. The second alternative consisted of an imposed partition. Western Bosnia and Serb-occupied Krajina (in Croatia) would merge. A Muslim republic would be formed with a Serb enclave (Romanija) within it. Semberija would be annexed by Serbia and eastern Herzegovina by Montenegro. Croatia would be given western Herzegovina and parts of Posavina. This scenario, or some variant of it, was very likely what Milošević anticipated, at least in broad outline and absent any provocative steps such as the premature merger of western Bosnia and Croatian Krajina. His experience in Croatia encouraged plans for war and ethnic cleansing in Bosnia, to be followed by a cease-fire under UN auspices and the freezing of Serbian gains. Yet his strategy for Bosnia remained flexible and opportunistic, as events were to show.

This did not mean that Milošević had given up plans for creating a greater Serbia. A UN-enforced cease-fire in Bosnia after a presumably short campaign there, and the continuing presence of a UN force in Croatia, would set the stage for realizing the Milošević variant of a greater Serbia. But that goal would not be allowed to jeopardize the creation of a new Yugoslavia consisting of Serbia and Montenegro. While in July 1991 Milošević and Jović appeared set on creating a greater Serbia, by late 1991/early 1992 Milošević appeared more committed to the idea of a new, less extensive Yugoslavia, for emotional as well as purely pragmatic reasons.[183] Serbs outside this new Yugoslavia would not be incorporated into this new state, but would exercise the right of self-determination in order to retain *de facto* independent status within Croatia and Bosnia. It followed from this—to repeat a point made earlier—that Milošević needed the cooperation of the international community. The international community had to accept the goal of a cease-fire without coercing the parties, economically, militarily, or politically, into a solution unfavorable to the Serbs because of their role as aggressors. The weakness in this strategy was apparent. It could easily be put in jeopardy by the actions of the Muslim forces, who consistently broke cease-fires engineered by the UN and welcomed by the Serbs. Moreover, it underestimated the determination of international actors, once they recognized Bosnia-Herzegovina, to see it survive.

The new Belgrade line laid out at the Convention for a New Yugoslavia in December 1991 ("Yugoslavia first, greater Serbia later") compelled the Bosnian Serbs to take a more flexible approach to the question of Bosnian independence. This was apparent when Karadžić addressed the opening session of the Bosnian Serb assembly a week after Germany recognized Croatia. Karadžić asserted that, as a result of Bosnia's decision to apply for recognition, "in a constitutional and legal sense Bosnia-Herzegovina has ceased to exist." But he went on to suggest that Bosnia-Herzegovina might be transformed into a confederation. The Serbs would have the right to be "federally" tied to Serbia and Sarajevo would have the status of an extra-territorial city.[184] This made it clear that any effort to negotiate a compromise would have to address not only the internal relationships among Bosnia's three main groups, but the external relations of the Serbs (and the Croats) with their neighboring homeland(s). The latter issue would come up repeatedly in international efforts to mediate a constitutional solution to the crisis.

Meanwhile, the closer that Bosnia-Herzegovina came to holding a referendum on independence, the more the internal divisions among the ethnic communities in Bosnia-Herzegovina came to the surface. The SDA, with the support of Europe and the United States, was determined to press ahead. Izetbegović announced that Bosnia would hold the referendum "even if the devil is knocking at our door."[185] The SDS made it clear that if Bosnia-Herzegovina declared independence the Serbs would exercise their right to self-determination and secede. Although it was no longer possible for the

Serbs to propose the union of Serb Bosnia with Yugoslavia, it was still possible to push for the formation of a confederation so loosely constructed that it would leave the Serb portions of Bosnia free to merge with the new Yugoslavia at some future date.

Such a solution to the Bosnian question—confederation followed by the eventual secession of the non-Muslim regions—was also attractive to the right wing of the HDZ, with its base in western Herzegovina. The radicals in the HDZ could advance their demands for autonomy for western Herzegovina, secure in the knowledge that President Tudjman of Croatia would support them. As we have noted, Tudjman and Milošević first discussed the partitioning of Bosnia in Karadjordjevo, in March 1991. In July, a senior advisor to Tudjman suggested in an interview with the London *Times* that the partitioning of Bosnia was the "only peaceful solution" to the Yugoslav conflict, and that Tudjman and Milošević had discussed such a solution in at least two prior meetings. A key part of the deal was to be the creation of a Muslim "buffer state" in the center of Bosnia-Herzegovina and a voluntary population exchange—a proposal that would have ruled out the inclusion of a truncated Bosnia in rump Yugoslavia, the solution favored by the Bosnian Serbs in their discussions with the MBO in summer 1991.[186] At the end of 1991, Tudjman espoused the partitioning of Bosnia publicly, provoking an angry letter in support of the integrity of Bosnia from a number of leading Croatian intellectuals in Sarajevo.[187] In the middle of January 1992, talks were held between Tudjman and Nikola Koljević (joined by Franjo Boras, one of the two Croatian members of the Bosnian presidency), signaling a rapprochement between the SDS and the HDZ.[188] Shortly thereafter Koljević came forth with a compromise plan that provided for regionalization of Bosnia. His plan called for each ethnic community to set up its own administration in cantons in which it had a majority. But cantons of like nationality would not necessarily be territorially unified.[189] The plan anticipated the proposals put forth by EU negotiators in March, about which we shall have more to say below.[190]

These discussions between the Serbs and Croats failed to produce an agreed plan for the future of Bosnia. It was in the interest of the Croatian government to support the unity of Bosnia, rather than the Serb proposals for its partition, if only as a means of detaching Bosnia from Yugoslavia; both as a prelude to later Herzegovinian secession and as a way to win Croatia the support of the international community for its own efforts to restore Croatian territorial integrity. Encouraged by the unstinting support of the international community for a referendum on independence, the Bosnian parliament met in late January 1992 to consider the wording of the referendum. The debate in parliament was then followed by a confrontation between the moderates and hard-liners within the HDZ over the wording of the referendum adopted by the parliament—a portent of the political divisions among the Bosnian Croats yet to come. These events were scarcely noted in the Western media. But they made it painfully clear that only a negotiated solution agreed by all three nationalist parties could avert the mounting crisis.

Independence

The future of Bosnia-Herzegovina was bound up with the fate of the referendum on Bosnian independence. Three outcomes were possible. First, the adoption of the referendum could have been accompanied by a constitutional agreement on the future of Bosnia. In this case, the referendum would have ratified an elite pact for the creation of a consensual system of government in Bosnia. Second, the Croats, who held the swing vote in parliament and in the electorate, could have defeated the referendum or insisted that it be reworded in such a manner as to preclude any hope that a central government could continue to function in Bosnia. In this case, the referendum would have legitimated and accelerated ethnic partition. Finally, the Croats could throw their lot in with the Bosnian government and the SDA, in which case the referendum would constitute a vote for Bosnian independence and legitimate the existing constitutional system, at the risk of provoking civil war with the Serbs.

The Parliamentary Showdown

The debate in parliament over the adoption of the referendum took place January 25, and ended when the Serb deputies withdrew after a majority consisting of Bosnian Muslim and Croat delegates turned down a Serb motion that the matter be placed before the not-yet-established Council for National Equality. When Momčilo Krajišnik, the Serb president of the assembly, attempted to adjourn the session, he was replaced by a member of the SDA and the proposal to hold a referendum was adopted in the absence of the SDS members in the form proposed by the Muslim deputies. The decision placed the Bosnian government and the Serbs on a collision course.[191]

The account of the debate given in *Oslobodjenje* nevertheless suggests that, over the seventeen hours that the assembly was in session, the deputies were groping for a compromise. The crux of the matter was whether an agreement on the regionalization of Bosnia could be adopted *prior* to the referendum on independence, in which case the referendum would both declare Bosnia's independence *and* establish the basis for a new constitutional order. The description of the debate given in *Oslobodjenje* merits quoting at some length:

> [During the course of the session] numerous consultations took place, leading to frequent pauses, and every time the session recommenced it seemed that a solution was near. Especially in the midnight hours, when the vice president [of the SDA] Muhamed Čengić suggested that a proposal for the regionalization of the republic be worked out first and then that the referendum take place within a specified period of time, [a proposal] to which the head of the SDS Radovan Karadžić, who at one point found himself on the podium with Čengić, agreed.
>
> "Never were we closer to agreement as at this time," said Karadžić, accompanied by applause from the deputies. But the next pause brought a new turn of events. Vlado Pandžić, president of the parliamentary club of the HDZ, expressed satisfaction at the narrowing of the gap over an agreement over the referendum. Only after Radovan Karadžić had requested that the commitment [*obaveza*] to regionalization be defined by a new constitutional act (first regionalization, then referendum) did the president of the Party of Democratic Action Alija Izetbegović refuse any kind of conditions being placed on the referendum, saying that "we shall remain with what we have already proposed, and as far as talks [following the vote] are concerned, we are ready to accept them. . . ."
>
> At that moment it was clear that the hope for a favorable outcome of the talks between Karadžić and Čengić was over. Vojislav Maksimović, president of the parliamentary club of the SDS, proposed that further discussion was superfluous and in the name of all the SDS deputies suggested that the proposal for bringing a decision to hold a referendum of citizens be sent to the Council for Equality Among the Nations [*Savet za Medjunacionalnu ravnopravnost*]. With this, the session of the Assembly was finished for the deputies of the SDS who, along with President [of the Assembly] Krajišnik, left the Assembly hall. It was exactly three-thirty [A.M.].[192]

How close the deputies were to real agreement remains a matter of debate. Critics of the SDS claimed that Karadžić was demanding *de facto* confederalization of Bosnia before a referendum could be held.[193] In any case, the Croats could not risk being seen voting with the Serbs and against the Muslims. Their support assured adoption of the referendum proposal. But the HDZ was in fact deeply divided. The moderate faction, headed by Kljujić, favored the version of the referendum proposed by the Bosnian government, that Bosnia-Herzegovina was a sovereign state of its citizens, not of its constituent national groups. The radical wing of the HDZ, with Mate Boban as its spokesman, favored a referendum that would declare the three main national groups as sovereign.

One might assume from the action of the assembly that the issue had been settled, and that the pro-Bosnian faction in the HDZ had carried the day. Instead, the factional struggle within Croat ranks intensified during February as the date for the referendum drew near. President Tudjman met with Boban and Kljujić in Zagreb to mediate the dispute. The result appeared to be a victory for the hardline faction. Boban publicly circulated an alternative version of the referendum—the so-called Livno Declaration. It defined Bosnia-Herzegovina as a "state community of its constituent and sovereign nations, Croats, Muslims, and Serbs, living on their national territories."[194] In early February, Kljujić was ousted as head of the HDZ by the radicals from western Herzegovina. Kljujić did not hide his bitterness. His letter of resignation was the occasion for what he believed was his parting shot at the nationalists within his own party: "Just let me tell you. Many who sit here and who support cantonization of Bosnia and Herzegovina will live in a Greater Serbia, and I shall depart for Australia."[195]

Kljujić's resignation was then delayed. But the issues dividing the HDZ remained. The campaign against Kljujić was followed by secret talks at the end of February in Graz between Karadžić and Josip Manolić, an adviser to Tudjman.[196] The Croatian position that emerged from these talks was not, on the surface, greatly different from that of the SDS. It called for a Bosnia-Herzegovina made up of sovereign constituent nations linked together in a confederal relationship. Given the confusion in Croat ranks, the degree to which the Croat population would turn out to support the referendum remained uncertain. Then, several days before the referendum was to be held, the Bosnian Catholic Church issued an appeal to the Bosnian Catholics to vote in favor of independence, in effect, to support the wording of the referendum adopted by the Bosnian parliament.[197] The event suggested that the Catholic Church in Bosnia had become a key player in the Bosnian government's push for the independence of Bosnia. But in the end the Croat vote for the Bosnian government's version of the referendum must be understood in the light of Zagreb's desire to see Bosnia separated from Yugoslavia. It was evident even to the hardline Croats that the only form in which the referendum could pass was that approved by the parliament and supported by the Muslims. As adopted by the Bosnian assembly, the referendum asked the people of Bosnia if they wished to live in a "Bosnia of citizens," carefully eschewing any reference to regionalization of the republic along ethnic lines. The dilemma for the Croats was partially resolved just prior to the referendum by the Lisbon negotiations among the three parties, mediated by the EC (discussed below). All three national leaders agreed that Bosnia-Herzegovina should be divided into ethnic units. The HDZ could then argue that the regionalization sought by the hardline Herzegovinians had been agreed to at Lisbon, and that Croats were therefore free to vote for the referendum as adopted by the Bosnian assembly.[198]

International concern over the upcoming referendum began to surface during February. The UN decided in early February to establish the headquarters for the UNPROFOR operation in Croatia in Sarajevo, out of concern over developments in Bosnia.[199] Vance was alarmed by the situation in Bosnia. He described it as a "time bomb," adding that the UN mission in Bosnia believed the referendum could trigger an eruption of violence.[200] On February 15 the *Süddeutsche Zeitung* reported on a speech by Stipe Mesić to the German Society for Foreign Policy in which he warned, to the displeasure of the audience, that holding the referendum would lead to war.[201] Prompted by these concerns, Carrington proposed that a peace conference on Bosnia be held prior to the staging of the referendum in order to allow a consensus to emerge on how sovereignty was to be exercised in an independent Bosnia.[202]

The Cutileiro Negotiations

The EC-sponsored talks on Bosnia opened on February 14 in the Villa Konak in Sarajevo. At the second session of the Bosnia conference, held in Lisbon February 22–23, the EC mediator, Jose Cutileiro, put forth a proposal that for the first time called for a state of national regions, while requiring the three national party leaders to pledge support for the independence of Bosnia-Herzegovina.[203] The assent of all three national parties to the EC Lisbon plan was received cautiously and largely ignored in the Western press. The agreement was a bitter disappointment to Izetbegović. The SDA wasted no time in convening a meeting of 250 "notables" in Sarajevo on February 25 to denounce the accord and in holding a press conference at which it announced that it opposed creating ethnic cantons in Bosnia, thereby repudiating the Lisbon agreement in no uncertain terms.[204] Karadžić, on the other hand, was triumphant, sensing that the parcelization of Bosnia-Herzegovina had begun. He then met with the Croats in Graz, where they agreed, in effect, to the partitioning of Bosnia. (The Graz agreement is discussed in more detail in chapter 5.) The Croat representatives to the talks in Lisbon kept a low profile, but had every reason to be satisfied with the Cutileiro proposals. They fulfilled the Croats' desire for autonomy for western Herzegovina while recognizing the inviolability of Bosnian borders, the latter point of utmost importance to Zagreb. Miro Lasić, who represented the HDZ at the Lisbon conference, announced that under the agreement the cantons in Bosnia would obtain sovereignty and on this basis urged the Croats in Bosnia to vote yes in the upcoming referendum when, in fact, the referendum made no mention whatsoever of dividing Bosnia along national lines.[205] However, no attempt was made to resolve the issue of where the ethnic regions, or cantons, would be located. The Lisbon agreement thus had the opposite effect from what had been intended by the EC. It deepened the gap between the three sides over the future of Bosnia. Each side rushed to exploit the situation, or to attack the accords, as the case might be.

A follow-up meeting held in Villa Konak at the end of February produced no results. On March 9, after strenuous negotiations in Brussels, a second version of the Lisbon agreement was produced. Secretary of State James Baker, meeting in Brussels with representatives of the EC in an attempt to win European backing for recognition of Bosnia-Herzegovina, met with Bosnian foreign minister Haris Silajdžić, informing him of U.S. support for the EC proposals.[206] It appeared that the EC effort also had the support of Belgrade. On March 10 the *Guardian* reported that the Serbian government was ready to accept the fact that Bosnia would not be included in the new Yugoslavia and quoted an EC diplomat as saying that the government in Belgrade was being very constructive. At the same time, the rump Yugoslav presidency refrained from attacking the principles for a settlement put forth by Cutileiro. The presidency called for a political solution in Bosnia based on agreement among the three nations "as the only way out."[207]

The reaction to the Brussels settlement among the Bosnian Serbs, in contrast, was highly negative, even among members of the democratic opposition in Sarajevo. *Borba* reported on March 10 that the Muslims and Serbs were still far apart.[208] Karadžić found the proposal inadequate, insisting that the Serbs of Bosnia would accept nothing less than their own state, linked with the two other ethnic communities through a loose confederal arrangement that permitted special ties to Yugoslavia (that is, to Serbia proper).[209] According to *Borba,* Karadžić had offered Cutileiro a map of Bosnia divided into mini-units with "corridors" joining them into some sort of archipelago, which Cutileiro rejected out of hand. Under immense pressure from the EC to approve the Brussels plan, the Serb delegation proposed to refer the matter to their assembly for approval—a tactic they would employ repeatedly during the Bosnian conflict to avoid agreeing to a settlement. On March 11 the Bosnian Serb assembly voted to reject the EC plan, arguing that it put too much power in the hands of the Bosnian central government.[210]

One final effort was made to settle the question of Bosnia-Herzegovina's constitutional structure prior to recognition in negotiations that took place March 17–18 at the Villa Konak in Sarajevo. The negotiations produced proposals for the restructuring of Bosnia-Herzegovina similar to those suggested at Brussels.[211] It was reported that the three delegations signed a "Statement on Principles of a New Constitutional Solution for Bosnia and Herzegovina," giving rise to the belief that the three parties were close to a settlement. But Cutileiro, in his press conference following the meeting, said only that the participants "agreed," not that they signed. The SDA representative said they did not sign.[212] According to the EC proposal, Bosnia was to be divided into three "constitutive units" defined primarily in ethnic terms, but also taking into account economic, geographic, and other criteria. (By early April, "other criteria" were defined as historical, religious, cultural/educational, and transport and communications, and the will of the inhabitants.) The map produced by these negotiations, but never finally agreed to by the parties, was in fact an ethnic map of Bosnia, in which the *opštine* were apportioned among the three ethnic communities by what appeared to be a simple rule of thumb—the ethnic community that constituted a plurality or majority according to the 1991 census. As a result, each of the three "constitutive units" consisted of noncontiguous regions: two Muslim, four Croat, and six (or possibly seven) Serb. According to Cutileiro, the agreement was to be submitted to the Bosnian assembly for approval, and then voted on by a referendum.[213]

The ambiguity surrounding the agreement reached at the Villa Konak was evident. No decision was reached over whether the army and police should fall under the jurisdiction of the federal or cantonal governments. The general principles supposedly agreed to at the meeting provided that the three constitutive units were to be represented by an equal number of delegates to the upper house of parliament, where key issues were to require a four-fifths majority for passage. This granted an effective veto to two-thirds of the delegates from any one of the three major groups. Thus, the EC plan for Bosnia-Herzegovina amounted to the "Yugoslavization" of the republic, and its *de facto* partition along ethnic lines.[214] By falling back on the Yugoslav formula, the EC attempted to preserve the fiction of a unified Bosnian state, while permitting as much devolution of authority to the ethnically defined units as could be achieved. As Ambassador Cutileiro characterized it, "The constitutional principles recognized a central point for the Muslims, and for the EC: that existing borders of Bosnia-Herzegovina would be inviolable, but that inside those borders Serbs and Croats would be guaranteed autonomy from Muslims and from each other."[215] Moreover, according to the constitutional principles agreed to on March 18, each "constitutive unit" was to be "allowed to establish and maintain links with other republics and their organizations providing their relations and links are in accordance with the independence and integrity of Bosnia-Hercegovina."[216]

The Muslims and the Serbs each sought to portray the Villa Konak

Map 3.2 **The Cutileiro Map, March 1992**

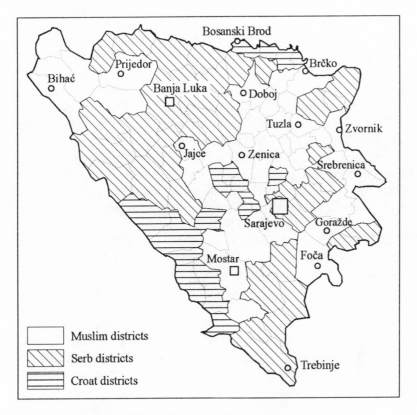

Muslim districts

Serb districts

Croat districts

Based on a document of the EC Conference on Yugoslavia (mimeo).

agreement as a victory for their own entrenched positions.[217] Karadžić asserted that the March 18 document set the seal on three separate Bosnias.[218] Irfan Ajanović, spokesman for the SDA, claimed that the document confirmed that Bosnia-Herzegovina would have all the attributes of a single state, including its own currency, a single system of defense, a single foreign policy, and a single legal-judicial system.[219] The Bosnian Croats at first supported the plan, most likely in the hope that it would effectuate the final divorce of Bosnia-Herzegovina from Yugoslavia and the Serbs, but also because the proposed settlement facilitated relations between Croat areas in Bosnia and Croatia proper, and provided autonomy for Croat-majority *opštine*. But the Villa Konak agreement was, in the end, repudiated by all three ethnic communities. On the critical issue of where the cantonal boundaries were to be drawn, there was almost total confusion.

It was reported in the media that the map prepared by Cutileiro was presented to the participants at the last minute, for further discussion. The participants were not allowed to voice their objections or to make changes. In his press conference following the meeting, Cutileiro characterized his map as a "beginning document," to show where people reside in the majority. He added that the three parties also submitted maps.[220] Radically differing maps, allegedly proposed by each of the three sides, were published in the Yugoslav media (see Maps 3.3, 3.4, and 3.5). The differences among them reflected the conflicting territorial ambitions that would soon lead to bloodshed. The SDA map looked very much like the EC map, except that two border districts in eastern Bosnia, Rudo and Čajnice, as well as the Šekovici enclave in eastern Bosnia, were assigned to the Muslims. The HDZ map showed the small *opštine* of central Bosnia—Bugojno, Novi Travnik, Jajce, Kotor Varoš, Travnik—as Croat, while the SDA map showed these areas as Muslim. The HDZ map also claimed Mostar, Konjic, and Jablanica, which were Muslim on the SDA map. The Serbs claimed all or part of the mixed provinces along the Drina—Foča, Rogatica, Goražde, Višegrad, and Bratunac—which were claimed by the SDA in their map. The mixed Serb-Muslim provinces on the border of Cazin and Bosanska Krajina regions also were claimed by both the Muslims and the Serbs. The Drventa district in the Posavina was claimed by all three parties.[221]

The Croats were the first to repudiate the EC map publicly.[222] Milenko Brkić, several days after agreeing to the Cutileiro plan, insisted that cantonal borders would have to be drawn on the basis of the 1961 census. This would have brought Mostar under Croat administration.[223] A few days later, the SDA also repudiated the agreement.[224] Izetbegović declared that he was opposed to ethnic cantons and had accepted the EC plan in order not to jeopardize the forthcoming recognition of Bosnia, and to avoid being blamed for the break-up of negotiations, since the Serbs and Croats had accepted. He asserted that he had accepted only "conditionally," pending approval of the EC proposal by the people of Bosnia in a referendum.[225] Izetbegović then changed his mind again, and was reported to be ready to accept the Villa Konak agreement within the framework of global agreements.[226] Meanwhile, Karadžić had taken advantage of the confusion over the SDA position to announce that, in light of the SDA renunciation of the Villa Konak agreements, the Bosnian Serb republic had adopted its own constitution and would settle for nothing less than the status of a sovereign and constituent unit in Bosnia.[227] At approximately the same time (the end of March), a group of ninety-three Croat intellectuals from Bosnia criticized the EC plan, asserting that it was contrary to the results of the referendum on independence and that 59 percent of the Croats in Bosnia would become national minorities if Cutileiro's map were adopted.[228]

Map 3.3 **The SDA Map, March 1992**

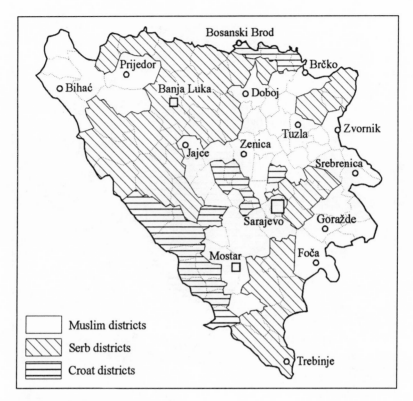

Adapted from *Politika,* March 19, 1992.

The possibility that the EC-sponsored talks could nevertheless have produced a positive outcome was later given credence by a dispatch that appeared in the *New York Times* in August 1993.[229] It suggested that Ambassador Zimmerman had encouraged Izetbegović to distance himself from the Cutileiro plan, concerned that the EC negotiations were undermining the U.S.-backed push to recognize Bosnia within its existing borders. Zimmerman was quoted as saying: "Our view was that we might be able to head off a Serbian power grab by internationalizing the problem. Our hope was that the Serbs would hold off if it was clear Bosnia had the recognition of Western countries. It turned out we were wrong." The *Times* account alleged that Izetbegović twice agreed to a partition during the course of the EC-sponsored negotiations but backed off when "he became aware of the U.S. plans to push through recognition of his government." It alleged that Izetbegović renounced the Lisbon agreement after Zimmerman visited Sarajevo in March.

Map 3.4 **The HDZ Map, March 1992**

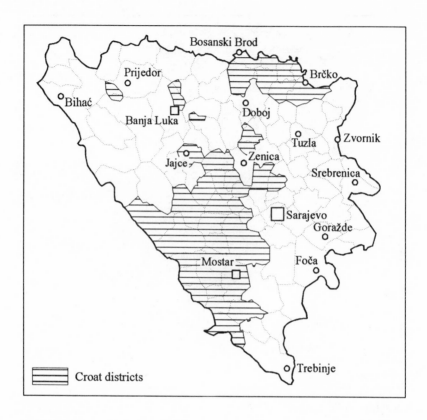

Adapted from *Politika*, March 19, 1992.

In a letter to the *New York Times* repudiating this report, Zimmerman suggested that U.S. policy had been supportive of the EC negotiations, and that he had urged Izetbegović to "stick by his commitments."[230] According to Zimmerman, Izetbegović confessed he was having second thoughts about the Lisbon agreement. Although Zimmerman asked Izetbegović why he had signed it, the ambassador reports he acted on standing instructions to support any agreement that the EC could broker, and did not encourage Izetbegović to go back on the agreement. In his account of this incident in his memoir, Zimmerman adds that he suggested to Izetbegović that the agreement was not final, "and there would be a further opportunity for him to argue his views."[231]

Although the ambassador's explanation hardly sounded like a ringing

Map 3.5 **The SDS Map, March 1992**

Adapted from *Oslobodjenje*, March 14, 1992.

endorsement for the Cutileiro plan, the United States was officially supportive of the EC efforts to find a constitutional solution to the Bosnian crisis. At the time of Izetbegović's visit to the United States in February, the State Department "expressed the support of the United States for the ongoing efforts, under the auspices of the EC Conference, to foster dialogue among all parties in Bosnia-Hercegovina, and the opposition of the United States to any attempt to disrupt the upcoming referendum on the independence of Bosnia-Hercegovina."[232] In remarks made at a policy think tank in Belgrade on March 11, 1992, Zimmerman spoke of the importance of supporting the integrity of Bosnia and Herzegovina and said that, with respect to EC efforts to negotiate a settlement in Bosnia, "whatever is agreed will get the full support of my government."[233] Secretary of State Baker, as we have seen, informed Silajdžić in Brussels that the United States supported the EC plan.

But it was also clear that the United States did not interest itself greatly in the details of discussions over the future constitutional order in Bosnia and that Baker did not use the opportunity at Brussels to meet with Izetbegović to put the maximum pressure possible on the Muslims to accept the EC proposals. American attention was focused on Milošević, not on the delicate negotiations that would be required to strike a balance between autonomy for the ethnic communities and maintaining the integrity of the Bosnian state. Zimmerman was skeptical of the claim that Bosnian Serbs' rights were being violated and was unsympathetic to the Bosnian Serb call for self-determination. He told Karadžić in October 1991: "It seems to me you're just angry that Serbs are a minority. But that's how elections come out, that's democracy. Your creation of autonomous regions is provocative, and your unilateral changes of Bosnia's borders are destabilizing." To Zimmerman, "It was growing increasingly obvious that Karadžić had no intention of playing by the rules."[234] Zimmerman reports he told Karadžić and Koljević in mid-January 1992,

> It's time to start dealing with reality. Since Europe has decided to recognize the Yugoslav republics, American recognition is inevitable, just a matter of time. Why don't you participate in the referendum on independence and come to terms with the fact that with 30 percent of the population Serbs can't expect to dictate the outcome? By participating you can at least affect the timing and content of independence.[235]

The Zagreb weekly *Danas* quoted Zimmerman as declaring that "the United States is very interested in a unified and integral B-H."[236]

A plausible case might be made that the United States missed an opportunity to facilitate a solution to the Bosnian question during the March EC negotiations. But the evidence that the United States and its ambassador to Yugoslavia deliberately sabotaged a possible agreement in March does not stand up to scrutiny. On the other hand, Izetbegović could not help but be aware of U.S. plans to push through recognition of Bosnia once the joint U.S.-EC declaration of March 10 (cited above) was made public. Nothing that Zimmerman could have said to Izetbegović could have made this clearer—or could have increased the Bosnian government's expectations of assistance from the West. With the U.S.-European commitment a matter of public record, it would seem that the Bosnian government had very little reason to take the ongoing EC-brokered talks seriously. Only if the United States and the EC had insisted on an agreement on constitutional issues as a condition for recognition would the Muslim side have been motivated to support the Cutileiro plan. But this would, in turn, have allowed the Bosnian Serbs to block recognition of Bosnia, or delay it, by obstructing the EC negotiations.

The sixth meeting of the EC conference on Bosnia-Herzegovina took place at the end of March in Brussels. On this occasion Cutileiro proposed a single president and an 18,000-man army for the Bosnian federal government.[237] One can only surmise that such a proposal, totally unacceptable to the Serbs, was a token gesture by the EC designed to win Bosnian support on the eve of recognition. A special commission was set up to address the problem of fixing the borders among the cantons. It was to report back May 15. Such delay in the face of a spreading civil war gave the impression that the EC had given up all hope of averting the conflict. More probably, the focus of the EC was beginning to shift, under U.S. pressure, away from the cantonization of Bosnia, and toward supporting the Bosnian government's efforts to halt Serbian aggression. A final session of the talks was held July 28 at which Silajdžić, representing the Bosnian government, refused even to read the proposals for a constitutional framework proffered by Cutileiro.[238]

Referendum and War

The EC negotiations described above took place largely after Bosnia declared its independence following the referendum of February 29–March 1, but before the United States and Europe extended diplomatic recognition to the new state. Although the SDS did not attempt to block the referendum, the Serbs refused to participate in it. They remained adamantly opposed to any declaration of independence made before Bosnia's transformation into some kind of confederation whose members would enjoy special relations with neighboring states. The referendum, by triggering the events that would result in independence and recognition, was from the Serb point of view a step toward war.

This interpretation is underscored by the events surrounding the staging of the referendum. The voting itself took place uneventfully. The official results showed that 62.68 percent of the total number of voters in Bosnia-Herzegovina voted in favor of independence; almost precisely the outcome one would expect if all the Muslims and Croats supported the referendum. There were charges that Serbs who might have wished to vote in favor of the referendum had been kept away from the polls by intimidation.[239] In fact, there were Serbs who looked favorably upon the establishment of an independent Bosnia. In a poll of Bosnian students conducted in November 1991, 43.38 percent of the Serbs approved of an independent Bosnia. However, only 8 percent thought that Bosnia could survive outside Yugoslavia.[240] At the same time, Croats who favored partition were under the pressure of the HDZ and the Catholic Church to vote for independence. Thus, the exact sentiments of the Bosnian population other than the

Muslims must remain in doubt. But the net change in the outcome had voters been entirely free to vote their consciences would likely have been small.

The day following the referendum, barricades went up in Sarajevo. The ostensible reason for this act was the shooting of several Serbs at a wedding over the weekend. The Serbs demanded that the negotiations over the future of Bosnia-Herzegovina be brought to a conclusion before the declaration of independence was adopted; that independent Sarajevo TV be replaced by national television channels; and that the Ministry of Interior be reorganized along national lines. These demands were first acceded to by Izetbegović, then repudiated after the JNA stepped in and the people of Sarajevo took to the streets to protest the terror.[241] Shortly thereafter, the Socialist Party organized a peace rally in Mostar that attracted 10,000 persons.[242] Encouraged by the support of the masses, and convinced that the Serb side had suffered a major political defeat, Izetbegović went ahead and declared the independence of Bosnia-Herzegovina on March 3. His actions were ratified by parliament (in the absence of its Serb members) the same night.

The motives of the Serbs in setting up the barricades on March 2 were the subject of considerable debate. Most commentators saw the move as a dry run for an eventual Serb takeover, orchestrated from Belgrade. It is also possible that the Serbs were seeking to paralyze the Bosnian government at this crucial juncture (in effect, to stage a coup), but were deterred by the actions of the army and the peace demonstrators. A Western media source quoted the commander of the Sarajevo military district, General Kukanjac, to the effect that what the Serb militants were doing was "sheer madness."[243]

At a minimum, the actions of the Serbs could be taken as a crude warning aimed at dissuading the Bosnian government from declaring independence prior to the successful conclusion of the EC-sponsored negotiations. If this was the intent of the maneuver, it failed. The majority of the people of Sarajevo repudiated the masked gunmen. On March 5, Vance met with party leaders in Sarajevo and expressed his concern with the situation in Bosnia, but left Sarajevo before the crisis was resolved. Vance also disappointed the Bosnian government with his announcement (on March 4) that UN troops would not be available for duty in Bosnia.[244] On March 6, the same day a large rally for peace was held in Sarajevo, Karadžić called for an army takeover, and warned that if the EC were to recognize Bosnia-Herzegovina before it was transformed, there would be civil war.[245] The army refused, just as it had turned down the offer of the Milošević forces to take power in Yugoslavia in March 1991.

The temporary victory of the democratic opposition in Sarajevo and the fact that, as we reported earlier, Milošević had already indicated in the context of the EC conference on Yugoslavia that he was ready to accept independence for Bosnia encouraged optimism in the West. The usually astute *Guardian* correspondent, Ian Traynor, and the veteran German journalist, Viktor Meier, for example, offered unusually positive analyses of the situation.[246] Meanwhile, during the month of March, all three national camps prepared for war.

Mostar was the scene of armed confrontations between JNA reservists and Croat irregulars. In early March, fighting broke out in the northern city of Bosanski Brod, in the ethnically Croat area of Bosanska Posavina on the Croatian-Bosnian border. Local Croats, with the support of the Muslims, tried to block the passage of JNA forces from Croatia to Bosnia.[247] According to Serb sources, the fighting in Bosanski Brod took on the dimensions of a full-fledged conflict when Croatian paramilitaries under the leadership of Ante Prkačić crossed the bridge linking Bosanski Brod with Croatia on March 26. According to Serb sources, the Croatians burned and pillaged the Serb village of Sijekovac.[248] Reports in the second week of March described a situation of near anarchy in the Doboj region.[249] In the third week of March, there were reports of fighting between Croatian irregular forces and the JNA in Herzegovina.[250] Fighting was reported in Derventa, as Croats tried to cut the link between Bosanska Krajina and Serbia.[251] The flight of the Serb and Croat populations from Kupres was reported on March 27, as the Croats occupied the town only to be evicted by the JNA.[252] The mayor of Goražde, Hadžo Efendić, declared a state of emergency, and Tanjug reported that Goražde had "sunk into darkness and fear."[253] At the same time, Serbs began the ethnic cleansing of Croat villages in Herzegovina, and Croats initiated the cleansing of Serb villages in the Posavina.[254] This first phase of the struggle was characterized by the breakdown of law and order, the takeover of power throughout the republic by the national parties and their "crisis staffs" (*krizni štabovi*), and local confrontations, mostly between Serbs and Croats, in anticipation of major battles to come.

The first engagement of Serbian forces from outside Bosnia occurred in Bijeljina on April 2 and 3, when an armed confrontation between the Muslim Patriotic League and local Serb territorial units took place. The fighting degenerated into sniping on the civilian population, and sparked the intervention of the paramilitary Serbian Guard, under the command of Željko Raznjatović (Arkan). A massacre of Muslims followed, the first of the war.[255] Arkan's incursion into Bosnia was a major factor in escalating tensions in Bosnia, and provoked an outraged reaction from the international community, as well as an agonized appeal from Izetbegović for a halt to the fighting. By April 6, when the EC granted recognition (followed by the United States the next day), Bosnia-Herzegovina was on the brink of full-scale war, and panic had seized the population.[256] Crisis committees had taken over. Western hopes that recognition would head off the civil war had clearly not been realized. In the view of *Borba*'s correspondent in Sarajevo, "If you recognize, war will spread, if you don't, it will spread."[257]

In the event, recognition sparked a Serbian invasion of eastern Bosnia. Serbian irregulars, including Arkan's forces and JNA reservists from Serbia, launched a full-scale attack on Muslim cities and towns along the Drina. Fighting broke out in Sarajevo on April 6, and on April 8 the Yugoslav army entered the fray. Instead of slowing or halting the war, as in the case of Croatia, recognition had apparently accelerated the pace of Bosnia's decline and destruction. The Bosnian crisis had become the Bosnian tragedy.

Could Bosnia Have Been Saved?

The preceding account suggests the difficulties that the international community faced at the time the Bosnian conflict began. First, Bosnia-Herzegovina was disintegrating from within. In the words of Ljiljana Smajlović, until the war a journalist for *Oslobodjenje:*

> A year before the war broke out Bosnia was, in effect, partitioned. The authority of the central government in Sarajevo extended only to the city's limits. Serb-dominated Banjaluka (sic) in northwestern Bosnia, for instance, refused to send tax monies to the government in Sarajevo. Muslim-dominated Zenica in central Bosnia refused to send army conscripts to the JNA. Croatian Listica, in western Herzegovina, refused to allow army convoys to pass through its territories.[258]

Second, the winding down of the war in Croatia freed up Croat and Serb forces, above all Croat units from western Herzegovina, to undertake operations in Bosnia. Third, reconfiguration of the JNA created a distinctively Bosnian Serb army. Milošević's decision to create a Bosnian Serb army was taken in anticipation of a civil war seen as inevitable in the light of the German move toward recognition. Milošević and his advisers were convinced that recognition of Croatia would lead to the recognition of Bosnia by the EC and the United States. Their response was to prepare for war, and to provide Belgrade with some basis for denying involvement once the war broke out. In any case, as our account makes clear, Serb preparations for war in Bosnia pre-dated the German decision.

Could the international community have done anything differently to prevent this terrible conflict before it broke out? Or, to state the question more provocatively, did international actors, singly or collectively, accelerate the trend toward war in Bosnia?

A full answer to this question would require us to consider the international response to the larger Yugoslav crisis as a whole. Given our more narrowly focused concern with Bosnia, we may begin with the debate over the recognition of Croatia and Slovenia. The decision has had its defenders and critics, but the latter far outweigh the former.[259] Those critical of German pressure to recognize Croatia call it a blunder of major proportions, in the absence of which the international community might have found a way of averting the Bosnian tragedy. Among the most outspoken critics of the German decision is Ambassador Zimmerman, who argues that recognition of Croatia necessitated the recognition of Bosnia-Herzegovina, which in turn sparked the conflict in Bosnia.[260] Yet the fact remains that it was the U.S. government, at Zimmerman's urging, that pushed the idea of recognizing Bosnia in March 1992. U.S. criticism of Germany for actions that led to an outcome—the recognition of Bosnia—which the United States then embraced with zeal seems disingenuous. The controversy is complicated by the fact that two different recognition decisions were at issue: the German and EC decision to recognize Croatia and Slovenia, and the U.S. decision to push for the recognition of Bosnia-Herzegovina.

The German campaign for recognition of Slovenia and Croatia appears to have influenced Milošević's decision of December 5 to redeploy JNA troops in Bosnia. Milošević grasped what Genscher seems to have ignored, but what Carrington and Vance feared; that recognizing one or two republics would necessitate recognizing them all, accelerating Bosnia's slide into war. Recognition, coming hard on the heels of the EC sanctions against Serbia, undercut any pretense of impartiality that the EC had tried to maintain up to that time. In light of the formal criteria for recognition adopted by the EC, recognition also meant that the EC accepted the claims of those they recognized to be democratic, respectful of human rights, and legitimate members of the international community. If a newly recognized state then found itself threatened, the international community was in principle duty bound to go to its defense.[261] A rational and consistent recognition strategy would have necessitated follow-up actions that went beyond simply punishing Serbia with economic sanctions. Recognition should in principle have been followed by military and economic aid to those recognized. Yet such aid was not forthcoming. The critics of recognition could therefore argue that the tangible results of recognition for the states concerned were small, while the expectations generated by recognition were immense, and cruelly disappointed.

It could be argued that the German initiative helped convince Milošević to give up the idea of achieving a greater Serbia through military means.[262] But, as we have demonstrated above, his abandonment of a greater Serbia came in response to a combination of factors: the military difficulties the Serbs were encountering in Croatia, the willingness of the UN to permit the Serbs to control occupied areas of Croatia, and the breakdown of the EC Conference on Yugoslavia. The risk of an aggressive Serb response to the recognition decision was real; judging from the facts that, in reaction to the recognition decision, the hard-liners in Belgrade urged that the borders of a greater Serbia be carved out of Croatia and Bosnia by force, and that there was an upsurge of fighting in the second week of December 1991. Although Milošević chose a different course of action—internationalizing the issue of the Serb-inhabited areas in Croatia—that outcome was far from certain at the time the recognition debate was going on. Thus, the argument that recognition dissuaded the Serbs from creating a greater Serbia, while not without merit, is by no means proven.

Meanwhile, those defending the recognition decision had a number of strong arguments to support their case. Recognition did seem to end any hope Milošević may have had to occupy all or most of Croatia and, in retrospect, sounded the death knell for the Serb strategy of a greater Serbia. On balance, recognition was a logical step—one that could have been taken even earlier—if the overarching priority of the West was to make sure that Serbia could not block the emergence of new states within the borders of the former Yugoslav republics. In the German view, Serbian aggression had been under way from the beginning of the conflict. Recognition could not be blamed for inciting the Serbs to an action to which their preparations for war in Bosnia suggested they were already committed.[263] The German argument was, in essence, that recognition was a show of firmness that would induce Belgrade to be more reasonable. If there was a failure, it was in not insisting on autonomy for the Serbs in Croatia; that is, in recognizing Croatia despite its failure to implement the recommendations of the Badinter Commission.

Did recognition of Croatia and Slovenia raise the issue of recognition of Bosnia prematurely, as Carrington and others feared? Bosnia's best hope for survival lay in the success of the EC Conference on Yugoslavia. The collapse of these negotiations marked a turning point for the Bosnian government. As we have seen, once these negotiations collapsed Izetbegović became less willing to delay recognition, in contrast to his earlier eagerness to see recognition postponed while the talks continued. The issue of Bosnia's future status thus assumed central importance at least a month before Germany recognized Croatia. In the light of what was happening within Bosnia itself, the sooner the Bosnian issue was resolved, the better. The mistake, then, was not in recognition of Croatia *per se,* but in the failure to tie recognition to agreement on constitutional reforms in Bosnia.

If, on the other hand, Serbia was determined to see Bosnia partitioned and to annex the Serb portions of it, then—absent any outside force that might constrain the Serbs—the republic's fate was already sealed, recognition or no.

Finally, the argument *for* recognition entailed an argument *against* continuing to seek a comprehensive solution to the Yugoslav crisis. Lord Carrington argued passionately against jettisoning the comprehensive approach, claiming that it offered the only hope of success in the long run. Opponents of recognition argued that a comprehensive solution would be rendered impossible by a decision to opt for selective recognition of the former republics. The problem with this argument was that it tied resolution of the war in Croatia to issues elsewhere, and allowed both Croatia and Serbia to complicate negotiations in the Hague in order to protect their own interests. Zagreb, for example, argued that Croatia could not accept any more autonomy for the Serbs in Croatia than Serbia would grant to the Albanians in Kosovo, knowing that Serbia had sharply limited the autonomy of Kosovo two years earlier. In the end, the comprehensive approach, in which the solution of any one problem depended on the solution of all of them, gave each party to the negotiations a cost-free veto; exercising this veto, the Serbs prevented any agreement as they consolidated their military position in Croatia in fall 1991, forcing the Europeans to bring the EC-sponsored talks to an end in November. As events were to prove, the only comprehensive solution that would have ended the confrontation between Serbia and Croatia was a deal between them to divide up Bosnia. This, in effect, is what happened at Dayton, as we shall see in chapter 7 and the conclusions to this study.

The second part of the recognition debate concerned the U.S. push to recognize Bosnia-Herzegovina in spring 1992. The Americans argued that Serbia was preparing aggression against Bosnia and that recognition would deter, not hasten, civil war. This was exactly what the Germans argued in respect to Croatia, and it is not unfair to surmise that the U.S. policy toward Bosnia was influenced by the apparent success of the German strategy toward Croatia. Yet the two situations were not strictly comparable, and the U.S. attempt to replicate the German move was a mistake (if, indeed, this was what the Americans were attempting). The progressive disintegration of Bosnia meant that Croatia and Serbia would be forced to intervene at some point, if only against each other. If recognition remained purely symbolic, and did not entail concrete steps to reverse the disintegration of Bosnia from within, it would fail to accomplish its purpose. Milošević was preparing for war in Bosnia, but it is not clear that he wished Serbia to become involved in Bosnia at just this moment. Milošević, after all, was waging a campaign for recognition of rump Yugoslavia as the legitimate successor to the old Yugoslavia. Important military assets, including military bases and weapons manufacturing plants, would be put in jeopardy if war broke out too soon in Bosnia; all the more so now that Croatia could be expected to enter the Bosnian conflict on the side of the Bosnian government.

According to one close observer of these events, the European diplomats at the Brussels meeting were confident that an agreement could be reached, and claimed that they had the backing of Milošević in this endeavor. It is not unreasonable to surmise that Karadžić and Milošević were not in complete agreement, and that Karadžić already feared that Milošević would sacrifice the Bosnian Serbs to serve his own interests just as readily as he turned on Babić and the Krajina Serbs. Miloš Vasić has argued, "It can be safely assumed that even by 1992 Milošević realized that the Bosnian Serbs were out of control."[264] The issue was whether Serbia could avoid a war and achieve its minimal objectives by adopting the EC plan while keeping the Bosnian Serbs in check. The possibility of exploiting the differences between Belgrade and the Bosnian Serbs dictated a policy of caution on the part of the international community in respect to the recognition of the Bosnian government. But, as we have argued above, it is not clear that Western policymakers recognized the nuances of Milošević's position, or the emerging differences between him and the Bosnian Serbs.

By the second week in March it appeared that all sides had resigned themselves to the fact that the timetable for recognition had been set by the United States, and that war was inevitable. One has the unsettling feeling that each of the nationalist leaders was now play-acting for the sake of the international community, intent simply upon placing the onus for the outbreak of war on someone else. The Americans could not argue that they were misled or uninformed about the threat of war inherent in recognizing Bosnia-Herzegovina before the nationalist parties reached an agreement over the country's future. On the contrary, U.S. and EC diplomats received numerous warnings from both official and unofficial sources in Serbia that recognition of Bosnia-Herzegovina would result in war.[265]

The problem was that the United States, which held the key to resolution of the Bosnian conflict, was not present at the EC negotiations. The apparent U.S. lack of interest in the constitutional issues surrounding the talks amounted to an endorsement of the integral Bosnia line taken by the Bosnian government. By spring 1992, however, it was clear that this position was unacceptable to Serbia. Yet, the United States did not press Serbia to compromise, not even by offering to exchange recognition of Yugoslavia for Serbia's agreement to the peaceful reorganization of Bosnia in a way that would not jeopardize the security of its constituent peoples. U.S. policymakers failed to perceive the basic difference between the wars in Croatia and Bosnia: The former was a straightforward territorial dispute; the latter a question of the existence or nonexistence of the state itself and, in the eyes of some, the survival of its peoples. José Cutileiro, for one, remained convinced that a chance for a peaceful solution had been allowed to slip away in spring 1992, alluding to advice from "well-meaning outsiders who thought they knew better" to explain Izetbegović's refusal to adopt the March 18 agreement.[266]

In defense of the U.S. reluctance to become involved in the constitutional issues surrounding the Bosnian crisis, it must be noted that the talks in Brussels and Sarajevo in March 1992 showed that the Serb and Muslim positions on the nature of a new Bosnian constitution were far apart. A realistic assessment of the talks might well have led the Americans to believe they would fail. Serbia's willingness to accept a compromise was contradicted by the reluctance of Serbia to offer Bosnia recognition if such a compromise could be reached. This suggested that Milošević wished to keep open the option of annexing Serb lands in Krajina and Bosnia, even at the risk of war.

To understand the dilemma facing the United States (and the international community in general), one must also appreciate the extent to which the Serbian leadership had, by this time, isolated itself within its nationalist rhetoric and debased its credibility by denying that it was directly involved in the war in Croatia and arming the Serbs in Bosnia. While other Serbs were warning the Americans of a war in Bosnia, Milošević took a totally different tack. He downplayed the urgency of the Bosnian question, and argued with Ambassador Zimmerman that the Bosnian Serbs—unlike the Serbs in Croatia—were not "threatened in existing conditions."[267] In the paranoic atmosphere of the time, which Milošević had done so much to create, Zimmerman took this to mean that the Serbs were intent on attacking Bosnia.[268] Zimmerman chose to overlook the warning in Milošević's words that other circumstances (recognition) could lead to a change in Serbia's purported desire to seek a peaceful solution. If the Serbian government was ready to compromise over Bosnia—that is, if Belgrade was sincere that a constitutional solution was possible—it lacked the language to communicate this message to a U.S. ambassador and State Department who were by now deaf to nuances.

The events of spring 1992 therefore allow several different interpretations of the motives that guided Milošević in his policy toward Bosnia. They do not, however, relieve Serbia from responsibility for invading eastern Bosnia in April 1992, and for encouraging the ethnic cleansing that followed. (The same should be said, of course, about the responsibility of the Croats for attacking Herzegovina at about the same time.) The mistake of the West was not in recognizing Bosnia-Herzegovina on April 7, 1992. The mistake came earlier, and consisted of its unqualified support for the holding of a referendum on independence before the three nationalist parties had agreed on a constitutional solution. The proper time for a referendum would have been after such an agreement, as foreseen in the Cutileiro plan. But was a constitutional solution truly possible, even assuming that the United States pressured both the Serbs and the Muslims? To achieve a peaceful outcome it was necessary, first, to persuade Milošević that his strategy of engaging the UN on his side, as had occurred in Croatia, could not be repeated in Bosnia. But developments in Croatia encouraged Belgrade to engage in a quick and bitter campaign of ethnic cleansing once Bosnia declared its independence, and then present the world community with a *fait accompli,* hoping the UN would then step in to ratify this change.

The means of diplomatic coercion that would have been necessary to dissuade Belgrade from this policy—in effect, to send a message that a cease-fire followed by a UN force would not be an acceptable way of dealing with the Bosnian conflict—depended crucially on the fate of Krajina. As we shall see in later chapters, once Milošević concluded that Krajina was lost, the Milošević version of a greater Serbia collapsed, and with it the need to prolong the war in Bosnia. The point to be made here is that Belgrade was riding a tiger in Krajina, afraid to assert outright its claims to the region, but unable to let go. But Belgrade's indecision over what to do about Serb claims to parts of Croatia drove Croatia and the Bosnian Croats to support Bosnian independence. This, in turn, encouraged the Bosnian Muslim inclination to forgo compromise and simply override Bosnian Serb offers to negotiate autonomy, the sincerity of which was therefore never put to the test.

In the end, it was not external factors that brought Bosnia to ruin, but internal ones: the profound clash of perception and principle among the Bosnians themselves concerning the fate of their country that made compromise impossible. In early 1992, in an interview with *Vreme,* Koljević expressed the dilemma inherent in this situation as follows:

> You know what, I told Alija Izetbegović one thing based on the Muslim demands. The Muslims want a sovereign Bosnia, the Serbs do not want it, and the Croats have said that they want it. The Muslims want a unified Bosnia, a Bosnia that will not split apart. I think that it is unrealistic to have both. I can understand the Muslim need or fear, if you wish, of Serbian or Croatian domination, and I can see that quite clearly. But you cannot make up for that by placing Serbs in the position of a minority. I say to them that it must be decided whether it will be a unified Bosnia that will not be absolutely sovereign, or a sovereign Bosnia that will not be absolutely unified,

meaning a Muslim Bosnia. Let a Muslim Bosnia be sovereign. Can Bosnia be both sovereign and unified, integral, at the same time? Hardly.[269]

The contrasting vision of the Bosnian Muslims was reflected in Izetbegović's address to the congress of the SDA in November 1991:

> Serbia and Croatia are national states. Bosnia-Hercegovina is not this and it can only be a civil [*gradjanski*] republic. (Applause) For it is not Muslims, Serbs, and Croats who live in Bosnia-Hercegovina, but a national mixture of these three peoples, including, of course, a smaller number of other peoples. If somebody wants to speak about ethnic self-determination of peoples in the ethnic sense of the term, he must explain how this otherwise indisputable principle is to be applied to a mixture of peoples found, for example, in Sarajevo or in Bosnia-Hercegovina in general.
>
> Therefore the right question for Bosnia-Hercegovina is not whether to carry out self-determination of peoples, but how to do so with a mixture of peoples. Nobody has so far given a decisive and clear theoretical answer to that. Of course, there is a practical answer, and it is the historical formula of Bosnia as multi-denominational, multi-national, and multi-cultural community.
>
> Why would one mar something that has been created by a fortunate combination of historical circumstances, has been functioning well, and also represents a humane, democratic, and one may also say, a European solution. Why would one change that even if it had been possible, and particularly why do so if it is impossible without violence and blood and if a retrograde concept of national autocracy is offered along with that change?[270]

CHAPTER 4

The War on the Ground, 1992–94

The war in Bosnia-Herzegovina involved an internal struggle among ethnic nationalists over the definition and control, indeed, the very existence of the state, as well as an international struggle between the government of Bosnia-Herzegovina and its neighbors. The intensity of emotions and perceived stakes of the struggle escalated as revelations of widespread abuses of civilians and charges of genocide made the brutal nature of the war apparent to all concerned. Complexity and emotion are the enemies of effective policymaking, and Western policies toward Bosnia reflected this. The United Nations, already involved in the unstable peace in Croatia, was drawn into the Bosnian conflict against the judgment of its leaders and suffered what may prove to be lasting damage to its peacekeeping capacity. The great powers, having at first underestimated the dangers in Bosnia, very quickly drew back from efforts by local actors and the UN to involve them more extensively. The British and French, who provided the bulk of UN peacekeeping troops, resisted any expansion of their role. The United States attempted to isolate and contain the war through sanctions and embargoes while policymakers struggled to find a solution. This left the three nationalist forces to pursue their own goals by whatever means they chose. It was the people of Bosnia-Herzegovina who paid the price.

As we shall see in the chapters to follow, Western responses to the fighting in Bosnia were crisis driven; that is, they were shaped by the need to "do something" rather than by carefully calculated policy objectives. Yet it should be kept in mind that the outraged response in the West to particularly egregious developments—reports of massacres, ethnic cleansing, and other atrocities—added an element of credibility to Western threats, directed almost exclusively against the Serbs. This enabled the United States to project power into the conflict under the NATO banner, but only as long as the feeling of outrage lasted. In each case the use of force was highly circumscribed, out of concern on the part of policymakers not to be drawn into commitments from which they would not be able to disentangle themselves. We shall analyze this "crisis-driven" diplomacy in more detail in the chapters to follow. Here, we present an overview of key developments on the ground in Bosnia that helped shape Western policy responses to the war.

The Onset of Fighting

The outbreak of fighting in Bosnia in March 1992 and the first few days of April were described in chapter 3. By the end of March 1992 Bosnia was in disarray. The definitive rupture between the Bosnian government and the Serbs took place on April 4, when Izetbegović ordered the mobilization of all police and reservists in Sarajevo, and the SDS issued a covert call for the Serbs to evacuate the city. As Serb government officials left, they told the Serbs remaining behind that they would be back in a few days.[1] On April 6 the Serbs began the shelling of Sarajevo. On April 7 and 8, following international recognition of Bosnia-Herzegovina, Serb forces crossed the Drina from Serbia proper and lay siege to the Muslim cities of Zvornik, Višegrad, and Foča. By mid-April all of Bosnia was engulfed in war.

As the violence spread, fear and panic grew, accelerating the ethnic polarization of the population noted in chapters 2 and 3. Yet, throughout Bosnia there were efforts in these first few weeks to stem the tide of ethnic violence. In Bijeljina, for example, a number of local Serbs tried to halt a massacre being perpetrated by Arkan's forces and, according to Bosnian sources, were killed by Arkan's men.[2] In Goražde, a "Citizens' Forum" was organized to ward off ethnic violence.[3] Thanks in part to the efforts of this group, the town remained calm during the initial Serb onslaught in eastern Bosnia. In Tuzla, prior to May 15, the antinationalist and civic-minded opposition parties controlled the municipal government. The defense of the city was organized independently of the Bosnian government; Muslims, Serbs, and Croats all participated. In Vareš, a moderate Croat administration cooperated with local Muslims to keep ethnic tensions under control. Robert Donia and John Fine have noted how Muslims and Croats were able to maintain ethnic harmony in Fojnica until 1993, with the support of the Franciscans.[4] In the Cazinska Krajina (Bihać) region an agreement was reached between the local JNA commander, General Spiro Niković, and local leaders in Bihać, Cazin, Bosanki Petrovac, and Velika Kladuša for a cease-fire. In Doboj, a Muslim mayor and an SDS police chief set up joint patrols before the city fell to the Serbs on May 2. In Sarajevo, an antiwar, pro-democracy assembly was formed and staged a sit-in in the parliament building the first week of April. The JNA in Sarajevo, under the command of General Kukanjac, participated in efforts to stem the violence, which the general blamed primarily on the Muslims, not the Serbs.[5]

These efforts went for naught, however; in part because all sides had been preparing for war well before hostilities commenced. Smail Čekić has documented, in great detail, preparations by the SDS and the JNA for war in Bosnia, ranging from arming the Serb population to relocation of military depots and bases.[6] According to Bosnian testimony, the JNA had set up siege positions around Sarajevo in advance of the fighting.[7] These efforts were facilitated by the fact that outlying districts surrounding Sarajevo were inhabited by Serbs who were, in the main, nationalist and anti-Muslim. They were quickly absorbed into the ranks of the Serb irregulars who took up the siege of the city.[8] The Bosnian Muslim Green Berets were organized in fall 1991. We have seen in chapter 3 that Izetbegović estimated their strength at between 35,000 and 40,000 when the conflict began.[9] Croat units from western Herzegovina returned home following the end of the fighting in Croatia, anticipating that war would soon break out in Bosnia. Serbs who were mustered out of JNA units in Croatia returned to the Prijedor area from Croatia, bringing their weapons with them despite the objections of the Muslim-controlled city assembly.[10] Thus, Bosnia was rapidly becoming an armed camp in spring 1992.

The Serbs were confident that they could prevail relatively quickly in a showdown with the Bosnian government. Koljević was reported to have suggested in April that the whole thing would be over within ten days.[11] During the critical first six weeks of the war, Serb irregular and paramilitary forces were supported by JNA troops brought into eastern Bosnia from Serbia, and by JNA units retreating from Croatia into western Bosnia, as well as by local JNA garrisons. Without the participation of the JNA, it is doubtful that the cities along the Drina where the Muslims were the majority would have fallen so rapidly, if at all.

The Bosnian government was at first hopeful of winning the JNA over to its side, but relations with the JNA deteriorated quickly. An effort was made to bring the two sides together at a meeting in Skopje, Macedonia, on April 26. Who initiated the meeting remains unclear. It was attended by Izetbegović, General Blagoje Adžić, and Branko Kostić for the Serb government. Kostić and Adžić called for a political settlement and a continuation of the EC talks; Izetbegović demanded the withdrawal of the JNA from

Bosnia or its radical transformation into an army of Bosnia-Herzegovina.[12] General Kukanjac, commander of the JNA forces around Sarajevo, insisted for his part that there would have to be a political agreement among the contending factions, all confrontations would have to end, and Croatian troops—which had crossed into western Herzegovina as well as the Bosanski Brod area in the north—would have to leave Bosnia before the JNA could be transformed into the army of a Bosnian state. On April 27 the Bosnian presidency issued an order that the JNA should be placed under civilian control or leave Bosnia. This was followed by a disastrous series of events in early May pitting the JNA against the government.[13]

The decisive battle for Sarajevo came on May 2, when a disorganized Serb attack aimed at cutting the city in two was beaten back by a handful of Green Beret troops and local gang members. On May 3, President Izetbegović was kidnapped by JNA officers at Sarajevo airport on his return from negotiations in Lisbon. They used Izetbegović as leverage to gain an agreement on the safe passage of JNA troops out of the barracks in downtown Sarajevo under UNPROFOR protection. But Muslim forces failed to honor the agreement and ambushed the convoy as it left the barracks, despite the personal presence of Izetbegović and his attempt to carry out the agreement. The incident left all sides—Muslim, Serb, and UN—embittered. On May 18 a cease-fire was signed, and an agreement reached on the evacuation of the JNA from Bosnia. On May 20 the Bosnian presidency declared the JNA an occupation force, ending, once and for all, any hope that the Yugoslav military could be won over to the Muslim side.

Šefer Halilović, who was then commander of the Bosnian army, claims in his memoirs that the kidnapping of Izetbegović was the occasion for a coup attempt. According to Halilović, Alija Delimustafić, minister of the interior, and Fikret Abdić, member of the presidency, came to him (Halilović) and proposed removing Izetbegović and reincorporating Bosnia-Herzegovina into Yugoslavia, leaving western Herzegovina to Croatia. Halilović claims he turned this proposal down, and the attempt collapsed.[14] Halilović's account, if correct, suggests the depth and political importance of the divisions within the Bosnian Muslim elite.

The Shelling of Sarajevo and the Opening of Sarajevo Airport

The war entered a new phase when General Ratko Mladić was made commander of the newly formed army of the (Bosnian) Serb republic on May 20. The event was preceded and followed by an escalation of violence all over Bosnia. On May 18 a Red Cross relief convoy was shelled on the outskirts of Sarajevo. On May 22 a UN convoy was hijacked. On May 24 the village of Kozarac, in the Banja Luka region, was overrun by the Serbs and its inhabitants massacred. On May 24 and 26, and again on May 28 and 29, Sarajevo experienced severe shelling by the Serbs. UN Secretary-General Boutros Boutros-Ghali, in his report to the Security Council of May 30, attributed these attacks to General Mladić.[15]

The escalation of fighting on the ground, and especially the increased shelling of Sarajevo, led to increased concern in the West—reviewed in greater detail in chapter 5—about the mounting humanitarian crisis in Bosnia; concern that was heightened by the shelling of a breadline in Sarajevo on May 27 that killed scores of civilians. This was the first of many such incidents around which controversy erupted over who had perpetrated the atrocious act. The nature of these controversies and their significance will be considered in more detail later in this chapter. Here, we note only that the incident of May 27 set the stage for the first decisive action of the West: the imposition of sanctions on Yugoslavia (Serbia and Montenegro) by the Security Council on May 30, 1992 (Resolution 757).

On May 30, Bosnian forces attacked the JNA barracks in Sarajevo. Heavy shelling of the city followed. On June 5 and 6, as street fighting raged and the last of the JNA personnel and dependents evacuated Sarajevo, the city suffered its worst shelling yet. In response to these events, the international community initiated efforts to open the Sarajevo airport to humanitarian relief flights. On June 20 a cease-fire, which was meant to set the stage for the UN takeover of the airport, was broken as both sides battled for control of the territory between the airport and the city.[16]

The crisis over the opening of the airport reached its climax on June 26 when Boutros-Ghali issued what the press described as an ultimatum. It gave the Serbs 48 hours to stop their attacks on Sarajevo. The secretary-general demanded that the Serbs allow the UN to take control of the airport and that they place their heavy weapons under UN supervision as provided for in a cease-fire agreement negotiated by Maj. Gen. Lewis MacKenzie, the Canadian UNPROFOR commander in Sarajevo.[17] At the same time, the media reported that President Bush was meeting with his advisors to consider the use of force in Bosnia. On June 28 and 29, President Mitterrand of France made his dramatic and improbable visit to Sarajevo. The end of this stage of the drama came when the Serbs, without incident, turned the airport over to an UNPROFOR contingent of Canadian troops on June 29. (The diplomacy leading up to the UN takeover of the airport, and the implications of this insertion of peacekeeping troops where there was no peace to keep, will be examined in greater detail in chapter 5.)

The events of the six weeks between May 20 and the end of June riveted the attention of the world on Sarajevo. The callousness of the Serb shelling and sniping from the surrounding hills provided a dramatic contrast to the courage of the Sarajevans under siege. It turned world public opinion decisively and permanently against the Serbs. The opening of the airport at the end of June ensured that the focus on events in Sarajevo would continue, as the city became easily accessible to the media. In effect, these extraordinary events created an instant bond between the "global village" served by mass media, and the people of Sarajevo.

The War Outside Sarajevo

Meanwhile, outside of Sarajevo, the fortunes of the combatants varied dramatically during the first year of the war. Within a matter of months the Serbs had seized the Muslim-majority cities along the Drina and Sava rivers and expelled the Muslim population.[18] Serb advances into Posavina in the north and into central Bosnia in the early weeks of the war were reversed by a joint Muslim-HVO (Croat Defense Council, or Bosnian Croat army) offensive in May. Taking advantage of the confusion resulting from the formal withdrawal of the JNA from Bosnia, Croat and Muslim irregulars occupied most of Posavina and advanced southward, placing Doboj under siege. As a result, Serb forces in Bosanska Krajina to the west were cut off from Semberija and Serbia to the east. In the middle of May Srebrenica, which had fallen to Serb irregulars on April 18, was retaken by Muslims under the command of Naser Orić. In May, the Serbs suffered their most costly defeat of the war in eastern Bosnia when, according to Serb accounts, Avdo Palić, a former captain in the JNA, ambushed a Serb force near Srebrenica, killing 400. According to a Western media account, by November 1992 almost 400 square miles of eastern Bosnia were under Muslim control.[19] On June 10–11 the HVO, strengthened by the addition of Muslim infantry to its ranks, launched an attack against the Serbs in eastern Herzegovina, forcing them to abandon Mostar in mid-June. In June and July Croat forces in central Bosnia were reported within artillery range of Sarajevo.

In June 1992 the Serbs launched their first counterattack of the war, most likely with the support of forces from Serbia, and won back areas seized by the combined Croat-Muslim force in central Bosnia in May. Bihać, which lay astride the rail line from Banja Luka to Knin (in the Serb-held Krajina region of Croatia) remained in Bosnian Muslim hands. The Serbs also failed to establish a secure corridor in the north between Banja Luka to the west and Semberija and Serbia to the east. They were unable to take the town of Gradačac, which lay to the south of the corridor, or the town of Orašje, to the north. The Croat population in Orašje remained loyal to the cause of the Bosnian government and put up a stiff resistance to the Serbs.

While Muslim towns along the Drina were overwhelmed in the first two months of the war, cities farther to the west such as Jajce, Bosanski Brod, and Bosanska Gradiška, did not fall to the Serbs until summer or autumn 1992. The fall of Bosanski Brod and Jajce in October came as a shock to the Bosnian government, and might have been avoided if there had not been a breakdown in cooperation between the Croat and Muslim defenders of these two cities.

In Herzegovina, regular army forces from Croatia moved well into Bosnia to secure an area overlooking the Serb-populated town of Trebinje, where they remained until the end of the war. Their deployment was designed to protect Dubrovnik, which lay just across the nearby Croatian-Bosnian border. In eastern Bosnia, Bosnian army guerrilla forces launched attacks during winter 1992–93 against the Serbs in the Tuzla-Zvornik area, at one point reaching the banks of the Drina and firing mortar rounds across the Bosnian-Serb border into the town of Bajina Bašta, east of Srebrenica. A significant role in the Muslim offensive was played by the sixteenth Bosnian Brigade from the area of Bratunac, which consisted of troops who had earlier escaped to Croatia, been re-equipped, and infiltrated back into Bosnia in August 1992. Most of these events went unnoticed in the Western press.

If a cease-fire had been negotiated in June 1992 at the time the UN took over the Sarajevo airport, it would have been on terms far more advantageous to the Muslims than several years later. On the other hand, the Serbs had already virtually encircled Sarajevo. Muslim-held areas in eastern Bosnia (Goražde, Srebrenica) had only the most tenuous links with the Bosnian government stronghold in central Bosnia. Cazinska Krajina (the Bihać enclave) was completely cut off from Sarajevo. It was the scene of fighting between the independent Muslim forces of Fikret Abdić and the Bosnian army's Fifth Corps. Hammering out a political settlement at this stage of the war would, therefore, have been an immense challenge—although perhaps no more so than three years later.

In January 1993, fighting broke out between Croat and Muslim forces in central Bosnia. The Muslims found themselves in a two-front war or, more accurately, a multi-front war against two adversaries. The causes of the conflict between the Muslims and the Croats were related to the division of Bosnia proposed under the Vance-Owen plan, and will be discussed more fully in chapter 5. Following publication of a proposed map by the international mediators in January, the Bosnian Croat serving as minister of defense of Bosnia-Herzegovina ordered Croat forces to take control of those provinces expected to be Croat-majority territories. His action was immediately opposed by the Muslim commander of the Bosnian army.[20] The fighting between Croats and Muslims began around Gornji Vakuf and then spread to the vicinity of Bugojno, Busovača, Konjic, and Jablanica. UN peacekeepers negotiated several cease-fires, but to no avail. On January 27, Izetbegović and Boban issued a joint statement calling for an end to the fighting. A lull in the fighting followed. But it broke out with renewed intensity in mid-April in the Lašva valley, to the north and west of Sarajevo. There were confrontations between Muslim and Croat forces throughout central Bosnia, especially around Vitez and Travnik; in the south-central districts of Konjic and Jablanica; and in the Neretva valley north and south of Mostar. Croat forces joined the Serbs in the siege of Tešanj and Maglaj, in the Bosna river valley. In south-central Bosnia and the Neretva valley, Serb units appear to have worked against the Croats by holding their fire against the Muslims.[21]

On May 9 the HVO attacked Bosnian government forces in and around Mostar. The Croat attack was met with outrage in the UN. The Croat offensive against the Muslims was accompanied by ethnic cleansing of the Muslim population in the Neretva valley. HVO forces laid siege to the eastern, Muslim sector of the city, shelling the area continually. It was estimated that more than 100,000 Croat shells fell on east Mostar in the nine-month siege that ended in January 1994.[22] In early June 1993 the Muslims seized control of Travnik. From this point on the initiative in central Bosnia lay largely with the Muslims, who eventually brought most of the Lašva valley—with the exception of Vitez—under their control. Croat forces were cleared from the vicinity of Konjic in south-central Bosnia.

In eastern Bosnia, a Serb offensive in spring 1993 reduced Muslim control to several remote enclaves. The Serb attack on Srebrenica in April 1993 is examined in more detail below. Its consequences for Western policy, including the demise of the Vance-Owen plan, are examined further in chapter 5. Later in the summer, the Serbs cut the link between Sarajevo and Goražde by seizing the town of Trnovo. Serb forces then pushed on to the heights overlooking Sarajevo from the southwest, cutting the Muslim supply route into the city. The result was a confrontation between NATO and the Serbs, brought on by fear that Serb forces might launch an assault on the city proper. The crisis over the "strangulation of Sarajevo" is examined below. A cessation of hostilities in summer 1993 would have left all three sides holding fragments of territory scattered north and south, east and west, across Bosnia. This fragmentation of territory among the combatants complicated the already difficult negotiations in summer and fall 1993 described in chapter 6, and remained a feature of the Bosnian conflict until summer 1995. The approximate situation on the ground in spring and summer 1993 is shown in Map 4.1.

Map 4.1 **Approximate Areas of Control, May–June 1993**

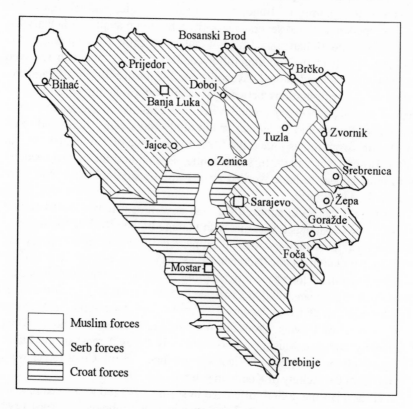

Based on UNHCR, *Information Notes: Bosnia and Herzegovina* 7 (June 30, 1993), n.p.

By the end of 1993, Muslim pressure on the remaining towns still under Croat control in central Bosnia—Kiseljak, Vitez, and Prozor—had increased to the point that Croatia dispatched regular army troops to central Bosnia. Croatian and Bosnian Croat forces engaged in ethnic cleansing, set up detention camps for Muslims, and laid siege to the Muslim quarters of Mostar. In response, the UN Security Council adopted a statement on February 3, 1994, threatening Croatia with sanctions.[23] Relations between the Croats and Muslims had deteriorated to the point that, according to the Belgrade magazine *NIN*, the Croats and Serbs had agreed to launch a joint offensive against the Muslims.[24] No such joint operation came to pass, however. The Markala marketplace shelling in February, discussed in more detail below, led instead to the formation of a Muslim-Croat–Croatian alliance under American sponsorship.

Foreign military observers of the fighting in Bosnia tended to downgrade both the Serbs and the Muslims for their lack of discipline, poor command and control, and, in the case of the Serbs, reluctance to take casualties. One Western military observer concluded in May 1994 that "if the Serbs had a real infantry, they would have finished with Bosnia a long time ago."[25] Western observers were no less blunt in pointing out that the Bosnian army was under the thumb of the SDA and poorly led by generals chosen for their political loyalty rather than their military skills.[26] These deficiencies led all sides to rely on irregulars and special units, the latter to make up for the lack of combat-ready infantry. The Croatian paramilitary organization HOS (*Hrvatske odbrambene snage,* or Croatian defense forces) operated in the Neretva valley and eastern Herzegovina in spring and summer 1992. Its operations were terminated by Zagreb, which considered it a political rival to the Bosnian Croat army, or HVO, which was made up entirely of irregulars. Special units often doubled as punishment squads, engaging in burning and plundering of villages and ethnic cleansing. All sides became skilled at subterfuge and deception, and both the Serbs and the Muslims scored major victories using these tactics.[27]

On the Muslim side, the most well known of the special units was the Black Swans, led by Hase Tirić. Based in Kakanj, the Black Swans were under the command of the Bosnian army general staff. The unit was made up of volunteers aged 20–22, orphaned by the war. It was employed in major or difficult operations. The Black Swans also served as a bodyguard for Izetbegović when he traveled in Bosnia outside Sarajevo.[28] The Seventeenth Krajina brigade, "the angry army of the dispossessed" under the command of Colonel Fikret Cuskić, was considered an elite force, although there are doubts about how effectively the unit performed.[29] On the Croat side, Mladen Naletelić-Tuta, who later became a gang boss in Mostar, led special HVO punishment squads that burned and pillaged Muslim villages in southwest Herzegovina. The most notorious of the Serb special units were based in Serbia. These included Arkan's Tigers and the Red Berets under the control of the Serbian Ministry of the Interior. These units were brought into the conflict in Bosnia when local forces proved wanting, most notably in the attacks on the enclaves in eastern Bosnia, where a group of irregulars known as the Yellow Wasps and led by Dušan Vučković committed widespread atrocities and sowed terror among the Muslim population.[30] In the closing days of the war, Arkan's forces reappeared in Bosnia as part of the Serb effort to halt the advance of the Croatian and Muslim forces toward Banja Luka. Even at that late date the Tigers remained true to their reputation from the earliest days of the conflict, engaging in ethnic cleansing and committing atrocities against the few remaining Muslims and Croats in the area.

In most regions of Bosnia the conflict retained a distinctly local character. Whole sectors of the front remained relatively untouched by the war, loosely defended by local militia. Nowhere was this localized form of conflict more evident than in the fighting between the Muslims and the Croats in central Bosnia in 1993. Christopher Collinson has described the tactics employed in the region.[31] Hostilities did not prevent profiteering by local officials as a means of personal enrichment and as a way of providing funds for prosecuting the war. One side would even sell arms to the other. In Cazinska Krajina, the Serbs from Krajina (Croatia) sold weapons to the troops of both the Bosnian Fifth Corps and Abdić's forces.[32] Alliances sprang up between the Serbs and the Croats during the fighting between the Muslims and the Croats in 1993. According to Safet Oručević, the mayor of the Muslim sector of Mostar, the Serbs and the Muslims in the Neretva Valley also entered into an alliance. Not far to the north, in the Konjic district, the Serbs provided assistance to the Croats against the Muslims.[33] Kasim Begić suggests that the Bosnian Croats and Bosnian Serbs concluded a military cooperation agreement on June 20, 1993.[34] According to Muslim sources, while Serb General Djorde Djukić was briefly held in captivity in Sarajevo after hostilities had ceased, he described to Muslim authorities an arrangement whereby the Serb armies were supplied with fuel by the Croats for eighteen months during 1993 and 1994. The termination of the operation in December 1994 might be taken as an early sign that the Croats were preparing their later offensive against the Serbs.[35]

Criminal gangs played an important role in the war, especially on the Muslim side.[36] Sarajevo owed its survival in the early days of the fighting to criminal gangs that assumed responsibility for the defense of the city. Serb forces surrounding Sarajevo had little taste for urban warfare, while the criminal elements who defended Sarajevo were in their element in such fighting. Among these criminal-soldiers, Jusuf Prazina gained fame as the commander of the Green Berets. The defense of Dobrinje was organized by Ismet Bajramović-Ćelo, who commanded the military police in Sarajevo and was in charge of the central prison. The Croat suburb of Stup was under the control of a local Croat, Velimir Marić. Mušan Topalović-Caco controlled the area from Skenderija on the left bank of the Miljacka eastward. The private armies of these groups remained intact for approximately eighteen months. "Ćelo" and "Caco," with the support of Bosnian Chief of Staff General Šefer Halilović, were pitted against Izetbegović and Jusuf Prazina.

In June 1993 Halilović was removed and replaced by Rasim Delić, who then brought the gangs under government control. In October 1993, just days before Haris Silajdžić was appointed prime minister (and possibly as a condition of his taking the office), government forces surrounded the headquarters of the opposition gangs in two separate operations. Caco was killed, and Čelo reportedly gave himself up. The ranks of the legendary criminal heroes of Sarajevo were further weakened when Prazina deserted the cause of the Bosnian government to the join HVO. He later fled abroad, where he was assassinated in January 1994. Nonetheless, independent local commanders remained a force to be reckoned with in Sarajevo until the end of the war. In January 1995, for example, *Oslobodjenje* ran an interview with Ismet Hadžić, commander of the Fifth Motorized Brigade defending Dobrinje. Brigadier Hadžić boasted of his iron-fisted control of the district and of his independence from the Bosnian government.[37]

There were also many unsung heroes who defended Sarajevo who did not belong to criminal bands. There were the young people of Dobrinje, about whom Zdravko Grebo wrote so movingly,[38] as well as the inhabitants of Butmir, west of the airport. The latter fought for their neighborhood as much as for the Bosnian national cause.

Western journalists in Sarajevo made the point that Bosnian fighting units included people drawn from all ethnic communities in the city. The situation appears to have been more complicated. Miloš Vasić reports that the number of Serbs in the Bosnian army had fallen from 13 to 5 percent by summer 1994.[39] Serbs of fighting age were subject to forced mobilization into the Bosnian army on the threat of having their property confiscated.[40] They were given dangerous duties on the front; digging trenches was the most common assignment. It was the practice of all three sides to give dangerous jobs to detainees or persons who were not thought trustworthy. Anyone, however, including on occasion even Muslim intellectuals, could get caught up in a *racija,* or sweep for forced labor.

The Croats of Sarajevo generally would not fight outside their own neighborhood of Stup. The Croats were on good terms with their Serb adversaries and protested strongly against Bosnian Muslim commando raids against Serb lines that led to retaliatory shelling of Croat neighborhoods by the Serbs. In November 1993 the Bosnian army command broke up the Croat units defending Sarajevo and integrated them into the predominantly Muslim Bosnian army.[41]

One gets the impression that in Sarajevo the truly mixed units with high morale were to be found in the front-line neighborhoods such as Butmir or Dobrinje. Bosnian defenses also were manned by mixed Muslim-Croat units elsewhere in Bosnia, such as in Usora[42] and Gradačac in central Bosnia. They were motivated by the same mix of local stubbornness and mutual trust that was present in some of the front-line neighborhoods in Sarajevo. A definitive account of how the Bosnian army incorporated Serbs and Croats into its ranks awaits the availability of more detailed evidence.

The Major Crises, 1993–94

Srebrenica, April 1993

The first of the crises to which the West responded was occasioned by the Serb attack on Srebrenica in early April 1993. Srebrenica had been in the vortex of the east Bosnian maelstrom from the start. It was overrun by the Serbs in April 1992 and recaptured by Muslim irregulars in May. Srebrenica was a jump-ing-off point for Muslim guerrilla activity against Serb towns and villages in eastern Bosnia in winter 1992–93.[43] Žepa, to the south, had been the scene of the ambush of Serb troops by Avdo Palić in May 1992, noted above. That the Serbs would seek to take Srebrenica, or neutralize it, was hardly surprising. But the bitter fighting in eastern Bosnia that provided the background of the campaign was not well known in the West. As a result, the Serb offensive in April 1993 was viewed as a deliberate provocation aimed at undermining the Vance-Owen plan, which we shall see in chapter 5 was then at a critical stage of negotiation, rather than as yet another round in one of the most brutally fought military contests in Bosnia. It probably was both. The fact that the enclave was packed with refugees provided the extra dimension that made humanitarian intervention a distinct possibility in the event the Serbs tried to overrun the town. Reports of the suffering of the refugees trapped in Srebrenica were some of the most dramatic and riveting of the war.[44] The UN commander for Sarajevo at the time, General Philippe Morillon, found himself in the thick of the battle. Acting on his own initia-tive, Morillon managed to cross Serb lines and raise the UN flag in Srebrenica, much to the delight of the refugees packed in the town, but to the dismay of his superiors in New York.[45]

The drama in the Srebrenica enclave unfolded against the backdrop of renewed fighting around Sarajevo, where more than 1,000 Serb shells a day were falling on the city at the height of the bombardment. On April 12, 1993, the Serbs unleashed artillery barrages on Sarajevo and Srebrenica. The attack on Srebrenica was devastating. According to press reports, at least fifty-six persons were killed in the densely packed streets of the town.[46] The attacks followed the sudden suspension of cease-fire talks by General Mladić at the Sarajevo airport, hours before NATO was to begin enforcing a no-fly zone over Bosnia adopted by the UN Security Council in October 1992 (Resolution 781 of October 9, 1992, the details of which are described in chapter 5). The Serbs' suspension of cease-fire talks and shell-ing of Srebrenica seemed a deliberate act of malice with political intent.

The emotions raised in the West by the Serb shelling of Srebrenica were expressed vividly by Larry Hollingsworth, an official of the United Nations

High Commissioner for Refugees (UNHCR), who had earlier led the first humanitarian convoys into Žepa:

> I hope that the military commander who ordered the firing on Srebrenica burns in the hottest corner of hell. . . . [Those] who loaded the weapons and fired the shells—I hope they have nightmares forever more, I hope their sleep is punctuated by the screams of the children and the cries of mothers.[47]

The anguish triggered by the spectacle of Sarajevo under siege and the reports of massacres and shelling of civilians in eastern Bosnia led the Clinton administration to propose tightening sanctions against Yugoslavia (Serbia and Montenegro), and lifting the arms embargo against Bosnia, as we shall see in chapter 5.

The shelling spread consternation among the diplomats tasked with negotiating a political settlement to the Bosnian crisis. Owen, who in February had cautiously conceded that air power might be used as a means of "tilting the balance of forces," now advocated bombing Serb targets if that was what was required to prevent them from seizing other Muslim-occupied cities.[48] In Washington the pressure to take action was heightened by the visit to the White House of Vaclav Havel, president of Czechoslovakia and an advocate of active opposition to the Serbs, and by the emotions surrounding the opening of the Holocaust Museum in Washington. U.S. threats to launch air strikes followed, although they were carefully hedged by qualifications (these are treated in more detail in chapter 5).

But, just as the mounting crisis increased the pressure to "do something," the easing of the crisis in the week of April 16–23 resulted in the drawing back from involvement on the part of U.S. policymakers. General Lars-Eric Wahlgren, the UN commander for Bosnia, received a phone call from Milošević informing him that Karadžić had agreed to allow UNPROFOR personnel into Srebrenica. A letter from Karadžić to this effect arrived at the Security Council the following day. Early on April 18 an agreement was signed between the Serbs and UN commanders which provided that the Serbs would withdraw from around Srebrenica if UN forces undertook to disarm Muslim forces in the city within seventy-two hours. The same morning a Canadian UNPROFOR unit, which had been halted by the Serbs outside Srebrenica, was allowed to enter the town.[49] On April 21 the UN announced that the turnover of Bosnian Muslim arms had been completed. In fact, the search for weapons had only been cursory, in anticipation of a visit to Srebrenica of representatives of countries in the Security Council that felt UNPROFOR should not, according to then UN Undersecretary-General for Peacekeeping Operations Kofi Annan, be "disarming the victims."[50]

Although tensions remained high in the region—only a small contingent of UN troops protected Srebrenica against the Serbs—the confrontation in eastern Bosnia wound to an uneasy close. The Serbs insisted that the terms of the agreement with the United Nations were not fulfilled. But they were not ready to re-ignite the crisis, having for the time being contained Muslim forces in the region.

The Strangulation of Sarajevo, July–August 1993

The crisis over the strangulation of Sarajevo was prompted by the capture of Trnovo by the Serbs in early July 1993, and the battle for Mt. Bjelašnica and Mt. Igman at the end of July. Humanitarian relief convoys had been prevented from reaching the city due to the fighting between the Muslims and Croats in central Bosnia. The Serb offensive raised fears in the West that the city might be cut off completely, and that a frontal assault on the city might be imminent. In early July a U.S. disaster relief team reported that Sarajevo was without electricity, water, or fuel, and was on the verge of collapse.[51] By the middle of July, the Clinton administration began to discuss ways of preventing the Serbs from overrunning Sarajevo. On July 12 a mortar shell landed in a crowd queued up at a water pump in Sarajevo, killing twelve. There were reports in the media that President Clinton was deeply disturbed by TV coverage of Sarajevo.[52] The Security Council, reflecting the growing mood of crisis, adopted a resolution on July 23 condemning the blockade of Sarajevo and demanding that utilities be restored. The role of the Bosnian government in preventing the restoration of services, which we shall examine below, was not common knowledge and was ignored in Western policy debates. In the course of the heavy fighting around the city, according to media reports at the time, the UN command recorded 3,777 shells falling in the city in a sixteen–hour period.[53] At about the same time, the CIA informed the Clinton administration that the Serbs were on the verge of total victory in Bosnia.[54]

Concern for the fate of Sarajevo led U.S. policymakers to argue more forcefully for the use of air power against the Serbs. On August 2 NATO ambassadors warned of that organization's "determination to take effective action," and initiated preparations for the use of air power to relieve the "strangulation" of Sarajevo and end interference with humanitarian relief efforts. But they set no deadline for action.[55] The NATO statement appeared, however, to commit NATO to the defense of Sarajevo. It may have been a factor leading Karadžić to inform international mediators on the same day that the Serbs would withdraw from Mt. Igman. His readiness to do so may also have been prompted by the conclusion of a cease-fire on July

30. But the crisis was not over. The cease-fire of July 30 quickly broke down. On August 4 General Mladić's forces seized portions of the supply road over Mt. Igman that linked Sarajevo to the outside world. Negotiations at Pale on August 5 between the Serbs and Belgian General Francis Briquemont, who had replaced Morillon as UN Sarajevo commander, produced a pledge from General Mladić to withdraw Serb forces if UN units occupied the vacated areas, and a promise from Karadžić to open access routes for relief convoys into Sarajevo. *Le Monde* suggested that the August 5 agreement called for the Serbs to withdraw to the July 30 lines, but no one could agree where they were.[56] According to Serb sources, however, General Mladić had agreed to withdraw Serb forces from the summit of Mt. Bjelašnica only to a distance from which they still would be able to maintain fire control over the positions handed over to the UN.[57] Negotiations between General Mladić and Bosnian General Rasim Delić the next day, August 6, broke down over General Delić's insistence that Bosnian government troops, accompanied by UN units, be allowed to reoccupy Igman and Bjelašnica.[58] In the end, an agreement was reached between Generals Briquemont and Mladić that the Serbs would withdraw from Mt. Bjelašnica, to be replaced by French UNPROFOR forces. The Serbs also were to permit the safe passage of humanitarian convoys. The Bosnian government, presumably, was not to use the Igman road for resupplying its troops.[59]

The seizure of the Mt. Igman road by the Serbs was a critical moment in the battle for Sarajevo. It appeared that Muslim forces had been drawn down prior to the battle, perhaps under the impression that the area was impregnable. Seasoned Bosnian government troops appear to have been sent—via a tunnel recently opened under the Sarajevo airport—to the central Bosnian battlefield.[60] What was seen at the time as a stunning victory by General Mladić thus may have been in fact only a temporary advantage that Bosnian forces could have reversed, given the opportunity. If so, the Serb decision to turn the mountain road over to UNPROFOR was not the concession it appeared to be. The Serbs may have been using the UN to do what they could not do on their own: deny this strategic ground to the Muslims. The Serb withdrawal was an acknowledgment that they could not force Sarajevo to capitulate using siege tactics, since turning the mountain over to the UN reopened a vital supply line into the city. But the establishment of at least formal UN control over the disputed territory may also have been seen by the Serbs as a step toward the territorial division of Bosnia-Herzegovina, to be enforced by the UN; a development that would likely have frozen the unbalanced distribution of territory between the warring parties then in force, shown in Map 4.2. Indeed, as we shall see in

Map 4.2 **Areas of Control, September 1993**

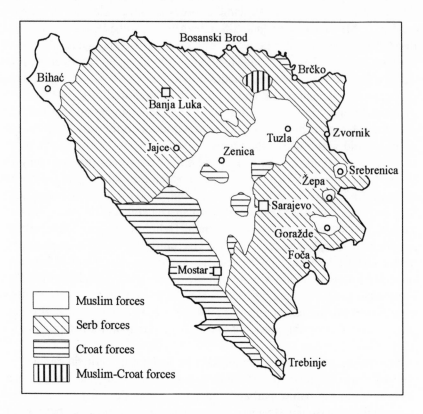

Based on U.S. Department of State map no. 2466 9–93 STATE (INR/GE).

chapter 6, just such a division of Bosnia among the Serbs, Muslims, and Croats was then under active negotiation.

Meanwhile, the introduction of UN forces onto Mt. Igman transformed these peacekeeping units into more direct participants in the Bosnian conflict. They were pitted against Bosnian government forces seeking to infiltrate and control the vital road link to Sarajevo, as well as against the Serbs. The situation in UN-patrolled territory on Mt. Igman was murky, and remained so. At stake was the question whether the Mt. Igman route into Sarajevo was to be open only to humanitarian convoys, as the Serbs hoped would be the case if the UN controlled the mountain roadway, or also to civilian and Bosnian military traffic. In the event, the actions taken by NATO in August 1993 did not result in the opening of Sarajevo. The agreements were not fully honored at the time they went into effect, and later were largely repudiated.

The Markala Marketplace Shelling, February 1994

With the definitive rejection of partition plans brokered by Owen and Stoltenberg in summer and fall 1993—treated in more detail in chapter 6—the Serbs began to step up their shelling of Sarajevo. The shelling of the Markala marketplace in downtown Sarajevo on February 5, 1994, produced heavy civilian casualties and was immediately presumed to have been the responsibility of the Serbs. The massacre came as the culmination of a month or more of shelling of Sarajevo. During this time a school yard as well as a stadium full of fans watching a soccer game had already been hit. Civilian casualties were heavy.[61] The mounting casualties had produced increasing pressure in the West for action. The French, in particular, had already been pressing their allies—including the Americans—for a more forceful response to the Serbs.

The event received extensive media coverage, discussed later in this chapter, and shocked the world. The ensuing NATO ultimatum to the Serbs to withdraw their artillery from around Sarajevo focused American policy on finding a political solution to the Bosnian crisis. The ultimatum also proved the most successful policy initiative taken by the international community in response to the recurring humanitarian disasters that had marked the Bosnian war up to that point.

The Europeans took the lead in responding to the incident. On February 7 the EU called for an immediate lifting of the siege of Sarajevo.[62] The following day, February 8, the United States demanded that Serb heavy weapons be moved outside the range of civilian targets. As we shall see in more detail in chapter 6, this change in the U.S. posture was taken in the context of a broad review of Bosnian policy that led to the emergence of a new U.S. strategy for ending the war. On February 9 NATO adopted an ultimatum demanding the withdrawal of Serb heavy weapons from a twenty-kilometer-wide "total exclusion zone" around the city and threatening to subject any heavy weapons that remained in this zone to air attack. The politics and negotiations surrounding these events are discussed in detail in chapter 6. In the course of the crisis, UN Sarajevo commander British Lt. Gen. Michael Rose negotiated a local cease-fire calling for the withdrawal of Serb weapons from around Sarajevo or their placement under UN control, and the deployment of Russian UNPROFOR troops to monitor the agreement. The Markala massacre thus produced the more direct involvement of NATO and the United States in the Bosnian crisis, as well as the increased involvement of the Russians—developments that would often work at cross-purposes over the next year and a half.

Bosnian Serb agreement to end the shelling of Sarajevo initiated the easing of tensions. An agreement concluded March 23 provided for the opening of Sarajevo to civilian traffic, increasing the flow of civilians and supplies into and out of the city. Families began to return to Sarajevo and a more plentiful supply of goods became available in the shops. As the cease-fire held, there was talk of the war "winding down."[63] The strategy of a "return to normalcy," which General Rose had outlined in February, seemed to be working.

On February 23 the Muslims and Croats in Bosnia signed a U.S.-brokered cease-fire ending the Muslim-Croat conflict in Bosnia and opening the door to cooperation between the Bosnian Muslims and Croatia. The creation of a Muslim-Croatian alliance was a key element in the emerging U.S. strategy for ending the war in Bosnia. This strategy, and the tortuous development of Croatian-Bosnian relations, will be described in detail in chapters 6 and 7. In Croatia, a temporary cease-fire was signed on March 29, 1994, between the Serbs holding Krajina (the self-declared Republic of Serb Krajina [*Republika Srpske Krajine*] or RSK) and the Croatian government. This step gave rise to talk that a comprehensive solution to the crisis might be found, encompassing both Croatia and Bosnia. On February 28/March 1, four Jastreb fighter planes crossed into Bosnian airspace from the RSK in violation of the no-fly zone and were shot down by NATO aircraft. NATO's forceful response contributed to the feeling that the UN/NATO partnership was proving effective in reining in the conflict.

In a speech on April 7 U.S. National Security Advisor Anthony Lake seemed to be preparing the American public for a U.S. presence in Bosnia once a political settlement was reached. Lake declared that U.S. troops would "go in strong" once a peace settlement was reached and would "establish a commanding presence with the numbers, equipment and robust rules of engagement they need to defend themselves and accomplish their mission."[64] That such a presence was far from reality will become clear from the detailed analysis of U.S. and Western policies in this period presented in chapter 6.

Goražde, March–April 1994

The Bosnian Serb attack on the Goražde enclave in eastern Bosnia in March 1994 dashed the hopes for peace raised by the success of the February NATO ultimatum. The attack began in late March and ended April 26, when the Serbs drew back from the city in the face of another NATO ultimatum. The Western media reported that the crisis had begun with a Bosnian Serb offensive against Goražde at the end of March. A contrasting version prepared by U.S. congressional staffers suggested that the origins of the crisis lay in a Bosnian government attack out of the enclave on March 20, the purpose of which was to upset peace negotiations and precipitate Western intervention in Bosnia.[65] Bosnian army forces had been on the offensive in central Bosnia since mid-March and, according to UN military sources, had transferred additional troops to Goražde. The origins of the battle, however, are of less importance than its consequences.

Events came to a head on April 10. Prior to this date, it appeared that the Serbs had set themselves limited objectives: to neutralize the Bosnian forces in the enclave and seize the north–south highway that followed the right bank of the Drina on the eastern outskirts of the city. On April 9 Bosnian Serb forces occupied the Gradina ridge overlooking the town. The Serbs then shelled Goražde on April 10. UN and NATO commanders, angered by the attack and fearing a Serb effort to take the town, launched a NATO air strike against Serb positions the same day. The strike received the support of Boutros-Ghali, who on April 9 had ordered UN forces in Bosnia to use "all available means" to obtain the Serb withdrawal from positions around Goražde. A second air strike took place on April 11. The Serbs continued their attack. Mladić threatened Rose that "one more attack and I will shoot down aircraft—cannot guarantee safety of UNPROFOR and will attack UNPROFOR and your headquarters."[66] By April 15 Bosnian Serb forces had breached the defenses of the town. A third NATO air strike on April 16 followed further shelling of the city by the Serbs. But air strikes appeared to have little effect. In fact, the Serbs fired upon NATO aircraft and downed a British Harrier jet. All three NATO air attacks were limited, or pinprick strikes against specific targets, intended to deter the Serbs, rather than broad-gauge attacks designed to neutralize Bosnian Serb military capabilities in the area. In response to the NATO air strikes, the Serbs began to take hostages. Within days, some 200 UN and civilian personnel had been detained by the Bosnian Serbs.

A frantic search for a peaceful solution to the crisis ensued as the Bosnian Serbs continued their attack. On April 16 the United States decided to adopt a policy of cautious moderation toward the Serbs, apparently in the hope that ongoing negotiations might bear fruit and that Russian efforts to broker a Serb pullback from Goražde might succeed.[67] But peacemaking efforts by Russian foreign minister Andrei Kozyrev and special envoy Vitaly Churkin collapsed amid bitter charges of Serb perfidy, reported in more detail in chapter 6. As the shelling continued, UN observers were evacuated from Goražde. At this point, as we shall suggest in chapter 6, the U.S. position hardened. Clinton's advisers urged the broadening of air strikes. A major change in U.S. policy seemed to be in the offing.

The immediate impetus for the change receded, however, after April

19. On that day the Bosnian Serbs agreed to a cease-fire and the entry of an UNPROFOR contingent into the town. They began releasing hostages and returning weapons seized from UN depots around Sarajevo. Kozyrev announced that the Serbs had once more promised that they would not occupy Goražde, and this assurance was repeated by Karadžić. Nonetheless, shelling of the city continued. On April 20 the Western media reported that Serb gunners had targeted the Goražde hospital. The description of the carnage was appalling. Dr. Mary McLaughlin reported on April 20 that they were "running out of words to describe what is going on. . . . It seems the Serbs are prepared to level east Goražde house by house in order to gain control over it. . . ."[68] A letter from two UNHCR doctors trapped in Goražde was distributed by Agence France Presse on April 22:

> Both residents and refugees are crowded into crumbling buildings waiting for the next shell. When it hits, many are killed as there are such crowds in each building. It is usually many from one family. The wounded lie for hours in the debris as it is suicidal to try and bring them to the hospital. . . . There is no safety or effective treatment in the hospital. Shells batter down the walls there and machine gun fire rakes the wards. Twenty people were confirmed killed in one of the hospital apartment [sic] yesterday. The Serb excuse for targeting it is that it is a military institution. I've been in all parts of the hospital a hundred times in the last month and can assure the outside world that this is a lie. The theaters and all sterilizing equipment were destroyed by a shell yesterday morning so no further operations can be carried out.[69]

No UN observers were present to witness the shelling, but UN officials expressed horror and indignation at developments in Goražde.

Almost unnoticed in the mounting political fury in the West was the fact that much of the fighting was focused on a struggle for control of the Pobjeda munitions factory complex, which, according to a brief report in the Western media, included a honeycomb of underground tunnels and storage bunkers. Local Bosnian commanders acknowledged that there was heavy fighting in the factory, and that the Serbs had taken 30 percent of the complex, rigged it with explosives, and were pounding it with artillery in an effort to destroy the munitions stored inside. One Bosnian liaison officer claimed the factory had enough explosives in it to "flatten a city." As the deadline for withdrawal approached, the Serbs continued to assault the factory, and Bosnian commanders in Goražde complained to UN observers that the Serbs were trying to buy time in order to blow it up.[70] No further discussion of this potentially crucial military dimension of the fighting was to appear.[71]

The U.S. proposed establishing total exclusion zones around the safe areas—including Goražde—analogous to the zone established around Sarajevo in February; that is, zones backed by the threat of NATO air strikes to ensure compliance. On April 22, as the fighting around Goražde continued, NATO issued an ultimatum to the Serbs attacking the city. The ultimatum allowed the Serbs two days to pull back three kilometers from the town. An exclusion zone extending twenty kilometers from the center of the city was declared, from which Serb heavy weapons had to be withdrawn by April 27. After a good deal of debate, NATO extended the same protection to Žepa, Tuzla, Bihaći and Srebrenica, which had been declared safe areas by UN Security Council Resolution 824 (May 6, 1993).[72]

As these events were unfolding Milošević summoned Karadžić and Mladić to Belgrade, where they met with Yasushi Akashi, the UN secretary-general's special representative and head of the UNPROFOR mission. On April 22 Akashi was able to report an agreement on the removal of heavy weapons from around the city, but not on the withdrawal of Serb troops three kilometers from the city center.[73] The Belgrade accord brokered by Akashi was not immediately honored. Fighting continued on April 23. The Western media reported a "withering infantry, tank and artillery attack" by the Serbs on Goražde. The ultimatum had given the Serbs until April 24 to withdraw their troops, but they were supposed to cease their attacks immediately. NATO Secretary-General Manfred Woerner wished to launch air strikes against the Serbs. Akashi rejected the request, insisting that the Serbs be given the opportunity to meet the deadline of April 24 before strikes were launched. Woerner was reported furious at the decision.[74] The defining moment of the crisis appeared to have arrived. NATO plans called for a massive strike against the Serbs that would "crush the besieging Bosnian Serb military units and force the Serb leadership back to the bargaining table."[75] At least two dozen Serb military installations were reportedly targeted. While the Americans reportedly favored hitting targets throughout Bosnia, the Europeans are alleged to have limited the area of attack to the twenty–kilometer exclusion zone around the city. One NATO officer suggested: "The plan is to bomb the crap out of them. The idea would be to make it something the Serbs would never, ever, want to experience again."[76]

The search for a solution to the Goražde crisis took place in an atmosphere of mounting tensions, triggered by the apparent determination of the Bosnian Serbs to press their attack regardless of international protests and the threat of air strikes. It appeared that the Serbs intended to seize the town. Such an outcome would have created a humanitarian crisis. In retrospect, and especially in light of what would happen in Srebrenica a year later, there was indeed cause for concern. Goražde had been a base for

Muslim forays into the surrounding countryside, and the combination of local Serbs eager for revenge and irregulars participating in the attack for plunder—not to speak of the military rationale for eliminating a Bosnian stronghold in eastern Bosnia—placed the town in great jeopardy. The willingness of UN commanders and others to accept assurances from the Serbs that they would not seize the town seemed, even at the time, naive.

The Akashi decision to block air strikes against Goražde was one of the most important actions taken by the UN during this phase of the war. Akashi may have been influenced by the accounts of what would happen to UN personnel in the event of such air strikes conveyed to him during his meeting in Belgrade.[77] The decision was all the more notable because Boutros-Ghali was reported ready to approve the NATO request for air strikes, despite the fact that they were opposed by the local UN commanders in Bosnia.[78] The effect of the projected NATO air strikes can only be surmised. If they had stunned or disabled the Serb forces around Goražde, they might have reasserted the dominant position of the UN–NATO alliance in Bosnia and led the Bosnian Serbs to negotiate a settlement along the lines developed later by the Contact Group (described in more detail in chapter 6). Alternatively, NATO air strikes might have led to a massive wave of hostage-taking by the Serbs, and a stand-off similar to that which occurred a year later, in May 1995. Either of these outcomes appeared possible, underscoring the uncertainties surrounding any decision to use force in the absence of a clear political strategy for ending the conflict.

Despite the failure to launch air strikes, the shelling of Goražde tapered off on the afternoon of April 23. UN forces were permitted into the town. By April 26 the fighting around the town had ceased. Bosnian government forces either departed or disengaged themselves from the battle. After a week-long review, a "senior UN military officer" concluded that reports by UN relief workers and others had substantially exaggerated the fighting and the casualties.

According to this officer, damage to the hospital and other buildings was not as great as had been suggested. Reports of 700 dead and up to 2,000 wounded were inflated. The officer, comparing earlier reports with his own direct examination of conditions in Goražde, concluded that the earlier reports had been

> deliberately exaggerated in order to shame the world into doing something. The attacks were not of the dimension suggested. A false impression was given to the international community to help stir the vision of the Bosnian Serbs as the enemy.[79]

He reported that the hospital, which had been described as virtually destroyed, was operative; with just one shell through the roof. There was no evidence of 700 corpses. He suggested that the UN military observers were of a low standard; that the relief workers were overly emotional in their accounts; and that the ham radio operators, who were the source of much of the information on what was taking place in Goražde, were not trustworthy. This assessment gained additional credence when UNHCR spokesman Peter Kessler reported that field personnel—without the knowledge of their superiors—had obtained their initial estimates from Bosnian government sources. General Rose was reported by *Borba* to have claimed that Muslim troops fled, leaving UN troops exposed to Serb fire, and that the Muslim wounded transported out of Goražde included youths who jumped off their stretchers once in Sarajevo.[80]

The debate over the damage done to Goražde illustrated the controversies surrounding media coverage of the war, discussed in greater detail below. It came as a tawdry aftermath to a humanitarian emergency. The angry tone of UN officials in response to reports of a humanitarian crisis in Goražde testified to the existence of profound differences concerning responsibility for the Goražde events; indeed, over the whole nature of the fighting. General Rose and his entourage were convinced that the Bosnian Muslims were bent upon drawing the West into the war, and that the United States was encouraging the Bosnians in this behavior. A UN civil affairs officer lashed out at the United States on the occasion of the opening of the U.S. embassy in Sarajevo a few days later. The ceremony was the opportunity for Madeleine Albright to declare "I am a Sarajevan," and "Your future and America's future are inseparable." The unidentified UN official made no attempt to conceal his anger:

> If anything emboldens the Muslim government to fight on, it's things like this. They can point to that and say, See, the Americans are with us. We can only hope that the failure of NATO to come to their aid around Gorazde will convince them that the U.S. cavalry isn't around the corner.[81]

These differences in perception are the subject of closer examination in our discussions of the UN mission and the media, later in this chapter.

The events at Goražde marked the beginning of a drift away from concern with humanitarian issues on the part of the Western powers. Force gradually came to be seen largely as a means to bring the Serbs to the negotiating table and later, as we shall argue in chapter 7, as a means to impose a solution. With this change, the justification for a UN presence in Bosnia increasingly was called into question. An additional 7,200 troops were authorized by the Security Council in March 1994. But this hardly began to meet the needs of the safe areas for additional UN forces. The exclusion zone around Goražde was never enforced. Serb "police" remained within the three-kilometer zone for an extended period. The first signs of a breakdown of the exclusion zone around Sarajevo can be traced to this period.[82] Over time, it proved impossible to implement the plans for creating such zones in the four remaining safe areas.

Tensions continued to rise between UNPROFOR and the combatants during summer 1994. In June Akashi undertook a major effort to get agreement on a lasting cease-fire in Bosnia. Immediately following the agreement, fighting broke out in Cazinska Krajina. The status of the demilitarized zone created on Mt. Igman as a result of the crisis over the strangulation of Sarajevo in July–August 1993 (described earlier) was put in jeopardy when the Serbs again closed the Mt. Igman route to overland traffic on July 27, 1994. The Serbs attacked a British convoy and killed a British soldier. Lord Owen, in a confidential letter to the European Union on July 29, threw his support to the policy of air strikes against the Bosnian Serb forces, and even went so far as to urge the withdrawal of the UN from Bosnia to permit these attacks to go forward.[83] Violations of the exclusion zone around Sarajevo by both sides multiplied. Bosnian government forces used heavy weapons positioned outside the exclusion zone to fire at Serb forces within. In response, General Rose warned the Bosnians on August 10 that they could face air strikes. Rose also proposed inserting UN forces between the combatants in the area of Vareš. The Bosnian government rejected Rose's proposal, however, remaining steadfast in its refusal to allow UN forces to serve as a buffer between the combatants (except in Sarajevo), so as to avoid creating conditions for *de facto* partition. The Serbs cut off electricity to Sarajevo on September 14. On September 18–19 Bosnian forces initiated an attack against Serb lines around the city, leading to the heaviest shelling of Sarajevo by the Serbs since the preceding February. The fighting ended only after General Rose threatened both sides with air strikes.[84] On September 22 NATO responded to a Serb attack on a French armored car by launching an air attack against an abandoned Serb tank outside Sarajevo, provoking a furious response from General Mladić.[85]

The Bosnian government also was angry with General Rose, above all for focusing on Bosnian transgressions in the exclusion zone around Sarajevo and not on the Serbs' closure of the city to civilian traffic and humanitarian aid. An incident in which the UN accused the Bosnians of firing a mortar shell on the Sarajevo airport produced an outraged reaction from the Bosnians.[86] Throughout the summer, the Bosnian government angrily rebuffed claims that it was breaking the cease-fire and escalating the fighting, arguing that they were defending themselves against an aggressor, and that they had every right to try to regain territories the Serbs had seized by force and subjected to ethnic cleansing. In the view of the Bosnian government, for example, the Fifth Corps attack on Abdić's forces in Cazinska Krajina in June 1994 (treated in more detail below) was an internal matter that did not fall within the purview of the cease-fire.[87] In an interview with *Oslobodjenje*, General Rasim Delić, the commander of the Bosnian forces, argued that the Bosnians lost more territory than they gained during the cease-fire of spring 1994; that the Serbs rejected Bosnian proposals for adequate supervision of the cease-fire; and that after the first 30-day cease-fire expired, the Serbs refused to renew it and called instead for mobilization of the Serb population. Delić insisted, finally, that the Bosnian army was not the first to attack during the summer campaigns.[88] In fact, all the fighting in spring and summer 1994 resulted in very little change in the distribution of territory between the warring parties. General Rose, in turn, was reported to have become exasperated with the Bosnian Muslim refusal to sign a long-term cease-fire. He was convinced that the Muslims simply wanted NATO and the United States to join the struggle on the Muslim side and were prepared to do anything to achieve this goal. In late September, he accused the Bosnian army of trying "to create images of war for the world, to get us to respond with air power," and warned that air power might be used against the Bosnians instead.[89]

The situation around Sarajevo continued to deteriorate through fall 1994. It proved impossible for the overextended French UNPROFOR forces to control the UN demilitarized area on Mt. Igman. Bosnian government forces infiltrated the area and refused to leave unless the French secured the supply route. On October 6 Bosnian guerrillas destroyed a Serb battalion headquarters, killing twenty, among them three female nurses.[90] On October 7, French forces took the unprecedented step of launching an attack on Bosnian units on Mt. Igman. The Serbs set their own deadline of October 20 for the Bosnian forces to leave the exclusion zone.[91] The fighting continued, however.

By the end of October the UN and NATO had lost control of the situation in Bosnia. Sarajevo and its environs were in complete disarray. Heavy fighting was in progress on a multitude of fronts across Bosnia. The Bosnian Muslims and Croats launched a joint offensive against Kupres, which fell to Croat control on November 3. The Bosnian Seventh Corps advanced up the Vrbas river from Bugojno in the direction of Donji Vakuf. The Croats launched a separate attack from their stronghold of Livno against the neighboring Serb towns of Glamoč and Bosansko Grahovo. At about the same time the Bosnian Fourth Corps attacked south from Sarajevo toward

Trnovo. However, none of these efforts resulted in major gains for the Bosnian government forces. On November 19 UNPROFOR shut down the Sarajevo airport after the Serbs refused to guarantee the safety of flights in and out of the city. The UN operation in Bosnia appeared no longer to be effective, raising the prospect of its withdrawal.

Bihać, November–December 1994

The heaviest fighting in 1994 took place in the Bihać pocket in the Cazinska Krajina region of northwest Bosnia-Herzegovina. The Serbs had made an effort to capture Bihać in 1992, but failed. Fighting in the area tapered off in 1993. But the stage was set for a resurgence of fighting when Fikret Abdić accepted the Owen-Stoltenberg partition plan (described in detail in chapter 6), declared the autonomy of the Cazinska region, and in October 1993 signed a pact of cooperation and friendship with the Bosnian Serb republic.[92] The Bosnian Fifth Corps under Atif Dudaković, which had defended Bihać against the Serbs, now turned on Abdić. After three months of fighting, most of the pocket was under the control of the Fifth Corps. A cease-fire was signed between the Bosnian army and the Muslim forces loyal to Abdić in January 1994. Fighting broke out again in early February when the Bosnian Serbs attacked the Fifth Corps in an effort to prevent it from seizing Abdić's stronghold of Velika Kladuša. The Serb attacks increased in intensity following the creation of the exclusion zone around Sarajevo in mid-February (described above), suggesting that Serb artillery may have been moved from Sarajevo to Bihać. Fighting was particularly intense on the Grabež plateau, a strategically important land mass which was to change hands several times during 1994. The fighting caught French UNPROFOR units in the middle. On March 10 the Serbs shelled a French observation post and, the following day, Serb snipers killed a French peacekeeper. NATO air strikes against the Serbs were authorized when tank rounds landed near the French barracks, but bad weather prevented them from taking place.[93]

The fighting in Cazinska Krajina continued through spring and summer 1994. In early June, Bosnian government units launched a fresh attack on the Abdić forces. A confused battle followed, stretching into summer. The Bosnian Serbs applied pressure on the Fifth Corps around Bihać while Abdić, whose forces had been pushed by Dudaković back toward Velika Kladuša, received artillery support from the Krajina Serbs located across the nearby border in Croatia. In July, Dudaković's forces scored a decisive victory over Abdić. By late August Abdić's forces were in full flight from Cazinska Krajina into neighboring Croatia. According to press reports, some 20,000 of Abdić's followers crossed into Serb-held Krajina in the third week in August.[94]

The Bosnian Serbs responded to the defeat of Abdić by launching an offensive against government forces in the Bihać pocket from Serb-held territory in Croatia in early September. According to Muslim accounts, General Mladić commanded the Bosnian Serb forces and was wounded on September 12 in the village of Majdan, inside Croatian territory.[95] The Serbs were defeated in this encounter. The Fifth Corps, against great odds, scored one of the most significant Bosnian victories of the war up to this point. Emboldened by his victory, Dudaković then attempted to break out of the Bihać pocket. He launched an offensive southward from Bihać on October 26.

The attack produced rapid Bosnian government advances. The tide of battle shifted dramatically in the second week of November, however, after the Serbs launched a counteroffensive. By November 11 Bosnian Serb forces, aided by an attack on the Bosnian government forces launched from the rear by the Krajina Serbs from across the Croatian-Bosnian border,[96] had reached the Grabež plateau overlooking the city of Bihać. By November 24, the day NATO met to decide whether to issue an ultimatum to the Serbs to withdraw from Bihać, the Serbs had pushed government forces back into the confines of the city and seemed intent upon inflicting a total defeat on the Fifth Corps.[97]

Whether the Serbs had violated the limits of the safe area around Bihać was difficult to determine. The safe areas had been created by Security Council declaration rather than by negotiation among the combatants on the ground. Hence, their borders were never established precisely. On November 14, when the Serb attack on Bihać was in full swing, the UN produced a map, but admitted that they did not know when it had been drawn. Whether the map had previously been made available to the parties to the conflict remained unclear.[98] A later report by the secretary-general makes it clear that the borders had been defined only in response to the crisis, on the basis of "tactical features, population density, and available UNPROFOR troops."[99] In any event, UN forces in the safe area did not have sufficient resources for the task. French UNPROFOR troops that had occupied the Bihać safe area the previous summer had been withdrawn, leaving in their place only 1,200 ill-equipped Bangladeshi troops.[100]

The Bihać crisis of November–December 1994 was potentially the most explosive of the Bosnian war up to that point. Cazinska Krajina, in which Bihać was located, was a battleground for six different military formations: the Bosnian Serb army, the Serb army of the RSK located across the Croatian border in Krajina, Abdić's breakaway Bosnian Muslim faction, the Fifth Corps of the Bosnian government army under General Dudaković, and the regular army of Croatia. The crisis over Bihać found the international community locked in debate over the future of the safe areas. At the height of the Bosnian government offensive out of the Bihać pocket in early November, the Russians raised the issue of Bosnian provocations and violations of safe areas. The Russians argued that while the Security Council resolutions creating safe areas did not require the Bosnian government forces to surrender their arms, Resolution 913 called on all parties to stop provocative actions. In case of violations, the UN was to use all possible means, including the use of air power, to halt such provocations. Earlier, according to a TASS report, the Russians had proposed, with the support of the secretary-general, that the anomaly in the UN rules governing security zones permitting them to be used as bases for offensive military operations be examined and corrected. The secretary-general had raised this issue himself in several earlier reports to the Council. But the effort was rebuffed by the Security Council. The U.S. media largely avoided the issue of Bosnian forays out of Bihać. The British *Guardian,* normally a staunch defender of the Bosnian cause, nevertheless chastised NATO for not insisting that the Bosnian government offensive out of the Bihać pocket be halted.[101] The Clinton administration failed to condemn the Bosnian attack, "reasoning that the Muslims were victims in the war and were trying to reclaim their own territory." British and French policymakers suggested the Bosnians were now acting as aggressors.[102]

On November 3 four converted surface-to-air missiles (SAMs) were launched at Bihać from Serb positions. The missiles could not be aimed. Each contained 250 pounds of explosives. Mercifully, no deaths resulted although one missile landed near a school.[103] One can speculate that had the missiles hit the school, there would have been a forceful reaction—and a very credible one—from NATO. The missile attack might have been a reaction to the capture of Kupres by the Croats and Muslims, or a provocation aimed at escalating the conflict. In any case, it was the kind of mindless and destructive action that had become characteristic of the Serbs during the war. In reaction to these events, U.S. policymakers decided on November 12 to push for the creation of an exclusion zone around Bihać, extending into Croatia proper. But the proposal was rejected by the Europeans, who were not convinced the Serbs would try to overrun Bihać.

Serb air strikes—the first air strikes of any consequence launched by the Serbs against a safe area—sharply increased the tension. On November 18 planes taking off from the Udbina airbase in Serb-held Krajina (Croatia) bombed Bihać. A second raid followed the next day. On November 19 the Security Council authorized NATO to attack Serb targets in Croatia. On November 21 NATO aircraft, in their largest operation up to that time, bombed the Udbina airbase. The NATO attack purposely rendered the runway unusable, but left Serb aircraft undamaged. On November 23 NATO planes struck at three Serb SAM sites in the Bihać area, apparently over the objections of General Rose—this, despite the fact that two more missile attacks on Bihać had occurred in the interim.[104] The Serbs reacted furiously to the NATO attacks. General Mladić, in a letter dated November 22, called the Udbina attack "brutal and merciless."[105] An advisor to Karadžić, in a phone conversation with General Rose's aide, threatened that another attack would mean "war."[106] The Serbs began seizing UN personnel, or restricting their movements.[107] In Europe and the United States, there were calls for the West to show its resolve. The Serbs were said to be "taunting" the international community, and the credibility of both the Security Council and NATO was alleged to be on trial.[108]

On November 23 and 24, there were reports in the Western media that the U.S. administration was studying options for the use of air power to prevent the collapse of Bihać. The United States was reportedly contemplating a massive NATO attack against Serb positions around Bihać in order to prevent the enclave from being overrun, and the British and French were reportedly close to agreement with the United States.[109] The November 23 raid had struck only the radars at the SAM sites under attack. The Americans were now eager to strike at the missile launchers themselves, and the French agreed.[110] With Serb forces reportedly penetrating into the heart of Bihać, the moment seemed ripe for a vigorous Western response to the Serbs, both as a means of protecting the safe area and bringing pressure on the Bosnian Serb leadership to rejoin the peace talks.

The Serbs, for their part, seemed to be in no mood to accept a local cease-fire. Mladić called a cease-fire "senseless."[111] On November 25, the Western media reported that the Serbs had demanded the surrender of the Muslim forces.[112] On November 24 General Rose reacted to the hard line of the Serb generals with one of his strongest statements directed against the Serbs. Rose asserted that they had "crossed the line beyond which the safety of the population of Bihać is now directly threatened. . . . It does seem extraordinary to me that they should be in such a flagrant and blatant violation of the United Nations designated safe area."[113]

The next day Rose called for NATO strikes against the Serbs and ten fighters were sent in. But they received no directions from ground spotters under UN command and thus made no attack. The failure of the spotters to communicate with the NATO craft was later attributed to an order issued by General Rose's command.[114] On November 26, Silajdžić demonstratively walked out of a meeting with Rose, angered over the general's failure to call in air strikes against the Serbs. As the crisis around Bihać eased, Rose steadfastly refused to authorize further air strikes, arguing that his mandate did not permit taking sides in the conflict unless UN troops or civilians were imperiled.

In the midst of these threats and counterthreats, Akashi met with Milošević and Milan Martić (president of the RSK) in Belgrade on November 23 in hopes of gaining agreement for a cease-fire. The talks were opposed by the Bosnian Serb leadership. Karadžić was not present at the meeting, and the Serbs in Pale rebuffed Akashi's suggestion for a meeting in Pale several days later, presumably to signal their displeasure with the talks in Belgrade.[115] The UN was finding that its ability to mediate among the combatants was diminishing as the war wore on.

A NATO meeting was called on November 24, when uncertainty over the course of events was at its highest, to determine the Western response to Serb actions. The United States proposed enlarging the Bihać safe area; the complete demilitarization of the enclave; and guarantees for the safe passage of Bosnian government troops, who would be required to leave the safe area.[116] The proposal addressed for the first time the Serb demand that the safe areas be demilitarized. It also opened the door to punishing air strikes against the Serbs. According to a media report, Bihać would be protected from the Serb attacks by wide-ranging NATO air strikes against Serb ammunition dumps and supply bases throughout Bosnia. The French resisted. They demanded that the Americans make clear who would police the demilitarized area. The point struck to the heart of the dispute between Europe and the United States over the failure of the Americans to contribute troops to the UN operation in Bosnia. If the United States was not willing to send troops to police such a high-risk undertaking, then the real purpose of the proposal, the French suggested, was to provide a rationale for air strikes against the Serbs to bring them to the bargaining table. The French feared that the Serbs would react by taking hostages. With the French and Canadians leading the way, the U.S. proposal was rejected; even after the U.S. delegate to the proceedings, Robert Hunter, agreed that the United States would not insist on "strategic strikes."[117] A strikingly low-key communique was issued instead, in which NATO urged the Bosnians and Serbs to seek a political solution to the conflict.

The media immediately sensed that NATO had "blinked" in front of the Serbs. One account suggested that the NATO statement "might merely prolong the war by suggesting that the alliance lacks resolve."[118] Once more, Western policy appeared adrift. Negotiations among the warring parties to end the conflict had stalled. The UN mission was increasingly under fire. NATO, instead of projecting power, had bowed to the concerns of the Europeans over the welfare of their troops in Bosnia. However, as we shall see in detail in chapters 6 and 7, these events in late 1994 marked the beginning of a complex reassessment of policy options by Western leaderships, especially in the United States.

While the outcome remained in doubt for several days more, a combination of events contributed to a lessening of tensions. First, Serb artillery encircling the city was not targeting civilians. The *New York Times* quoted Major Koos Sol, a UN military spokesman, to the effect that Serb artillery had been careful not to target the safe area; in the major's words, "almost nothing has been falling into the safe area."[119] Second, on November 24 (the day of the NATO meeting described above) the Serbs allowed the first UN aid convoy into Bihać. Third, the other parties in the conflict also exercised restraint. A Croatian threat to intervene against the Krajina Serbs did not materialize, and the Krajina Serbs bowed to demands by Milošević that they cease their provocations. Fourth, the Bosnian government, faced with a choice between destruction of the Fifth Corps or escape, chose the latter. By November 24, the Western media reported, there were barely 400 Muslim soldiers left in Bihać.[120] Sporadic shelling of the city continued, but Serb efforts to capture the city ceased. The Serbs ignored a statement by the president of the Security Council calling on them to adhere to a UN-brokered cease-fire already accepted by the government.[121] But the Bihać crisis had for the moment been defused. The end result was very little change in the territory controlled by each side.

The UN Mission Under Attack

The end of the Bihać crisis coincided with a hardening of Serb behavior toward UNPROFOR. The Bosnian Serbs continued to hold UN personnel hostage long after the Bihać crisis had passed. The Serbs installed additional SAMs around Bihać and Sarajevo (the missiles first began appearing in October), and they prevented humanitarian convoys from moving through Serb-held territory. A convoy was allowed through to the Bihać pocket on December 8 (the first one since November 24). Another convoy was permitted to reach the Srebrenica enclave in eastern Bosnia on December 11, the first in six months. Serb belligerence culminated on December 13 with an attack on a UN armored vehicle in the Bihać pocket. One of the soldiers wounded in the incident died when the Serbs refused to allow him to be helicoptered out of the area. The incident led the Western media to conclude that the UN operation had lost its direction, purpose, and credibility.[122]

The first two weeks in December 1994 were perhaps the worst UNPROFOR had experienced in two and a half years of the war. A UN official in New York, Thant Myint-U, used some of the frankest language ever by a UN representative when he declared on December 5:

> The international community should understand clearly that the Bosnian Serbs are not only waging war against the Bosnian government in Bihać. They are targeting UNPROFOR; detaining its personnel and denying others essential supplies. This is a deliberately designed, carefully calculated insult against the United Nations.[123]

Several days later another UN spokesman declared: "We need to do something immediately. This is a critical point and our options are strictly limited."[124]

Bosnian Serb pressure on UNPROFOR eased following negotiations between Akashi and Karadžić in mid-December. The underlying reason for this change in behavior was not immediately apparent. In hindsight, it appears that the Serbs may have been influenced by the possibility of a NATO mission to Bosnia to evacuate the UN. On December 7 President Clinton had announced that the United States was prepared to send troops to effect the withdrawal of UN forces if this step proved necessary. From this point onward, the dynamic of the Bosnian crisis began to change. In effect, the deterioration of the humanitarian effort in Bosnia had itself created a tangible interest—ensuring the security of a UN withdrawal—that represented a credible basis for Western intervention. Both the Bosnian government and the Bosnian Serbs had much to lose and little to gain if the UN withdrawal took place. It was the growing threat of this withdrawal that provided the catalyst in 1995 for the American effort to end the fighting.

The decline in trust between UNPROFOR and the Bosnian government contributed to the growing pressure to withdraw from Bosnia. The lack of trust in the UN displayed by the Bosnian government was exacerbated by the feud between the media and UNPROFOR. The feud began with attacks by the media on the first UN commander in Sarajevo, General Lewis MacKenzie, culminating with the Herak case in spring 1993. The government had persuaded the Western press to accept its version of the confessions of Borislav Herak, a Bosnian Serb captured by the Bosnians, imprisoned, and then convicted of heinous crimes in March 1993. The *New York Times* made Herak's confession of rape and other atrocities front-page news.[125] Herak later recanted his confession. Some sleuthing by journalists after Dayton revealed that two Muslims whom Herak's companion, Sretko Damjanović, had been accused of murdering were in fact alive and well.[126] Herak had also charged that General MacKenzie and his troops favored a Serb brothel where Muslim women were kept captive.[127] (This part of Herak's confession was not repeated in the *New York Times* dispatch cited above.) The charge could easily have been challenged as a transparent attempt by the government to discredit MacKenzie, who was an outspoken critic of Muslim (as well as Serb and Croat) behavior. The charge seemed an open-and-shut case of the worst kind of slander, but few Western journalists came to the general's defense, setting the stage for further confrontations between the media and UN commanders. It finally became necessary for the UN secretary-general to defend General MacKenzie publicly against these charges.

The perception was widespread among journalists in Sarajevo that UNPROFOR personnel were indifferent, and even callous, in the face of Muslim pleas for greater help. Personnel within the UNPROFOR operation in Sarajevo who shared this view would leak information to the media, who would confront the UN command with demands to take more decisive action against the Serbs. Many well-informed analysts outside Bosnia, most notably those associated with the journal *War Report,* shared a negative view of the UNPROFOR operation in Bosnia.[128] As a result, a sentiment bordering on contempt for the UN infused a great deal of journalistic reporting. Chuck Sudetic's remarks in an article published in *Rolling Stone* in early January 1995 captured the feeling of the press corps toward the UN quite well, if somewhat crudely:

> U.N. officials even went so far as to blame the Bosnian government for prolonging the war and accused its army of shooting at its own civilians to prompt Western intervention. One Canadian peacekeeper from Quebec spoke, as Bosnians would say, "with no hair on his tongue": "The United Nations is helping the Muslims keep this war going, and their leaders don't give a fuck about their own civilians. We could all get the fuck out of this place and go home if these Muslims surrendered."[129]

The fact that some UN officers openly expressed their admiration for the professionalism of the Serb forces, and even spoke of General Mladić in flattering terms, added to this hostility on the part of the media toward UN efforts at peacekeeping.

On the other hand, UN commanders felt that the media did not understand the nature of the war in Bosnia. It seemed apparent to UNPROFOR officers that the Bosnian government was not only exaggerating the suffering of civilians in order to win sympathy, but contributing directly to that suffering. One notable example, which was reported in some detail in the West, were the obstacles the government placed in the way of the project to supply fresh drinking water to the people of Sarajevo. The reluctance with which many in the West treated this phenomenon was reflected in the account in the *Washington Post.*[130] An otherwise first-class job of investigative reporting by John Pomfret pulled its punches by attributing the

refusal of Bosnian authorities to allow the water purification project to proceed to bureaucratic bumbling rather than to a conscious policy of manipulation. That it was, indeed, the latter is reported more directly in a later
documentary film account of the humanitarian relief efforts of Fred Cuny.[131]

Even more serious, some UN commanders remained convinced that the
Bosnian government condoned incidents in which Muslims shelled their
own people or directed sniper fire against them to gain sympathy in the
West. This view found some support among U.S. officers. General Charles
G. Boyd, the recently retired deputy commander-in-chief of the U.S. European Command, criticized the Bosnian Muslims for such actions openly in
a widely noted article in *Foreign Affairs*.[132] Others in UNPROFOR and in
the intelligence community challenged this belief. The result was a striking
disparity of viewpoints within UNPROFOR—even among personnel from
the same country—concerning the behavior of the combatants and their
culpability for some of the more egregious actions against the civilian population. Inevitably, this contributed to the feelings of frustration, and of being
misunderstood, that characterized the attitudes of many participants in the
UN operation in Bosnia. It was difficult even for a seasoned observer of the
Bosnian war to accept suspicions that the Muslims were targeting their own
people. Indeed, as we shall see below, this was an issue that divided even
the journalists reporting it. Determining the truth in these matters constituted one of the most thorny—and consequential—issues of the war.

Media, Public Opinion, and Western Policy

Western media became one of the most important battlefields of the war in
Bosnia. The Bosnian government attempted to influence and manipulate the
media both on the spot in Bosnia and through public relations professionals
in the West. For the most part, Western coverage of the war in Bosnia
focused on the plight of the Bosnian Muslims, and especially on the shelling of Sarajevo, out of genuine concern for and identification with the
victims rather than as the result of manipulation. As early as August 1992,
for example, one editorial writer for the *Boston Globe* noted that reporters
felt a duty to help what they perceived to be a defenseless civilian population under attack. "These people in Sarajevo are not in a position to defend
themselves," one journalist told him. "They're fighting a war for the conscience of the world."[133]

The compelling nature of the story of Muslim victimization deterred
most reporters from any effort to examine the complex issues underlying
the war. Even if they had, one respected journalist with experience in
Bosnia noted in fall 1993 that most lacked the training necessary to under-

stand the events they were forced to interpret. They were, in this journalist's view, like "scouts without compasses."[134] Most investigative reporting during the war thus consisted of efforts to expose Muslim victimization more completely. The emotional nature of the Western attachment to the Muslim cause led some journalists to dispute vigorously interpretations and reports inconsistent with this story line and, according to some accounts, led some editors to suppress such reports.[135] At the same time, the media did send back copious and accurate dispatches on the war. These provide a large portion of the sources used in this work. Laura Silber's dispatches for the *Financial Times,* for example, culminated in the first in-depth account of the Yugoslav crisis and the initial stages of the war in Bosnia, *Yugoslavia: Death of a Nation,* a volume Silber co-authored with Allan Little.

The failure of much of the Western media to understand fully the dynamics of the war in Bosnia, to examine dramatic events with a more critical eye, or to resist manipulation, distorted popular perceptions of the war, but did not generate popular enthusiasm for involvement in it. U.S. public opinion, for example, while concerned about Bosnia and supportive of ending ethnic cleansing and the war, tended not to support direct involvement of U.S. ground forces. A review of public attitudes toward the use of force compiled in August 1994[136] revealed that the American public was not deeply concerned by the wars in Yugoslavia. Surveys conducted through 1993 revealed that relatively small proportions of the public were following events closely, and that those who felt the United States had a responsibility to do something about the fighting were far outnumbered by those who felt it did not. When asked in January 1993 specifically whether U.S. forces should be used to end the fighting, 55 percent said no. (Forty-seven percent opposed their use even when the question was worded more provocatively, in terms of preventing the Serbs from taking over.)

Majorities of the public opposed the use of air strikes against the Serbs through spring 1993. In June large majorities of the public favored their use to protect UN forces; in August majorities of the public favored their use to defend Sarajevo. A study published in November 1993, however, made it clear that the American public did not view the war in Bosnia as a matter of high priority for the United States. It ranked well behind "stopping international drug trafficking," "strengthening the domestic economy," "stopping the flood of illegal aliens," "protecting the global environment," and other issues in importance.[137]

A year later, in November 1994, 62 percent of those surveyed continued to believe that the United States did not have a responsibility to act in Bosnia. In June 1995, 64 percent of Americans continued to believe the United States had no responsibility to act. But, at the same time, 71 percent did support using U.S. forces to defend peacekeepers if they were to come under attack. Overall, however, ending the warfare in Bosnia continued to rank in importance well behind the issues cited a year earlier.[138]

While popular opinion thus placed little pressure on Western policymakers to act, the intensity of media coverage of developments in Bosnia did. As Michael Beschloss has argued,[139] intense media coverage, such as that extended to the events described in this chapter, helped to create a crisis atmosphere for policymakers. The analysis of media coverage and its effect on policy carried out by Nik Gowing provides evidence that media coverage *by itself* did not substantially alter the policies considered by decisionmakers. Indeed, Gowing's interviews with individuals involved in U.S. policymaking in 1992 underscore the fact that government intelligence sources usually provided policymakers with information about unseen developments long in advance of the media.[140] But his account also suggests that dramatic and intensive coverage of events did produce pressure on policymakers to "do something."

The Three Massacres

Media coverage of the war in Bosnia, like Western policy, was driven by crises. In part, the sense of crisis surrounding certain events was the product of media coverage itself. Three events were the subject of intense coverage that assumed crisis proportions, and were central to the escalation of Western involvement in the war: the breadline massacre of May 27, 1992; the Markala marketplace massacre of February 5, 1994; and the second shelling of the Markala marketplace on August 28, 1995. The breadline massacre occurred as Western leaders were convening in Lisbon to consider their next steps in Bosnia. Both sanctions against Yugoslavia (Serbia and Montenegro) and direct military intervention to stop the fighting in Bosnia were under consideration when the attack occurred. As we shall see in chapter 5, disgust over the deaths of innocent civilians played a role in pushing the West toward rushing sanctions through the Security Council on May 30, and becoming more directly involved on the ground. The Markala marketplace massacre of February 1994 came at a point when, as we reported earlier in this chapter, the Serbs and Croats appeared on the verge of undertaking a joint offensive against the Muslims, and the United States—as we shall see in more detail in chapter 6—was under great pressure from the French to act decisively to end the conflict. The massacre galvanized the West into action. The second, August 1995, Markala marketplace massacre provided the trigger that, as we shall see in chapter 7, the United States was looking for in order to launch the massive NATO air campaign that helped bring the fighting to an end. In each instance, the importance of the event, and uncertainties in the evidence of what transpired, aroused heated debate over whether Bosnian Muslim forces might have carried out attacks on their own people as part of an effort to induce Western military intervention.

The predominant assumption in the Western media, that the Bosnian government simply could not have engaged in such inhuman acts, does not stand up to scrutiny. Incidents in which the Muslims fired on their own people did occur. We have already noted the reports of such incidents by General Boyd. In November 1994, in the midst of the Bihać crisis reported earlier in this chapter, the UN provided a detailed public report of evidence that the Bosnian army had launched a mortar attack against a Sarajevo neighborhood under its own control, killing a child.[141] Another such case occurred in December 1994 when two persons were killed and seven wounded in Sarajevo. Former UNPROFOR military sources have described how the incident was blamed by the Bosnian government on a Serb tank firing from a UN-controlled weapons depot outside the city. A UN investigation of the incident determined that the shell could not have been fired from Serb positions, and that the explosives involved were a mortar shell and a satchel charge, findings that implicated the Muslims.[142] In late July 1995 an UNPROFOR anti-sniping team isolated a sniper under Bosnian government control who had been attacking civilians in Sarajevo.[143] Whether responsibility for any of the three key massacres lay on the Bosnian Muslim side—government or otherwise—was less clear.

The UNPROFOR contingent was hardly anticipating problems of this kind when it arrived in 1992. The breadline massacre took the UN by surprise, and no official investigation of the incident was ever launched. General MacKenzie, in his account of the incident, quotes an entry from his diary that leaves the question of responsibility for the incident open, but notes that there were a number of unusual circumstances surrounding the explosion:

> The street was blocked just before the incident. Once the crowd was let in and had lined up, the media appeared but kept their distance. The attack took place, and the media were immediately on the scene. The majority of people killed are alleged to be "tame Serbs."[144]

His conclusion left the question of guilt unresolved: "Who knows?" he wrote. The American journalist Tom Gjelten later argued that MacKenzie had been traumatized by the kidnapping of Izetbegović and subsequent ambush of the JNA convoy under his protection, noted earlier in this chapter, and never forgave the Muslims.[145]

The Yugoslav government demanded that an investigation be carried out by UNPROFOR, arguing that the explosion and resulting casualties could not have been caused by four rounds from artillery or mortars, regardless of caliber.[146] Several months later the *Independent* ran a story in which an unnamed UN official asserted that "we believe it was a command-detonated explosion, probably in a can," and explained that the impact was not as large as would be expected from a mortar round landing on a paved surface.[147] Prior to the report in the *Independent,* the Belgrade weekly *Vreme* carried out its own investigation of the incident and disputed the charge that the Bosnians were responsible. *Vreme* reported that the UN neither carried out an investigation of the blast scene nor interviewed survivors. *Vreme* suggested that the evidence the Muslims were responsible came entirely from Serb sources.[148] A lengthy and critical analysis of the event published in December 1993 by Tom Gjelten also cast doubt on key elements of the argument that the incident was manufactured by the Muslims, but at the same time left the question of responsibility unresolved. He argued passionately that "no physical evidence has ever been found that suggests Muslims purposely shoot themselves, and at this stage the notion is as preposterous as it is insulting to Bosnian honor."[149]

The Markala marketplace massacre of February 5, 1994, was investigated three separate times by UN officers within hours of the explosion.[150] Only one of the three investigations implicated the Muslims. Although the investigations of the first day left the question of who was responsible in doubt, the report implicating the Muslims nonetheless retained currency.[151] On February 7, two days after the explosion and two days before NATO established an exclusion zone around Sarajevo and confronted the Serbs with an ultimatum to withdraw from it, Secretary of State Christopher asserted that the explosion was the work of the Serbs.[152] NATO acted without certain knowledge of the origin of the mortar shell, but in the conviction that the Serbs had committed the deed. On February 10, Boutros-Ghali, acting on the basis of the early reports, informed Christopher that the Muslims were the most likely perpetrators. Christopher rejected this conclusion. On February 11, UNPROFOR finally initiated a thorough investigation of the incident. Although there were a total of ten crater analyses, the investigation was hampered—perhaps botched would be a better description—by the first investigating team, which removed the tail fin of the mortar shell but did not analyze the shell's fuse furrow, which was then obliterated. The final report on the incident, dated February 14 and distributed in summary form to the press on February 16, concluded that the calculated trajectory of the shell placed its origins within two and a half square kilometers of territory that encompassed both Muslim and Serb sites.[153] In other words, either side could have launched the shell.

The Western media had no such doubts, however. Almost instantaneously, television journalists conveyed the judgment that the Serbs were responsible. Fueled by the terrible carnage wrought by the explosion, the electronic and print media helped build the incident into a crisis. In the meantime, however, the conviction that it was the Muslims who were responsible had taken root within the ranks of UN officers. The incident thus served to reinforce the remarkable split in perceptions of the combatants both among UN officers and between the UN and the Western media. But the most important consequence of the shelling in the short term was that it brought NATO into direct involvement in the war, in establishing an exclusion zone around Sarajevo. In the longer run, as we shall argue in chapter 6, the incident brought the United States into more direct involvement in efforts to end the war. It is this post-event development, more than anything about the event itself, that made culpability for the first Markala marketplace massacre such a significant—and contentious—issue.

The second shelling of the Markala marketplace, on August 28, 1995, took place at a moment when, as we noted above and shall see in more detail in chapter 7, Western policymakers appeared already to have decided to use force—air power—against the Serbs and were waiting only for an appropriate "trigger." The shelling provided this, and was offered as one of several justifications for the NATO bombing campaign that began on August 30. Here, we are concerned only with the fact that, once again, the attribution of culpability for the incident was surrounded by controversy.[154] That controversy arose out of the fact that while the first four of a series of five shells were determined to have come from the same—Serb—origin, the fifth shell appeared to have originated elsewhere. It was the fifth shell that resulted in civilian casualties.

A crater analysis performed by a British and a French officer placed the first four shells on trajectories pointing to Serb responsibility. They placed the fatal fifth shell on a different trajectory that suggested it "might easily have been not the Bosnian Serbs but the Bosnian government army" that was responsible.[155] A Canadian officer asserted that "anomalies with the fuse" suggested the fifth shell had not been fired from a mortar at all, a suspicion reinforced by the absence in this case—reported by an U.S. official—of the distinct whistle characteristic of an incoming mortar shell.[156] These doubts were overruled by a senior U.S. officer at UNPROFOR headquarters in Sarajevo and, by the end of the day, the UN announced officially that the Serbs were responsible. Within forty-eight hours, NATO officers had decided Serb responsibility for the shelling was "beyond all reasonable doubt"[157] and cited the incident as justification for initiation of the air campaign against the Serbs. According to a later Western media analysis, however, "Neither NATO military nor civilian authorities reviewed the evidence [—other than the hastily written report submitted to General Smith and then classified by the UN in New York—] before committing the alliance to a massive counterpunch."[158] Two days later the artillery officer commanding the Russian UNPROFOR contingent in Sarajevo, Colonel Andrei Demurenko, went on Sarajevo television to denounce the UN report as a "falsification."[159]

The authors have talked to a number of former UN military officers and civilian officials who have vehemently defended the integrity of the official UN report, which—unlike that of February 1994—was never released. From their accounts it appears that the fifth shell did have an angle of descent different from the first four. The evidence, our sources argue, was clear that the first four were fired from Serb positions. The report, we are told, concluded that the fifth shell originated from the same position, but its angle of descent had apparently been affected by some anomaly such as hitting a building on the way down. Yet, this version of the UN report seems to contradict the account of the U.S. officer at UNPROFOR headquarters—cited above—who claimed to have found traces of the "fuse tunnel" or "furrow" overlooked by the British and French officers first on the scene. It was on this basis that the U.S. officer claimed the fatal shell had been fired from the same location as the first four. Thus, the evidentiary picture surrounding the August 28 incident remains confused. It will be cleared up only when the classified UN report and other evidence is made public.[160]

The uncertainties surrounding these three events do not negate the evidence of disproportionate attacks and atrocities committed against Muslim civilians by the Bosnian Serbs. While the Serbs engaged in atrocities of this kind "out of spite" (*iz inata*), the Bosnian Muslims appear to have been trying to wring another round of sympathy from the West or to affect the outcome of specific meetings or decisions by Western policymakers. Regardless of their purpose or perpetrators, of course, the attacks on defenseless civilians were wretched acts.

A striking aspect of these incidents from the analysts' perspective is the general reluctance on the part of policymakers to pursue the matter of who was responsible before responding to them. Policymakers already intent on certain actions, it can be argued, needed clear and persuasive justifications for their actions and thus simply suspended their critical judgment in order to use such incidents as justification to pursue preferred options. In the three cases presented here, policymakers imposed sanctions on Yugoslavia, created the exclusion zone around Sarajevo and threatened to use air power against the Serbs, and, finally, used air power on a massive scale. A statement by U.S. ambassador to the UN Madeleine Albright at the time of the first Markala massacre expresses openly the degree to which policymakers simply ignored uncertainties that called into question their preconceived ideas about the conflict:

> It's very hard to believe that any country would do this to their own people, and therefore, although we do not exactly know what the facts are, it would seem to us that the Serbs and the Bosnian Serbs are the ones that probably have a great deal of responsibility.[161]

The shaky reasoning reflected in this statement nonetheless reflects a real dilemma confronting Western policymakers as they attempted to cope with the challenges thrown up by the conflict in Bosnia-Herzegovina: the need to reconcile morality and interest. The prominence gained by these three events—indeed, by the many tragic incidents in which large numbers of civilians were killed—reflected the interconnectedness of sometimes conflicting moral and pragmatic-political considerations in Western approaches to the war; the desire of policymakers and the public alike for morality and interest to coincide; and the tendency toward cognitive dissonance when, as was often the case, they did not. In no case was the clash between morality and interest as difficult to cope with as in the challenge raised by ethnic cleansing and other atrocities, and the debate over genocide in Bosnia.

Ethnic Cleansing and Genocide

War Casualties

The civilian population bore the brunt of the war in Bosnia. The number of casualties is a matter of debate. The figure of 200,000 (or more) dead, injured, and missing was frequently cited in media reports on the war in Bosnia as late as 1994.[162] The October 1995 bulletin of the Bosnian Institute for Public Health of the Republic Committee for Health and Social Welfare gave the numbers as 146,340 killed, and 174,914 wounded on the territory under the control of the Bosnian army.[163] Mustafa Imamović gave a figure of 144,248 perished (including those who died from hunger or exposure), mainly Muslims.[164] The Red Cross and the UNHCR have not, to the best of our knowledge, produced data on the number of persons killed and injured in the course of the war. A November 1995 unclassified CIA memorandum estimated 156,500 civilian deaths in the country (all but 10,000 of them in Muslim- or Croat-held territories), not including the 8,000 to 10,000 then still missing from the Srebrenica and Žepa enclaves.

This figure for civilian deaths far exceeded the estimate in the same report of 81,500 troops killed (45,000 Bosnian government; 6,500 Bosnian Croat; and 30,000 Bosnian Serb).[165]

These data were challenged by George Kenney, in an article appearing in spring 1995.[166] Kenney asserted that the Red Cross and other international agencies estimated the number of casualties in the tens of thousands. Kenney himself argued for a figure of between 25,000 and 60,000.[167] The yearbook of the Stockholm International Peace Research Institute gave the figure of 25,000 to 55,000 total deaths in the fighting, excluding casualties in the fighting between the Bosnian Serb army and the Bosnian Croat army.[168] According to a Bosnian Serb publication as disseminated by electronic mail in early 1997, the Bosnian Serb republic suffered 18,392 deaths in the military, and 36,543 wounded. This figure apparently does not include Serbs from outside Bosnia who died in the fighting in Bosnia.[169] On the basis of these data, not only the Kenney and Stockholm Peace Institute estimates, but the CIA estimate of casualties from the war, appear too low.

The issue of the number of rapes committed during the war was the focus of a furious controversy. It appears that information on rapes initially was being either concealed or held back by international agencies.[170] Then, in a rush to condemn Serb actions, unsubstantiated claims were made that 20,000 or more women had been the victims of rape by Serb forces in Bosnia.[171] The UN Commission of Experts was able to identify 1,600 actual cases of rape.[172] A study of rape victims in hospitals in Croatia, Serbia, and Bosnia carried out by experts attached to the UN Human Rights Commission produced evidence of approximately 12,000 cases of rape, the majority of which had been committed by Serbs.[173] The Commission experts estimated the number of rape cases on the basis of pregnant rape victims in hospitals. The figure was a conservative estimate, based only on data available at selected hospitals.

The very nature of the crime, and the circumstances under which it was committed, suggest that the precise number of rapes will never be known. The charge that rapes were committed by the Serbs in such a fashion as to constitute "genocidal rape" must be approached with caution.[174] A cautious approach should not, however, be allowed to obscure the fact that large numbers of Muslim women were incarcerated and repeatedly raped, and that incidents of rape of Serb and Croat women did not approach the scale of victimization of Muslims. The UN Human Rights Commission report of August 4, 1995, sums up the state of knowledge as follows:

> It is difficult to assess the actual numbers of individuals who suffered rape or sexual abuse; victims are often reluctant to report such experiences owing to

social stigma and fear of reprisals. Available information indicates that rape has been committed by all sides to the conflict. However, the largest number of reported victims have been Bosnian Muslims, and the largest number of perpetrators have been Bosnian Serbs. There are few reports of rape and sexual assault among members of the same ethnic group.[175]

After only a month of fighting the UN estimated some 520,000 persons—12 percent of the population—had been displaced.[176] The unclassified CIA memorandum of November 1995 estimated that 900,000 to 1.2 million refugees had fled Bosnia to other countries, and an additional 1.3 to 1.5 million individuals still inside the country had been displaced from their homes.[177] This amounted to more than half the total pre-war population of the country. Only a portion of this can be attributed directly to the fighting. Much of it was the result of fear, ethnic cleansing, or an effort to find security. Inhabitants of rural areas, for example, fled in large numbers to the cities, seeking safety. At the center of this web of motives was the policy of ethnic cleansing; that is, forcing an ethnic community to flee its traditional place of residence—most often by extensive violence or the threat thereof—for the purpose of creating an ethnically homogeneous population as a basis for claiming political control over the territory.

Ethnic Cleansing

There are no precise data on ethnic cleansing, but estimates of the total number of displaced persons range from one-third to two-thirds of the total population. The number of Muslims who were expelled from their homes in Serb-occupied areas of Bosnia is usually placed at between 700,000 and one million.[178] According to a study of the Bosnian Institute of Public Health, the number of displaced persons in the territory controlled by the Bosnian Federation on December 31, 1994, was 1.025 million out of a total population of 2.214 million—almost one out of every two persons living in federation territory.[179] Mustafa Imamović suggested that 60 percent of the population of Bosnia was displaced, and 1,245,000 were abroad at the end of the war. Halilović has reported that there was a massive movement of Serbs out of Muslim-held areas (notably Zenica) into Serb-held areas of Sarajevo, which was carried out with the cooperation of the Bosnian government.[180] A Serbian demographer, Srdjan Bogosavljević, estimated the total number displaced in Bosnia at over 1.4 million—roughly one-third of the total prewar population.[181] The number of Bosnian Muslims who fled Bosnia by the end of 1994 was estimated by Bogosavljević at around 720,000. He estimated the number of Serb refugees at about 460,000, and the number of Croats at about 150,000. In Bosnia as a whole, Bogosavljević estimated that by the end of 1994, taking into account both those who had left Bosnia and the refugees who had recently arrived (largely Serbs), the ethnic composition of Bosnia stood at roughly 40 percent Muslim, 34 percent Serb, and 26 percent Croat. (The OSCE estimated the population in 1996 at 48 percent Muslim ["Bosniac"], 39 percent Serb, and 12 percent Croat.)[182]

These data do not capture the great differences in the conditions under which displacement and ethnic cleansing took place. The Muslim population in Serb areas was not encouraged by its own leaders to leave. On the contrary, the claim of the Muslim-dominated government in Sarajevo to all of Bosnia was strengthened by the continued presence in Serb-held areas of Muslims (and others) who remained loyal to the idea of a unified Bosnia-Herzegovina. It is an understatement to say that these persons left under duress. By way of contrast, the Serb aim was to partition Bosnia and exchange populations. Consistent with this policy, the Bosnian Serb leadership pressed Serbs to leave areas under the control of the Bosnian government *en masse*. The Croat nationalists did likewise.

The distinctions among motivations for flight must also be considered in any discussion of ethnic cleansing in Bosnia. It is difficult to distinguish among refugees, displaced persons, and those who moved for other reasons. Muslims were subject to coercion, even terror, designed to force them out of Serb-held territory. It is important to distinguish this from the voluntary decisions of Serbs to flee Muslim- or Croat-held territories in anticipation—right or wrong—of such measures being applied against them, or in the belief that they could not live under ethnically alien rule. Yet, ethnic "self-cleansing" sometimes was a prudent step, as the excesses committed by the Croatians against the mostly elderly and defenseless Serbs who remained behind in Krajina in 1995 attest. The departure of the Sarajevo Serbs after Dayton and the exodus of Serbs from Krajina further illustrate the difficulty of distinguishing between coercion and voluntarism.

As far as the Croats are concerned, they appear to have left towns such as Vareš voluntarily, but in fear of retribution (in this case from the Muslims). Croat motives for leaving Sarajevo, or Zenica, or Tuzla were undoubtedly mixed, and not always the consequence of direct pressure by the Muslims. In Serb-controlled areas such as Posavina, the displacement of Croats can safely be attributed to coercive ethnic cleansing.[183] Sorting through all these factors, and separating those who were ethnically cleansed from those who left, or were displaced but not ethnically cleansed, could be a statistician's—not to mention a moral philosopher's—nightmare.

The cruelties that were committed in the course of Serb ethnic cleansing are significantly better documented than those committed against the Serbs or the Croats, and for this reason, comparisons of degree or of the nature of the atrocities committed must be made with care. Keeping this in mind, the fact remains that Serb ethnic cleansing was particularly devastating in its impact.[184] In the last analysis, given the number of Muslims expelled from Serb-controlled territory and the brutality that accompanied the expulsions, the sum total of atrocities committed by the Serbs was in a category by itself.

A massive campaign of ethnic cleansing was initiated by the Bosnian Serbs in April, May, and June 1992 in eastern Bosnia, parts of eastern Herzegovina, the Sava river valley, Bosanska Krajina, and the suburbs of Sarajevo. These operations were carried out by local militia and SDS activists following the occupation of predominantly Muslim cities by paramilitary forces. As we noted earlier, the paramilitary troops were aided by JNA units from Serbia. The Serb campaign of ethnic cleansing established a pattern that was to be followed on other occasions and by other groups throughout the war, but nowhere else on such a large scale. Muslim women and children were usually forced across the battle lines into Bosnian territory or transported out of Bosnia to the Sandžak, and even on occasion to Macedonia. Most women and children were spared incarceration and death, but were totally at the mercy of their tormentors. As we noted above, many women became the victims of rape. Refugees trying to escape the fighting ran the risk of being shelled. Men, women, and children fell victim to atrocities perpetrated by paramilitary groups and others. Men and boys were interned, and many were killed outright, either upon capture or during incarceration in the worst of the Serb detention camps. In a practice reminiscent of World War II, local political Muslim leaders, teachers, and professionals were selected out and executed by the Serbs.[185] We do not know how many of the Muslim intelligentsia were killed in Serb-occupied areas of Bosnia. Nor can we say for sure whether executions of local Muslim intelligentsia were widespread or concentrated in certain areas. When asked by the prosecutor at the Hague tribunal about the number of missing Muslim teachers, politicians, and professionals in the Prijedor region, Hanna Greve, a Norwegian judge who gathered evidence on events in the region for the Commission of Experts of the UN, replied that "most of those key people from other parties than the SDS—from other parties than the Serb parties and outside the Serb group—are dead."[186]

The first wave of ethnic cleansing climaxed in the Kozarac tragedy noted earlier in this chapter. Between May 24 and 26 several Muslim villages in the Prijedor region, including Kozarac, were surrounded and shelled, and a sizable number of their inhabitants massacred.[187] From the few reports available, it appears that the ethnic cleansing of Muslims in northern Herzegovina carried out by the Serbs was especially brutal. Ethnic cleansing continued in Serb-held areas for the next three years until only several thousand Muslims and Croats were left in all of the territory under Serb control.[188] Even these few were subjected to ethnic cleansing by Arkan's forces in Bosanska Krajina—the area of Banja Luka and Prijedor—at the end of the fighting.[189] The Serbs, furthermore, were guilty of the complete eradication of Muslim cultural monuments—mosques, libraries, and the like—in territory under their control. The apparent scorched-earth approach of the Serbs to Muslim cultural and religious structures suggests either a total lack of control by Serb leaders over extremists, or an obsession with removing all signs of Muslim presence.

Local Serbs were not, as a rule, eager to be part of ethnic cleansing. Various stratagems were used by the organizers of cleansing operations to involve the local population in the anti-Muslim campaigns, usually by playing on fears that the Muslims would initiate ethnic cleansing of the Serbs if the Serbs did not act first. Deliberate efforts were made to sow fear and distrust. Ejub Štitkovac, in his excellent account of the ethnic cleansing of the Muslims, recounts how the story of the murder of a farmer's wife by Muslims was spread far and wide in the area around Bihać in order to turn the Serb population against the Muslims. The stratagem worked even though the woman was probably the victim of Serb extremists.[190] The instigators of ethnic cleansing were usually—but by no means always—outsiders to the cities and towns about to be cleansed. These outsiders included paramilitary forces and irregulars, some of them "weekend warriors" from Serbia. The allocation of responsibility for these atrocities among local criminal elements, nationalist extremists, and paramilitary forces under external control is extremely difficult, and will have to await the more comprehensive gathering of evidence concerning the atrocities committed by the Serbs during the war.[191]

Once ethnic cleansing had occurred, it appears that local Serbs would usually close ranks against their former Muslim neighbors. The local Serb population was stiffened in its resolve by the influx of Serbs fleeing from adjacent Muslim-held areas, and by the fear of retribution, should the Muslims ever return. Ethnic cleansing thus achieved a two-fold objective: creating largely irreversible facts on the ground, and enlisting the local population in a cover-up of its operation and consequences. This of course was true for ethnic cleansing throughout Bosnia. The entire surviving population of an ethnically cleansed area was traumatized by its consequences, but not in a manner that made it possible for those cleansed to return to their homes.

The goal of Serb ethnic cleansing was to secure, by force, Serb claims to the territory occupied in the first months of the war. There is little doubt that Belgrade supported the campaign in its early stages. The paramilitary forces that sparked the terror along the Drina in April were armed and supplied by the Ministry of the Interior in the Belgrade. According to an investigation carried out by a *Guardian* journalist, the ethnic cleansing campaign was directed by "a small group of men from the State Security Department of the Serbian interior ministry, appointed by Milošević and totally loyal to him," and coordinated by a network of Serbian state security agents.[192] Milošević appeared blind to the risks he took by encouraging excesses against the Muslims, an action bound to enrage public opinion outside Serbia and at the same time undercut the effort to rehabilitate Serbia that he had begun in January and February 1992 (described in more detail in chapter 3). The negative reactions came quickly. Reports of ethnic cleansing and atrocities in Serb-controlled territory began appearing in the Western media in April. Milošević played a dangerous game of denial, informing Cyrus Vance as well as U.S. Ambassador Warren Zimmerman that there were no irregular forces in Bosnia at a time when Arkan was boasting on Belgrade television of his military prowess in liberating Bijeljina.[193] A few weeks later Milošević was forced to acknowledge indirectly the presence of the paramilitary groups in Bosnia. At a hastily called meeting with European ambassadors he announced that irregular armed forces were no longer permitted to enter Bosnia from Serbia.[194] Reports of atrocities nevertheless continued, setting the stage for the imposition of sanctions on Yugoslavia at the end of May 1992.

In July and August 1992, during the run-up to the International Conference on the Former Yugoslavia in London (reported in more detail in chapter 5), Western journalists revealed the existence of Serb-run detention camps for Muslims in which prisoners were held under abysmal conditions. Torture and execution of inmates was common in the worst of these camps. Nik Gowing suggests that the United States and the UN, among others, had knowledge of the existence of the camps as early as June, and that policymakers at higher levels engaged in heated internal debate about the information.[195] The Bosnian Serb leadership finally bowed to international pressure. They allowed the media limited access to the camps, and released a number of their inmates.[196] The result was more revelations of torture and ill-treatment of Muslims. These accounts were then incorporated into the reports of human rights organizations and findings of the Special Rapporteur of the UN Commission on Human Rights, Tadeusz Mazowiecki. The news of these camps could not have come at a worse time for Milošević, who was hoping to get the international community to ease sanctions against Serbia and facilitate an end to the fighting in Bosnia on Serbian terms. When ethnic cleansing continued into the fall, international outrage deepened. In the report of the Special Rapporteur issued in November 1992, Mazowiecki concluded that:

> The continuation of ethnic cleansing is a deliberate effort to create a *fait accompli* in flagrant disregard of international commitments entered into by those who carry out and benefit from ethnic cleansing. The continuation of this policy presumes the inability or unwillingness of the international community to enforce compliance with solemn agreements adopted under the auspices of the United Nations, and thus undermines the credibility and authority of international institutions. The international community cannot allow the London and Geneva agreements to continue to be systematically ignored and violated.[197]

Mazowiecki recommended a robust application of the London accords adopted in August 1992; including concentrating Serb heavy weapons under international supervision, disarming irregulars, and broadening the UN mandate in Bosnia. But, as we shall see in chapter 5, these steps were not taken.

Ethnic cleansing was not restricted to Serb-occupied territory. It took place in various forms throughout Bosnia after the outbreak of war. Serbs also were the targets or victims of ethnic cleansing. Serbs from villages in the vicinity of Odžak in the Posavina region were rounded up in spring 1992 by the local Croat authorities, detained, and ultimately transported to Croatia in the face of advancing Serb forces.[198] These actions were accompanied by armed confrontations between Serbs and Croats.[199] This was followed by a massive exodus of Serbs from the Posavina region, apparently organized by local Serb authorities after the war broke out in April.[200] There were reports of rapes of Muslims in the Posavina region by Croat irregulars.[201] In eastern Herzegovina, the combined Croat-Muslim offensive of May 1992 that followed the departure of the JNA was accompanied by the burning of Serb villages and the expulsion of their inhabitants.[202] A Yugoslav government account of atrocities committed against Serbs in Herzegovina claimed that 45,000 Serbs were forced out of the Neretva valley and the city of Mostar at the time of the Croat-Muslim attack.[203] Croat forces consisting of the Bosnian Croat army (HVO) and Croatian defense forces (HOS) expelled Serbs from their villages, forced Serbs to cross mined front lines, dragooned Serbs into work details, and sent them to the front to dig trenches.[204]

Croats also were victims of ethnic cleansing in the early stages of the war. In March 1992 the Serbs took control of the area around Bosanski

Brod. According to Croatian sources, local Serb paramilitary forces engaged in atrocities and ethnic cleansing against the Croats. Croats and Muslims both felt the brunt of Serb ethnic cleansing in Bosanska Krajina. The occupation of Posavina by the Serbs in late spring 1992 led to ethnic cleansing of the Croats and atrocities against Croat villagers.[205] Croats were the victims of massacres perpetrated by the Muslims in the Konjic area; notably in the village of Doljani, where forty-two Croat civilians were reported killed in April 1993.[206] Croats were forced to flee Travnik, Vareš, and other cities and towns in central Bosnia during the 1993 Croat-Muslim war.[207] In Vareš the Croat population was persuaded to flee by Croat extremists on the eve of the Muslim takeover of the town.

The dispatches of Western journalists early in the war tended to dismiss or minimize accounts of the ethnic cleansing of Serbs or the imprisonment and torture of Serbs in Sarajevo, although John Burns of the *New York Times* gave an accurate, if limited, description of the plight of the Serbs in Sarajevo in summer 1993.[208] The first authoritative account of the situation in Sarajevo, by Belgrade-based *Vreme* journalist Miloš Vasić, suggested that for the first year and a half—when, as noted earlier in this chapter, criminal gangs ruled Sarajevo—Serbs were at substantial risk.[209] Vasić's account is corroborated by the accounts of Serbs who were jailed, then exchanged for Muslims later in the war,[210] and further verified by revelations after the war of mass graves of Serbs killed by "Caco's" men.[211] General Jovan Divjak, the highest-ranking Serb in the Bosnian army, asserted that the total was no more than 500; the Bosnian Serbs put the number at 1,500.[212] The battle for Sarajevo in May 1992 noted earlier in this chapter resulted in the slaughter of Serb civilians who lived in the Pofalići neighborhood. Muslim accounts describe the fighting as an effort by the Serbs to split Sarajevo in two, and the victory of the Muslims as decisive for the defense of the city, as we noted earlier in this chapter. Halilović reports that the battle began when the Serbs, breaking a neighborhood cease-fire, attempted to take control of Pofalići. He reports that the Muslims suffered only one casualty in the fighting, which suggests that the Serbs offered little resistance.[213] Serb accounts, in contrast, describe a massacre in which Serb homes were burned, and Serbs were killed fleeing to higher ground.[214] We have already noted forced mobilization (by all sides) for dangerous work at the front. According to Serb witnesses in the Bosnian-held suburb of Hrasnica, this amounted to forced labor of virtually the entire Serb male working-age population.[215] Serbs caught trying to leave Sarajevo were punished with lengthy prison terms by the Bosnian authorities.[216]

The picture painted by Serbs who experienced persecution by the

Muslims in Sarajevo is—not surprisingly—grim and replete with accounts of torture, arbitrary arrests, and abuse. But Serbs also testify to the help they received from Muslim friends and neighbors. Gaining a balanced picture of the situation of the Sarajevo Serbs under Muslim control is therefore extremely difficult. Many Serbs who remained in the city, especially the cultural and political elite who supported the Bosnian cause, managed to escape persecution. Helsinki Watch reported in spring 1994 that there had been no widespread eviction of Serbs from their apartments.[217] The presence of Serbs in the charitable organizations active in Sarajevo suggested a degree of tolerance for the Serbs by the Muslim authorities that was absent in the treatment of non-Serbs in the Serb-held areas of Bosnia. The Helsinki Watch Report concluded:

> Non-Muslim civilians in government-controlled parts of Sarajevo are not generally persecuted by government forces. The most violent crimes against Serbs, Croats and other non-Muslims have been perpetrated by local gangs, some of which were disbanded in early 1993 and their members killed or imprisoned by the government, and some of which still continue to operate, albeit on a smaller and less savage scale.[218]

In Tuzla, often considered a model of Muslim-Serb ethnic cooperation within the Bosnian republic, a purge of Serbs from responsible positions took place after May 15, 1992, the day that a JNA convoy was attacked outside the city and its weapons seized by local forces. Regulations issued in Sarajevo called for the confiscation of apartments of persons not physically present in Tuzla. The decree was enforced against the Serbs following the events of May 15, and many Serbs in Tuzla found that they had become second-class citizens overnight.[219] The position of Serbs in Tuzla worsened in subsequent years as their number dropped and Muslim refugees from the countryside encouraged fundamentalist currents within the city. Serbs who fled the city paint an unhappy, even grim picture of Serbs losing their jobs and apartments, being forced to join the army, imprisoned, and persecuted. According to one Western media account in October 1994, however, the government "struggled hard to protect non-Muslims and persuade them to stay, even distributing arms to reassure Serbs in isolated villages."[220] Mazowiecki, in his sixth report of March 1994, noted that Serbs and Croats in Tuzla were not subjected to harassment at levels comparable to other groups in Bosnia.[221] An accurate picture of the Tuzla situation would have to take these quite different views into account, as well as the impact of the influx of Muslim refugees on attitudes toward the Serbs in the city.[222]

Local authorities in Bosnian Muslim-held areas in the vicinity of Sarajevo also engaged in ethnic cleansing of Serbs. A study of ethnic cleansing by *Médecins du Monde* included the account of a young Serb driven out of the town of Pazarić, near Sarajevo. He reports that the town was blocked off by Muslim forces, Serb homes were torched, and Serbs killed. Serbs from the area were placed in a makeshift camp, and tortured by Croat extremist paramilitary and Sandžak Muslims.[223] Tarčin, a predominantly Muslim town, was the point of contact between the Serb forces besieging Sarajevo and Muslim-held areas to the south. To avoid the potential problem of hostile Serbs in their rear, the local Muslim authorities in Tarčin arrested men of military age and placed them in a large, windowless grain silo. The arrests began in mid-May 1992 and were completed in June. Conditions were abominable. Prisoners might not see daylight for months at a time; some died of starvation. The silo structure held some 600 persons when full, according to Serbs incarcerated there. Conditions improved after the Red Cross visited the camp in November 1992, but more than 100 prisoners still remained in the camp after the Dayton agreement in 1995. Even then Bosnian government authorities were slow to release their captives. In the district of Konjic, southwest of Sarajevo, local Muslim officials carried out ethnic cleansing first of Serbs, then of Croats, who were far more numerous in the district.[224] According to Serbian sources, ethnic cleansing of the Serbs in the region began as early as April 1992.[225]

In the rural areas of eastern Bosnia no quarter was given by either side in savage fighting in which the Bosnian Muslims more than held their own during the first year of the war.[226] One incident, the ambush of Serb civilians fleeing Goražde in August 1992, came at a delicate moment in the efforts to implement the confidence-building measures agreed to at the London conference (detailed in chapter 5), and was widely reported in the Western press.[227] Serbian sources claim that in the period May–October 1992 Muslim forces destroyed all but one of thirty-three Serb villages in the vicinity of Goražde, as well as the Serb quarter of Goražde itself. Bratunac was the scene of Serb massacres of Muslims in spring 1992 and of Muslim atrocities against Serbs in winter 1992–93.[228]

The region around Srebrenica was also the scene of brutalities committed by both Serbs and Muslims. According to a Serbian source,[229] Serbs began to flee the Srebrenica area in spring 1992. Almost no Serbs, according to this account, were left in the area after May. The intensity of the conflict in eastern Bosnia is reflected in a proposal made in February 1993 by a delegation to Sarajevo from Srebrenica. They proposed that the Bosnian government arrest and execute a Serb from Sarajevo for every Muslim killed at Srebrenica.[230] As a result of the mutual savagery, eastern Bosnia was largely depopulated of both Muslims and Serbs, and its villages destroyed. The main perpetrator of massacres in Serb villages was Naser Orić, mentioned earlier.[231] In an interview with the *Washington Post,* Orić came across as ruthless, showing videotapes of the Serb villages he had sacked and burned. He fled Srebrenica (or was removed by the Bosnian government) shortly before the Serb attack in July 1995. The culmination of this barbarity was the massacre of unarmed Muslim men and boys seeking to escape Srebrenica in July 1995 by Serb forces under the command of General Mladić. We shall consider this event, the worst massacre of the war—and the worst that Europe had seen since World War II—in chapter 7.

Central Bosnia escaped communal violence and ethnic cleansing until 1993. Earlier in this chapter we described the Muslim-Croat war that started in central Bosnia in 1993. Here, we wish only to note that atrocities were carried out by both sides in what Western observers called a war of "village against village."[232] The Muslim offensives in the Lašva valley in spring 1993 were accompanied by ethnic cleansing.[233] The result was the flight of civilians, often in anticipation of a battle, and a reshuffling of the ethnic composition of the region. In March 1993 Muslim authorities in Konjic initiated a campaign to drive out the local Croats, many of whom were then detained in the Muslim detention camp at Celebići. Reports of conditions at Celebići, where Serbs and later Croats were interned in a former JNA oil storage depot, were strikingly similar to the accounts of Western journalists and others who visited camps in Serb-held territories, although it appears that the scale of the abuses was smaller.[234] The lawlessness of the Muslim officials in the Konjic district was reported in the Bosnian press, but Sarajevo was slow to act, finally removing a number of local leaders in the district in 1994.[235]

In Herzegovina, Croat authorities initiated state-sponsored ethnic cleansing of Muslims in conjunction with the attack on Mostar in May 1993. On June 14–15 there was a massive eviction of Muslims from the city west of the Neretva river (the Croat section), accompanied by the ethnic cleansing and internment of Muslims from the Neretva valley and Croatian-occupied areas of eastern Herzegovina. Muslim towns in Herzegovina—Stolac and Čapljina—were ethnically cleansed.[236] Detention camps were set up by the Croats to house Muslims, many of whom had at one time or another fought on the Croat side. When detainees were set free in August, they told stories of torture, abominable living conditions, and humiliation at the hands of the Croat prison authorities.[237] A Serb source alleges that in August 1992 Muslims massacred Serbs from five villages in northern Herzegovina east of Kalinovik.[238]

To attribute such acts to all sides has been criticized as "moral equivalence," or as an effort to minimize the differences among the combatants as a means of ignoring the special responsibility of the Serbs for the destructiveness and brutality of the war.[239] Our account makes clear that one side—the Muslims—was the aggrieved party; fighting for its survival as a political community, if not for its very existence. But, at the same time, the evidence we present here makes it clear that all three parties—including the Muslims—were behaving in ways that undermined any claim to moral superiority. Each side had a view of the war that was peculiarly its own, a factor that we shall explore in more detail in chapter 5 when we deal with the political context of the war. We cannot say whether these behaviors derived from ethnic, national, or Balkan culture; or from the exigencies of waging war; or, as is most likely, from the interaction between them. But it is clear that the perspectives of Muslim, Serb, and Croat leaders accommodated policies, behaviors, and tactics that clashed with the principles guiding Western policymakers and mediators as they engaged in efforts to negotiate an end to the war. The result was a "reality gap" between conditions on the ground and the formulas proposed by the West for ending the war. Nowhere was this gap more evident than in the contrast between the persistence of ethnic cleansing on the ground, and the adherence to the multi-cultural ideal in the proposed solutions to the conflict. This is a problem to which we return in the conclusion to this study.

Genocide

Serb actions early in the war—including ethnic cleansing, the executions of leading Muslims in the Prijedor region, mass rape, and other atrocities—gave rise to the charge that the Serbs had committed genocide against the Muslims of Bosnia. This charge was sustained by actions committed right up to the closing weeks of the fighting, above all by the killings at Srebrenica in July 1995. The charge is one of the most sensitive and important aspects of the conflict. We do not propose to resolve this controversy here. To do so would require a separate and more detailed study; focused not only on ascertaining exactly *what* happened, but as we shall see from the discussion below, also on determining *why* it happened. Instead, we hope to demonstrate here the enormous complexity of the issue that confronted Western policymakers, and thereby give the reader some insight into the difficulty policymakers faced in formulating policy responses to it.

The determination of genocide depends on one's definition of the phenomenon. Totten and Parsons's discussion[240] suggests that the term can be applied to a very broad range of acts. But it seems clear that intention to exterminate the target people, *as such,* is central to the definition, although Helen Fein has argued for a sociological definition of intent as the performance of deliberate acts with foreseeable consequences.[241] The scope or magnitude required for such acts to be considered genocide is, however, undefined. The UN Convention on Genocide applies to destruction of peoples "in whole or in part" and thus leaves open the question of threshold, suggesting that small-scale acts of the type specified therein—that is, destruction of "part" of a people—might qualify. The questions of intent and threshold are therefore central to the determination of whether genocide has taken place in Bosnia-Herzegovina.

Helen Fein has identified five conditions that distinguish genocide from other forms of warfare:[242] (1) "A sustained attack, or continuity of attacks, . . . to physically destroy group members"; (2) "The perpetrator is a collective or organized actor or a commander of organized actors"; (3) "The victims are selected because they are members of a group"; (4) "The victims are defenseless. . ."; (5) "The destruction of group members is undertaken with intent to kill and the murder is sanctioned by the perpetrators." With respect to events in Bosnia-Herzegovina, it is important to note that Fein argues the existence of a legitimating ideology by itself does not constitute evidence of genocide. It is the specific pattern of behaviors that constitute such evidence. Reference to a legitimating ideology is, rather, a means by which to *account for* genocide. This makes the stipulation of intent much more difficult—and still more central to determining whether genocide has taken place.

Third parties (non-governmental organizations, interested governments, and multinational organizations) have accumulated enormous amounts of forensic evidence and eyewitness testimonies, many of which we have cited above. These testimonies chronicle events from the beginning of the war in 1992 right up to the last stages of the fighting before the cease-fire in 1995. Journalists and independent organizations have provided additional details of events. On the basis of this evidence, it is clear—as we tried to demonstrate above—that the early months of the war witnessed atrocities, ethnic cleansing, and population displacements on a massive scale. They occurred everywhere in Bosnia, but their impact was felt above all by the Muslim population in Serb-occupied areas. On the other hand, many Muslims incarcerated in Serb detention camps in the early days of the war were released, as the data cited by Michele Mercier in her work on the International Committee of the Red Cross (ICRC) in Bosnia make clear.[243] Entire units in the Bosnian army were made up of ethnically cleansed and formerly incarcerated young men from the regions under Serb control. The release of prisoners rather than their execution may constitute critically important evidence of the absence of an intent to exterminate the Muslim people, *as such*—although it does not, to be sure, mitigate the horrors of what went on in these camps or free their perpetrators from charges of crimes against humanity.

The case for genocide rests on the fact that the killings, rapes, and other abuses against the Muslim civilian population correspond to activities described in the UN Genocide Convention, and on the argument that they were committed in a manner that fulfills *all* the conditions identified by Fein as distinguishing genocide from war crimes. Available evidence makes it clear that Serb forces carried out sustained or continuous attacks against the Muslim civilian population from the beginning of the war in 1992 right through the takeover of the Srebrenica enclave in July 1995. It appears unquestionably to be the case that the victims of killings were selected because they were Muslims even though, as we have noted, violence was applied even to ethnic Serbs who refused to submit; that in the overwhelming proportion of cases the victims were defenseless; and that the killing was intentional. It is clear that Serb paramilitary units constituted "a collective or organized actor" and played a major role in the killing. There is also increasing evidence that high-level Bosnian Serb and Serbian military commanders and political leaders authorized such activities. Stronger evidence of the direct authorization of such acts by Bosnian Serb and Serbian police, military, and political leaders—if such authorization were couched in terms of the destruction of the Muslim people, *as such*—would strengthen the case for genocide.

Such evidence of intent appears crucial to making the case for genocide. But, even in the absence of such evidence of intent, it is clear that once widespread media coverage of this issue began in summer 1992 it was impossible for Bosnian Serb and Serbian leaders not to have been aware of the violations that were occurring in the field. Their failure to stop them constitutes a basis on which to argue at the very least for their culpability in crimes against humanity.

The case against the charge of genocide rests on the fact that, in the absence of clear evidence of intent to destroy the target group *as such,* the ethnic cleansing carried out by the Serb side clearly constitutes a crime against humanity, but may not constitute genocide. The intent of the Bosnian Serb and Serbian leaderships to cleanse non-Serbs from the territories to which they laid claim is painfully clear. But the practice of expelling Muslims from Serb-controlled territories and the tendency to single out men and boys for execution—while in themselves despicable—seem contrary to an intent to destroy the Muslim people *as such*. The close correspondence between actions carried out in an effort to establish control by force, create a homogeneous population, and impose a nationalist regime—ethnic cleansing—and actions that might be motivated by an intent to exterminate the target people as such—genocide—underscores the difficulties raised by the requirement of intent, and the stipulation in the Genocide Convention that genocide may be directed against "part" of a people. When might ethnic cleansing be considered to have passed the threshold of genocide; and how, in light of the "in whole or in part" clause, might that threshold be defined? Is it simply numerical? Or are certain categories of action to be considered genocidal regardless of the number of victims involved? And, if so, should not the charge of genocide also be directed against other participants in the conflict? These are difficult, but centrally important questions.

The issue of whether one side or another committed genocide must also be seen against the background of the debasement of the concept and, therefore, significance of genocide, not only by the participants in the conflict, but by outside observers as well. The accusation of genocide, unlike the charge of war crimes, fixes guilt on one party, and by implication, absolves the other (the victim). The charge of genocide is almost always accompanied by demands that the alleged perpetrator(s) be punished—not only for the alleged act(s) of genocide, but for all actions surrounding the genocide. The charge of genocide thus becomes a vehicle for negating and denying all other issues surrounding the conflict.

Jean Manas has argued:

> Opposition to the means should be decoupled from opposition to the goal. Mass killings and forced expulsions would be objectionable even if the goal they were intended to serve was noble. Alternatively, a goal might be noble (or at least acceptable) even if the means utilized to effectuate it was illegitimate. Thus, a right to statehood cannot be extinguished (assuming it is applicable) simply because some of its advocates and beneficiaries have committed wrongs in an effort to vindicate that right.[244]

In Bosnia, focusing international debate on the means through charges of genocide became a vehicle for delegitimating discussion of the ends. Yet, it was the mutually exclusive ends pursued by each party in Bosnia, and the conflicting international principles to which each side appealed, that had to be addressed if the conflict was to be resolved.

Whichever argument one wishes to make, the gravity of the accusation of genocide demands precise charges and precise evidence. Up to now, although the International Criminal Tribunal for Yugoslavia at the Hague has indicted Serb leaders for genocide, it has not identified the difference between acts of genocide and crimes against humanity in its indictments. Nor has it grappled with the problems of threshold and intent. It is precisely in this regard that the Hague Tribunal can make an important contribution to understanding. By compelling prosecutors and their expert witnesses to define thresholds and present evidence of intent—and providing judgments as to their validity—the Tribunal can build a basis for deciding why certain crimes must be considered genocide, while others should not. By doing so, the judges of the Tribunal will move the process of determining whether genocide has taken place in Bosnia-Herzegovina onto firmer ground.

Conclusion

By the end of 1994, almost three years of war had produced only a stand-off. The Bosnian Serbs were much more vulnerable than it appeared at the time. The Bosnian Serb republic was depopulated and the leadership at odds with Serbia over the contact group plan proposed by the great powers under U.S. leadership (treated in detail in chapter 6). Bosnian Serb military forces were stretched thin. In June General Mladić and the Bosnian Serb military argued to no avail that the Bosnian Serb republic would have to prepare for a long and difficult struggle in which the military would be compelled to take power over from the civilian government.[245] In August 1994 a revealing interview appeared in the Belgrade weekly *NIN* with a Serb commander on Mt. Ozren,[246] an area that was to be turned over to the Bosnian government in the event of a peace accord despite the fact that it was inhabited by Serbs. The Serb officer, Milovan Stanković, noted the catastrophic loss of population in the region—from some 90,000–120,000 before the war, to only 30,000–40,000 (not counting military formations). He blamed this on the Bosnian Serb politicians. His view of Serb war aims was biting:

> Our policy has never defined the basic aims of the struggle—political, national, economic, military or regional aims. It has never been clearly said what state it is, of what size, and what cities are to be taken. The policy that says that the border is as far as the army boot can reach is, to say the least, frivolous. A boot can easily slip. When we took Doboj during the first days of the war, we formed an operational group on Ozren with the aim of guarding the corridor and the Doboj–Zvornik railway line. I could not understand that we could give up that route.

When asked if there was dissatisfaction among the soldiers, the officer replied:

> Today there are three categories of Serbs: those not at war, those at war but not fighting it, and those who are fighting it. Those who are fighting it are the abject poor. They are dissatisfied for many reasons. There are many problems of morale, problems in the organizations and in the front lines. There are no mummy's and daddy's boys among them. They are either drivers in the rear lines, or somewhere in the artillery. These people see injustices everywhere they look. Look at Doboj, look at who holds all the businesses, look at who has usurped power. The bars are full, the shops are full, everyone is relaxed

and having a good time. If a soldier is to be satisfied, then he must be motivated, he must have clothes, shoes, a good salary, and he must know that he is fighting for a country in which there will be room for him.

In response to the question of why he was embittered, the officer answered:

> I am not embittered, I am disappointed. My efforts have lost their meaning. A man who is fighting has to know where he is going and what his aim is. . . . I know I am a thorn in the side of some in the state-political leadership. . . . I am afraid that—at a given moment—they will sacrifice the Serb republic, the corridor, and all the rest for the sake of Žuč hill [in Sarajevo], or Foča, or Herzegovina. . . .
>
> Military defeat is a cover-up for policy. I will give you one example that staggered me: I said that, out of common interests, we should hand over some territories to the enemy, but let it be after the war, and only under the condition that our people are compensated. One people's deputy, I will not name him, says to me: "Do you think it is in the interests of the state for a man to wait until the end of the war, and then you have to go to him with a committee and say that his house is worth 150,000 German marks? It works out much better if he moves out with only his shirt on his back, then he will be happy with whatever he gets in the end." I cannot reconcile myself to such games.

This officer's lament captured the weaknesses of the Bosnian Serb position: the lack of political leadership, absence of clearly defined goals, demoralization of the troops, corruption on the civilian front, and the realization that territorial concessions were inevitable and would entail great political costs.

The Bosnian government, on the other hand, was in a stronger position by the end of 1994 than a year earlier. The cease-fire with the Croats, the demonstrated ability of the Bosnian army to take the offensive, and the continued sympathy and support of the international community all strengthened the government. As we shall see in chapters 6 and 7, the Muslims also were circumventing the embargo and receiving arms and financial support with the tacit blessing and, according to some sources, participation of the United States.

But in some respects the position of the Muslim-led government had worsened. None of the offensives staged by the Bosnian army had succeeded; the Muslims did not seem capable of winning back on their own the territory they had lost to the Serbs. U.S. involvement had not led to militarily significant air strikes against the Serbs. The most immediate consequence of U.S. involvement was the coordination of efforts to end the war by the Western powers and Russia through the Contact Group. Its proposals were not well received in Sarajevo, as we shall see in chapter 6. By the end of 1994 relations with the United Nations mission in Bosnia had deteriorated to the point that it appeared the UN might withdraw. For this the Serbs were primarily to blame. But the Bosnian government, which repeatedly accused the UN of failing to come to the aid of the beleaguered Bosnian state, had ignored cease-fires negotiated by UNPROFOR commanders, and had fired on its own civilians, was also responsible.

Would Western military support for the Bosnians have shortened the war, or merely intensified it? The more pessimistic view was, as we shall see in the chapters to follow, that arming the Muslims would have increased the slaughter in eastern Bosnia without changing the fundamental relationship of forces there. The more optimistic view was that the addition of U.S. air power would at least have allowed the Muslims to occupy the strategic northern corridor (which, on occasion they did) and hold it (which they could not). But even those who advocated the use of U.S. air power feared that fighting would intensify as a result, a development that would almost certainly have led to the breakdown of the humanitarian effort, and raised the prospect of a UN withdrawal from Bosnia well before 1995—that is, well before the United States was prepared to act to prevent it.

Whether one was a pessimist or an optimist, Western military intervention would have required the United States and its European allies to heal the political rift that had opened between them in the course of 1993 and 1994. And, it would have required Western policymakers to solve the daunting challenges of military involvement raised by their military professionals. If Bosnia was to be saved, it would have to be saved by a combination of political and military means, not by arms alone.

The political differences between the United States and its allies and the effort to overcome them are a central theme of the chapters that follow, as are the debates surrounding the question of Western military intervention. We examine these issues in the context of the larger search for a political solution to the conflict. These efforts required Western policymakers and international mediators assigned the task of negotiating a settlement to overcome the reality gap between the West and the warring parties evident in the discussions earlier in this chapter. Intervention in the absence of a political formula for settling the conflict that recognized and managed the new realities created by the war, as we shall argue in the chapters to follow, could result only in a prolongation of the fighting, or a hasty and ill-conceived partition.

The complexity of the crisis for Western policymakers lay in the fact that those who argued for intervention did so on behalf of the idealized, multi-ethnic Bosnia described in chapter 2. They were, for the most part, unwilling to give in to the tragic new realities created by the war. Yet, given the realities of the war on the ground described in this chapter, military intervention on this basis would have required the West to end the humanitarian effort and acquiesce (if not participate) in a much more intense conflict, aimed at the military defeat of the Serbs and—at least until March 1994— the Croats. Even then it was not self-evident that the idealized Bosnia could be preserved. The analyses of international involvement in the war presented in the next two chapters demonstrate clearly that no Western government would undertake the risks of such action in the absence of a political formula for ending the conflict in Bosnia and a compelling national interest in imposing it.

CHAPTER 5

The International Community and the War

The Vance-Owen Plan

The outbreak of the war in Bosnia-Herzegovina in March 1992 came at a moment when the cease-fire in Croatia was barely two months old and UNPROFOR troops were just starting to deploy to the four United Nations Protected Areas (UNPAs) in Croatia. Over the course of the next two and three-quarter years, from March 1992 to the end of 1994, the international community was to meet setback after setback in Bosnia while desperately searching for a political solution to the crisis. This was a period when, as we have seen in chapter 4, a series of crises kept the Bosnian conflict in the public eye, and imposed a sense of urgency on the efforts of the international mediators to find a political solution.

International responses to the war in Bosnia-Herzegovina were dominated by the great powers. Britain, France, and Germany, as well as the United States and Russia, played critical roles in shaping collective responses to the crisis. Throughout, each of these actors pursued their own, often conflicting, national interests. But, they also acted in concert. They dominated the activities of the multilateral organizations and institutions most directly involved in the conflict. Through these organizations, they attempted to define the political framework within which the war in Bosnia-Herzegovina had to be fought, and within which its solution had to be found. They imposed limits on the actions of the warring parties, on each other, and on other interested parties. But even within these limits they faced resistance and even opposition; from within the UN, from other states that viewed the war quite differently, and especially from the warring parties themselves, who sought at every turn to manipulate outside intervention to suit their own goals. Differences among the great powers themselves, and especially the differences between the United States and its European allies, created another obstacle to ending the war through international action.

The difficulties of finding a solution to the war in Bosnia-Herzegovina were further compounded by the conceptual turmoil of the post–Cold War international system. Key principles of international order in the Cold War era were proving inadequate or even mutually contradictory in the effort to resolve conflicts arising out of competing nationalisms. There were as yet no guidelines for dealing with the complexities surrounding the collapse of a state. Nor was there any consensus among the great powers or in the United Nations about how to resolve the apparent contradictions between the traditional rights of states to protect their territorial integrity and those of peoples or nations to self-determination, or between state sovereignty and the right of multilateral actors to inquire into, if not intervene in, the domestic affairs of states.[1] This lack of consensus around crucial principles complicated the task of negotiating a political settlement to the conflict in Bosnia, as each of the warring parties and its supporters viewed the conflict differently, and turned to different principles to justify their positions. These difficulties were compounded by growing differences among the perceived national interests of the major powers—differences that became especially acute in the course of negotiations to end the fighting in 1993.

The Political Context

From the outset, the nature of the war in Bosnia-Herzegovina was subject to conflicting interpretations. These were rooted not only in objective facts on the ground, but in the political interests of those articulating them. For external actors, to accept any one interpretation as definitive was to constrain one's policy choices, or even to mandate certain policies and actions on moral or political grounds. Hence, Western policymakers rapidly found themselves as deeply embroiled in the dispute over defining the war as the warring parties themselves. Unlike the Bosnians, however, Western actors could—and did—change their view of the war in order to suit the policies they chose to adopt. Thus, ultimately, it was interest—and the policies that flowed from interest—that defined the war in Bosnia for Western policymakers.

From one perspective, the war in Bosnia-Herzegovina could be viewed as a clear-cut case of civil war—that is, of internal war among groups unable to agree on arrangements for sharing power. Some of the parties in this civil war, like those in many other such wars, enjoyed substantial political and military backing from neighboring states. From the perspective of international diplomacy and law, in contrast, the international decision to recognize the independence of Bosnia-Herzegovina and to grant it membership in the United Nations provided a basis for defining the war as a case of external aggression by both Serbia and Croatia. With respect to Serbia, the further case could be made that the Bosnian Serb army was under the *de facto* command of the Yugoslav army and was therefore an instrument of external aggression. With respect to Croatia, regular Croatian army forces violated the territorial integrity of Bosnia-Herzegovina, lending further evidence in support of the view that this was a case of aggression.

To interpret the war as a case of external aggression simplified the choices facing Western policymakers, although it did not make them any easier. If the conflict were viewed as a civil war, the factors that would have to be taken into account by outside actors intent on bringing peace to the region became far more complex. The question of intervention immediately became linked to the necessity of finding a solution to the underlying political conflict among the warring groups, rather than the more simple—but not easy—act of opposing aggression. If the war was not only a civil war but ethnic in character, then the putative right to self-determination of ethnic minorities in a newly established state could not be overlooked. The claims of the central Bosnian government then had to be weighed against the competing claims to statehood of the Bosnian Serbs and Bosnian Croats as constitutive national groups in the old order. Finally, any effort to end the war was complicated by a still deeper problem: The war in Bosnia was being waged by actors who for the most part had neither the inclination nor the experience to make concessions for the sake of peace.

The Bosnian Serbs

As we have shown in chapters 3 and 4, the Bosnian Serbs were from the outset opposed to Bosnian independence, preferring instead that the republic remain part of Yugoslavia. Failing in this, the Bosnian Serbs pursued a three-way partition of Bosnia-Herzegovina. As the war unfolded, they sought to ensure ethnic domination of the territory under their control through a brutal campaign of ethnic cleansing against the Muslims, seen by some Western analysts as genocide (discussed in more detail in chapter 4). Thus, the ideology and behavior of the Bosnian Serbs was anathema to the liberal democratic West.

Map 5.1 **The Graz Map, May 1992**

Adapted from a map supplied by "interior ministry of the Serbian Republic of Bosnia-Herzegovina" (May 1994). This source showed shaded areas without precise boundaries.

Despite their insistence on partition, however, the Bosnian Serbs were wary about producing maps of precisely where and how partition should be achieved. The Bosnian Serb map that emerged around the time of the Villa Konak meeting of March 1992 (Map 3.5 in chapter 3, page 115) was crudely drawn and insensitive to Muslim claims for a viable state. More can be learned concerning Serb claims at the start of the war by examining another map that appeared following talks in the first week of May 1992 in Graz, Austria, between Radovan Karadžić and the Bosnian Croat leader, Mate Boban (Map 5.1). We present it here only as evidence of the Bosnian Serb perspective, not as definitive evidence of what was agreed between the Serbs and the Croats.

The Graz map indicated that the Serbs expected to bring 70 percent of Bosnia under their control, of which perhaps 10 percent constituted areas under dispute with the Croats. Another 20–30 percent was contested with the Bosnian Muslims. The Serbs and Croats disagreed over control of Mostar.[2] The Serbs defined the Neretva river as the border between their respective holdings—splitting the city in two along its north–south axis and dividing the largely Croat western sector from the largely Muslim old city and its Serb hinterlands to the east. The Croats maintained that all of Mostar fell under Croat control. According to a Croatian radio report, the Croats defined their claim south of Mostar explicitly in terms of the border established by the 1939 *Sporazum,* cited in chapter 2 (Map 2.1, page 22). Elsewhere, Jajce, Doboj, and possibly Trnovo, were allocated to Muslim control on the Graz map. (All of these towns were in Serb hands by the end of 1992.) The key areas of conflict between the Serb claims and the claims of the Muslims were eastern Bosnia, the Sanski Most and Prijedor areas in the west, and the city of Sarajevo. Sarajevo, like Mostar, was shown on the map as a border town, partitioned between the Serbs and the Muslims. According to the Croatian report, Kupres was allocated to the Croats "for strategic reasons." In exchange, Posavina was assigned to the Serbs. This suggests a deal between the Serbs and the Croats, and may explain the ease with which the Serbs were able to regain the territory won by the Muslims and Croats in the early weeks of the war (as reported in chapter 4).

The Graz map also suggests that a settlement satisfactory to the Serbs in the early stages of the war would have reduced the area held by the Bosnian Muslims to an enclave in central Bosnia. During later negotiations, the Serbs would demand even more territory, notably an outlet to the Adriatic sea. As we shall report below and in chapter 6, the Bosnian Serbs would agree to some territorial concessions under pressure from international mediators and from Belgrade. But on certain issues, the Bosnian Serbs would not budge. These included their claims to eastern Bosnia and the predominantly Muslim towns along the Drina, the districts of Prijedor and Sanski Most, and those parts of Sarajevo which they envisaged as the capital of the new Serb state.

The danger of reducing the Muslims to a rump state populated by angry refugees expelled from Serb-held territory seemed to be of no import to Bosnian Serb leaders. They professed not to be concerned whether this enclave formed a federation with the Croat part of Bosnia, and did not oppose this move when it took place under U.S. urging in March 1994. The Bosnian Serbs focused instead on gaining international recognition for their own state (the Bosnian Serb republic, or *Republika Srpska),* and its eventual union with Serbia. As we shall see below, when this prospect materialized in fall 1993, the Serbs seemed ready to make limited territorial concessions in return for independence. But when the international community refused to consider independence for the Bosnian Serb republic, the Serb leadership reverted to its earlier demands. The Bosnian Serb political leadership remained surprisingly united in pressing their claims, even as the war dragged on and it became clear that the Serbs would have to settle for far less than the 70 percent they had initially controlled or seized by force.

The Muslims

The Bosnian government and the ruling SDA were internally divided between those who wished to put their trust in the West (and to turn the other cheek to Croatia), and hardliners concentrated in the military and the "Sandžak faction"—persons from the Sandžak region of Serbia and Montenegro who had settled in Sarajevo—who wished to take on all comers. It was the former who eventually prevailed. Bosnian chief of staff Gen. Šefer Halilović, who belonged to the Sandžak faction, claimed after the war that he was dismissed in June 1993 because he proposed that the Muslims should be prepared to fight the Serbs and the Croats at the same time. Equally important for explaining his dismissal is the fact that Halilović sought to subordinate the SDA to a military-dominated popular front for the defense of Bosnia.[3] Of course, leaders of the Sandžak faction did not differ from their more moderate colleagues in one key respect: They attempted by all means at their disposal to involve the West in the war on the Bosnian government's side.

There was a second, more profound division within the Bosnian leadership, between the secularists and the more conservative Muslims in the SDA. We have already described the basis of this division in chapter 2. The consequences of these divisions for the political strategy of the Muslims with respect to the war were muted. For example, Ejup Ganić, who figured prominently in both the Sandžak faction and the conservative Muslim faction, and Haris Silajdžić, the personification of the "secularist" position, both demanded preservation of the existing Bosnian borders. But the former was identified with the effort to establish a Muslim-dominated state, while the latter hoped to preserve a multicultural state. Izetbegović, in contrast, while sympathetic to the conservatives and committed to protecting the Muslim nation in Bosnia, was willing to accept some form of partition of Bosnia as a means of achieving this goal.

The Muslim-dominated Bosnian government argued that the war was a case of aggression against an internationally recognized state by Serb nationalist militias from Serbia and elements of the Yugoslav Army, working in alliance with local Bosnian Serbs. The Bosnian Muslim claim to statehood and legitimate government control rested on formal diplomatic and legal foundations. As we suggested in chapter 3, the international community extended legal and diplomatic recognition to Bosnia in an attempt to avert conflict. The Bosnian claims were not subjected to critical analysis on their own merits. The tenuous state of the government's control over its own territory; the competing claims of the Bosnian Serbs and Croats to statehood; the reluctance of the Muslims to share power after the 1990 elections; and the tactics leading to the declaration of Bosnian sovereignty were not considered by the international community to have undermined the Muslim claim. Given international recognition of the Bosnian state, the Muslim-led government of Bosnia-Herzegovina argued that individual states acting alone, or the international community acting in concert, had the right—and even a moral obligation—to come to its assistance. At the very least, the international community could not obstruct the exercise of Bosnia-Herzegovina's most fundamental right as a sovereign state: the right to self-defense. The Bosnian government therefore appealed to the West to make a choice: either to take action to oppose aggression and reverse ethnic cleansing, or to lift the arms embargo. In Izetbegović's words, on the occasion of his address to the United Nations Security Council in September 1993: "Defend us or let us defend ourselves. You have no right to deprive us of both."[4]

The contrast between the Serb and Croat positions on the one hand, and the Bosnian government's position on the other, assured the Muslims that their cause would receive widespread sympathy in the West. But two factors worked against the Muslims in this regard. First, they proved unable to formulate a political ideology outside of the Muslim national idea. The options before the SDA were familiar ones, drawn from the competing currents in Bosnian political history outlined in chapter 2. The SDA could have chosen simply to identify Muslim culture and Muslim history with the state of Bosnia, in which case the Muslims would take on the status of the titular nationality, with all that implied. They might have chosen instead to adhere to the notion of Bosnians as "Bošnjaks" (Bosniacs) regardless of nationality. Alternatively, they might have embraced the doctrine of a genuinely secular civic culture. Although a congress of the SDA held in December 1992 supported the notion of a civic culture for Bosnia, in practice the SDA leadership seemed to waver between the first two options—with the assertion of Bošnjak identity gaining prominence only in the American-drafted documents of the Bosnian (Muslim-Croat) Federation (discussed in chapter 6) and the Dayton accord (discussed in chapter 7).

The notion of "Bošnjaks" was, in fact, introduced into common usage during the war, but failed to take hold as a term designating all nationalities in Bosnia. It became identified instead with the Muslims. The SDA leadership did not define Bosnia explicitly as a state of the Muslims in political discourse with the West. But this view did emerge in views expressed in the Islamic world. Izetbegović, for example, presented himself to the Arab world as a Muslim nationalist for whom the state and the Bosnian, Muslim nation were one. In an address to "Bosnian fighters–Pilgrims at Mecca," this feeling came through in a heartfelt, unambiguous fashion:

> We, if God allows, will continue our battle for Bosnia, for our people. We want to have our own state. . . . God forbid that we should be a stateless people! We are determined, if God allows, to create our own state, to have a home of our own to protect us. . . . In our own state we will live as we see fit. No one will give us instructions how to organize our lives, as was the case before. One thing is for sure: in that state Islam will be respected.[5]

As the war impelled the Bosnians toward deeper ties with the East, the tendency for them to present themselves—as Izetbegović did in Mecca—as the titular nationality of a state committed to respecting Islam raised immense problems for relations with the Bosnian Croats and Croatia. And it surely hardened the Bosnian Serb leadership against any effort to reconstruct a common state.

The third option—that of a civic culture—found support primarily among the intellectuals of Sarajevo such as Zdravko Grebo, perhaps the most respected member of the non-SDA Muslim democratic intelligentsia in Sarajevo during the war.[6] It was absent among the SDA leadership, with the notable exception of Haris Silajdžić. Popular support for a civic culture proved relatively weak against the appeal of Muslim nationalism, especially as the population transfers wrought by war and ethnic cleansing eroded the prospect of preserving a multicultural population anywhere outside of Sarajevo. Thus, the Bosnian Muslim leadership could not develop a liberal democratic program with popular appeal.

The second obstacle to unrestrained Western support for the Bosnian government was the growing influence of Islam on Bosnian society and the close connection between the SDA and the Muslim clergy. These had been features of the Bosnian regime from its inception. But they became more evident as the war dragged on and the government was compelled to deepen its relations with Islamic states in an effort to garner political and military support. The latent authoritarian tendencies within the SDA, inherited from the communist period, began to reappear in those areas under the control of the Bosnian government, but in a new Islamicized form.[7] The Muslim clergy grew more assertive. Its more conservative spokesmen came out publicly against mixed marriages. The Bosnian government introduced religious teaching in the schools. Izetbegović is reported to have spoken out in

December 1993 in a speech in Zenica—an Islamic stronghold—against the possibility of a "common life" in Bosnia, and to have backed away from this view only under pressure from the United States.[8] The conservative Islamic character of the emerging regime was underscored for the West by the close connections it forged with Iran, which (as we shall see in chapter 7) became a major supplier of arms and volunteers for the Bosnian Muslim cause.

The Muslim hope that the West would participate wholeheartedly in the defense of Bosnia against Serb aggression was never to be realized. As we shall note below and in the chapters to follow, many in the West interpreted this as a failure of will, even a case of appeasement by Western governments. Yet the Muslim leadership could not offer any formula for ending the war short of the capitulation of the Serbs, a goal to which the West would not commit itself. The chief diplomatic triumph of the Muslim leadership was to regain Sarajevo at Dayton. But this was due primarily to unexpected support from Milošević, rather than Western insistence that the city had to be turned over in its entirety to the Muslims.

The Bosnian Croats

The divisions within the HDZ in Bosnia have been recounted in chapter 3. With the onset of fighting in spring 1992, relations between the Muslims and the Croats, both within Bosnia-Herzegovina and between Bosnia-Herzegovina and Croatia, were for the most part overshadowed by the conflict between the Serbs and the Muslims. Yet Muslim-Croat relations played a critical role in shaping the crisis in Bosnia. The drive among Herzegovinian Croats for autonomy and union with Croatia, noted in chapter 3, led their representatives in international negotiations to oppose Bosnian government efforts to preserve a unitary state, and to align themselves with Bosnian Serb efforts to impose a highly decentralized formula—or even partition—on Bosnia. The Croats of central Bosnia and Sarajevo, where the moderate Franciscan tradition was strongest, took precisely the opposite view. They supported the Bosnian state and made every effort to nurture a close relationship between Croats and Muslims.

The democratic opposition in Croatia proper also favored preservation of the Bosnian state. In part, this reflected their support for the right of all the post-Yugoslav republics to territorial integrity—a right that was essential to Croatian efforts to win back control of the Krajina from the Serbs. But it also reflected their principled commitment to the creation of a civil society in Bosnia based upon tolerance among all three national communities. The far right in Croatia, represented by Paraga's Party of Rights and its paramilitary formation, the HOS, also opposed the partitioning of Bosnia, but for quite different reasons: They favored an alliance of Croats and Muslims against the Serbs, and the creation of a republic made up of Croats and Muslims that would eventually be absorbed into a greater Croatia.

Serbs, Croats, and Muslims: The Triangular Relationship

It was against this backdrop that the politics of the triangular relationship among the Muslims, Croats, and Serbs unfolded. The Serb-Croat relationship was ambiguous and paradoxical. Enmity between the two nations had been fueled by the war in Croatia and the seizure of almost one-third of Croatia by the Serbs of the Krajina. At the same time, Milošević and Tudjman appeared eager to exploit the breakup of Yugoslavia and the outbreak of the conflict in Bosnia-Herzegovina to create a greater Serbia and a greater Croatia at the expense of the Bosnian Muslims. The retreat of the Croatians from Bosanski Brod in October 1992 coincided with the withdrawal of JNA troops from the Prevlaka peninsula, in Montenegro, leading to speculation that Serbia and Croatia were conspiring at the expense of the Bosnian Muslims.

Yet relations between Serbia and Croatia remained hostage to the issue of the Krajina and eastern Slavonija. Croatia's overriding interest was to regain territories under Serb occupation. Croatia sought to consolidate its influence in those parts of Bosnia it considered vital to its interests, while cultivating its ties with the United States in an attempt to win support for retaking the areas in Croatia under Serb control. All of these considerations weighed against an outright alliance with Serbia.

For the Bosnian government, good relations with Croatia were a matter of life and death, both as an assurance that arms would reach the Bosnian forces and as a guarantee that Bosnia would not be partitioned. During summer and fall 1992 the Croatian and Bosnian leaderships attempted to forge a stronger relationship between their governments and, especially, their armed forces. But, as we shall see below and in chapter 6, a series of formal agreements came to naught. By October 1992 relations had sunk to the point where the Bosnian government was sharply divided between its moderates, including Izetbegović, and the more belligerent faction described above.[9] The Izetbegović strategy, which might be called "sink or swim with Croatia," won the day and relations between Bosnia and Croatia improved. We will examine these relations in greater detail in chapter 6.

The International Community

The war in Bosnia was characterized by an unprecedented degree of organizational involvement on the part of the international community. Western involvement in the war took several forms, each reflecting not only the character and mission of the organization or institution involved, but also the understanding of the war that motivated involvement in it. In addition, a whole host of international non-governmental organizations became involved in efforts to relieve the human suffering that accompanied the war. International multilateral organizations became involved in both political efforts to end the fighting and humanitarian relief efforts. The humanitarian operation, launched by the UNHCR under the shield of UNPROFOR, was the largest in the history of the UN. By the end of 1994, more humanitarian aid had been airlifted into Sarajevo than into Berlin in 1948–49. One might have anticipated that this would have engendered respect for the UN, allowing it to stand above the conflict, as was the case with most of the non-governmental organizations that provided humanitarian relief in Bosnia. But this did not happen. Instead, the UN became deeply enmeshed in, and tarnished by, the politics of the war.

Direct UN involvement came first in March 1992, with the transfer of UNPROFOR headquarters from Banja Luka to Sarajevo, and subsequently in response to the mounting violence in April and May 1992, especially the severe shelling of Sarajevo by Serb artillery in the surrounding hills. As we reported in chapter 4, the kidnapping of President Izetbegović on May 3 and subsequent ambush of the JNA convoy drew UNPROFOR commanders into the direct line of fire as they attempted to mediate the confrontation. We have already described in chapter 4 how the shelling of a breadline in downtown Sarajevo on May 27 led to the imposition of sanctions on Yugoslavia (Serbia and Montenegro), and how the fighting in Sarajevo and concern for the survival of its civilian population led the UN to seek and gain control over the Sarajevo airport in June. The UNPROFOR deployment grew from 1,500 troops in August 1992 to 23,000 troops by the end of 1994. These troops performed traditional UN peacekeeping functions in arranging cease-fires, interposing themselves between the combatants as part of cease-fire arrangements, and assisting in the delivery of humanitarian aid. At the same time, however, the Security Council, acting in a highly politicized environment, adopted resolutions calling for the use of all available means to assure delivery of relief supplies and the use of force to defend UN troops in the safe areas, or mandated action such as cooperation with NATO in the use of air power against the Serbs, that cast UNPROFOR troops in the role of peace enforcers. UN commanders found it difficult to implement these resolutions without jeopardizing their ability to function as peacekeepers. Hence, UN commanders often opposed them. The consequences of attempting to combine peacekeeping and peace enforcement actions in Bosnia were catastrophic for the UN. In the words of Paul Diehl:

By choosing to send peacekeeping troops, the United Nations limited its option for enforcement actions; contributing states were reluctant to support coercive actions for fear of retaliation against these troops. The neutrality of U.N. personnel was also called into question when the organization was imposing harsh sanctions on Serbia, threatening air strikes against Serbian military positions, and delivering food and other supplies to Bosnian Muslims; the expectation that the U.N. peacekeeping personnel could be perceived as impartial in this context was unreasonable.[10]

The UN occupation of the Sarajevo airport, which allowed humanitarian intervention to go forward, showed how important it was that the UN was actively engaged in Bosnia. But that intervention, and the broader UN presence that followed, also worked against those trying to find a political solution, since it created a deterrent to more decisive involvement by the great powers, and injected a new factor into the crisis that could be—and was—manipulated for military and political advantage by the warring parties.

The decision by Western leaders to go ahead with a humanitarian relief effort in Bosnia-Herzegovina in the absence of a broader political settlement made it clear that they did not expect such a settlement to come quickly. The decision not to use force to deliver relief reflected both Russian opposition and the unwillingness of some European and American policymakers to become more deeply involved in the conflict. The U.S. military had opposed intervention from the beginning of the fighting. According to Robert Hutchings, then director of European affairs at the National Security Council, "The Department of Defense and the Joint Chiefs were at pains to exclude the military option *a priori* and, fresh from the military triumph in the Gulf, their opinions carried even more weight in administration councils than usual."[11] The military believed that the use of force would inevitably lead to ground combat.[12] Opposition in the Pentagon would provide a major obstacle to direct U.S. involvement in the war, and to support for a negotiated settlement of the war that might require the deployment of U.S. troops to implement or enforce it.[13] But the most fundamental explanation for the lack of direct U.S. involvement in the early stages of the war was the view held by key policymakers that the fighting did not threaten U.S. national interests.

Hutchings reports that policymakers "never decided whether important U.S. interests were at stake. We never decided whether Yugoslavia mattered enough to invest considerable American leadership and, if need be, to place substantial numbers of American men and women in harm's way to halt or at least contain the conflict."[14] David Gompert, another senior policy staffer at that time, states the case more directly: "Clearly, and correctly, American leaders did not see 'vital' national interests imperiled by the

Yugoslav conflicts."[15] Then Secretary of State James Baker reports, from the perspective of the Bush Administration: "Our vital national interests were not at stake. The Yugoslav conflict had the potential to be intractable, but it was nonetheless a regional dispute." At the same time, Baker reports, there "was an undercurrent in Washington, often felt but seldom spoken, that it was time to make the Europeans step up to the plate and show they could act as a unified power."[16] Indeed, the Europeans themselves had declared in June 1991, at the outbreak of fighting in Slovenia, "It is the hour of Europe," and "If anybody can achieve things it is the European Community."[17]

Those in Washington who viewed the crisis in the former Yugoslavia as a civil war, as did the secretary of defense, argued that it did not threaten international peace or require Western intervention. Those who came to see the conflict as a case of aggression by Serbia against a sovereign state (Bosnia-Herzegovina), as did the secretary of state, eventually pressed for more direct Western intervention. Secretary Baker, for example, was reported to have suggested that "the only way to solve [the situation in Bosnia-Herzegovina] is selective bombing of Serbian targets, including Belgrade."[18] But in the absence of a clearly perceived threat to the national interest and in light of the judgment among policymakers that "this was a problem with no good, feasible solutions,"[19] the president's principal foreign policy advisors remained deeply divided over what to do in Bosnia-Herzegovina. There was a "growing sense" among some of them that President Bush might suffer "political damage" in the upcoming election if the administration failed to act. Some feared that failure to oppose perceived Serbian aggression against Bosnia-Herzegovina might encourage Serbian moves against Kosovo and Macedonia and thereby threaten a wider Balkan war.[20] When they gathered to discuss the crisis at the end of June 1992, the meeting was, in the words of Secretary Baker, "one of the most spirited I had ever attended," with the military opposing Baker's effort to increase U.S. involvement in support of humanitarian relief efforts.[21]

President Bush made it clear that the United States would act only as part of a UN-sanctioned multinational effort aimed at humanitarian relief. The United States would not attempt to solve the political conflict unilaterally or by force. The Bush administration thus appeared to be moving in May and June 1992 toward an effort to find a diplomatic solution to the war. But the United States remained aloof from international efforts to negotiate an end to the fighting. As one unnamed "senior U.S. official" put it in May: "We are willing to help, to add our voices to the Europeans. . . . But we are not about to get out in front of the Europeans. They must define the distance and set the pace for the international community in dealing with Yugoslavia."[22] Revelations in the media in August 1992 of the abuses associated with the ethnic cleansing carried out by the Serbs against the Muslims in Bosnia-Herzegovina, and the ensuing controversies over whether these acts could be considered genocide, intensified the American moral commitment to the Muslim-dominated government and opposition to the Serbs. But it did not move the U.S. government to become directly involved in the search for a solution, or to commit its resources to enforcing a solution once it was found. According to a former State Department official, policymakers had had "credible and verified reports of the existence of the camps—Serbian-run camps—in Bosnia and elsewhere as of June, certainly July 1992, well ahead of the media revelations."[23]

U.S. policymakers were sensitive to public opinion. But it would be a mistake to see U.S. policy simply as a response to media pressure. Policymakers intent on pursuing a particular course of action can themselves generate media pressure in support of their preferences. Secretary Baker reports, for example, that in April 1992 he instructed his press secretary, Margaret Tutwiler, to talk to Bosnian foreign minister Haris Silajdžić, "about the importance of using Western mass media to build support in Europe and North America for the Bosnian cause." Baker also had Tutwiler "talk to her contacts at the four television networks, the *Washington Post,* and the *New York Times* to try to get more attention focused on the story."[24] One month later, Baker would cite "mounting public concern and criticism" to pressure the British—who feared an open-ended commitment analogous to that in Northern Ireland—into supporting humanitarian intervention.[25] The Bosnians undertook the kind of efforts to influence the media suggested by Baker by hiring two public relations firms to press their cause with congressmen, policymakers, the media, and other opinion-making elites.[26]

International efforts to end the conflict were further hampered by the lack of coordination among international actors, and the ongoing unwillingness or inability of local leaders to fulfill their commitments. The warring parties, for example, apparently agreed during July 1992 talks in London to a truce, and to place their heavy weapons under UN supervision. They further agreed to begin indirect talks on future constitutional arrangements for the republic and to allow refugees to return to their homes. British foreign secretary Douglas Hurd cautioned that "where there is no will for peace we cannot supply it."[27] And, as was the case with previous agreements, no cease-fire was actually established. UN Secretary-General Boutros Boutros-Ghali objected to the proposal to place heavy weapons under UN supervision agreed to by the parties in London, which he noted had been put forward by EC mediators without UN authorization. Thus, by July 1992 the effort to negotiate an end to the conflict in Bosnia-Herzegovina seemed to require greater coordination among international actors, a more comprehensive approach to the region as a whole, greater pressure on local actors to reach agreement, and a commitment on the part of outside powers to enforce any such agreement.

The negotiation of a solution to the conflict was also made more difficult by the fact that any meaningful settlement required the active cooperation of the leaderships of both Serbia and Croatia; without them, a settlement was impossible. Elections to the parliament of the newly declared Federal Republic of Yugoslavia (Serbia and Montenegro) in June 1992 produced an even more nationalist body than before. The Socialist Party led by Serbian president Slobodan Milošević won a majority of seats, and the extreme nationalist Serbian Radical Party led by Vojislav Šešelj became the second-largest parliamentary party.[28] In Croatia, President Franjo Tudjman was also under pressure from more extreme nationalist forces. In December 1991, one of his senior advisors had alleged that the government was eager to make political concessions to end the fighting, including granting local autonomy to Serb areas within the Croatian state. But, according to this official, "no one in Croatia would survive politically" the surrender of territory.[29] By July, the Tudjman government appeared to be less willing to make any such concessions. Elections in August 1992 consolidated Tudjman's hold on the Croatian presidency and produced an overwhelming parliamentary majority for the HDZ. But greater domestic political security produced no greater inclination in Zagreb to compromise the Bosnian Croat goal of establishing their own state in Herzegovina.

The International Community Is Drawn In

The onset of the war in Bosnia found international actors unprepared to become involved. The tone was set by UN policymakers in New York, who refused entreaties by Izetbegović, as early as March 1992, to station UN troops in Bosnia. Undersecretary-General for Peacekeeping Marrack Goulding, in his May 1992 study of the feasibility of a peacekeeping mission to Bosnia, argued that a UN force could not carry out its duties in Bosnia unless there was a political settlement. Goulding was skeptical that even a limited mission sent to protect humanitarian convoys, or to take over the airport, would be feasible. In Goulding's words:

> The situation in Bosnia Herzegovina is tragic, dangerous, violent and confused. . . . Without an agreement of some sort, a workable mandate cannot be defined and peace-keeping is impossible. . . . The United Nations personnel are routinely harassed, the Organization's property stolen and its emblems and uniforms misappropriated by the various parties. These are not the condi-

tions which permit a United Nations peace-keeping operation to make an effective contribution.[30]

Secretary-General Boutros-Ghali rejected Izetbegović's entreaties, and was supported in his decision by his special envoy, Cyrus Vance. Vance, however, argued for an activist UN role in negotiating an end to the conflict, while Boutros-Ghali argued that the EC should be responsible for finding a political solution to the crisis.[31]

The failure of the Security Council to send UN forces to Bosnia in spring 1992 has since been questioned on the grounds that the conflict might have been brought under control if an international force had intervened at an early stage.[32] It is sufficient to read the Goulding report to realize the risks that any such operation entailed unless it was launched as a full-scale military operation. In the absence of any interest on the part of Western powers in intervening in this way, the immediate problem lay in achieving the political settlement upon which the success of any peacekeeping effort would depend.

The reluctance of UN policymakers to be drawn into the conflict was matched by the reluctance of the great powers. Their policymakers were prepared to support measures such as Security Council Resolutions 749 of April 7, 1992 (calling for a cease-fire and negotiated settlement), and 752 of May 15, 1992 (calling for a cease-fire, the withdrawal of Yugoslav and Croatian troops, the disbanding and disarming of irregular forces, the negotiation of a constitutional agreement under the auspices of the EC Conference on Yugoslavia, and an end to ethnic cleansing). But they were not prepared to act directly. A senior U.S. official declared unambiguously in mid-April that "there is no possibility that the United States would intervene militarily."[33]

The first discernible change in Western attitudes toward the Bosnian conflict came in the third week in May, when the United States began to focus on the humanitarian crisis in Bosnia. On May 23 Secretary of State Baker declared the situation in Bosnia-Herzegovina "unconscionable," and a "humanitarian nightmare." The change in the U.S. position appears to have been linked to the shelling of an ICRC (International Committee of the Red Cross) relief convoy on May 18.[34] On May 24 Baker urged the EC to become more active in resolving the crisis. He made it clear, however, that there would be no unilateral use of force by the United States, which "cannot be the world's policeman." "Before we consider force," he suggested, ". . . we ought to exhaust all of the political, diplomatic, and economic remedies that might be at hand."[35] By May 26 the United States and the EC had agreed to a plan for graduated sanctions against Serbia.[36] Russian opposition to the plan nevertheless made it uncertain that a resolution calling for sanctions would receive the approval of the Security Council.

The shelling in Vaso Miškin street on May 27 galvanized the Security Council into action. According to press dispatches, the pictures in the press and on television had an electrifying effect on Baker.[37] President Yeltsin expressed his anger at the incident and withdrew Russian objections to imposing sanctions against Serbia.[38] On May 30, Resolution 757 was adopted by the UN Security Council. Invoking the coercive authority of Chapter VII, the resolution instituted an economic embargo against Yugoslavia (Serbia and Montenegro) and affirmed that borders could not be changed by force. It renewed the Security Council's demands for an immediate cease-fire as well as an end to outside interference, the withdrawal or disarming of JNA and Croatian military units in Bosnia-Herzegovina, and the disarming and disbanding of all irregular units. The Security Council also called for an end to forced expulsions of local populations and for the establishment of a "security zone" around Sarajevo airport to facilitate a humanitarian airlift effort. It demanded that all resolutions adopted by the Security Council be honored by Belgrade.[39]

The vote on sanctions in the Security Council was taken in haste and without the benefit of the secretary-general's May 30 report to the Security Council. The May 30 report gave a sobering assessment of the situation in Bosnia, and stressed the virtual impossibility of carrying out the provisions of Resolution 752. The report concluded that responsibility for the shelling of Sarajevo lay not with the JNA, but the newly formed Army of the (Bosnian) Serb republic (BSA in UN parlance), and that only a political agreement among the warring parties in Bosnia could end the conflict. Despite Milošević's part in directing the ethnic cleansing campaign carried out by Serbian paramilitary forces (discussed in chapter 4), Boutros-Ghali's analysis of the situation raised doubts about the exclusive culpability of Serbia for the deteriorating situation in Bosnia, and about the ability of Yugoslavia to take the actions demanded of it in Resolution 757 (above all, implementation of Resolution 752).[40]

Carrying out the sanctions decision raised a host of problems for the international community and for the Security Council, which was split over how harshly the sanctions should be implemented and under what conditions they should be lifted. Russia favored a lifting or amelioration of the sanctions once Yugoslavia (Serbia and Montenegro) formally withdrew its forces from Bosnia. The United States saw sanctions as a punitive measure which would isolate Serbia and, possibly, lead to the overthrow of the Milošević regime. It soon became obvious that the economic blockade was hurting the least fortunate in Serbia and Montenegro the most, and that

Milošević's hold on power was not weakened, but strengthened.[41] The economic impact of the embargo on Yugoslavia's neighbors in the Balkans was particularly harmful and led to widespread "sanctions-busting."

The imposition of sanctions on Yugoslavia nevertheless did give the international community leverage on Serbia in the political negotiations for a settlement of the Bosnian crisis. It meant that Milošević could not put off settling the Bosnian question indefinitely. From that point onward, Milošević's efforts were bent toward getting the sanctions lifted. Such comprehensive sanctions could only have been imposed by the UN Security Council, whose cooperation was essential as long as neither Europe nor the United States was willing to use force in the region on their own. At the same time, effective implementation and enforcement of the sanctions—and especially the financial sanctions imposed later—required U.S. participation.

The imposition of sanctions on Yugoslavia was therefore a major step in involving the international community in the Bosnian crisis. What was particularly striking was the fact that the adoption of this measure was a reaction to an event whose origins were, as we have noted in chapter 4, at the time obscure—possibly the result of a deliberate Serb attack, but perhaps the result of a stray shell, or even an elaborate deception carried out by the Bosnian Muslims. The reaction of the international community to the May 27 "breadline massacre" established what was to become a familiar pattern, alluded to in chapter 4. The international community would be galvanized into action by a tragedy that aroused the feeling that "something must be done." The impulse to act was the product of shock and of fear that something worse might be just around the corner. Because failing to act was felt to be a sign of weakness or—worse—callousness, the policies springing from such reactions sometimes were made hastily and quickly. But because the effect of such shocks, and the commitment to "do something," would wear off quickly, in some cases nothing was done at all.

Western policymakers appeared not to be inclined to act in response to the heavy shelling of Sarajevo that began in late May and continued into June 1992. On June 8, 1992, the Security Council adopted Resolution 758, calling on all parties to respect their agreement to establish a cease-fire and turn control of Sarajevo airport over to the United Nations "for humanitarian purposes." But no action was taken. As President Bush remarked on June 4, "Prudence and caution prevents military action."[42]

Nevertheless, the continued shelling contributed to mounting tensions and created a crisis atmosphere in Washington and the European capitals. In testimony to the Senate Foreign Relations Committee on June 23, Secretary Baker called the shelling of Sarajevo an "absolute outrage," and refused to rule out the use of force, if undertaken multilaterally.[43] But when President

Bush and his principal foreign policy advisers met in the White House in late June to consider further responses to the Yugoslav crisis they were told that it would require the deployment of some 35,000–50,000 troops to reopen Sarajevo airport by force and establish a security zone around it.[44] The establishment of a ground corridor through which larger quantities of supplies could be transported would require an even greater commitment, since it would involve 125-mile-long journeys through "God-given terrain for guerrilla operations."[45] Defense planners feared that "the Serbs would wage a costly campaign of attrition against foreign intervention."[46]

American internal differences over the use of force were matched by differences among the Europeans.[47] They differed not only over the substance of policy, but over how it would be implemented. The French, for example, pressed for a European response carried out through the WEU. The British opposed greater involvement and sought to direct it through NATO so as to involve the United States.[48] The Russians not only opposed the use of force, but were themselves internally divided.[49]

Thus, the Western powers again appeared to be backing away from involvement in the war. Yet, as we have seen in chapter 4, within the next few days, Secretary-General Boutros-Ghali issued an ultimatum to the Serbs to turn the airport over to the UN; French president Mitterrand made a dramatic visit to the city; and, on June 29, the Serbs relinquished the airport to UN peacekeepers.

On balance, and until further evidence is available, the immensely important decision by the Serbs to turn over the airport to UNPROFOR would seem to have been influenced most by two considerations. The first was Belgrade's reaction to the imposition of sanctions and its desire to accommodate the international community as a means of gaining a cease-fire and a political solution in Bosnia favorable to Serb interests. The second factor, which became more important as the crisis deepened, was the threat of U.S. intervention. U.S. threats were limited to providing air support for humanitarian operations. Secretary of Defense Richard Cheney had ruled out the use of U.S. ground forces.[50] But, if the airport remained in Serb hands it could have become a U.S. target, perhaps tipping the nearby battle over the access route from the airport to Sarajevo—which had been raging for most of June—in favor of the Bosnian government.

We have seen that the Bosnian Serb leadership in Pale resisted international pressures. We know as well that the threat of air strikes held less weight there than in the Serbian capital. The critical question to be addressed in this connection is, therefore, how Belgrade reacted to the veiled U.S. threats. Milošević appeared ready to make concessions over control of the airport as early as the first week in June, on the eve of the Serbian elections. On June 2, a week after Bosnia-Herzegovina was admitted into the UN, Milošević offered to end the siege of Sarajevo and called on the international community to take over the airport. He also suggested that foreign observers could be stationed with Serb units to monitor Serb compliance. On June 3, the rump Yugoslav presidency called for the takeover of the airport by the UN.[51] Also on June 3, Belgrade suspended flights to Banja Luka, isolating Western Bosnia, since Croat and Muslim troops had in the meantime blocked the northern corridor. This sequence of events suggests pressure from Belgrade on the Bosnian Serbs to accede to international demands to turn over the airport to the UN. The timing of these actions in early June—before Secretary of State Baker's threatening testimony to the Senate—suggests that Belgrade was acting more out of its interest in ending the sanctions and negotiating a favorable end of the war than out of a fear of U.S. air strikes. To a certain extent, Milošević appeared to be following the same tactics he had pursued earlier in Croatia: In response to the granting of international recognition and UN membership to Bosnia, he began in early May to advocate the deployment of UN troops so as to achieve the *de facto* partition of the country.

Despite the pressure from Belgrade, the Bosnian Serbs did not concede until June 11, when Karadžić offered an unconditional turnover of the airport to the UN.[52] General Mladić, on the other hand, resisted the proposed move and escalated the fighting. For Mladić, the policy of relinquishing the airport must have seemed a betrayal of the Bosnian Serb cause, a move that would drive a wedge into the Serb siege lines and which could be exploited by the West to supply the Muslims with arms as well as humanitarian aid. While Mladić may not have believed that NATO strikes were imminent, the totality of the crisis—including the threat of Western intervention—gave Belgrade the leverage it needed to impose its will on the Bosnian Serb military. A key role also was played by the UN. It provided a neutral force on which the Bosnian Serbs, suspicious of the consequences of any withdrawal, might rely to police the airport and the flow of aid into Sarajevo against abuse by the Muslims.

By July 1992 international efforts to avert the impending conflict in Bosnia-Herzegovina were in disarray. The EC effort led by Ambassador José Cutileiro to negotiate a Bosnian settlement, described in more detail in chapter 3, collapsed after recognition of Bosnia by the EC and the United States in the first week of April. The impression that Bosnia was descending into anarchy was reinforced by the kidnapping of Izetbegović and the ambush of a JNA convoy that followed. This incident poisoned relations on all sides of the issue and strengthened the resolve of U.S. decisionmakers to remain aloof from the conflict. A further effort to convene the Cutileiro negotiations in late May failed under the impact of the breadline massacre and the ensuing heavy shelling of Sarajevo in June. The establishment of an international presence at Sarajevo airport in support of a humanitarian relief effort had been achieved without resorting to the force levels required by U.S. military estimates. But the international community failed to follow up on this success by increasing its pressure on the warring parties to stop the fighting, resume their negotiations, and conclude an agreement.

The hopes of the Bosnian government that they could receive Western aid following recognition proved illusory. The British warned the Bosnian government that they should not expect Western assistance. The message was delivered on July 17 by Foreign Secretary Hurd to President Izetbegović personally in Sarajevo. While they met, the presidency building came under mortar fire, an attack attributed by some to the Serbs and by others to the Muslims.[53] The Hurd visit coincided with a meeting of representatives of the Bosnian Serbs, Bosnian Croats, and the Bosnian government in London under the sponsorship of Lord Carrington, and may have been intended to facilitate an agreement. Nonetheless, each of the three parties refused to meet directly with the others in London. They communicated with each other through an EC mediator. Bosnian government officials revealed what little interest they had in seeking a negotiated solution when they admitted that "the only reason the Government signed the accord in London was that failure to do so would have allowed the Serbian leaders to present the Government as the party obstructing peace."[54]

Thus, the EC-mediated negotiations had ceased to function as a means of achieving a political settlement and an end to the fighting. They had deteriorated into a means by which each warring party sought to gain political advantage over the others and to strengthen the position of its fighting forces on the ground. In some circumstances, local leaders had to be coerced into participating.

Following the occupation of the Sarajevo airport, the first concerted reaction to the war in Bosnia took the form of a humanitarian response to the cruelties of ethnic cleansing and internment described in chapter 4. On August 6 the Bosnian Serb republic, under international pressure, opened some of its detention camps to Western journalists. In the furor that resulted from exposure of the abuses in these camps, the UN Security Council was seized with the issue of ethnic cleansing by the Serbs. The debate in the Security Council found the United States and Britain sharply divided over how far the Security Council should go in threatening the use of force against the Serbs if they did not curb ethnic cleansing and permit humanitarian aid to flow to the Muslim cities freely.[55] President Bush was reported to be seeking allied support for the use of force to deliver humanitarian supplies to Sarajevo by deploying European ground troops in a more aggressive role than UN peacekeepers, and using NATO air power to protect them. But Secretary-General Boutros-Ghali cautioned that the threat of force might make UN troops already in Sarajevo the direct targets of attack. The British reminded the Americans publicly that "the only objective that would justify the massive use of force would be the achievement of a peace settlement."[56] Thus, Security Council Resolution 770, adopted in August 1992, carefully limited the authorization to use "all measures necessary" solely to the delivery of humanitarian assistance, not to the imposition of an overall settlement.

The Bush administration may have been responding to domestic political pressure from the Democratic candidate for president, Bill Clinton, who on August 5 called on Bush to "do whatever it takes to stop the slaughter of civilians" and suggested "we may have to use military force."[57] Former British Prime Minister Margaret Thatcher weighed in the next day with a call for the use of air power against both the Bosnian Serbs and Serbia.[58] Within days, Deputy Secretary of State Lawrence Eagleburger dampened any American enthusiasm for the use of force by raising the specter of "another Lebanon or Vietnam."[59] Eagleburger's pessimism reflected the prevailing military estimates of the scale of the commitment that would be required. A senior aide to the chairman of the Joint Chiefs of Staff told Congress in August that 60,000–120,000 troops would be necessary to secure a land route from the Croatian coastal city of Split to Sarajevo and to establish a twenty-mile secure zone around the Sarajevo airport for the protection of relief flights. As many as 400,000 troops would be needed to impose a cease-fire throughout Bosnia-Herzegovina.[60] British military analysts offered different estimates: 10,000 troops with strong air support to open a land corridor; 30,000 troops to secure Sarajevo, and 100,000 troops to secure all Muslim-held territory.[61] In the absence of a political settlement among the warring parties, however, even intervention on this scale held out little promise of settling the conflict. Moreover, under such conditions it would be difficult to define the specific mission of an intervention force and therefore impossible to determine when its mission had been completed and it could be withdrawn. The experience of UNPROFOR in Croatia suggested that a traditional peacekeeping mission, including even a formal cessation of hostilities, would only lead to an unstable de facto partition of the republic. Given the reluctance of the Bush administration to become involved on the ground in Bosnia, the prospect that intervention would become an open-ended commitment ensured that such an effort would not be undertaken.

The absence of a credible threat of force clearly reduced the incentive for the Bosnian Serbs, who enjoyed military superiority, to make concessions in the interest of achieving a settlement with the Muslims and the Croats. At the same time, the Muslim-dominated Bosnian government continued to hope and work for outright Western military intervention while it violated cease-fires that would have allowed the Serbs to consolidate their victories. The hope for intervention was kept alive by incremental increases in Western involvement such as that represented by the August Security Council resolution, by continued discussions of intervention within the U.S. administration, by media pressure to intervene, and by the sympathy of some U.S. congressional actors. This reinforced the resistance of the Bosnian government to conceding military victory to the Serbs, and made it unwilling to agree to any settlement that might institutionalize Serb (or Croat) gains.

The ICFY

Unwilling to impose a settlement by force, the great powers had little choice but to pursue negotiations among the warring parties, even though it was clear that neither the Serbs nor the Muslims were much interested in negotiating. It was under these conditions that the United Nations and the European Community convened the International Conference on the Former Yugoslavia (ICFY) in London at the end of August 1992.[62] Initially, the participants in the struggle were reluctant to attend. The Bosnian government was not prepared to enter into negotiations for a political settlement. Milošević attended reluctantly, at the urging of Cyrus Vance. The night before the meeting, August 25–26, Serb forces around Sarajevo, in a reckless display of spite, shelled and completely gutted the National and University library in Sarajevo, the *Večnica,* provoking sharp attacks at the London meeting against their behavior. The Serbian government's position at the London meeting was further undermined by the presence of a delegation from the Yugoslav federal government, led by Milan Panić, which was openly hostile to Milošević.

The discussions at London revealed the great differences in positions among the participants, and provided little basis for optimism that a mutually agreed settlement could be reached easily. Although some participants advocated direct military intervention by an international force, none sought to circumvent the recognized authority of the UN Security Council to legitimate any such action. At the same time, it was clear that none of the permanent members of the council were as yet ready to support such action. Rather, they appeared intent on achieving what the British foreign secretary called a "political solution" that preserved the existing borders of Bosnia-Herzegovina, but also "satisfies all three ethnic communities."[63] Thus, the conference actually signaled all the parties that, at least in the short term, outside powers were unlikely to use force to bring the fighting to an end.

At the same time, the conference attempted to isolate and threaten Serbia, and Milošević personally, for aggression against Bosnia. A document severely critical of Serbia was circulated among conference participants. According to a member of Panić's delegation, Milošević was ready to sign the document, but Čosić and Panić resisted, and the document was withdrawn. If accurate, this account suggests Milošević's indifference to, and perhaps contempt for, any document that did not commit him to a specific course of action.

Few new positions were revealed at the two-day London meeting. The Bosnian government delegation requested that it be exempted from the arms embargo established by the United Nations, arguing that in the absence of direct military support from outside powers Bosnia should be permitted to exercise the right of self-defense. The French foreign minister, in contrast, called for strengthening the arms embargo. The delegates to the conference thus took no action on the Bosnian request. Similarly, the conference refused to adopt the Bosnian government's definition of the conflict as one between the Bosnian government and an "aggressor," continuing instead to define the conflict as one among three ethnic communities—a definition that suggested a certain degree of doubt about the wisdom of having recognized the Bosnian state only three months earlier.

The conference adopted a statement of general principles for the negotiation of a settlement that included calls for the cessation of fighting, an end to the use of force, nonrecognition of gains won by force, recognition of the sovereignty and territorial integrity of states, and the inviolability of recognized borders. The conference stressed respect for individual rights as embodied in existing international conventions, implementation of constitutional guarantees of the rights of minorities, and the promotion of tolerance, rather than the principle of national self-determination. In this way, the conference left open a basis for both preserving the territorial integrity of Bosnia-Herzegovina and recognizing the distinctiveness of the Muslim, Serb, and Croat communities within it. The conference explicitly condemned forced expulsions and called for the closing of detention camps, the safe return of refugees, adherence to the Geneva Conventions, and for questions of state succession to be settled by consensus or arbitration. The conference insisted that it would not recognize the results of "ethnic cleansing."

The London meeting appeared briefly to have gotten the process of negotiating a settlement off to a positive beginning with an agreement among the warring parties on humanitarian actions, an end to ethnic cleansing, a cessation of hostilities, the international supervision of heavy weapons, and respect for human rights. Consistent with the reluctance of the great powers to embark upon the use of force, however, the London declarations contained no enforcement provisions. According to one source with direct access to the Bosnian government delegation, the absence of such provisions was the cause for some hesitation on the part of some members of the delegation to agree to the conference documents. Ensuing events on the ground in Bosnia-Herzegovina, and the difficulty of negotiations in Geneva, revealed that the London agreements were, indeed, empty commitments on the part of all involved in them. But the Bosnian government delegation nonetheless signed them, resigning itself to the fact that the specification of principles was the most they could hope to achieve for the moment. Izetbegović made a point of using the documents to affirm his claim to represent the legitimate government of Bosnia by adding his official title under his signature by hand. The fact that he had to do so, however, reflected the still-uncertain commitment of the international community to his state.

The London meeting established the like-named International Conference on the Former Yugoslavia, or ICFY, to continue the effort to negotiate a peaceful end to the Yugoslav conflicts. The ICFY was based at UN headquarters in Geneva and was co-chaired by former U.S. secretary of state Cyrus Vance (in his capacity as personal envoy of the secretary-general of the United Nations) and former British foreign secretary Lord David Owen (for the European Community). It immediately became the focus of coordinated international efforts to resolve the conflict. The ICFY process was from the outset more closely connected to European governments than to that of the United States. This was the result of both U.S. unwillingness to participate in or support the negotiations, and the direct integration of the ICFY into the European diplomatic network. Lord Owen consulted intensively with European governments, and the ICFY organization was integrated into the EC intergovernmental confidential communications network. Policymakers in the UK and France, major troop-contributing countries whose governments therefore had strong interests in the negotiations, remained particularly well informed. American and Russian policymakers, in contrast, appeared, at least according to accounts prepared by Lord Owen and ICFY staff, to be less well informed with respect to the details, and unwilling, at first, to participate in the mediation effort.[64]

The aftermath of the meeting in London attested to its ineffectiveness. Whether by coincidence or as a consequence of the empty gestures of the international community, the fighting in Bosnia escalated sharply at the end of August. On August 30 the Alipašino Polje market in Sarajevo was shelled, apparently by the Serbs. Fifteen persons were killed and 100 wounded. An Italian civil aircraft was shot down over Bosnian airspace, in a location suggesting that either the Muslims or the Croats were responsible. Efforts to implement the confidence-building measures adopted at London went forward nevertheless. On September 1, the Serb side agreed to concentrate its artillery around Sarajevo. On September 6, following a visit to Sarajevo by Marrack Goulding, Vance and Owen issued an "ultimatum" to the Serbs requiring them to place Serb artillery around Sarajevo, Bihać, Jajce, and Goražde under UN supervision by September 12. On that date, Karadžić announced that the artillery around Sarajevo was under UN observation. But sharp fighting broke out the same day. Serbs began shelling the city, using both artillery hidden from the UN and weapons under UN observation. The fighting and shelling continued into the following week. As a result, Izetbegović refused to attend the ICFY negotiations in Geneva, much to the anger of Cyrus Vance.

The August meeting in London also deepened the rift between Secretary-General Boutros-Ghali and the European states directly involved in negotiations and events on the ground. As we have seen, the rift had been evident in July, prior to the London conference, when Boutros-Ghali had expressed anger over the July 17 agreement to commit UN forces to Bosnia, and when the secretary-general turned down a proposal by UNPROFOR General Nambiar to deploy UN observers in Bosnia. Boutros-Ghali laid out his position in no uncertain terms: It was the responsibility of regional organizations, not UN forces, to engage in peace enforcement (in contrast to peacekeeping, the traditional role of the UN).[65] Plans nevertheless went ahead before and during the London conference for the dispatch of UN troops. The British offered to send a modest contingent of 1,800, and plans were laid for a total of 6,000 UN personnel to implement the agreements reached in London.[66] Events would prove that the pessimistic assessment of the secretary-general that UN forces were not sufficient to police a cease-fire and oversee the concentration of Serb artillery was well founded.

The Vance-Owen Plan

The ICFY negotiators led by Vance and Owen attempted, through diplomatic efforts, to find a solution to the multiple conflicts in former Yugoslavia by balancing recognition of the sovereignty and territorial integrity of the post-Yugoslav states defined by former republic borders, with respect for individual rights, implementation of constitutional guarantees of the rights of minorities, and the promotion of tolerance. This approach rejected the Serbs' (and the Croats') insistence that they were a "constituent nationality" of Bosnia, not a "minority," and therefore enjoyed a right to state formation that they wished to exercise autonomously. The ethnic definition of the state inherent in the concept of a "constituent nation" contradicted the civil definition of the state which lay at the core of the negotiators' commitment to preserving the territorial integrity of Bosnia-Herzegovina.

Unfortunately, as we argued in chapter 2, civil society in Bosnia and the civil definition of the state that it supported was only in its infancy when Yugoslavia disintegrated. Beginning with the 1990 elections, it had eroded rapidly, a process accelerated by the outbreak of the war. There was little basis for Serb (and Croat) nationalists, already hostile to the idea of a civil state, to trust Bosnian Muslim leaders not to attempt to impose their own national identity on the state, thereby reducing Serbs (and Croats) to a "minority." But, as the data presented in chapter 2 made clear, whereas in Slovenia, Croatia, and Macedonia the Slovenes, Croats, and Macedonians were healthy majorities, in Bosnia-Herzegovina, the largest group—the Muslims—constituted less than half the population, and some Muslim leaders were among the strongest advocates of the civil idea.

The options available to Vance and Owen for solving the conflict in Bosnia thus were extremely limited. The failed EC effort had established Serb and Croat expectations of ethnic autonomy that would be difficult to ignore. But efforts to accommodate these expectations would be opposed by the Muslim-dominated Bosnian government and by the United States. Furthermore, the London conference had gone on record as opposing any solution that endorsed ethnic cleansing, placing the ICFY in the position of either demanding that the Bosnian Serbs give up territory where the Muslims had been a majority, or offering a plan that would drastically limit the powers of the Serb authorities in Bosnia, rendering the question of ethnic boundaries moot. Few negotiating teams had ever been given a more difficult mandate.

In early October 1992, the ICFY staff presented Vance and Owen with five options for Bosnia-Herzegovina: (1) a centralized state; (2) a centralized federal state with significant functions carried out by 4–10 regions; (3) a loose federal state of three ethnic units, not geographically contiguous; (4) a loose confederation of three ethnically determined republics with significant independence, possibly even in the security field; and (5) a Muslim state, created through partition, with Serb territory becoming part of Yugoslavia (Serbia and Montenegro) and Croat territory becoming part of Croatia. According to Owen, he and Vance chose the second option as the basis for their peace plan, but redefined it as a decentralized state.[67] It would be more accurate, however, to characterize the plan that evolved under Vance and Owen simply as a highly decentralized state of ten regions.

From the beginning, negotiators recognized that the views of the three parties diverged widely. The Muslim-dominated Bosnian government "advocated a centralized, unitary State, arranged into a number of regions possessing merely administrative functions."[68] The Serbs opted for "three independent States, respectively for the Muslim, Serb, and Croat peoples, with each of these states having its own international legal personality." These might form a loose confederation. Negotiators recognized that there was no way to create "three territorially distinct States based on ethnic or confessional principles." "Such a plan," they argued, "could achieve homogeneity and coherent boundaries only by a process of enforced population transfer." They therefore rejected the Serb model. But they also rejected the unitary, centralized state model. They opted instead for a decentralized state in which the central government "would have only those minimal responsibilities that are necessary for a state to function as such, and to carry out its responsibilities as a member of the international community." From the perspective of the co-chairs, this solution coincided with the expressed preferences of all three parties. But the course of negotiations would demonstrate that there was, in fact, little agreement among them.

The negotiations were at first carried out bilaterally, between the ICFY and each of the three parties. The Muslim-dominated government delegation continued to oppose the decentralization plans put forward by negotiators, as well as the willingness of negotiators to consider ethnic factors in shaping their proposals. The negotiators determined that the boundaries should be "drawn so as to constitute areas as geographically coherent as possible, taking into account ethnic, geographical (i.e., natural features, such as rivers), historical, communication (i.e., the existing road and railroad networks), economic viability, and other relevant factors." They acknowledged that "it is likely that many of the provinces (but not necessarily all) will have a considerable majority of one of the three major ethnic groups, and most will have a significant representation of minorities."[69]

The Bosnian government's negotiating position was weakened by a series of severe military defeats at the hands of the Serbs in October, brought about by the withdrawal of Croat military support (described briefly in chapter 4). Izetbegović, in order to reach an accommodation with Croatia, announced on October 24 that he would reconsider the question of an ethnic division of Bosnia. On the same day Mate Boban staged a coup against the moderate leadership in the Bosnian HDZ, leading to the final ouster of Stjepan Kljujić from the leadership of the HDZ. This made the task of the mediators even more difficult. The Boban faction in the HDZ demanded virtually unlimited autonomy for Herzeg-Bosnia (*Herceg-Bosna*). The group was persuaded to muffle its claims for a semi-independent state only after meeting with Vance, Owen, and Tudjman in Zagreb in mid-December. According to a Serbian source, Boban gave up demands for autonomy in exchange for assurances that the Bosnian Croats would be treated generously when the co-chairs drew up the provincial boundaries of the new Bosnian federation.[70] Izetbegović resumed his previous opposition to the creation of ethnic entities within Bosnia.

In the negotiations in Geneva the Bosnian Croat delegation insisted on demilitarization of the common, Bosnian state; the establishment of three "constituent units" composed of ethnically like provinces; and the introduction of decision making in state institutions based on consensus among the three constituent groups. The Croats also opposed most of the provisions for international oversight of Bosnian state institutions. The Bosnian Serbs continued to propose the establishment of three distinct, sovereign, ethnic states with international legal status, loosely confederated to form the state of Bosnia-Herzegovina, which would enjoy a more limited international legal status. The Serbs also sought to impose consensual decision rules and to exclude international oversight.[71] Thus, there was close correspondence between the Serb and Croat negotiating positions, and these differed dramatically from those of the Muslims, or Bosnian government.

While the Serbs continued to insist on dividing the country into three ethnically defined entities, the Bosnian government eventually proposed the creation of 6–18 provinces. The ICFY negotiators proposed that 7–10 geographically coherent provinces might be established whose borders could be determined on the basis of ethnic, geographical, communications, economic, and other relevant factors. The Bosnian government opposed overt recognition of the ethnic factor in determining the structure of the state, while both the Croats and the Serbs insisted that the three main ethnic groups traditionally recognized as "constituent peoples" play a dominant role in government. ICFY negotiators attempted to address these demands for recognition and empowerment of ethnic groups by providing for the rotation of key offices among representatives of the three groups, and by incorporating extensive provisions for the protection of group or minority rights into the peace plan, including international supervision.

The ICFY developed a comprehensive set of draft proposals in October 1992. Negotiators proposed a bicameral parliament consisting of a lower house elected directly on a countrywide basis according to proportional rules of representation, and an upper chamber appointed by the provincial governments. The national executive, or presidency, would consist of the chief executives of each of the provinces. Most governmental functions were to be carried out at the provincial level. This applied especially to the police. The national government was precluded from organizing a uniformed civil police force. Devolution was the watchword, and "almost all activities in which individuals are directly affected by the government" were assigned to local authority.[72] Although governmental arrangements for these provincial authorities were left unspecified, they were required to be fully democratic. The ICFY proposals left open the question whether decisions taken by democratically elected bodies at the national, provincial, and local levels would be taken by a majority vote, or on the basis of super majorities to protect national and minority rights. In this initial draft proposal, the military was to be under the control of the Bosnian government. By January 1993, however, a crucial change had occurred: The concept of a unified national military under central government control was deleted from the proposal and replaced by "the progressive demilitarization of the country."[73]

The settlement proposed by negotiators, which came to be known as "the Vance-Owen plan," called for the establishment of a Human Rights Court. A majority of the judges of this court were to be Europeans appointed by the president of the European Court of Human Rights and the president of the European Commission on Human Rights. The plan also called for the establishment of four ombudsmen to investigate all questions relating to the implementation of human rights, one for each of the four constitutionally recognized groups (Muslim, Serb, Croat, and "other"). A separate Constitutional Court was to handle disputes between state bodies over the exercise of the presidential appointment power and other constitutional questions. It, too, was to have a majority of foreign judges, appointed by the ICFY. The constitutional and other political arrangements finally agreed on by the parties also had to comply with international human and civil rights standards as defined by 17 international conventions and agreements specifically enumerated in the October 1992 "proposed constitutional structure for Bosnia and Herzegovina" put forward by the ICFY co-chairs.[74] In order to ensure compliance, the ICFY itself was to establish an International Commission on Human Rights for Bosnia-Herzegovina. The ICFY approach appeared to amount to the establishment of a *de facto* international trusteeship over the country, although negotiators consciously avoided the use of such terminology.

As a security and confidence-building measure, negotiators also provided for an indeterminate transitional period during which there would be extensive, direct participation in and oversight of domestic institutions by international actors. The duration of some of these arrangements was limited to a specific period. The duration of others was to be determined by the ICFY or its successor. The duration of some was to be determined by "objective factors." Some arrangements were to remain in place until the existing constitution could be amended, "for which high enough majorities should be set so that they can only be obtained by a substantial consensus of the groups."[75]

Although the parties remained far apart, all seemed to agree that a settlement would include some form of internal reorganization of the republic. Negotiations became focused on defining these internal divisions. In December the ICFY considered competing Bosnian government and Serb maps. The Croats submitted a map (Map 5.2) indicating six areas in which Croats were alleged to constitute a majority of 60 percent of the population or greater, and explained that they "would expect to end up with two provinces."[76] The fact that the Croat-majority provinces in the map eventually put forward by the co-chairs corresponded closely to this Croat proposal, and that the co-chairs' allocation of territory in central Bosnia clearly favored the Croats, lends additional weight to the Serbian report cited earlier that a deal over the map had been struck in December between the Bosnian Croats and the co-chairs. The Muslim-led government proposed thirteen ethnically diverse provinces of varying population size (Map 5.3). The boundaries proposed by the government were clearly designed so as to dilute Serb majority areas.[77] The Bosnian Serbs proposed a map that claimed "about 75 per cent of the area of the country" for themselves (Map 5.4). It included all areas in which they alleged that Serbs constituted a majority or owned the greatest percentage of the land, plus areas "in which they would have constituted such a majority except for the genocide committed during World War II and the policies of the subsequent Titoist regime," as well as other areas simply under their military control.[78]

In view of these differences, the co-chairmen came forward in talks held January 2–4, 1993—the first joint meeting of all the delegations since the co-chairs had begun their work on September 3—with a map of their own. They also put forward revised proposals for the future constitutional and political organization of the postwar state and an agreement for peace that included an ambitious schedule for the cessation of hostilities, separation of forces, demilitarization of Sarajevo, and opening of land routes to the city.[79] Most international attention was drawn to the map proposed by the ICFY. It called for the establishment of ten provinces whose boundaries, the co-chairs reported, were drawn on the basis of ethnic, geographic, economic, and politico-military considerations. The proposal can be seen in Map 5.5.

Of the ten provinces in the initial Vance-Owen proposal, there was a Muslim majority in three provinces, a majority of Serbs in two provinces, and a majority of Croats in one. Of the remaining four provinces, the Serbs were a plurality in one, the Croats in two, and the Muslims in one. The ethnic distribution of the population of the ten provinces, based on 1991 census data, is given in Table 5.1 (page 224).

Map 5.2 **The Croat Map, December 1992**

Adapted from *Oslobodjenje,* January 2, 1993.

The co-chairs still called for a decentralized state in which most govern-ment functions would be exercised by the provinces. All matters of vital concern to the parties were to be regulated by the constitution, which could be amended with respect to these matters only on the basis of a consensus. Ordinary central governmental decisions, however, were not to be subject to the veto of any one of the three parties, thereby rejecting a major Serb (and Croat) demand. The presidency of the country would consist of three repre-sentatives from each of the three main groups, rather than the governors of each of the provinces, and would be elected directly by the population rather than appointed by the upper house of parliament. This change ap-peared to be yet another effort to introduce democratic accountability in the hope that this would dilute the power of nationalist leaders. The introduc-tion of an ethnic principle of representation in the presidency was counter-balanced by the stipulation that the presidency was to have no executive

Map 5.3 **The Bosnian Government Map, December 1992**

Adapted from *Oslobodjenje,* January 2, 1993.

functions, and no unanimity or consensus rule in decisionmaking. Its primary function was to make senior appointments to government and these, in turn, were to be guided by ethnic proportionality with key posts rotating among groups.[80]

According to this January 1993 version of the plan, Bosnia-Herzegovina was to be progressively demilitarized, including Sarajevo. A cease-fire was to go into effect within seventy-two hours of an agreement. In December 1992, however, NATO had ruled out sending troops to Bosnia.[81] As a consequence, mediators were compelled to devise a plan for implementing a cease-fire and later demilitarization that could be carried out through action by the warring parties themselves, under UN supervision. The co-chairs acknowledged that no agreement had yet been reached on the actual separation and withdrawal of forces. Sarajevo (province Seven) was to be

Map 5.4 **The Serb Map, December 1992**

Adapted from *Oslobodjenje,* January 2, 1993.

demilitarized. The co-chairs "envisaged" that Serb forces would be withdrawn to provinces two, four, and six; Croat forces to province three; and "the remaining forces would hopefully reach agreement as to their deployment in provinces 1, 5, 8, 9 and 10."[82] No deadlines were set for the withdrawal of troops, although it was hoped that the retreat of troops to "their" provinces could be carried out within forty-five days. These formulations left the status of forces in the two key Croat provinces encompassing western Herzegovina and central Bosnia (eight and ten) to be decided by further negotiation between the Croats and the Muslims. The latter were as likely to resist any withdrawal of their forces from central Bosnia as the Croats were likely to insist on complete military control of these provinces. The January 1993 plan also left control over the strategic province encompassing eastern Bosnia and the Tuzla region (province five) unsettled, in dispute between the Muslims and the Serbs.

Map 5.5 **The Initial Vance-Owen Map, January 1993**

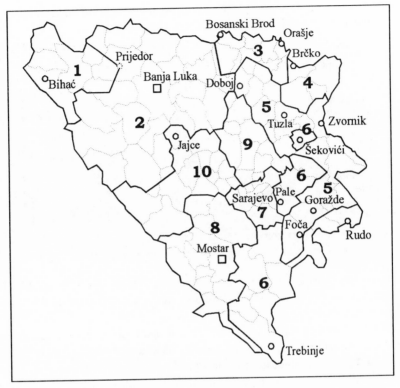

Based on UN Security Council document S/25050 (January 6, 1993), p. 19.

Owen reports that "the strongest resistance" to the demilitarization of Sarajevo and the conclusion of a cessation of hostilities agreement came in December 1992 from the hardline Muslim faction, led by Ejup Ganić.[83] One possible reason for this resistance was the imminent arrival of a new American administration, some of whose senior figures had taken much more aggressively pro-Bosnian Muslim or anti-Serb positions on the conflict during the presidential election campaign and since the November election. The Clinton administration was not, however, united on the issue. Those advocating military action against the Serbs included Vice President Al Gore and Ambassador to the United Nations Madeleine Albright. The national security advisor, Anthony Lake, also advocated more forceful action. While Albright linked calls for action to U.S. interests in Europe, Lake appears to have approached the issue from a broader geopolitical perspective. According to one account, he argued that forceful defense of the

Table 5.1

Approximate Ethnic Composition of Provinces, Initial Vance-Owen Proposal, January 1993 (based on 1991 census)

Province (no. and capital)	Ethnic Composition of Population (in percent)		
	Muslim	Serb	Croat
1. Bihać	74.0	18.4	3.7
2. Banja Luka	20.2	62.7	9.0
3. Bosanski Brod	17.9	28.2	47.3
4. Bijeljina	38.3	49.7	3.6
5. Tuzla	63.9	24.5	4.6
6. Nevesinje	25.1	70.0	0.6
7. Sarajevo (city)	50.1	26.2	7.4
(suburbs)	56.2	26.2	11.5
8. Mostar	28.7	10.9	54.4
9. Zenica	55.8	15.7	20.1
10. Travnik	38.3	12.7	43.8

Source: Based on data from the 1991 census.

Muslims in Bosnia-Herzegovina would strengthen the administration's claim that its efforts to contain Iran and Iraq were not motivated by anti-Muslim sentiments.[84]

After presenting their proposals, the co-chairs recessed the negotiations to allow the delegations to consider their positions. The rest of the month of January 1993 was devoted to efforts to secure their agreement. The Croat delegation was the most cooperative, largely because most of its territorial aspirations were satisfied by the proposed map. Hence, Mate Boban signed the proposed constitutional principles, which included the proposed map, and the agreement on implementing a cessation of hostilities. The Bosnian government raised several objections to the proposal. In a formal response developed on January 20 and 21 and published on January 22,[85] the government argued that the map favored the ethnic principle, and sanctioned the results of aggression by legalizing occupation of territory taken by force and amnestying war criminals. The government also protested that Muslim-majority counties (*opštine*) were included in the Croat-majority provinces. It demanded that Konjic, Jablanica, Gornji Vakuf, Donji Vakuf, Bugojno, and Travnik be included in either the proposed Zenica province, the proposed Sarajevo region, or a new region that incorporated both the Zenica and Sarajevo regions. According to the 1991 census (see Table 2.2 page 30), Bugojno was only 42.1 percent Muslim, while Busovača was 44.9 percent and Fojnica 49.4 percent Muslim. Yet the latter two *opštine* were not among those demanded by the government. Perhaps the large Croat populations of these counties (48.1 percent and 40.9 percent, respectively) precluded such demands. Similarly, the strategically important Vitez and Pucarevo *opštine* contained more Croats than Muslims and were not included in the government's demands.

The Sarajevo province, in the Bosnian government's view, should have the "same status" as the other provinces—thereby converting it into a Muslim-majority province instead of one in which all three groups would participate in local government on an equal basis. The government demanded special rights in the Croatian port of Ploče; provisions for the return of refugees; redefinition of the UNPROFOR mission as creating peace (*uspostavljanja mira*) rather than implementing the agreement (*provodjenja sporazuma*); region-wide demilitarization rather than demilitarization of Bosnia alone; and significant expansion of the proposed competencies of the central government. In light of these objections, President Izetbegović "accepted" the constitutional principles and cessation of hostilities agreement, but did not sign them. He continued to object to the map, stating in early February that "it had the effect of rewarding the ethnic cleansing that had taken place as it would leave military forces in areas from which populations had forcibly been removed and to which they could not return unless such forces were removed."[86] This question of the disposition of forces would be a vexing one for the negotiators. The territorial demands put forward by the Bosnian government in January 1993 are indicated in Map 5.6.

The Serbs were divided. On January 9 Milošević confronted a Bosnian Serb delegation in Belgrade and, according to a participant in the meeting, demanded that they accept the Vance-Owen plan. No agreement was reached, and the debate carried on to Geneva, where Milošević, Yugoslav president Dobrica Ćosić, and Panić again demanded that the Bosnian Serbs agree to the plan. According to the same participant, the argument dragged on into the early morning hours. Milošević threatened the Bosnian Serb delegation, but to no avail. Owen also reports witnessing such a confrontation in Geneva, perhaps the same one.[87] In the end, the Bosnian Serbs refused to agree to any of the proposals, informing the mediators of their stance on January 10.

The Bosnian Serbs accepted the Vance-Owen map only "as a basis for starting negotiations." Karadžić rejected outright the proposed constitutional principles because they precluded the establishment of a state-within-a-state for the Serbs and because the principles explicitly forbade the provinces from having any sort of "foreign relations," thereby preventing the Bosnian Serbs from one day claiming "special relations" with Serbia. The Bosnian Serbs also rejected the cessation of hostilities agreement. The

Map 5.6 **Bosnian Government–Proposed Changes to Vance-Owen Map, January 1993**

Adapted from *Oslobodjenje,* January 7, 1993; includes demands enumerated in *ibid.,* January 22, 1993.

co-chairs then set a deadline of January 12 for Karadžić to accept the plan. To their dismay, he announced his rejection of the plan on that day instead. Milošević then intervened once more, with the support of Čosić.[88] Within hours, Karadžić announced his acceptance of the plan, subject to approval by the Bosnian Serb Assembly. On January 20 the Assembly met and ostensibly approved the plan, but made clear that it had not changed its demands for a corridor linking Serb-held areas in the west and the east, and for Serb control over eastern Bosnia. One journalist characterized the meeting as "political theater."[89]

On January 23 Karadžić accepted the constitutional principles, but made clear his opposition to the map. He suggested that the population of disputed areas be consulted to determine the borders of the provinces. Because ethnic cleansing of these areas had already taken place, any referendum of the population in these areas would, of course, have ratified Serb control over them. For this reason, the co-chairs rejected this suggestion.[90] The support Milošević had shown for the plan now vanished, to be replaced by a calculated silence. The federal government of Yugoslavia, under the direction of Panić and Ćosić, continued to support the plan.

As the plan was modified under U.S. pressure to accommodate the Muslims, the support of Milošević became crucial to persuading the Bosnian Serbs to accept it. Milošević's motivations and intentions remained opaque during this period. The risk of intervention, if the plan was rejected by the Serbs, was slight. On the other hand, outrage and hostility toward the Serbs following reports of mass rapes, obstruction of the humanitarian effort, and the murder of the deputy prime minister of Bosnia at an illegal Serb roadblock in Sarajevo on January 9 had intensified. At the same time, a review of U.S. policy could be expected once the new administration assumed power in Washington later in January, raising the prospect that harsher sanctions might be applied against Yugoslavia. Accepting the Vance-Owen plan as proposed in early January thus posed few risks for Milošević and some potential political and public relations benefits. Accepting the plan also created opportunities for him to delay its implementation, a goal made clear as the result of the discussions at the Serb Assembly.

The co-chairs secured the agreement of all three sides to a set of constitutional principles late in January only by separating them from the map. The Croat and Serb leaders—Boban and Karadžić—also signed the military agreement. But Izetbegović now refused to do so, rescinding his earlier support and arguing that arrangements for the control of heavy weapons were inadequate.[91]

The failure to reach agreement on military issues reflected the unwillingness of each side to concede control over any territory. Discussions between the Muslims and the Croats over military cooperation, and even possible unification of their respective armies in Bosnia, had been taking place since June 1992.[92] Establishment of a joint command had been part of a July 1992 agreement on friendship and cooperation between Bosnia and Croatia, but no actual progress toward this goal had been achieved by the end of 1992. In January 1993, the Croats sought to resolve the issue of military deployments under the Vance-Owen plan by proposing that all military units in the provinces designated as Croat-majority provinces be placed under the control of the Bosnian Croat army (HVO) provincial command structures, and that these be unified under a single HVO command for all Croat-majority provinces. A parallel arrangement would be established in Muslim-majority provinces. The unified HVO and Bosnian army commands would then be integrated under a single military command for the republic as a whole, in Sarajevo. Such arrangements would clearly have accelerated the consolidation of Croat control over provinces eight and ten, and the *de facto* partition of the country. For this reason, the Muslims insisted that only a single unified command for all of Bosnia-Herzegovina be established above the level of the provinces.

While the disputes over the map and the military continued, the ICFY added important details to the plan for peace. At the insistence of the Muslim-dominated government, which—according to a participant in the negotiations—feared it might otherwise be replaced in any transitional period, the ICFY negotiators drafted arrangements for an interim government in Bosnia, for the period between the conclusion of the peace agreements and the holding of free and fair elections.[93] None of the proposed provinces was to be given over to the exclusive control of one or another group during the interim period. The January 1993 proposed Vance-Owen plan called for the distribution of leading government offices among all three groups in each of the provinces during the interim period, in rough accordance with their proportion of the population in 1991 (as indicated in Table 5.2). In Sarajevo province, each of the groups would enjoy equal representation. Interim governments would then be expected to draft local constitutions "by consensus" and prepare free and fair elections "on the basis of proportional representation," but take ordinary decisions on the basis of a "simple majority."[94] While it is clear that proportional representation was intended to ensure the representation of all groups, the specific provisions of the electoral law—on which the actual outcome of any elections would depend—remained to be worked out later. The plan for the interim period called for allowing existing local, or *opština*-level, authorities to remain intact.[95] To do so, however, would make implementation of the Vance-Owen plan extremely difficult in the absence of a powerful agency of enforcement.

An interim central government for Bosnia-Herzegovina as a whole, consisting of three representatives nominated by each of the three parties to the agreement, would take over the powers and authority of the Bosnian presidency until free and fair elections could be conducted. Confirmation of the nine members of the interim central government would be subject to the approval of the ICFY co-chairs. The January plan specified that the interim government (but not the future central government) would make its decisions on the basis of consensus, a change from the early draft of October 1992. In the event that the interim government could not reach a consensus, the issue in question would be referred to the co-chairs for resolution. The co-chairs would assist in the preparation of a new constitution for Bosnia-Herzegovina, and be available to assist the interim central government in its work.[96]

While the final shape of the provincial and republic governments could

Table 5.2

Vance-Owen Formulas for Ethnic Representation in Interim Provincial Governments

Province (no. and capital)	Governor	Vice-Governor	Distribution of Seats in Government		
			Muslim	Serb	Croat
1. Bihać	Muslim	Serb	7	2	1
2. Banja Luka	Serb	Muslim	2	7	1
3. Bosanski Brod	Croat	Serb	2	3	5
4. Bijeljina	Serb	Muslim	4	5	1
5. Tuzla	Muslim	Serb	5	3	2
6. Nevesinje	Serb	Muslim	2	7	1
7. Sarajevo	[none]	[none]	3	3	3
8. Mostar	Croat	Muslim	3	1	6
9. Zenica	Muslim	Croat	6	2	2
10. Travnik	Croat	Muslim	5	1	4

Source: UN Security Council document S/25221 (February 2, 1993), pp. 41–43.

be determined in important ways by decisions yet to be made about electoral laws and other important details, it was clear that negotiators were seeking to end the conflict through the application of principles of extreme devolution and consensual decision-making. By requiring consensus on constitutional principles and applying principles of proportionality to elections and to government offices, negotiators seem to have been seeking to encourage the kind of power-sharing arrangements described in chapter 1 and often cited by political scientists as solutions to ethnic conflict, but which had already failed in Yugoslavia.[97] The only basis for believing that this might succeed in Bosnia-Herzegovina appears to have been the co-chairs' insistence on imposing democratic accountability on Bosnian elites—and the hope that the mass population in Bosnia still remained less nationalistic than its leaders. But the co-chairs were unwilling to rely on such provisions alone. The interim arrangements for Bosnia-Herzegovina established the ICFY co-chairs as *de facto* international trustees of the Bosnian state. Consistent with this role, the co-chairs would appoint a representative who would reside in Sarajevo. The plan further called for international oversight or control over a number of civil functions, from civil police to road and railway administration.

The Vance-Owen plan represented an attempt to create internal boundaries that might satisfy demands for ethnic autonomy and make future attempts at secession more difficult. For example, they specifically avoided ceding all of eastern Bosnia to the Serbs, but did assign to them areas that separated Muslim Bosnia from the Muslim-populated Sandžak region of Serbia and Montenegro. At the same time, territories assigned to the Serbs in the west, around Banja Luka, remained separated from those in the east—in the initial proposal by a Croat-majority province and, in the revised plan (discussed below), by both the Croat province and a Muslim corridor to the Sava. Overall, the plan assigned 43 percent of Bosnian territory to Serb-majority provinces—substantially less than the approximately 70 percent of the republic held by the Bosnian Serb army at that time. The plan thus called for the Serbs to relinquish nearly 40 percent of the territory they were then holding.[98] The proposed formulas for creating interim governments in the provinces—if implemented—assured a Muslim-majority government in the strategically critical province five, in eastern Bosnia. Only the Croats, who were most heavily concentrated in western Herzegovina, directly bordering Croatia, were left well positioned by the Vance-Owen plan to secede—a result of the facts of Bosnian geography rather than the provisions of the plan or the political calculations of international negotiators.

Unlike the Cutileiro plan reported in chapter 3, the Vance-Owen plan limited the extent to which provinces might establish relations with neighboring states. They would be "allowed to enter into administrative arrangements with each other or with foreign States as long as the subject of the agreement was one within the exclusive competence of the province concerned and did not infringe on the rights of any other provinces or of the central Government." Given the broad powers of the provinces, this limitation was not as severe as it appeared at first glance. But, only the Republic of Bosnia-Herzegovina—not the provinces—was to have "international legal personality." Provinces would not be able to conclude "formal international treaties."[99] Thus, the Vance-Owen plan was designed to deny, or to lay the groundwork for reversing, what appeared to be the four most important war aims of the Bosnian Serbs: first, to establish a Serb entity or state-within-a-state in Bosnia-Herzegovina, consisting of a single, continuous territory that shared a common border with Serbia; second, to legitimate the "ethnic cleansing" of this territory; third, to win the right for this entity to unite with Serbia; and fourth, to reduce the powers of the central Bosnian government to insignificance.

Nonetheless, when the provisions of the plan became public, it was severely attacked in the United States for allegedly having given too much away to the Serbs. A former assistant under secretary of defense for policy planning in the Bush administration, Zalmay Khalilzad, argued that the plan "amounted to appeasement." *New York Times* columnist Anthony Lewis warned Washington to "beware of Munich,"[100] an analogy raised the previous day by Izetbegović.[101] Such criticisms reflected the frustrations felt by advocates of using force to put an end to the continuing abuses of the war—most of them being committed by the Serbs—rather than a realistic assessment of the plan itself or the constraints under which it was being negotiated. The most important deficiency of the Vance-Owen plan was the continuing absence of provisions for enforcement of its territorial, institutional, and legal provisions against those who might not comply with them. The plan was, after all, anathema to the Bosnian Serbs, who still dominated the military situation on the ground. However, the absence of enforcement provisions reflected the fact that those international actors capable of providing such support remained unwilling to commit themselves to implementing the plan, let alone enforcing it. Indeed, without direct and forceful pressure from the international community the warring parties would never agree to any enforcement provisions in the first place. Thus, the negotiators remained hampered most of all by the unwillingness of the United States to become involved in any form of intervention at this time.

Intensification of the international diplomatic effort to achieve a settlement in Bosnia took place during the last stages of the 1992 presidential election campaign in the United States and the prolonged period of transition between the November elections, in which the incumbent was defeated, and the inauguration of Bill Clinton as president in January 1993. U.S. policy, which under the Bush administration had opposed any U.S. involvement in the use of force in Bosnia, thus became temporarily frozen in place. In an interview featured prominently in the *New York Times* in September 1992, the chairman of the Joint Chiefs of Staff, Gen. Colin Powell, had effectively ruled out U.S. military involvement in Bosnia. In response to criticism of the Bush administration's inaction leveled by candidate Clinton, Powell argued that military force should be used only when a decisive victory is possible. He contended that it would be difficult to locate and destroy all of the Serb artillery, that by intervening Washington would be seen as taking sides in the conflict, and that the warring parties might respond by retaliating against personnel carrying out the UN relief effort. However, by ruling out the use of force in advance, General Powell also reduced the prospects of a political settlement. In the words of a former State Department official for human rights critical of the general's position, "In order to get the Serbs to negotiate seriously, we and our allies have to be prepared to use force."[102] But, while force might hasten the signing of a political agreement, it would not assure its implementation, short of a full-scale occupation of Bosnia by UN or NATO forces. Furthermore, hasty intervention in support of an unworkable plan might hasten partition rather than prevent it. The conflicting logic of these views thus seems to have created a "catch-22" dilemma for U.S. policymakers concerning the use of force.

A month later, the Bush administration reportedly did consider providing the Muslims with additional arms as a means of counterbalancing Serb military superiority, but it could not do so unilaterally without violating the UN arms embargo that the administration had itself helped to establish. The United States sought Security Council authorization to establish a "no-fly zone" over Bosnia, but this was essentially irrelevant in view of the nature of the conflict on the ground. At the December 1992 meeting of the ICFY Steering Committee in Geneva, the United States called for the convening of a Nuremberg-like tribunal to prosecute war crimes committed in Bosnia, a demand put forward by the United States and other participants at the London Conference in August. U.S. Secretary of State Lawrence Eagleburger identified a number of Croats, Muslims, and Serbs as war criminals, Milošević among them.[103] While this move could be justified on moral grounds, it complicated the ongoing negotiations still further, and contributed to the difficulties confronting the Clinton transition team, which was already planning the incoming administration's responses to the conflict.

As we noted earlier, Bill Clinton had argued for more forceful action in Bosnia-Herzegovina during the presidential campaign. Immediately upon taking office in January 1993, he ordered a full policy review by his principal foreign policy advisors. The review was animated by doubt that the ICFY negotiations could, in the words of Secretary of State–designate Warren Christopher, "find an agreement, find a solution that's peaceful that the parties would, in fact, agree to."[104] The administration may also have concluded that the complicated plan was unworkable—although this was not the publicly articulated reason for rejecting it. A long list of options was considered; some new, most already considered and rejected under the Bush administration. These included lifting the UN arms embargo in order to allow the United States and others to arm the Bosnian government, enforcement of the UN flight ban over Bosnia, more aggressive delivery of humanitarian aid, establishment of safe havens for refugees within Bosnia, tightening economic sanctions on Serbia, punitive air strikes against Serbian forces, establishment of a military cordon around Serbia to enforce sanctions, and various levels of direct military intervention.[105] According to a former deputy assistant secretary of defense for Europe and NATO, the administration also considered and rejected a proposal to permit border changes and population transfers—with compensation by an international agency. Policymakers rejected this approach because "it would aid and abet ethnic cleansing, while rewarding and legitimizing Serb aggression."[106]

The Clinton administration's early opposition to the Vance-Owen plan appeared to be based on a belief that the plan ratified ethnic partition.[107] It may also have been based on domestic political considerations on the part of the Clinton advisors, who, according to Owen, viewed Vance as "an 'old-style Democrat' and just what Clinton's 'new Democrats' want[ed] to put behind them."[108] Moreover, Owen's criticism of the new administration during a trip to the United States in early February 1993, which had been intended to influence American policymakers and public opinion in favor the Vance-Owen plan, backfired. It increased the new administration's resistance to the plan.[109]

In the end, however, a six-point plan announced by Secretary of State Christopher in mid-February did not substantially change U.S. policy, although some took it as a commitment to implement the Vance-Owen plan. Although the Clinton administration remained vocal in its criticism of the Vance-Owen plan, it was reluctant to become involved militarily on the ground in Bosnia and offered no viable alternative of its own. According to Secretary Christopher, the administration decided "to become actively and directly engaged in the multilateral effort to reach a just and workable resolution to this dangerous conflict" out of both humanitarian and strategic concerns. Humanitarian concerns included "the human toll" of the war associated with "Serbian 'ethnic cleansing'," and "atrocities . . . committed by other parties." Strategic concerns included the American interest in defending the principle that internationally recognized borders should not be altered by force, in preventing the conflict from becoming "a greater Balkan war," and in defending the rights of minorities.[110] The president appears also to have been concerned that a failure to act "would be to give up American leadership."[111]

According to Christopher, the six-point plan consisted of the following: First, the United States would participate actively in the ICFY process, by appointing an envoy to the talks. Second, the president would communicate to all three parties that "the only way to end this conflict is through negotiation." Third, the United States would tighten economic sanctions and increase political pressure on Serbia, which Christopher identified as an aggressor in the war. Fourth, the United States would address humanitarian needs. The fifth point concerned the crucial issue of enforcement, and the U.S. position was very carefully hedged. According to Secretary Christopher:

> The United States [is] prepared to do its share to help implement and enforce an agreement that is acceptable to all parties. If there is a viable agreement containing enforcement provisions, the United States would be prepared to

join with the United Nations, NATO, and others in implementing and enforcing it, including possible U.S. military participation.[112]

Clearly, the administration was fearful of being drawn into an open-ended
military commitment.[113] The secretary reported that the president had already "consulted widely with our friends and allies" and was seeking close
cooperation with the Russians, actions that constituted the sixth point of the
U.S. initiative.

According to a senior diplomat, the U.S. formally refused in the Security
Council to "endorse," "welcome," or "support" the Vance-Owen plan. This
blunt expression of opposition increased Bosnian government resistance to
a settlement. A European analysis argues that "signals coming from the
incoming Administration promising a firmer U.S. line and increased U.S.
involvement encouraged Izetbegović to wait for U.S. intervention."[114] In
negotiations in Geneva in late January, Izetbegović and Silajdžić seemed to
avoid opportunities to come to agreement. For example, the Bosnian Croats
and Serbs both signed the cessation of hostilities agreement that had been
hammered out in direct negotiations among the military commanders of all
three sides under the auspices of the Mixed Military Working Group of the
ICFY. But, as we noted earlier, although Izetbegović had previously agreed
to sign it, he now refused to do so.[115]

The co-chairs moved negotiations to New York in early February 1993
in order to increase their access to U.S. policymakers and bring the influence of supportive Security Council member states to bear on the parties.
Nonetheless, the Bosnian government delegation refused to meet with the
other two parties, or to discuss issues surrounding the map and the interim
central government.[116] The Clinton administration's stance led the negotiators to offer the Bosnian government important territorial concessions as an
incentive to negotiate. The co-chairs revised the proposed map so as to
grant the Muslim demand for access to the Sava river in the north by
extending the territory of a Muslim-majority province (number five, the
Tuzla province) northward.[117] According to a senior diplomat involved in
the negotiations, the Bosnian Muslims argued that they needed land on the
Sava river in order to enable them to export their products by sea. Since,
however, the Sava river flows through Belgrade, it is difficult to accept this
argument as explaining the Muslim position. Rather, it seems more likely
that, although the Serbs' vital northern corridor was already cut by a Croat-
majority province under the proposed Vance-Owen map, the Bosnian government was seeking a means to prevent the linkup of Serb territories even
if the Serbs and Croats were to "swap" territories they held inside Bosnia-
Herzegovina. This revised map (Map 5.7)—not the widely reproduced ini-

Map 5.7 **Revised Vance-Owen Map, February 1993**

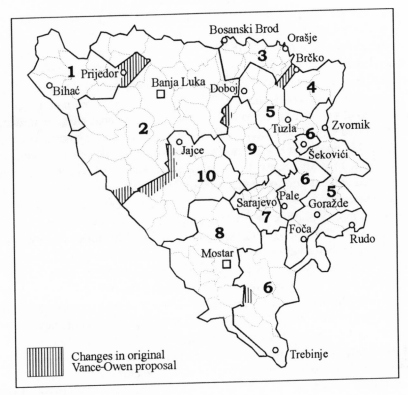

Based on UN Security Council document S/25248 (February 8, 1993), p. 9.

tial map (Map 5.5)—became the basis for further negotiations.[118] This decision by the co-chairs to sever the so-called northern corridor ensured that the Bosnian Serbs would reject the plan.

Milošević was equivocal. He persuaded the Bosnian Serbs to accept the constitutional principles, but did not pressure them publicly, at this stage, into accepting the map and other provisions of the agreement. Indeed, the position of the Yugoslav government and the Bosnian Serbs on the fate of province five—eastern Bosnia—was evasive, suggesting that both Belgrade and Pale were determined to keep the area, regardless of the fact that it would have a Muslim majority under both the initial and revised maps. This impression was reinforced when the Bosnian Serbs, with Belgrade's assistance, launched a major offensive in eastern Bosnia in March, designed to ensure Serb control of the area. Clearly, the fate of province five was a major unresolved issue, although one that none of the parties, including the negotiators, chose to parade in front of the media.

As we have seen, the decision by the United States finally to participate in the ICFY negotiations contributed to a stiffening of the Bosnian government position. The appointment of a special envoy, Ambassador Reginald Bartholemew, constituted a U.S. attempt to influence the outcome of the negotiations so as to make them more acceptable to the Muslims.[119] A European analysis reports that the U.S. envoy "was much more prone to act as a conduit for Izetbegović to put requests to the co-chairmen, thus giving them implicit U.S. backing," and "showed much greater enthusiasm for striking deals between Boban and Izetbegović than for negotiations with the Serbs." In early March, the U.S. envoy held direct talks with Izetbegović, conducted without prior consultation with U.S. allies or the ICFY co-chairs, over measures to be taken in the event that no settlement was reached. These measures included lifting of the arms embargo in case the Muslims signed but the Serbs did not. This further encouraged the Muslims to attach such conditions to their assent so as to ensure that the Serbs would not sign.[120]

ICFY negotiators had great difficulty overcoming the fundamental differences among the parties over the proposed interim arrangements for governing Bosnia. The Muslim-led government delegation formally objected to the provisions for consensual decisionmaking contained in the January draft cited earlier, arguing that they failed to provide "any solution to overcome blockades when consensus cannot be reached." They proposed instead that the existing (enlarged) presidency be ethnically "balanced" and that it then use the powers granted it by amendment LXXIII (1990) of the existing constitution to appoint an interim government.[121] The Serbs rejected any proposal that ratified the existing Bosnian constitution or government.[122] On March 3, under heavy pressure from the co-chairs, the Muslims and Croats reached agreement on a proposal calling for restructuring the existing presidency into a nine-member body with three representatives from each of the three constituent peoples that would

> take its decisions by consensus of nine, by a qualified majority of seven, or by a simple majority of five depending on whether the question relates to a constitutional principle, or specially important questions, or to normal business of the Presidency.[123]

This established Muslim-Croat agreement on a major issue. The Serbs, however, continued to resist any effort to preserve the existing presidency.

A formal agreement on interim arrangements, including the presidency and government, was signed by the Muslims and Croats on March 25, 1993, but rejected by the Serbs.[124] The agreement called for Bosnia and its provinces to be "governed under the prevailing legal system," a formulation that hedged on a commitment to preserve the existing constitution that was reported on March 12,[125] and left the question whether the interim presidency represented a continuation of the existing presidency open to conflicting interpretation. The March 25 agreement seemed to imply that the parliament elected in 1990 would be reinstated, as demanded by the Bosnian government. But both the Croats and the Serbs remained opposed to such a move.[126] The interim presidency would be composed of three representatives of each of the parties. As had been agreed on March 3, the presidency would have a limited role, and make its decisions on the basis of consensus (concerning constitutional principles), a qualified majority of seven (on "specially important questions"), and simple majority (in cases of "normal business"). The co-chairs retained the role of arbiters of presidential decision-making principles. The interim government would be composed of three ministers from each of the three constituent peoples. It would remain subject to extensive oversight by international actors (outlined above) to ensure application of the seventeen international human rights treaties and other instruments specifically enumerated in the plan. The revised plan called for the holding of free and fair elections within two years,[127] thus defining more precisely the anticipated duration of the interim arrangements. It was expected that this period would allow time for the return of refugees and displaced persons.

In the view of the co-chairs, the position of the Bosnian Serbs hardened in the period from January to March. By the time of the Croat-Muslim agreement of March 25, the Serbs opposed the creation of any central government at all and argued instead for the creation of three separate states.[128]

The agreement on interim arrangements of March 25 also called for a further revision of the map of provincial boundaries. The main result of this revision to the map (see Map 5.8) was to enlarge the province of Sarajevo, giving it a majority-Muslim population. The agreement called for an independent interim executive for the province, to be appointed by the three parties in proportion to their population. This ensured Muslim political control over the Sarajevo province.

The Bosnian Serbs objected to the proposed Vance-Owen map from the beginning, contending that "many predominantly Serb areas had been excluded from Serb majority provinces." They continued to propose that the populations of these areas be consulted as to border issues, but the co-chairs again rejected this on the grounds that "there had been so much ethnic cleansing and displacement of population in Bosnia and Herzegovina that it

Map 5.8 **Second Revised Vance-Owen Map, March 1993**

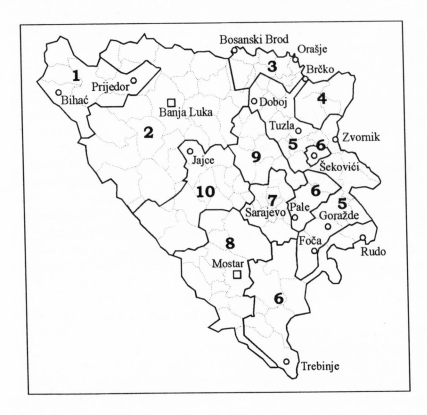

Based on UN Security Council document S/25479 (March 26, 1993), p. 24.

would be wholly impractical" to base decisions on the will of those currently residing in disputed areas. The Serbs also proposed "wholesale
changes" in eastern Bosnia. They proposed expanding province four to
encompass parts of five and the Šekovići enclave that was detached from,
but part of, province six; and they proposed expanding province six to
include the southern portion of province five (Map 5.9). It seems clear that,
despite the fact that the co-chairs considered the Serb proposal to expand
province four as having transformed a Serb-majority province into a
Muslim-majority province, the Serbs had no intention of giving up control
of the proposed new province, especially not after launching a major mili-

Map 5.9 **Bosnian Serb–Proposed Revisions (Eastern Bosnia), February 1993**

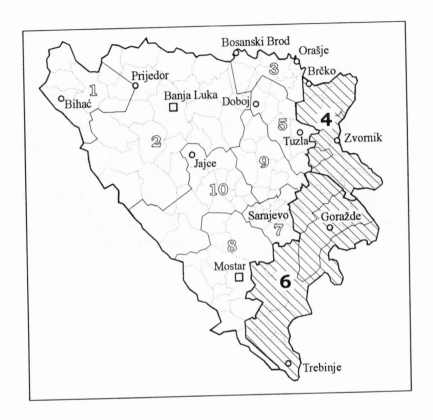

Based on UN Security Council document S/25248 (February 8, 1993), p. 8.

tary campaign against Bosnian forces in eastern Bosnia. The intent of the Serb proposals seems to have been to create consolidated—and militarily more easily defended—borders in the east, and to lay the basis for the creation of a large, territorially continuous Serb entity.[129] Despite increasingly strident Serb objections, negotiators in March 1993 defined the twice-modified map as the "basic document" to which "only marginal changes" could be made.[130]

The co-chairs rejected Serb efforts to legitimate the creation of three distinct, ethnically defined entities within Bosnia-Herzegovina by merging the Serb-majority provinces, as well as Serb efforts to prevent the establishment of central state institutions for all of Bosnia. They noted that such positions "would have the effect of convincing any fair-minded person that they [the Serbs] had no intention of living within the single state of Bosnia and Herzegovina." In light of Bosnian Serb opposition to key elements of the plan, the co-chairs concluded that "it was clear . . . that the position of the Bosnian Serbs had hardened appreciably since the Geneva round of negotiations in January on many of the political aspects of an overall settlement."[131] In mid-April, the co-chairs again opposed a Bosnian Serb effort to consolidate their holdings. The co-chairs cut short an attempt by Karadžić to initiate a swap with the Croats that would have broadened the territories assigned to the Serbs in the northern corridor.[132]

The interim arrangements agreed to by the Muslims and Croats on March 25 called for the withdrawal of armed forces to the respective provinces of each side. The co-chairs insisted that "there was no escaping the need for withdrawal of the Bosnian Serb armed forces from those parts of the territory of Bosnia and Herzegovina which they at present claimed for themselves and which lay outside the three provinces . . . in which the Serbs could expect to be the majority in the provincial government." They "rejected the Bosnian Serb suggestion that United Nations forces should be invited into the territory which they at present occupy outside these provinces but from which they would withdraw their forces." But they noted that "the territories involved would, under the proposal, remain under the administration and control of the Bosnian Serbs, with Serb police remaining."[133] What this potentially major concession to the Serbs would mean in practice, however, was initially unclear.

The military status of territories to be relinquished by the Serbs under the plan was a difficult and critical issue. Clearly, if Bosnian government troops were to be allowed to occupy these territories, the Bosnian Serbs would be denied any opportunity to create the territorially continuous entity they sought. At the same time, Bosnian government control over areas previously occupied by the Serbs seemed critical to the survival of Bosnia-Herzegovina as a state. In order to make the plan more palatable to the Serbs, the co-chairs now appeared to be promising them that they could retain local authority even inside a Muslim-majority province, a promise that seemed on its face consistent with the earlier stipulation that local (opština) authorities would remain in place. But, according to the text of the March 25 version of the interim arrangements, local police units were to be subordinated to provincial authorities, and were to reflect the ethnic composition of the province as a whole—presumably, as recorded in the 1991 census. This meant that in Muslim-majority provinces from which Serb forces were to be withdrawn, local police would be under the control of the Muslim-majority provincial government, while local governments would remain in the hands of the Serbs wherever they constituted a local majority.[134] The reassurances offered by the co-chairs to the Bosnian Serbs thus seemed to contradict the actual provisions of the plan.

The provisions of the interim arrangements dealing with military withdrawal called for province seven (Sarajevo) to be "immediately demilitarized." Serb forces were to withdraw into provinces two (the Bosanska Krajina, or Banja Luka region), four (the Bijeljina region in northeast Bosnia), and six (eastern Herzegovina). Croat forces were to withdraw into province three (the Posavina, or northern corridor region). In provinces five (eastern Bosnia), eight (western Herzegovina and south-central Bosnia), nine (north-central Bosnia), and ten (western Herzegovina and central Bosnia), both Bosnian and Croat forces were to be deployed, "under arrangements agreed between them."[135] These formulations left the Muslims without undisputed control over any province into which they could withdraw their troops from Sarajevo. They suggested that little progress on a withdrawal agreement had been achieved since January, and that neither the Croats nor the Muslims were willing to give up territory, regardless of what province it fell to under the Vance-Owen plan. Indeed, publication of the revised Vance-Owen map on March 26 was followed on April 15 or so by the resumption of fighting between the Muslims and the Croats in central Bosnia.

The Croats would have agreed to Bosnian Muslim military control over province five in exchange for Muslim agreement to cede military control of provinces eight and ten. But the Serbs would have been unlikely to accept such an arrangement. It would have led to the entry of primarily Muslim government forces into areas earmarked, according to the assurances of the co-chairs noted above, for Serb police and civilian administration. Thus, it seemed as though the distribution of forces among the provinces would have depended heavily on arrangements made among the parties themselves; hardly a reassuring prospect if the interim arrangements for Bosnia were to function as intended.

The Bosnian Croats and Muslims could not come to any agreement on their own. Immediately following the signing of the March version of the interim plan, Izetbegović traveled to Zagreb for additional negotiations to work out unresolved issues with the Croats, including military cooperation. Once again, the Croats pressed for control over the military in Croat-majority provinces and the creation of a separate HVO command for these provinces. Now, however, according to one account in the independent Croatian press, it appeared that their proposal enjoyed the backing of Vance and Owen—a position that would have been consistent with the pattern of favoring Croat interests that began to emerge in December 1992. Nonetheless, the Bosnians rejected it.[136] Thus, by early April, the March 25 agreement between the Croats and Muslims was already unraveling.

The Muslim-dominated Bosnian government was no more enthusiastic about the Vance-Owen plan in March 1993 than the Serbs, but for quite different reasons. The government qualified its acceptance of the March 25 interim arrangements by entering into the record its reservations.[137] The government stated that "regardless of the fact whether or not all parties will sign the documents today, the Delegation of Bosnia and Herzegovina considers that the International Community was and will remain obligated to protect the independence and the territorial integrity of Bosnia and Herzegovina as an attacked country." It stipulated that "our signatures on the proposed documents will become invalid and will be considered null and void if . . . all interested parties, especially the aggressor side does not sign the documents without any alterations or reservations within a reasonable time frame" and "[if] the International Community does not undertake, within [sic] a timely fashion the [sic] effective measures of implementation of the signed agreement." It further affirmed that Bosnia-Herzegovina "will not surrender its legitimate right to self defense in accordance with Article 51 of the UN Charter," an affirmation made more significant by the fact that the interim agreement appeared not to grant the Muslims undisputed military control over any of the provinces. The Bosnian government warned that if the plan failed it would "undertake all necessary measures to defend its people, and . . . expect the Security Council without further delay to lift the arms embargo on Bosnia and Herzegovina." Such an expectation may have been encouraged by Izetbegović, who told the Bosnian government that he had "received assurances that the United States will do everything . . . in their power to help lift the arms embargo if the aggression continues."[138] Thus, confident that the Serbs would not agree to the plan, the Bosnian Muslims extended only qualified agreement to it.

The Bosnian government may also have been encouraged to sign on to the plan by the February statement of U.S. willingness to participate in implementing and enforcing an agreed plan, and by the evidence of NATO preparations to do so. Secretary-General Boutros-Ghali was resisting UN involvement in an enforcement mission, and arguing for the deployment of a U.S.-led multinational force instead.[139] Former senior officials of previous administrations were publicly pressuring the Clinton administration to take unilateral military action in Bosnia.[140] The United States was reportedly urging NATO to prepare a force of 50,000–70,000 for deployment,[141] despite the fact that the co-chairs had estimated that implementing their plan would require the deployment of only 15,000–25,000 troops.[142] The Bosnians' agreement also appears to have been secured under pressure from the Croats. Owen reports that the Bosnian Croats threatened Izetbegović that they would withdraw their military support for the Muslims if the government did not sign.[143]

While the Americans focused their efforts on representing Muslim interests, the French attempted to encourage Serbian president Milošević to support the plan. French president Mitterrand met with Milošević in Paris in March and, according to Owen, promised that if the map were accepted, "then sanctions must and should be lifted as soon as technically feasible." According to this account, Mitterrand assured Milošević that France would convince others, such as German Chancellor Kohl, to support this position: "France would 'fight and win the battle to lift sanctions'."[144] By April, Milošević appeared to be ready to accept the Vance-Owen plan. His actions appear to have been motivated by clear self-interest: the desire to have existing sanctions lifted, and to avoid implementation of more stringent transport and financial sanctions, eventually adopted as Security Council Resolution 820 of April 17 and scheduled for implementation on April 26. Yet, as we shall see, Milošević refused to commit himself publicly to supporting the plan until the status of eastern Bosnia and other Muslim-majority areas ethnically cleansed by the Serbs was resolved in further negotiations with Lord Owen.

The United States sought to pressure the Bosnian Serbs into agreeing to the Vance-Owen plan by strengthening economic sanctions against Serbia. The Russians, however, opposed the American inclination to act against the Serbs. Russia abstained from the vote on Resolution 820, which called for the tightening of sanctions against Yugoslavia, and made clear its opposition to the use of force against the Serbs. During the Vancouver summit in early April the Russians argued that to act against the Serbs would strengthen Russian nationalist opposition to the Russian constitutional referendum scheduled for April 25. In deference to Yeltsin, the United States agreed to delay implementation of UN sanctions against Yugoslavia until April 26. Thus, the economic incentives for Milošević to back the Vance-Owen plan increased in April.

Still, Milošević stopped short of giving his public support to the Vance-Owen plan. In the meantime, in the first three weeks in April, the battle for Srebrenica brought NATO into the Bosnian crisis. Lord Owen, in his frustration over Serb attacks in eastern Bosnia, was moved to call on April 16 for air strikes against Bosnian roads and bridges to interdict supplies coming from Serbia.[145] Several days later, the media were reporting that full-scale war had broken out between the Muslims and Croats in central Bosnia. At about the same time, Karadžić queried the Croats as to the territory they might accept in exchange for turning control of the Posavina, or northern corridor, over to the Serbs—a deal that Vance and Owen moved quickly to prevent.[146] In his reports on central Bosnia, John Burns of the *New York Times* concluded that Vance-Owen was now a dead letter.[147] It was under these circumstances that Milošević agreed, in a meeting with Lord Owen on April 25, to throw his support behind the plan.

Milošević's behavior at this point requires explanation. The increase in Muslim-Croat fighting in central Bosnia in April would seem to have presented the Serbs with an unprecedented opportunity to expand their grip over most of Bosnia. One would have anticipated increased Serb intransigence in dealing with the ICFY. In fact, however, the Serb strategy called for gaining international acceptance of what they had won already, not further territorial aggrandizement. Milošević's delay in openly supporting the Vance-Owen plan could be explained by the Serbian president's unwillingness to take a politically unpopular step until he could demonstrate that the international community had left him no choice. Milošević may also have waited to the last moment in the hope that the Russians would block imposition of tougher sanctions on Yugoslavia. Owen was of the opinion that U.S. threats of military action might have concentrated Milošević's mind, but it was the threat of economic sanctions that finally persuaded him to go along with the plan.[148] But, while Milošević faced multiple pressures to make concessions, so did Lord Owen: the prospects for the Vance-Owen plan were unraveling both because of the fighting in central and eastern Bosnia and because of the continuing lack of U.S. support. Thus the stage was set for a deal between Owen and Milošević.

This seems to be the background for what transpired on April 23. Silber and Little report that Owen met with Milošević in Belgrade on April 23 and assured him that "a serious UN force" (later specified as Russian) would be deployed to police the strategically important northern corridor and, more important, assured him that territories then under Bosnian Serb control but destined under the plan to become part of Muslim- or Croat-majority provinces would be policed by UN, and not Muslim or Croat, forces. Silber and Little also suggest that Owen assured Milošević that—contrary to the provisions of the agreement between the Muslims and Croats brokered by the ICFY (detailed above)—decisions of the interim Bosnian presidency would be taken by consensus, thus giving the Serbs a veto.[149] Owen himself reports that the co-chairs were also prepared to agree that "in areas where the Serbian army had to be withdrawn and where they had been defending Serbian villages, as far as practical we would ensure that there was no deployment of the opposing military whether the Bosnian army or the [Croat] HVO."[150] He also reports that in a meeting with Milošević, Ćosić, and Mladić in Belgrade on April 23 he reminded them of "the idea of allowing only UN troops to go into areas where Serb forces had to withdraw from Serb villages and thus prevent the entry of Bosnian Muslim soldiers into previously fought over territory." According to a report by Mirko Klarin of *Borba,* the deal was closed on April 25, after Owen returned to Belgrade from discussions in Zagreb with the Bosnians and the Croatians. Milošević then gave his blessing to the Vance-Owen plan.[151]

The April 25 accord represented a major concession to the Serbs in comparison to the actual provisions of the March 26 version of the plan, but was close to the position expressed by the co-chairs at that time, cited earlier. The deployment of UN forces to police territories "relinquished" by the Bosnian Serbs but still administered by them would have prevented the deployment of Bosnian army troops to much of province five and thereby would have left eastern Bosnia, much of the northern corridor, and Serb-occupied areas of Sarajevo province under *de facto* Serb control. (Whether this meant that UN troops would take the place of Serbian police is unclear.) At that time (April 1993), the consequences of the UN deployment in the UNPAs in Croatia would have provided strong evidence to support such an interpretation on the part of the Serbs. Milošević's support for the Vance-Owen plan thus may very well have reflected such an assessment. According to Silber and Little, Karadžić reported at the time that Milošević told him the plan could be accepted because it would be impossible to implement.[152] Indeed, the complexity, and apparently contradictory nature, of these formal and informal arrangements regarding the military status of disputed and strategically critical territories provided good reason to believe that the plan could not have been implemented easily, even if all parties had agreed to it. With the fierce fighting between the Muslims and Croats in central Bosnia in April, it increasingly appeared that partition was becoming inevitable.

Owen attempted to bring the fighting between the Muslims and Croats to an end. Following his meetings in Belgrade on April 23, Owen traveled to Zagreb on April 24 to meet with Boban and Izetbegović and their military commanders, Milivoj Petković and Šefer Halilović. With Tudjman present, Owen negotiated a cease-fire, and an agreement to begin military cooperation between the Muslims and Croats in Bosnia.[153] However, the agreement to establish a joint Muslim-Croat command called for the preservation of "separate identities and command structures" for the Bosnian and Croat (HVO) armies, and the establishment of military districts "whose areas will be related to the operational requirement for joint operations and not to provisional provincial boundaries. Their areas will not overlap."[154] Thus, neither side agreed to relinquish control over any territory, and fighting between the Muslims and Croats continued.

The Bosnian Serbs took a much harder line toward the Vance-Owen plan than Milošević. At a meeting of their parliamentary assembly April 2 in Bijeljina, Karadžić had argued that the map was unacceptable because "the lack of communication between the various Serbian components and with Yugoslavia itself would create a series of Serbian 'Nagorno Karabakhs,' surrounded by enemies and a constant source of instability and war." He had also questioned the economic viability of the Serb-designated provinces. According to Karadžić, they included only 43 percent of the republic and none of the important river basins, excluded areas where the population was predominantly Serb, and denied the Serbs important economic resources, including power stations.[155]

Karadžić's objections closely paralleled the conclusions of an independent Slovenian analysis of the plan, first published in Ljubljana and republished in Sarajevo in mid-March.[156] The Slovenian analysis predicted that the Bosnian Serbs would not accept the plan because (1) the territories assigned to them were geographically discontinuous; (2) they were denied the main industrial and mining areas, including defense industries, as well as hydroelectric power plants; (3) they were left without coherent transport and communications networks; (4) they would have to give up 24 (in fact, almost 40) percent of the land they then occupied; (5) they would lose control of militarily strategic locations and most of their territory would be subject to strategic encirclement by the Muslims and Croats; (6) they would lose control of the heavy weapons that allowed them to counterbalance manpower and geostrategic advantages of the Muslims and Croats; and (7) the plan called for them to allow the return of refugees to ethnically "cleansed" areas.

The Bosnian Serb assembly then voted decisively to reject the Vance-Owen map, even after Karadžić warned that rejection might lead to the use of force by the international community. Secretary of State Christopher's February 1993 statement had made it clear, however, that the commitment of U.S. ground troops to Bosnia was contingent on the conclusion of a viable agreement acceptable to all the warring parties. Ironically, therefore, the Bosnian Serbs could prevent Western intervention by rejecting such a settlement. Indeed, despite reports in early March that the United States was urging NATO to prepare for a large-scale intervention,[157] and despite the fact that U.S. military personnel in NATO had already been "quietly" carrying out "serious planning for implementation" for some time,[158] no action was taken as the Bosnian Serbs pursued their military offensive in March and April and overran besieged Muslim towns in eastern Bosnia.

The Serb offensive against Srebrenica, described in chapter 4, led some influential figures in the West to urge abandoning the Vance-Owen plan and to call for the use of force against the Serbs instead. In late April, former national security advisor to President Carter, Zbigniew Brzezinski, attacked the plan as "appeasement" and called for bombing the Serbs as aggressors.[159] Some may have discounted this criticism as a possible reflection of past enmity between Brzezinski and Vance, dating back to their roles in the Carter administration. But, a few days later, former secretary of state George Shultz called for bombing the Serbs in both Bosnia and Serbia, arguing that "when you try to conduct diplomacy without power and the other side is using force, you wind up making a fool of yourself."[160] These and other advocates of the use of force directed their fury exclusively against the Serbs, an understandable response to the ethnic cleansing and atrocities being carried out by the Serbs. But they ignored the three-dimensional character of the conflict made clear by the continuous fighting between Bosnian Croats and Muslims. Such public pressure and, perhaps, the increasingly complex situation on the ground, undoubtedly helped to push the administration into abandoning the Vance-Owen plan.

As we have seen in chapter 4, at the height of the Srebrenica crisis, the United States made threats to use force. President Clinton first confirmed that air strikes were under consideration if the Serbs did not halt their attacks on Srebrenica on April 16, then again on April 23, and finally on May 2, giving the impression to many observers that air strikes might be imminent. In his testimony to the Senate Appropriations Committee on April 27, Secretary of State Christopher set four conditions on the use of force: an exit strategy, clearly stated goals, strong likelihood of success, and public support.[161] As we noted above, the Serb attack on Srebrenica had also prompted Owen to call on April 16 for air strikes against the Serbs.[162] But his call for the use of force should be understood primarily as a plea to impose the Vance-Owen plan on the warring parties. While the Clinton administration was apparently moving toward a decision to use force, it was at the same time finally abandoning the Vance-Owen plan. Hence, it would have to come up with a political strategy of its own for ending the conflict if the use of force was to be effective. But no such American alternative to the Vance-Owen plan was proposed. In the end, therefore, the administration backed away from using air power.

The Serb assembly, meeting once again in Bijeljina, voted against the Vance-Owen plan again early in the morning on April 26, after a long debate. They did so despite a lengthy letter from Milošević, Montenegrin president Momir Bulatović, and Yugoslav president Dobrica Ćosić urging them to accept the plan. The letter was drafted late the night before, after a six-hour meeting with Owen, Karadžić, and Krajišnik. It reported on the results of the "detailed, lengthy and very difficult talks" with Lord Owen on April 23. It confirmed the concessions on consensual decision making in the Bosnian interim presidency intended to assuage the Bosnian Serbs. On the critical issue of troop deployments the letter stated that units of the HVO and Muslims would not be permitted on territory where Serbs live outside Serb provinces. Only UN forces would enter these areas. The letter suggested, however, that the northern corridor issue remained unresolved.

In a reflection of the importance of sanctions in Milošević's calculations, the letter asserted that the Bosnian Serb leaders had "no right to expose to danger and international sanctions 10 million citizens of Yugoslavia merely because of the remaining open issues, which are of far lesser importance than the results achieved so far." The three presidents claimed the "same right" as the Bosnian leaders "to pass decisions of significance for the Serb nation," and reminded the Bosnians that the proposed plan represented an "honorable peace."[163] But their efforts remained fruitless, as the Bosnian Serb assembly voted 77–0 to reject the Vance-Owen plan.[164]

In a final effort to salvage the plan, following a telephone call from Milošević on April 29, negotiators convened a meeting with all the Bosnian parties plus Milošević, Ćosić, and Tudjman in Athens on May 1–2. Karadžić was subjected to intense pressure throughout the night and into the early morning from Milošević, Bulatović, and Ćosić. Vance is reported to have told Karadžić that "this is the last chance café, that the US air force is all prepared to turn Bosnia and Serbia into a wasteland."[165] Karadžić gave in to this pressure and agreed to all elements of the proposal. Owen attempted to reconcile the disparities between versions of the interim arrangements previously agreed between the Muslims and the Croats and the assurances he had given privately to Milošević.[166] Owen declared that the interim presidency would adopt its rules of procedure by consensus while voting majorities would vary with the subject matter. When the presidency disagreed over the procedure to be followed, the choice of voting rule would be left to the ICFY co-chairs. Owen thus qualified the commitment to a consensus rule he reportedly gave to Milošević in Belgrade, and Milošević gave to the Bosnian Serbs in the letter cited above. With respect to the disposition of forces, Owen promised that UN troops would protect Serb towns and villages in areas from which the Bosnian Serb army would be withdrawn. While no major changes to the map were possible, the Athens agreement provided that "it will be possible for villages or towns that feel they have been wrongly placed on one side or other of the provisional boundary to have their positions reviewed"; and that the northern corridor would consist of a UN-controlled throughway flanked on either side by a five-kilometer-wide, UN-controlled demilitarized zone and manned by mobile combat-ready troops drawn from Europe, North America, and the Russian Federation.

Despite these "clarifications" to the plan intended to address Serb concerns, Karadžić's signature was nullified within days by the Bosnian Serb assembly, the third time they had rejected the plan in little more than a month. Milošević personally argued with members of the assembly in support of the plan, but was unable to overcome the opposition. The delegates turned decisively against the plan when Mladić displayed a series of maps highlighting the extensive amount of territory the Serbs would have to relinquish if the plan were implemented, and reassured the delegates that "his men were not afraid of Western intervention."[167] The assembly then decided to hold a referendum on the fate of the plan. When the referendum was held May 15–16, the Bosnian Serbs voted overwhelmingly to reject the Vance-Owen plan.[168]

Milošević's support for the version of the Vance-Owen plan that emerged from his talks with Owen at the end of April suggests that he still saw support for the plan as a means by which to secure the lifting of sanctions against Yugoslavia (Serbia and Montenegro), although Karadžić alleged that Owen had made it clear during meetings in Belgrade with Bosnian Serb and Serbian leaders that agreement over Bosnia-Herzegovina would not bring an end to sanctions.[169] At a minimum, Milošević hoped to prevent tighter sanctions from going into effect. By supporting the plan personally in the Bosnian Serb Assembly, Milošević seems to have demonstrated his commitment to it. That he failed to win the day suggests that he either underestimated the depth of Bosnian Serb sentiments, or had been misled by Mladić. If, however, Milošević himself did not actually support the plan, or understood in advance that it would be rejected, he may have chosen to sacrifice some of his personal prestige in the mistaken belief that by doing so he would gain Western support for the lifting of sanctions, or prevent their tightening, despite rejection of the plan. Bosnian Serb rejection of the plan still left him free to pursue Serbian interests in Bosnia and Krajina.

The former, less cynical, view seems more persuasive in light of the progressive deterioration in relations between Milošević and the Bosnian Serb leadership that began in January, and Milošević's later abandonment of support for both the Croatian and the Bosnian Serbs in the hope of lifting sanctions against Yugoslavia. Following rejection of the Vance-Owen plan by the Bosnian Serb assembly, Belgrade instituted a partial embargo against the Bosnian Serb republic, and called for the Bosnian Serbs to cancel the referendum. On May 14, a meeting of Serb legislators from all regions except Bosnia was held in Belgrade in support of the peace plan.[170] Bitter attacks on Karadžić began to appear in the regime press in Belgrade.[171] Following rejection of the Vance-Owen plan by the Bosnian Serbs in the May 15–16 referendum, Belgrade's campaign against the Bosnian Serbs slackened. Milošević, backed by Čosić, rejected the plan to deploy UN monitors to observe the Serbian blockade of the Bosnian Serb republic.[172]

Although it was hardly noticed in the heat of the debate over sanctions, air strikes, and the fate of the Vance-Owen plan, the United States was finally able, in the crisis atmosphere that prevailed, to gain UN approval for implementation of UN Resolution 781 prohibiting the use of Bosnian airspace by the combatants. The resolution had been adopted October 9, 1992. Efforts to implement the ban had been resisted by the Europeans and Russians. Initially the Serbs failed to comply with Resolution 781, but when President Bush announced that the United States would participate in enforcing the no-fly resolution, the Serbs grounded their aircraft. Still, the Serbs remained defiantly opposed to active implementation of the ban. On December 24, Karadžić had threatened a "declaration of war" against UNPROFOR if the ban was enforced.[173] General Lars-Eric Wahlgren, commander of UN troops in the Balkans, expressed opposition to enforcement of the ban on the basis that such a step could endanger the humanitarian aid program.[174]

The Europeans, in response to the Serb offensive in Eastern Bosnia, dropped their objections to the implementation of the ban on military flights over Bosnia in the middle of March 1993.[175] The Russians gave way soon thereafter, setting the stage for adoption of Security Council Resolution 816 on March 31, which authorized active implementation of the flight ban. Resolution 816 allowed NATO craft to shoot down planes violating the no-fly zone over Bosnia; following adoption of appropriate measures by NATO on April 2, enforcement was to go into effect April 12. Under the rules adopted by NATO, those violating the flight ban would first be warned, and Serb ground forces could not be attacked. The Serb response—the shelling of civilians in Srebrenica—has been described in chapter 4.

The Death of the Vance-Owen Plan and the U.S. Proposal for "Lift and Strike"

Even before the Serbs finally rejected the Vance-Owen plan, the Clinton administration had decided to support lifting the arms embargo against the Bosnian government. In late March senior policymakers had begun to debate lifting the arms embargo as "a cost-free way for the United States to have an effect on the war." Chairman of the Joint Chiefs Gen. Colin Powell was reportedly against any use of U.S. ground troops, and challenged the use of air power by asking, "If we bomb Serb military targets in Bosnia and that doesn't bring them to the conference table, then what?" This proved impossible to answer.[176] In mid-April, senior policymakers refined their options, leaving the administration with a choice between lifting the arms embargo and using air power to protect the Muslims while they were armed, and a cease-fire with protection of Muslim enclaves.[177] As we have already noted, the president confirmed publicly on April 16 that air strikes were, in fact, under consideration. But no decision had yet been made.

Owen warned that a confrontation with the West was inevitable, and that the Bosnian Serbs would be punished economically, politically, and "in my view, militarily, within the context of the UN Charter." Indeed, British and French officials were reported by U.S. media to be ready to go along with President Clinton's call for "a stronger policy," which one senior U.S. official defined as a program of limited bombing designed to achieve a cease-fire in place and a new round of negotiations. But several options were reportedly "on the president's desk."[178]

President Clinton remained undecided as to the precise option to pursue and was receiving contradictory advice from congressional and military sources.[179] In the end, the president's closest advisers, including Gen. Powell, were reported to support arming the Bosnians and using air power to protect them while they received weapons and training.[180] After an apparently vigorous internal debate that culminated in a five-hour-long meeting of senior policymakers on May 1,[181] the administration adopted this option—a strategy that was to become known as "lift and strike."

This approach was controversial even within the U.S. military, and brought to the fore differences in views between ground and air force commanders. Air Force Chief of Staff Gen. Merrill A. McPeak testified to the Senate Appropriations Committee in late April that there would be "virtually no risk to American pilots." But Army Lt. Gen. Barry McCaffrey, the new strategic planner for the Joint Chiefs of Staff, testified that air strikes would "be quite a severe challenge for the use of air power," and that he saw no military solution. Marine Corps Maj. Gen. John Sheehan told the committee that he did not see how victory could be achieved without ground troops. Air Force Maj. Gen. Michael Ryan warned that after the first air attack Serb artillery would go into hiding, taking advantage of the terrain and making the task of destroying them much more difficult; without follow-up by ground forces they would just ride out any bombing.[182]

Lifting the embargo was strongly opposed by the Russians and the French. French foreign minister Juppé made it clear that France would withdraw its troops from UNPROFOR in the event the embargo were lifted. The military option was also fraught with domestic political risks for the administration. Meeting with congressional leaders on April 30, President Clinton was advised that there would be no politically acceptable way to withdraw from engagement. Once the United States enters a war, he was warned, it becomes a U.S. war and the United States cannot afford to fail. One Democratic lawmaker reported after the meeting that the president was told: "The republic will survive, but his presidency will be badly damaged. If you decide to go, you have to prevail. And if the steps you take are insufficient to achieve your objectives, then you have to increase the steps you take." Republican Senator Richard Lugar reported that he and Republican Senator Robert Dole warned that there was no such thing as a no-cost or low-cost war: "We took a very strong position that the United States must not lose. As Republicans our advice was that the President was going to suffer substantially if in fact this doesn't work out well, that people will not be generous and he ought to anticipate that."[183] Indeed, a later account of this meeting suggests that one Democratic leader cautioned the president that the Republicans would use any negative outcome—even the damage inflicted on civilians that inevitably accompanies any bombing campaign—to domestic political advantage.[184]

Nonetheless, the president was reported to have "decided in principle" on May 1—while the Athens meeting was in progress and before the Bosnian Serbs had again rejected the plan—"to commit American air power to help bring an end to the fighting."[185] The U.S. proposal was characterized by one of the president's "chief advisors" as "the least bad thing we could come up with in a situation where we think we have to do something."[186] One "top policymaker" described the decision to Elizabeth Drew in the following terms: "The basic strategy was, this thing is a no-winner, it's going to be a quagmire. Let's not make it our quagmire. That's what lift the arms embargo, and the limited air strikes, was about."[187]

What, precisely, the administration was proposing to use force *for* was clouded in ambiguity.[188] The president referred in his May 1 statement to both humanitarian and national interest concerns, but did not clarify the conditions under which air strikes might be launched.[189] Secretary of State Christopher, declaring that "the Serbs know that they have exhausted the patience of the international community," announced that the "clock is ticking." He demanded that the Serbs stop shelling cities, honor the cease-fire to which they had already agreed, and allow humanitarian aid to move freely. He suggested that the decision to use air power was motivated by "issues of conscience and humanitarian concerns," but "fundamentally" by "the strategic interest of the United States . . . to limit the risk of a widening instability that could lead to a greater Balkan war."[190]

The *New York Times* reported on May 4 that Clinton had confirmed U.S.

readiness to commit troops to implement Vance-Owen; according to the *Times*, the first such explicit commitment made by the Clinton administration.[191] Both the *Washington Post* and the *New York Times* published detailed reports of alleged NATO plans for deployment.[192] These called for 60,000 troops, one-third of which would be American. They were to engage in aggressive use of force, including the suppression of opposition. The alleged NATO plans also called for reconstruction of physical infrastructures and social and political systems. The NATO plan estimated that deployment would last one year, despite warnings from the CIA that it would likely become an open-ended commitment. The UN commander in Bosnia was reported already planning to hand over operations to NATO.[193] But the U.S. commander of NATO's Southern Command reported that troops would not be dispatched until organized fighting had stopped.[194]

The linkage between Serb actions and the level of force the United States would employ was made explicit by an administration official who reported that if there was a "good faith effort" by the Bosnian Serb parliament to enforce the agreement in the next few days, then the Security Council could authorize the use of force and NATO would be ready to arrive in Bosnia within seventy-two hours. If this did not pan out, the official continued, then the United States would go back to the "stronger military steps option." Christopher warned that if the Serbs accepted the Vance-Owen plan, but continued to attack Žepa in eastern Bosnia, the Europeans would be ready to back sterner measures proposed by the United States.[195] In light of the debate within the administration aired in the media, one could reasonably assume that were the United States to have embarked on the use of force at this time, it would have lifted the arms embargo against the Bosnian government while launching air strikes at Bosnian Serb military targets, although this was not spelled out in the president's statement of May 1, or in the explanations that accompanied the announcement.[196]

Confusion over what air strikes were meant to achieve was compounded by the fact that the policy of "lift and strike" had been roundly denounced by the British and the French, who were concerned that its implementation would not only expose their peacekeeping troops to retaliatory attack, but would also widen the war. If the proposed steps failed to deter the Serbs, or encouraged the Muslims to launch new offensives, this would escalate and prolong the conflict, and increase the likelihood of spillover into neighboring countries. Outside powers, including NATO member states, might be drawn into the fighting. The European Community appeared willing to accept the *status quo* rather than become more deeply involved militarily, or risk escalation and spillover. Moreover, the U.S. proposal did not appear to be defined in terms of a particular outcome, the achievement of which would signal the end of Western military involvement.[197] Fear of becoming tied down in a prolonged conflict with no clear strategy for disengagement would lead to later demands by U.S. congressional actors for the articulation of a clear "exit strategy" as part of any proposal for U.S. involvement.

Secretary of State Christopher traveled to Europe immediately after the conclusion of the May 1 policy meeting. His trip came after the Athens talks had concluded, but before the Bosnian Serb assembly had the opportunity to reject the Vance-Owen plan once again. He presented the U.S. "lift and strike" proposal to the European allies. The Europeans proposed instead to establish and defend "safe areas" in Bosnia-Herzegovina, a proposal rejected by Christopher. In the American view, "safe areas" would facilitate ethnic cleansing by encouraging Muslims to abandon Serb-held territories. Moreover, they would require additional ground troops to provide protection. The Europeans already were pressing Christopher for U.S. troops to participate in existing operations. The adoption of a "safe areas" approach would increase that pressure and raise the prospect of U.S. troops being drawn into ground combat, which the Clinton administration sought to avoid.[198]

The failure of Christopher to convince the Europeans to adopt the "lift and strike" approach undermined the credibility of the U.S. threat to use force against the Serbs. By the time the Serb parliament met on May 5–6 it was clear that the U.S. was not ready to act unilaterally against the Serbs, and that the Europeans were resisting any effort to use air strikes, if only out of concern for their own forces on the ground. Responsibility for the failure of the Christopher mission was placed on the secretary of state by those who argued he lacked forcefulness. Yet the U.S. administration was far from clear on what the commitment to use force was meant to achieve, other than to respond to the pressure "to do something." Nor did the administration make clear what the consequences would be for the Serbs if they failed to take the steps demanded by Washington. Under these circumstances, the European proposals for creating safe areas, however distasteful to the Clinton administration, appeared to offer a means of avoiding a situation in which the Western powers committed themselves to the use of force with no clear-cut political objective in mind.

The establishment of safe areas seemed to retreat from efforts to solve the conflict, and to acquiesce to partition on the worst possible grounds for the Muslim-led Bosnian government. It provoked intense opposition from the Bosnian government. Izetbegović declared the plan "absolutely unacceptable" and characterized it as putting Muslims on "reservations."[199] The Organization of the Islamic Conference denounced the plan as accepting ethnic cleansing.[200] Non-permanent members of the UN Security Council opposed it, and it provoked dissension among NATO member states.

NATO, under the authority granted in paragraphs 10 and 11 of Resolution 836 (June 4, 1993), undertook the task of protecting UNPROFOR units in the safe areas. But the use of NATO air power for this purpose was subjected to the dual control of NATO and the UN. This "dual key" arrangement became the source of additional friction between the two organizations.

Thus, more than a year after the war in Bosnia broke out, the international community was still in disarray. Owen, in his memoirs, has strongly criticized the United States for its failure to back his negotiating efforts. U.S. policymakers seemed enamored of air strikes, but unsure as to when and how to use them. At the heart of the dilemma facing the Europeans and Americans was the disjunction between those attempting to negotiate a settlement—the ICFY—and those with the power to implement it—the United States and NATO. While this disjunction may have led, as Owen claimed, to the loss of an opportunity to resolve the conflict in Bosnia, it had the obvious advantage that the party ultimately capable of projecting power into the region was not bound to a plan not of its own making—a potential source of failure in any intervention effort. Thus, two issues—the merits and defects of the Vance-Owen plan as the only hope for preserving even a vestige of multicultural Bosnia, and the question whether intervention should or could have occurred earlier—are intimately connected, and must be considered together.

Vance-Owen: An Assessment

Of the several proposals that preceded the Dayton accords and dealt directly with the Bosnian issue, the Vance-Owen plan stands out as the most fully articulated peace plan, the one that made the fewest concessions to partition, and the one that included the most specific provisions for international supervision of the outcome. As we shall see in chapters 6 and 7, later settlements proposed by Owen-Stoltenberg and by the Contact Group laid the basis for the Dayton settlement. Many of the key constitutional issues and territorial issues, such as the division of Bosnia according to the ratio 51–49 (51 percent of Bosnian territory to the Muslim-Croat federation, 49 percent to the Serb republic), were hammered out in negotiations conducted during 1993 and 1994, after the Vance-Owen plan was dead. The creation of the Bosnian (Muslim-Croat) Federation under U.S. sponsorship in March 1994 was an essential building block of the Dayton process. It allowed partition to go forward without the stigma that would have been attached to an agreement creating an isolated, rump Bosnian Muslim enclave. But the contact group plan and the plan for a Union of

Three Republics brokered by Owen and Stoltenberg also represented *de facto* partition plans. Thus, to ask whether a significantly "better" opportunity to settle the conflict was missed is to ask whether the Vance-Owen plan could have worked if it had not been rejected by the Clinton administration and the Bosnian Serbs.

In assessing the Vance-Owen plan, it is necessary to confront first the most fundamental question about efforts to negotiate a settlement: Were the parties negotiating in good faith? This question addresses not only the warring parties themselves, but international actors, as well. Were international actors prepared to fulfill the oversight and enforcement functions called for by the plan? The long record of promises broken and agreements violated by all three sides in the conflict suggests very clearly that international negotiations and the plans they produced—beginning with the European Community's Conference on Yugoslavia and continuing with the ICFY— were viewed by the warring parties as arenas for advancing their respective military and political agendas, rather than as means by which to end the war. Nationalist leaders used their access to international actors to legitimate their claims to authority and to gain international political advantage.

As early as January 1993, for example, it was reported that Bosnian government participation in such negotiations was motivated primarily by the desire to "avoid alienating the West," and that Muslim hardliners hoped simply to continue the fighting until the West was compelled to intervene.[201] Similarly, the Bosnian Croats agreed to the Vance-Owen plan primarily because of the territorial gains it awarded them in western Herzegovina and, especially, central Bosnia. They continued to fight—both politically and militarily—to secure their claims to territory in central Bosnia even after signing on to the plan. The Bosnian Serbs simply refused to accept any plan that did not recognize and legitimate the existence of a distinct Serb entity, and continued to engage in "ethnic cleansing" operations designed to consolidate their hold over all the territories they controlled. All three sides ignored cease-fire and other provisions of signed agreements with impunity.

This lack of good faith in the negotiations was encouraged by the lack of commitment on the part of international actors to enforce any agreement that might have been reached. The reluctance of outside powers—particularly the United States—to commit troops to an enforcement mission was reinforced by the lack of good faith on the part of the warring parties. Because of this reluctance, the detailed and complex provisions for military disengagement included in the Vance-Owen plan included almost no mention of enforcement. The plan called for the deployment of international forces as part of the provisions for withdrawal of forces from front lines and the creation of a demilitarized zone between them. But, in the absence of any commitment on the part of international actors to provide the necessary troops, the formal estimate of how many would be required was probably deliberately minimized. As we noted above, the co-chairs told the Security Council in February 1993 that 15,000–25,000 troops would be required to implement—not enforce—the plan.[202] But this estimate was far lower than those offered by U.S. military planners in congressional testimony, and less than half the number being estimated by NATO military planners. Media reports suggested the Americans were at that time urging NATO to prepare for a force of 50,000–70,000 troops, while NATO planners were preparing to deploy up to as many as 150,000 troops, depending on the anticipated level of local resistance.[203] When talk circulated of mounting an international intervention force to compel the parties to agree, congressional resistance to any such effort was immediate.[204] Estimates of the size of the effort that would be required and the strength of domestic political resistance, contributed to the continuing reluctance of the new Clinton administration to deploy ground troops to Bosnia under any but the most carefully specified conditions.

Thus, the Vance-Owen plan could not overcome the fundamental lack of credibility of the commitments entered into by the warring parties, and suffered from the absence of a clear international commitment to provide the military resources that would be necessary to implement the plan if the parties were to reach agreement. There appeared to be no possibility that international actors would even attempt to impose a settlement by force. These conditions compelled negotiators to draft provisions for the withdrawal of forces that lacked specific deadlines and for which no enforcement mechanism was specified. Moreover, the plan called for a new interim government in which each of the three warring parties would be represented equally, and which would make its decisions by consensus. In light of these provisions, absent powerful enforcement action by the international community the January version of the plan was likely to produce no more than a cease-fire in place—because none of the warring parties would voluntarily give up control of territory—and a political stalemate. Such an understanding explains why Milošević appeared willing to accept the plan in January; why, as the co-chairs fleshed-out and stiffened the political provisions of the plan in February and March, Milošević became less enthusiastic; and why, after the concessions of April, he chose to support it again. It may also explain why the United States was so reluctant to support the plan. But the weaknesses of the plan and the absence of international support for it were mutually reinforcing conditions.

Political opposition to the plan on the part of the Clinton administration played an important role in leading the Bosnian Muslims to reject the plan. This opposition was rooted in a belief on the part of key actors in the administration that the plan amounted to "appeasement" of the Bosnian Serbs, who were viewed as aggressors and perpetrators of genocide; in spite of the fact that the Serbs were, as our analysis has made clear, the most vehement opponents of the plan. In assessing the Vance-Owen plan, it is necessary to separate the issue of genocide from the issue of appeasement, and to ask whether implementation of the plan—with the military and political backing of the great powers, to be sure—might have brought peace to Bosnia-Herzegovina without necessarily satisfying the Bosnian Serbs.

The most difficult issues surrounding the Vance-Owen plan involved delineation of the boundaries of the proposed ten provinces. First, as we have seen, the configuration of these boundary lines, and especially the modification introduced in February 1993 that cut the Serbs' northern corridor, were consciously designed to deny to the Serbs the single, continuous territorial entity they were seeking. Second, the territory designated as Serb-majority provinces represented a reduction of almost 40 percent from the amount of territory they held at the time of the negotiations. Third, eastern Bosnia and the cities along the Drina were to be part of a Muslim-majority province (province five), despite the fact that the Serbs had demonstrated through ethnic cleansing, military operations, and intransigent negotiation their intent to hold on to this territory. These three factors explain the rejection of the plan by the Bosnian Serbs, and argue strongly against the view that the plan constituted "appeasement." But, what of the provisions for internal governance of a postwar Bosnia contained in the plan?

In support of the Vance-Owen plan, it can be argued that its provisions reflected a fundamentally realistic approach to conflict management. They were detailed and complex. Indeed, some criticized the plan as overly complex. The international monitoring arrangements specified in the plan were highly intrusive, and thus more difficult for some of the parties to accept. But the complexity and intrusiveness of the plan suggest that negotiators recognized very clearly that the warring parties could not be expected to engage in even the most minimal cooperative behavior in the absence of close international supervision. Hence, rather than simply creating power-sharing arrangements and naively relying on the parties to conform voluntarily to the formal and informal rules of behavior that would be required for them to work, the Vance-Owen plan called for international actors to play direct and, in some cases, dominant roles in the operation of many Bosnian institutions.

Although detailed and complex, the Vance-Owen plan as articulated in Security Council documents remained far from a complete blueprint for the successful operation of a Bosnian state. An enduring, unresolved issue on which both the Croats and the Serbs aligned themselves in opposition to the Muslims, for example, was the status of the parliament elected in 1990. While the Muslim-led government argued for—and won—recognition by Vance and Owen of the legal status of the existing constitution and parliament, it seems clear that an entirely new set of rules of procedure would have had to be drafted if that institution was to function. That drafting process would almost certainly have been a contentious one. Similarly, the Vance-Owen plan provided only the most basic rules of procedure for the interim presidency, and it left definition of its relationship to the government to a later date. The plan included general principles for a constitution for Bosnia, and the outline of a constitutional structure for the state, but not an agreed constitution. It called for free and fair elections, but contained no agreement as to how these were to be achieved. The plan left the details of drafting a constitution and electoral laws to a later date. These were also certain to be highly contentious processes. In the absence of trust—indeed, in the presence of a high level of inter-group animosity—it appears that these processes would have required the continued close involvement of the negotiators if they were to be concluded successfully.

Direct international involvement appeared to be critical if the plan was to address the legitimate demand of the Bosnian government that the rights of refugees driven from their homes should be protected. Extensive implementation and enforcement guarantees were important in order to protect the rights of all individuals. But they were especially crucial for those whose homes were located on the "wrong" side of ethnic boundaries—that is, in a province expected to have a majority of another ethnic group. Although the plan clearly called for proportionality in local government institutions, including the civil police, in order to protect ethnic minorities, the settlement also called for intrusive, extensive, and prolonged international involvement in the internal administration of the post-war Bosnian state and its subunits. Such provisions could only be as effective as the strength of the international commitment that lay behind them, however. Absent strong support from the international community at the local level, each group would almost certainly carry out ethnic cleansing in the provinces under its control. Thus, in the end, the efforts of negotiators to devise institutional and procedural provisions to protect minority participation in decision-making, to impose formulas for proportional representation in key positions, to ensure both ethnic proportionality and international oversight of the civil police, to incorporate specific guarantees of rights into the constitutional agreement, and to create special courts and other institutions to safeguard these rights and ensure the democratic functioning of the postwar Bosnian state all were futile. They reflected the gap between Western ideas about a multicultural society in a civil state and the realities on the ground in Bosnia, identified in chapter 4. Bosnian Muslims, Serbs, and Croats could not be expected to cooperate unless they were compelled to do so. And, they could be compelled to do so only by the presence of a considerably superior outside force willing to engage directly in the political process, if need be, by removing those opposed to the type of settlement envisaged by the plan.

To succeed, a settlement would not only have required sufficient force to ensure compliance, but would have had to address the real political interests and concerns of all three warring parties as a means of creating incentives on all three sides for upholding the settlement. The public record of the negotiations provides ample testimony—only part of it cited in this chapter—of the difficulty of reconciling these interests and concerns. On a number of key issues, including control of the northern corridor, the status of Sarajevo, and the fate of the eastern enclaves, compromise between the parties appears to have been impossible. Any concession to the interests of one side effectively discredited the proposal in the eyes of the other(s). And, any concessions to Serb interests threatened to discredit the negotiations in the eyes of U.S. policymakers, whose support was crucial to the success of any implementation/enforcement effort. Vance and Owen appeared unable even to facilitate an exchange of concessions between the parties themselves as long as the Bosnian Serbs remained unconvinced that they confronted a military threat, and as long as the Bosnian Muslims remained hopeful that outside assistance would eventually enable them to overcome Serb military superiority and take control of all of Bosnia-Herzegovina. The latter hope was fueled by U.S. statements and actions throughout the effort to negotiate a settlement.

The question of military deployments in province five was not only of strategic importance to the warring parties, it also was of defining significance for the Vance-Owen plan itself. Under the provisions of the plan as it had evolved up to April 1993, Serb forces were required to withdraw from province five. But it was not clear who would replace them. Absent any agreement with the United States or commitment by NATO to supply troops to occupy the province (or, at least, Serb-majority villages and towns within it), it seems unlikely that the Serbs could have been persuaded to withdraw, and it would have been impossible to prevent Muslim troops from moving into this territory if the Serbs did withdraw. A settlement that disregarded Serb interests could only be imposed by the use of force on a level that international actors remained unwilling to employ even in the course of the fighting that led up to the Dayton agreement in 1995. Hence, as we have described above, provisions of the plan concerning the occupation and control of territory by UN forces were modified in April and May 1993 in ways that seemed to allow the Serbs to retain local control in strategic territory assigned to Muslim-majority provinces. It appeared that some territories in the strategically important province five might be left under the local administrative control of the Serbs. But it was unclear whether they would be subject to civil police under the control of Muslim authorities, continue to be policed by Serbs, or be policed by UN forces. If implemented, the uncertainties of these provisions promised to create an unstable and even highly volatile situation of competing claims to strategically critical territory. This, as developments in Croatia in 1994 and 1995 would demonstrate, would have been a formula for future war.

These changes do not, however, justify the charge of appeasement leveled at the plan and its architects. These changes occurred long *after* the initial charges had been made against the co-chairs in January. Those charges contributed to undermining support for the plan, especially in the United States. The concessions made by Owen to the Serbs in late April came when it seemed that the alternative to agreement was an uncontrolled escalation of the fighting. April–June 1993 was a period of intense fighting between Muslims and Croats in central and eastern Bosnia. Both the Croats and the Serbs were engaged in offensives to consolidate their hold on territory. By the time the co-chairs secured the March version of the plan, and especially by the time Owen met with Bosnian Serb and Serbian leaders in Belgrade in late April, it was clear that none of the parties was willing to give up control of the territories they then held, regardless of the definition of provincial boundaries.

The concessions to the Serbs proposed in April represented an approach no different than that taken by the co-chairs in February and March when, faced with the Bosnian Muslims' refusal to agree, they modified the map to meet Muslim demands at the expense of Serb interests. In the absence of the April concessions, neither Milošević nor Karadžić would have agreed to the plan. Although the United States was an advocate of "improving" the plan to favor Bosnian Muslim interests, it was as yet unwilling to address Serb or Croat interests as a means of winning their agreement. At the same time, it remained reluctant to commit itself to the use of force to compel the Bosnian Serbs to accept the plan, preferring instead to rely on the pressure of tightened sanctions against Serbia. Faced with intransigence, Vance and Owen seem to have used concessions with respect to the control of territory as an incentive to agreement. Had the co-chairs had the capacity to coerce an intransigent party into agreement, then the charges of appeasement leveled against them might have been justified. But coercion was an option that simply was not available to them.

The necessity of allowing the Serbs to retain control over province five and the failure to broker a military agreement between the Muslims and Croats suggests that the apparent agreement of all three parties to the Vance-Owen plan, however fleeting, represented little more than their interest in a cease-fire, which would allow them to prepare for the prolonged fighting that now seemed inevitable. It did not represent agreement on a political solution to the conflict. The continuing opposition to the plan by the Bosnian Serbs made such a solution impossible.

In retrospect, Vance and Owen may be criticized more fairly for their unwillingness to give up on their plan when it was clearly no longer viable. Their last-minute concessions to Serb interests failed to secure the agreement of the more hard-line Bosnian Serbs, led by General Mladić. The rejection of the plan by the Bosnian Serb assembly made it clear that political incentives to accept a negotiated settlement had to be accompanied by a credible threat of force to convince hard-liners to accept it. For the duration of the Vance-Owen negotiating effort, however, Western advocates of using military force refused to recognize the legitimacy of the competing political claims of the warring parties, preferring instead to align themselves with one side in the conflict. Thus, the Vance-Owen plan never received the support necessary to make it a realistic basis for settlement. At the same time, those who recognized the need to accommodate conflicting claims in a political settlement appeared to rule out the use of force. With the demise of the Vance-Owen plan, the strategy of addressing the real political interests of the warring parties was quickly transformed into a strategy of conceding to Serb and Croat demands for partition. Until the use of force and the recognition of real interests could be integrated in a single approach, international actors could not hope to bring the conflict to an end. That integration appears not to have been achieved until 1995; that is, until the chief proponent of the use of force—the United States—became convinced of the need for a realistic political settlement that addressed Serb interests, and then only after a basic alteration in the balance of forces on the ground had taken place.

CHAPTER 6

The International Community and the War

Negotiating Partition, 1993–94

The demise of the Vance-Owen plan in May 1993 was followed by efforts to negotiate an agreed partition of Bosnia-Herzegovina. During summer and fall 1993, ICFY mediators worked directly with the three warring parties, as well as with the Croatian and Serbian leaderships, to develop a plan acceptable to all sides. The United States, still holding itself aloof from the talks, did not oppose *de facto* partition in principle, but sought to shift the content of each proposal in favor of the Bosnian Muslims. This complicated, but did not, by itself, subvert these efforts. With the formation of the Contact Group in spring 1994, the Americans took over leadership of the diplomatic effort to find such a solution, but proved as ineffective as their European allies had been, and for much the same reason: despite the increasing involvement of NATO and occasional limited use of air power in 1994, the Americans and Europeans both remained unable to project power into the conflict in a way that was both credible and free from unacceptable risks. American rhetoric calling for the use of greater force was not supported by action—because such actions were opposed and even prevented by European and UN officials, and because U.S. policymakers were unable to define the goals of such action and not yet convinced that their pursuit was worth the risk. By the end of 1994, however, these obstacles to forceful action began to recede—in part, as a result of the conscious decisions and actions of policymakers intent on bringing the conflict to an end, but also because of the uncontrolled nature of the events themselves; above all, the prospect of the United States having to deploy troops to protect a UN withdrawal from Bosnia.

The *Status Quo* Prevails

Following the failure of U.S. efforts to win European support for a strategy of lift and strike, the Clinton administration reluctantly accepted the proposal for establishing safe areas first put forward by Austria in 1992, then picked up by the Russians, and later adopted by the Europeans. Creating safe areas did little to hasten an end to the conflict, but was consistent with a strategy of containment, which Secretary Christopher defined in testimony before the U.S. Congress in mid-May as "one of the prime goals of President Clinton."[1] The goal of U.S. policy became "to contain and stabilize the situation" and "to put the brakes on the killing," an approach characterized by an unnamed senior administration official as putting "first things first."[2] Most important, following a meeting with the Russian, French, British, and Spanish foreign ministers in Washington on May 22 the United States signaled its willingness to accept the territorial gains achieved by the Serbs, rather than impose a reduction in those territories as called for by the Vance-Owen plan. The ministers agreed to a "Joint Action Program" to safeguard humanitarian shipments and otherwise "freeze" the *status quo* on the ground.[3] French foreign minister Alain Juppé underscored Western reluctance to use force to "push back all those who make territorial conquests in defiance of international law." He asserted: "It would take 200,000 men. I don't know of a single state in the world who is ready to do that. It is necessary for the hypocrisy to cease."[4]

On June 7 the Bosnian government also reluctantly accepted the safe area concept, but demanded a number of modifications. It insisted that the protected zones be enlarged and connected with government-held regions; that Serbian heavy weapons near the zones be withdrawn; that monitors be placed on the border between Bosnia and Serbia; and that the Yugoslav government and the Security Council reaffirm their commitment to the Vance-Owen plan.[5] But the safe areas approach never received unqualified support in Washington. Within weeks of the Washington agreement, an unnamed "senior administration official" criticized the approach as "unmanageable" and as creating "six little West Banks in Western Europe." Most tellingly, this official predicted that the most likely outcome of the fighting in Bosnia would be partition, with Muslim-held areas forming a state alliance with Croatia to counterbalance the power of the Serbs.[6] This signaled the approach soon to be adopted by the Europeans and the Americans.

The U.S. decision to accept the territorial *status quo* in Bosnia-Herzegovina appears to have been rooted in a decision that, as Secretary Christopher put it during a televised interview in June, the war in Bosnia-Herzegovina "involves our humanitarian concerns, but it does not involve our vital interests."[7] Christopher is alleged again to have asserted that the war was "not central to our vital interests" in a confidential letter to U.S. ambassadors later in the month.[8] Yet, the administration persisted in its half-hearted, and perhaps merely symbolic, support for arming the Muslims. It voted, for example, along with a minority of the Security Council in favor of a resolution calling for the lifting of the arms embargo.[9] Even though the resolution failed to pass, U.S. support for it further undermined efforts to negotiate an end to the fighting.

During the May meetings in Washington, the United States had already signaled its dissatisfaction with the ICFY by proposing the establishment of a "Contact Group" comprising the United States, Russia, and the three main troop-contributing countries of the EC: France, Britain, and Spain. The Contact Group would take over the task of ending the fighting in Bosnia-Herzegovina. While not opposing the Contact Group, the Europeans supported continuation of the ICFY negotiations.[10] The Washington meeting thus failed to heal the basic rift between the United States and its European allies. French foreign minister Juppé pointedly observed that "I haven't agreed with the so-called division of labor between those who are in the sky and those who are on the ground" in Bosnia-Herzegovina. He wished "that all the great powers involved in the painful drama will assume their responsibility."[11]

The collapse of the Vance-Owen plan, the acceptance of the *status quo* embodied in the Washington Joint Action Plan, the continued refusal of the United States to supply ground troops for Bosnia (in contrast to its deployment of troops to Macedonia), and the inability of the United States and its European allies to heal their rift had dramatic consequences for negotiations. International mediators henceforth shifted their efforts toward accepting the Croatian-Serbian approach of partitioning the republic as a means of bringing the fighting to an end. On June 16, negotiations resumed in Geneva with Milošević and Tudjman in attendance. With the rejection of the Vance-Owen plan, Cyrus Vance had resigned in May as co-chair of the ICFY. He was replaced by former Norwegian Foreign Minister Thorvald Stoltenberg, who also had once served briefly as UN High Commissioner for Refugees. Owen continued to defend the Vance-Owen plan up to the eve of the Geneva meeting. But on June 16 Owen left the negotiating initiative to Milošević and Tudjman, who put forward a joint Serbian-Croatian proposal to solve the Bosnia crisis.

The Serbian-Croatian proposal, as it emerged in this and subsequent meetings in Geneva, borrowed portions of the Vance-Owen plan in its provisions for a transitional government while providing for a final settlement that partitioned Bosnia-Herzegovina into a confederation of three independent republics.[12] Milošević submitted a map on June 23. It would have left the Bosnian Muslims with only 23 percent of Bosnia.[13] Mirko Klarin, diplomatic correspondent in Brussels for the independent Belgrade newspaper *Borba,* observed that a veritable diplomatic revolution was now in progress as the international mediators abandoned the effort to preserve the Republic of Bosnia-Herzegovina, and focused instead on a partition that could only come at the expense of the Bosnian Muslims.[14] Media accounts reported that "the Muslim-led government delegation was shocked and angered at Owen and Stoltenberg and felt they had abandoned their position as neutral mediators to put forward an ethnic-partition plan already supported by the Serbs and Croats."[15]

European leaders were divided over what approach to take in the wake of the collapse of the Vance-Owen plan and the surfacing of the Serbian-Croatian proposal for partition.[16] The views expressed at a meeting of foreign ministers in Copenhagen in June 1993 ranged from French support for preserving as much of the institutional structures of the Vance-Owen plan as possible even if the map had to be redrawn, to Italian support for shifting the focus of attention to the Serbian-Croatian proposal for partition and concern for the protection of minorities. The rapidly shifting political conditions led the Dutch foreign minister to remark that he felt "like Alice in Wonderland."[17]

Bosnian hopes of Western intervention were sustained by the repeated resurfacing of the U.S. proposal to lift the arms embargo and provide air support for the government, and from their continued success at securing weapons on the international arms market.[18] As reports of the "strangulation" of Sarajevo and its near collapse reached Washington at the end of July (examined in chapter 4), the president was reported to have asked his advisors for "new military options aimed at preventing the fall of Sarajevo and protecting humanitarian deliveries." According to a "senior official" at the Pentagon, however, it was not clear that either the United States or NATO was yet "willing to use force to stop the killing and force an endgame on the [basis of the] partition peace plan." The dilemma inherent in the use of force for such a purpose was clear:

> Any U.S. air strikes, officials say, need to be harsh enough to convince the Serbs they would be better off reaching a peace agreement and perhaps ceding some territorial gains. At the same time, the military action must avoid leaving the Muslims with the impression that they could gain by continuing to hold out.[19]

Secretary Christopher then appeared to rule out any use of force by the Americans when he declared that "the United States is doing all it can consistent with our national interest."[20] But, within a week, as the crisis over Sarajevo intensified, the vice president acknowledged that the administration was again considering the use of air power against the Serbs, and that U.S. Bosnian policy was "under intensive review."[21]

The Clinton administration came under intense pressure to act following a UN Security Council resolution on July 23 condemning the Serb blockade of Sarajevo. While a new round of negotiations resumed in Geneva the third week in July, the United States attempted to convince the French and the British to agree to a strategy of graduated air strikes against the Serbs to protect Sarajevo. But the French resisted. After the French UNPROFOR base in Sarajevo was shelled,[22] the French dropped their objections. But French Defense Minister Francois Leotard, speaking in Washington only a few days after the attack, insisted that the use of air power be restricted to the defense of UN troops.[23] The principal foreign policy advisors of the Clinton administration are reported to have considered a unilateral military operation to relieve the siege of Sarajevo, but to have rejected it when they learned of the scale of the effort that would be required:[24] "There was no way you could do ground forces; the number would just be too big . . . off the chart, in terms of what you could get politically."[25]

On July 31 the White House opted for a policy of air strikes against the Serbs as a means of ending the shelling and strangulation of the city. The U.S. plan went well beyond the authorization provided by Security Council Resolution 836, which limited air strikes to protection of UN personnel, and represented a sharp break with past U.S. policy. While the threat of air strikes was not directly tied to winning Serb approval for the political settlement authored by Tudjman and Milošević and supported by the ICFY—which in fact favored the Serbs—it was the first of many U.S. efforts to press the use of air power to influence Serb behavior rather than in the tit-for-tat fashion preferred by the UN. In keeping with the American approach, the plan called for NATO to launch strikes on its own initiative, without prior UN approval.[26] America's allies vehemently opposed the plan as endangering their forces in Bosnia.

On the eve of the NATO ambassadorial meeting of August 2, U.S. State Department spokesperson Michael McCurry told reporters that "air strikes could begin within the next few days."[27] News of this statement "raised the flagging spirits of the [Bosnian] governmental delegation" at the Geneva talks. Izetbegović "froze" his participation in the talks and demanded the withdrawal of Serb forces from strategic positions around Sarajevo.[28] At the NATO meeting, however, countries with troops on the ground in

Bosnia, including both Canada and Great Britain, continued to oppose the U.S. call for air strikes against the Serbs. The debate, according to one Canadian diplomat, was "as bitter and rancorous a discussion as has ever taken place in the alliance."[29] The NATO members with troops in Bosnia, led by the Canadians and the French, wished air power to be used in defense of UN forces. They feared Serb retribution if a NATO attack went beyond the UN guidelines of "proportionate response." They found support from UN Sarajevo commander Lt. Gen. Francis Briquemont, the ICFY mediators (Owen and Stoltenberg) and influential figures such as General Powell and General MacKenzie,[30] all of whom warned of the danger that air strikes could lead to Serb reprisals and undermine the negotiations then under way in Geneva.

As we noted in chapter 4, the statement adopted by NATO on August 2 threatened future action against those who attacked UNPROFOR or obstructed humanitarian aid, but authorized no immediate action against the Serbs. NATO ministers retained the "dual key" arrangement that gave the UN secretary-general final authority over the use of air power. UN officers in Sarajevo reported that the Bosnian Serbs concluded from these developments that the threat of air strikes had receded.[31] The aftermath of the NATO decision, nevertheless, was the withdrawal of the Serbs from Mt. Igman, and an end to the immediate threat to Sarajevo. The assessment of the Western media was that the Serbs had retreated in the face of a show of force.[32]

Negotiating Partition

The United States and its NATO allies, meanwhile, had to pressure the Bosnian government to return to the talks after its hopes had been raised that NATO was preparing to intervene in Bosnia.[33] As we have noted, the Bosnian government decried the decision of the ICFY to focus the talks in Geneva on partition. Yet, not to participate in the negotiations posed the risk of political isolation at a time when the Bosnian government was under unprecedented military and diplomatic pressure. It would give a green light to the bilateral negotiation of a deal between Serbia and Croatia over Bosnia, largely in direct talks between Tudjman and Milošević. The first of a series of meetings between the Serbian and Croatian leaders took place in the third week in June, and resulted in the joint Serbian-Croatian proposal noted earlier. In the second week in July, Tudjman and Milošević proposed that the Muslims receive 30 percent of Bosnia. This figure served as a baseline for the negotiations over partition carried out by the mediators in the months that followed.

Under pressure from the negotiators, the Muslims resumed their participation in the ICFY talks in late July. Media accounts of the U.S. decision to participate in the Geneva talks reported that the administration intended to show its support for "the disadvantaged Muslim side in the negotiations" and to "counter European pressure on the Muslims to make a deal."[34] But a European participant in the negotiations reports that the United States worked "behind the scenes to persuade Izetbegović to negotiate a settlement," although it "remained extremely paranoid about appearing to put any form of public pressure on him."[35]

In a letter to Lord Owen on July 7, Izetbegović conveyed his belief that the realities in Bosnia had now changed, implying his readiness to consider some kind of partition plan.[36] On July 9, in an interview with Sarajevo radio, Izetbegović noted that concessions would have to be made for the sake of peace and declared: "My intimate preoccupation is with saving the Muslim nation. Serbs and Croats will somehow survive. I am worried that the bare survival of Muslims is threatened."[37] This was a note that Izetbegović was to strike throughout the negotiations that followed, even as he demanded more territory and an outlet to the sea, effectively blocking a final agreement.

Meanwhile, the Muslims more than held their own in increased fighting with the Croats. While Croat forces consolidated their hold over the Mostar valley, the Bosnian army advanced into central Bosnia. On June 10, Travnik fell to the Bosnians. On June 29, Muslim forces managed to break the siege of eastern Mostar. On August 1, Bugojno fell, and approximately a week later a large Muslim offensive was launched in central Bosnia, setting the stage for the re-entry of regular Croatian armed forces into the war, this time in central Bosnia. (We noted in chapter 4 that Croatian forces had already entered Bosnia in March 1992.) The fight against the Serbs, on the other hand, went from bad to worse. On June 23, the Maglaj-Tesenj region was cut off from the rest of Bosnia by a combined Serb-Croat force. On July 12, Trnovo fell to the Serbs, cutting Muslim links to eastern Bosnia and opening the door to the Serb attack on the mountains south of Sarajevo, Bjelašnica and Igman, which resulted in the crisis over the strangulation of Sarajevo in July, noted above and in chapter 4. For their part, the Croats in the area of Orašje in the Posavina maintained a purely defensive position, enabling the Bosnian Serbs to more than double the width of the strategic corridor between eastern and western Bosnia.[38]

At the moment that the Bosnian government was forced into negotiations over partition, the focus among hardliners in the SDA leadership appeared to shift toward accommodation with the Serbs and continuing the struggle against the Croats. They sought to use the negotiations to obtain an outlet to the Adriatic, freeing Bosnia from dependence on Croatia for the delivery of arms. This can be said, at least, about Ejup Ganić (and in all likelihood, his Sandžak faction). In a remarkable interview with a Slovenian newspaper in July, Ganić suggested that "the Muslims are Islamized Serbs, and the biggest mistake we made was at the beginning of the war when we concluded a military alliance with the Croats."[39] He then amplified on his remark in an interview in Zagreb, adding: "We are related much more closely with the Serbs than with the Slovenes and the Croats. We speak a dialect that is more similar to Serbian than Croat. The same goes for mentality, habits, and customs."[40] The bottom line for Ganić was that the Serbs were stronger. "Our situation is hopeless," Ganić continued in the version of his interview published in the Hamburg newspaper *Die Woche.*

> We can only choose between two enemies. We will decide in favor of the Serbs. The English say: If you can't beat them, join them. The Serbs have achieved everything and they are even supported by the world in their war of conquest. . . . Thus, we keep to the stronger. And these are the Serbs. We have already had secret talks with them, but I do not want to elaborate on this.[41]

A month later, in the course of vehement protests against partition, Ganić was quoted by *Der Kurier* in Vienna as claiming, "We would win the war if we had 20 kilometers free access to the sea."[42] This position, while conciliatory toward the Serbs, raised the issue of why Croatia and the Bosnian Croats should even entertain the thought of granting the Muslims access to sea. To do so would likely mean that future attacks on Croat forces by the Bosnians would be carried out by better-armed troops.

Even among the most dedicated supporters of Bosnian territorial integrity there was doubt that the Republic of Bosnia-Herzegovina could be saved. In an interview with Cairo radio on August 4, Silajdžić sounded a pessimistic note that echoed Ganić's views, confessing that "the other side is stronger."[43] Later in the month, Mirko Pejanović, a Serb member of the Bosnian presidency, came out—albeit with great reluctance—for the peace plan proposed by the mediators, on the grounds that this was the only way to halt the bloodshed in Bosnia.[44] Silajdžić, in his August 4 interview, focused on the need to compromise with the mediators to preserve the state of Bosnia, which he made clear included not only Muslims, but others as well. He supported the notion of a federal Bosnia, a position the Bosnian presidency had spelled out in Geneva on July 11, and which Izetbegović had endorsed.[45] The presidency's plan called for the establishment of a federal state in which only the federation would exercise the powers traditionally associated with statehood, including the retention of international legal status, security affairs, and management of the economy. Each of the three national groups would participate on a "parity" basis in executive organs, and on an equal basis in representative institutions. The constituent units of the federation would not, however, be defined exclusively in ethnic terms and would number anywhere from four to twenty-two. In the event this proposal was rejected, the presidency suggested it would propose that the Security Council establish a UN protectorate over Bosnia.[46]

The Owen-Stoltenberg Proposal

It was under these circumstances that the negotiations resumed in Geneva on July 27. According to a Bosnian source, the presidency's proposal was immediately rejected by all other parties and talks proceeded on the basis of the Serbian-Croatian proposal.[47] While Tudjman and Milošević had proposed that the Muslims be given 30 percent of Bosnia, Karadžić would not agree. The issues of Sarajevo and an outlet to the sea for the Muslims also remained unresolved. Unable to reconcile these differences, the mediators were able to gain agreement on constitutional principles through the approval of a document that called for the establishment of a "Union of Republics of Bosnia and Herzegovina."

The Union was a *de facto* confederation consisting of three constituent republics, each with its own constitution and democratic government. All powers would reside in the republics. The presidency of the Union would consist of the presidents or appointees of the republics and would make its decisions on the basis of consensus, with the chairmanship rotating every four months. The presidency would appoint the prime minister, foreign minister, and other government ministers. The Union would retain a Court of Human Rights with international participation to guarantee such rights as contained in the nineteen international human rights instruments incorporated in the constitutional agreement. Under the provisions of Article 1, the Union would be a member state of the UN, a stipulation that addressed directly an objection raised by the Bosnian government. Each constituent republic would be allowed to apply for membership in an international organization or become a party to an international treaty as long as such membership "would not be inconsistent with the interests of the Union." No republic could withdraw without the prior agreement of all the republics. If a republic withdrew from the Union, it was obligated to return to the Union those territories within its boundaries necessary to provide Sarajevo (that is, the Muslim republic) with access to the Adriatic and to the Sava, as well as all properties of the common, Union institutions located in Sarajevo. Neither the republics nor the Union government was permitted to have a standing army.[48] In other words, it was a plan for tripartite partition.

In the negotiations that followed the signing of the Union agreement, the

Map 6.1 **Bosnian Presidency Proposal for Partition, June 1993**

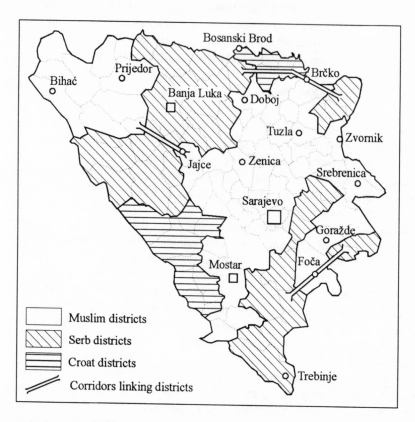

Adapted from *Oslobodjenje* (European edition, August 6–13, 1993).

focus was on three issues in particular: the fate of Sarajevo, the nature of the map that would determine the boundaries of the new republics, and the amount of territory each republic was to receive. The Muslims and the Serbs were deadlocked over the future status of Sarajevo. The Serbs proposed an exchange of territories that would have resulted in the partitioning of the city. They proposed giving up the Grbavica neighborhood of Sarajevo in order to include all of the inner city in the Muslim-majority republic, in exchange for which they sought Dobrinja. They also proposed consolidating Muslim and Serb holdings by exchanging Vogošća in the north for Butmir and Hrasnica in the south, with the airport to be available to both the Muslim-majority and the Serb-majority republics by dividing it down the center of the main runway. The prospect that Sarajevo would be partitioned

Map 6.2 **Serbian-Croatian Proposal for Partition, June 1993**

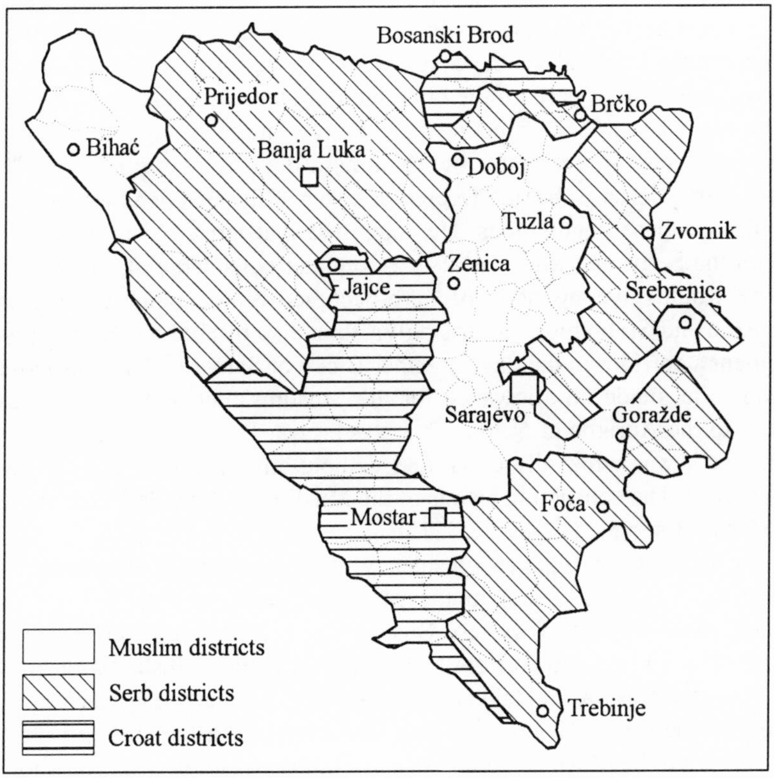

Adapted from *Borba,* August 13, 1993.

was strenuously resisted by the Bosnians. A preliminary agreement on Sarajevo was nevertheless reached on August 18. Sarajevo was to be placed
under UN administration, the nature of which was to be spelled out in a
peace treaty among the three sides. The Sarajevo region would be demilitarized. All ten prewar districts were to be included in the new region, with
the exception of Pale.[49] The agreement was clearly a stopgap measure.
While Owen subsequently spoke of "UN administration," it appears that
each side was to be responsible for the territory it then controlled, leaving
the ultimate fate of the city unresolved.

Where the borders of the three republics would be drawn and the amount
of territory each would receive were the focus of additional discussions.
Facing the prospect of partition, the three sides had begun to explore the
possibilities of territorial swaps even before the negotiations got under way

at the end of July. In early June, the Bosnian Serbs had put forth the demand for an outlet to the Adriatic near Čilip, on the Montenegrin border. Tudjman signaled that he would be willing to consider an exchange of territory that would allow the Serbs access to the sea and provide for Croatian annexation of parts of the hinterland of Dubrovnik that lay in Bosnia. Following the June 17 meeting in Geneva, Tudjman suggested that the Bosnian Croats might grant the Muslims a duty-free zone in Ploče.[50] In early July, Aleksa Buha, the foreign minister of the Bosnian Serb republic, confirmed these negotiations. He suggested that territorial exchanges between the Serbs and Muslims also were under consideration, in which the Serbs would give up parts of Serb-occupied Sarajevo in exchange for Goražde and Srebrenica. Surprisingly, Buha also offered the Bosnian government a corridor to the Sava at either Brčko or Šamac.[51] These proposals, meanwhile, made no allowance for the Muslims' demands for their own outlet to the Adriatic at Neum. This was prewar Bosnia's one outlet to the sea. But it was ethnically Croat and without any economic potential as a future port. The conflicting claims of the Muslims and the Serbs can be seen in Maps 6.1 and 6.2 (pages 272–273).

The map of the Bosnian presidency gave the cities of the Drina river (Zvornik, Višegrad, Foča) to the Muslims; reclaimed the Prijedor and Sanski Most regions of western Bosnia for the Bosnian government; proposed a broad Bosnian corridor to the Sava; affirmed Muslim control over all of central Bosnia; and laid claim to the entire Mostar valley, including an outlet to the sea at Neum. The map was evidently a bargaining ploy, far beyond what the Muslims could hope to achieve. Yet it was still far short of a viable state. The Serbian-Croatian map published by *Borba* August 14–15 was based on previous positions taken by Tudjman and Milošević. The Sana river was now the eastern border of Muslim territory in western Bosnia. Incredibly, the map indicated that Muslim territory extended all the way to the Sava, leaving unclear whether the Serbs would retain any part of Brčko or the Posavina corridor. Eastern Bosnia remained largely in Serb hands, but was cut off from eastern Herzegovina by a Muslim corridor stretching from Trnovo and Sarajevo to the Serbian border. Central Bosnia and the Neretva valley were to go to the Croats. The Muslims were denied access to the sea. The proposal thus strongly favored the Croats over the Muslims in central and southern Bosnia. At the same time, the inclusion of Srebrenica and Goražde in a Muslim corridor that stretched across eastern Bosnia to the border of Serbia and its Sandžak region was a major Serbian concession to the Muslims, but almost certainly unacceptable to the Bosnian Serbs. Neither the Bosnian presidency nor the Serbian-Croatian map made allowance for a special Sarajevo region.[52]

Map 6.3 **Owen-Stoltenberg Proposal for Partition, August 1993**

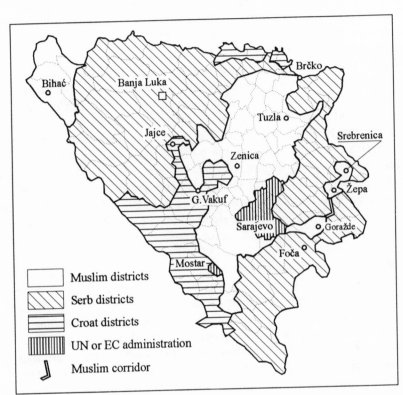

Muslim districts

Serb districts

Croat districts

UN or EC administration

Muslim corridor

Based on UN Security Council document S/27337 (August 20, 1993), p. 4.

On August 21 the mediators presented a complete package of agreements on a take-it-or-leave-it basis. The major provisions of the plan included the agreement for a Union of Republics; a military agreement; and a map of the proposed partitioning of Bosnia-Herzegovina.[53] The map produced by the negotiators and offered to the parties to the conflict is shown here as Map 6.3.

In eastern Bosnia, the mediators bowed to Bosnian Serb demands and cut the proposed territorial link between the Srebrenica enclave and Goražde. The Bosnian Muslim state was to include territory on the east bank of the Neretva reaching south to Stolac, a Croat-majority province under the Vance-Owen plan. This failed to meet the Muslim demand for an outlet to the sea at Neum. In central Bosnia, the Muslims would retain the Lašva valley, including Travnik. The line between Muslim central Bosnia and Croat western Herzegovina would run along the Vrbas river, dividing the river towns of Bugojno and Donji Vakuf. Jajce, farther to the north and downstream on the Vrbas, was at the time occupied by the Bosnian Serbs. Croats and Muslims had been equally represented there before the war. The mediators' map awarded it to the Croats. To the west, the border between the Muslim Cazinska Krajina and the Serb Bosanska Krajina followed the Una river, an obvious concession to the Serbs. The towns along the Una were divided. Bihać was to remain in Muslim hands, while Bosanska Krupa (a heavily Muslim town before the war) was to be partitioned between the Muslims and Serbs, according to an account published in *Borba*.[54] The Bosnian republic was denied access to the sea, but Croatia agreed to grant the Bosnian republic access to the ports of Ploče and Rijeka, as well as freedom of transit to members of the Union.[55] Mostar was to be placed under EC administration for two years. The dispute over Brčko and the Muslim demand for a corridor to the Sava was resolved by partitioning the city and granting the Serbs sovereignty over an east–west corridor, through which a Bosnian north-south corridor (spanned by a Serb overpass) was to run.[56]

When all the territories of the respective republics were added together, the Bosnian Muslim republic was to receive 30 percent of Bosnia-Herzegovina (including that part of the Sarajevo region mediators calculated was Muslim);[57] 54 percent went to the Serbs; and 16 percent fell to the Croats.[58] An appendix to the agreement provided for the establishment of an "Access Authority" that would have responsibility for controlling the protected corridors and highways that were to fall under UN supervision.

Enforcement of the plan, according to Stoltenberg, would require "at least 40,000 troops from the United Nations," and, during a press conference in Geneva, "he pointedly noted that the Clinton administration has pledged to be an on-the-ground player once peace is declared."[59] Planning for such a force had already been under way for some time at the NATO Southern Command in Naples, Italy. An unnamed senior administration official conceded that "ground troops are certainly under consideration."[60] Indeed, elements of a NATO plan leaked to the press in May had called for the participation of 20,000 U.S. troops in a multinational force of some 60,000 troops.[61] According to media reports, on August 19 Secretary of State Christopher urged Izetbegović to accept the Owen-Stoltenberg plan and pledged that the United States stood ready to help put the plan into effect.[62] President Clinton, however, stipulated in August that the deployment of U.S. troops would depend on his being "convinced the agreement is fair, fully embraced by the Bosnian government, and is enforceable"; and on knowing "whose responsibility it is to stay for how long."[63]

The main virtue of the Owen-Stoltenberg plan lay in its effort to recognize the reality of Bosnia's now deep ethnic and military divisions. Although the Serbs were required to give up approximately 20 percent of the territory they then held—including the ethnically Serb Mt. Ozren region to the west of Tuzla—the map clearly favored the Serbs in the west and the east. Drawing internal boundaries along Bosnia's rivers—the Una, the Neretva, the Vrbas—had long been a Serb idea. The plan represented the maximum the international community could hope to demand from the Bosnian Serbs in the absence of additional military leverage. On the other hand, the Muslims were placed in a position that could only be characterized as disadvantageous in the extreme. Access to the sea and the Sava river depended entirely on the goodwill of the Croats and Serbs, respectively. Ethnically cleansed Muslim areas in eastern Bosnia and the Prijedor–Sanski Most area were included in the Bosnian Serb republic. Sarajevo, although demilitarized, remained divided. Local opposition within Bosnia in areas adversely affected by the map was vocal on all sides.[64] The rules governing the administration of the UN-protected corridors and highways were left undefined. Notably, the Owen-Stoltenberg plan was subjected to far less criticism in the United States for allegedly rewarding Serb aggression or for sanctioning ethnic cleansing than the earlier Vance-Owen plan, which had been far less generous to the Serbs.

Even more ominous from the Muslim perspective, perhaps, was the fact that the plan called for all treaties entered into by Bosnia after November 18, 1990 to be approved by the new parliament. Parliamentary approval, in turn, required a majority vote by each of the three republic delegations. This appeared to give each group a veto power that could be used to dismantle the state that had been established in the interim.[65]

It was no surprise, therefore, that the plan which the mediators had labored through July and August to fashion was rejected by the Muslims. Lawyers for the Bosnian government appeared before the World Court to ask that any agreement on the division of the republic be declared "null and void on the basis that any signature was coerced under the threat of continuing genocide."[66] The Bosnian ambassador to the UN repudiated the agreement by asserting that his government had been under "unprincipled pressure" to participate in the negotiations.[67] Izetbegović presented the plan to an assembly of the remaining (mostly Muslim) members of the Bosnian parliament and several hundred Bosnian public figures, but opposed its adoption. Members of parliament voted 65–0 to continue the negotiations, but rejected the mediators' plan in its present form.[68] In addition to seeking an outlet to the sea, the assembly demanded a special resolution of the UN Security Council that would provide effective guarantees for implementing the agreement, and guarantees that the United States and NATO would participate in implementation.[69] Izetbegović, in rejecting the plan, struck a pessimistic note. He no longer believed that a unified Bosnia was possible—". . . it looks like we must partition," he told the meeting[70]—but he could not accept the plan, which was unjust:

> Our army has done what it could. And others, you well know, never wished to come at all. The Americans told me—we support you in everything, but do not expect that we are ready to send a single soldier and have him return in a coffin. . . . The Americans wish to remove this war from their agenda.[71]

On August 31 Izetbegović returned to Geneva with a set of demands for additional territories to be included in the proposed Muslim-majority republic in the Prijedor and Sanski Most districts to the west, in eastern Bosnia, and southward to the Adriatic. His demands received the backing of the Clinton administration, which called on the Serbs and Croats to make "the adjustments that the Bosnian government has asked for." The president warned that "the NATO military option is very much alive." Secretary of State Christopher sent messages to both Milošević and Tudjman urging them to accede to Muslim demands, and threatening to hold Serbia and Croatia "responsible" if their "intransigence" led to a breakdown in the negotiations.[72] These comments were offered against the background of renewed public pressure on the administration to act. One hundred prominent individuals, led by Margaret Thatcher and George Shultz and including leading figures from politics, philanthropy, education, science, and culture from the United States and abroad, published an open letter to the president on September 3 urging the United States to lead a military intervention against the Bosnian Serbs and Serbia.[73]

Shortly thereafter, President Izetbegović appeared before the Security Council to call for NATO air strikes and the lifting of the arms embargo against Bosnia-Herzegovina. He received a very cold reception, however. After a speech by the U.S. ambassador supporting the Muslim demands, the Council is reported to have "lapsed into a rare, heavy silence" and to have adjourned abruptly, developments that left the U.S. ambassador "visibly shaken."[74] Izetbegović then traveled to Washington to lobby Congress for direct U.S. military involvement in defense of his government.[75]

The Clinton administration continued to produce contradictory signals with respect to the negotiation of a settlement. President Clinton met Izetbegović at the White House September 8 and, according to media reports, stressed for the first time the need for congressional approval for the participation of U.S. troops in any enforcement operation. One account reported that Clinton mentioned this four times during "a brief photo opportunity at the start of his meeting."[76] Despite continued pressure in Congress to lift the arms embargo, it remained clear that there was little enthusiasm in Congress for the deployment of U.S. ground forces. Members of the House Foreign Relations Committee reportedly "advised Izetbegović not to expect any military support from the United States that might turn the tide of war and help his bargaining position."[77] By raising the issue of congressional approval, the president appeared to be backing away from any willingness to commit troops to Bosnia. A U.S. government official involved in policymaking on the Bosnia issue reported privately on the same day Izetbegović visited the White House that the president was supposed to have been telling Izetbegović that there was "no chance" of U.S. intervention and urging him to come to terms in Geneva. This message was confirmed by Izetbegović in remarks in Sarajevo in October.[78] Bosnian representative to the UN Muhamed Sacirbey, was reduced to remarking, when asked about the president's behavior, "I was pleased by something I saw in his eyes."[79]

International efforts to mediate an agreement continued in the form of bilateral talks among some of the parties, as well as between the co-chairs and each of the parties. The middle of September witnessed lengthy discussions between Izetbegović and Krajišnik. The result was an agreement for a cease-fire between the Muslims and the Serbs, to take effect September 18, and a pledge that the Serb republic could stage a referendum within a two-year period to decide whether to stay in the Union, providing prior agreement had been reached on the fate of Sarajevo, presumably in a manner favorable to the Muslims. If the Serb republic did secede, the Bosnian republic would retain the Union's seat in the UN.[80] The agreement, initiated by Owen and signed in Geneva, was meant to provide the Bosnian Serbs with an opportunity to achieve full independence in return for surrendering their claims to Sarajevo. Izetbegović explained in an interview on Sarajevo radio September 18 that no referendum could be held in the Serb republic unless there had been a satisfactory territorial settlement.[81] A somewhat similar agreement had already been signed September 14 in Geneva between the Muslims and the Croats, leading the mediators to claim a breakthrough in the talks. But, according to the Zagreb press, the agreement stipulated that secession could take place only with the approval of the other two states in Bosnia, thus making it impossible for the Serbs to secede without approval of the Croats and Muslims. [82] Yet the logic of pursuing a cease-fire, absent a political settlement, once again proved false, as Bosnian forces in the Lašva valley continued their offensive against the Croats throughout the month of September.

The Invincible *Proposal*

Direct multilateral negotiations were resumed September 20 at Sarajevo airport, only to be transferred the following day to the HMS *Invincible,* where the mediators met with Tudjman, Milošević, Bulatović, and the representatives of the three warring parties.[83] The *Invincible* negotiations produced an amended version of the August agreement and a new map (Map 6.4), providing the Muslim-majority republic of the future Union of Republics of Bosnia and Herzegovina with access to the Adriatic sea through Croatian territory.[84] This required Croatia to grant the Muslim republic guaranteed use of, as well as uninspected access to and transport from, a port to be constructed at the Croatian town of Ploče, located at the mouth of the Neretva river, under a ninety-nine-year lease arrangement. It also required the Bosnian Serbs to cede to the Muslim republic territory on the Neretva river—previously slated for inclusion in the Serb-majority republic—for construction of a new permanent port facility. These concessions, while significant, were far outweighed by the political gains to be achieved by the Croats and the Serbs as the result of the *de facto* partition called for by the package. The agreement also included a provision that once relations between Croatia and the Federal Republic of Yugoslavia (Serbia and Montenegro) were normalized (that is, once the Krajina issue was resolved), a three-way exchange of territories among the Union, Croatia, and Yugoslavia would be negotiated so as to enhance the strategic security of both Dubrovnik and the Bay of Kotor, and grant the Serb republic in the Bosnian Union its own access to the sea.

Despite Serb and Croat concessions, the agreement was opposed by Muslim hardliners. An assembly of Bosnian public figures meeting September 27 insisted that the Serbs cede more territory to the Bosnian republic, in effect killing the plan. The rump Bosnian parliament then adopted a resolution on September 28 in support of the position taken by the assembly of notables.[85] A certain number of the delegates rejected the proposals of the mediators on principle, because they legitimized the destruction of a multicultural Bosnia. The Western media also noted a hope among the delegates that "the tide in the war was beginning to shift."[86] Muslim military leaders were alleged to have wanted to continue fighting, especially against the Croats, against whom they had scored significant recent victories.[87] Some "Muslim officials" were reported to have been "almost gleeful at the results" of the voting.[88]

Muslim rejection of the plan could also be attributed, in part, to U.S. support for their demands. The new U.S. envoy to the ICFY, Charles Redman, attended the Bosnian parliamentary session that considered the pack-

Map 6.4 **Map Negotiated Aboard HMS *Invincible*, September 1993**

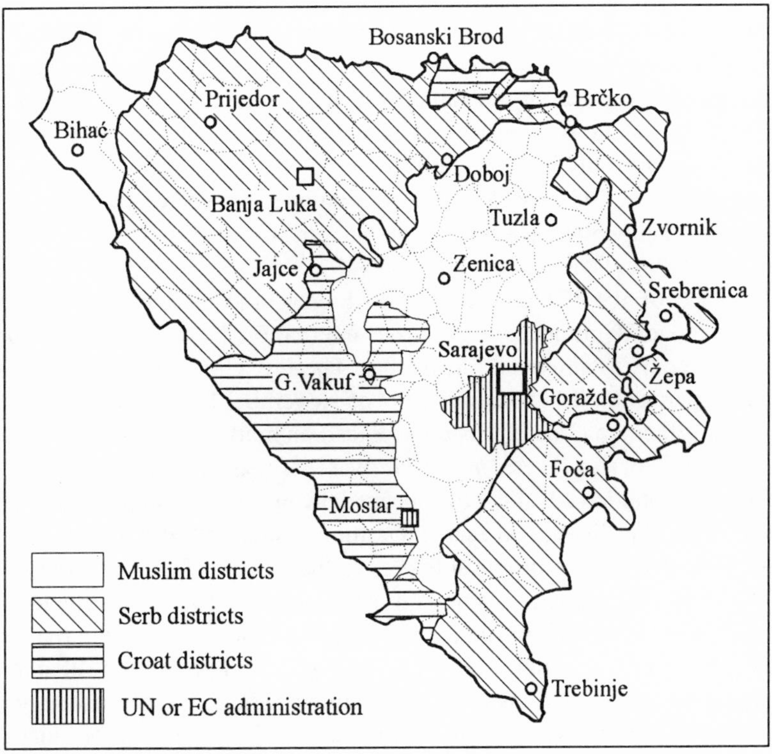

Based on unclassified CIA map 731482 (R00855) 3–94.

age. He did not criticize the Bosnians' decision. Instead, he called for more flexibility on the part of the Croats and the Serbs.[89] He approved of the vote as "democracy in action," and asserted that the United States shared their concern to get "a peace pact that could be carried out."[90] But the administration remained unwilling to act in pursuit of such a pact. In testimony before the Senate in October, a senior State Department official described a set of conditions for U.S. participation in any implementation effort that established a series of impossibly high thresholds for participation. The administration's position was attacked by both those senators opposed to involvement and those supportive of the use of force.[91]

The EU Action Plan and the Demise of the ICFY

By September 1993 the failure to produce a settlement was placing the ICFY under increasing pressure to end the war before winter, when it was feared the people of Bosnia could face starvation. Rejection of the *Invincible* package led the ICFY co-chairs to consider pursuing a comprehensive solution to the crisis, encompassing not only Bosnia, but Krajina (in Croatia) and the Serbian province of Kosovo, as well. Several of the European governments proved skeptical of such an approach.[92] Owen nevertheless urged that the lifting of sanctions against Yugoslavia be tied to a solution to the issue on Krajina, which in his view would provide the momentum for an agreement on Bosnia. Secret talks on Krajina were initiated in Norway, but collapsed when Tudjman publicly stated the Croatian position on November 3, limiting the Serbs to "local and cultural autonomy."[93]

In place of the ICFY strategy, the French and German governments launched a joint initiative to increase international pressure on all three parties to come to agreement in Bosnia. The French-German initiative became known as the EU "Action Plan" of November 8. The solution of the Krajina problem in Croatia was to be placed on hold. The package proposed by the mediators on HMS *Invincible* was defined as a starting point for renewed negotiations. But the Europeans now proposed to explain clearly to · the Muslims the likelihood that international support for them would decline if they rejected a proposal that gave them most of the territories they sought. The Europeans also agreed to offer incentives for the Serbs to give up territory to the Muslims, including suspension of sanctions, international recognition, and assistance for reconstruction.[94] The Action Plan contradicted the U.S. insistence on maintaining sanctions until all regional problems had been resolved. Russia, on the other hand, argued for sanctions to be lifted in advance of a settlement if the Serbs were not responsible for lack of progress in the negotiations. But the negotiations based on these proposals, which were carried out in meetings between the EU foreign ministers and the conflicting parties in November 1993, also failed, as the Bosnian government took an increasingly hard line.

Izetbegović demanded the use of force to protect aid convoys, the opening of Tuzla airport, the return of occupied territories including Neum, and the stationing of international peacekeeping forces only on Bosnian government-controlled territory as a means of permitting the government a five-year period in which it might develop the means of self-defense. The territorial demands effectively reiterated earlier positions that had prevented conclusion of an agreement, and appeared to constitute yet another effort by the Muslim government to prevent an agreement that might freeze the *status quo*. Croatian President Tudjman accepted the European proposal. He reiterated the Croatian offer to allow the establishment of a Muslim-controlled port at Ploče, suggesting the Croats would not offer any additional flexibility on territorial issues. The Serbs were even less agreeable. Milošević attacked the application and continuation of sanctions against Serbia, asking how they could be expected to end a civil war between Muslims and Croats. He argued that continuation of the sanctions encouraged the Muslims to believe that time was on their side and, therefore, to resist any settlement. Karadžić, .in bilateral discussions with the French, flatly rejected the demand that Tuzla airport be reopened, arguing that it would be used to deliver military supplies, not an unreasonable suspicion in view of the fact that the European proposal called for the international community to control only one of the three existing runways. The unenthusiastic response of all three parties to the proposed EU Action Plan opened up political rifts among the Europeans. According to one European report, "The follow up meeting in Brussels on 22 December 1993 degenerated into an undignified shouting match as individual foreign ministers broke ranks when Karadžić failed to agree to their proposals."[95]

The abject failure of the November negotiations highlighted the fact that the Muslim leadership, after its initial bout of extreme pessimism in July, had grown more confident in its ability to survive on its own. As late as the meeting of the Bosnian assembly on September 27, Izetbegović was displaying characteristic self-doubt and indecision, outlining all the factors that were working against the Bosnians, and suggesting that the very biological existence of the Muslim people was at stake if the war was not ended soon—yet rejecting the settlement offered on the *Invincible* as unjust. Meanwhile the Bosnian army thanks to its successes in central Bosnia, was increasingly opposed to a settlement. On November 4 Muslim troops forced the Croats out of Vareš, one of the oldest Catholic bishoprics in the Balkans. On November 7, in a government shakeup, Silajdžić was made prime minister, cementing the alliance between the liberals and the military in opposition to partition. The sum of these developments was, according to Western observers, the emergence of a nascent nationalism among the Muslims, a push toward self-reliance, and a determination to fight on.[96] By the November 1993 negotiations, both the Muslims and the Croats were pursuing a hard line, especially against each other. The Croats, perhaps fearing a Muslim-Serb rapprochement, were insisting that the Bosnian Serbs could not leave the Union without the agreement of the Bosnian Croat republic-to-be.[97] The Muslim offensives in central Bosnia continued into December, when Vitez came under siege. Grbavica, the Serb-held suburb of Sarajevo, came under attack the first week in January.[98]

European contacts with Muslim leaders in December made it clear that the Muslims were "much more self-confident" and "believed they could make more military progress," and thus were less interested in an immediate negotiated settlement.[99] Even the generally sympathetic Western media noted that the lack of progress at Geneva suggested the Bosnian government had little interest in actually reaching a settlement.[100] Talks scheduled for early January were delayed by Muslim reluctance to participate, and by a shelling of Sarajevo airport attributed at the time to the Muslims. By the beginning of 1994, if not earlier, the Muslims had lost interest in negotiations to end the war, the intensive efforts of the ICFY mediators notwithstanding.

In the event, it was left to Tudjman and Milošević to try and close the gap between the parties, presaging the role they were to play at Dayton two years later. They met in December 1993, and agreed to a map that would increase the Muslim share of Bosnia to 33.5 percent, with the Serbs receiving 51 percent and the Croats 17.5 percent. The Bosnian Serbs initially resisted the proposal, but in the first week in January agreed that the Muslims could receive 33.6 percent, on condition that the Bosnian Serb republic be granted immediate independence.[101] As the EU Action Plan faded, Milošević and Tudjman (as well as Montenegrin president Bulatović) met for two days of talks with Izetbegović, Karadžić, and the Bosnian Croat Mile Akmadžić in Geneva on January 18–19, 1994. The map proposed by the Bosnian Serbs (Map 6.5) provided the basis for the negotiations.

The Bosnian Muslim position remained firm despite warnings of Serb-Croat military cooperation in the coming spring (detailed in chapter 4). If Bosnia was to be partitioned, the Muslims demanded 40 percent of the territory of the republic, access to the sea at Neum, a linkup of the eastern enclaves, and access to the Sava river. None of these demands was unreasonable, with the possible exception of the requirement that the Muslims receive 40 percent of Bosnia. But none could be realized under a negotiating framework based on the ICFY, whose leverage on the Serbs was weak. The negotiating impasse was in certain respects a catch-22: the major enticement to the Serbs to give up territory—Sarajevo, for example—was a promise of immediate independence, no strings attached. But it was precisely this prospect that fueled Muslim demands for more, and more viable, territory for their state; which in turn hardened Croatian resistance to granting the new, and militarily more confident Muslims, an outlet to the sea.

As the prospect of a successfully negotiated end of the conflict receded, governments with peacekeeping troops on the ground were growing increasingly concerned about the vulnerability of their troops, as well as the open-ended nature of their commitment. The fighting in Bosnia appeared to be escalating rather than winding down. Mounting evidence suggested that all three sides were preparing for new offensives. The prospect that Croatia and Serbia would be drawn into direct involvement in the war, with untold consequences in Kosovo, Macedonia, and beyond, also was increasing.[102] Key officials in the Clinton administration were growing concerned that

Map 6.5 **Bosnian Serb Proposal for Partition, January 1994**

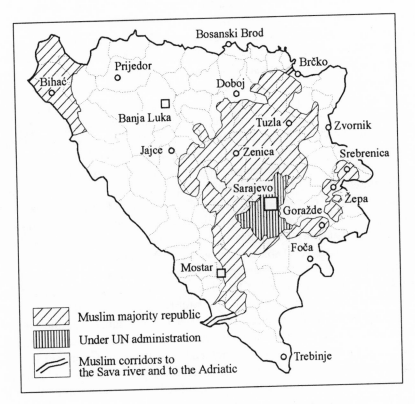

Based on UN Security Council document S/1994/64 (January 21, 1994), p. 5.

continued U.S. inaction would jeopardize the credibility and coherence of the NATO alliance and destabilize the fragile new democracies elsewhere in Eastern Europe.[103] The French were growing increasingly frustrated by the U.S. refusal to pressure the Muslims into accepting an agreement.[104] Yet President Clinton himself appeared unsure of the international community's ability to stop the fighting, saying that he did not think it "has the capacity to stop people within that nation from their civil war until they decide to do it."[105]

It was under these circumstances that the French launched a campaign to pressure the United States into making a commitment to Bosnia. The French pressed their European allies to persuade Washington to throw its support behind the political solution backed by the EU and to back a French proposal to employ air strikes to open the airfield at Tuzla to the UN.[106]

The urgency of French calls for intervention appears to have been motivated, at least in part, by concerns raised by the escalating military activity of the Bosnian army. The United States resisted French pressure for deeper involvement in Bosnia. The differing French and American views of the war led to a bitter public dispute between Foreign Minister Juppé and Secretary of State Christopher in January 1994 over the "morality" of their respective governments' positions.[107] The intensity of the debate reflected, perhaps, the growing sense that a new outbreak of more intense fighting was imminent. UN officials were at this time reporting openly on the movement of Croatian and Yugoslav (Serbian) regular army equipment and troops into Bosnia-Herzegovina in apparent preparation for renewed fighting.[108]

The debate was further fueled by fighting around Sarajevo, and the unwillingness of the Serbs to allow humanitarian convoys into eastern Bosnia. Serb shelling of Sarajevo following the Muslim attack on Grbavica once again raised the issue of NATO's obligation to prevent the strangulation of Sarajevo. On January 10—a day marked by the fierce shelling of Sarajevo by the Serbs—a NATO summit convened in Brussels to consider the Bosnian crisis. The result was a resolution that authorized NATO to use air strikes to protect Sarajevo, but fell short of meeting the French demand for opening the Tuzla airport.[109] The possibility of air strikes dimmed when UN Secretary-General Boutros-Ghali, after initially supporting the NATO resolution, issued a statement on January 18 criticizing NATO's proposals on the grounds that they would not facilitate the delivery of aid to UN peacekeepers in the safe areas in eastern Bosnia. He called for "other military assets" (more ground troops) to meet the UN's needs.[110] In issuing his assessment, Boutros-Ghali was adopting the position of his special representative in Bosnia, Yasushi Akashi. Akashi was in a position to veto air strikes under the dual key system agreed to the previous summer. There was little prospect, therefore, that NATO would undertake air strikes any time soon, either around Sarajevo, or in order to open the airport at Tuzla. On the contrary, the opposition of the British, and especially the Canadians, to air strikes only highlighted the contradiction between positioning UN troops in safe areas—where they risked being taken hostage—and pursuing a policy of attacking Serb military targets from the air.

Toward Reluctant U.S. Leadership

Against the background of a renewed, contentious debate fought out in the media among Western policymakers over what should be done to end the fighting, the explosion of a mortar shell in the central marketplace in Sarajevo in early February—the Markala marketplace massacre described in more detail in chapter 4—sparked a public outcry for action. Worldwide coverage of this event, and the accompanying background reporting on the war and the failure of international efforts to bring it to an end, intensified the pressure on Western policymakers. It lent added urgency to a conclusion allegedly reached by President Clinton's senior national security advisers even before this event: that it was time for the United States to undertake a new initiative.[111] The president began to participate directly in his advisers' deliberations on Bosnia and to lobby other NATO leaders to take direct action—activities that he had for the most part declined to undertake up to this time.[112]

After extended debate, NATO issued an ultimatum on February 9 that reflected a compromise between the U.S. and French positions. It ordered the Serbs to cease their attacks on Sarajevo and to withdraw their heavy weapons from an exclusion zone around the city or face NATO air attack, and admonished Bosnian government forces not to launch assaults of their own from within the city.

The warning to the Bosnians was widely viewed as a cosmetic attempt at evenhandedness. At the time, media coverage attributed NATO action solely to the marketplace shelling, and interpreted Western intervention as an effort simply to restrain the Serbs. The NATO response was, indeed, intended to restrain the Serbs. But the warning to the Bosnian government reflected the intense sensitivity of those with experience on the ground to the Bosnian government tactic of launching military assaults against Serb positions from the safe areas, which had never been demilitarized and whose borders had never been firmly established.[113] At the time of the NATO meeting, for example, responsibility for the marketplace shelling had not yet been definitively determined.[114] Regardless of the culpability to be established for this event, in order for the NATO effort to achieve a meaningful cease-fire, the well-established pattern of attack and counterattack, or provocation and response, which contributed to the continuous violence had to be broken.

The NATO ultimatum set a ten-day deadline for the Bosnian Serb forces to withdraw their heavy weapons and mortars twenty kilometers from the center of the city. (Heavy weapons were permitted within two miles of Pale, which fell within the exclusion zone.) The prohibition was extended to the far smaller number of heavy weapons in the hands of the Bosnian army in Sarajevo. Any such weapons in the "total exclusion zone," along with "direct and essential military support facilities," were to be subject to NATO attack if not under UNPROFOR control after the deadline.[115] In a series of exchanges between Boutros-Ghali and NATO, which had begun before the mortar incident, the secretary-general confirmed UN support for NATO action, while the authority to order air strikes was transferred from Boutros-Ghali to Yasushi Akashi. Once the go-ahead was given, both the UN and NATO commanders in Bosnia were to agree before further strikes could take place. This dual key arrangement continued to be the source of controversy between NATO and the UN in the months to follow.[116]

The following week was one of tension and confusion. The Geneva talks convened February 10 but broke up a day later after the Bosnian government refused to participate.[117] The Russians initially opposed the NATO ultimatum,[118] while making desperate efforts behind the scenes to get the Serbs to agree to pull back their weapons. In Sarajevo, General Rose was able to cobble together a cease-fire that went into effect February 10. Although the agreement was not signed, the Serbs agreed to place their heavy weapons under UNPROFOR control (not simply observation). Still, the issue of just what kind of control UNPROFOR would exercise over Serb weapons, and whether any could remain in the exclusion zone, remained unclear due to disagreements between General Rose and NATO.[119] On February 17, in a key move aimed at resolving the crisis, Russia's special envoy Vitaly Churkin and Karadžić announced that the Serbs had agreed to Russian proposals for a withdrawal of Serb forces and that the Russians would contribute troops to monitoring a cease-fire.[120] On the same day, the details of an agreement over the control of heavy weapons were worked out between UN staff and the Serbs.[121] The Serb pull-back of heavy weapons began that day, in conjunction with the appearance of Karadžić and Churkin in Pale.[122]

This fortunate outcome had been far from certain. The Serb military, led by General Mladić, had vigorously opposed the removal of heavy weapons from the exclusion zone.[123] Mladić was won over on February 17, thanks in part to pressure from the Russians.[124] The differences between General Rose and NATO over whether the Serbs should be allowed any leeway in abiding by the February 9 ultimatum delayed implementation of the agreement to the last possible minute. In fact, both the Bosnian Serbs and the Bosnian government were unhappy with the agreement establishing the exclusion zone. The Serbs argued in vain for a larger UNPROFOR troop presence to secure the cease-fire. The Bosnian government was openly hostile to the cease-fire engineered by General Rose, and dismayed and shocked when NATO air strikes against the Serbs in response to the marketplace massacre were not forthcoming.

Washington's choice of NATO as the venue for debating the use of force—a move designed to permit the United States to retain close political and military control over any eventual operations—effectively minimized the role of Russia in policy deliberations. The ICFY mediators were pushed to one side during the crisis, a clear sign that they had outlived their usefulness. Owen, who opposed the air strikes, tried vainly to forge a plan that would take Sarajevo out of the war as an alternative to the NATO ultimatum.[125] Russia opposed the use of force against the Serbs and resisted extending Security Council authorization for any NATO action.[126] NATO was thus obliged to justify its actions on the basis of existing Security Council resolutions and, despite the objections of the Russians, no effort was made to seek explicit Security Council authorization for the use of air power.

The fact that the Serbs finally did withdraw their heavy weapons (or place them under UNPROFOR control) could be seen as a response to Western firmness, as Anthony Lake, President Clinton's national security adviser, was to argue the following fall.[127] However, perhaps the most dramatic signal of the administration's readiness to use force—a somber radio address by President Clinton on February 19 reiterating the threat to use force against the Serbs if the deadline for withdrawal was not met[128]— came *after* the February 17 agreement had been concluded. Alternatively, the Russian role in supplying forces to police the cease-fire could be seen as critical to the outcome. Their presence prevented Bosnian government forces from using the opportunity to break out of the city. Our own surmise is that both factors contributed to the decision of the Serbs to abide by the NATO ultimatum. It was important, in addition, that the agreement was one that fit the Serb goal of keeping alive negotiations for a cease-fire that would consolidate Serb gains. The Serbs were even willing to consider the demilitarization of Sarajevo, as long as those areas under Serb control were not turned over to the Bosnian government.

President Boris Yeltsin pointedly remarked on February 15 that Russia would "not allow" the Bosnian question to be resolved "without the participation of Russia."[129] The injection of Russian forces secured the importance of Russian participation in any international effort to achieve a settlement. The Russian commitment to deploy troops in areas strategically important to the Bosnian Serbs was accompanied by increased Russian pressure on the Serbs to withdraw from the NATO exclusion zone.[130] Russian participation in negotiations tended to counterbalance U.S. support for the Muslim-dominated government. Owen implies that the increased prominence and influence of the Russians resulting from their involvement in implementing the Sarajevo exclusion zone finally prompted the United States to take a more active role in efforts to negotiate a solution to the conflict.[131] At the very least, the Russian actions took most key members of the Clinton administration by surprise,[132] and may have increased the pressure they felt to act.

The creation of a NATO-enforced weapons exclusion zone around Sarajevo and a similar, later action applied to Goražde and the four other safe areas established by earlier Security Council actions highlighted the differences in philosophy and practice between UN peacekeeping operations and the kind of coercive diplomacy advocated by the United States and some other—but not all—NATO countries. The inclinations of peacekeepers to maintain strict neutrality and to afford warring parties ample opportunities to "save face" in the interest of establishing voluntary compliance clashed with the U.S. inclination to respond to force with counterforce, or at least with the threat of counterforce. Akashi was drawn into a particularly bitter dispute with the Americans, arising out of his inclination to negotiate a settlement rather than resort to force and his criticism of the Clinton administration's unwillingness to contribute troops to the peacekeeping effort.[133] What was becoming increasingly clear was that neither the Clinton administration, nor UN officials, nor the NATO leadership appeared to be guided by a coherent strategic concept for the settlement of the conflict. Washington appeared to be motivated primarily by the desire to reaffirm the effectiveness of U.S. leadership in NATO and the broader international community, as well as by the wish to bring the war to an end. Indeed, four of the seven U.S. interests in the war defined by President Clinton at the time involved relations with Europe and NATO; none concerned the substance of the conflict itself.[134]

The president repeatedly ruled out the use of U.S. ground troops to impose a settlement. Otherwise, his administration was issuing somewhat conflicting signals. Unnamed senior officials reported in media accounts that the administration was ready to press the Muslims to accept partition and to lift sanctions against Serbia in exchange for cooperation. But Undersecretary of State Peter Tarnoff was reported to have told European allies that the United States would not pressure the Bosnian government to sign an agreement.[135] Secretary of Defense William Perry, appearing on a TV talk show on February 10, said NATO would consider widening and intensifying air strikes to compel Serb compliance with the NATO ultimatum. But that threat was toned down by Deputy Undersecretary of Defense Walter Slocombe, who on the same day said, "We are not embarking on a policy of generalized air strikes across Bosnia either to affect the military outcome or to propel the parties to settle."[136]

Nonetheless, the prospect that more extensive air strikes might be launched against the Serbs, the increased involvement of NATO in the fighting, and U.S. political support probably contributed to the escalation of Muslim territorial demands in Geneva in February 1994.[137] The Bosnian government refused even to discuss the issue of Sarajevo, raising instead the status of fifteen other disputed areas. The Bosnian delegation was reported to be "going through the motions," hoping for NATO air strikes against the Serbs;[138] a hope sustained, perhaps, by such forceful rhetoric as that employed by Ambassador Albright at the Security Council on February 14. "The objective of peace cannot be achieved by diplomacy alone," she argued.

> Our diplomacy must be backed by a willingness to use force when that is essential in the cause of peace. For it is only force plus diplomacy that can stop the slaughter in Sarajevo and break the stalemate in Geneva.

Albright warned the Bosnian Serbs that they "should not doubt our will, nor that of our NATO partners, to carry out the February 9 decision."[139] Indeed, as we noted in chapter 4, on February 28 NATO aircraft downed four Yugoslav jet fighters over central Bosnia—NATO's first combat action since its establishment in 1949.[140]

The United States embarked on an effort to identify the Bosnian government's "bottom line" in the negotiations. The U.S. envoy to the ICFY, Charles Redman, declared in Sarajevo on February 11 that the United States intended "to reinvigorate the negotiations and produce the kinds of results the Bosnians have been looking for."[141] Secretary of State Christopher testified later in the month to the Senate that the United States considered the Serbs aggressors and was not going to impose a solution on the victims, another sharp reversal of both the substance and the rhetoric of American policy.[142] Yet, Redman was reported to be "pushing the Bosnians not to expect to win a war they have lost through negotiations or even through NATO air strikes."[143] He extracted from Silajdžić the astonishing concession that the Bosnian government would accept "complete autonomy for the territory under Serb control."[144] It seemed, from the responses of Bosnian Ambassador to the UN Muhamed Sacirbey in an interview on American television on February 19, that the Muslims were indeed moving toward accepting the idea of partition.[145]

At the same time, the Americans had begun to pursue a separate settlement between the Croats and the Muslims that would end the fighting in central Bosnia, provide a counterweight to Serb military power, and lead to an overall settlement based on the creation of two rather than three entities within Bosnia-Herzegovina.[146] The step was a major diplomatic initiative. It took place, however, against a backdrop of failure and frustration in the Croat-Muslim relationship, despite the common interest of Zagreb and Sarajevo in defeating the Serbs.

Croat-Muslim Relations and the Establishment of the Bosnian Federation

Croat-Muslim relations were to prove the key to ending the war in Bosnia. But, for the first year and a half of the war, these relations were strained by Croatian overtures to Belgrade and by the conflicting Muslim and Croat claims to territory in central Bosnia and the Neretva valley. An alliance between the Croats and Muslims was first negotiated by Tudjman and Izetbegović in May 1992, but never implemented.[147] A number of subsequent efforts were made by international negotiators at the ICFY to get the Muslims and the Croats to halt the fighting between them. December 1992– January 1993 saw repeated efforts by Vance and Owen in this regard. Both the Croats and the Muslims realized that they were suffering a serious loss of credibility in the eyes of the international community while allowing the Serbs to consolidate their hold over almost three-quarters of Bosnia. Nonetheless, cease-fires failed to hold. On May 18, 1993, international mediators convened a meeting of Muslim and Croat leaders in Medjugorje, two days after the referendum in Serb-held territories had rejected the Vance-Owen plan.[148] Their intention was to forge an agreement implementing the plan in the provinces designated as either Muslim-majority or Croat-majority, with the exception of province five. But, as we have noted, the Muslims and Croats were unable to agree on military control. The project died when the Croats insisted at a meeting held in Geneva on June 14 that a "coordinating body" for the union include Karadžić as well as two other Serbs.[149]

In January 1994, amid reports that regular Croatian troops were involved in the fighting in central Bosnia, further attempts were made by the international community to reconcile the Bosnian government and the Croatians. The foreign ministers of the Bosnian government and Croatia—Haris Silajdžić and Mate Granić—met under the auspices of ICFY mediators in Vienna in early January. Some progress appears to have been made. It was agreed that Mostar would be placed under EU administration for two years. There were also discussions in Vienna of a cease-fire, and an eventual cessation of hostilities. On January 9, 1994 Izetbegović and Tudjman met in Bonn at German urging. The discussions were held in the shadow of negotiations between Belgrade and Zagreb aimed at improving relations between Serbia and Croatia. At the Bonn meeting, Tudjman proposed the formation of a loose union between two Bosnian states, the Croat Herzeg-Bosnia and a Muslim Bosnian republic. Predictably, Izetbegović rejected the offer. The two also failed to resolve their conflicting claims to territory in central Bosnia.[150]

The failure of the Tudjman-Izetbegović talks in January 1994 may have convinced the Americans that an end to the Muslim-Croat conflict could not be reached through negotiating boundaries between them. It may have shaped the U.S. strategy of trying to get around the territorial issues by pushing for a formal federation between the Bosnian Muslims and Bosnian Croats first, leaving ethno-territorial boundaries for later resolution. But the underlying territorial issues would not go away. Croatia had occupied Neum, and central Bosnia remained effectively partitioned by the Muslim-Croat fighting of 1993 and subsequent cease-fire.

Later in January 1994, Belgrade and Zagreb agreed to set up "representative offices" in each other's capitals. The move took place amid renewed talk that Milošević was ready to jettison the Krajina Serbs for the sake of an agreement with Croatia.[151] As we noted in chapter 4, rumors circulated in European capitals of a combined Croat-Serb offensive in Bosnia that might endanger UN forces.[152] The Bosnian government, despite its growing military confidence, found itself beleaguered. It was fighting a two-front war, and contending with the diplomatic offensive launched by the Europeans for concessions to Belgrade as part of their action plan to hasten a political settlement. The Croats, for their part, were hardly better off. Their credibility and prestige had suffered drastically from the ethnic cleansing in Herzegovina, while sanctions loomed if Croatian regular army troops were not withdrawn from central Bosnia. Both the Croats and Muslims, then, had much to gain from a cease-fire and an end to the fighting between them, which in any case had more or less already determined the territorial division of central Bosnia and the Neretva valley.

Thus, under intense diplomatic pressure from the United States, the Croats agreed to a U.S.-brokered plan calling for formation of a joint Muslim-Croat federation in those Bosnian territories held by Muslim and Croat forces—about one-third of the country.[153] On February 8, one day before the NATO ultimatum that followed the Markala marketplace massacre, Mate Boban was removed from his post as president of Herzeg-Bosnia and replaced by a relative moderate, Krešimir Zubak.[154] This tightened Zagreb's control over the Bosnian Croat leadership. On February 18, the Bosnian and Croatian foreign ministers met in Germany under American auspices to work out the "normalization" of relations between the two states and discuss the creation of a Muslim-Croat federation in Bosnia.[155] These talks led to agreement on a cease-fire between Muslim and Croat forces in Bosnia on February 22.[156] Bosnian Croat forces (the HVO) complied with the agreement only under pressure from Zagreb.[157] According to Tudjman, the Americans secured Zagreb's support only after offering their assurances for Croatian territorial integrity and promising Croatia an international loan for reconstruction, membership in the Partnership for Peace program of

NATO, and membership in the Council of Europe.[158] According to a Western media account, Tudjman had been subjected to immense pressure from the Americans, including a direct threat by President Clinton of sanctions and isolation.[159] Tudjman himself acknowledged that the United States "insisted and persisted that we must reach agreement with the Muslims."[160]

On March 1 an agreement on the principles of a Bosnian (Muslim-Croat) Federation, and a preliminary agreement on a confederation between the Bosnian Federation and Croatia, were initialed in Washington by Silajdžić and Zubak. This immediately came to be known as the "Washington agreement."[161] On March 4 an agreement on further details of the Washington agreement was hammered out in Bonn under German supervision and initialed by Zubak and Ejup Ganić.[162] This was followed by intensive talks in Vienna between the two protagonists, held in the American embassy. The Vienna negotiations produced a draft constitution on March 13.[163] On March 12 an agreement on integration of the Bosnian Croat and Muslim armed forces was signed in Split in the presence of retired U.S. General John Galvin.[164] A constitution for the federation was formally signed in Washington on March 18. The agreement signaled that the Croats had given up—at least formally—their demands to divide Bosnia into three entities, Croat, Muslim, and Serb. The Bosnian (Muslim-Croat) federation was to be a single entity composed of a number of cantons yet to be determined. On March 28–30 the rump parliament of the Republic of Bosnia-Herzegovina met and adopted the constitution of the federation.[165]

The Muslim-Croat agreement marked a sharp change in Croatian strategy. As reported on Zagreb TV, Tudjman informed Akashi "that the entire geopolitical situation has changed as a result of [the Washington agreement] and Croatian efforts would now be directed towards the solving of the problem of the reintegration of the [UN] protected areas [in Croatia] into the constitutional and legal system of the country."[166] Tudjman appeared to have abandoned the tripartite partition of Bosnia in exchange for securing the territorial integrity of Croatia, and a bilateral partition of Bosnia. The Croats could accept the Bosnian (Muslim-Croat) Federation proposed by the Americans because the fighting between Muslim and Croat forces had resolved a number of the military control issues concerning western Herzegovina in favor of the Croats; because the agreement provided extensive local control for ethnic minorities within cantons, thus delaying the inevitable confrontation between Croats and Muslims over control of the mixed cantons; and because by accepting the agreement Croatia would get the United States behind partition. In addition, by accepting the agreement Croatia could secure significant economic and political support from the United States.

Under the American plan, a Bosnian Federation would be established in the territories under Muslim and Croat control, which would then enter into a confederative relationship with Croatia; a clear victory for Zagreb and a step in the direction of fulfilling historical Croatian territorial aspirations in Bosnia and Herzegovina. Creation of the federation would contribute to the economic and political isolation of the Bosnian Serbs. Muslim and Croat military forces were to be integrated under a single joint command, increasing the pressure on the Bosnian Serbs to agree to a settlement, although existing command structures were also allowed to remain in place. The Washington agreement left the most difficult territorial and political issues unresolved, however.[167] Similarly, it applied unspecified principles of proportionality to elections for representative office, and established "consensual" principles of decision-making on unspecified critical issues. It provided the federation with access to the sea by adopting arrangements similar to those developed as part of the *Invincible* package that had been rejected by the Muslims. Most important, it made no effort to provide for the eventual inclusion of Serb-majority territories. Although unnamed senior officials in the Clinton administration reportedly acknowledged that a stable settlement would require exchanges of territories and would have to allow the Bosnian Serbs at least some form of association with Serbia that paralleled the relationship between the federation and Croatia, the formal initiative seemed to reflect a U.S. determination to ignore Serb interests.[168] Following the signing of the Washington agreement, U.S. national security advisor Anthony Lake characterized the positions of Serbia and the Bosnian Serbs as intransigent.[169]

The constitution of the federation adopted in Washington on March 18, 1994, reaffirmed the sovereignty and integrity of Bosnia-Herzegovina. The constitution was to apply to those districts which, in 1991, were in the majority Muslim or Croat (Article 1). Constitutional arrangements for those areas which were Serb would be defined in the context of a peace settlement for Bosnia. The status of those Serbs who found themselves inside the borders of the federation was left unresolved. Only the Bosniacs (the newly adopted label for the Muslims) and Croats were identified as constituent peoples of the Republic of Bosnia-Herzegovina. This formula excluded "others" (presumably Serbs and other ethnic groups), who helped form the federation but were not constituent peoples.[170] In mixed Muslim-Croat cantons, the constitution called for the devolution of control over education, culture, and the media to municipalities whose majority differed from that of the canton as a whole. Until a peace settlement took effect, the Republic of Bosnia-Herzegovina (that is, the existing Muslim-dominated government) would continue to exercise key functions of the federation, including the conduct of foreign affairs.

Notwithstanding the adoption of a constitution, the final form of the

Map 6.6 **Bosnian Federation (Without Serb-Held Territory)**

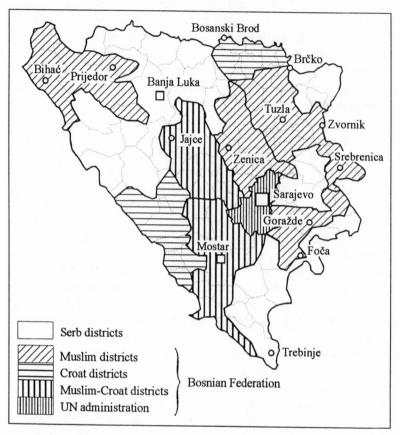

Serb districts

Muslim districts

Croat districts

Muslim-Croat districts

UN administration

Bosnian Federation

Based on a document of the Vienna meeting, May 11, 1994.

federation remained unresolved. The assembly (the rump Bosnian parliament, with Croats participating) remained deadlocked over the choice of the president of the federation and the delineation of the boundaries of its cantons. In mid-April, the EU met in Brussels to discuss the future of Mostar, and to draw up a plan of assistance for the city.[171] In the second week of May, further negotiations were carried out in Vienna under the watchful eye of Charles Redman, now the U.S. ambassador to Germany. It was agreed that the constitution of the federation would guarantee the equality of the constituent peoples in mixed cantons, thereby implying that in these territories power would be devolved to local ethnic communities.[172] Two different maps were agreed to by Silajdžić and Granić (Maps 6.6 and

Map 6.7 **Bosnian Federation (Proposed Serb Canton)**

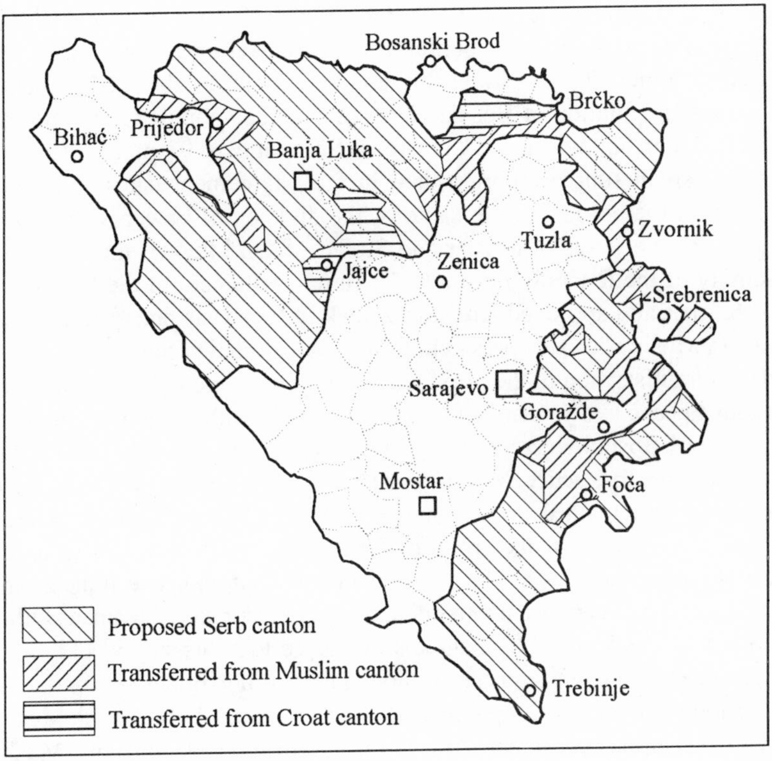

Based on a document of the Vienna meeting, May 11, 1994.

6.7). The first consisted of a map of the federation that included those territories held by the Muslims and Croats, as well as areas in which the prewar population included a Muslim-Croat plurality. This amounted to 58 percent of the republic. It excluded territories held by the Serbs. In the unlikely event that the Bosnian Serbs decided to join the federation, a second map defined the cantons for all of Bosnia-Herzegovina. Interestingly, the Serb cantons defined in this latter map included a corridor between the Banja Luka region and Serb cantons in eastern Bosnia. Both the expansiveness of the claims inherent in the first map, and the limited but strategic concessions to the Serbs in the second map—heretofore resisted tenaciously by the Muslims—suggested that neither the Croat nor the Muslim side was genuinely committed to including the Serbs in the federation.

The first map was made public on May 14, in Geneva, in the presence of the foreign ministers of the Contact Group.[173] The map divided the federation into eight cantons, two of which were "mixed," two Croat, and four Muslim. The Sarajevo region was to fall under UN administration.[174] Based on prewar census data, the borders of the federation announced in May would have included an estimated 2,844,00 people, or about 65 percent of the prewar population of Bosnia-Herzegovina. The population would have been 51.1 percent Muslim, 24.1 percent Serb, and 16.93 percent Croat.[175] But a Bosnian source reported that, in fact, agreement had not yet been reached on the borders of the cantons, the division of power within mixed cantons, or the status of Mostar and Stolac.[176] On May 31, the constituent assembly of the federation (in fact, the rump parliament of the Republic of Bosnia) met and approved Krešimir Zubak (a Croat) as president and Ejup Ganić (a Muslim) as vice president for the transitional period.[177]

UN administration of the province of Sarajevo could not be implemented without a peace treaty. Until then, the city remained the responsibility of the Republic of Bosnia-Herzegovina. Mostar, on the other hand, fell under EU administration. In practice, Mostar remained divided, and the powers of the EU administration remained strictly limited.[178] The problem of Bosnian access to the sea was resolved by the promise of a customs union with Croatia and the lease of harbor facilities at Ploče once the confederation between the Bosnian Federation and Croatia went into effect. That confederation remained stillborn, however. It was blocked by Zagreb's insistence that this step would have to await a peace settlement and clarification of the position of the Serbs.

Although never fully implemented, the agreements between the Muslims and Croats brokered by the Americans in spring 1994 did end Muslim-Croat fighting and made it possible to establish a common Muslim-Croatian military effort against the Serbs. Croatia became more open to the Bosnian government's circumvention of the arms embargo, and Bosnian military commanders appeared to be encouraged further in the belief that they would eventually defeat the Serbs. Roadblocks were removed in some areas of central Bosnia, and a trickle of refugees began to return to their homes. Living conditions also improved. These were modest but real achievements. But the main consequence of the federation was to make it possible for the United States to accept the partition of Bosnia. As one senior diplomat put it privately, formation of the Bosnian Federation was "the first shoe"; the second shoe was to drop at Dayton.

Formation of the Contact Group

Despite the relative peace that prevailed in Bosnia in spring 1994, neither the establishment of a Muslim-Croat federation nor the halfhearted coercive diplomacy pursued by the United States and NATO offered much hope of achieving an overall political settlement. As we noted earlier, the NATO ultimatum designed to end the siege of Sarajevo produced a corresponding hardening of the Bosnian government's negotiating positions and the breakup of the ICFY talks in Geneva in February.[179] In April 1994 Izetbegović told the ICFY co-chairs: "To be honest, if we could we would take land by force but we don't have the means. We are only negotiating because we don't think we can win militarily."[180] Indeed, one journalist has suggested that the Muslims agreed to the U.S. plan for a federation only after the United States threatened to withdraw its support for the Bosnian government.[181]

The outbreak of fighting around Goražde in April 1994 threw all hope of negotiating a cease-fire to the wind. The use of NATO air power in "pin-prick" attacks against Serb forces attacking the city (described in chapter 4) shifted the burden of finding a political settlement to the United States. The Clinton administration, although still internally divided, was becoming frustrated by the lack of progress in the ICFY negotiations and by the opposition of UN officials to the use of force against the Serbs.[182] Secretary of State Christopher declared, "I feel very strongly that this is a time when even a cautious Secretary of State, which perhaps I'll always be, feels the need to vindicate the United States leadership." He nevertheless suggested that the goal of U.S. leadership should be "to take a strong robust position to ensure that this conflict does not spread and to ensure that we maintain the credibility of NATO as well as our own forces,"[183] rather than to resolve the conflict itself. But the administration was coming under increased domestic political pressure to lift the arms embargo and to use air power as a means of forcing concessions from the Serbs. Former U.S. Ambassador to Yugoslavia Warren Zimmerman laid out the case for using air power against the Serbs in the *Washington Post* on April 24. He argued that the crisis in Goražde had brought the Bosnian conflict to a "defining moment." Speaking of President Clinton, Zimmerman warned:

> If, for whatever reason he comes up short on the use of U.S. force, that failure will bring him most of the blame. If, on the other hand, he is successful in a major expansion of air strikes, then he has an excellent chance of driving the Serbs to a negotiated settlement that preserves a viable territory for the Bosnians.[184]

The administration was also coming under some pressure from the Europeans to join in an effort to impose a settlement on the warring parties. French Foreign Minister Juppé warned in mid-May, for example, that the Europeans considered their position in Bosnia untenable and that "there is no question of going through another winter there."[185] In a speech in the United States, he warned that, unless there was a "swift diplomatic breakthrough," France would have to consider withdrawing its troops. He urged the United Sates to pressure the Muslims to this end.[186] Thus, a combination of factors appeared in spring 1994 to push the Clinton administration toward reliance on force as a means to end the fighting—through more extensive use of air power, lifting the arms embargo, or direct intervention.[187]

In order to draw the United States more directly into the task of finding a political solution, and to preserve a central role for the Europeans, the co-chairs of the ICFY proposed establishing a "Contact Group" of U.S., Russian, French, German, and British representatives in late April 1994 in London to hammer out a solution that all could support and enforce. This revived the idea first broached by the Americans in May 1993 in connection with the short-lived "Joint Action Program" (reported earlier in this chapter). The proposal also reflected the increased tendency since February for the great powers to negotiate among themselves rather than participate in the ICFY. A meeting of U.S., Russian, European, and UN officials had already taken place in Bonn in February, and had agreed on a division of labor between the Russians—who were expected to bring the Serbs to agreement—and the Americans—who "promised" to deliver the Muslims.[188] The establishment of the Contact Group conceded leadership of the peace effort to the United States and, indirectly, to the Russians. It effectively circumvented the ICFY on the Bosnia question and ended its role as the locus of efforts to mediate a settlement.[189]

Formation of the Contact Group also transformed the character of the international effort to achieve a settlement. The Contact Group would not attempt to conduct direct, multilateral negotiations among the warring parties. Representatives of the group met with each of the parties separately for consultations. But even this was largely to preserve appearances.[190] These meetings provided yet another forum in which the warring parties would present their demands. In a meeting with Contact Group representatives at the end of April, for example, Izetbegović expressed his regret that the opportunity had been missed at Goražde to destroy the Serb "war machine," and argued that only this would create the conditions for peace in Bosnia. He also set out two conditions for a settlement: respect for the sovereignty and territorial integrity of the Republic of Bosnia-Herzegovina, and the withdrawal of Serb troops from Muslim and Croat areas. He also stressed that a settlement in Bosnia could not be separated from a comprehensive peace settlement for all former Yugoslav areas, including specifically (and provocatively) the Sandžak.[191] His concern for the Sandžak reflected the pressure coming from the extremist faction of the SDA. Ejup Ganić (as we noted earlier, a Muslim originally from the Sandžak), for example, later claimed openly that the Sandžak was part of Bosnia.[192] The Contact Group, however, decided in mid-May that the Muslim-Croat federation would receive 51 percent, and the Serbs 49 percent of the territory of Bosnia-Herzegovina as part of an eventual settlement.[193]

The Contact Group met with all the parties in late May in Talloires, France, to present their initial proposals. The Contact Group members attempted to devise a plan that all members of the group would be willing to impose on the parties. High priority was assigned to preserving unity among the members. According to one close observer,

> At times the driving force appeared to be the will to maintain European/Russian/American solidarity, even if this meant unwelcome compromises at potentially crucial stages of the peace process. A strong adverse reaction from one participant often resulted in the other representatives, even if they saw merit in the proposals, acquiescing in the interests of maintaining solidarity.[194]

The main issues confronting the Contact Group, and the positions of the warring parties on them, were little changed from those that had developed over the course of 1993 and early 1994.[195] There was also little change in the positions of the great powers themselves. The United States continued to seek the application of greater military pressure against the Bosnian Serbs and the tightening of sanctions against Serbia, while the Russians resisted.

The Russians were particularly critical of the use of NATO air power against the Serbs at Goražde without prior consultation, although they, like the Americans, appeared to be internally divided over the issue.[196] While Russian military leaders still appeared sympathetic to the Bosnian Serbs, the events surrounding Goražde in April had hardened attitudes toward the Bosnian Serbs in the Russian foreign ministry.[197] The Bosnian Serb attack on Goražde appears to have been sustained despite attempts by Russian Foreign Minister Kozyrev and Special Envoy Vitaly Churkin to persuade the Serbs to end the attack. Churkin, following a meeting with Bosnian Serb leaders, declared that

> The Bosnian Serbs must understand that in Russia they are dealing with a great power, not a banana republic. Russia must decide whether a group of extremists can be allowed to use a great country's policy to achieve its own aims. Our answer is unequivocal: "never."[198]

Russian Defense Minister Pavel Grachev, however, explicitly disagreed with Churkin and argued that "it would be wrong to put all the blame on the Bosnian Serbs."[199]

The European members of the Contact Group advocated lifting sanctions on the Serbs in return for compliance, while the Americans sought to maintain sanctions until all outstanding conflicts in the former Yugoslavia were resolved. This was to become a key issue in future negotiations. The Group finally agreed on "phased suspension of the sanctions" in return for compliance, including "withdrawal to agreed territorial limits" as defined by a map under preparation by the Group.[200]

The warring parties remained deeply divided over the map. They disputed the territories around Prijedor and Sanski Most in western Bosnia, the whole of eastern Bosnia, the northern corridor at Brčko, and the establishment of a land corridor between the Bihać pocket in the northwest and territories under at least the nominal control of the Muslim-Croat federation. A Muslim proposal to establish a land corridor between the Bihać pocket and central Bosnia raised the prospect that by agreeing to such a plan the Bosnian Serbs would be effectively isolating the Serb-populated Krajina region in Croatia. They rejected it out of hand. The parties also disputed control of Sarajevo. The Bosnian Serbs offered to exchange the suburbs of Ilijaš and Vogošća for the enclaves in eastern Bosnia, an offer which the Bosnian government turned down. The Serbs demanded access to the sea. Despite the fact that negotiators conceived of opportunities to settle these disputes through land swaps, they declined to put forward any such proposals themselves for fear of the public outcry that would ensue, particularly if they were to propose that the Muslims give up the eastern enclaves in exchange for territory around Sarajevo. The U.S., Russian, and European envoys did, however, engage in the trading of disputed territories on their own in an apparent effort to represent the views of their respective clients while forging a proposal that would be acceptable to all concerned. The difficulty of convincing the Bosnian Serbs to concede to Muslim demands led Russian diplomat Alexei Nikiforov to observe in June that only a federation (Muslim-Croat) military victory could get the Serbs to give up territory.[201]

Akashi attempted in early June to mediate cease-fire talks in Geneva. The importance that the Serbs placed on these negotiations was indicated by the presence in Geneva of General Mladić, who, according to press accounts, left the Geneva conference furious at Bosnian government opposition to a formal cease-fire.[202] The failure of these negotiations was a political defeat for Akashi, and from this point on, the UN ceased to play a significant role in resolving the Bosnian crisis. On June 8 the Bosnian government grudgingly agreed to a cease-fire of one month, but then promptly violated the agreement.[203] Taking advantage of the relative calm in eastern and central Bosnia, government forces launched an offensive against Fikret Abdić's Muslim forces in Cazinska Krajina (the Bihać pocket). The prolonged and inconclusive fighting that resulted has been described in detail in chapter 4.

Despite reluctance on the part of the United States, the Contact Group did finally produce a map in July 1994[204] and presented it to all three parties along with a "peaceful ultimatum" to accept it. The map (Map 6.8) expanded the territories assigned to the Muslims and Croats (now formally linked in the Bosnian Federation) over those allocated to them under the August Owen-Stoltenberg agreement—but this was still less territory than they would have received under the Vance-Owen plan. The map also provided direct access for the federation to Brčko. Most of the city was to go to the federation, with the Serbs' east–west corridor reduced to a bridge over a north-south highway.[205] The map established a 51 percent–49 percent division between the Muslim-Croat federation on the one hand, and the Bosnian Serbs on the other. This represented rejection of Muslim demands for 58 percent that had appeared to enjoy the backing of the United States, especially since the map of the federation agreed to in May (Map 6.6 page 296) laid claim to 58 percent.[206] Although the Muslim-led government remained dissatisfied with the territorial division and immediately renewed their demands for still more territories,[207] Izetbegović made it clear that the government would accept the contact group plan so as to throw the onus of rejection onto the Serbs. "If we evaluate that the Serbs will say no," he stated, "then we will say yes. So I emphasize that we will be saying yes, since the Serbs will be rejecting it."[208] Indeed, Karadžić is reported to have been relieved when he saw the map for the first time. "I thought the maps would present a problem," he is reported to have observed. "But there is no problem. There won't be a single Serb who would accept this." In his view, "the maps had been drawn so the Serbs would reject them and be blamed for the continuation of the war."[209]

The constitutional arrangements proposed by the Contact Group were not made public. They appear to have been based largely on those proposed as part of the *Invincible* package. According to a Bosnian analysis,[210] the contact group plan consisted only of a three-page "working proposal" calling for the establishment of two entities (the Bosnian [Muslim-Croat] Federation and a Serb entity). It called for a presidency composed of one representative of each of the three groups, which would make its decisions on the basis of consensus. Leadership of the presidency would rotate among the groups every four months. The parliament would make its decisions on the basis of a two-thirds majority that had to include a majority of the delegates of each group. Despite the federation agreement brokered by the Americans, a European source[211] reports that the Croats opposed the divi-

Map 6.8 **Contact Group Map, July 1994**

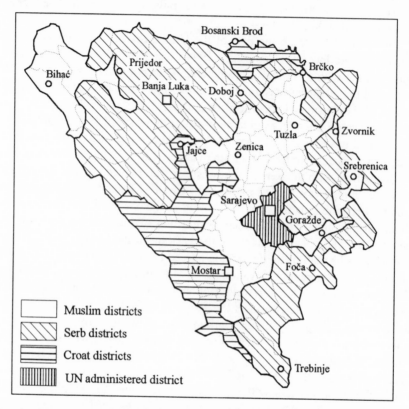

Based on UN Security Council document S/1994/1081 (September 21, 1994), p. 2.

sion of Bosnia into two entities, preferring three. The Serbs continued to pursue the creation of an entirely separate Serb entity. They argued that the formation of a Muslim-Croat federation claiming 58 percent of Bosnia, and the refusal to allow the Serb republic to establish closer ties with Serbia when Bosnian Croats were permitted to establish ties to Croatia through the federation, precluded their participation.

The contact group members disagreed sharply over the incentives and disincentives to be attached to their proposal. A U.S. proposal to develop graduated military options to pressure the Serbs into acceptance met with strong resistance. The Russians in particular were concerned that too great a reliance on such military measures as exclusion zones might encourage provocations by the Bosnian government designed to trigger military intervention. They argued that a proposal to lift sanctions would be more effective than a threat to lift the arms embargo. Lifting of the arms embargo also was opposed by the British and the French, who made it clear that they would not keep their troops in Bosnia-Herzegovina if the embargo were lifted.[212] The Clinton administration, however, remained under intense domestic political pressure to support lifting the embargo. In June the House of Representatives voted to lift the embargo by a substantial majority that included many members of the president's own party. In July the Senate failed by only one vote to adopt such a measure.[213]

The contact group map, if accepted by all three parties, would have required the deployment of an international military force to ensure its implementation. The United States agreed that it would supply about half the troops necessary, or about 20,000 troops. If the map/plan were to be rejected, senior administration officials predicted that U.S. involvement in the war would escalate. Secretary of Defense William Perry suggested that in either case NATO would have "an expanded role" in Bosnia and "the United States would be an important part of that." Another official suggested that the United States would use air power more aggressively to defend the safe areas.[214] The prospect that the failure of the plan would lead to an escalation of the fighting and the wider involvement of NATO led UN Secretary-General Boutros-Ghali to return to a theme he had first broached in the summer of 1993: that regional powers should take over responsibility for peacemaking in Bosnia. He argued that the contact group countries, "with all the political weight and the readily deployable human and material resources which they possess, [ought] to assume responsibility for implementing what they have negotiated." He recommended the withdrawal of UNPROFOR from all of the former Yugoslavia.[215] The United States, for its part, was committed to using air strikes as a means of forcing the Serbs to sue for peace. Thus, by mid-1994, greater U.S. involvement in the fighting appeared inevitable, although the president remained opposed to the deployment of U.S. ground troops in combat operations.

On July 19 the Bosnian Serb parliament voted against the contact group map/plan, attempting to present its vote as a "yes, but. . . ." The vote was received by the contact group members as an unequivocal "no," although the Russian response was less negative.[216] Because of the continuing opposition of the Europeans and Russians to the use of force,[217] however, no threat to compel the Serbs to accept the plan was forthcoming. At the public unveiling of the plan in Geneva in July, Kozyrev characterized it as a "peaceful ultimatum," and noted that lifting the embargo was "an extreme measure" that would become "a very strong possibility" only "at the end of the day."[218] After the Bosnian Serbs rejected the plan, the contact group foreign ministers were unable to agree on specific measures by which to implement their threats.[219] The result was a continuing stalemate between the U.S.-led Contact Group and the Bosnian Serbs.

The Bosnian Serbs ignored efforts by British and Russian diplomats, working "in utmost secrecy," to draft a Serb response to the plan that would be acceptable to the Contact Group.[220] The Bosnian Serbs also ignored heavy pressure from Milošević, who argued at the end of July 1994 that peace was of "paramount national interest for the Serbs" and that no one had the right to reject it, even if "compromise is necessary."[221] Part of Milošević's motivation could be found in a pledge by the contact group foreign ministers to introduce a Security Council resolution relieving sanctions on Yugoslavia (Serbia and Montenegro) if the Bosnian Serbs accepted the plan, and to tighten sanctions if they rejected it.[222] "Creating conditions for lifting the sanctions is the least the citizens of the FRY [Federal Republic of Yugoslavia (Serbia and Montenegro)] have the right to expect from the citizens and the leadership of the [Bosnian] Serb republic," Milošević argued.[223] Although Milošević did not attack Karadžić directly, the Belgrade press began a campaign against the Bosnian leaders (General Mladić excepted), indicating that Milošević was now ready to confront the Bosnian Serb leadership, and possibly seek their removal, if they did not accept the contact group proposal. Secretary of State Christopher increased the incentive for Milošević to abandon the Bosnian Serbs in early August, when he stated that sanctions could be eased if Belgrade applied a blockade against the Bosnian Serb republic. And, in September, the Contact Group agreed to ease sanctions if international monitors were permitted to verify that Belgrade had halted the flow of arms to the Bosnian Serbs.[224]

The Bosnian Serbs may have been emboldened in their opposition to the plan by the ambiguity of an effort by Russian military leaders to get them to accept the plan. According to Silber and Little, Karadžić reported that Grachev had told the Serbs on July 27 that they must accept the plan "because if they attack you we will have to defend you, which could cause problems for us." Karadžić interpreted Grachev's statement—not unreasonably, if this is an accurate account of what was said—as a message of support rather than as a warning of the uncertainty of Russian intervention.[225] The Bosnian Serb assembly proceeded the next day to reject the contact group plan for the second time by calling for additional "adjustments," "clarifications," and negotiations.[226]

The failure of the contact group "peaceful ultimatum" can be attributed to a number of interrelated factors: First, it appears not to have addressed the Bosnian Serbs' political demand for autonomy or their territorial demands for security. Thus, the plan offered them no compensatory gains that might lead to voluntary acceptance of an overall reduction in territory.

Second, any effort to offer the Serbs such positive incentives to accede to the plan would have required the United States to pressure the Bosnian Muslim leadership to agree, something it appeared still unprepared to do. Third, the plan was not accompanied by a credible threat of the use of force to compel the Serbs to accept it. U.S. policymakers attempted to present the ultimatum as an effort at coercive diplomacy, but there was no coercive power behind it. Finally, the members of the Contact Group were themselves divided over the plan, and especially over the consequences if it were to be rejected. The warring parties thus continued to receive mixed signals that strengthened their resistance to any compromise.

Toward Coercive Diplomacy

With the Bosnian Serb rejection of the contact group map/plan, President Clinton came under increased domestic pressure to act unilaterally to lift the arms embargo against the Bosnian government. The U.S. Senate adopted two different measures directing the president to do so, although these were not binding.[227] The administration remained reluctant to take unilateral action in violation of Security Council sanctions for fear of setting a precedent for others openly to violate future UN sanctions supported by the United States.[228] Thus, it proposed instead that, if the Bosnian Serbs did not accept the plan by October 15, it would introduce a UN resolution lifting the arms embargo.[229] The Russians, however, made it clear to the administration that they would not agree to a formal lifting of the embargo, and would use their veto in the Security Council if necessary.[230] The administration appeared confused and undecided as to how to proceed with respect to the embargo, and finally opted to withdraw from efforts to enforce it. This decision caused consternation in Europe, and reminded U.S. policymakers that the crisis in Bosnia was undermining the unity of the NATO alliance.[231] Unable to lift the embargo, the administration turned instead to covert means for evading it.

Presidential security advisor Anthony Lake acknowledged later, in the midst of congressional inquiries into administration actions, that the United States had learned in 1992 that Iran was smuggling arms to the Bosnian Muslims with Turkish assistance, but took no action. Bosnian government officials reported that by 1993 arms and money for arms were also being supplied through the Turkish pipeline by Saudi Arabia, Malaysia, Brunei, and Pakistan, and that other shipments came from Hungary and Argentina. The Clinton administration, contrary to its publicly stated support for the arms embargo, apparently knew of most of these shipments but took no action.[232] Some reports suggest that the administration became more actively involved in circumventing the embargo in 1994 and 1995 rather than merely turning a blind eye to the actions of others.

In April 1996 it was revealed that President Clinton had "directly participated" in a decision two years earlier to inform Croatia that the United States would not block Iranian arm shipments to Bosnia across Croatian territory. An unnamed official of the National Security Council reported that a decision was made "at the highest levels" to direct U.S. Ambassador to Croatia Peter Galbraith to inform Croatian President Tudjman that he had "no instructions" with regard to Tudjman's request for American approval. This amounted to a clear signal that the United States would not block such shipments and, therefore, *de facto* support for them.[233] By early 1995, reports appeared in the media of Iranian shipments of "hundreds of tons of weapons" over previous months, and the arrival in Bosnia of Iranian Revolutionary Guards to provide training in their use, as well as U.S. knowledge and tacit acceptance of these actions.[234]

The newly appointed assistant secretary of state charged with overseeing efforts to end the Bosnia conflict, Richard Holbrooke, is reported to have begun searching for ways to circumvent the arms embargo immediately upon taking office in summer 1994.[235] The Bosnian government is reported to have pressed Holbrooke in September to urge friendly third countries to ship weapons to the Bosnians, in exchange for the Bosnian government's ending its pressure to lift the embargo. Such a shift in the Bosnian position did, in fact, take place in September 1994, but was explained at the time in terms of less Machiavellian calculations.[236] Holbrooke, allegedly with the approval of his superiors, is reported to have proposed such action to policymakers. A later, retrospective account of these events, which appeared when the Clinton administration was facing congressional accusations from its domestic political opponents that its support for third-party arms shipments constituted an unauthorized covert operation and that its denials of involvement amounted to "misprision of a felony—failing to report a crime,"[237] reported that Holbrooke's proposal was rejected by Lake and Christopher in early November 1994, allegedly because it "seemed too close to a covert operation" and because it would be viewed by allies with troops on the ground "as a betrayal."[238] Indeed, in November 1994, Undersecretary of State Peter Tarnoff (Holbrooke's direct superior) was compelled to travel to Paris to deny in person reports that the United States was secretly arming the Muslims, a denial which French Foreign Minister Juppé merely acknowledged, but did not accept.[239] In early 1995 reports of covert arms shipments multiplied, along with allegations of U.S. involvement in them.

In February 1995, UN military officers reported several unidentified flights by helicopters and C-130 aircraft into the Bosnian-controlled Tuzla airport. UN and NATO officials disputed the nature and origin of these flights, which fueled speculation that a covert operation to deliver arms to the Bosnians was under way, and that NATO was at the very least ignoring it.[240] By July, European intelligence sources were suggesting that the United States was "orchestrating" arms shipments to Bosnia by allies in the Muslim world. U.S. officials continued to deny direct involvement in covert actions, but one unnamed American diplomat who was serving in the region at the time acknowledged that a supply operation was being run out of Turkey by "Turkish or private contractors using special funding the U.S. knew about," with U.S.-supplied information on scheduling the flights and advice on when "the coast is clear."[241] These efforts were part of a much broader pattern of illegal arms shipments to the region by several states, and of covert involvement in the fighting on the part of the Western powers.[242]

After the Bosnian Serbs rejected the contact group ultimatum, Milošević increased his rhetorical attack on the Bosnian Serbs, accusing them of "treason" and "crimes against their own people," as well as challenging their right to endanger "the fate of Yugoslavia."[243] He characterized Bosnian Serb objections to the plan as "senseless and absurd" and "the greatest betrayal of Serb interests ever," attributing them to "insane political ambition" and "greed."[244] On August 4 the Serbian government formally broke off economic and political relations with the Bosnian Serb republic (*Republika Srpska*) and closed the Yugoslav-Bosnian border to all traffic bound for the Bosnian Serbs except food, clothing, and medicine.[245] On the same day, Milošević issued a blast at the Bosnian Serb assembly for its decision to call a referendum on the contact group map/plan.[246] The Yugoslav Army backed Milošević in his dispute with the Bosnian Serbs, albeit reluctantly.[247] The rupture finalized the tensions between Belgrade, for which territorial issues in Bosnia were of secondary importance to lifting sanctions, and Pale, for which the territorial concessions demanded by the contact group map appeared to be matters of life and death.

The fact that Milošević was ready to pressure the Serbs into giving most of Brčko to the Muslims, thus cutting the east–west Serb corridor in Bosnia, was a sign that Belgrade had withdrawn its support from the cause of the Serbs outside of Serbia proper. Paradoxically, this probably strengthened Milošević's hand in dealing with the Bosnian Serbs, as well as the Serbs in Croatian Krajina. It set the stage for the negotiations at Dayton, when Milošević negotiated a settlement of the Bosnian crisis without consulting the Bosnian Serbs.

In September 1994 the ICFY established a civilian border-monitoring mission in Yugoslavia to observe, examine, and report on cross-border traffic. In October the ICFY co-chairs submitted a report to UN Secretary-

General Boutros-Ghali concluding that Serbia and Montenegro had cut off all non-humanitarian shipments to the Bosnian Serbs. This triggered the partial lifting of sanctions. The United States disputed these findings, telling NATO defense ministers at about the same time that the Bosnian Serbs continued to receive weapons and other military equipment from Serbia. But the United States did not oppose acceptance of the ICFY report or the partial lifting of sanctions. According to media accounts, the United States declined to oppose the report because the evidence was not dramatic enough, because there was no clear-cut evidence of Milošević's involvement, and because of disagreement within the administration over whether the sharing of intelligence would compromise sources and methods.[248] According to Owen, one reason that the border appeared not to be closed could be found in the fact that Milošević never agreed to block transit traffic across Serb-held Bosnia destined for Serb-held territories in Croatia.[249] Thus, international monitors might certify Serbian compliance even while strategic materials continued to cross the Serbian-Bosnian border, ostensibly bound for Krajina but vulnerable to diversion to the Bosnian Serbs. Whether Milošević continued to supply the Bosnian Serbs or not, however, it seemed clear that by late 1994 the divergence of interests between them— already evident in the course of negotiations over the Vance-Owen plan— had grown even wider as the potential benefits for Milošević of turning more openly against the Bosnian Serbs had become more tangible. This created an important opportunity to exercise diplomatic and political pressure on the Bosnian Serbs through Belgrade.

The political isolation experienced by Pale was complicated by divisions between the military and civilian leadership of the Bosnian Serb republic. Its outward manifestation was a growing rift between Karadžić and General Mladić. That Mladić and Karadžić were often in disagreement had been obvious from the time of the UN takeover of Sarajevo airport in June 1992, and became apparent again during the Srebrenica and Goražde crises described in chapter 4. Mladić played a decisive role in the Bosnian Serb assembly in securing the defeat of the Vance-Owen plan in May 1993 after Karadžić had accepted it at Athens. These differences between the two Bosnian Serb leaders may have been little more than a "good cop–bad cop" charade for Western consumption. But they appear to have reflected the genuine reluctance of Mladić to follow the more moderate line that Karadžić had been compelled to adopt under pressure from Belgrade. In summer 1994 Mladić dropped out of sight. Rumor had it that he had sided with Milošević in the rift between Belgrade and Pale.[250] Yet General Mladić, despite his quarrel with the civilian leadership in Pale, remained a consistent hawk, opposing the contact group settlement[251] and affirming his willingness to engage in a prolonged conflict rather than capitulate to the West. The rift between Mladić and Karadžić revealed the strain on the Bosnian Serbs of more than two years of war, and the absence of any coherent Bosnian Serb strategy for bringing the conflict to an end.

The immediate effect of Milošević's crackdown on the Bosnian Serb republic was to increase the intransigence of the Bosnian Serb leadership. On August 5 the Serbs staged a raid on a UN storage depot, prompting General Rose to authorize an air strike against a Serb target in the Sarajevo exclusion zone.[252] On August 6 the Bosnian and Croatian Serbs met and proclaimed their backing for the unification of the Bosnian Serb republic and the republic of the Krajina Serbs. The two self-declared entities were to unite to form a Principality of Serb States—in effect, a Western Serbia.[253] This was only one of a number of such unification proposals, all of which remained stillborn in the face of opposition from Belgrade, and due to the fact that such a state would never receive recognition from the international community.

In sum, after more than two years of war, the international effort to mediate the Bosnian crisis had failed and the war itself seemed locked in a stalemate. However, although it was not obvious at the time, the sequence of events which was to alter this impasse had already begun in fall 1994, with the attack of Dudaković's Fifth Corps out of the Bihać pocket, described in chapter 4. As we noted there, the Muslim offensive was initially successful, but was beaten back by a Serb counterattack, which by November had pushed Dudaković's forces back across the Una river. In November, the Serbs completed the encirclement of Bihać. Once more, there were accounts of civilian casualties from Serb shelling, although civilian casualties, on the Bosnian side were not great. The subsequent NATO air attacks, described in chapter 4, constituted the first use of air power—under the pretext of defending a safe area—to force the Serbs to the bargaining table. The inclination to do so was already clear in late September, when a senior White House official was quoted by the *Guardian* to the effect that "without a major increase in pressure there is no prospect that the Bosnian Serbs will change their tune." The *Guardian* account suggested that White House officials wanted to use air power not only to protect safe areas, but more broadly, while the Bosnian army was armed and trained during the winter.[254] If this interpretation is correct; the Bihać crisis marked the first effort of the United States to use air power (if indirectly) for broader political purposes—the "marrying of force with diplomacy," as a dispatch in the *Washington Post* called it at the time.[255]

But this approach faced opposition from U.S. allies. Russian Foreign Minister Kozyrev suggested that the Muslims had launched their fall offensive "with the clear intention of involving NATO and other third forces in fighting on its side, achieving the lifting of the arms embargo and, of course, ensuring air strikes."[256] Even more important, the French, acutely aware of the military resources that would be required to implement U.S. calls for the defense of a safe area around Bihać, demanded to know what troops would be available to carry out such a task. The events surrounding Bihać led UN Secretary-General Boutros-Ghali to submit a report to the Security Council that highlighted the political and military deficiencies of the safe area concept and to call for their demilitarization.[257]

The U.S. approach was rejected. As we reported in chapter 4, NATO issued only a low-key communiqué urging the Bosnians and the Serbs to seek a political solution to the conflict.[258] Opposition to the use of NATO air power and to the defense of a safe area around Bihać on the part of both the British and the French led American policymakers to conclude that their insistence on using force was damaging NATO cohesion without achieving a significant change in the course of the war.[259] The French president and prime minister issued a statement warning that lifting the arms embargo would only intensify conflict, and observing that

> the tragic events in Bihac show that any encouragement given to the recon-quest of territory by force—and notably the prospect of lifting the arms embargo—is vain or dangerous. It only fuels the cycle of violence to the detriment of the search for a negotiated peace settlement, which is the only durable solution to the conflict among the Bosnian communities.[260]

That U.S. policymakers came to a similar conclusion was reflected in a number of public statements and diplomatic activities. Secretary Christopher, for example, conceded that the administration would no longer rely on force to reach a settlement, and stressed the need for diplomacy and incentives to persuade the Serbs.[261] Similar efforts to downplay the use of force in Bosnia were undertaken by the White House and by the secretary of defense.[262] The communiqué issued following the meeting of NATO foreign ministers on December 1 had Bosnia in twentieth place. The maintenance of alliance unity and cohesion was given higher priority.[263] Even more telling, in early December, Charles Redman, the U.S. envoy for Bosnia-Herzegovina, engaged in direct discussions with the Bosnian Serb leadership in Pale. He conveyed American willingness to consider the possibility of confederation between the Bosnian Serbs and Serbia, as well as changes in the contact group map, as long as the overall 51–49 percent division of Bosnia between the Muslim-Croat federation and the Serbs was preserved.[264]

Thus, the Americans appeared, at the end of 1994, to be moving toward the realization that outside actors could not simply impose a settlement on the parties by force. Settlement would require both military and political initiatives. Serb military power would have to be counteracted on the ground. At the same time, however, at least some Bosnian Serb interests would have to be accommodated if a political settlement was to be reached. Such coordination of accommodation and force is the essence of coercive diplomacy.

From the U.S. perspective, such a change of strategy may have become urgent. The French now saw Bosnia as a "total dead-end" and, following the lead of Secretary-General Boutros-Ghali, called upon the UN and NATO to prepare for the withdrawal of UNPROFOR.[265] The Clinton administration might therefore have been compelled to deploy U.S. ground troops to Bosnia in order to protect UN peacekeepers as they withdrew from the country. Planning for such a withdrawal had, in fact, already been under way for several months within NATO.[266] From the outset, U.S. policymakers feared that such an operation might, in effect, substitute U.S. forces for UNPROFOR under even more hostile conditions. As one U.S. official put it in August, "the game is not to be left holding the bag."[267] Plans called for the participation of 10,000 American troops in a NATO force.[268] Pentagon officials estimated that as many as 25,000 American troops might be involved in an operation that would last "several weeks."[269] The risk that these troops might become enmeshed in an escalation of three-way fighting in Bosnia-Herzegovina appeared very high.

By the end of 1994, therefore, the political and military dimensions of international efforts to end the fighting in Bosnia-Herzegovina seemed for the first time to be converging around an as-yet tacit, but coordinated, strategy.[270] The United States had embarked on an effort to arm the Bosnian army through covert arms shipments by third parties and, the evidence suggests, U.S. forces. It had already begun open efforts earlier in the year to strengthen the Croatian military and encourage closer coordination of Croatian, Bosnian, and Bosnian Croat forces. These efforts, which may have increased European fears of escalation, aimed at creating a credible military counterbalance to Serb forces on the ground.[271] The Americans appear to have concluded that by covertly aiding the Bosnian government and encouraging Muslim-Croat cooperation, the tide of battle could eventually be turned in favor of the Bosnian government. Lifting the arms embargo appears, by the end of 1994, to have been considered too great a risk to be included as part of this strategy. The possibility that prolonged warfare could lead the United Nations to withdraw from Bosnia, however, posed a real threat to this approach. For the U.S. strategy to succeed, the United States required some diplomatic "breathing space" in which to bring the military and political dimensions of Bosnian policy into coordination. A four-month cease-fire secured by former U.S. president Jimmy Carter in December 1994 appeared to provide precisely such a respite.

Conclusion

With Bosnian Serb rejection of the Vance-Owen plan in spring 1993, the Western powers were divided over strategy in Bosnia. The Europeans placed a higher priority on finding a political solution that would allow them to withdraw their troops from harm's way than on redressing the violations of moral and political principles committed during the course of the war. This led the Europeans away from the complex plan for a unified Bosnia contained in Vance and Owen, to the more straightforward plans for partition negotiated and then abandoned in summer and fall 1993. The United States, viewing the conflict from afar, initially condemned partition and placed higher priority on redressing the violations of the war; an emphasis that led them inevitably to withhold their support from the Tudjman/Milošević and *Invincible* plans for partition in 1993, and to call for the use of force against the principal violators, the Serbs. Unwilling to commit troops to the ground, the United States called for the use of air power against the Serbs and the lifting of the arms embargo against the Bosnians.

Our account suggests deficiencies in both the U.S. and the European arguments. U.S. support in 1993 for what was labeled "lift and strike" ignored the fact that the only sure way the Bosnian government could hope to receive arms and level the playing field was through cooperation with the Croatians. The Croatians, we have argued, held the key to the outcome of the conflict in Bosnia. Thus, lifting the embargo would have had little impact in the absence of a Bosnian-Croatian alliance. If the events of spring 1993 were any guide, the Bosnian Croats would welcome the lifting of the embargo only if they could prevent arms from reaching the Muslims, and then use the opportunity to attack the Muslims with the assistance of Croatia—exactly the reverse of what the policy was meant to achieve. The further danger in linking "lift" with "strike" was that the Bosnian government—understandably—would likely have taken this pledge as a green light to launch attacks against the Serbs, expecting U.S. air support. The resulting escalation of the conflict would have squeezed the UN out of Bosnia. This was the danger foreseen by General Powell at the time of the debate over lift and strike in summer 1993. The U.S. strategy also offered no clear political solution to the conflict. It posited as an outcome only a "level playing field"; that is, further military conflict. Without a clear political settlement in advance, Bosnian Muslims would attempt to recover all Bosnia.

European fear of the Serb reaction to a lifting of the arms embargo was probably exaggerated. The Serbs were constrained by their lack of manpower. They probably could not have mounted a major offensive against the Muslims. The Serbs could have stepped up their attacks on the eastern enclaves in response to U.S. air strikes, but they had already done so in Žepa and Srebrenica. Both the UN and the Europeans had a record of overestimating the Serb response to forceful actions by the West, as events in Croatia and in Bosnia itself—such as the opening of Sarajevo airport, the withdrawal from Mt. Igman, the enforcement of the no-fly zone over Bosnia, and the imposition of an exclusion zone around Sarajevo in 1994— had demonstrated. The fear that UNPROFOR troops would be taken hostage was well grounded. Their vulnerability might have been reduced by redeployment or reinforcement prior to the onset of an air campaign. But, as we shall see in chapter 7, such an action had far reaching diplomatic and military implications.

The escalation of NATO, Russian, and U.S. involvement in Bosnia after the February 1994 marketplace massacre highlighted the degree to which the warring parties were able to manipulate outside powers and international organizations, and the negotiations they sponsored, to advance their own political and military agendas rather than to move toward peace. U.S. officials, for example, repeatedly defined their participation in ways that handed the Muslims veto power over U.S. proposals and encouraged Bosnian government claims that appeared to be designed to ensure the failure of negotiations and draw the West into more direct military involvement. At the same time, Washington was unwilling to acknowledge publicly that no settlement could be negotiated without the participation of the Serbs, and that such an agreement could be achieved only by recognizing at least some of the Serbs' territorial and political goals. On condition of anonymity, administration officials conceded that an eventual settlement would have to accommodate Bosnian Serb demands.[272] The value of the U.S. approach, however, lay in the creation of a Muslim-Croat military alliance for the purpose of counterbalancing Serb power on the ground—regardless of the prospects for Serb acquiescence to the approach or even post-war Muslim-Croat cooperation. The U.S. decision to forge a Muslim-Croat alliance was a crucial element in creating the basis for a turn toward coercive diplomacy in 1995.

Until the Americans took over leadership of the Contact Group in 1994, the Europeans had provided the diplomatic initiative, as well as most of the UN commanders, troops, and logistical backup. Following the nineteenth century pattern, one might have expected the European Community (later, Union), as the putative hegemon in the region, to take the lead in determining how the war in Bosnia would be resolved and, when necessary, to project power into the region. This the Europeans did not do. They did not act in the tradition of geopolitical balance-of-power politics to which local actors in the Balkans had long been accustomed. The Europeans avoided significant military involvement on one side or the other, and refrained from any effort to impose a settlement on local actors. Instead, it was the United States that finally emerged as the decisive actor in the Bosnian conflict.

It was the United States that ultimately took on the role of hegemonic actor in the Balkans: taking sides, projecting power in the form of air strikes (in NATO guise), and isolating the local violator of the preferred *status quo*. The United States assumed this role only gradually. It proposed the use of force divorced from diplomacy in 1993. It proposed the use of diplomacy divorced from force as part of the Contact Group in 1994. Both approaches failed. U.S. policymakers appear to have been struggling during the latter half of 1994 to achieve the fusion of diplomacy and force, but were unable to do so without a further catalyst: the prospect of a complete collapse of the international effort to end the war—for which the United States would be blamed—and the withdrawal of UN forces under fire, an operation for which the United States would be compelled to commit ground troops to combat. This delayed the entry of the decisive actor onto the scene, with the result that actions that might have restrained the violence were taken later rather than sooner.

That the United States played this role ran counter to historical precedent, according to which the global or more detached power (such as Germany in 1878) stood to one side, mediated the conflict, supported the regional powers in their efforts to find a political solution, and provided a check on those who might seek to upset the approved balance in the region. In effect, by the end of 1994, the United States and Europe reversed the historical roles of distant and regional powers in the Balkans. This reversal of roles between Europe, the preeminent regional actor, and the United States, the more global and distant power, had important consequences. Most important, it gave primary responsibility for settling the conflict to an actor whose interests in the region were less direct and more tied to global interests and perspectives than those of the putative regional hegemon. Concretely, this meant that initially the United States was far less concerned with ensuring long-term regional stability in the Balkans than in satisfying its own short-term, distant interests. The Balkan crisis was seen by the United States primarily through the prism of domestic and global politics and only secondarily through the lens of local and regional ramifications. When the U.S. leadership was compelled to deal with these ramifications, it imposed a settlement shaped as much by U.S. concerns as by the requisites of stabilizing the region.

CHAPTER 7

Imposing the Dayton Agreement

The four-month cease-fire negotiated by former U.S. president Jimmy Carter ended most, but not all, of the fighting in Bosnia-Herzegovina, and provided an opportunity for the United States to attempt to coordinate diplomatic and military resources in an effort to reach a more lasting negotiated settlement. The diplomatic dimensions of this effort required the United States to negotiate directly with the Bosnian Serbs and to accommodate, at least partially, their interests—an approach eventually supplanted by direct talks with Milošević. It also required the United States to pressure the Bosnian Muslims to agree to a settlement that entailed a *de facto,* and perhaps permanent, partition of the country—something they had adamantly opposed from the very beginning of international negotiations.

The U.S. decision to use force initially was taken in response to the danger that the UN would withdraw, raising the prospect that U.S. ground forces would be drawn into the conflict under the worst conditions possible. The actual use of U.S. air power to help bring the war to an end occurred only after dramatic changes in both the military situation on the ground and the political position of the Clinton administration. Most important, it required U.S. policymakers to commit themselves to a political settlement based on partition, a solution that Washington had heretofore resisted and condemned. We shall argue in this chapter that these changes came about not as the result simply of a change in political "will," but as the result of clear changes in the interests perceived at stake by U.S. policymakers.

The military dimension of the U.S. effort included direct and indirect

317

efforts—both open and covert—to arm, train, and encourage the Bosnian and Croatian armies to wage war against the Serbs. The Croatian takeover of Krajina was a critical element in bringing the war to an end. But this was not sufficient to bring about a negotiated settlement. In the end, the United States had to intervene directly in the fighting by launching an extensive air campaign against the Bosnian Serbs in order to create the conditions necessary to get all three sides to commit themselves to negotiations. The United States also was forced to acquiesce in the use of counterforce by the Serbs against the Muslims and Croats in order to prevent them from exploiting U.S. air power to escalate the conflict by threatening Yugoslav (that is, Serbian) strategic interests. Finally, the United States was compelled to offer political concessions to the Bosnian Serbs to induce them to enter into negotiations; most notably, institutionalization of the Bosnian Serb republic and the consequent *de facto* partition of Bosnia-Herzegovina.

The combination of political concessions and military force—what might be called a strategy of coercive diplomacy—hastened the conclusion of a settlement. The diplomatic dimension of the U.S. effort to end the war brought the United States more closely into alignment with the approach taken earlier by its European allies and, in the end, produced an agreement that closely resembled earlier European and contact group proposals for *de facto* partition. But this was not accomplished without a number of serious setbacks along the way, as the Serbs exploited UN and NATO weaknesses in summer 1995 to try to seize the safe areas. As a result, the West continued to practice crisis diplomacy even as steps were taken to project power into Bosnia and bring diplomacy and force into closer coordination.

The Dayton agreement reflected the interest of the U.S. administration in bringing the fighting to a halt, rather than the readiness of the three warring parties to settle their political differences. Thus, it produced an unstable peace under which the parties continued their pursuit of fundamentally incompatible goals by other than military means, while they prepared for what appeared to be an inevitable resumption of fighting. A U.S. commitment to arm the Bosnian government was an essential condition for achieving the Dayton agreement. But it may very well have hastened the day when Muslim leaders will decide to take by force what they believe they lost in the early rounds of fighting and later at Dayton. Thus, for the foreseeable future, the tenuous peace established by the Dayton agreement can be expected to last only as long as the international military force deployed to support it remains in place, and the military strength of the parties remains in approximate balance. Neither of these conditions promises to be long-lasting.

The Political Dimension of Western Policy

The record of earlier efforts by the ICFY and the Contact Group to negotiate a political settlement of the conflict made it clear that if the United
States was to assume leadership of a serious effort to bring the fighting to
an end, U.S. officials would have to negotiate directly with Bosnian Serb
leaders and with Serbian president Slobodan Milošević. The need to accommodate Bosnian Serb interests had been the subject of debate within the
administration, and between the administration and its European allies,
since the beginning of international efforts to negotiate a settlement, in
1992. Efforts to negotiate an agreement in 1993 seemed to offer the greatest chance of success when Milošević was actively engaged in the process,
and to offer little hope when he was not. The U.S. effort in 1994 to create a
Muslim-Croat federation on those portions of Bosnia-Herzegovina with
Muslim and Croat majorities inevitably raised the question of the eventual
status of the remaining Serb-majority territories of Bosnia-Herzegovina.

The hostility of the Americans toward the Serbs was reflected in the
"take-it-or-leave-it" approach adopted by the U.S.-led Contact Group in
1994. The U.S. administration consistently opposed conceding to the Bosnian Serbs a right to confederate with Serbia that would parallel the confederation between Croatia and the Muslim-Croat federation. But the
Europeans favored giving the Bosnian Serbs such a parallel right, and U.S.
officials admitted from the start, in unattributed statements to the press, that
such a parallel arrangement represented a highly probable outcome. They
remained adamantly opposed, however, to any outright annexation of Bosnian Serb territory by Serbia—a scenario described pejoratively as "An-
schluss."[1] Moreover, U.S. policymakers remained under intense public
pressure from both Congress and political supporters of the Bosnian
Muslims not to make any concessions to Serb interests at all, and to undertake instead efforts to ensure an outright military victory for the Bosnian
Muslims.[2]

The landslide victory by the Republicans in the November 1994 congressional elections in the United States placed further pressure on the Clinton
administration to act. Republican Senator Robert Dole, the majority leader
in the Senate and undeclared candidate for the presidency in opposition to
Clinton, had long been an advocate of lifting the arms embargo on the
Bosnian Muslims and using air power against the Serbs. Now he and the
new Republican Speaker of the House, Representative Newt Gingrich, intensified efforts in both houses of Congress to lift the embargo; efforts that
were gaining support even among Democrats.[3] By mid-1995, concern grew
in the White House that Bosnia would become a campaign liability for the

president in the 1996 elections. In order to avoid domestic political defeat, the conflict would have to be resolved before the winter of 1995.

The Europeans viewed the failure of NATO air strikes in November 1994 to deter the Serbs from counterattacks against Bosnian army forces that violated the UN-declared safe area around Bihać as further evidence of the futility of relying on military power alone to end the conflict. We have already noted in chapter 6 that French president Mitterrand and Prime Minister Balladur reacted to the events in Bihać by rejecting the use of force in favor of negotiations, which they called "the only durable solution to the conflict."[4] European negotiators had consistently treated the recognition and accommodation of the conflicting political interests of all three parties—including the Bosnian Serbs—as essential to negotiating an end to the fighting. The Clinton administration appears finally to have been persuaded of this in November and December 1994.

The failure of NATO air strikes in November 1994, and the ensuing discord among NATO allies, led to a major reconsideration of the U.S. administration's Bosnia policies, initiated by the president's national security advisor, Anthony Lake. The administration's senior policymakers concluded that the use of force alone was futile. Secretary Christopher stressed the need for diplomacy and incentives to persuade the Serbs to end the war and accept the contact group plan and map.[5] If force were to be used, it would have to be used in support of a political settlement to the conflict.[6] To achieve a settlement through diplomacy and incentives, however, required that the United States negotiate directly with the Serbs. The administration therefore reopened direct discussions with the Bosnian Serb leadership in December 1994.

As we noted in chapter 6, Charles Redmond, the U.S. ambassador to Germany and former envoy for Bosnia, was sent to Pale. This ended official U.S. ostracism of the Bosnian Serbs. The ambassador allegedly underscored for the Serbs the possibility of altering the division of territory between the Muslim-Croat federation and the Bosnian Serbs contained in the contact group map proposed in July, as long as the 51- to 49-percent ratio of Muslim-Croat to Serb territories was preserved.[7] The administration's support for former president Carter's mission to Bosnia, and his direct negotiations with the Bosnian Serb leadership over a cease-fire agreement, also reflected the Clinton administration's decision to become more directly involved in negotiating a political settlement. The administration insisted, however, that Carter also emphasize the contact group plan as the basis for such negotiations,[8] thereby clearly signaling that it would insist on basing any settlement on the general framework contained in that plan, or at least on the 51–49 territorial division of Bosnia contained in it. This position was made explicit in January 1995 in a letter from Secretary of State Christopher to Bosnian president Izetbegović.[9] The seriousness of the administration's effort also led to the removal of the U.S. ambassador to Bosnia—an ardent supporter of the Bosnian Muslims who opposed making any concession to Bosnian Serb interests—and his replacement by a deputy more amenable to negotiating with the Serbs.[10]

Revising the Contact Group Plan

A meeting of NATO foreign ministers in early December 1994 provided the context for a meeting of the contact group foreign ministers that produced the necessary change in the "take-it-or-leave-it" definition of the group's proposals: the contact group ministers declared that "the territorial proposal [the 51–49 division of Bosnia] . . . remains the basis for a settlement . . . [but] can be adjusted by mutual agreement between the parties." They also declared that "constitutional arrangements agreeable to the parties will need to be drawn up which preserve the integrity of Bosnia and Herzegovina and allow equitable and balanced arrangements for the Bosnian [Muslim]-Croat and Bosnian Serb entities."[11] "Equitable and balanced arrangements" was the NATO code expression for Bosnian Croat and Bosnian Serb special relations with Croatia and Serbia, respectively. This subtle but significant change in the position of the Contact Group reflected the change of approach on the part of the United States outlined above, and brought the U.S. position into alignment with the position taken on this issue by Britain and France since the earliest stages of negotiations over Bosnia. It seemed to signal more flexibility than was suggested by a letter President Clinton sent to Izetbegović, pledging U.S. support for Bosnia-Herzegovina "as a single state within its existing borders," reported in the U.S. media at about the same time.[12] And, it came amid rumors that the Contact Group would look favorably upon the exchange of Bosnian government-held enclaves in Goražde, Žepa, and Srebrenica for Serb-held land around Sarajevo.[13]

The administration's apparent willingness to revise the contact group proposal in order to accommodate Serb interests was, understandably, opposed publicly by the Bosnian government. When Assistant Secretary of State Richard Holbrooke, at a press conference in January 1995, defined the Contact Group's goal as gaining "acceptance of the . . . plan as the starting point for negotiations," for example, Bosnian prime minister Silajdžić responded by saying: "That's your position, Mr. Holbrooke. But for Bosnia-Herzegovina it was take-it-or-leave-it." President Izetbegović insisted that "the Serb side must accept the plan" before negotiations could resume.[14] On a visit to Washington in January 1995 Silajdžić called publicly for setting a deadline for Serb acceptance of the contact group plan. "If this deadline is not met," he said, "we demand a multilateral lifting of the arms embargo, and if not a multilateral, then a unilateral lifting."[15] He made a more extensive argument in support of lifting the embargo in an opinion piece in the *Washington Post* in February.[16] In this way, the Bosnians encouraged efforts on Capitol Hill, led by Senator Dole, to pressure the administration into abandoning the UN-imposed arms embargo and providing the Bosnian army with arms. Holbrooke insisted that the Bosnian objections were "disingenuous," as he alleged that the Bosnian government had agreed privately in advance to discussions with the Serbs.[17] Nonetheless, it appears that the United States was attempting at this time to uphold the contact group plan in talks with the Muslim-led Bosnian government, while suggesting to the Serbs that it would be changed.[18] By mid-February 1995, however, it appears that the U.S. effort had stalled. The Bosnian Serb parliament again rejected the contact group plan and map on political grounds, arguing that it required them to become part of a unified Republic of Bosnia-Herzegovina and declaring that no external pressure could force them to accept it.[19]

The French responded to Bosnian Serb opposition by proposing further concessions to the Serbs, including the lifting of sanctions against Belgrade in exchange for recognition of Bosnia-Herzegovina.[20] The French proposal provoked a "heated debate" among senior U.S. policymakers, in which UN ambassador Albright and Vice President Al Gore continued to oppose making concessions to the Serbs.[21] Milošević's willingness to hold out for a better deal was not surprising in light of the differences among the great powers, the low cost of saying no, and the Bosnian Serbs' continued opposition. Indeed, one unnamed U.S. diplomat acknowledged that "the West is trying to sell Milošević a house and each time they offer it to him at a lower price. Why should he buy now and agree to a peace plan when he knows that in a few months he's going to get a better deal?"[22] At the heart of the debate was the issue of lifting sanctions against Yugoslavia (Serbia and Montenegro). It appeared at this time that Milošević would not cooperate in ending the war without gaining concessions on this issue. The absence in the West—or even within the U.S. administration—of a consensus on this issue contributed to the confusion that marked the diplomatic scene between May and July 1995.

The U.S. Decision to Use Force

Several closely related factors impelled the Clinton administration to act more decisively in Bosnia. The most important factor influencing the administration's actions was the fact that the outbreak of fighting in

March—even before the Carter cease-fire had expired—and the apparent certainty that it would escalate raised the very real prospect that United Nations forces would have to be withdrawn from Bosnia. The administration is reported to have begun considering the possibility of U.S. involvement in a withdrawal operation soon after Croatian president Tudjman threatened in mid-January not to renew the UN mandate in Croatia.[23] Secretary-General Boutros-Ghali, speaking at an international conference on peacekeeping in early March 1995, raised the prospect of a UN withdrawal even higher than he had in his report of July 1994 (noted in chapter 4). He stated pointedly, "If there is not the political will among the protagonists, we cannot achieve peace." He asked, "[M]ust we stay for an indefinite period, like Cyprus, for 30 years?"[24] The sniping death of a French peacekeeper in April led French defense minister Leotard to warn that France would not "send soldiers *ad infinitum.*"[25] The ineffective use of air power against the Serbs by NATO in late May 1995 and the ensuing hostage crisis (described in more detail below) raised the prospect of a withdrawal even higher.

The withdrawal of UNPROFOR would require the United States to commit substantial ground forces and logistical support to Bosnia in an effort to protect allied troops as they were withdrawn. President Clinton acknowledged, in a speech to the Air Force Academy on May 31, that the United States had "a longstanding commitment to help our NATO allies . . . to take part in a NATO operation to assist them in a withdrawal if that should ever become necessary."[26] While the president had already signed the authorization for such a mission in December 1994, Richard Holbrooke argues in his memoir that it was not until the administration was briefed in early June 1995 on the operational plan for the mission that U.S. policymakers realized the mission raised the almost certain prospect that U.S. troops would become directly involved in the fighting.[27]

The character and extent of U.S. participation in the reconfiguration or withdrawal of the UN mission in Bosnia, or whether there was to be any U.S. involvement at all, remained a matter of debate within the administration. Secretary of Defense Perry, Chairman of the Joint Chiefs of Staff Gen. John Shalikashvili, and Ambassador Albright all pushed for more forceful action. But Secretary of State Christopher continued to oppose any expansion of the U.S. role, arguing that neither Congress nor the American public would support it.[28] The president was forced immediately to backtrack on his Academy speech in the face of domestic political opposition to any involvement of U.S. forces on the ground in Bosnia.[29] In Congress, both Democrats and Republicans criticized the administration, calling instead for lifting the arms embargo on the Bosnian government.[30] In Britain and

France, a "considerable constituency" opposing deeper military involvement was reportedly building up.[31] At the same time, however, the costs of withdrawal were perceived as very high. Thus, the Europeans appeared to be facing much the same dilemma as the Americans.[32]

NATO planning for a withdrawal of UN troops from Bosnia had begun in mid-1994.[33] Preliminary planning was completed in mid-December, with a worst-case scenario that called for deployment of 40,000–50,000 troops. By mid-March NATO planners were preparing for "all eventualities from a peaceful extraction of UN forces to a fighting withdrawal in the face of attacks from Bosnian Muslim and Croat and Bosnian Serb forces."[34] By this time, too, the Americans were expected to provide about half of the forces necessary, or about 25,000 troops, a figure confirmed by Secretary of Defense Perry in late May.[35] A later media account reported that NATO planners had concluded that such an operation would be at best messy, at worst a bloodbath, with both Serbs and Muslims trying to seize equipment and perhaps taking hostages.[36] This view was underscored in late May, when the Serbs seized 400 UN troops as hostages and shelled civilian targets in Tuzla in response to the limited use of NATO air power against them. Not surprisingly, the speech by the president at the Air Force Academy on May 31 set off a firestorm of controversy, and open opposition to U.S. involvement, including opposition from both Republicans and Democrats in Congress. Yet, as one British journalist put it in June, "If the Europeans are forced to fight their way out of Bosnia and the United States leaves them to it, the Atlantic alliance will suffer a blow from which it may not easily recover."[37] Not surprisingly, the administration was reported "desperate" to avoid such an operation.[38]

By March 1995 the Bosnian army had gone over to the offensive, conducting operations in Tuzla and Travnik in violation of the Carter cease-fire. It also was active in the exclusion zone around Goražde, using the UN safe area as a base of operations in an apparent effort to draw Serb artillery fire into the safe area and thereby direct international attention away from their own violation of the cease-fire and, perhaps, to draw Serb troops away from Tuzla and Travnik. In mid-June the Bosnian army launched an effort to break out of Sarajevo. The Bosnian Serb army then launched attacks against the eastern enclaves of Srebrenica, Žepa, and Goražde. They entered Srebrenica on July 8, overrunning UN positions. The West tried vainly to deter the Serbs from overrunning Srebrenica by carrying out an isolated air strike on July 11—which was widely denounced in the West as a mere "pinprick." On July 12, the takeover of Srebrenica was complete. It was followed by the mass slaughter of thousands of Muslims who fell into the custody of Serb soldiers under the direct command of General Mladić. The precise number of victims is as yet unknown, but the killings at Srebrenica constitute the largest such incident in Europe since World War II and are central to the charges of genocide against the Serbs, and the personal culpability of General Mladić.[39] Despite the threat of further air strikes, the Bosnian Serbs proceeded to attack and overrun the smaller safe area at Žepa.

An unnamed senior official in the Clinton administration later reported that policymakers concluded they were "faced with the worst possible outcome: we were going to have to initiate the evacuation of the United Nations forces in Bosnia—a move that would be very risky to American life, and expensive, and would lead to a wider war. The fall of Žepa and Srebrenica crystallized this fear." Holbrooke reported that, with these developments, "even the most marginally informed person finally realized that the policy was headed for a crash, and that we were headed for military involvement either way."[40] A media account at the time of the Srebrenica and Žepa takeovers in July reported that talks among U.S., British, and French officials about what actions to take in response were imbued with a "sense of urgency verging on desperation."[41] Once again, senior policymakers in the Clinton administration felt, in the words of the president, that "we've got to try something."[42] The prior decision to negotiate with the Serbs and at least partially accommodate their interests was now accompanied by a decision to use force to prepare the way for a settlement by deterring the Serbs from further attacks on the safe areas until the balance of forces on the ground had shifted against them.

Holbrooke, in a March 1996 account, is quoted to the effect that a decision to use force was reached on July 15, when Clinton administration policymakers realized that their commitment to support a NATO withdrawal made U.S. involvement on the ground inevitable. "At that point," Holbrooke reported, "the President saw the degree to which involvement was now inevitable, and how much better it would be to have involvement built on success rather than failure."[43] The administration therefore embarked on a concerted effort to ensure that the involvement of U.S. troops would take place under the most favorable circumstances possible. Hence, the U.S. decision to use force in Bosnia was driven by concern that the events in Srebrenica were a prelude to a withdrawal of the UN that would trigger the deployment of U.S. ground forces in Bosnia.

The ineffective use of NATO air power against the Serbs in May 1995 and the ensuing hostage crisis, followed little more than a month later by the attack on Srebrenica and its fall to the Serbs, seemed to signal the end of the UN mission's usefulness in Bosnia-Herzegovina. The British appeared to reject any increase in their own military involvement. Foreign Secretary Malcolm Rifkind, who had earlier served as defense minister, warned in

June that the UN would not wage war in Bosnia and suggested that if the parties no longer consented to its presence then UNPROFOR should be withdrawn.[44] In mid-July Prime Minister Major declared in parliament that "unless the warring parties are prepared . . . to return to some form of discussion to reach a political settlement, there is no doubt that continuing fighting would put the continuing presence of the UN at risk."[45] Secretary Rifkind made the point even more explicit by telling parliament "withdrawal must remain an option."[46] Thus, the U.S. decision to use force to avert a UN withdrawal, reported by Holbrooke to have taken place at this time, appeared to put U.S. and British policymakers on distinctly different paths.

However, the election of Jacques Chirac as president of France in April had introduced a more forceful supporter of the use of force into allied leadership councils. Chirac called for strengthening UN forces in Bosnia during the May hostage crisis. Following the fall of Srebrenica in July, he called for the Security Council to approve its recapture by force. He also called upon the United States and Britain to join France in a military operation to protect besieged areas. Significantly, however, French officials warned that failure to act would lead to the withdrawal of French troops from Bosnia.[47] President Chirac's calls for the use of greater force may have represented his genuine policy preference. If they did, then both U.S. and French policymakers appeared to be moving away from British policymakers. But President Chirac's statements may have been only a bluff intended to set the stage for laying the onus of a withdrawal on U.S. inaction, as suggested by Clinton administration officials.[48] Nonetheless, Chirac's calls for action had the effect of convincing U.S. policymakers that they had to act. Much of this effect can be attributed to the positive media reaction to Chirac's stance, and the effect of that reaction on President Clinton.[49] But the split between Britain and France clearly threatened to lead to withdrawal, an option that could be avoided only if the United States assumed a forceful leadership role in bringing the allies together around a common strategy to end the conflict.

Changes on the ground as the result of continued fighting in spring and summer 1995 in Bosnia were critical to the U.S. effort. These altered the political-strategic balance among the warring parties. Thorny territorial issues that had blocked political settlements in the past were being settled by the parties themselves, by force. One unnamed Clinton administration official observed candidly in August, after Srebrenica and Žepa had been overrun by the Serbs, that "while losing the enclaves has been unfortunate for Bosnia it's been great for us."[50] The prospect that a viable line of demarcation between the Serbs on one side and the Muslim-Croat federation on the other might be established as the result of the renewed fighting in 1995 raised the possibility that U.S. air power could be used effectively in support of a political settlement without a commitment of U.S. ground troops—an important sticking point in all earlier debates over the use of air power to end the fighting. U.S. involvement on the ground could then be restricted to policing of a settlement agreed to in the wake of U.S. bombing.

U.S. policymakers thus made no effort to discourage Croatia from using force to take Krajina from the Serbs, or from undertaking offensive operations with the Bosnian Muslims inside Bosnia against the Bosnian Serbs. According to media accounts, senior policymakers in the Clinton administration met repeatedly in July and August to discuss how to bring about a settlement in Bosnia. In the days preceding the Croatian offensive against the Serbs in Krajina, the U.S. president approved what one official characterized as a "yellow light" and another as "an amber light tinted green" approach with respect to Croatian intentions, rather than a "red light."[51] In October 1995 the U.S. envoy to the Bosnian (Muslim-Croat) Federation, Ambassador Charles Thomas, acknowledged that "you'd have to say we gave the green light for the Krajina offensive because our admonitions were at best half-hearted."[52] Even before the operation against Krajina, British sources reported that the United States had "given the green light" for Croatian offensive operations.[53] Croatian troops provided the heretofore missing ground forces necessary to ensure the success of a U.S. air campaign. But, as we shall see below, the emergence of the Croatian military did not occur without U.S. involvement. It was the product of the approach adopted by the United States in early 1994: to strengthen Croatia as a strategic counterweight to Serbia and forge a Croatian-Muslim alliance as a military counterweight to the Bosnian Serbs.

Finally, the apparent eagerness of Milošević to force an end to the war in Bosnia raised the prospect that he might finally compel the Bosnian Serbs to accept what they had refused to accept in the past. As the analysis in chapter 3 suggests, Milošević had long been ready to subordinate the interests of the Croatian and Bosnian Serbs to his own personal interests as well as those of Serbia. But, political concessions offered by the West were not enough, by themselves, to persuade him to sign on. Until the Americans combined an offer to lift sanctions against Yugoslavia (Serbia and Montenegro) with a credible threat of extensive and prolonged use of force against the Bosnian Serbs, in the context of a major military defeat at the hands of the Croats and Muslims that threatened to upset the larger strategic balance between Croatia and Yugoslavia, Milošević refrained from imposing his will on the Bosnian Serbs.

Coercive Diplomacy

Milošević had met with representatives of the Contact Group in February and March 1995 to discuss the French-initiated proposal, noted earlier, to lift some of the sanctions on Yugoslavia (Serbia and Montenegro) in exchange for Yugoslav recognition of Bosnia-Herzegovina and Croatia. These meetings included contact with U.S. Deputy Assistant Secretary of State Robert Frasure, who had assumed responsibility for negotiations over Bosnia in February, when the administration concluded that direct talks with the Bosnian Serbs were unproductive and shifted its attention once again to Milošević.[54] As the May 1 expiration of the Carter cease-fire approached, the contact group representatives continued to press Milošević to agree to their modified map and plan, which now seemed to permit the possibility that the proposed borders might be "adjusted" and a future Bosnian Serb entity might be allowed to establish some relationship to Serbia. Neither these modifications nor the fact that the Bosnian Serbs now appeared to be on the defensive proved persuasive, however.

As we noted above, fighting had already resumed in Bosnia in March 1995, six weeks before the scheduled expiration of the Carter cease-fire, with an offensive by Bosnian government troops. Over the next several months, military and political conditions in Bosnia changed radically. With the formal expiration of the Bosnian cease-fire in early May, Croatia moved immediately to retake the UN-protected area in western Slavonija by force. The ease with which the Croatian army carried out its task led to speculation among usually reliable Yugoslav journalists that this reflected some sort of deal between Milošević and Tudjman, concluded as early as their meeting in Karadjordjevo in 1991.[55] But the area was not strongly defended, as relatively few Serbs were left in the territory. Croatian troops also took the offensive inside Bosnia, advancing up the Livno valley toward both the Bihać pocket and, more important, to within striking range of Knin—thereby positioning themselves for an assault on Serb-held territories in Croatian Krajina.

According to UN military and political sources, the Bosnian army had undergone a complete reorganization during the cease-fire period and had moved away from reliance on opština-based units best suited to local warfare and toward more mobile formations better suited to offensive operations. Muslim offensives against the Serbs around Travnik and Tuzla in March and around Sarajevo in June, noted earlier, involved larger-scale troop movements and increased levels of artillery and mortar exchanges than had taken place earlier in the war, signaling at least an improvement in Muslim military capabilities,[56] and perhaps even a shift in the military balance between the Muslim and Serb armies. At the same time, the Bosnian Serbs stepped up their shelling of Sarajevo. The continued escalation of the fighting thus seemed almost certain.

The contact group members continued to pursue a negotiated settlement even after the May cease-fire ended and the fighting in Croatia and Bosnia escalated further. As we have seen, both the French and British renewed their threat to withdraw their troops if no progress was made.[57] French prime minister Juppé criticized the Russians for failing to pressure the Serbs, and the Americans for failing to pressure the Bosnian government to accept the contact group plan, and warned that "this share-out of the roles between those who are doing the hard graft and the others who are pulling the diplomatic strings cannot continue for very much longer."[58] The credibility of the French threat to withdraw was underscored for the other members of the Contact Group by the rapidly deteriorating relationship between French peacekeepers and the Muslim population in Sarajevo, and the mounting French casualties.[59] Hence, pressure either to act decisively or withdraw entirely began to build. The United States responded to increased Serb shelling of Sarajevo and a May 9 incident that produced the worst civilian casualties since the February 1994 marketplace massacre by calling for air strikes against the Bosnian Serbs, a response also called for by UN military commanders on the ground in Sarajevo, but rejected by senior UN officials.[60]

On May 25 UNPROFOR commander Lt. Gen. Rupert Smith elected to back up an ultimatum to the Serbs to withdraw weapons from the exclusion zone around Sarajevo and to return those weapons they had removed from collection sites by calling for NATO air strikes against a Serb ammunition dump in Pale. In response, the Serbs shelled Tuzla, hitting a cafe and killing seventy-one civilians. After a second NATO attack on the Pale ammunition dump, the Bosnian Serbs seized 400 UN troops as hostages, using many of them as human shields at other potential targets of NATO attack.[61] This confrontation led to intensified talk in the West of both escalated military involvement and UN withdrawal. Over the next two weeks, the Serbs released some hostages, but seized others.[62] Holbrooke noted in a later press interview that he had recommended that the United States "tell the Serbs to free the hostages in 48 hours or we will bomb the daylights out of them." But, his interviewer reported, no one took him seriously; other senior officials noted that "the tirade had a kind of 'for my memoirs' quality to it."[63] The hostages finally were released following an announcement by the UN command on June 10 that it would "abide strictly by peacekeeping principles until further notice," thereby effectively fulfilling Serb demands that the UN renounce the use of force.[64]

Meanwhile, the United States continued to negotiate with Milošević. Frasure met repeatedly with him in May. Just as Milošević appears to have supported the Vance-Owen plan in 1993 primarily because of his interest in alleviating onerous sanctions against Yugoslavia (Serbia-Montenegro) and a belief that agreement would inevitably lead to partition, it seems clear that his cooperation in spring 1995 also hinged on the promise of lifting sanctions and the preservation of some political gains in Bosnia. The members of the Contact Group, however, appear to have been divided over precisely these issues. One unnamed senior U.S. State Department official, noting that the Russian ambassador in Belgrade maintained direct contact with Milošević during the latter's talks with Frasure, seemed to imply that Milošević's resistance to signing on to the plan may have been stiffened by Russian support: "I wouldn't say they sabotaged [the talks] but they certainly sometimes have their own ideas." The State Department's official spokesman acknowledged that "we sometimes have tactical differences with Russia" and asserted that the United States would "let the Russians know that the only offer the contact group can accept is the offer Frasure put on the table."[65]

The United States appears to have offered Milošević the suspension of UN-imposed sanctions against Yugoslavia in exchange for Bosnian Serb agreement to the 51–49 partition contained in the contact group map and Yugoslav recognition of Bosnia-Herzegovina. But Milošević insisted on the lifting, or complete end, of sanctions. He also appeared to be willing to recognize only the state borders of Bosnia-Herzegovina, not its government. The United States remained unwilling, for its part, to forgo entirely the option of reimposing sanctions if the agreement failed to achieve U.S. goals. The United States may have agreed to give the secretary-general rather than the Security Council the authority to determine whether Yugoslavia was fulfilling its commitments, a concession that would have eliminated the U.S. veto over such a determination. However, it appears that the United States was, in any case, unwilling to suspend the most important, financial sanctions against Yugoslavia.[66] The Russians, in contrast, argued that "there are no longer any grounds for continuing to maintain the sanctions against Yugoslavia."[67] But they appear not to have had much influence on the approach taken by Frasure, despite the fact that formally he was representing the Contact Group in his negotiations with Milošević.

Frasure appears to have narrowed the differences with Milošević to a single issue: how and when sanctions, once lifted, could be reimposed. Nonetheless, the administration abandoned its talks with Milošević in early June, calling Frasure back to Washington.[68] The hostage crisis made the continuation of such talks difficult. Divisions within the administration itself may also have contributed to the decision to break off these talks. U.S. ambassador to the United Nations Madeleine Albright, an increasingly influential advocate in policy debates of stronger measures against the Serbs, is alleged to have threatened to resign over the concessions offered to Milošević, something the administration could ill afford in light of the domestic political controversy over its handling of Bosnia. Holbrooke, in contrast, suggests in his memoir that the talks were broken off in order to allow the Europeans "to take the lead for a month or two."[69]

The political and military situation changed dramatically during the course of the summer. We have already noted that the Serbs overran the government-held safe areas of Srebrenica and Žepa in eastern Bosnia in July, and that the Bosnian army had earlier gone on the offensive both to the north and to the south of Sarajevo. By early July, the Bosnians had scored significant gains against the Serbs. Regular Croatian army troops were also active in Bosnia and together with Bosnian Croat troops carried out a successful offensive against the Serbs in the Livno valley, in western Herzegovina. This put Croatian artillery and troops within striking distance of Serb-held Knin, just across the nearby Bosnian-Croatian border. The Croatian army launched a full-scale offensive against the Serb-held Krajina region on August 4, and regained complete control of the region in a matter of days. The Krajina Serb military put up no resistance. Hundreds of thousands of Serbs fled Croatia in the face of the Croatian offensive, creating a flood of Serb refugees in Serb-held Bosnia and Serbia.

Like the earlier Serb takeovers of Srebrenica and Žepa, the Croatian victory in Krajina solved a heretofore intractable territorial issue. While NATO conducted air strikes against the Serbs in late August (discussed in more detail below), the Croatian army proceeded to mount offensive operations in western Bosnia in September, in cooperation with the Bosnian army, routing the Serbs from Cazinska Krajina (the Bihać region) and much of Bosanska Krajina (western Bosnia). As suggested by Maps 7.1 and 7.2, these developments produced a radical redistribution of the territories under Croat, Muslim, and Serb control, bringing them more closely into line with the formulas that had been under negotiation since 1994 and shifting the military and political balance decisively in favor of the Croatian–Bosnian Muslim–Bosnian Croat alliance. The areas controlled by each of the warring parties in May 1995 are shown in Map 7.1; changes in the areas of control between May and October are shown in Map 7.2.

Nonetheless, Milošević continued to play a critical role in the U.S. effort to end the war. Circumstantial evidence suggests that the successful Croatian offensive to retake Krajina had been preceded by indirect discussions between Milošević and Tudjman and a possible agreement on Milošević's

Map 7.1 **Areas of Control, May 1995**

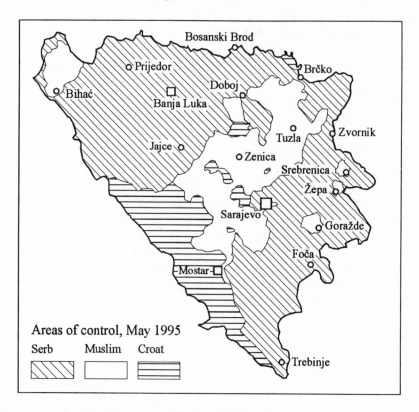

Areas of control, May 1995

Serb   Muslim   Croat

Based on unclassified CIA map no. 735935 (R00855) 5–95.

part not to oppose the Croatian effort. A senior advisor to Tudjman traveled to Belgrade to meet with Milošević shortly before the Croatian offensive.[70] Earlier, a deputy chief of the Yugoslav army general staff was dispatched from Belgrade to Knin to take over command of the Krajina Serb military. General Mile Mrkšić is reported to have brought 50 Yugoslav army officers with him and to have organized an elite mobile strike force within the Serb forces in Krajina, including both artillery and armor.[71] Yet, the forces under his command offered no organized resistance to the Croatian effort to retake Krajina, encouraging instead the massive exodus of the Serb population from Croatia. According to UN military and political sources, the withdrawal was "well orchestrated and orderly." They reported that 10,000–15,000 Krajina Serb troops with hundreds of tanks, artillery pieces, and other heavy equipment crossed into Bosnia. The absence of concerted Serb

Map 7.2 **Changes in Control, May–October 1995**

Based on unclassified CIA maps 735935 (R00855) 5–95 and 737414 (R00855) 10–95.

military resistance to the August 1995 Croatian offensive to retake Krajina and the subsequent combined Croatian-Muslim offensive inside Bosnia that overran large swaths of Serb-held territories intensified speculation that what was taking place reflected an agreement reached behind the scenes among the Croatian, Bosnian, and Serbian leaderships on the partition of Bosnia-Herzegovina. Such speculation received further impetus from a report on August 8 that Mrkšić had ordered his troops to retreat without a fight.[72] Karadžić, in an open letter read on Bosnian Serb television on August 8, accused Milošević of treachery against the Krajina Serbs, and thousands of demonstrators gathered in Belgrade to accuse Milošević of treason.[73]

The Bosnian Serbs refused to give in to diplomatic pressure from the United States or political pressure from Milošević. On August 1 Milošević had sent a letter to both Mladić and Izetbegović—bypassing Karadžić—urging them to conclude a peace treaty immediately. The letter seemed to reflect Milošević's commitment to ending the war, possibly in response to U.S. insistence that the Bosnian Serbs had to cease their attacks before a diplomatic solution could be agreed on.[74] The appeal to Mladić reflected Milošević's growing inability to control Karadžić, as well as the growing differences between Mladić and Karadžić. Mladić, although a ruthless military leader, had been pressing the political leadership under Karadžić to come up with a political formula for ending the conflict. In April 1995 Mladić warned them that "if a political solution at the negotiating table is not found, the war will be long and exhausting."[75] As we shall see below, Mladić would prove to be a hard negotiator even under military pressure from NATO. But in the end he seemed to understand that the Bosnian Serbs could not win a military contest on their own.

The Bosnian Serb leadership did not bow to military pressure from the combined Croatian–Bosnian Muslim offensive alone. They entered negotiations only after the United States created a credible threat that a wide-ranging bombing campaign would be mounted against them, and after Milošević had seized control over their negotiating positions. Equally important, by mid-August the United States had signaled its willingness to offer a number of important concessions to the Bosnian Serbs to get them to enter into negotiations. Reports of an August 16 meeting in Belgrade between Milošević and an American delegation that included both Frasure and Holbrooke suggest the United States was offering an exchange of the Bosnian government-held Goražde enclave for territory around Sarajevo, a widening of the strategic northern corridor, and most important, some form of confederation between a Bosnian Serb entity and Serbia itself—changes in the U.S. approach that one unnamed European official characterized as "pure American Realpolitik."[76] But the exact details of these concessions remained unclear. Karadžić remained unwilling to enter into negotiations on the basis of the 51–49 division of territory called for by the Contact Group. Nor was it clear that the Bosnian government could be persuaded to accept the U.S. approach.

While Croatia and the Bosnian government were reported in late August also to be resisting the U.S. initiative,[77] Holbrooke and the Americans reserved the threat to use force for the Serbs alone. In a television interview on August 27, Holbrooke warned that "if this peace initiative does not get moving—dramatically moving—in the next week or two, the consequences will be very adverse to the Serbian goals," and the same day a senior White House official threatened that the arms embargo would be lifted and the Serbs subjected to six to twelve months of "compensatory" air strikes.[78]

Unlike previous occasions, however, this threat followed a decision to make significant political concessions to Bosnian Serb interests. It also reflected not only a decision on the part of the Americans to use force, but a consensus to do so among the Americans, British, and French. Once taken, the decision to mount an extensive air campaign did not allow for last-minute acquiescence by the Bosnian Serbs. Hence, the U.S. campaign was launched despite a last-minute announcement from the Bosnian Serb parliament on August 29 that it had accepted the U.S. proposal and agreed to negotiate.[79] In a letter to former president Carter delivered on August 29, Karadžić accepted the U.S. peace initiative, including the creation of a union between the Bosnian (Muslim-Croat) Federation and the Serb republic[80]—a concession that piqued the interest of U.S. policymakers.[81] However, in light of the numerous Bosnian Serb declarations in the past that had proved of little consequence for Serb behavior, simply accepting the U.S. proposal would probably have had little effect on the U.S. approach even in the absence of a prior decision to use force. But now, according to one State Department official, "the game will basically be just to wait for the trigger for air strikes and the trigger would be Sarajevo or Goražde—some of the things that have been going on right now."[82]

In the face of the U.S. threat to use force, and in an effort to win the lifting of sanctions, Milošević imposed an agreement on the Bosnian Serb leadership on August 29 establishing a joint Bosnian Serb–Yugoslav (Serbia and Montenegro) delegation to conduct all further negotiations. The delegation would consist of three Yugoslavs, including Milošević, and three Bosnian Serbs. The agreement gave Milošević the authority to resolve any deadlock in the delegation, and made all decisions of the delegation binding on the Bosnian Serbs.[83] It followed several days of intensive meetings in which Milošević appears to have pressured the Bosnian Serbs to agree to the U.S. initiative.[84] By this arrangement Milošević took direct responsibility for the further conduct of negotiations with the United States. Holbrooke later characterized this agreement as "the breakthrough that ended sixteen months of stalemate."[85]

Another aspect of that breakthrough was an agreement on September 1 between Holbrooke and Milošević to exchange Yugoslav diplomatic recognition of Bosnia-Herzegovina in its existing borders for *de facto* U.S. recognition of the Bosnian Serb republic. According to Holbrooke's memoir, the September 1 meeting with Milošević produced a draft "Joint Agreed Statement of Political Principles" which stipulated that Bosnia would "continue in its legal existence with its present borders and continuing international recognition." It is not clear from this or any other account of this meeting what Milošević received in exchange for this important political concession, other than inclusion in the draft of the name "Republika Srpska" for the Serb entity within Bosnia.[86] Despite Milošević's clear interest in the permanent lifting of sanctions, for example, these remained in place.

Holbrooke followed up on the September 1 talks by meeting Izetbegović in Ankara, Turkey, on September 4 to urge him to accept constitutional status for the Bosnian Serb republic, and to grant it the right to establish relations with a neighboring state, that is, Serbia. This represented an extremely important U.S. concession to the Serbs. Holbrooke may also have been exploring the possibility of exchanging Goražde for territory around Sarajevo as part of the settlement. But, according to Holbrooke's account of the meeting, the "central issue" was the name of the country itself, and of the Serb entity within it. Izetbegović refused to give up the name "Republic" to describe the country as a whole, and vehemently opposed using the name "Republika Srpska."[87] According to a later U.S. press account, Bosnian opposition to Republika Srpska was overcome only when, during a meeting between Holbrooke and Bosnian leaders in Split, Croatia, on September 6, Secretary of State Christopher telephoned Izetbegović to reassure him that the proposed constitutional arrangements did not imply U.S. recognition of Bosnian Serb sovereignty, and Holbrooke "threatened" Bosnian foreign minister Sacirbey with "a crisis in U.S.-Bosnian relations" and a halt to the NATO bombing then under way.[88]

Yet another aspect of the diplomatic breakthrough in August–September 1995 may have been an apparent decision by the Americans and Milošević to attempt at the same time to settle the outstanding issues between Croatia and Serbia which, in the wake of the restoration of Croatian control over Krajina, now consisted primarily of the status of eastern Slavonija, the last Serb-held piece of Croatian territory. On October 3, the Erdut agreement was concluded, providing for the return of eastern Slavonia to Croatia after a transitional period.[89] These diplomatic developments took place against the background of NATO air strikes that provided the coercive force missing from earlier efforts to negotiate a settlement. This combination of force and diplomacy paved the way for the agreement reached on September 8 in Geneva among the foreign ministers of Croatia, Bosnia, and Serbia, calling for Croatia and Serbia to recognize Bosnia-Herzegovina in its existing borders and establishing that Bosnia-Herzegovina will consist of two autonomous entities: the (Bosnian) Serb Republic (referred to as *Republika Srpska* in the document) and the Federation of Bosnia-Herzegovina (Muslim-Croat).

Milošević would again play a critical role two weeks later in brokering the agreement between Holbrooke and the Bosnian Serbs ending the NATO bombing campaign in exchange for an end to the Bosnian Serb siege of Sarajevo and the withdrawal of their heavy weapons from the exclusion zone around the city. That agreement opened the door to an eventual cease-fire and the negotiation of a comprehensive settlement. Milošević would play an even larger role in the later negotiations over that agreement at Dayton. None of these developments, however, would likely have occurred in the absence of, first, a credible threat to use force—made possible in large part because the successful Croatian and Croatian-Muslim offensives lent credibility to the U.S. threat to use air power; second, the use of air power in ways that signaled a willingness to impose a settlement on the warring parties; and third, the willingness of the United States to offer compensatory political concessions to the Serbs.

The Military Dimension of Western Policy

It is clear that the Clinton administration embarked on a strategy of strengthening the Croats as a military counterweight to the Serbs as early as March 1994, about the same time that it brokered the Muslim-Croat federation agreement.[90] It is also clear that the United States made no effort to discourage and, through its military assistance and political support, encouraged and may even have assisted in Croatian efforts to regain control of the Serb-controlled areas of Croatia by force and to exert additional military pressure on the Bosnian Serbs. Meeting with Croatian president Tudjman in Copenhagen in March 1995, for example, Vice President Al Gore not only declared "full U.S. support for restoring Croatian sovereignty to all parts of Croatia," but also went so far as to suggest that "President Tudjman cannot sit idly by as chances fade for people driven from their homes in Serb-held areas to return safely. The legitimate frustration of the Croatian people makes it impossible to continue the status quo."[91] In late July, on the threshold of the Croatian offensive against the Krajina Serbs in August, Croatian and Bosnian military and political leaders met in Split and concluded a military cooperation agreement.[92] U.S. Ambassador to Croatia Peter Galbraith was an unannounced participant in the meeting and may have conveyed a U.S. commitment to support them.[93] But it does not appear to be the case that U.S. policymakers had yet decided on using the Croatian military as a surrogate ground force to complement U.S. air power and bring the war to an end. The speed and ease with which the Croatian offensives in Krajina and Bosnia advanced seemed to take at least some U.S. officials by surprise. Secretary of Defense Perry, for example, was later reported to have judged the Croatian timetable for victory "too optimistic" and to have anticipated "prolonged fighting that would pressure Milošević to intervene."[94]

U.S. policymakers appear still to have been confused, divided, and undecided on Bosnian policy in early July 1995. The reinforcement of UN-PROFOR through deployment of a more heavily armed rapid reaction force in June (treated in more detail below) now appears in hindsight to have been part of a strategy of increasing military pressure on the Serbs either to force negotiations or shift the tide of battle. But it may also have been seen by policymakers at the time as laying the groundwork for a different set of outcomes: the possible withdrawal of UNPROFOR under hostile fire and the military disengagement of the West. A recent Bosnian analysis attributes formation of the rapid reaction force to a desire to save UNPROFOR rather than to confront the Serbs.[95] Indeed, NATO plans for such a withdrawal had already received provisional approval at a meeting of the North Atlantic Council in June.[96] In short, rather than having planned in advance the precise sequence of events that led to Dayton, the Americans appear to have reacted to developments as they unfolded; first by refusing in July to negotiate with Milošević until the Bosnian Serbs halted their attacks on the safe areas, then by moving quickly to exploit the diplomatic opportunities created by the Croatian takeover of Krajina from the Serbs. They utilized the new position of strength held by NATO to pressure Milošević to restrain the Bosnian Serbs politically. They used air power to expand Croatian military successes as a means of pressuring the Bosnian Serbs militarily into agreeing to negotiations and pulling back from Sarajevo. They pressured the Bosnian Muslims to accept a negotiated settlement. And, finally, they conceded to Bosnian Serb political interests where necessary.

Prior to its 1995 change of strategy, the United States had pressed for one or another form of the "lift and strike" approach first articulated in 1993 (described in chapter 5). France, Britain, and Russia had opposed lifting the arms embargo, making it unlikely that any such action would pass the Security Council. Indeed, lifting the embargo appeared certain to trigger the immediate withdrawal of French and British troops, and draw the United States into deploying forces on the ground. The United States could not, therefore, act unilaterally, at least not openly. As early as November 1994, however, the United States was compelled to deny reports that it was secretly arming the Bosnians.[97]

As we noted in chapter 6, United Nations military observers reported flights of transport aircraft in February 1995 that suggested a major covert operation to supply arms to the Bosnian army was under way at Tuzla airport.[98] NATO disputed these reports, with a U.S. officer claiming that the flights in question were either NATO air patrols or commercial aircraft in Serbian airspace. One UN official retorted, however, that "the idea that trained officers could mistake a low-flying transporter over Tuzla for a commercial aircraft flying at 35,000 feet in Serbian airspace is frankly ludicrous and insulting."[99] Later media reports suggested that these flights had been part of a larger covert U.S. effort to supply the Bosnian army, involving sympathetic third countries.[100] In April, the media revealed that Iran had for months, perhaps for more than a year, been delivering "hundreds of tons" of weapons and ammunition to the Bosnian army via Croatia, "with the Clinton administration's tacit acceptance."[101] In July, the media reported that senior U.S., French, and British officials all acknowledged that the Europeans had raised the issue of U.S. violations of the arms embargo in high-level meetings.[102] In February 1996 Saudi officials reported that they had provided $300 million in arms supplies (as well as $500 million in humanitarian aid) to the Bosnian government in violation of the arms embargo and with the knowledge of the United States.[103] The Saudis reported that U.S. involvement "was more than just turning a blind eye. . . . It was consent combined with a stealth operation." The Saudi effort also was channeled through Zagreb. But Saudi sources acknowledged that some supplies were delivered by night flights into Tuzla and other airfields controlled by the Bosnian government. The administration's precise actions with respect to Iranian arms shipments later became the subject of a congressional inquiry as to whether they constituted an illegal covert operation.[104]

The deniability of direct U.S. government involvement in the effort to build up the Muslim and Croatian militaries was preserved through the use of ostensibly private military contractors to provide the necessary training and advice. A request for military assistance from the Croatian minister of defense in March 1994, for example, was referred by the Pentagon to a private contractor, Military Professional Resources, Inc. (MPRI). MPRI sent a former U.S. Army chief of staff and a former commander of U.S. forces in Europe, among other retired officers, to Croatia as part of a program of assistance to the Croatian military. The vast improvement in Croatian military performance achieved within less than 18 months, as evidenced by the successful campaign to retake Krajina in August 1995, suggested to some Western military analysts that the Croatian forces were the beneficiaries of U.S. military planning and advice. A Croatian journalist reported that in the days immediately preceding the Krajina attack, former U.S. Army Chief of Staff Gen. Carl Vuono met ten times with senior Croatian officers involved in planning the attack to discuss "computer scenarios." But a spokesman for MPRI denied that any "wargaming" had taken place.[105]

In other instances, official U.S. involvement in advising the Muslim and Croat militaries was more open. According to one media account, retired Maj. Gen. John Sewall, who formally served as an adviser to secretaries Christopher and Perry on the military affairs of the Muslim-Croat federation, was cited by the French and British governments as having advised the

Bosnian Army on combat tactics and assisted in supplying it with weapons. Sewall himself acknowledged that the UN commander was "very nervous" about his activities, and admitted that "there may be private Americans advising the Bosnian army."[106] Indeed, one media inventory of U.S. involvement cited the presence of veterans of U.S. special operations units as advisers to the Bosnian Army.[107] Insistence on the private status of an organization such as MPRI or on the "retired" and "former" status of high-level U.S. military personnel involved provided only the thinnest of veils over what was a clear administration effort to assist and strengthen the Croatian and Bosnian Muslim militaries.

The escalated fighting in spring 1995 compelled UN military and political officials to undertake a formal review of their mission in mid-May.[108] This review resulted in publication at the end of May of a report by the secretary-general outlining four options for the future role of UNPROFOR:[109] (1) withdrawal, (2) continuation of the *status quo,* (3) greater use of force, and (4) revising the mandate to include "only those tasks that a peace-keeping operation can realistically be expected to perform in the circumstances currently prevailing in Bosnia and Herzegovina." Boutros-Ghali rejected both withdrawal and continuation of the *status quo.* Reliance on greater force, he argued, would require "substantial reinforcement" of the UN presence. It would also require replacing UNPROFOR with "a multinational force authorized by the Security Council but under the command of one or more of the countries contributing troops to it." Boutros-Ghali had favored the fourth option,[110] calling for a scale-down and redeployment of the UN force and limiting its operations to "good offices, liaison and negotiation; monitoring cease-fires . . . ; maintaining a presence in the safe areas, after negotiating appropriate regimes for them but without any actual or implied commitment to use force to deter attacks against them; operation of Sarajevo airport with the consent of the parties;" and other humanitarian activities. This option limited the use of force, including the use of air power, to self-defense. But the third option, to rely on greater force by replacing UNPROFOR with a multinational force, became more attractive in the days immediately preceding publication of the report, when the limited use of air power against the Serbs in late May produced another hostage-taking crisis—the third in just over a year.

U.S. policymakers, fearing the breakdown of the UNPROFOR mission and a decision to withdraw, pressured their European allies and UN officials to use force against the Serbs in spring 1995.[111] U.S. ambassador Albright opined publicly that "we do not understand why air power is not appropriate at this time." She noted that the *status quo* could not be maintained, and suggested "we are at some kind of major decision point."[112] It was partly in response to this pressure that UNPROFOR commander Lt. Gen. Rupert Smith called for the May 25 air strike that set off the hostage crisis described earlier in this chapter. Neither the United States nor its allies had a strategic plan for how to proceed from that point. French prime minister Juppé angrily criticized the attacks as "not well prepared" and for exposing peacekeepers to "thoughtless risks." He argued that "ultimatums and air strikes must be used after reflection and preparation."[113] One unnamed U.S. official suggested in a later media account that the approach amounted to little more than "drop a few bombs and see what happens." At a closed session of the Security Council, according to the same account, "countries providing the bulk of the troops" (a phrase that clearly suggests Britain and France) demanded that the air strikes be halted.[114]

In response to the deteriorating situation on the ground, the contact group foreign ministers agreed to expand, strengthen, and re-deploy UN troops in Bosnia-Herzegovina, and give them more aggressive rules of engagement.[115] These decisions were soon followed by a decision to establish rapid reaction forces in Bosnia and Croatia under UN command.[116] The deployment of two thousand U.S. marines and their equipment to ships in the Adriatic in late May raised the prospect that the United States might participate in this reconfiguration of the UN mission.[117] Indeed, British sources reported that a decision to this effect had been agreed on.[118]

The purpose of the rapid reaction force, as defined by its European architects in a proposal to Secretary-General Boutros-Ghali in early June,[119] was "to reduce the vulnerability of [UNPROFOR] personnel and to enhance its capacity to carry out its existing mandate" by providing it with 15,000 well-armed and mobile troops. The new force would become an integral part of UNPROFOR, under the existing UN chain of command and the operational control of UN commanders. It would, however, be something of a hybrid; for it would "operate under national uniform, under the United Nations flag and insignia but without blue helmets and without painting its vehicles white. It would operate under existing United Nations rules of engagement."[120] These guidelines suggested a European decision to move toward the creation of a peace enforcement capacity. But the European proposal specifically stated that deployment of the rapid reaction force "would not change the United Nations role to peace-enforcement." The proposal also acknowledged that this was no substitute for political negotiations to end the war.

These moves seemed to suggest that both the Americans and the Europeans were being drawn more directly into an escalating conflict; precisely the outcome that U.S. policymakers had intended to avert by the use of air power. But these actions were also consistent with preparation for a withdrawal of UN forces. Hence, use of air power in a very limited fashion and in the absence of a clear political strategy for bringing the war to an end served only to divide the Americans and the Europeans. It appeared to increase the likelihood of a UN withdrawal and direct U.S. involvement in it, rather than contribute to a negotiated solution and the military disengagement of the West.

While Western policymakers debated their next moves, military developments on the ground in Bosnia in July increased the pressure to use force more decisively. As we have already noted, Bosnian Serb forces overran the Bosnian government–held enclaves of Srebrenica and Žepa, which had earlier been declared UN safe areas. Croatian forces were reported massing in preparation for an attack on the Krajina.[121] The Bosnian Serbs threatened to attack Goražde. Indications that the seizures of Srebrenica and Žepa were accompanied by large-scale atrocities lent a "sense of urgency verging on desperation" to the policy debate among the Western allies.[122] That debate juxtaposed two options: withdrawal of UN forces to permit the warring parties to continue to fight on their own, versus a deliberate escalation of Western military involvement to end the war.[123] NATO plans for withdrawal appear to have been completed by the fall of Srebrenica. They assumed the worst: a wintertime withdrawal under hostile conditions. Moreover, they did not provide for humanitarian relief or support for refugees, tens of thousands of whom were likely to take to the same roads NATO forces would need to secure to carry out their rescue mission.[124] Not surprisingly, therefore, Clinton administration officials appear to have been seized by concern to avoid the withdrawal of UN forces and to avoid having to commit U.S. ground forces to an operation that appeared to promise significant American casualties.

The president appears to have been confounded by developments in Srebrenica. On the one hand, Clinton responded to the Serb attack by telling reporters in the White House rose garden that UN forces should "go back in there and re-establish the safe area," a statement administration officials later called a mistake. On the other hand, he seemed to suggest that withdrawal of the UN mission ought to be followed by joint Western action to lift the arms embargo on the Bosnian government.[125] Following the fall of Srebrenica, an unnamed senior State Department official characterized Clinton as "bewildered" by recent developments.[126]

As we noted earlier, French president Chirac responded to the fall of Srebrenica by calling for joint military action to retake the enclaves. But senior U.S. military officials are reported to have concluded that the French proposal would have brought the United States and its allies to the brink of war with the Bosnian Serbs. In part, this may have been a product of the military's penchant for proposing more extensive use of force than envisaged by civilian policymakers so as to ensure the security of an operation.[127] Indeed, a retrospective media account of Clinton administration policy on Bosnia reported that General Powell, a particularly outspoken advocate of using force only on an overwhelming scale and only when U.S. interests were clear-cut, had been a major obstacle to any decision by senior policymakers to use force in Bosnia for the duration of his service as chairman of the Joint Chiefs. However, Powell had been replaced by General John Shalikashvili in October 1993. Shalikashvili was reported to have opposed the deployment of U.S. ground troops to Bosnia, but to have supported the use of U.S. air power against the Serbs.[128] Thus, Clinton administration officials were reported in July 1995—at the time Holbrooke would later claim the decision to use force had been made—to be focusing on the more aggressive use of air power against the Serbs instead of the French proposal to use ground forces.[129] In Britain, the options divided even the ruling party. Tory backbenchers demanded withdrawal, while other Tory MPs warned against such action as a "policy of betrayal and despair."[130] The British government opposed escalating Western involvement, warning that any decision that UN forces required reinforcement would trigger withdrawal. Hans van den Broek, speaking during a pause at a meeting of European foreign ministers on July 17, reported "a general feeling that going to war in Bosnia can never be the objective."[131] Yet, behind the scenes, European ministers were reportedly warning the British and the French that "equivocation in the Balkans simply would not do for much longer. . . . Some ministers were talking of a collapse of international power in the Balkans."[132]

Top military officials from the United States, France, and Britain met in London on July 16 to consider the reinforcement of Goražde, the last remaining government-held enclave in eastern Bosnia and the apparent next target of the Serb offensive.[133] Senior Clinton administration officials reportedly were convinced that unless Goražde were protected, it should be abandoned. A senior British official characterized the inclination to defend Goražde as "a large touch of the Dien Bien Phus [sic]."[134] The French opposed the U.S. proposal to rely on air power, but proposed instead that ground troops be sent into the enclave—to be transported by U.S. helicopters.[135] The differences between the British and the French appeared to some senior U.S. policymakers as "irreconcilable." "One of our closest allies wants us to jump in hard, and our other closest ally says it won't be necessary," one senior official said. "There is no consensus here to base a policy on."[136]

The U.S. case for using air power to protect Goražde was made still more difficult by Russian opposition. The Russians opposed mixing human-itarian, peacekeeping, and hostile military functions as "very unrealistic and certainly very dangerous." Russian foreign minister Kozyrev asked whether those proposing NATO action were "prepared to really fight a war, not to play the high moral ground or play with public opinion, but conduct a huge military operation which will inevitably involve huge casualties, including civilian casualties."[137] Kozyrev remained opposed to military action even after conferring with Secretary Christopher in London.[138]

Russian resistance was evident in the results of a multilateral conference in London on July 21. The participants failed to agree on a joint conclu-sion, allegedly because Kozyrev refused to sign a joint communiqué advo-cating air strikes to protect Goražde. Representatives of the major powers thus met separately with the press following the conference, and offered somewhat different interpretations of its result. Secretary Christopher stressed that the Bosnian Serbs were "now on notice that an attack against Goražde will be met by substantial and decisive air power." Moreover, he asserted that "any air campaign in Goražde will include significant attacks on significant targets. There will be no more pinprick strikes." These state-ments were consistent with the report that the administration had decided on the use of force on July 15, and indicated that that force would be used to deter further Serb attacks on the safe areas. Christopher also announced that "existing command and control arrangements will be significantly adjusted to ensure that responsiveness and unity of purpose are achieved." This appeared to indicate that the allies had agreed to abandon the "dual key" arrangement whereby the approval of UN political leadership was required before any decision by military commanders to use air power could be implemented. Indeed, Holbrooke suggests in his memoir that the United States proposed both to draw a "line in the sand" around Goražde and to end the "dual key" arrangement.[139]

But the "chairman's summary" read out by British foreign secretary Malcolm Rifkind said only that a Serb attack on Goražde would be "met with a substantial and decisive response." Moreover, Rifkind acknowledged that while there was "strong support" for this there was also "great concern" over it. Christopher, in contrast, asserted that "today's participants are fully aware of the risks" of hostage-taking and that "we're determined that the taking of hostages will no longer be allowed to prevent the implementation of our policies." Kozyrev and Russian defense minister Grachev reported that they had rejected both the air strikes and a proposal to use the rapid reaction force to open a ground supply route into Sarajevo. Yet, this was precisely how the rapid reaction force would soon be used. Grachev re-ported that they had proposed alternative, unspecified, measures to prevent safe areas from being used "as a springboard to launch attacks," but that these had been rejected.[140] Significantly, the "chairman's summary" reported that participants had agreed that "if the arms embargo were lifted, UNPROFOR would have to withdraw," and that "the departure of UNPROFOR would involve activating national plans to protect such a withdrawal."[141]

Thus, the July 21 conference in London appears to have made it unmistakably clear to American policymakers that they could not lift the arms embargo without triggering American involvement in a withdrawal operation. The Clinton administration remained under intense domestic political pressure to act, pressure which had already led to the decision on July 15 to use force, identified earlier in this chapter. Within days of the conference, the U.S. Senate voted in favor of directing the administration to lift the embargo, with or without approval from the Security Council. But the British and French responded immediately by threatening to withdraw their troops in response.[142] The *de facto* end to the arms embargo and consequent escalation in fighting seemed inevitable, however. Soon after the London conference, Islamic states began declaring their intention to supply weapons to the Bosnian government in open defiance of the UN embargo.[143] Thus, paradoxically, the divisions revealed at the London conference, combined with the impending collapse of the arms embargo, may have reinforced the U.S. administration's decision finally to use extensive air power against the Serbs—and the European willingness to accept its use. It remained unclear, however, how far the United States was prepared to go in altering the contact group plan to meet Serb interests or the extent to which it was prepared to impose such a plan on the Muslims; that is, the diplomatic elements of the coercive diplomacy strategy were not yet in place. Moreover, negotiations with Belgrade over lifting sanctions were still stalled.

Indeed, a discordant note was struck when it was announced by French foreign minister Hervé de Charette on July 21 that EU mediator Carl Bildt had reached agreement with Milošević on recognition of Bosnia in exchange for the conditional suspension of sanctions against Yugoslavia.[144] This suggested that the Europeans were taking a "soft" approach to Belgrade that contradicted the harder line emerging from the meetings then under way in London.

Senior administration sources in Washington reported that a plan for extensive bombing of Serb targets in Bosnia had already been drafted, but that the goal of the planned operation remained unclear.[145] The July 21 conference appears to have produced an agreement among the Americans, British, and French to use the threat of air power to deter Serb action against Goražde despite Russian objections. The key to this agreement was a reversal of the British position on the use of force, brought about in the days leading up to the conference under intense pressure from the United States. According to a British account at the time,[146] events in Srebrenica and Žepa had raised the government's concerns about the fate of their troops in Goražde. The British military had made clear to Foreign Secretary Rifkind and to Defense Secretary Michael Portillo the potentially enormous costs of an attack on British forces in Goražde. If the Serbs were to be deterred from such an attack by air power, the military argued, "then the ministers had to accept that the West had gone to war." Rifkind then flew to Washington to seek U.S. support for the protection of Goražde. In a series of meetings with Secretary of State Christopher, the foreign secretary was compelled to agree to the U.S. demand to use "massive and overwhelming force," and to cut UN civilian officials out of the authorization process. In effect, Rifkind "had to concede that if the United States was to use its awesome air power then the U.S. government would insist on its own terms for doing so." The United States and Britain agreed that the use of air power would be triggered only if the Bosnian Serbs attacked.

The reaction in Belgrade to the fast-moving developments in July was swift: On July 21 the Yugoslav prime minister appealed to the Bosnian Serbs "not to attack the Muslim enclave of Gorazde, because an escalation of military operations—apart from causing loss of life and civilian suffering—would have a powerful negative effect on the successful outcome of the peace process."[147] Whether this move came in response to the "soft" approach proffered by Bildt, or the "hard" approach emerging in London and becoming manifest on the ground as the result of more determined responses by UN forces (noted in more detail below), is unclear.

Bildt's announcement of a deal quickly proved premature.[148] Following the July conference a delegation of U.S., British, and French air force generals met with the Bosnian Serb military commander, General Mladić, in Belgrade on July 23 to reinforce the hard approach. They warned Mladić that an assault on Goražde would result in air attacks at "unprecedented levels" and demanded an end to attacks on all safe areas. They warned that the allies and the UN would take "any steps which may become necessary" to resupply UN troops in Bosnia and warned specifically against any further hostage-taking. At the same time, however, they asserted that the allied goal remained a negotiated political settlement of war and that "there is no military solution to this conflict."[149] But a very different message may have been conveyed simultaneously to the Croats and the Bosnians. The meeting of Croatian and Bosnian military and political leaders, including Tudjman and Izetbegović, in Split—noted earlier—took place on July 22. As we also noted earlier, the meeting was attended by U.S. Ambassador Galbraith. It produced the first effective Croat-Muslim military cooperation agreement and laid the foundation for coordinated operations against the Serbs in August and September. The precise U.S. role in the talks is not a matter of public record, but a close observer of these events has suggested that the United States encouraged offensive military operations against the Serbs and signaled its likely support for them. This would have been consistent with the tenor of political discussions going on at the time among senior policymakers in the administration and with the U.S. strategy of coercive diplomacy emerging at the time. It remains unclear, however, whether the United States offered any specific commitment to support Croat-Muslim operations militarily beyond the training and, possibly, covert supply efforts already under way.

The allies remained reluctant, however, actually to use air power. A meeting of NATO military planners on July 24 failed to reach consensus on how to deal with the "dual key" issue. According to one participant, "the central issue" was "whether we can go bomb on our own," adding that "the dual key right now is intact."[150] Meanwhile, events on the ground seemed to be coming to a head. France responded to the killing of two of its UNPROFOR troops in a Serb attack on July 22 by shelling Serb positions with heavy mortars positioned on Mt. Igman. At the same time, the French redeployed rapid reaction forces nominally under UN command to Mt. Igman,[151] but without consulting the UN.[152] British forces serving as peacekeeping troops also redeployed with their heavy weapons to Mt. Igman to become part of the rapid reaction force. This gave UNPROFOR, or perhaps NATO, the capacity to inflict heavy damage on Serb gun emplacements within a 10-mile radius. The French had demonstrated their capacity to do so on July 22 by destroying three of these emplacements—a sure signal to Milošević and the Bosnian Serbs of the credibility of Western warnings.[153]

The prospect of a well-armed and mobile European force on the ground in Bosnia was unsettling for all three warring parties. The French were pressing to use the force to relieve and defend Goražde, a proposal rejected by the British and Americans, but which helped prompt the U.S.-led decision to rely on air power to protect the enclave against the Serbs.[154] The Croats feared that the combat capabilities of the force might be used in behalf of the Bosnian government. They blocked the passage of new troops and equipment out of Ploče and across the Croatian-Bosnian border in an effort to win a commitment that the force would be used only to protect UNPROFOR and to implement the contact group plan for partition.[155] The Bosnian Muslims, in contrast, feared that the force would not be used in their behalf.[156] The Croats and the Muslims each feared that the rapid reaction force might be used against them.[157] Hence, both Croats and

Muslims impeded deployment of those elements of the force that passed through Ploče, while the Bosnian Serbs moved to seize as much as they could in eastern Bosnia before the force was brought up to full strength.

The rapid reaction force did reopen the land route into Sarajevo over Mt. Igman, but it was not used to oppose the Serb takeover of Žepa or to defend Goražde. The British insisted that it would be used only to secure the land route and to protect UN peacekeepers.[158] Indeed, by the end of August French president Chirac complained of "the relative impotence of the rapid reaction force."[159] As we have already noted, Žepa fell to the Bosnian Serbs on July 25. On July 27, the Bosnian Serb–populated towns of Glamoč and Bosansko Grahovo in Western Bosnia fell to the Croatian offensive up the Livno valley.[160] This isolated Knin from Bosnia, strengthened Croatia's hand for an attack on the Krajina Serbs, and positioned the Croats for an attack on the strategic city of Jajce to the northeast—whose hydroelectric generators supplied the power for Serb-held Banja Luka.

NATO officials reported on July 25 that British and French representatives to the alliance were still pressing to preserve the role of the UN secretary-general in any decision to use force, and thereby reduce the likelihood air power would actually be used against the Serbs. French officials were suggesting that U.S. statements following the London conference had been exaggerations of the decisions of the meeting.[161] British sources were suggesting that the allies had reached consensus on using air power to defend Goražde and had only to devise a means of unlocking the dual key arrangement for authorization without entirely undermining the authority of the UN.[162] NATO ambassadors convened in Brussels for a two-day meeting on July 25 that ended in an agreement to respond to Serb actions with a wider use of force.[163] The solution to the dual key dilemma was found by delegating authority to initiate the use of air power to the local UN commander in Bosnia, British Lt. Gen. Smith, thereby shifting the *de facto* locus of control over the decision from the UN chain of command to the NATO allies.[164] NATO then duly committed itself on August 1 to use air power to defend not only Goražde, but Bihać, Sarajevo, and Tuzla, as well.[165] The more forceful approach of the British and French troops on the ground (as well as the apparent reversal of the British position on the use of force), and the Croatian gains against the Serbs were cause for "cautious optimism" among Western policymakers that an evacuation of UNPROFOR might not be necessary after all.[166]

The Military and Political Dimensions Are Integrated

The success of the Croatian offensive in Krajina, which began in early August and was completed in only four days, dramatically altered both the military situation on the ground and the political balance among the allies. The U.S. administration was openly sympathetic to the Croatians, offering only the mildest criticism of the action in Krajina, a reaction that stood in sharp contrast to the strong condemnations from all other members of the Contact Group.[167] Key players in the administration, including National Security Advisor Lake and Ambassador Albright, supported the action, arguing that Croatian success would improve the possibility of a negotiated settlement of the war in Bosnia.[168] The British and French viewed the action as accelerating the need to choose between decisive action to end the conflict, or withdrawal. A decision to withdraw, they informed Washington in early August, would have to come by the end of the month. A majority of the British cabinet, which presumably had approved of the agreement to support American demands to use air power only two weeks earlier, now appeared ready to vote for withdrawal.[169] Within days of the Croatian action, and in face of the European pressure to decide, weeks of internal policy debate in the Clinton administration were brought to an end with the adoption on August 8 of a proposal for a more straightforward *de facto* partition of Bosnia-Herzegovina.[170]

Unlike the contact group map, the American proposal now conceded the recent Serb gains in eastern Bosnia, included the exchange of Goražde for territory around Sarajevo, and according to Holbrooke's memoir, provided for the widening of the Serbs' northern (Posavina) corridor. But it preserved the 51–49 division of territory. Holbrooke reports that it also called for "the full lifting of all economic sanctions against Yugoslavia if a settlement was reached."[171] The U.S. media reported that if the Bosnian Serbs rejected it, the U.S. proposal called for lifting the arms embargo and using "robust air strikes" to protect the Muslims while they armed themselves.[172] This was, in effect, the lift and strike proposal described in chapter 5 and put forward by the Americans off and on since 1993. Anthony Lake and Undersecretary of State Peter Tarnoff traveled immediately to European capitals, including Moscow, to present the new American proposal to the allies.[173] It remains unclear whether this proposal included a U.S. decision actually to use air power against the Serbs. Holbrooke later claimed that it did not, and that that decision was made by President Clinton only after the shelling of Sarajevo on August 28 led to large numbers of civilian casualties. Holbrooke reported in October 1996 that "the attack angered President Clinton, and he told the UN and our NATO allies that we would wait no longer; it was time to 'hit the Bosnian Serbs hard'." In his later memoir, Holbrooke explains the impact of the August 28 shelling by suggesting that, because it came in the midst of a U.S. diplomatic effort to end the war, the attack was "the first direct affront to the United States."[174] But, as we have noted, Holbrooke himself had threatened the Serbs with air strikes in a television interview the previous day. The August 28 shelling of the Sarajevo marketplace thus appears only to have provided a justification, or "trigger," for actions already decided upon earlier. Other accounts suggest a decision to use force had been made—at the urging of Lake and Albright—prior to the Lake-Tarnoff mission to Europe on August 9. This interpretation is lent additional weight by the fact, revealed later, that at about this time NATO had quietly taken control over the decision to use air power out of the hands of the UN entirely.[175]

The French and British were ready, without prompting from the United States, to agree to changing the contact group map to accept the Serb takeover of the eastern enclaves. They appeared ready to support a proposal that gave the Bosnian government control of Sarajevo in exchange for Goražde, the last enclave in eastern Bosnia under government control.[176] But they also were still threatening to withdraw their troops at the end of September.[177] The U.S. initiative thus took on additional urgency.

The Bosnian government still held out against further concessions to the Serbs, especially after revelation of the atrocities committed by General Mladić's troops in Srebrenica. More arm-twisting from the Clinton administration was required. That process appears to have gotten off to a false start in Split on August 15, when Holbrooke met with Bosnian foreign minister Sacirbey to discuss the new U.S. proposals. Once again, the Americans displayed acute sensitivity about publicly pressuring the Muslims to make concessions. Although it appears clear that the U.S. proposal included the exchange of Goražde for Sarajevo, Sacirbey told the press that "Dick Holbrooke said to me 'we're not asking you to give up Gorazde, and I want you to tell the press'."[178] But British and UN officials displayed no such reluctance to pressure the Bosnian government into acceding to the emerging U.S. proposal. The UN announced on August 18 that British forces would withdraw from Goražde.[179]

The Russians remained openly opposed to the use of force against the Serbs. Russian president Boris Yeltsin, meeting Milošević in Moscow, warned that further Croatian "aggression" against Serb-held territory might lead Russia unilaterally to abandon international sanctions against Yugoslavia.[180] Yeltsin's meeting with Milošević reflected the diplomatic isolation of the Russians that resulted from the emergence of a U.S.-imposed consensus to use force: Tudjman had declined to attend the Moscow meeting, possibly as the result of U.S. efforts to prevent the Russians from encouraging a Serbian-Croatian deal at the expense of the Muslims, whom Yeltsin had failed to invite. Even as the U.S./NATO air campaign was being carried out against the Serbs later in August and September, the Russians continued to insist that NATO had no mandate for such action.[181] The NATO air campaign was criticized by Yeltsin as a foretaste of conflict between two military alliances in Europe—an enlarged NATO, and Russia and its allies. Aside from criticism of the broader geostrategic implications of joint U.S.–British–French action against perceived Russian interests in the Balkans, the Russians also objected to at least one specific feature of the emerging settlement: they insisted the Bosnian Serbs be allowed to establish links to Yugoslavia (Serbia and Montenegro) that paralleled those established between the Bosnian (Muslim-Croat) Federation and Croatia.[182] This would, in fact, become a key concession in the emerging agreement that eventually ended the fighting.

As we noted earlier, the return of Krajina to Croatian control and the elimination of the Srebrenica and Žepa enclaves in eastern Bosnia removed major and difficult issues from the negotiating table. According to one U.S. official, "Now that it has happened, the Bosnian problem is less a moral issue and more a matter of traditional balance-of-power diplomacy, which offers a prospect of successful negotiation."[183] The American media reported a "clear atmospheric change" toward optimism.[184] U.S. officials began to talk openly of negotiating a partition of Bosnia.[185]

Despite resistance to the U.S. initiative from all three warring sides, the Americans strategically placed the blame for the continuing difficulties in negotiating a settlement squarely on the Bosnian Serbs.[186] However, determined resistance to negotiating a partition also came from the Bosnian Muslims. On August 18 Izetbegović put forward a series of 12 demands.[187] He demanded preservation of the sovereignty and territorial integrity of the Republic of Bosnia-Herzegovina; control of Sarajevo; mutual recognition between Serbia (sic) and Bosnia; a settlement that facilitated rather than obstructed reintegration of all of Bosnia-Herzegovina; and implementation of any agreement by troops of the contact group countries, including the United States. Izetbegović refused to recognize, extend any rights to, or deal with the Bosnian Serb government ("the Pale regime"); and, he insisted on Milošević's assuming leadership of the Serb side in any negotiations. Izetbegović further demanded that, in the event the Serbs rejected the plan or failed to carry it out, the arms embargo be lifted. Of these demands, insistence on the sovereignty and territorial integrity of the Republic of Bosnia-Herzegovina presented the greatest stumbling block to an agreement.

On August 28 Bosnian army commander Rasim Delić openly rejected the new U.S. initiative, characterizing it as a plan "without a head and without a tail" and declared that "we have only one direction and that is to continue fighting."[188] Izetbegović, meeting with U.S. and French officials in Paris on August 28 and 29, plaintively declared that the government could not negotiate with "a pistol on our temple" and would not participate unless air power was used against the Serbs.[189] The Bosnian insistence that the Americans make good on their threat to use air power against the Serbs intensified in the wake of the mortar attack on August 28 and may have been an additional influence on the U.S. decision to launch the NATO air campaign two days later. According to one Western media report, Holbrooke struck a deal with Izetbegović in Paris on the evening of August 29: the use of extensive force against the Serbs by NATO and the UN in exchange for Bosnian agreement to negotiate on the basis of U.S. proposals and not to exploit the bombings to gain ground against the Serbs.[190] But events already unfolding on the ground, reported earlier in this chapter, made it clear there was little chance the Muslims would adhere to the latter part of this bargain.

Thus, if a negotiated settlement was to be reached, it would require the application of significant pressure on all three of the warring parties, particularly on the Bosnian government, to get them to accept the partitioning of their country. The exercise of military muscle against the Serbs was now seen by the Americans and the Europeans—but still not the Russians—as the means through which to exert that pressure.

As we noted above, on August 29—the day after the mortar attack and less than 48 hours after Holbrooke's televised threat to use air power against them—the Bosnian Serb parliament accepted the U.S. peace initiative and Milošević seized personal control over Bosnian Serb negotiating positions so as to facilitate a settlement.[191] In doing so, Milošević fulfilled at least one of the demands put forward by Izetbegović, noted above; we shall see below that he would fulfill others, as well. But the division of territory in Bosnia was still far from agreement, and the Bosnian Serbs had not yet agreed to withdraw from around Sarajevo when NATO launched a prolonged air campaign against Serb targets in Bosnia on August 30—less than 48 hours after the last UN forces had withdrawn from Goražde, leaving no UNPROFOR troops vulnerable to hostage-taking.[192] The air campaign attacked a wide range of Serb military targets across Bosnia, hitting command and control facilities, especially air defenses.

The air campaign was at first justified as a specific response to the mortar attack of August 28. But, as we noted in chapter 4, according to a later media analysis, "Neither NATO military nor civilian authorities reviewed the evidence before committing the alliance to a massive counterpunch."[193] The air campaign also was justified as an effort to put an end to the siege of Sarajevo. But, despite persistent denials by the principals, including Holbrooke,[194] the attacks appear almost certain to have been undertaken in an effort to alter the military balance among the warring parties (although not to the extent that the emerging territorial balance would be threatened), allow the Muslims and Croats to seize additional territories, compel the Bosnian Serbs to pull back from Sarajevo, and facilitate a negotiated end to the war. Holbrooke, as well as NATO Secretary-General Willy Claes, suggested as much in comments to the press at the time.[195] The NATO air commander in Italy, Lt. Gen. Michael E. Ryan, later acknowledged that "by battering the communications web and . . . Serb military infrastructure. . . ," he believed he could "inflict enough pain to compel Serb compliance."[196] Ambassador Albright reportedly played a key role in the decision to use force in this way by drafting a memo in early August calling for the use of U.S. military force in support of the compromise settlement advanced by National Security Advisor Lake.[197]

The air campaign was accompanied by an artillery assault on Serb positions around Sarajevo from the French and British rapid reaction forces that had, as noted earlier in this chapter, been redeployed to Mt. Igman. On the initiative of UN commander General Bernard Janvier, a "pause" in the NATO campaign was declared on September 1 in order to allow the Serbs to withdraw their heavy weapons from the exclusion zone around Sarajevo. According to a later account of these events, Janvier was responding to a suggestion by Milošević that the Bosnian Serbs might be ready to withdraw.[198] Janvier met with Mladić to negotiate. Even though Bosnian Serb political leaders declared they were ready to give in,[199] Mladić refused to withdraw unless the UN prevented the Muslims from exploiting the withdrawal to seize territory.[200]

After four days and the failure of the Serbs to comply, the NATO air attacks were resumed on September 5 at a higher level of intensity and against a broader range of targets.[201] The decision to resume the attacks came at the insistence of the Clinton administration. According to a British media account, Holbrooke favored continuing the bombing while talks continued, so as to create a "pincer movement" against the Serbs. Pressure to do so also came from "the heart of the presidency . . . as well as the State Department and the Pentagon."[202] Cruise missiles were used against air defense and other targets surrounding Banja Luka on September 10. According to Holbrooke, use of the missiles came in response to a threat by Mladić to attack the remaining safe areas. Holbrooke reports that one of the missiles "knocked out the main communications center for the Bosnian Serb Army in the west, with devastating consequences."[203] The last air strikes were carried out on September 12. The air campaign weakened the Bosnian Serb military by disrupting its communications and, therefore, its command and control. They contributed to the success of the joint Croatian-Muslim offensive. While NATO continued to attack Serb targets, the Croatian-Muslim offensive gained control over much of central and western Bosnia. The precise military consequences of the bombing remain unclear, however. One Canadian military intelligence source, for example, suggested to the authors that the effect was "more psychological than military," and that Serb communications were down for only 24 hours.

The initial decision on September 14 to "suspend" the bombing campaign came in response to Bosnian Serb agreement to withdraw their heavy weapons from the exclusion zone and end the siege of Sarajevo. This was achieved by Holbrooke and a team of U.S. negotiators who traveled to Belgrade on September 13 for discussions with Milošević. Milošević, in turn, insisted that the Americans negotiate directly with the Bosnian Serbs. Holbrooke and his aides negotiated directly with Karadžić and Mladić only after stipulating that the latter were to be considered part of a delegation headed by Milošević, in accordance with the agreement imposed on the Bosnian Serbs by Milošević two weeks earlier. The negotiations with the Bosnian Serbs appear to have been less than "diplomatic": Holbrooke is reported to have cut Mladić short, shouting: "Look, either we can negotiate an agreement on the removal of your guns around Sarajevo or we can all go home. There's nothing more to say." The Bosnian Serbs came under intense pressure from Milošević to agree to the demands dictated by the United States, although the final documents were presented as a Serbian proposal.[204] The United States extracted an agreement on the withdrawal of Serb heavy weapons from around Sarajevo, a cease-fire, and the cessation of U.S. air strikes. The agreement left some NATO and UN officials dissatisfied over the weapons the Serbs were permitted to retain.[205] Izetbegović was reportedly unhappy over this, and over "the underlying assumption in Mr. Holbrooke's plan that Sarajevo inevitably will be divided."[206]

One key to securing Serb acquiescence appears to have been Western assurances that the Bosnian army would not move against territories around Sarajevo from which Serb forces were to withdraw their weapons.[207] To ensure against this, Russian peacekeeping troops were to be deployed to Serb-held areas of Sarajevo.[208] Another factor may have been recognition on the part of NATO "that some of Mladic's concerns are genuine."[209] The impact of the cruise missile attack, as well as the mounting Serb losses on the ground—Donji Vakuf and the key city of Jajce had fallen to the Croatian offensive on September 13—must also have been factors. A later media account suggests that Mladić decided he could not stop the Croatian-Muslim offensive while NATO air strikes continued.[210] When the Serbs began implementing their commitment to withdraw, the September 14 decision to suspend NATO bombing was extended.[211]

The Croatian-Muslim offensive threatened to overrun the largest Serb-populated city in Bosnia, Banja Luka, and contributed to raising Croat and Muslim ambitions. This was more than the Americans appear to have bargained for: Several administration officials were cited in media reports at the time to the effect that the bombing campaign might become counterproductive if it convinced the Bosnians they might be able to achieve all their goals on the battlefield.[212] Croatian and Muslim ambitions were reined in only when Holbrooke "bullied" Tudjman and Izetbegović in a meeting in Zagreb on September 19 to stop the offensive against Banja Luka,[213] and Serb counterattacks that included air strikes against Croatian and Muslim forces raised the potential cost of proceeding further.[214] The Serbs' use of air power was in direct violation of the no-fly zone that had, up to then, been enforced by NATO, at least against Serb fixed-wing combat aircraft. But, in September 1995 there was no NATO attempt to prevent the Serbs from using air power to defend Banja Luka. Owen observes that such restraint was "a clear indication that NATO and UN commanders did not want the military balance tilted so sharply that the Contact Group's 51–49 per cent split was put in jeopardy."[215]

The NATO air campaign did not by itself bring the conflict closer to a negotiated settlement. By September 9 military planners were admitting that they had underestimated the Serbs' will to resist.[216] Military officials in Washington argued that restrictions on the range of targets limited the effectiveness of the campaign. NATO was, for example, reportedly avoiding hitting targets in "contested areas" where the Bosnian army might take advantage of such attacks to seize territory, and had restrained the Muslims from launching offensive operations out of Sarajevo.[217] By September 13, NATO commanders were reporting "that they are rapidly running out of military targets in southeastern Bosnia," yet they had "not achieved the result we hoped it would with Mladic."[218]

The fact that the air campaign was accompanied by significant efforts by the United States to forge a political solution that balanced Serb, Croat, and Muslim interests was vital to the emerging settlement. As we noted earlier in this chapter, the foreign ministers of Croatia, Bosnia, and Yugoslavia had met in Geneva under the sponsorship of the United States to sign an accord on "basic constitutional principles" for Bosnia-Herzegovina on September 8, while the NATO air campaign was still in progress. That document[219] called for mutual recognition of the existing borders of the former Yugoslav republics including Bosnia-Herzegovina. It also called for the Bosnian state to be composed of two "entities": the Bosnian (Muslim-Croat) Federation brokered by the Americans in 1994, and a *Republika Srpska* ([Bosnian] Serb Republic)—the name used by the Bosnian Serbs to describe their self-declared state but until then rejected by the West. The recognition implied by use of this name was a major concession and was vehemently resisted by the Bosnian government, which relented only under heavy pressure from the United States.[220] When the agreement became public, many in Sarajevo were dismayed.[221] Furthermore, each of these entities was granted "the right to establish parallel special relationships with neighboring countries." This represented the first formal recognition by the United States of the Bosnian Serb political claim to autonomous status, one of the Serbs' major war aims. As we noted earlier, this brought the U.S. position closer to that taken by the Europeans and their international negotiators— and much maligned by the Americans—since 1992. It represented a large step toward the *de facto* partition of Bosnia into ethnic states: a Serb state, and a binational Muslim–Croat state.

The September 8 agreement implemented the deal negotiated between Holbrooke and Milošević a week earlier in Belgrade, cited earlier in this chapter, in which Milošević agreed that Yugoslavia would recognize Bosnia-Herzegovina in exchange for *de facto* recognition of the Bosnian Serb Republic.[222] The September 8 agreement represented a clear reversal of position on the part of the Bosnian government. Only a week earlier Bosnian Prime Minister Silajdžić had declared that, while a Serb entity might be allowed within Bosnia-Herzegovina, it would not be allowed to call into question the territorial integrity or sovereignty of the state as a whole.[223] The September 8 agreement defined the basic shape of the later Dayton agreement. The concessions demanded by the Bosnian Serbs as a condition of agreement help explain their later resistance to aspects of Dayton that seem to undermine or contradict these concessions.

Securing agreement among all three parties required the Americans to pressure the Bosnian Muslim leadership into accepting the existence of the Serb republic, which the Muslims did only after their meetings with U.S. negotiators in Ankara on September 4 and in Split on September 6, noted earlier in this chapter. As we have already noted, it was during the latter meeting that Secretary Christopher telephoned Izetbegović to reassure him that the proposed agreement did not imply that the United States recognized Bosnian Serb sovereignty, and Holbrooke threatened a crisis in U.S.-Bosnian relations and a halt to the NATO bombing then still under way.[224] Although the agreement signed in Geneva on September 8 amounted to a *de facto* agreement to partition Bosnia, it still left unsettled the crucial questions of how territory was to be divided, the status of Sarajevo, and the degree of autonomy to be granted to the Serb entity. Moreover, it established no cease-fire, and both NATO bombing and fighting between Bosnian Serb and Muslim and Croatian forces continued.

The growing uneasiness of the British and French with the U.S. escalation of the air campaign signaled by the use of cruise missiles led to a shift in emphasis from coercion to diplomacy. According to one British media account, both the British and the French were warning the United States "that their troops will not be used to wage war on behalf of the Muslim-led government."[225] The Russians, too, were uneasy. They sponsored a Security Council resolution calling for an immediate suspension of the bombing, but could not secure its adoption.[226] Russian defense minister Grachev warned that the bombing jeopardized Russian participation in the "Partnership for Peace" program of NATO and, more important, Russian compliance with unspecified arms control agreements.[227] The British and French, in contrast, were merely seeking "tangible signs of diplomatic progress" as a condition for keeping their troops in Bosnia.[228]

The agreement of September 14 suspending the NATO bombing campaign in exchange for a Serb pullback from around Sarajevo, described above, provided the progress that the Europeans were seeking. It also included provisions to open roads into Sarajevo for UN and humanitarian relief traffic, and to open Sarajevo airport to all traffic. But the Bosnians were not happy about the agreement. The end of the bombing, restraints imposed on the Bosnian army in Sarajevo—it had been massing troops for an apparent attempt to break out of the city[229]—and the deployment of Russian troops represented important new concessions to the Serbs. According to one senior Clinton administration official, Izetbegović asked Holbrooke, "Why aren't you continuing to bomb these people?"[230]

By late September 1995 the warring parties had established another, more consolidated, but still unstable front line that divided Bosnia approximately in half between the Serbs and the Croatian-Muslim alliance. The Bosnian Serbs transferred some of the heavy weapons they withdrew from Sarajevo to the defense of Banja Luka, contributing to their ability to halt and partially reverse the Muslim-Croatian offensive against their principal city.[231] Nonetheless, the balance of military power had been shifted in favor of the Muslim-Croatian alliance. This led the Bosnian government to harden its negotiating positions, and the Croatian government to be drawn toward the prospect of expanding the portion of Bosnian territory under *de facto* Croatian control.[232]

On September 25 all three sides were reported still making new demands and resisting the conclusion of a further agreement defining the functions of the Bosnian presidency and parliament, and the relationship between the Republic of Bosnia-Herzegovina and the Republika Srpska. Bosnian Muslim leaders continued to object to the concessions being offered to the Serbs. A Bosnian analysis reports that they were reluctant to proceed with negotiations, most of all because in their view the draft document under consideration did not preserve the status or legal continuity of Bosnia-Herzegovina as a state.[233] A senior U.S. official reported that "the Bosnian government, confronted for the first time with the opportunity to create a viable state, has become virtually paralyzed because of [internal] battles between the president and the prime minister"; that is, between Izetbegović and Silajdžić. Such differences would characterize all further negotiations over a settlement. Meanwhile, Croatian president Franjo Tudjman again declared that the ideal solution would have been to create three Bosnian states, and that "the problem of how Muslims and Croats will live together there remains open—a problem we shouldn't underestimate even though cohabitation is desirable and possible."[234] This blunt, but ominous assessment was downplayed by U.S. negotiators and the media alike. Indeed, in the midst of their common offensive, Croatian and Muslim troops fell to fighting each other for strategic cities and towns in western Bosnia, including Bosanski Petrovac, Jajce, and Mrkonjić Grad.[235] Tensions between them may have been intensified by further evidence of a deal between the Croats and Serbs over the partition of Bosnia-Herzegovina. According to UN military and political sources, Bosnian Serb counterattacks in western Bosnia in October were focused against the Bosnian army's Fifth and Seventh Corps. Serb troops engaged the Bosnian Croat and Croatian forces in only sporadic fighting.

Nonetheless, the Bosnian, Croatian, and Yugoslav foreign ministers signed a second agreement on "basic principles" in New York on September 26.[236] These included

> (a) freedom of movement, (b) the right of displaced persons to repossess their property *or receive just compensation,* (c) freedom of speech and of the press, and (d) protection of all other internationally recognized human rights in order to enhance and empower the democratic election process.

"Just compensation" was diplomatic code for acknowledgment that many refugees or displaced persons were not likely to return to their homes. According to a central participant in the international diplomacy surrounding the Bosnian conflict, this was the first time the wording had appeared in a joint document and its appearance reflected the fact that all involved recognized that many refugees would not be able, or even willing to return to their homes.

The agreed principles also included the holding of free and democratic elections (but did not call for the direct election of the presidency demanded by Sarajevo); the establishment of a parliament and presidency, each of whose memberships would be apportioned between the Muslim-Croat federation (two-thirds) and the Serb republic (one-third); and the granting of a limited veto power over government decisionmaking to each of the two entities. The September 26 document contained some gains for the Muslims, as it preserved attributes of statehood for the Republic of Bosnia-Herzegovina as a whole. But it also seemed to allocate substantial autonomous power to the two entities ostensibly "within" it. In Silajdžić's hopeful view, these provisions "confirm[ed] that the minimum of the state structure will remain . . . , that Bosnia has . . . all the attributes of the state." Izetbegović said only that the agreement was "a step in the right direction."[237] This was only a minor difference in an otherwise growing gulf between the two Muslim political leaders, a gulf opened up by the prospect that the war would be ended by a negotiated partition imposed by the United States, rather than by the military defeat of the Serbs.[238]

The September 26 agreement was followed within days by a NATO decision to provide troops to implement a Bosnian peace deal once it had been adopted and a cease-fire established, as well as the start of efforts by President Clinton and his top policymakers to overcome domestic political opposition to U.S. participation in such a mission.[239] But the September 26 agreement still left a number of important issues unresolved, including how a new central Bosnian government would function, and the relationship between the two internal entities established under the terms of the first Geneva agreement. The three parties disagreed over how to carry out almost all of the functions that defined statehood—including the conduct of foreign trade, customs and border administration, citizenship and passport controls, and representation in international institutions. These were left for future negotiations.

Open hostility between the negotiating parties, as well as perceived opportunities on all sides to make further gains in ongoing fighting, made it impossible for negotiators to conclude a cease-fire.[240] Contrary to the situation in August and early September, when Bosnian Serb intransigence was blamed for negotiating difficulties, Holbrooke now charged that it was "primarily the Muslim side" that opposed a cease-fire.[241] On October 4 Holbrooke warned Izetbegović that he was "playing craps with the destiny of his country" by refusing to agree to a cease-fire, and added, "If you want to let the fighting go on, that is your right, but do not expect the United States to be your air force."[242]

The effort to negotiate a cease-fire dragged on into October. Even after a cease-fire agreement and plans for holding proximity talks among the three parties in the United States on a comprehensive agreement were announced in early October by President Clinton at the White House,[243] the parties were unable to implement a cease-fire until they became convinced that the opportunities for additional short-term gains on the battlefield had been exhausted.[244] The Bosnian Muslims would not accept a cease-fire or agree to go to a peace conference until the United States agreed to provide military assistance to the Bosnian army. Such assistance was opposed by the Pentagon, and the commitment was made only after the president decided to do so.[245] But the Bosnian government did not actually halt its offensive operations in northwestern Bosnia until it appeared that Belgrade might be preparing to enter the fighting.[246] By this time, another key piece of the U.S. strategy for ending the conflict seemed to fall into place: On October 3 Thorvald Stoltenberg and U.S. Ambassador to Croatia Peter Galbraith negotiated an agreement for the reintegration of eastern Slavonija into Croatia.[247] This was the last Serb-held territory (formally, UN Protected Area) in Croatia. Milošević signaled his support for the plan, which removed the last obstacle to Croatian approval of a cease-fire in Bosnia. The cease-fire was announced on October 5. Agreement on the return of eastern Slavonija was finalized on November 12.

The great difficulty with which the three parties came to any agreement reflected the extent to which they remained in fundamental conflict, and the degree to which even their modest achievements could be attributed to pressure from the United States. The continuation of fighting on the ground in Bosnia after the onset of negotiations, after the announcement of a cease-fire agreement, and after that agreement was finally signed on October 12,[248] fueled domestic opposition in the United States to the administration's plans to deploy American troops as part of an international force to implement a comprehensive settlement.[249] On the eve of the proximity talks at Dayton, the U.S. House of Representatives passed a "sense of the House" resolution by an overwhelming vote of 305–103, stating that the administration should not send, or even pledge, U.S. troops to such a mission without first securing permission of the Congress.[250]

The Dayton Agreement

The proximity talks among the three parties in Dayton, Ohio were characterized by the same difficulties and disagreements that had characterized earlier international efforts to broker a settlement of the conflict. But they also differed in two critical respects: the willingness of the United States to exert substantial pressure on the parties, especially the Bosnian Muslim leadership, to agree; and the fact that neither the Bosnian Serbs nor the Bosnian Croats—the parties least susceptible to U.S. pressure—were a direct party to the negotiations. The Dayton negotiations in November 1995 represented the continuation of the U.S. strategy of combining military and political pressure with key political concessions, which had emerged in July and August 1995. The United States took direct control over the peace process at Dayton, relegating other Western actors to subordinate roles. According to the leader of the British delegation at Dayton,

> The US negotiator, supported by a very large team, . . . organise[d] the agenda and [ran] the negotiation as he wished, with the acquiescence of the rest. They were informed but not consulted, and their primary role was to assist so far as needed, witness and ratify the outcome. But they were not to interfere.[251]

The success of this strategy depended on the willingness of the United States to undertake the kind of commitment that U.S. policymakers—and especially the Pentagon—had been seeking to avoid since the start of the war: the indefinite deployment of U.S. troops on the ground in Bosnia to participate in an international force to monitor the agreement and patrol the cease-fire lines. It also required that the Bosnian Croats and Bosnian Serbs submit to representation by Tudjman and Milošević, respectively, whose designs for the partition of Bosnia were integral to the outcome of the negotiations.

Long-standing differences in the basic war aims of the three warring parties that had been the source of conflict in earlier negotiations re-emerged at Dayton.[252] The Croats and the Muslims, for example, disagreed from the outset over how power was to be allocated in Bosnia. The Muslims continued to advocate proportionality rules based on population, while the Croats (represented by Croatia) insisted on apportioning power on the basis of equality among all three "constituent nations." The Croats, extending the logic of the September "Basic Principles" and the Washington accords of 1994, argued for lodging most state power in the Bosnian (Muslim-Croat) Federation rather than in the central government of Bosnia-Herzegovina in Sarajevo. This reflected the long-standing Croat war goal of establishing a distinct entity for Croats; a goal they were already well on their way to achieving on the ground with the assistance of the Croatian army. Their resistance to sharing power with the Muslims was already transforming the federation into two distinct ethnic states. The Croat preference for ethnic separation within the federation paralleled precisely the Bosnian Serb preference for strengthening the Bosnian Serb republic at the expense of the central state. Bosnian Muslim negotiators, in contrast, argued for a unified Bosnian state. These were political differences that had persisted from the very beginning of international negotiations over constitutional and institutional formulas for Bosnia-Herzegovina.

Unlike previous negotiations, however, significant differences emerged among Bosnian Muslim leaders in response to the opportunities and pressures of the negotiations. A Bosnian source observed:

> the delegation of [Bosnia-Herzegovina] was not homogeneous and arrived at unified positions with great difficulty, which naturally had negative implications ... during the course of the negotiations, ... in regard to the acceptance of its proposals and suggestions because the strongest counter-argument of the mediators was [to ask] whether a position was the position of the delegation of [Bosnia-Herzegovina] (which was very rarely the case, and was a generally known fact).[253]

According to other accounts, Bosnian prime minister Silajdžić continued his advocacy of a centralized, unified, multiethnic state. Bosnian president Izetbegović again proved more willing to compromise the unity of the state in exchange for securing control over a compact territory for the Bosnian Muslims; just as he had during the Owen-Stoltenberg negotiations in summer 1993, described in detail in chapter 6. In effect, Izetbegović was willing to accept ethnic partition—at least as an interim solution—in order to secure Muslim power over a definable territory.

As had been the case in all previous negotiations, it was agreement on a map designating the precise lines of that *de facto* partition that proved the most difficult to achieve. Media accounts of the talks in Dayton focus almost exclusively on the disputes over the map, although it is apparent from the contents of the final agreement[254] that much of the three weeks of negotiation had to have been consumed in discussion of military and governance issues. The fact that the agreement ultimately authorized the existence of a distinct Bosnian Serb army, for example, represented a major concession by U.S. negotiators and a significant political defeat for Izetbegović and the Bosnian central government.

The Map

Going into Dayton, the key points of contention with respect to the map constituted a familiar list: control of Sarajevo; the status of the northern corridor and the Posavina region, including the choke point between eastern and western Serb territory at Brčko; the area of Prijedor and Sanski Most, now under Croatian-Muslim control; and the status of the last remaining government-held enclave in the east, Goražde, and the corridor of territory by which it would be connected to government-held territory in central Bosnia. All these issues had been visited repeatedly in past negotiations. There was, however, one vital difference this time with regard to territory. In all previous negotiations the Serbs had been in the driver's seat, since they had controlled about two-thirds of Bosnia. Now, as a result of the combined Croatian-Muslim offensives in summer 1995, the Serbs controlled somewhat less than 50 percent of Bosnia.

In the past, the parties had been unable to reach agreement on territorial issues because of Bosnian Serb dominance on the ground. Now, however, Milošević and Tudjman acted together to resolve these issues, and their solutions were accepted and supported by the United States. The final map appears to have been defined largely without Muslim participation. According to one account, "the Bosnians ... ended up being badgered into agreement,"[255] and according to another they were simply "broken."[256] The active roles of Milošević and Tudjman, and the imposition of territorial solutions on the Muslims, reinforced earlier suspicions that much of what transpired during the fighting in 1995 reflected not only the underlying convergence of Serbian and Croatian interest in the partition of Bosnia-Herzegovina, but possibly even a prior secret deal between them.

Milošević made all the decisions for the combined Yugoslav–Bosnian Serb delegation. This reflected not only the formal authority granted him by the agreement imposed on the Bosnian Serbs in late August (described earlier in this chapter), but also the new strategic reality on the ground in Bosnia: the losses suffered by the Bosnian Serbs weakened them politically, and heightened the interest of Serbia (Milošević) in reaching an overall settlement with Croatia. Milošević decided the issue of Sarajevo unilaterally by conceding to Izetbegović that the Muslims deserved to control both the city and a portion of the surrounding hills, thus transferring to Muslim control militarily, politically, and symbolically important territories that had been at the center of Muslim-Serb disagreement and under Serb control since the onset of fighting. While such a transfer had earlier been conceived by U.S. policymakers as part of an exchange in which the Muslims would cede Goražde to the Serbs, Milošević appears to have accepted much less than this in return: unspecified concessions at Lukavica and Pale. Similarly, Tudjman is reported to have overridden Bosnian Croat demands for the return of lands in the Posavina to Croatian control, and ceded this territory to the Bosnian Serb republic. His decision seemed to confirm Milošević's assertion that "President Tudjman and I have already agreed that the Bosnian Posavina will be part of Republika Srpska." Close observers of the talks noted that this statement again fueled speculation about a "Zagreb-Belgrade deal" and left the Bosnian Muslim delegation "too stunned to react."[257]

It was Milošević's turn again to concede territory when the corridor to

Goražde was defined. Silajdžić was compelled by U.S. negotiators to abandon his demand that the Goražde enclave be extended to the existing Bosnian-Serbian border[258]—a demand recognized by Milošević as designed to split the Bosnian Serb republic. But Milošević was persuaded by the Americans, who insisted on a corridor that used the topography of the region to enhance security, to accept a corridor five miles wide rather than only two miles wide. The creation of this corridor introduced an obvious source of future conflict between the Muslims and Serbs. A Western media report in December 1995[259] cited Serb objections that the corridor cut the main road between Višegrad and Foča, and that it appeared to reflect Muslim interest in seizing the Sandžak region across the border in Serbia.

When Milošević learned that his concessions had reduced the Serb republic to 45 percent rather than 49 percent of Bosnian territory, he demanded that Serb territory be increased. "I was very flexible in my desire to approach peace," he argued, "but I cannot go back to Belgrade with less than 49 percent."[260] He sought to acquire additional territory in the strategic Posavina corridor. But Silajdžić proposed instead that territory under the control of the Croats be transferred to the Serbs. This was the origin of the egg-shaped territory in western Bosnia at Mrkonjić-Grad, captured by the Croats in the September fighting, but assigned to the Serb republic at Dayton. The Croatian delegation accepted this change only after President Clinton telephoned Tudjman urging him to be flexible. The differences between the areas controlled by each group at the time of the October cease-fire and the allocation of territory between the Bosnian (Muslim-Croat) Federation and the Republika Srpska agreed at Dayton is depicted in Map 7.3.

The initial resistance of the Croats to ceding the territory around Mrkonjić-Grad to the Serbs—Croatian foreign minister Granić had declared upon hearing it that there was no chance his government would accept the proposal[261]—led Christopher to demand that the Bosnian Muslim delegation come up with concessions of their own territory to meet Milošević's insistence on 49 percent. However, the Bosnian delegation was less willing to be flexible than Tudjman. Izetbegović, for example, is reported to have become "happier" as it appeared the settlement would collapse.[262] The Bosnian delegation came forward instead with a new map of their own that revived claims to territories previously assigned to the Serbs, including the city of Brčko at the choke point in the northern corridor. This appears to have been a reprise of a familiar Bosnian negotiating tactic: faced with an agreement they had negotiated but could not bring themselves to accept, they rescinded earlier territorial concessions and raised new demands at the last moment in an effort to force the Serbs (or the Croats) to bear the onus

Map 7.3 **November 1995 Areas of Control and Dayton Inter-Entity Boundary Line**

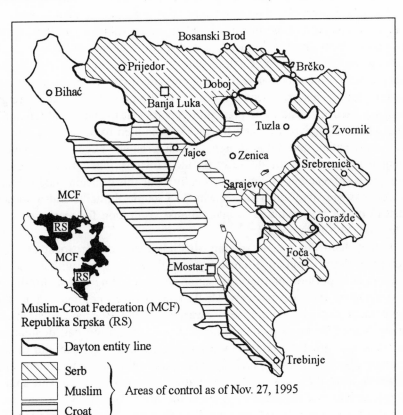

Based on unclassified CIA maps 737785 (R00389) 11–89 and 737760 (R00855) 11–95.

of having blocked an agreement. In the past, the Muslims had been able to scuttle European-brokered agreements in this way because they enjoyed the support of an outside power that shared their dissatisfaction with the agreement: the United States. Now, however, it was the United States that had brokered the agreement, and it would not bow to Bosnian pressure. Instead, Holbrooke threatened to abandon the parties to their own devices.

Ensuing discussions narrowed the territorial issues to the status of Brčko. But final agreement on the status of that city could not be achieved, raising the real prospect of the collapse of the entire negotiation. As we reported in chapter 5, the fact that the revised Vance-Owen map had assigned Brčko

and surrounding territory to the Bosnian government was a key factor leading the Bosnian Serbs to reject the Vance-Owen plan. At Dayton on November 20 Holbrooke threatened that "the U.S. government would no
longer be involved in the Bosnian problem, and a solution would be up to
the parties themselves."[263] Indeed, later that day Secretary of State Christopher delivered to Izetbegović a draft statement announcing the failure of the
talks, clearly a means of increasing the pressure on the Bosnians to give in
on this issue. This statement was leaked to the press by Bosnian foreign
minister Sacirbey, leading to premature reports that the talks had failed.[264]
That failure was averted when Milošević attempted to persuade Tudjman
and the Croatian delegation to issue a joint Croatian-Yugoslav announcement blaming failure of the talks on the Muslims. The Croats—sources
disagree as to whether Tudjman personally made this decision—argued that
Brčko was too small an issue on which to scuttle the talks and proposed
instead that it be submitted to international arbitration for resolution at a
later date. Milošević agreed.[265]

If they held out for Brčko, the Muslims faced the prospect of a renewed Serbian-Croatian alliance against them, and the withdrawal of
their most important international supporter. According to a senior diplomat close to the negotiations, Muslim negotiators pointed out to the
Americans that Brčko had been awarded to the Bosnian government
under Vance-Owen, a plan that the U.S. administration had denounced
as weak and pro-Serb. But they argued to no avail. By the end of the
Dayton process, "American officials spoke with disappointment and
anger at what they saw as the vacillation, internal conflicts and sometimes cynical maneuvering of Bosnian officials." Secretary Christopher,
for example, was uncharacteristically reported to have "exploded" at
Izetbegović in the closing hours of the process.[266] Not surprisingly,
therefore, the Bosnian delegation accepted the decision on Brčko and
agreed to the overall map. By acceding to the Dayton agreement, however, the Bosnian Muslims were able to hold the Americans to their
earlier commitment to provide military assistance: Holbrooke reported
later in Senate testimony that the United States had given the Bosnians a
verbal agreement to "lead an international effort to ensure that the
Bosnians have what they need to defend themselves adequately."[267] This
resulted in establishment of the U.S. "train and equip" program that has
since supplied the Bosnian army with large quantities of equipment,
including heavy weapons. That program is creating a more realistic military foundation for the continuing ambitions of the Bosnian Muslims to
regain control over more of Bosnia-Herzegovina. It seems clear that it
would not have happened in the absence of an agreement at Dayton.

Thus, for the Muslims, the deficiencies of the Dayton agreement likely represented a necessary, if bitter, step.

The final map also represented a political defeat for the Bosnian Serbs, especially in the Sarajevo area, and it was imposed on them without their participation. One account reports that Bosnian Serb members of the Yugoslav delegation, who had effectively been excluded from negotiations by Milošević, went "berserk" when they were shown the map shortly before the signing ceremony.[268] Another account reports that Koljević "was so stunned that he fainted."[269] Following Dayton, Milošević met with Bosnian Serb leaders in Belgrade to pressure them into carrying out the agreement. The meeting lasted 12 hours and reportedly was at times "explosive."[270] The next day, Karadžić publicly accepted the agreement, as well as the fact that the military struggle was over. The Bosnian Serbs would now, he remarked, have to pursue their goals by political means.[271]

The Constitution

The Dayton constitution redefines "the Republic of Bosnia and Herzegovina" as a state ("Bosnia and Herzegovina") composed of two entities, the Federation of Bosnia-Herzegovina (the Bosnian [Muslim-Croat] Federation) and the Republika Srpska (the [Bosnian] Serb Republic). It is the legal continuation of the Republic of Bosnia-Herzegovina. Not only is the Republika Srpska recognized as a distinct entity, it (as well as the federation) is granted "the right to establish special parallel relationships with neighboring states"[Art. III.2(a)]. Thus, the very definition of the post-Dayton state institutionalizes the political concessions to the Bosnian Serbs that were essential to the U.S. strategy for halting the fighting. Indeed, the Dayton process itself conceded to the Bosnian Serbs something that U.S. negotiators had up to then resisted: a formal status in the negotiations equal to that of the federation and Bosnia-Herzegovina as a whole. The Serb republic was an equal signatory to the agreements on the military, regional stabilization, the inter-entity boundary, elections, the constitution, arbitration, human rights, refugees, monuments, public corporations, civilian implementation, and the international police task force. It was excluded only from the general framework and initialing agreements, which constituted a tripartite agreement among Croatia, the (soon-to-be-former) Republic of Bosnia-Herzegovina, and Yugoslavia. Thus, while the Bosnian Serbs had been dominated by Milošević at Dayton, the Bosnian Serb republic and its leadership gained enhanced formal legal status in the post-Dayton environment.

The constitutional agreement establishes "Bosnia-Herzegovina" as an extremely decentralized state, in which the central government retains only very limited powers [Art. III.1]. It enjoys international legal status and therefore is responsible for external relations, including foreign policy, foreign trade, customs, immigration and relations with international police authorities. Consistent with the principle that Bosnia-Herzegovina is to constitute a single, undivided market economy, the central state is also responsible for monetary policy and international financial relations, as well as transportation, communications and air traffic control. Article III.3(a) reserves for the entities "all governmental functions and powers not expressly assigned" to the common state. This formulation underscores the predominance of the entities over the central government, and the *de facto* partition of the state. Representative and decision-making principles and procedures prescribed for the common political institutions of Bosnia-Herzegovina also reinforce the division of the state into two distinct entities, rather than its unity. Moreover, they include *de facto* recognition of the internally divided nature of the (Muslim-Croat) federation, thus introducing elements of a tripartite partition. This, in fact, was the preferred solution of the Bosnian Croat members of the Bosnian government delegation. According to a Bosnian account,[272] the Croat members of the government delegation put forward their own proposal for transformation of the Republic of Bosnia-Herzegovina into a "Union of Bosnia-Herzegovina" composed of two entities, but in which each of the three nations would be represented equally and exercise a veto over state decisionmaking. It was, in this Bosnian view, a proposal for "a union without content."

While the provisions of the Dayton constitution give the appearance of ethnic power-sharing along the lines suggested by well-known theories of ethnic conflict management, they are not constructed in ways likely to encourage power-sharing behavior. This becomes clear when one examines the provisions dealing with the parliament and presidency. The Parliamentary Assembly of Bosnia-Herzegovina established under the Dayton agreement consists of two chambers. The House of Peoples is composed of 15 delegates, 10 from the federation and 5 from the Serb republic. The delegates of the federation consist of 5 Croats and 5 Muslims, who are to be selected by the Croat and Muslim members of the federation parliament, respectively. The five delegates from the Serb republic are to be Serbs [Art. IV.1(a)]. In this way, the constitution institutionalizes the ethnic division of the state, and excludes all other groups from participation in one of its parliamentary institutions. Nine delegates are defined as a quorum for the House of Peoples, providing there are at least three Muslim, three Croat, and three Serb delegates present [IV.1(b)]. Thus, three delegates from any one of the ethnic groups can paralyze the chamber merely by refusing to attend, thereby denying it a quorum. This would effectively paralyze the government as well, for the constitution stipulates that all legislation requires the approval of *both* chambers [IV.3(c)]. The second chamber of parliament is the House of Representatives, which comprises 42 members; 28 from the federation, and 14 from the Serb republic, to be determined by direct elections [IV.2(a)]. There is no ethnic criterion for election to this chamber, thus allowing for the election of members of other ethnic groups, an ethnic imbalance among members from the federation, or the election of Muslims or Croats from inside the Serb republic. A simple majority of the members of the House constitutes a quorum [IV.2(b)]. This provision prevents the 14 members from the Serb republic from paralyzing the work of this chamber. But it does allow 22 of the members from the federation to constitute a quorum in the absence of all other members.

Decisionmaking in both chambers is to be based on simple majorities of those present and voting [IV.3(d)]. If a majority does not include at least one-third of the votes from each entity, the constitution requires efforts to secure such votes. These provisions offer little protection against action in the House of Representatives in the absence, for example, of either nine members from the Serb republic or 18 members from the federation. The affirmative vote of just five members from the Serb republic legitimates any majority vote by deputies from the federation. Only 12 votes are required to achieve a majority of a 22–member quorum. But the one-third rule appears to require at least 15 affirmative votes to adopt any decision if it is interpreted as referring to the total number of delegates instead of only those present and voting. Regardless of which way this provision is interpreted, however, if the leadership is unable to secure the support of one-third of the members from the entity in question within three days, a simple majority of those present and voting will nonetheless suffice for adoption. The only secure veto is provided by a vote of two-thirds or more of the delegates or members in a chamber from either entity [IV.3(d)]. There is no procedure in the Dayton constitution for overriding such opposition.

These provisions create a formally limited, but in practical terms unlimited veto for each of the major ethnic groups. In the case of the Serb republic, they provide the potential equivalent of an ethnic veto for the Serbs in each chamber. Four Serb delegates from the Serb republic are sufficient to veto action in the House of Peoples (three are sufficient to deny it a quorum), and nine Serb members are sufficient to veto action in the House of Representatives. If five Muslims (or Croats, or Serbs supportive of a unified Bosnia, or combination thereof) won election as members of the House of Representatives from the Serb republic, they would be able to block a Serb veto in this chamber. But in the case of the federation, the Muslims and Croats each control only one-half the delegates to the House of Peoples (insufficient to veto, but sufficient to deny a quorum), and neither the Muslims nor the Croats are likely to control two-thirds of the members of the House of Representatives from the federation. If the Muslims or Croats wish to veto action in the House of Representatives, they have to act in alliance with each other—or with the Serbs.

Each ethnic group may also attempt to veto parliamentary acts by declaring them "destructive of a vital interest" [IV.3(e)]. A majority (3 of 5) of the delegates in the House of Peoples from any one of the three groups can make such a declaration, but its approval requires support from a majority of the delegates from each of the three groups present and voting. Thus, this route is easily blocked by three delegates from either of the other two groups. In such an instance, if the parliamentary leadership is unable to resolve the issue, "the matter will be referred to the Constitutional Court, which shall in an expedited process review it for procedural regularity" [IV.3(f)]. This formulation suggests that the Court cannot rule on the substance of the matter and thus cannot provide relief for any group that feels aggrieved by the proposed parliamentary action. This effectively nullifies the Court as an avenue of appeal. The apparent ethnic veto provided by this procedure is thus no veto at all. In the absence of goodwill among the three groups represented in the House of Peoples, this procedure appears instead to promise the inevitable escalation of conflict over any proposal perceived by any one of them as destructive of its vital interests.

Ethnicity as the basis of political identity, representation, and decision making is further institutionalized in the presidency of Bosnia and Herzegovina. The presidency is composed of three members, one from each of the ethnic groups. The constitution stipulates that the Croat and Muslim members are to be elected from the federation, the Serb members from the Serb republic [V]. The presidency is to attempt to make decisions by consensus, but may adopt decisions supported by only two members. However, an ethnic veto is provided for any dissenting member who declares a decision of the presidency "destructive of a vital interest of the Entity from the territory [sic] from which he was elected" [V.2(d)]. In such cases, the decision is then to be referred to the parliament of the Serb republic (if the Serb member has taken this action), to the Muslim delegates of the House of Peoples of the federation parliament (in the case of the Muslim member), or to the Croat delegates of the House of Peoples of the federation parliament (in the case of the Croat member), wherein a two-thirds vote will nullify the presidential decision. Each of the ethnic communities can thus veto presidential decisions required to implement parliamentary actions. Again, however, if non-Serbs (or ethnic Serbs supportive of the unity of a multicultural Bosnia-Herzegovina, or some combination thereof) gain more than one-third of the seats in the parliament of the Serb republic, the ability of the Bosnian Serbs to veto actions of the presidency would be blocked. Hence, the ethnic veto provided by the Dayton constitution is, at least in theory, limited. How likely this is to occur remains uncertain.

Thus, the provisions of the constitution institutionalize the ethnic partition of the country by establishing ethnic qualifications for membership in key institutions and ethnicized processes of decisionmaking within them. At the same time, they do not seem to create counter-balancing institutional incentives for interethnic cooperation. On the contrary, they create multiple incentives to engage in conflictual behavior. The mixture of ethnic and simple territorial criteria for participation/eligibility and decisionmaking encourages ethnically defined competition for parliamentary seats. The requirement that a two-thirds vote be secured for the parliament of the Serb republic to exercise the limited veto rights contained in the constitution creates an especially strong incentive for the Muslims to compete for seats in that parliament—and to insist on implementation of all those provisions of the Dayton agreement that would permit them to do so. Provisions for ethnic outvoting and override schemes, and a relatively easy mechanism by which any one group may paralyze one parliamentary chamber and, therefore, the common government, create incentives to compete for seats on an ethnic basis and, for those who secure seats, not to compromise. In an atmosphere of extreme intergroup hostility including, especially, hostility between elites such as exists in Bosnia-Herzegovina today, it is not unreasonable to expect each group to exploit every opportunity in the constitution to block actions it does not like. In the view of a British participant at Dayton, the constitution "is excessively complex and . . . at the same time does not—because no agreement could be obtained—contain a means of breaking political deadlock."[273]

Perhaps the harshest critic of the Dayton constitution, Robert Hayden, has pointed out a number of opportunities for confrontation beyond those outlined above.[274] The constitutional court consists of nine members: four selected by the federation parliament, two by the parliament of the Serb republic, and three by the president of the European Court of Human Rights after consultation with the presidency of Bosnia and Herzegovina [VI].

Although there is no ethnic qualification attached to judicial seats, it seems safe to assume that the court will be composed of two Muslims, two Croats, two Serbs, and three Europeans. A majority of its members shall constitute a quorum. It must adopt its own rules by a majority vote of its members. Presumably, it will make decisions by majority vote, as well. The court is specifically empowered to decide "whether an Entity's decision to establish a special parallel relationship with a neighboring state is consistent with this Constitution, including provisions concerning the sovereignty and territorial integrity of Bosnia and Herzegovina" [VI.3(a)]. The composition of the court and the potential elasticity of the concepts of sovereignty and territorial integrity create a potential avenue by which Muslim judges—if they are able to secure the support of Croat or foreign judges—might move to limit the ability of Republika Srpska actually to establish any formal relationships with a neighboring state, let alone the full range of relationships already established—*de facto* and *de jure*—between Croatia and the federation. At the same time, however, the same avenue might be exploited by Serb and Croat judges able to win at least some support among the European judges to prevent Bosnia and Herzegovina, or the central government, from expanding its authority. Some European judges might support efforts by the entities to expand their relationships with neighboring states. The probability of the latter scenario increases to the extent that the Muslim-Croat federation begins to splinter along ethnic lines and the Croats move to establish a formal tripartite partition of Bosnia. Under such conditions, two Croat judges would be likely to secure the support of two Serb judges and would then need only the support of one European judge to construct a judicial majority.

The U.S. negotiators who drafted the Dayton constitution, like international negotiators since the very beginning of efforts to draft a Bosnian constitution, seem to have been influenced by the logic of ethnic power-sharing schemes.[275] As we noted in the introduction, such an approach calls for the establishment of a secure "mutual veto" among ethnic groups as a means of compelling ethnic leaderships to compromise. But the provisions of the Dayton agreement do not provide such a secure veto. On the contrary, they create numerous opportunities for one group to subvert efforts by another to exercise such a veto. Moreover, the extremely high levels of animosity in the system preclude the kind of cooperative behavior that advocates of the power-sharing approach concede is necessary for it to succeed. The likelihood that two of the three groups in Bosnia will exploit opportunities to dissolve the state into three distinct entities, while the third attempts to undermine the autonomy of the entities, seems far greater than the likelihood of intergroup cooperation. Under such conditions, the international community, acting through the Office of the High Commissioner, might assume the authority granted it under the Dayton agreement to make decisions the government is unable to make because of divisions among the three groups. This, indeed, seems to have taken place.

The Bosnian (Muslim-Croat) Federation After Dayton

Agreement on the constitution for Bosnia was preceded at Dayton by an agreement between the Croats and the Muslims over the division of authority between the (soon-to-be-former) Republic of Bosnia-Herzegovina, and the (Muslim-Croat) Federation of Bosnia-Herzegovina. Since the creation of the federation in 1994, the Muslim leadership of Bosnia, and the Croats of both Bosnia and Croatia had been engaged in a political struggle for supremacy within those areas of Bosnia under their respective control. The Muslim leadership had resisted permitting the federation to assume a meaningful role in territories under the control of the Bosnian army, and the Croats had resisted sharing authority with the Muslims in areas under their control. Every outside observer of conditions in Croat-controlled areas of the federation agreed that they were moving rapidly toward full integration with neighboring Croatia, rather than toward integration into a common Muslim-Croat half of a Bosnian state.

By late 1994, the early momentum that led to the formation of the federation had been reversed. Wrangling between the Bosnian Croats and Muslims over the distribution of leading positions in the federation produced deadlock. It was symptomatic of the deep distrust between the Croats and Muslims that Krešimir Zubak, the president of the federation, could suggest that Muslim officials were preventing federal organs from assuming responsibility, not only "to extend their life, but to put them[selves] into a superior position in relation to federal institutions and bodies of power, which we cannot accept."[276] Izetbegović and Silajdžić, and the divergent factions of the Muslim SDA to which they belonged, also struggled over the distribution of power in the federation.[277] Efforts to create a functioning joint military command came to naught, despite intensive efforts by the United States to support military integration over the course of 1994.[278] This failure was paralleled by a lack of progress in other areas vital to the success of the federation: the return of refugees; the creation of *opština* and canton governments; the adoption of basic legislation for the federation in areas such as taxation, energy, defense, and internal affairs; and the reunification of Mostar under the aegis of the EU. In Mostar, successes in repairing damaged infrastructure and the like were offset by a deepening divide between the two halves of the city, increased crime, and a growing sense that the objective of restoring the prewar multicultural society of Mostar was failing. The Herzegovinian Croats, whose national-separatist tendencies were described in chapter 3, regarded Mostar as the capital of "their" state and resisted integration with the Muslims.

When the joint Croatian-Muslim offensive forced the Serbs out of western Bosnia in September 1995, underlying tensions rose to the surface once more. When the combined offensive captured the key city of Jajce, the Croatians took control of the city and refused to allow Muslims to return. The Muslims were reportedly also incensed by the Croatian occupation of the town of Mrkonjić Grad, which, like Jajce, lay across the main road link between the Bihać pocket and central Bosnia. There were scattered reports of fighting between Muslim and Croatian troops. These conflicts prompted a hasty trip to Bosnia by General John Sewall, special advisor to Secretary of State Christopher, in late September. But the American general apparently could do nothing to soothe tempers on either side.[279]

The Dayton agreement was built on the assumption that the federation would function as one of the two "entities" in Bosnia-Herzegovina. The document on implementing the federation agreement signed in Dayton on November 9, 1995,[280] granted the federation a wide range of authority, including defense, internal affairs, justice, finance, commerce, agriculture, education and culture, and public health. The agreement calls for the federation to assume "exclusive governmental authority on the federation, cantonal and municipal levels in the entire federation territory within the areas of its responsibilities." This formulation effectively excluded the central government of Bosnia-Herzegovina from any role in the internal affairs of that half of its own state. Under the provisions of the November 9 agreement, the federation would become a hyper-decentralized state along ethnic lines. It would even have two capital cities; Sarajevo and Mostar. This reflected the Croats' insistence on differentiating the federation from the Muslim-controlled government of Bosnia and Herzegovina, and their long-standing desire to establish Mostar as the capital of an autonomous Croatian state.

The federation agreement of November 9 required the Muslim-dominated Bosnian government, which had insisted up to this point on maintaining its legal identity as the sole legitimate representative of the people of Bosnia-Herzegovina, to eviscerate itself; turning over the control of domestic affairs to the government of the federation, whose decisions would be subject to a veto by either of its two "constituent nations." The danger, from the Muslim perspective, was that the nationalist Herzegovinian Croats who controlled the Bosnian HDZ would intentionally deadlock the federation assembly if they were not granted virtual independence for western Herzegovina. It therefore seemed completely out of character for the Bosnian government to surrender its powers to a federation government.

Indeed, the Bosnian Assembly, upon ratifying the Dayton accords, adopted a constitutional law which provided that, if the Dayton agreements were not implemented in a timely fashion, the constitution of the federation would be invalidated and all power would revert to the republic parliament; that is, to the pre-existing Bosnian government.[281] Since there were many provisions of the Dayton accords that could not be implemented in a timely fashion, even with the best of intentions, the Bosnian Assembly's move clearly was calculated to put down a marker for the Muslim-dominated central government to renege on its agreement. This action repeated the tactic adopted in March 1993, reported in chapter 5, when the government appended "Annex V" to the Vance-Owen plan. This action suggested that the Muslim leadership still had not actually accepted the partition presaged by the Dayton agreement.

The borders of the eight federation cantons delineated in the Vienna map of May 1994, reproduced in chapter 6 (Map 6.6, page 297), now had to be revised in light of the territorial changes that had taken place in summer and fall 1995. Posavina canton was, under the Dayton accord, to remain in the Republika Srpska except for the area around the town of Odžak. Odžak remained part of the Bosnian (Muslim-Croat) Federation, but was linked physically to Croatia, just across the Sava. Areas taken from the Serbs in the 1995 offensives were largely under Croatian control, yet claimed by the Muslims as well. Organization of the federation's local governments was also fraught with problems. It was agreed that the prewar *opština* borders would not be retained, presumably because they did not accurately reflect the ethnic distribution of the population before the war. Yet the vast displacement of the Muslim and Croat populations during the war seemed to rule out any redrawing of district boundaries based on the preconflict situation. The explosive political implications of allowing freedom of movement within the federation was shown by a Croat proposal in spring 1994 to permit Muslims displaced from Serb-held areas to settle only in cantons where Muslims were then in a majority.[282] The cantonal borders within the Bosnian Federation, as of May 1996, are shown in Map 7.4.

In Mostar, the federation agreement signed at Dayton foresaw the creation of six districts over which a city assembly was to function. The composition of the districts was to reflect their ethnic makeup at the time of the 1991 census.[283] On the face of it, the statute seemed to repeat all the

Map 7.4 The Bosnian (Muslim-Croat) Federation, May 1996

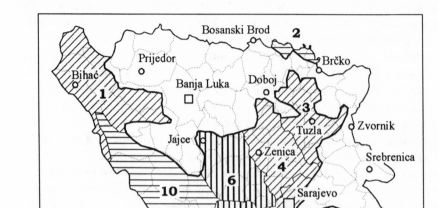

Based on U.S. Department of State, map no. 3533 2–96 STATE (INR/GGI) and OSCE map at www.oscebih.org/images/canton.jpg.

formulas of earlier documents, from the Cutileiro plan to the Dayton agreement, by harking back to the Bosnia of the prewar era. The difficulties of implementing the agreement in Mostar since the Dayton accord, and especially the continuing violence between Croats and Muslims, have demonstrated the contradiction between the diplomatic/political fiction of ethnic integration and the reality on the ground of ethnic partition imposed by war and reinforced by postwar political decisions and popular enmity. A late 1997 analysis of the conditions in Croat-controlled areas of Bosnia, prepared for the OSCE mission in Mostar but disavowed by the OSCE and leaked to the *New York Times,* concluded that rather than becoming integrated into the federation, Croat-controlled territory is "a region that in every respect, from military and security matters to business ties, is part of Croatia."[284] Such was the reality in the Muslim-Croat federation two years after Dayton. The future of the Bosnian Federation hardly seemed promising.

It appears likely that neither federation nor central institutions can prevent the three national parties (and their factions) and the multitude of local authorities from continuing to do pretty much as they please. These informal power structures had become deeply entrenched following the collapse of communist power in Bosnia in 1990. The Dayton agreement, by sanctioning the partitioning of Bosnia while blocking the secession of Herzeg-Bosnia and the Serb republic, unintentionally served to strengthen these local power centers. Experience has shown that it is not enough to adopt constitutions drawn up by foreign advisers, or appoint foreign ombudsmen and the like. Pre-existing centers of power have to be eliminated, and replaced by institutions with popular backing and operating in a democratic environment. This could have been accomplished in at least two ways. One was simply the military takeover of Bosnia by NATO; the "occupation scenario" that appeared imminent in May 1993 when all sides momentarily agreed to the Vance-Owen plan. A second approach, favored by the international community and finally adopted at Dayton, was to hold elections and push for the establishment of democratic institutions, however weak their social foundations.

The Military

The military and regional stabilization provisions of the Dayton agreement (contained in annexes 1A and 1B) put an end to the fighting in Bosnia-Herzegovina. An implementation force (IFOR) of some 60,000 NATO and other troops was deployed to Bosnia in December 1995, following the formal signing of the agreement in Paris and the adoption of Security Council Resolution 1031 (December 15, 1995) authorizing NATO to implement the agreement. IFOR operated under robust rules of engagement to enforce the military aspects of the agreement, consistent with the Chapter VII authority of Resolution 1031. The IFOR mission included ensuring compliance with the cease-fire, ensuring the withdrawal and separation of forces, ensuring the relocation of all heavy weapons and military forces to cantonment areas or barracks and the demobilization of remaining forces, and controlling Bosnian airspace. Implementation of these activities rendered all local military forces subject to close observation and control by IFOR.

IFOR also ensured the safe withdrawal of those UN forces not trans-ferred to IFOR. The confidence- and security-building measures called for by the regional stabilization provisions of the agreement were spelled out in detail in an OSCE-negotiated agreement in January 1996. This agreement instituted measures that limited the scope of allowable mili-tary activities on each side, and rendered all military activities transpar-ent. This agreement also called for the disbandment of all special operations and armed civilian groups in Bosnia.[285] Implementation of this agreement would make it extremely difficult for local forces to mount any sizable military action by surprise. According to a well-informed U.S. military official, these military and stabilization measures elimi-nated any immediate threat of a military confrontation in Bosnia. Local forces cannot mount any action that cannot be suppressed by interna-tional forces already on the ground in Bosnia, and forces outside Bosnia that can be called upon to support them. This guarantee against the renewal of fighting depends, however, on the continuing presence of international forces.

In December 1996 international forces were reduced to about 31,000 troops and renamed (Stabilization Force, or SFOR), and their mission was extended for an additional 18 months.[286] In December 1997 the Clinton administration decided once again to extend the commitment of U.S. troops to participate in the international force in Bosnia; this time for an indefinite period.[287] The administration seemed to have little choice but to do so. The European states have made it clear that if U.S. forces were to leave, their troops would be withdrawn from Bosnia, as well. Withdrawal of the inter-national military presence in Bosnia would seriously weaken the deterrents to a renewed outbreak of hostilities.

The Dayton agreement also included provisions for arms reductions and the establishment of a military balance among Yugoslavia (Serbia and Montenegro), Croatia, the Bosnian (Muslim-Croat) Federation, and the Republika Srpska [Annex 1–B]. But, according to the leader of the British delegation at Dayton, the arms control negotiation

> had received virtually no prior preparation and reliable data were few and far between. Such a lack of information made it difficult, but not impossible, to decide the depth of the arms reductions it was sensible to demand. No at-tempt was made to establish real coherence between reductions and the rear-mament involved in "equip and train," which was discussed in the shadows exclusively among Americans.[288]

The arms control provisions of Dayton have allowed the Bosnian govern-ment to build up its military capacity. The United States has undertaken to fulfill its commitment to arm the Muslims, entered into as part of the negotiations that ended the fighting in Bosnia, through its "train and equip" program.[289] The program calls for the United States to provide $100 million in U.S. military equipment, including rifles, machine guns, light anti-tank weapons, armored personnel carriers, and tanks, as well as communications equipment and helicopters, to the Bosnian (Muslim-Croat) Federation. Additional support pledged by Turkey and a group of Islamic states including Saudi Arabia and Kuwait increased the size of the program to $400 million. An extensive military training program is being conducted by MPRI under a separate civilian contract. In addition to efforts to improve the organization and fighting capacity of the federation army, the MPRI program includes an effort to integrate the Muslim and Croat armies into a single unified force under civilian control.[290]

Even the most outspoken supporters of the Bosnian government argue, however, that "such integration will, of course, never happen." They argue that, from the Muslim perspective,

> The administration is demanding an integration that, if genuinely effected, would require that Bosnian President Alija Izetbegovic relinquish sole control over his people's primary defense against forces that, for four years, sought to destroy the Bosnian state and kill or purge much of its Muslim population. Furthermore, it would mean sharing control with the Bosnian Croat militia, one of the very forces that led the genocidal assaults, and thereby potentially leaving a rump, predominately Muslim Bosnia undefended from attack by Croatia, the patron of the Bosnian Croat separatists.[291]

The Muslim leadership is thus likely to seek to subordinate Croat military forces rather than integrate them, while the Bosnian Croats are just as likely to resist any diminution in the autonomy of their military. In January 1997 Bosnian Croat leader and federation President Krešimir Zubak reported that a separate Croat corps will be maintained "in peace-time," with recruits being allowed to choose the unit in which they will serve. He explained, "A Croatian component will exist in the federation Army because we learned from experience with the Yugoslav Army that they turned against anyone who was not a Serb." This suggests that the Bosnian Croats expect the Bosnian Muslims to turn against anyone who is not a Muslim.[292] In late May 1997 the Muslim and Croat forces were reported still "largely unintegrated."[293]

Although the train and equip program is formally aimed at assisting the federation, the U.S. intent seems to be to strengthen Muslim forces. Ambassador James Pardew, the U.S. special representative for military stabilization in the Balkans, reported at a July 1996 press briefing:

The distribution of weapons will be based on objective military consideration. We don't think that this should be done on the basis of a percentage or "somebody gets some first," and so forth. . . . The greatest weakness—shortage of weapons—is in the Bosniac [Muslim] brigades. The Croatian brigades are a little better equipped. So it's logical that the Bosniac brigades will receive help more quickly.[294]

Indeed, U.S. government sources reported privately in September 1997 that the train and equip program and military training programs in other countries were benefiting primarily the Muslims.

The train and equip program does not preclude the Bosnian government from securing additional arms from other sources. Nor does it preclude the United States from supplying additional arms, outside the program. In May 1997, for example, Ambassador Pardew announced that the United States was sending heavy artillery and heavy equipment transports to the federation as "excess defense articles" rather than as part of the train and equip program.[295] The Bosnian government, like the other parties to the Dayton agreement, does remain subject to the arms control provisions of the agreement. This limits the range of weaponry that it can acquire openly. Covert shipments of arms, however, appear to be continuing. In November 1996, for example, an unnamed NATO official alleged in a Western media account that the Bosnian government was importing heavy artillery with the assistance of Turkish and Malaysian troops participating in IFOR.[296] A year later, in October 1997, the Western media reported that the government was "intensifying a clandestine program to arm and train its military" that involved continued military cooperation with Iran and other Islamic states.[297] The train and equip program, therefore, represents only a part of the Bosnian Muslim effort to build up their forces in anticipation of another round of fighting. Although the precise content of the assistance provided by MPRI remains cloaked in secrecy, it is certain that, as in the earlier case of Croatia, this training is producing significant improvement in the Bosnian army's capability to wage war. By October 1997 "senior NATO officials" in Bosnia were suggesting that the military balance already decisively favored the Muslims.[298]

Despite such improvements in its military, the Bosnian Muslim leadership's ability to pursue its goals by force is constrained by geopolitical realities. An attack on the Bosnian Serb republic could well provide the opportunity for Herzegovinian Croats to attempt to secede. Such an attack might draw Serbia into the fight and, soon thereafter, Croatia. Serbia and Croatia might enter such fighting as allies rather than opponents, seeking to dismember Bosnia-Herzegovina and reduce it to a rump Muslim state, if not partition it entirely according to plans discussed by Tudjman and Milošević on several occasions since 1991. Nonetheless, Charles Boyd reported in January 1998 that he found a "consensus" among those he interviewed in Bosnia that "if NATO withdraws, fighting will resume; and the Muslims, confident and spoiling for a rematch, will almost certainly initiate it." As a result, NATO "may now have to stay, if only to prevent them from restarting the war." He concludes, therefore, that "nothing the United States is doing in Bosnia today is so clearly destabilizing or unlikely to foster an enduring peace as [the train and equip] program."[299]

Conclusion

The suppression of fighting in Bosnia-Herzegovina and successful imposition of the Dayton agreement reinforces the central conclusion drawn from earlier, failed efforts to bring the war to an end: that the commitment and support of the United States was critical to the success of any such effort. At the conclusion of the Dayton agreement, a British official offered the following back-handed compliment to the Americans:

> The Bosnian crisis shows this alliance stands or falls with American leadership. A lot of the bickering for the past three years could have been prevented if Washington had taken this kind of assertive approach much earlier.[300]

The use of force against the Serbs was crucial to the success of the U.S. effort to end the fighting. But, as the analysis presented earlier in this chapter suggests, the steps by which the United States came to use force in Bosnia were far more complex than is generally understood, and included serious mistakes and setbacks before success was achieved.

The air strikes undertaken in late May 1995 at the urging of the United States were not only ineffective; they also weakened the deterrent effect on the Serbs of Western threats, and provoked a hostage crisis that ended UNPROFOR's ability to deter the Serbs. This came at a crucial moment for the Bosnian Serbs, when the Carter cease-fire had expired and both the Croats and the Muslims were mounting successful offensives against Serb positions in Bosnia. The European decision in early June to deploy a rapid reaction force to Bosnia raised the further danger that the Bosnian Serbs might soon also have to face Western combat troops deployed to protect UN safe areas. These developments increased the incentives for Mladić to move quickly against the Muslim-held enclaves in eastern Bosnia—while UNPROFOR was still weak and the West still inhibited from using its air power against him—so as to free Serb forces for redeployment elsewhere.

Indeed, General Rose had warned in November 1994 that any shift toward a more aggressive stance by UN forces would lead the Bosnian Serbs to attack the enclaves.[301]

At the same time—early June—the United States broke off Frasure's negotiations with Milošević. This appeared to end the opportunity for Milošević to trade moderation in Bosnia for an end to sanctions, and thereby eliminated the primary reason for him to restrain the Bosnian Serbs. Thus, by mid-June neither force nor diplomacy was providing any deterrent to Serb military action against the eastern enclaves. Although Milošević would later deny to Holbrooke that he had authorized the Srebrenica campaign, it seems clear that Mladić could not have attacked Srebrenica without at least the acquiescence of Milošević. According to Misha Glenny,[302] Mladić received explicit permission to attack in early July from JNA commander Momčilo Perišić. No such direction could have been given without the explicit approval of Milošević.

As we noted earlier in this chapter, the fall of Srebrenica on July 12 and the ensuing massacre sent shock waves through the Clinton administration. It responded by attempting to restore the credibility of the Western threat to use force against the Serbs; by applying that threat to the defense of Goražde and to a demand that the Serbs respect the safe areas; and by signaling that negotiations could be resumed only if the safe areas were respected. The U.S. decision on July 15 to use force, reported earlier, was followed by the intensive diplomatic effort in the period July 15–25 (also described earlier) to unify the allies around the use of force to defend the safe areas. The credibility of this threat was underscored both by the dispatch of NATO generals to meet with Mladić in Belgrade on July 23, and by the forceful response of the rapid reaction force on Mt. Igman to Serb provocations on July 22. But the threat was balanced by the generals' clear message that the allies still sought a negotiated end to the war.

As late as August 1 the diplomatic side of the coercive diplomacy still remained stalled. U.S. insistence that the Serbs cease their attacks before negotiations could resume may have led Milošević to send his August 1 letter to Mladić and Izetbegović (noted earlier) urging them to conclude an immediate peace. This may have been an indication that the intensive U.S. effort undertaken after July 15 was about to bear fruit. But events on the ground quickly overtook the U.S. initiative. The retaking of Krajina by Croatia ended the Serb threat to the safe areas still under Muslim control. It also demonstrated to U.S. policymakers that the ground forces some senior U.S. military officials had long insisted were necessary to make air strikes effective were now in place.[303] The enhanced credibility of the U.S.

threat—now that the Croatians had put the Serbs on the defensive—may have led the Bosnian Serb parliament to agree to the U.S. proposal for peace in late August. It may also have prompted Milošević's decision to wrest control away from the Bosnian Serb leadership and negotiate directly on their behalf. But the threat of force, by itself, was not sufficient to compel the Bosnian Serb military to withdraw its heavy weapons from around Sarajevo. That, as we have seen, was achieved only after the United States demonstrated that bombing would continue until the Serbs had withdrawn—by halting the bombing for a few days on September 1 to give the Serbs an opportunity to withdraw, and then resuming the bombing at a higher level when they did not. Holbrooke underscored this threat when he confronted Mladić directly in Belgrade on September 13 and won his commitment to withdraw. But the coercive force of air power had to be accompanied by the persuasive force of diplomatic and political concessions to convince Mladić to withdraw. The willingness of the United States to meet Mladić's demand that Serb-held territories be protected against a Muslim takeover once he had withdrawn, reported earlier in this chapter, appears to have been crucial to concluding this key agreement.

In order to compel all three parties to conclude the series of partial agreements that brought the fighting to an end, and to accede to the Dayton agreement, the United States had to alter its approach to the political issues underlying the war. Earlier European- and UN-led efforts to negotiate an agreement had failed in part because the United States had openly encouraged the Muslim-dominated Bosnian government to seek a more favorable settlement. The end of the fighting in 1995 and conclusion of the Dayton agreement required the United States to accommodate—at least partially—Serb political interests in the formulation of a settlement, and to compel the Bosnian Muslims to compromise.

Paradoxically, the use of U.S. air power against the Serbs may have given U.S. negotiators the leverage against the Bosnian government they needed to extract concessions from it, and the political protection against any negative public response in the United States to concessions to the Serbs. The Americans thus adopted positions they had earlier criticized European and UN negotiators for adopting. These included negotiating directly with the Serbs; sanctioning the *de facto* partition of Bosnia-Herzegovina by giving the Bosnian Serb republic geographic coherence while denying the same to Muslim-populated areas of the Bosnian Federation, and by granting each group a veto over the actions of the central government; and pressuring the Muslims to accept that partition. At the end of the Dayton negotiations, French officials chastised the United States for having blocked earlier solutions and pointed out the similarities between Dayton and earlier, European proposals.[304] Thus, for the first time since the beginning of the war, the U.S. insistence on the use of greater force was accompanied by a U.S. acceptance of a compromise—concessionary, from the Muslim point of view—political formula for ending the conflict. It was this formula that defined the goals and limits of military intervention as well as the general political characteristics of the settlement to be pursued through negotiations, thereby making both intervention and negotiation possible.

The intensified U.S. effort to bring the war to an end appears to have been motivated primarily by domestic American political considerations, and secondarily by concern for the cohesion of NATO, rather than by the publicly stated goals of punishing Serb aggression and reversing ethnic cleansing. Dayton did not accomplish very much with respect to the latter. The two real concerns of the Clinton administration merged by mid-1995, when the administration faced the prospect of having to commit U.S. ground troops to the withdrawal of the UN mission from Bosnia. By then, UNPROFOR had become a largely NATO-staffed operation. The concern of senior members of the Clinton administration to prevent the disintegration of NATO (and avoid an operation that would inevitably have been characterized in the media as "Dunkirk") required that the administration act to protect UNPROFOR troops from NATO countries against the dangers of a withdrawal operation. We have already noted that senior officials in the administration realized following the fall of Srebrenica that U.S. involvement in the conflict had become unavoidable. The imposition of a settlement through coercive diplomacy—even one that disadvantaged the Muslims—represented a clearly less risky option than withdrawing UN forces. But, as we have seen, the fighting in Bosnia-Herzegovina, and the former Yugoslavia as a whole, was not perceived as threatening U.S. strategic interests directly.

The U.S. approach to ending the war was shaped by concern for the military-strategic balance between Croatia and Serbia. The moral force of arguments in favor of helping the Bosnian Muslims secure a military victory evaporated in August and September 1995. In the face of the possible threat to regional stability inherent in allowing the broader Croatian-Serbian military balance to be overturned by a total defeat of the Serbs in Bosnia, the United States opted for the Milošević-Tudjman partition solution; thereby preserving the Serbian-Croatian regional balance.

As our account of the negotiations at Dayton suggests, the conclusion of an agreement depended more on negotiations and the exchange of concessions between the two regional powers—Croatia and Yugoslavia (Serbia and Montenegro)—than on the actions of the three Bosnian parties. The United States did not impose its own settlement at Dayton as much as it provided support for a resolution of the Bosnian question—partition—first pushed by Milošević and Tudjman as early as 1991. None of the Bosnian actors appears to view the Dayton agreement as a permanent, or "preferred" outcome. Each had to be compelled to accept it. None appears yet to have given up the possibility of achieving their preferred—and incompatible—outcomes by other means.

Ensuing Bosnian Croat actions in Mostar reflected their continuing unwillingness to share power with the Muslims. Bosnian Serbs continued to expel non-Serbs from their republic. Muslims refused to let Croats return to their homes in central Bosnian towns taken from the Croats by the Bosnian army, or to let Serbs return to Sarajevo. Both the Croats and the Serbs, as well as the Muslims, manipulated voter registration regulations in the September 1996 elections to ensure ethnic majorities in the communities they seek to control. Those elections produced a victory for the three nationalist parties: the Muslim SDA, the Croat HDZ, and the Serb SDS,[305] whose fundamental incompatibility was defined in chapter 2, and whose contributions to perpetuating conflict were chronicled in the subsequent chapters. As a result of the 1996 elections, the SDA achieved a secure majority and assumed a dominant role in Bosnian (Muslim-Croat) federation institutions. In elections to the House of Representatives of the parliament of Bosnia-Herzegovina, the SDA secured a majority of 16 of the 28 seats from the federation. The SDS secured a majority of the seats in the parliament of the Serb republic. The SDA secured 14 of the 82 seats in the Bosnian Serb republic parliament by taking advantage of absentee balloting by displaced Muslims. But, neither the Muslim SDA nor the Serb SDS controlled the two-thirds of its republic parliament required to exercise the regional veto provided for in the Dayton constitution.

The election for the presidency produced the expected results. Alija Izetbegović dominated the voting for the Muslim seat, with 80 percent of the vote. His main competitor, Haris Silajdžić, polled only 13.6 percent. The small turnout for Fikret Abdić, only 2.7 percent, reflected the damage done to his standing among Muslims by his actions during the war. Krešimir Zubak secured 88.7 percent of the Croat vote. Momčilo Krajišnik secured only 67.3 percent of the Serb vote. Mladen Ivenić, a candidate of the Bosnian Serb opposition to the SDS, secured 30 percent of the vote. Within the Serb republic, Biljana Plavšić stood for the republic presidency in place of Radovan Karadžić—who, as an indicted war criminal, had been prohibited from holding public office. Plavšić won 59.7 percent of the vote.

Of the four other candidates, none secured as much as 20 percent. Thus, the presidency of Bosnia and Herzegovina was, as anticipated, divided among the three nationalist leaderships.

The Bosnian Muslim leadership proceeded with the tasks of creating a government for the overall state, Bosnia and Herzegovina. From the first step, the Bosnian Serbs proved resistant to actions intended to strengthen the Bosnian state, and exploited the provisions of the Dayton agreement to block progress whenever possible. The convening of the first session of the Bosnian presidency, for example, became the subject of intense negotiation between the Serbs and the Muslims. On the Muslim side, the split between Izetbegović and Silajdžić was papered over, and Silajdžić assumed the post of prime minister. The Muslim split with the Croats, however, proved resistant to solution. The conflict over Mostar, for example, continued to erupt periodically into violence. Nonetheless, the Muslims have proceeded with the reconstruction of the Bosnian state.

The combination of an internationally supervised cessation of hostilities and the opportunities to arm and train created by the Dayton agreement allows the Bosnian Muslims to pursue a strategy defined by Croatian experience. The Croatians accepted a negotiated peacekeeping plan in January 1992 that left parts of their country under the *de facto* control of hostile Serbs intent on establishing their autonomy. But it also brought an end to large-scale fighting and created a breathing space of more than three years, during which Croatia was able to build up its military sufficiently to retake all its territories by force. As we have noted, President Izetbegović argues that the Bosnian Muslims were compelled to accept a disadvantageous and unjust peace plan at Dayton. But that peace plan has created an opportunity for the Muslims to build up the military capacity required to carry out their own campaign to retake territories they view as rightly theirs. Unlike the Croatians, they are able to pursue this goal in the open, freed from the constraints of even a porous arms embargo, and aided by the U.S. program to train and equip their army. Indeed, even as they negotiated, Bosnian Muslim leaders acknowledged that in the long run they might have to resort to war to achieve their goals.[306] Maintaining an effective international military presence on the ground in Bosnia to enforce the military and confidence- and security-building measures associated with the Dayton agreement is thus essential to prevent the outbreak of renewed fighting. Paradoxically, it is now the weakened and divided Bosnian Serbs who are the principal beneficiaries of that presence.

The power of the Muslim leadership remains dependent on appeals to nationalism and to the desire of displaced populations to reclaim territories now under Serb (and Croat) control. The Bosnian Muslim leadership will therefore sustain its claims to all of Bosnia, and the political incentives to restart the war will remain high. Indeed, those incentives increase as the Bosnian army accumulates more weapons and training. Not all analysts agree that the balance of military power will shift decisively in favor of the Muslims.[307] But, to the extent that the Bosnian army improves in strength, weaponry, and training, the original rationale for maintaining U.S. and European troops in Bosnia is being transformed. As the Bosnian army achieves the capacity to wage war against the Bosnian Serbs in pursuit of the Muslim leadership's claims to authority over all of Bosnia, the rationale for deployment of Western troops becomes prevention of a Bosnian offensive. More than two years after Dayton, there has been no reduction in the strength of the nationalist parties, and little evidence of either grassroots ethnic reconciliation or the kind of interethnic elite cooperation that would be necessary to make power-sharing work and avert a return to war in the event Western troops are withdrawn.

Chapter 8

Dilemmas of Intervention

The conflict in Bosnia-Herzegovina was the first major test in the post–Cold War period of the ability of the international community to resolve ethnic conflicts. These efforts failed to prevent a catastrophic war or to establish the conditions for a stable peace once the war was ended. As a result, Bosnia remained haunted by the contradiction between integration and partition. With the U.S. decision in December 1997 to keep troops in Bosnia indefinitely, it appears that a peacekeeping operation of indefinite duration is in the making; one more ambitious and costly than its closest counterpart, in Cyprus.

In this conclusion we address three compelling questions that arise out of the tragedy of Bosnia. The first is whether the catastrophe that has befallen Bosnia could have been averted; that is, whether the West—or the parties themselves—could have acted sooner, and how. To answer this, we examine whether the West missed opportunities for preventive engagement, and whether early intervention in the conflict might have succeeded. The second is whether the Bosnian experience offers any lessons for the more effective management of future conflicts. Based on the analyses in the preceding chapters, we offer some conclusions about humanitarian intervention, the use of force, and the role of diplomacy in conflict management; and we suggest some refinements to the dominant understanding of how such conflicts are brought to a negotiated end. The third question is whether, despite the shortcomings of the Dayton accord and the apparent difficulties of implementation, there still remains a way to resolve the contradiction between ideals and reality that haunts Bosnia in the post-Dayton period.

Was Preventive Action Possible?

Preventive action is widely understood as requiring the discovery of political solutions to the conflict at hand. A recent comprehensive report by the Carnegie Commission on Preventing Deadly Conflict[1] distinguishes between "structural prevention," consisting of "measures to ensure that crises do not arise in the first place," and "operational prevention," consisting of "measures applicable in the face of immediate crisis." In our view, the Bosnian experience suggests that there really are three broad categories of action available to policymakers for dealing with deadly ethnic conflicts. First, genuinely preventive action that addresses the sources of conflict before it turns to violence. This corresponds to what the Commission calls "structural prevention." For such action to be effective, it must come early. It does not involve—indeed, it should avoid—the use of force. Because it requires those seeking to avert conflict to become fully engaged in the civil and political functions of the society facing crisis, such action may be called preventive engagement.[2] With the Bosnian experience in mind, we suggest the Carnegie Commission's category of "operational prevention" should be further refined. We suggest distinguishing between early intervention, undertaken in response to the outbreak of violence and aimed at stopping its escalation before the costs of intervention rise and ethnic cleansing alters the political and demographic balances in society, and crisis intervention, which takes place after violence has escalated and the actors are committed to violence.

Early intervention is likely to be driven primarily by the importance of the conflict itself or the issues—including moral issues—that it raises. Early intervention involves the threat of force, implicit or explicit, to prevent escalation and compel the parties to negotiate their differences among themselves. The nature and extent of the force employed will be contingent on the circumstances. The focus of early intervention will be to solve the conflict itself. The conflicting parties themselves must therefore agree on a political formula for resolving the conflict if such intervention is to work. Crisis intervention, in contrast, takes place after the escalation of violence and is associated with higher levels of perceived potential costs to those intervening. Because of the perceived costs of intervening, crisis intervention will usually take place only when policymakers perceive important implications in the conflict for the international community, for key international actors, or for their own national interests.

The analyses presented in preceding chapters suggest that, in the Bosnian case, crisis intervention (as contrasted to early intervention) went through three stages. As we argued in chapter 5, the first stage consisted of humanitarian intervention, and the search for a diplomatic settlement that would return Bosnia to the *status quo ante* under international supervision (Vance-Owen). More direct involvement on the part of the Western powers was precluded by the judgment on the part of policymakers that no vital Western interests were at stake in the conflict. The second stage consisted of the attempt to negotiate a modified partition. This stage began in 1993 following the collapse of the Vance-Owen plan, with the United States still remaining aloof from, and hostile toward a largely European effort. It concluded with the United States leading the effort, through the Contact Group. As we reported in chapter 6, the motivations of the great powers involved at this stage were varied, and sometimes contradictory. With the entry of the United States into the diplomatic effort in early 1994, the groundwork began to be laid for backing up this effort with the use of force. The third stage of crisis intervention by the West consisted of the reliance on force to impose a settlement. It began with the tentative and failed effort at coercive diplomacy launched by the United States in May 1995. It began to succeed only when Croatia used force to regain control over Krajina. Decisive intervention by the West, led by the United States, thus depended in part on the complex developments surrounding the Croatian offensive, described in chapter 7. Nonetheless, Western intervention was driven by the perception of a clear threat to national interests; and focused primarily on alleviating the perceived threat to international actors and their interests, rather than on solving the conflict itself.

The Bosnian case thus suggests very clearly that when an escalating conflict is not perceived as having implications for the international community or key international actors, crisis intervention to end the fighting will not take place. Tentative efforts at intervention, such as in May 1995, may produce a backlash by one of the parties. When international actors perceive the stakes as high enough, they will impose conditions that eliminate the threat to their interests, either through disengagement or more forceful intervention. But the conditions imposed as the result of crisis intervention may not solve the underlying conflict.

Preventive Engagement: A Missed Opportunity?

The opportunity for preventive engagement in Bosnia began with the collapse of the Yugoslav League of Communists in January 1990, and the onset of ethnic and factional struggle over shaping the emerging Bosnian state. It ended with the outbreak of fighting in Slovenia in June 1991. Preventive engagement in Bosnia during this period was foreclosed both by factors external to Bosnia and the former Yugoslavia, and by conditions within the former Yugoslavia and Bosnia.

The competition for power in Bosnia that followed the breakup of the League, and the campaign leading up to the elections at the end of 1990 in Bosnia provided numerous opportunities to support non-nationalist parties. Our study confirms the enormous importance of elections for determining whether the population of a newly emerging state will be mobilized in the direction of democratic civil society or toward ethnic exclusivity. In Bosnia, conservative communist party leaders had reined in reform-minded communists during the 1980s, leaving the party unable to forge the kind of liberal reform coalition with noncommunists that provided the key to transitions in Slovenia, Macedonia, and other postcommunist states. In the absence of any outside help, this left the Bosnian reform communists weak and ineffective in the face of competition from the nationalists for popular support. The lack of Western efforts to support democratic parties in Bosnia and the other former Yugoslav republics represents a missed opportunity for preventive engagement.

In the aftermath of the elections, there appears still to have been some chance to get the three conflicting—but not yet warring—leaderships to implement genuine power-sharing arrangements. As long as it appeared that Yugoslavia might survive, even under a drastically altered constitutional arrangement, the Serbs, Muslims, and moderate Croats continued to engage in power sharing at the highest levels. Territorial "autonomy" took the form of local governments dominated by one group or another. In effect, noncontiguous ethnic enclaves were taking shape, but without ethnic cleansing. A slim opportunity existed to transform this rudimentary power-sharing arrangement into something that might survive the collapse of Yugoslavia. Such a solution appeared blocked, however, by three developments in (former) Yugoslav and Bosnian politics.

First, those who might have wished to pursue a peaceful solution to the crisis in Bosnia were faced with two authoritarian regimes, in Serbia and Croatia, that were prepared to use force to achieve their ends in Bosnia. Both harbored ethno-territorial claims against Bosnia and were ready to resort to ethnic cleansing (and ethnic self-cleansing) to achieve these claims and, in the process, to create a greater Croatia and a greater Serbia. Moreover, each was prepared to pursue their claims alone, or in cooperation—more precisely, collusion—with the other. The ambitions of these regimes would have had to be reined in if a peaceful solution to the conflict in Bosnia was to be achieved. Second, in the absence of a comprehensive strategy, the compromises that probably would have been necessary to achieve the peaceful dissolution of Yugoslavia even with the cooperation of moderate regimes in Croatia and Serbia would have worked at cross-purposes with the goal of constituting Bosnia-Herzegovina as one of the successor states.

Third, as we have shown in chapter 3, the nationalist regimes in Serbia and Croatia spawned Serb and Croat nationalist parties in Bosnia, and these were matched (and even preceded) by the rise of a Muslim nationalist party. As a result, Bosnia was already undergoing rapid ethnic polarization in 1990. The opportunity to establish power sharing was lost when the non-nationalists who could have played the role of balancer and mediator were excluded from power. As the case of Tuzla demonstrated, the non-nationalists were eager, willing and capable of sharing power—and relatively resistant to ethnic conflict. But none of the nationalist leaderships was willing to work with them, except where local ties proved strong enough to overcome nationalist passions and distrust.

Our study suggests that the victory of the nationalists in 1990 was intimately connected to developments in the broader, Yugoslav political context. No effort to save Bosnia could have succeeded in the absence of an effort to move the growing crisis in Yugoslavia onto the path of peaceful settlement. It seems clear that preventive engagement in the Bosnian conflict would have required the international community to commit its resources to facilitating the peaceful dissolution of Yugoslavia. Unfortunately, that effort came well after the elections in Bosnia. As we pointed out in chapter 3, once the nationalists came to power, Bosnia entered a downward spiral of ethnic conflict that outside actors could halt only through intervention. But engagement to achieve the dissolution of Yugoslavia peacefully was foreclosed by four perceptual barriers among Western policymakers: First, after the rise of Gorbachev and his renunciation of the Brezhnev doctrine in 1988, Yugoslavia was no longer perceived as of strategic importance to the West. Second, Western policymakers were unable to reconcile their commitment to existing borders with the realities of a disintegrating multinational state that threatened to spawn smaller and even more unstable multinational states. The hopes for a peaceful outcome voiced in Western capitals, and the intentions of the nationalist leaders to push forward with consolidating their control over territory through force and ethnic cleansing were fundamentally in conflict.

Third, Western policymakers were unable to identify peaceful means by which to reconcile their seemingly contradictory commitments to existing borders on the one hand, and principles of self-determination on the other; and to do so in a manner that did not incite nationalist leaders to push forward with their efforts to consolidate control over territory through force. Fourth, just as concern in the U.S. intelligence community began to focus on Yugoslavia in late 1990, when strategies of preventive engagement might still have made a difference, Western policymakers were focused instead on instability in the USSR and the Gulf War crisis. While the Gulf

War diverted them, instability in the USSR led policymakers to avoid any action that might have been viewed as setting a precedent for the dissolution of the Soviet Union.

To ask whether the tragedy of Bosnia could have been averted, therefore, is to ask whether the West could have intervened after the Gulf War had been concluded, and after the Soviet Union had disintegrated peacefully on its own accord; that is, after the dissolution of Yugoslavia had already turned violent. This was no longer a case suitable for preventive engagement. It called for early intervention.

Early intervention would have required the West to implement a comprehensive strategy for dealing with the several dimensions of the crisis suggested above and detailed in chapter 3; one in which the realities of the region and its politics could be reconciled with the legalistic and relatively enlightened outlook of Western diplomats and negotiators. Their failure to implement a comprehensive strategy may be explained in terms of a failure to comprehend the complexities and interrelatedness of the conflicts before them, and their inability to develop a coherent response to them. It may also be explained in terms of the lack of Western interests at stake in the conflict. The decision by Western policymakers not to use force to end the crisis cannot be explained in terms of a simple lack of "will." It must be explained in terms of the democratic policymaking process itself; the nature of force and the consequences of its deployment; and, finally, in terms of the requisites of using force successfully to resolve ethnic conflict.

The Difficulties of Early Intervention

The opportunity for early intervention in Bosnia-Herzegovina began with the conflict in Croatia, and ended with the outbreak of fighting in Bosnia in April 1992. After April, when the Bosnian Serbs initiated the takeover of territory by force and started to carry out ethnic cleansing, any effort to avert further catastrophe would have to have taken the form of crisis intervention. The analysis in chapter 3 of the relationship between events in Croatia and later events in Bosnia suggests that early intervention would have required the West to devise a strategy that included a definitive settlement of both the war between Croatia and Serbia and the conflict between Croatia and its Serb population, in a fashion that created incentives for both Belgrade and the Bosnian Serbs not to resort to force in Bosnia. This would probably have required coercive diplomacy to induce all sides in Croatia to settle. And this would not have been an easy task.

Mediation alone could not—and, as the experience of the EC Conference on Yugoslavia (the Hague conference) demonstrates, did not—work. The

Serbs were convinced of their right to exercise self-determination through secession, they had the military power to pursue their goals, and they were willing to use it. The analysis presented in chapter 3 makes it clear that the leadership of the United States was essential if Serbian aggression against Croatia was to be halted in a manner that would lend itself to the peaceful solution of the Bosnian crisis; not only because the United States commanded the resources necessary to carry out such a task, but because the Serbian leadership was acutely sensitive to U.S. reactions. The conflict in Croatia would have to have been solved first, but with an eye toward its implications for Bosnia. Unlike the comprehensive approach advocated by Lord Carrington and others, a successful strategy of early intervention would have avoided placing all the issues in the Yugoslav crisis on the table at once. Rather, it would have approached them sequentially, but on the basis of a consistent set of principles. Furthermore, in order to establish a common framework for solving the Croatian and Bosnian crises early, a strategy of early intervention would have had to include political solutions to the conflicts over internal relations among ethnic groups in Croatia and Bosnia. This was something that European mediators did not attempt in Bosnia until the Cutileiro negotiations; by which time it was too late.

The EC was not able, as the account in chapter 3 makes clear, to develop a strategy that adequately accounted for the differences between the border war in Croatia and the war of dissolution in Bosnia-Herzegovina. Understanding and addressing these differences was essential to successful early intervention. The solution of the Bosnian question revolved not around minority issues, as could be argued was the case in Croatia, but around the rights—constitutional and territorial—of three "nations" making mutually contradictory claims to autonomous statehood. This issue could be resolved within existing borders only through some form of power sharing, not an agreement on minority rights. The Europeans recognized this dilemma too late; only after sanctioning a majoritarian-rule referendum in February 1992 whose result made the negotiation of a constitutional agreement defining the nature of the Bosnian state and relations among the three national communities even more difficult to achieve. The United States remained unpersuaded that power sharing was the proper course of action, and remained wedded to the idea that mutual recognition of the six republics—without requiring prior agreement over constitutional issues—would somehow resolve the conflicts. It pressed neither for power sharing in Bosnia nor for territorial rights for the Serbs in Croatia. Indeed, the United States agreed to recognize Croatia at just the moment the Croatian government reneged on promises to the EC to provide minority rights to the Serbs—requiring only that Croatia recognize Bosnia.

The EC strategy also failed because it did not take into account the relationship between the conflict in Croatia and the developing crisis in Bosnia. With hindsight it became clear that, contrary to logical expectations, ending the fighting in Croatia simply helped to ignite the conflict in Bosnia. Croat irregulars from Herzegovina who had been engaged in the fighting in Croatia now moved back to Bosnia. Serb nationalist irregulars also moved from Croatia to Bosnia as the war wound down in spring 1992. The JNA, disengaged in Croatia, no longer needed to preserve the peace in its rear areas—Bosnia. At the same time, implementation of a cease-fire in Croatia did nothing to accelerate peace talks between Croatia and Serbia. On the contrary, these talks largely ended, as the Serbs sought to exploit and institutionalize the new *status quo* in Croatia, and the Croatians prepared to fight again.

A strategy of early intervention linking the settlement of the Croatian conflict to prevention of a conflict in Bosnia thus would have required a definitive settlement of the Croatian crisis in a manner that favored the Croatian claim to territorial integrity while it institutionalized ethno-territorial autonomy for the Krajina Serbs. At the same time, such a strategy would have called for institutionalizing ethno-territorial autonomy in Bosnia in a way that favored the Bosnian Serbs and the Bosnian Croats. As long as the possibility existed that Serb-held territories in Croatia might win their independence from Croatia, the Bosnian Serbs resisted any formula for preserving the Bosnian state. As long as the Muslim-led government of Bosnia believed that it could achieve recognition of its claim to all of Bosnia—and, later, military intervention by the West—without making any constitutional concessions to ethno-territorial autonomy, it resisted doing so. As our accounts of the Cutileiro, Vance-Owen, and subsequent negotiations make clear, an agreement that preserved the Bosnian state became possible only after the territorial integrity of Croatia had been affirmed and the Muslim government was persuaded that its claims would not be supported unless it agreed to autonomy for the Serbs and Croats. By waiting for the Krajina problem to be solved by Croatia in 1995—militarily, and at the cost of the ethnic cleansing of the Serbs—the West made it difficult to prevent autonomy in Bosnia from becoming the ratification of ethnic cleansing by the Serbs.

The recognition of Croatia, discussed in chapter 3, remains controversial. On the one hand, as we have seen, recognition led to Milošević's decision to halt the war in Croatia. This encouraged the belief—false, in the event—that recognition was the right approach to Bosnia. If it was, indeed, necessary to resolve the Croatian conflict first by aiding Croatia in its war with Serbia, then one might argue that recognition was the right step and that the mistake lay in the fact that it was initiated by Germany and the EC, rather than by the United States and the NATO countries acting in concert. To defend the territorial integrity of Croatia required recognition of Croatia. But neither recognition nor military defense should have been granted in advance of Croatia's having fulfilled all criteria of recognition, including the establishment of territorial autonomy for the Serbs. Similarly, pressure on the Serbs in Bosnia to accept autonomy within Bosnia instead of independence did not necessitate quick recognition of Bosnia. In fact, as we reported in chapter 3, until March 1992 the EC was urging the United States to put off recognition of Bosnia-Herzegovina, to allow talks under Cutileiro on constitutional issues to go forward. After March 10, these talks were held against the background that recognition was scheduled for the first week of April, regardless of the outcome of the talks. Thus, there was little reason for any of the Bosnian parties to negotiate in good faith. Both Cyrus Vance and Lord Carrington argued that recognition deprived the international community of a critical means of inducing the would-be successor states to settle their internal disputes, as well as their disputes with one another, peacefully. But recognition could have served these purposes only if it had been linked to a credible promise of defense as suggested above.

While Germany was, as we reported in chapter 3, a strong advocate of recognition, it was ill suited to carry out a strategy balancing recognition and force. German leaders were under too much domestic pressure to recognize, and too eager to do so; and Germany was in no position to threaten to use force. Neither France nor Britain could have played this role either; the former because of its still pro-Serbian position, the latter because of its opposition to the use of force. Acting collectively, the EC considered sending troops to Croatia, but rejected the idea. Only the United States had the capacity to integrate force and diplomacy. Moreover, it was, as we already suggested, the United States to which the Serbs looked to estimate the reactions to any move on their part. But, as our account makes clear, U.S. policymakers were opposed to any involvement in Yugoslavia; their attention and commitment were focused on Kuwait.

Would an alternative strategy of early intervention of the kind described here have avoided war in Bosnia? Even a settlement that preserved the borders of Croatia and Bosnia would not have protected Bosnia-Herzegovina from Serb control of much of its territory, or from *de facto* Croatian control of western Herzegovina. The granting of autonomy to the Serbs in Croatia and in Bosnia might have resulted in the creation of two contiguous autonomous Serb areas—in Krajina and western Bosnia—straddling the Croatian-Bosnian border. This might have created a new, even more challenging "Serb problem," since these states would undoubtedly have fallen under the control of nationalist leaders who were only too eager to proclaim the existence of a

"Western Serbia" rather than remain in Croatia and Bosnia. Territorial autonomy might very well have tempted Serb and Croat nationalist forces to escalate the crisis in Croatia and Bosnia, or tempted Tudjman and Milošević to move on to the outright partitioning of Bosnia between them, although they would have had to settle an even more difficult Krajina problem. To avoid the *de facto* partition of both Croatia and Bosnia-Herzegovina, and a coordinated attempt by the Serbs to secede from these republics and form their own separate state, Western actors would have had to engage in extensive peacekeeping and peacebuilding activities in Croatia and Bosnia-Herzegovina, including actions designed to preserve the Croatian-Bosnian border. This would have involved peacekeeping forces directly in the politics of the two republics, and in the relations between the central government and the autonomous regions, not an easy task in light of the sensitivity of governments to intervention in their internal affairs. Unlike the conditions that prevailed later in Bosnia, however, all three Bosnian parties as well as the Zagreb and Belgrade leaderships had agreed that, following a constitutional agreement in Bosnia, peacekeeping operations would have been welcomed.[3]

Unlike the post-Dayton situation, an early intervention force—and especially one that followed a constitutional agreement in Bosnia—would not have had to deal with large numbers of displaced persons and massive damage to the economy and the physical infrastructure. Most important, large proportions of the multicultural and civil society would still have been intact, providing an important constituency for efforts to build peace. To launch an intervention before violence had broken out in Bosnia would have been unprecedented, but not impossible. But public and political support in the West for such an intervention would have required widespread understanding of the complexities and interrelatedness of both Croatian and Bosnian politics; something that at the time apparently eluded even most policymakers in the West. And the presence of a UN peacekeeping force in Croatia and/or Bosnia would not have halted centrifugal forces at work within the two republics.

The underlying dilemma for the West in contemplating early intervention lay in the vast gulf between Western images of and preferences for Bosnia, and the nature and goals of the conflicting forces themselves. Statesmen and policymakers consistently underestimated the lengths to which participants in the conflict would go to achieve their goals. The two sides were separated by what we have called a "reality gap." Western diplomats and peacekeepers focused on the legalistic dimensions of the crisis, and focused their negotiations on a search for consensus and the creation of goodwill. The combatants, however, were deeply marked by the conviction that they were locked in a struggle for survival. They were profoundly distrustful of their opponents in the conflict and disdainful of the legal and diplomatic agreements drawn up by mediators.

The options available to policymakers could not easily have bridged the gap between the democratic civil state supported by the West and the nationalist state(s) sought by the warring parties. Early intervention thus might not have prevented the dissolution of Bosnia-Herzegovina. It might not have prevented the formation of a new Serb state in Croatia and Bosnia. But it might have averted the catastrophic killing that took place in Bosnia after April 1992 and strengthened the hand of those forces in Bosnia committed to preserving the multicultural ideal; and it would have created a peaceful alternative by which all parties might have pursued their goals. Thus, it might have achieved the primary goal of such intervention. The disengagement of the West, however, would have depended on whether a peaceful settlement could have been negotiated. This, in turn, depended primarily on the willingness and ability of those involved in the conflict to agree on a political solution; something they seemed neither willing nor able to do.

Crisis Intervention

Humanitarian Intervention

Up until virtually the end of the conflict, the international presence in Bosnia was characterized by efforts at humanitarian intervention; that is, by efforts to ameliorate the impact of the war on the civilian population without taking sides in the conflict. The successes and failures of this humanitarian effort have been the subject of considerable controversy. Central to this controversy is the question of whether humanitarian aid actually prolonged the war, by feeding the combatants and deterring military intervention by the Western powers.

The decision to embark upon a humanitarian intervention was, as we have suggested in chapter 4, one of a series of crisis-driven decisions by Western policymakers. It was made in response to the perceived need to provide humanitarian assistance at a time when negotiations to find a political solution to the war had made little progress, and the assessment of expert observers such as Marrack Goulding was that no military solution was in sight—an assessment that proved correct. Policymakers attempted, as the analyses presented in chapters 4 through 6 make clear, to address humanitarian concerns independently of the military and political conflict. This was not possible.

Because the humanitarian effort itself became focused on countering the effects of Serb excesses, it became virtually impossible for humanitarian aid workers to remain impartial, or to preserve the appearance of impartiality. The presence of Western troops on the ground as part of UNPROFOR represented an irresistible opportunity to try to influence Western opinion, to gain leverage on Western policymakers, and to draw the West directly into the conflict. In the absence of a political-military solution, humanitarian intervention became an open-ended commitment, which policymakers accountable to electorates wary of involvement in the fighting found politically untenable. As a result of sniping and other casualties among the UN troops, persistent criticism by the Bosnian government of their performance, and the taking of UN troops as hostages by the Serbs, humanitarian concern on the part of troop-contributing states was quickly displaced by a desire to end the fighting and reduce the risk to their troops. This brought the troop-contributing states into direct conflict with the major actor not contributing troops, which had a hegemonic world outlook rather than a regional one—the United States. The United States pressed its troop-contributing allies to take more forceful action against the Serbs. The strain of simultaneously trying to carry out humanitarian relief and implement the "safe areas" policy on the one hand, while on the other hand using force against one side, contributed to the degradation of the UN mission.

The Bosnian experience thus suggests that humanitarian intervention in the midst of a violent conflict is difficult (if not impossible) to sustain without addressing the political-military conflict that makes intervention necessary in the first place. If the political-military conflict continues, the humanitarian relief operation is likely to be drawn into the conflict; and extraction of humanitarian forces from harm's way will become the overriding concern of the contributing states and the sponsoring international organization(s). Yet, we must exercise great care before writing off the humanitarian effort in Bosnia. No political solution was in sight until the closing months of the conflict, and moral as well as political pressure to alleviate the suffering was enormous. We seriously doubt that the Bosnian Muslims would have been better off, or less vulnerable to a political solution at their expense, had there been no humanitarian intervention in 1992.

In fact, the relief effort in Bosnia was a success by humanitarian standards. It helped to avert starvation, provided emergency health and medical care, and supported civilian living conditions. As UNHCR officials have often remarked, no one starved during the war in Bosnia. The greatest success of humanitarian intervention came at the outset of the war, when UNPROFOR took control of the Sarajevo airport. The takeover had an immense impact on the war, even if it did not end the siege of Sarajevo as some had hoped it would. As we noted in chapter 4, UN control of the airport allowed Western journalists into the city. Their reports dramatized the plight of the Muslims, and their reporting helped elicit a commitment in the West to the defense of Sarajevo that became evident in August 1993. Because the Serbs were unwilling to turn the airport over to NATO forces, the UN was the only actor that could assume this responsibility. As we have seen, the harsh media criticisms of UN commanders in Bosnia ignored the vital role these actors played in arranging cease-fires following the 1993 Croat-Muslim war, and the February 1994 crisis. These criticisms also ignored the critical role UNPROFOR played in getting humanitarian supplies to populations in need, including the use of force to do so.[4]

The initiation of a peacekeeping and humanitarian operation *before* the achievement of a peace agreement violated the approach widely seen as essential to the success of such an operation. Yet, early deployment of a NATO peace enforcement operation was not possible. A realistic assessment of the Bosnian crisis must take into account the deep antipathy of the Bosnian Serb leadership toward NATO. This antipathy was shared by both the Croats and the Muslims. As we noted in chapter 7, for example, the latter obstructed deployment of the rapid reaction force partly out of fear of allowing the West a free military hand in the conflict. In the end, the presence of UNPROFOR facilitated the projection of Western power into Bosnia in 1995. NATO, in effect, infiltrated and took over the UN command structure as a means of projecting its power into Bosnia quickly.

Nonetheless, the question remains whether the presence of UN forces engaged in humanitarian relief actually delayed crisis intervention by the West. The analyses in chapters 5, 6, and 7 demonstrate that the presence on the ground of Western troops as part of the humanitarian relief effort contributed to deterring the West from using air power earlier in the fighting. It complicated the use of air power later in the war, and exacerbated political differences among the Western allies over ending the fighting. But humanitarian intervention can be said to have delayed crisis intervention only if such intervention otherwise would have been possible. As we will argue below, a whole host of other factors also stood in the way of crisis intervention. When these were removed, the humanitarian effort ceased to deter the West.

The Use of Force

Once the crisis in Bosnia turned violent and ethnic cleansing began, the use of force became hotly debated in the West. There were many advocates of earlier, more forceful Western intervention to stop the fighting in Croatia and Bosnia. These appeals tended to focus on the use of force to stop the fighting or roll back Serb gains, but they did not offer any formulas for resolving the political issues that underlay the fighting.[5] In chapter 3 we reported that WEU proposals for military intervention by tens of thousands of European troops to stop the fighting in Croatia in August and September 1991 were rejected by the EC. We noted in chapter 5 that the Bush and the Clinton administrations also considered and rejected intervention in Bosnia in late 1992 and early 1993. At that time, neither the Europeans nor the Americans were interested in, or able to impose a political solution by force.

Some analysts have characterized these decisions not to intervene as a failure of "will." James Gow, for example, attributes the failure of the West to end the war in May 1993 on the basis of the Vance-Owen plan to "bad timing, bad judgment, an absence of unity and, underpinning everything else, the lack of political will, particularly with regard to the use of force."[6] But democratic leadership calls for both responsibility and accountability, as well as "will." To argue that intervention could be based on "will" alone ignores the responsibility of democratic leaders to consider the costs of intervention to their citizens in terms of "blood and treasure." The public discourse on Bosnia in the West reported in chapters 5 and 6 makes it clear that up to the end of 1994 policymakers were receiving contradictory advice from their military professionals concerning the costs of intervention. At the same time, neither policy analysts in the national policy making establishments of the Western powers nor the mediators directly involved in negotiations to end the war had identified any clear political solution to the conflict. The deficiencies of the Vance-Owen plan were magnified by the lack of political agreement or "good faith" among the warring parties. Even Gow, while continuing to attribute the lack of Western action to "a lack of the political will to act forcefully," acknowledges that the situation in Bosnia "appeared to be both laced with risk and not absolutely indispensable."[7] Yet it was not clear that force alone could have overcome the problems posed by implementation of the Vance-Owen or succeeding plans. Under these conditions, the refusal to intervene appears to reflect responsible democratic leadership, rather than a lack of will.

The most compelling calls for the use of force were based on moral argument. Anthony Lewis, the *New York Times* columnist, mounted a moral appeal for military intervention from as early as August 1992.[8] Leslie Gelb, a *New York Times* editor and columnist, as well as a former senior foreign policy official in the Carter administration, constructed a particularly blunt moral argument in December 1992.[9] He characterized the lack of Western action as "an abdication of our humanity" and argued that "our souls" were in question. He even went so far as to charge Western leaders with "crimes against humanity." Such appeals were repeated on many subsequent occasions by both European and American intellectuals appalled at the atrocities being committed by the Serbs in Bosnia. Their worst fears were confirmed at the time of the Srebrenica massacre.

Policymakers refused to heed such calls, or accept that the Serbs were committing genocide, because to do so would force them to intervene at great cost and with unpredictable consequences. According to a former State Department desk officer, Richard Johnson, senior officials believed that the Serbs were engaged in genocide against the Muslims, but resisted acknowledging this publicly for fear that this would generate additional pressure for U.S. action.[10] In any case, the moral argument for intervention, however well-intentioned, did not fully address the moral dilemma of whether the lives of Western soldiers were worth less than the lives of the Bosnians the West would be trying to save; and whether, in fact, genocide was taking place.

The dangers of intervention were, as we have reported in chapters 5 and 6, subject to conflicting assessments within and between the national military establishments of the Western powers. The analyses presented in the preceding chapters suggest, however, that the risks of using force were in many cases exaggerated. The U.S. military overestimated the means necessary to accomplish certain missions, beginning with the pessimistic estimates by the Pentagon of the forces necessary to open the Sarajevo airport and the argument (which events were to prove had a basis in fact) that air power alone could not make a difference in tipping the balance between the fighting capabilities of the combatants. The UN, too, erred in this direction. UN officials strenuously objected to implementation of the no-fly zone. They argued that the Serb response to this decision would undermine UN peacekeeping efforts, only to be proven wrong. Akashi opposed deployment of the European rapid reaction force to Bosnia in summer 1995, concerned that its presence would lead to a showdown between the UN and the Serbs. General Janvier pushed for an end to NATO air strikes in September 1995, fearful that their continuation might provoke Serbia's intervention in the war.

These and other events in the course of the fighting suggest to us that the Serbs were, in fact, responsive to—if not entirely cowed by—credible threats of force. The NATO ultimatum of summer 1993 concerning the Serb threat to Sarajevo, for example, resulted in an easing of the crisis produced by the Serb occupation of Mt. Igman. The NATO ultimatum of February 1994 led to the pullback of Serb heavy weapons from Sarajevo. From the Serb perspective, there is no doubt that a NATO military presence in Bosnia would have seriously undermined Serb military superiority. Karadžić is said to have remarked that one NATO unit used as a blocking force in the corridor around Brčko would have been sufficient to undermine the Serb war effort. Yet it appears that such limited use of ground troops while fighting was still in progress was not considered by Western policy-makers wary of an open-ended commitment.

These observations do not mean, however, that the use of force could bring the Serbs to the bargaining table in the absence of other pressures, or that force alone could assure victory for the Bosnian Muslims. In view of the cautious approach prevailing among military establishments in the West, it seems certain that any decision to engage in crisis intervention would have involved tens, if not hundreds, of thousands of troops, and would have focused on ending the fighting and preventing further ethnic cleansing at the least possible cost to the West rather than a permanent solution to the crisis. The U.S. decision in 1994 to create and rely on a local surrogate (Croatian) army to confront the Serbs makes it clear that Western policymakers viewed the costs of becoming engaged in direct ground combat to alter the territorial division of Bosnia as unacceptable. The consequences for Bosnia of any such early intervention in the absence of a political agreement between the warring parties thus seem equally clear: military intervention would almost certainly have meant partition largely along existing lines of confrontation—an outcome that favored the Serbs and was widely opposed in the West in 1992 and 1993.

In addition, policymakers had to weigh the potential reaction of General Mladić to any use of force. Throughout the war Mladić was adamant in his resistance to threats of force. Even in the waning moments of the war, he resisted relinquishing control over territory around Sarajevo in the face of massive NATO air strikes. Mladić, it can be suggested, recognized the importance of air power in the war, but also believed that the Serbs could challenge NATO's air supremacy by a combination of threats, stubbornness, and the taking of hostages, if necessary. From both the military and symbolic points of view, therefore, the capitulation of Mladić in September 1995 was a decisive moment in the Bosnian crisis, confirming the necessity of combined ground and air operations to achieve effective coercion, and removing a major obstacle to a negotiated end to the fighting and the opening of peace talks.

But were combined ground-air operations, by themselves, enough to end the fighting? Mladić's acquiescence may also be seen as confirming the importance of force as an instrument of diplomacy rather than simple coercion. Mladić had acknowledged as early as mid-April 1995—before the radical military and political changes of the spring and summer—that "if a political solution at the negotiating table is not found, the war will be long and exhausting for the Bosnian Serbs."[11] The United States now was offering such a political solution. As we argued in chapter 7, the political concessions made by the United States to the Serbs, including the later U.S.

acquiescence in the use of Serbian air power to stop the Muslim-Croat offensive against Banja Luka, were important—and necessary—elements in the effort to bring the fighting in Bosnia to an end and avert the risk of that fighting escalating to a confrontation between the regional powers.

The futility of projecting power into an ethnic conflict without tying its use to a political solution devised in advance was made dramatically evident in May and June 1995. As we saw in chapter 7, the ineffective NATO air strikes against the Bosnian Serbs carried out in late May under U.S. pressure produced a hostage crisis that compelled the UN to forswear the use of air power against the Bosnian Serbs. This effectively ended the UNPROFOR humanitarian operation. In early June U.S. policymakers, under domestic pressure not to deal with Milošević while the Bosnian Serbs held UN hostages and facing congressional pressure to lift the arms embargo, backed away from a compromise political solution negotiated by Frasure. Together, these actions amounted to forgoing both diplomacy and force, and helped set the stage for the tragic events in Srebrenica in July.

The projection of power absent any plan for a political solution to end the war was to invite the kind of open-ended intervention in Bosnia that U.S. and other Western military planners were so adamantly against. It was precisely the inability of the international community to come up with a political solution to which all sides could agree—or be pressured into accepting—that undercut those who wished to use force to end the war. As long as this remained the case, the use of force had to be channeled into humanitarian intervention and the establishment of "safe areas." Thus, any analysis of the Bosnian crisis must explain why a coherent policy stance was so long in developing—first under the ICFY, then in the Contact Group, and finally at Dayton.

Diplomacy

Humanitarian intervention was undertaken on the mistaken assumption that it could be separated from the political and military dimensions of the conflict. The advocates of using force to end the war failed to address the political issues that had given rise to the conflict in the first place. Similarly, diplomatic intervention in 1992 to negotiate a settlement and restore elements of the earlier *status quo* lacked the backing of the threat or use of force as a means of achieving and implementing an agreement. Indeed, it might be argued that the August 1992 London Conference and the resulting ICFY negotiations under Vance and Owen were initiated by the great powers primarily as a means to avoid becoming involved in the use of force in Bosnia. As the analysis of the Vance-Owen plan in chapter 5 makes clear, knowledge that the Western powers were not yet ready to undertake more forceful crisis intervention in Bosnia undermined the credibility of the mediators. Their task, in the words of the deputy co-chairman of the ICFY, Ambassador Herbert S. Okun, was "like playing baseball without a bat."[12]

Okun's metaphor is provocative. While it is clear from the analyses of preceding chapters that the West could not simply have bombed the Serbs into accepting a plan that did not address their interests, Okun reminds us of the desperate need for forceful implementation if any plan to end the fighting was to succeed. Yet, herein lies the dilemma surrounding the Vance-Owen plan; if it had been clear in advance that the West would implement the plan with force—an approach that might be characterized as imposing a settlement—the Serbs would likely have rejected it outright. The Serbs had fought too hard to take control of eastern Bosnia and the northern corridor—and committed too many atrocities in the effort to do so—simply to hand this territory back to the Muslims. It seems clear, therefore, that it was the probability that the Vance-Owen plan would *not* be enforced that first led Milošević to support it in January 1993, and to urge the Bosnian Serbs to do likewise. By the same token, it was the prospect of a U.S.-led intervention to implement the plan that led Milošević to dissociate himself from the plan in February–March 1993.

Nonetheless, when Vance and Owen began their effort in September 1992, negotiators did have certain cards to play that were not available to EC negotiators in 1991 or early 1992, in what we have called the stage of early intervention. First, Serbia was suffering under draconian economic sanctions. As a result, Milošević seemed ready to strike a deal on Bosnia. The price of that deal was, of course, the *de facto* partitioning of Bosnia. Second, contrary to Serb expectations, the fighting had not ended with a quick Serb victory. Third, Serb efforts to achieve a UN-monitored cease-fire in Bosnia akin to that which had been established in Croatia had gotten nowhere, largely due to the resistance of the Bosnian Muslims, backed by the United States. Thus, Milošević and the Bosnian Serbs faced the prospect of a drawn-out struggle and were not averse to a settlement that would ratify their gains in Bosnia, even if it required acknowledging the existence of a loosely constructed Bosnian state and forbade the Bosnian Serb republic from seceding. Belgrade remained interested in the plan as long as it remained consistent with its strategy of seeking a cease-fire and partition.

The Vance-Owen plan was attractive to international actors because, while it accommodated demands for ethno-territorial autonomy, it refused to legitimate ethnic cleansing. Moreover, it refused to entrust operation of post-settlement state institutions to the three warring parties alone. The highly intrusive involvement in implementation on the part of the international community called for by the Vance-Owen plan was similar to arrangements that Hampson argues have been crucial to the success of other peace settlements.[13] Finally, the Vance-Owen plan reserved ultimate authority for an international representative, acting in the capacity of *de facto* caretaker for the Bosnian state.

At the same time, we have suggested some of the deficiencies of the plan in chapter 5. From the perspective of crisis intervention, perhaps the most important defect was found in the military provisions of the plan. These were of critical importance because Vance and Owen proposed to rearrange the areas under the control of the combatants, as well as the administrative map of prewar Bosnia, in ways that would challenge ethnic cleansing and the power of the nationalist parties. As we pointed out in chapter 5, the January 1993 version of the plan did not contain an agreement on the withdrawal of opposing forces to their respective provinces, and had not resolved the territorial dispute in central Bosnia between Croat and Muslim forces. Combined with provisions for the separation of forces calling first for the establishment of a UN-protected cease-fire line, the uncertainties surrounding the withdrawal of forces threatened to reduce the plan—once implemented—to little more than a cease-fire in place. Hampson argues, for example, that "if the parties fail to abide by rigidly established timetables for demobilization of forces, the peace process can quickly become unhinged."[14] Yet, no further agreement on these crucial issues was reached.

The goals to be pursued by NATO ground troops tasked to implement the Vance-Owen plan remained unclear. If all three parties had accepted the Vance-Owen plan, it is possible that Western troops might have been deployed to enforce its implementation. But how would such troops have implemented such ambiguous provisions as those concerning the withdrawal of forces? If these troops were to engage in the aggressive use of force, as suggested in contemporary media reports on the NATO plans cited in chapter 5, it seems likely that they would have been drawn into firefights with forces on all three sides. Alternatively, what would the political fallout have been of allowing the Serbs to remain in control of eastern Bosnia as provided in the April Owen-Milošević agreement when the area was part of a province in which the Muslims were the putative majority? In light of the well-established interest of the great powers in minimizing their own casualties, it seems likely that ground troops would not have been asked to compel local forces to withdraw, with the result that crisis intervention in the form of ground troops deployed in May 1993 would have produced a partition on the basis of a cease-fire in place rather than implementation of the actual provisions of the Vance-Owen plan, and would not have reversed the effects of ethnic cleansing. A political solution—even the one outlined in Vance-Owen—would have remained as distant as ever.

This was an outcome widely opposed in the West. Indeed, an explicit, detailed argument for intervention to effect a straightforward partition published in June 1993[15] received widespread attention, but was bitterly criticized, and rejected by U.S. policymakers. Partition pure and simple laid bare the underlying impossibility of dividing Bosnia into three parts. Outright partition made sense only if the Bosnian Muslims were permitted a more generous territorial settlement in exchange for allowing the secession of the Bosnian Serbs and the Bosnian Croats. Yet this option was doubly impossible; both the United States and the Bosnian government rejected it out of hand, and the international community was unprepared to accept the destruction of the Bosnian state it had only recently recognized and seated in the UN. It was only when the United States became more fully engaged in the conflict, beginning in early 1994, that the partition solution began to find support in Washington; and then only after the formation of a federation between the Bosnian Croats and Muslims provided camouflage for that partition.

The Road to Dayton

Ending the conflict involved intense negotiations between U.S. diplomats and the warring parties, as described in chapter 7. But these masked a fundamental shift away from negotiation, or mediation, as the means of ending the war, and toward imposition of a solution. The lack of good faith—even duplicity—on the part of the warring leaderships, noted in our assessment of the Vance-Owen negotiations in chapter 5, reflected not only the moral deficiencies of the individuals concerned and, perhaps, certain Balkan cultural characteristics, but the nature of violent ethnic conflict itself. The coercive diplomacy adopted by the United States after May 1995 appears to have been a conscious effort to break out of the prior pattern of negotiations and impose a solution on the combatants that fit Western priorities; above all, to prevent a humiliating and costly Western retreat in the form of a UN withdrawal from Bosnia.

This change in U.S. strategy was the key element on the road to Dayton. But changes in the relationship between the two regional powers—Croatia and Serbia—played an equally important role in making Dayton possible. The restoration of Croatian control over Krajina removed a major obstacle to Serbian-Croatian cooperation. The Croatian offensive in Bosnia, and especially the threat that Banja Luka might fall to Croatian control, created additional pressure on Milošević to relinquish control over eastern

Slavonija—the last Serb-held territory in Croatia. Serbia and Croatia thus agreed on November 12 that control over eastern Slavonija would be returned to Croatia. This affirmation of Croatian territorial integrity set the stage for Croatian-Serbian collusion at Dayton. In the end, the common interest of Croatia and Serbia in achieving the *de facto* partition of Bosnia had a greater impact on the shape of the Dayton accords and their aftermath than the interests of any of the three warring parties.

Cultivating Ripeness

As the analyses in chapters 4 and 6 made clear, the war in Bosnia had reached a stalemate by the end of 1994. The United States had by this time become deeply involved in the search for a settlement. It had, in conjunction with the other members of the Contact Group, put forth a plan for ending the war—the contact group plan—that was to serve as the basis for the Dayton settlement. Serbia, suffering under sanctions, had supported the contact group plan and contributed to the growing isolation of the Bosnian Serbs. Still, there was little sign that an agreement to end the conflict was near. In large part, this was due to the resistance of the Bosnian Serbs to a settlement that would have limited their access to the vital east-west corridor at Brčko. At the same time, the establishment of safe areas took the pressure off the Contact Group to press for an immediate solution, while persistent differences over the use of air power divided the United States and the Europeans. The stalemate was thus not only military, but diplomatic. As late as July 1995, pessimism, not optimism, was the prevailing mood among international actors involved in Bosnia.

The apparent suddenness with which this situation changed led some analysts viewing the war through the lens of conflict resolution theory to suggest that the ability of the United States to broker the Dayton agreement in 1995 reflected the "ripening" of the conflict.[16] George Rudman makes the same argument concerning the Muslim-Croat federation agreement in February–March 1994.[17] In effect, so this argument goes, conditions on the ground became conducive to a settlement in late 1995 and the United States therefore acted. But this perspective views conditions on the ground in Bosnia-Herzegovina as far too independent of the actions of the main outside actors.

There is little evidence to suggest that any of the parties to these agreements actually was ready for a negotiated solution to the conflict in 1995. No "hurting stalemate" of the kind that William Zartman has suggested is conducive to a negotiated settlement existed. It was not the case that "the countervailing power of each side, though insufficient to make the

other side lose, prevents it from winning."[18] Rather, the situat
the contrary. As we reported in chapter 7, Muslim and Croatia
making substantial territorial advances as NATO carried out
paign in fall 1995, with the prospect of even greater gains. The Bosnian
Serbs had overrun Srebrenica and Žepa and were threatening Goražde. The
prospect that Muslim and Croatian forces might once again turn on each
other, or that Serbia might enter the war, suggested the real possibility of
escalation. It seems clear that action by the United States was decisive in
preventing this, and making agreement possible. And, contrary to the "ripening" thesis, changes in the dynamic of the conflict itself had their origins
in U.S. actions that began long before Dayton and were directed toward
achieving a reconciliation between the Muslims and Croats.

The accounts of Muslim-Croatian relations presented in chapters 4 and 5
make it clear that cooperation between the two sides became possible only
after each had carried out ethnic cleansing in central Bosnia and the Mostar
valley and secured control of their respective territories as part of the 1993
Muslim-Croat war, and after the failed negotiations conducted by Owen and
Stoltenberg in summer and fall 1993 had demonstrated to Croatia and the
Bosnian Croats that they could not achieve the straightforward tripartite
division of Bosnia they and the Serbs had been seeking. But, as we reported
in chapter 6, Croatian acquiescence to the 1994 federation agreement came
only under considerable pressure, and with the promise of considerable
rewards, from the United States. With the establishment of the Bosnian
(Muslim-Croat) Federation, the United States created a "fig leaf" with
which to cover partition, making it possible for the United States to take the
lead in bringing the fighting to an end. As we have argued in chapters 6 and
7, the United States undertook efforts beginning in 1994 to build up the
Croatian army as a counterweight to the Serbs, and to strengthen Muslim
forces through both open and covert means. By doing so, the United States
obviated the need to deploy U.S. ground troops against the Serbs, thus
altering the calculations underlying domestic political and professional military opposition to the use of air power. At the same time, the United States
began a long and difficult process of negotiating with Milošević as a means
of exerting pressure on the Bosnian Serbs, while accepting the need to
accommodate at least some of the Bosnian Serbs' political demands.

The key to success was to craft a compromise political settlement while
waiting for the proper moment to apply pressure to the combatants in order
to assure that they would negotiate under hard constraints to end the fighting. Timing was all important, and it must be said that everything did not
fall into place for U.S. policymakers until July 1995. By then, the Americans realized they would have to exert pressure on the Bosnian Muslims to

accept what amounted to a plan for the partition of Bosnia-Herzegovina. This realization brought the United States into close political alignment with its allies, facilitating agreement among them on the use of force and on the goals of that use.

The most important consequence of these changes in U.S. policy was that they allowed the United States—a distant power—to enter the fray on its own terms, in support of a strategy it had devised for itself in response to its own perceived interests. The United States was able to avoid the trap of attempting to implement a plan it had not authored, and for which there would be little domestic support in the United States—the situation it faced in connection with the Vance-Owen plan in 1993.

The NATO air campaign of 1995 was, as we argued in chapter 7, part of the effort to integrate what had up to then been two distinct dimensions of Western policy—political and military—rather than simply a response to the dramatic changes on the ground in summer 1995. As we pointed out in chapter 7, agreement among the Western allies to use force in support of a specific formula for ending the fighting was achieved after the twin debacles of ineffective NATO air strikes followed by the taking of UN troops as hostages by the Serbs in May 1995, and the fall of Srebrenica and Žepa in July. There is little doubt that the hostage crisis finally created a clear and pressing U.S. interest in Bosnia—averting a messy withdrawal of UN forces—and that the fall of Srebrenica and Žepa made the formula for partition advanced by the Contact Group easier to implement. But these events were preceded by months of intensive diplomacy among the great powers that began in late 1994 and culminated in the decisions agreed on among the Americans, British, and French in July 1995. As we have suggested in chapter 7, it was this diplomacy, and especially the evolution of the U.S. position in this period described in chapter 7, that brought the use of force into the service of an agreed formula for ending the conflict and thereby created the strategy of coercive diplomacy that led to Dayton. Thus, it would be more accurate to say that crisis intervention and the NATO air campaign reflected the "ripening" of Western—and particularly American—policies, rather than the "ripening" of the conflict itself. As Hampson has suggested, "ripeness is a cultivated, not inherited condition."[19]

The Ripening of U.S. Policy

U.S. policymakers entered the conflict without a clear understanding of how, in the absence of geostrategic competition with the Soviet Union for influence and power in the Balkans, conflict in Yugoslavia affected U.S. interests. Traditional, or "realist" conceptions of national interest focused the attention of policymakers on the consequences of the war for U.S. power. Because no such consequences were evident, U.S. policy remained passive. U.S. policymakers inclined to view the conflict in Bosnia in larger, geostrategic terms saw it as a factor affecting Balkan stability, relations between Greece and Turkey or the United States and Turkey, and U.S. relations with the Islamic world.[20] The failure of reports of atrocities and accusations of genocide to galvanize policymakers into action underscored the fact that, for so-called "realists," moral concerns remained secondary to concerns about relative national power. Because the fighting was not perceived as affecting national power, policymakers settled upon a strategy of "containment" that appeared to allow them to isolate the fighting and prevent it from destabilizing the region as a whole.

At lower levels of the policymaking community, in contrast, what might be called a "moralist" perspective appeared to dominate. The clash between "realism" and "moralism" led to several well-publicized resignations of lower-level functionaries who were persuaded of the moralist interpretation of the war.[21] As the reviews of conflicting interpretations of the war presented in chapters 3 and 5 suggest, the conflict between realism and moralism created a false dichotomy in the policy debate between "interest" and "morality." It is not that realist approaches to understanding and managing conflict are wrong; it is that they are, by themselves, an insufficient basis for resolving conflicts. Realist solutions tend to focus on establishing military balances, without regard for the willingness of parties actually to use their weapons; this is a self-defeating approach in the face of ethnic conflict. At the same time, moralists' emphasis on justice creates a confrontation between the "best" and the "good." Yet, as Hampson has argued, "Without peace there can be no justice. . . . [C]oncern for justice must be tempered by the realities of negotiation and the parties' interests in reaching a political settlement."[22] The war in Bosnia challenged Western (European and U.S.) interests and Western (if not universally human) morality. But Western policymakers could not meet the moral challenge of ethnic cleansing and atrocities, perhaps even genocide, successfully without taking into account interests calculated on the basis of realist formulas; just as they could not entirely ignore morality in the pursuit of interests.

Only the perception of clear threats to strategic interests provided effective counterweight to the disincentives to crisis intervention present in Bosnia up to the end of 1994. None of the interests articulated by Western, and especially U.S. policymakers before 1995 required intervention to fulfill. The interests defined by President Clinton in 1993 and 1994, and reported in chapters 5 and 6, could be—and were—adequately served by a strategy of containment rather than intervention. The accountability of U.S.

leaders to a public reluctant to see U.S. ground troops become involved in combat was an important and legitimate constraint on U.S. action. As we have argued in chapter 7, U.S. policymakers intervened only when they perceived developments in Bosnia as threatening strategic national interests with respect to the Western alliance, and the domestic political interests of the administration itself.

With time, concerns about the indirect effects of the fighting on a broader range of U.S. interests began to emerge. Some U.S. policymakers became concerned about the potential consequences for postcommunist and other new democracies of allowing ethnic conflict to go unchecked. By July 1993, for example, senior U.S. intelligence officials were seeking guidance from the scholarly community as to whether the relationship between ethnic identity and war in the former Yugoslavia was a portent of wider chaos in the post–Cold War world, especially in the Balkans and former Soviet Union. Other analysts, both inside and outside the government, became concerned about the repeated failure of the United States and its allies to follow up on their warnings and threats to the Serbs. The interest of the United States in preserving its credibility, and in maintaining the coherence of NATO, gradually came to be perceived as at risk in Bosnia-Herzegovina.[23] All these factors may have played a role in redirecting U.S. policy. But we have argued in chapter 7 that it was the danger of involvement in a UN withdrawal operation and the implications of Bosnian involvement for the upcoming presidential election that finally led U.S. policymakers to act. Thus, the characteristics of the settlement imposed on the warring parties reflect primarily the interests of the United States and its allies in ending the fighting, rather than the requirements of establishing a stable peace.

Imposing Agreement

Once engaged, the United States dominated the negotiations that led up to the Dayton accords. There is a temptation to see this as a naked exercise of power, and to raise the question of why the United States did not use force sooner. But the ability of the United States to impose the Dayton accords reflected the emergence of U.S. interests, the fruition of intensive U.S. diplomacy among its allies, and favorable military developments on the ground in summer 1995 that had their origins in U.S. actions that began in early 1994. The success of the U.S. effort to impose an agreement on all three warring parties also depended, finally, on four other critical factors.

First, as we noted earlier, the two local powers—Croatia and Serbia— were once again able to act together on their common interest in partitioning Bosnia-Herzegovina. This interest was consistent with the plan put forward by the United States. Their interest in partition led each of them to control their respective client groups in Bosnia and pressure them into accepting the U.S. proposals. Hampson's analysis of five different peace settlements led him to conclude that

> a combination of international and regional intervention strategies is the pre-requisite for conflict termination and that the success of a peace settlement is inextricably tied to the interests of neighboring regional powers and their overall commitment to the peace process. Where such a commitment is lacking, the risk of failure is higher.[24]

Dayton, too, was in large part an agreement forged between two regional powers—at the expense of the lesser regional actors—with the coercive backing of the distant great power. To overlook this fact is to misunderstand and to underestimate the crucial importance of regional powers in resolving ethnic conflicts.

The United States's ability to influence the key parties to the agreement—Croatia, Serbia, and the Bosnian Muslims—and its willingness to pressure each of them into compliance was the second key factor that made Dayton possible. As we noted in chapter 7, bringing all three parties to the table required the United States to control Croatian territorial ambitions by allowing the Serbs to use air power to stop the Croatian offensive against Banja Luka in the closing days of the war; to negotiate directly with Milošević over ending sanctions against Yugoslavia (Serbia and Montenegro) and with the Bosnian Serbs over ending the fighting; and, finally, to pressure the Bosnian Muslims into acquiescing to political concessions to the Serbs, including relinquishing ethnically Muslim territory in eastern Bosnia and recognizing the Republika Srpska.

Such pressure had heretofore been nearly impossible politically for U.S. policymakers. They were able freely to pressure—and, as we reported in chapter 7, even threaten—the Muslims only after they had committed themselves to bombing the Serbs. The NATO air campaign protected U.S. policymakers from the charge of having given in to the Serbs, at least in the short run. But U.S. policymakers paid a price for achieving an end to the fighting—the tacit recognition and partial institutionalization of partition and of ethnic cleansing. This has rendered the post-Dayton efforts to reconstruct Bosnia immensely difficult; notwithstanding the pledges of all three formerly warring parties to allow refugees to return to their homes, and the creation of institutions meant to bind Bosnians of all nationalities into one state.

In exchange for their agreement, the Bosnian Muslims extracted from the United States a commitment to provide the Bosnian army with arms and training. The U.S. commitment to arm and train (officially, "train and equip") the Bosnian government army was the third critical factor that made the Dayton agreement possible. But it, too, undermines the long-term stability of the Dayton arrangements. As we have argued in chapter 7, the arming of the Bosnian Muslims through both open programs and covert activities— rather than undertaking determined efforts to impose deep arms reductions on the Bosnian parties and neighboring states so as to reduce their warmaking capabilities—makes the renewal of war more likely, if not inevitable, should the international force leave Bosnia.

The fourth factor that made it possible for the United States to impose an agreement was the expectation of all parties that it could be counted on to enforce an agreement in an impartial fashion. In this there was something of an irony. The United States had, during the course of the war, angered or alienated virtually all of the actors in the Bosnian drama, beginning with its own allies. The Europeans were relegated to the role of secondary actors in the negotiations at Dayton, although the plan itself borrowed a great deal from earlier efforts by the Europeans to negotiate a solution. The Clinton administration had ignored the pleas of the Bosnian government to lift the arms embargo. At the moment military victory seemed imminent to the Muslims, the Americans compelled the Bosnian government to accept a peace that threatened to leave them with a nonviable state. U.S. negotiators even denied them Brčko, a strategically located, formerly Muslim-majority city that had been allocated to the Bosnians under Vance-Owen. The Serbs, for their part, had suffered under draconian sanctions initiated and enforced by the United States, and then watched the United States side with Croatia while the Serb population of Krajina was cleansed, and its remnants subjected to systematic abuse and murder on a scale that might raise the question of genocide. Perhaps only Croatia had no reason to feel offended by the United States. Nonetheless, the United States was able to command more authority, and ultimately to engender more trust in its word, than any other actor in the conflict.

The U.S. role in ending the Bosnian conflict thus resists easy analysis. As we noted earlier, it was inconsistent with the historical role of the distant great power in the Balkans. The U.S. intervention also developed in apparent contradiction to the established norms of peacekeeping; according to which peace enforcement through the projection of power into a conflict is the role of regional powers, while the task of peacekeeping is carried out by the UN. The contradiction may be only apparent, however. The UN forces were deployed to Bosnia in 1992 to facilitate humanitarian relief, not to carry out a traditional peacekeeping operation. Peacekeeping roles emerged quickly out of this basic mission, and out of the gradual expansion of tasks—"mission creep"—imposed on the UN forces by the Security Council; the creation of safe areas and the increased responsibilities associated with them being the most obvious examples. Regional powers were active in the conflict from the beginning, but as predators, not peacemakers or peacekeepers. Finally, the task facing the international community after Dayton was not peacekeeping, but the reconstruction of a failed state, a task the UN could not carry out on its own. Viewed in this light, the conflict in Bosnia and the role assumed by the United States in its resolution may well be a harbinger of conflicts yet to come in other parts of the world, and the challenges they will present to Western policymakers.

Beyond Dayton: Cease-Fire, Peace, or Partition?

The Dayton process consisted of adversarial negotiations, mediated by the United States. The result was that Dayton resembled an armistice between warring states more than a social compact for the rebuilding of Bosnia. The obvious vulnerability of the common Bosnian institutions designed at Dayton to paralysis at the hands of one or another determined party (as discussed in chapter 7) reflects the failure of the Dayton plan to resolve the fundamental conflict over the definition of the state—indeed, over whether the Bosnian state should exist at all—that lay at the base of the fighting. As a Bosnian Croat politician remarked in summer 1997, "The key issue that led us into this war is, What kind of Bosnia and Herzegovina? The three sides give us completely different answers." The politician Mate Franjević went on to explain that by denying the Croats their own state, depriving Muslims of a truly unified Bosnia, and establishing a Bosnian Serb state-within-a-state, "Dayton has virtually assured that peace must fail."[25]

The key issue with respect to assessing whether early intervention might have produced a more desirable result than the crisis intervention that produced Dayton is, however, not one of institutions, or of borders. It is whether ethnic cleansing could have been prevented or reversed by earlier intervention, and whether ethnic cleansing will be reversed as a result of the Dayton accords. Earlier intervention could only have resulted in partition. While the institutional formulas for preserving the integrity of Bosnia-Herzegovina contained in the Vance-Owen plan may have been superior to those contained in the Dayton agreement, our earlier analysis makes it clear that there was almost no chance that intervening troops would have implemented them fully. Later plans, as we argued in chapter 6, offered only partition as a solution. Only the reversal of ethnic cleansing through the rebuilding of inter-ethnic and inter-entity links, and the eventual resettlement of refugees, can prevent the distinct entities created at Dayton—as

well as the Bosnian (Muslim-Croat) Federation—from dissolving into separate ethnic states.

Yet, refugee return is a process fraught with danger—both for the
individuals involved and the future of peace in Bosnia. If refugee return
is imposed on unwilling communities, or if it is used by one side or the
other as a means of military infiltration of the receiving community, it is
certain to become a source of future conflict. If refugee return is
achieved only because it is backed up by the implicit threat of the international troops in Bosnia, then it will be undone immediately upon the
departure of those troops; probably by force. Hence, relying on international troops alone to impose refugee return may create conditions that
will make it difficult for those troops to be withdrawn. This is the paradox of the forceful approach to refugee return, and the probable reason
why it has not been pursued up to now.

This paradox is rooted not only in the intense differences between the
formerly warring parties, but in the profound "reality gap" to which we
made allusion earlier in this study between the Western model of what
Bosnia ought to be that has driven Western policies since Dayton, and
what Bosnia has become in the aftermath of catastrophe. The Western
model presumes respect for legal norms, the benevolent effect of enlightened self-interest in guiding social relations, and tolerance and understanding among different ethnic groups. It presumes that the multicultural ideal
can be revived. But Bosnia has become a land characterized by a struggle for survival rooted in ethnic solidarity, disillusionment with ethnic
coexistence, and the predominance of narrow ethnic self-interests over
the commonweal. The contradiction between the Western vision of Bosnia
as a civil state and the nationalists' desire to define the state in ethnic
terms remains unresolved.

The gulf between these clashing realities cannot be overcome by force
alone. It may, however, be bridged through efforts to cultivate the emergence of a new generation of "post-nationalist" Croats, Serbs, and
Muslims who will be willing to cooperate—at least when mutual benefits are to be gained. To achieve this, international support for the rebuilding of Bosnia must be constructed in a manner that encourages the
reintegration of its infrastructures and local economies. The nurturing of
individuals and groups whose interests cut across the artificial boundaries created by war and the Dayton accord may lead to the emergence
of what John Paul Lederach terms a "peace constituency."[26] It is through
limited, self-interested cooperation across ethnic boundaries that, over
what may be a very long term, a culture of trust and enlightened cooperation among the three ethnic communities may re-emerge among some

social sectors at the grass roots in Bosnia.[27] The effort is certainly worth making.

Until civic organizations and institutions are stronger, until economic relations of mutual interest that cut across ethnic boundaries are more widespread, and until peace constituencies emerge among all three national groups, elections and electoral politics are unlikely to lead to democratization in Bosnia. On the contrary, they are likely to contribute to the consolidation of nationalist power. The re-emergence of civil society in Bosnia, of economic interests that cut across inter-ethnic boundaries, and especially of peace constituencies may also make it possible to achieve the arrest and prosecution of war criminals at far less cost to the West and to peace in Bosnia than is now possible. Strong civic institutional networks that include independent media and strong, autonomous economic actors, backed up by a continuing international military and police presence on the ground, may provide political counterweights to the criminal networks operating on all sides in post-Dayton Bosnia that support and protect indicted and suspected war criminals. When the strength of "interest" and the demands of "justice" coincide, arrest and prosecution will follow.

Like the Dayton agreement itself, genuine peace in Bosnia will depend greatly on Croatia and Serbia. The establishment of democratic regimes in these states—processes that also may take many years—will contribute to the process of ethnic reconciliation in Bosnia. While the democratization of Croatia and Serbia will not guarantee peace in Bosnia, the failure to democratize these states almost certainly guarantees further conflict. Here one is reminded forcefully of the fate of Bosnia-Herzegovina following the collapse of Yugoslavia. Efforts at reconciliation in Bosnia may be destroyed overnight as the result of developments in Serbia or Croatia. This is why the task of the international community is so unenviable; one can never really be sure when the task of democratization is complete; that is, when an apparently functioning society can safely be left to its own devices. Disengagement of the international community cannot come precipitously lest it undercut any progress toward a *modus vivendi.*

Western policymakers, who will be required to support efforts to build constituencies for peace in Bosnia, to democratize Bosnia and its neighbors, and to convince their constituents to support these efforts, therefore face a difficult task. They must realize that if they rely on the power of economic interest and the impact of grassroots efforts at reconciliation, it will take many years to establish genuine peace in Bosnia. If peace is to be achieved in any reasonable timeframe, the goals of Western policy must be redefined; the idealized vision of a multicultural state must be replaced by a more practical and achievable vision of an integrated, but still multinational community. They must not mistake the reaching of certain "targets" under pressure—for example, the adoption of a common currency—for the genuine reintegration of Bosnian society. U.S. policymakers, in particular, must abandon the attempt to remake Bosnia in the image of the United States and look instead to the integrated, democratic, and still multinational European Community of its allies as a model by which to define the Bosnian future. By doing so, they will not make their task any less difficult. But they will close the gap between Western policies and Bosnian realities.

Notes

Chapter 1: Introduction

1. For useful syntheses of this literature, see Joseph Rothschild, *Ethnopolitics: A Conceptual Framework* (New York: Columbia University Press, 1981), and Donald L. Horowitz, *Ethnic Groups in Conflict* (Berkeley: University of California Press, 1985).

2. See Saul Newman, *Ethnoregional Conflict in Democracies: Mostly Ballots, Rarely Bullets* (Westport, CT: Greenwood Press, 1996).

3. *New York Times,* November 1, 1995, p. A1.

4. Scott Reid, *Canada Remapped: How the Partition of Quebec Will Reshape the Nation* (Vancouver: Pulp Press, 1992), p. 34.

5. For a brief discussion of these two literatures, see Timothy D. Sisk, *Power Sharing and International Mediation in Ethnic Conflicts* (Washington, DC: United States Institute of Peace Press, 1996).

6. For explication of this view, see Barry R. Posen, "The Security Dilemma and Ethnic Conflict," in *Ethnic Conflict and International Security,* Michael E. Brown, ed. (Princeton: Princeton University Press, 1993), pp. 103–24.

7. Horowitz, *Ethnic Groups in Conflict* and *idem, A Democratic South Africa?* (Berkeley: University of California Press, 1991).

8. Robert Cooper and Mats Berdal, "Outside Intervention in Ethnic Conflicts," in Brown, ed., *Ethnic Conflict and International Security,* p. 203.

9. Lori Fisler Damrosch, "Changing Conceptions of Intervention in International Law," in *Emerging Norms of Justified Intervention,* Laura W. Reed and Cal Kaysen, eds. (Cambridge, MA: American Academy of Arts and Sciences, 1993), p. 98.

Chapter 2: Bosnian Political History

1. Colin Heywood, "Bosnia Under Ottoman Rule, 1463–1800," in *The Muslims of Bosnia-Herzegovina,* Mark Pinson, ed. (Cambridge: Harvard University Press, 1994), p. 24.

2. Xavier Bougarel, "Yugoslav Wars." Paper presented to the annual meeting of the American Association for the Advancement of Slavic Studies (September 1988), pp. 8–9.

3. Muhamed Hadžijahić, Mahmud Trajlić, and Nijaz Sukrić, *Islam i muslimani u Bosni i Hercegovini* (Sarajevo: Starješinstvo Islamske zajednice, 1977), pp. 19ff.

4. Muhamed Hadžijahić, *Od tradicije do identiteta: Geneza nacionlnog pitanja bosanskih Muslimana* (Sarajevo: Svjetlost, 1974), pp. 84–85. For a further discussion of Muslim national identity see Sabrina Ramet, "Primordial Ethnicity or Modern National-ism: The Case of Yugoslavia's Muslims, Reconsidered," in *Muslim Communities Re-emerge,* Andrea Kappeler, Gerhard Simon, and Georg Brunner, eds. (Durham, NC: Duke University Press, 1994), pp. 111–38.

5. Hadžijahić, *Od tradicije do identiteta,* p. 88.

6. *Ibid.,* pp. 69–70; and Salim Ćerić, *Muslimani srpskohrvatskog jezika* (Sarajevo: Svjetlost, 1968), pp. 119, 122–23.

7. Hadžijahić, *Od tradicije do identiteta,* pp. 107, 213–16.

8. Hadžijahić, et al., *Islam i muslimani,* pp. 124–26, and Hadžijahić, *Od tradicije do identiteta,* pp. 107, 213–16.

9. Ćerić, *Muslimani srpskohrvatskog jezika,* pp. 169ff.

10. For a similar argument, see Robert Donia and William G. Lockwood, "The Bosnian Muslims: Class, Ethnicity, and Political Behavior in a European State," in *Muslim-Christian Conflicts: Economic, Political and Social Origins,* Suad Joseph and Barbara L. K. Pillsbury, eds. (Boulder: Westview, 1978), pp. 185–207.

11. For a description of the division of Bosnia in 1939, see Ivo Banac, "Bosnian Muslims: From Religious Community to Socialist Nationhood," in Pinson, ed., *The Muslims of Bosnia-Herzegovina,* p. 140.

12. *Ibid.*

13. For a good description of Communist policy toward Bosnia before and im-mediately after World War II, see Wolfgang Höpken, "Yugoslavia's Communists and the Bosnian Muslims," in Kappeler, et al., *Muslim Communities Reemerge,* pp. 214–47; and Noel Malcolm, *Bosnia: A Short History* (New York: New York University Press, 1994), pp. 180–81.

14. Enver Redžić, *Nacionalni odnosi u Bosni i Hercegovini 1941–1945 u analizama jugoslavenske istoriografije* (Sarajevo: Akademija nauka i umjetnosti Bosne i Hercegov-ine, 1989), p. 103.

15. Ljiljana Smajlović notes that Tito offered Bosnia-Herzegovina a port at the end of the war, but the offer was turned down by Djuro Pucar ("From the Heart of the Heart of the Former Yugoslavia," *Wilson Quarterly* [Summer 1995], p. 106).

16. For an example of regions defined entirely in geographic terms, see Stjepko Golubic, Susan Campbell, and Thomas Golubic, "How Not to Divide the Indivisible," in *Why Bosnia?* Rabia Alia and Lawrence Lifschultz, eds. (Stony Creek, CT: Pamphleteer's Press, 1993), pp. 209–32, especially the map on p. 223.

17. Redžić, *Nacionalni odnosi u Bosni i Hercegovini,* p. 91; and Vera Kržišnik-Bukić, *Cazinska buna 1950* (Sarajevo: Svjetlost, 1991), pp. 24–27.

18. *The Fall of Yugoslavia: The Third Balkan War* 3rd rev. ed (New York: Penguin Books, 1996), p. 152. See also Kržišnik-Bukić, *Cazinska buna 1950.*

19. *Ibid.,* pp. 152–53.

20. Robert J. Donia and John V.A. Fine, Jr., *Bosnia and Hercegovina: A Tradition Betrayed* (New York: Columbia University Press, 1994), p. 118.

21. An account of village life and of relations among the Croats and Muslims in central Bosnia may be found in Tone Bringa, *Being a Muslim the Bosnian Way: Identity and Community in a Central Bosnian Village* (Princeton: Princeton University Press, 1995). An excellent account of the persistence of traditional values in the countryside

can be found in William G. Lockwood, *European Muslims in Western Bosnia* (New York: Academic Press, 1975).

22. Avdo Sučeska, "Osnovne osobenosti položaja Bosne u Osmansko-turskoj državi," in Dubravko Lovrenović, et al., *Istina o Bosni i Hercegovini* (Sarajevo: Altermedia, 1991), pp. 29–41.

23. Data on the rural and urban distribution of the ethnic communities are available only for 1981. Savezni zavod za statistiku, "Stanovništvo prema nacinalnom sastavu i tipu naselja," *Popis stanovništva 1981* Knjiga I, Podaci po naseljima i opštinama (Belgrade: Savezni zavod za statistiku, 1991), pp. 17–22. Harry Bauer and Thomas Kimmig ("Frieden um jeden Preis," in *Bosnien und Europa: Die Ethnisierung der Gesellschaft,* Nenad Stefanov and Michael Werz, eds. [Frankfurt: Fischer Taschenbuch Verlag, 1994], p. 48), assert that 70 percent of the Bosnian Muslims lived in the cities. It is not clear where this figure comes from. If it is based on unpublished data from the 1991 census, it represents a drastic redistribution and urbanization of the Muslim population between 1981 and 1991.

24. The exact number of *opštine* in Bosnia-Herzegovina depends on whether those of the Sarajevo region are included in the count individually or as a group.

25. Calculations based on data in Savezni zavod za statistiku, *Statistički Bilten* no. 1295, "Nacionalni sastav stanovništva po opštinama" (Belgrade: Savezni zavod za statistiku and Savremena administracija, 1991).

26. Steven L. Burg and Michael L. Bernbaum, "Community, Integration, and Stability in Multinational Yugoslavia," *American Political Science Review* 83, no. 2 (June 1989), pp. 535–54. Cf. Dusko Sekulic, Garth Massey, and Randy Hodson, "Who Were the Yugoslavs? Failed Sources of a Common Identity in the Former Yugoslavia," *American Sociological Review* 59 (1994), pp. 83–97.

27. In urban areas in 1981, 40.2 percent of the population was Muslim, while in all of Bosnia-Herzegovina, 39.5 percent of the population was Muslim. Serbs made up 27.8 percent of the urban population in 1981, and 32 percent of the population of the republic as a whole. Savezni zavod za statistiku, *Nacionalni sastav stanovništva SFR Jugoslavije,* Knjiga I, "Podaci po naseljima i opštinama" (Belgrade: Savezni zavod za statistiku, 1991), Table 2, p. 17.

28. Xavier Bougarel, *Bosnie: Anatomie d'un conflit* (Paris: La Découverte, 1996), pp. 92–93. A map of the voting in Sarajevo by nationality was prepared by the CIA, "1990 Election Results in Sarajevo Opstina by Ethnic Compositions of Political Parties," IMF 027 (R00480) 11/09/95.

29. Enver Redžić, *Nacionalni odnosi u Bosni i Hercegovini,* p. 27.

30. Noel Malcolm insists that the periods of disorder were an exception in the history of Bosnia. *Bosnia: A Short History,* p. xxi.

31. Ibrahim Tepić, "Položaj Bosne i Hercegovine u osmanskom carstvu," in Lovrenović, et al., *Istina o Bosni i Hercegovini,* p. 49.

32. *Ibid.*

33. Kržišnik-Bukić, *Cazinska buna 1950.*

34. *Black Lamb and Grey Falcon: A Journey Through Yugoslavia* (New York: Viking Press, 1968), vol. I, p. 327.

35. For the Serbian question, see Dušan T. Bataković, *Prelude to Sarajevo: The Serbian Question in Bosnia and Herzegovina, 1878–1914* (Belgrade: Serbian Academy of Sciences and Arts, 1996).

36. Ibrahim Tepić, "Državnopravni i politički položaj BiH za vrijeme austrougarske vladavine 1878–1914," in Lovrenović, et al., *Istina o Bosni i Hercegovini,* p. 57.

37. Robert J. Donia, *Islam Under the Double Eagle* (New York: Columbia University Press, 1981), p. 39. Cf. the discussions in Hadžijahić, et al., *Islam i muslimani;* Hadžijahić, *Od tradicije do identiteta;* and Ćerić, *Muslimani srpskohrvatskog jezika.*

38. Donia, *Islam Under the Double Eagle,* pp. 168ff.

39. Donia and Lockwood, "The Bosnian Muslims," p. 193.

40. Wayne S. Vucinich, "Yugoslavs of Muslim Faith," in *Yugoslavia,* Robert J. Kerner, ed. (Berkeley: University of California Press, 1949) p. 270.

41. Tepić, "Državnopravni položaj BiH za vrijeme austrougarske vladavine," pp. 48–49.

42. Autonomy of religious institutions was suppressed in 1929 but restored in 1935 under a deal in which the JMO re-entered the government. In the 1938 elections the JMO participated in the government coalition, but for the first time did not obtain a majority of the Muslim vote in Bosnia. See Bougarel, *Bosnie: Anatomie d'un conflit,* p. 33.

43. Vlado Azinović, "Bosna i Hercegovina u državnoj zajednici jugoslavenskih naroda," in Lovrenović, et al., *Istina o Bosni i Hercegovini,* p. 167.

44. Vucinich, "Yugoslavs of Muslim Faith," p. 271. Vucinich quotes Spaho: "If Bosnia and Hercegovina cannot get autonomy then we cannot at any price allow the region to be divided, but let the whole of it go to Serbia."

45. Hadžijahić, *Od tradicije do identiteta,* p. 227.

46. Redžić, *Nacionalni odnosi u Bosni i Hercegovini,* pp. 117–19. See also Höpken, "Yugoslavia's Communists and the Bosnian Muslims," p. 224, and Azinović, "Bosna i Hercegovina u državnoj zajednici," p. 167.

47. Azinović, "Bosna i Hercegovina u državnoj zajednici," p. 73.

48. Höpken, "Yugoslavia's Communists and the Bosnian Muslims," p. 225.

49. Safet Bandžović, *Ratne tragedije Muslimana* (Novi Pazar: Udruženje pisaca Sandžaka, 1993), p. 20.

50. Paul Shoup, *Communism and the Yugoslav National Question* (New York: Columbia University Press, 1968), pp. 66ff. The best overall treatment of the Muslims in World War II is to be found in Yeshayahu A. Jelenik, "Bosnia-Herzegovina at War: Relations Between Moslems and Non-Moslems," *Holocaust and Genocide Studies* 5, no. 3 (1990), pp. 275–92.

51. See Robert Hayden, "Recounting the Dead: The Rediscovery and Redefinition of Wartime Massacres in Late- and Post-Communist Yugoslavia," in *Memory, History and Opposition Under State Communism,* Rubie S. Watson, ed. (Santa Fe, NM: School of American Research Press, 1994), pp. 167–84.

52. Kržišnik-Bukić, *Cazinska buna 1950,* p. 23.

53. Bandžović, *Ratne tragedije Muslimana,* p. 25.

54. Jozo Tomasevich, *War and Revolution in Yugoslavia 1941–1945: The Chetniks* (Stanford: Stanford University Press, 1975), pp. 256–61. See also Vladimir Dedijer and Antun Miletić, *Genocid nad Muslimanima, 1941–1945: Sbornik dokumenata i svjedočenja* (Sarajevo: Svjetlost, 1990), chapters 2–4. For a Muslim view of these events, see Smail Čekić, *Agresija na Bosnu: Genocid nad Bošnjacima 1991–1993* (Sarajevo: Ljiljan, 1994), chapter 1. For an account by Adil Zulfikarpašić, who at the time was a Partisan, see "Put u Foču," in Adil Zulfikarpašić, *Članci i intervjui* (Sarajevo: Bošnjački institut, 1991), pp. 12–23.

55. Kržišnik-Bukić, *Cazinska buna 1950,* p. 27.

56. Enver Redžić, *Muslimansko Autonomaštvo i 13. SS Divizija* (Sarajevo: Svjetlost, 1987), pp. 176–82, and Redžić, *Nacionalni odnosi u Bosni i Hercegovini,* pp. 88–89.

57. Bogoljub Kočović, *Žrtve drugog svetskog rata u Jugoslaviji* (London: Veritas Foundation Press, 1985), p. 70.

58. Tomasevich, *War and Revolution in Yugoslavia,* pp. 226–27.

59. Lucien Karchmar, *Draza Mihailovic and the Rise of the Chetnik Movement* (New York: Garland Publishing, 1987), p. 493. For more on the efforts of the Nedić government to annex eastern Bosnia during World War II, see Redžić, *Nacionalni odnosi u Bosni i Hercegovini,* p. 48.

60. Karchmar, *Draza Mihailovic and the Rise of the Chetnik Movement,* p. 446.

61. Vladimir Ćorović, *Političke prilike u Bosni i Hercegovini* (Belgrade: Politika, 1939), p. 69.

62. Enver Redžić, *Tokovi i otpori* (Sarajevo: Svjetlost, 1970), p. 109.

63. Atif Purivatra, *Nacionalni i politički razvitak Muslimana* (Sarajevo: Svjetlost, 1972), p. 128n. The Croatian and Serbian parties grudgingly acquiesced in this decision three years later. See Zachary T. Irwin, "The Islamic Revival and the Muslims of Bosnia Hercegovina," *East European Quarterly* 17, no. 4 (January 1984), p. 444.

64. Hadžijahić, *Od tradicije do identiteta,* p. 223.

65. *Ibid.,* p. 82.

66. *Ibid.,* p. 177.

67. *Ibid.,* p. 121.

68. Ethnic composition of marriages is calculated from data presented in Savezni zavod za statistiku, *Demografska statistika 1981* (Belgrade: Savezni zavod za statistiku, 1986), pp. 228–29. Srdjan Bogosavljević has calculated that 16.8 percent of all married couples in Bosnia in 1981 were of mixed or "Yugoslav" nationality, and 15.8 percent of all children came from mixed marriages, in "Bosna i Hercegovina u ogledalu statistike," in *Bosna i Hercegovina izmedju rata i mira,* Dušan Janjić and Paul Shoup, eds. (Belgrade: Dom Omladine, 1992), pp. 32, 33.

69. *Ibid.,* p. 32. Bogosavljević also notes that of all the children of mixed marriages, by far the largest group (80,000) had at least one parent who was a Yugoslav. About 17,000 out of almost 230,000 children of mixed marriages whose parents were of different nationalities were of Serb-Croat origin. Only 6,000 were of Muslim-Serb origin and 4,000 of Muslim-Croat origin. Without citing sources, Bauer and Kimmig ("Frieden um jeden Preis," p. 47) assert that there were less than 1 percent mixed marriages in the villages in Bosnia.

70. These and data to follow are from Bogosavljević, "Bosna i Hercegovina u ogledalu statistike," pp. 24–29.

71. Dušan Miljković, ed., *Yugoslavia 1945–1985: Statistical Review* (Belgrade: Federal Statistical Office, 1986), p. 198.

72. Marie-Janine Calic, *Der Krieg in Bosnien-Herzegowina: Ursachen, Konfliktstrukturen, International Lósungsversuche* (Frankfurt: Suhrkamp Verlag, 1995), p. 74. See also Irena Reuter-Hendrichs, "Jugoslawiens Muslime," *Südosteuropa Mitteilungen* 2 (1989), pp. 111–12, 113.

73. For data on the growth of the Islamic community, see Steven L. Burg, "The Political Integration of Yugoslavia's Muslims: Determinants of Success and Failure," *The Carl Beck Papers in Russian and East European Studies* 203 (1983).

74. For a hostile reaction to this argument, see Salim Ćerić, *O jugoslovenstvu i bosanstvu* (Sarajevo: Oslobodjenje, n.d.), pp. 49–84. See also Esad Ćimić, "Osobenosti nacionalnog formiranja muslimana," *Pregled* 4 (April 1974), pp. 389–408.

75. For the trials, see Irwin, "The Islamic Revival and the Muslims of Bosnia Hercegovina," and Reuter-Hendrichs, "Jugoslawiens Muslime," pp. 105–15.

76. Steven L. Burg, "Research Note: New Data on the League of Communists," *Slavic Review* 46, 3–4 (Fall/Winter 1987), pp. 553–67.

77. *Borba,* February 11, 1989, p. 4. See also *Nova Hrvatska* no. 4 (1989), p. 6.

78. *NIN,* February 18, 1990, pp. 12–15. In February 1990 the only party that had begun to organize was the Greens.

79. Suad Arnautović, *Izbori u Bosni i Hercegovini '90* (Sarajevo: Promocult, 1996), p. 11 (note 2).

80. Xavier Bougarel, "Bosnia and Herzegovina: State and Communitarianism," in *Yugoslavia and After: A Study in Fragmentation, Despair and Rebirth,* David A. Dyker and Ivan Vejvoda, eds. (London: Longman, 1996), p. 96.

81. For an excellent summary of the views of the national parties, see Calic, *Der Krieg in Bosnien-Hercegovina,* pp. 68–82. A retrospective view of the 1990 elections and the positions of the national parties is provided by Arnautović in *Izbori u Bosni i Hercegovini '90,* pp. 39ff.

82. Milan Andrejevich, "Bosnia-Herzegovina: Yugoslavia's Linchpin," *Report on Eastern Europe* 1, no. 49 (December 7, 1990), p. 24.

83. Arnautović, *Izbori u Bosni i Hercegovini '90,* p. 44, note 16.

84. *Borba,* October 23, 1990, as translated in Foreign Broadcast Information Service, *Daily Report: Eastern Europe* (henceforth: FBIS, *EEU*), October 30, 1990, p. 57.

85. *Borba,* November 12, 1990, p. 4, as translated in FBIS, *EEU,* November 19, 1990, pp. 78–80.

86. Arnautović, *Izbori u Bosni i Hercegovini '90,* p. 42, note 10.

87. *Ibid.,* p. 45.

88. *Ibid.*

89. *Ibid.,* p. 43.

90. Vladimir Goati, "Politički život Bosne i Hercegovine," in Janjić and Shoup, eds., *Bosna i Hercegovina izmedju rata i mira,* p. 55.

91. For analyses of why the anti-nationalist parties did so poorly, and the nationalists so well, see Christian Promitzer, "Die Einebnung der Vielfalt: Nationen und Nationalismus in Bosnien-Herzegowina und im ehemaligen Jugoslawien," in Stefanov and Werz, eds., *Bosnien und Europa,* p. 20; and Bougarel, *Bosnie: Anatomie d'un conflit,* pp. 46–47.

92. For a partial list of these parties, see Tanjug, October 8, 1990, as translated in FBIS, *EEU,* October 10, 1990, p. 59.

93. Arnautović, *Izbori u Bosni i Hercegovini '90,* p. 113.

94. *Ibid.,* p. 12.

95. *Ibid.,* p. 21.

96. All calculations are based on data published in the Sarajevo daily *Oslobodjenje.* The most detailed, district-by-district preliminary results are to be found in the issues for November 20–24, and December 2, 4, and 5, 1990.

97. Calculated on the basis of results reported in Arnautović, *Izbori u Bosni i Hercegovini '90,* pp. 118–120.

98. *Oslobodjenje,* December 6, 1990, p. 3.

99. For intimations of difficulties, see *ibid.,* December 13, 1990, p. 3, and December 14, 1990, p. 3.

100. *Ibid.,* December 21, 1990, pp. 1, 3.

101. *Ibid.,* December 22, 1990, p. 3.

102. *Ibid.,* December 22, 1990, p. 4.

103. *Ibid.,* December 25, 1990, p. 4 and December 27, 1990, p. 4.

104. See, for example, *ibid.,* December 25, 1990, p. 5. For a broader discussion, see Hayden, "Recounting the Dead."

105. Arnautović, *Izbori u Bosni i Hercegovini '90,* pp. 47ff, but especially graphic B, p. 51, and Table 1, p. 57.

106. Smajlović, "From the Heart of the Heart," p. 111.

107. Arnautović, *Izbori u Bosni i Hercegovini '90,* p. 13.

108. See Arend Lijphart, *Democracy in Plural Societies* (New Haven: Yale University Press, 1977), and "The Power-Sharing Approach," in *Conflict and Peacemaking in Multiethnic Societies,* Joseph V. Montville, ed. (Lexington, MA: Lexington Books, 1990), pp. 491–509. Cf. Kenneth McRae, ed., *Consociational Democracy: Political Accommodation in Segmented Societies* (Toronto: McClelland and Stewart, 1974).

109. Kemal Kurspahić, "How Not to Save Bosnia," *East European Reporter* (Novem-

ber/December 1992), p. 63. For another forceful argument of the case against partitioning Bosnia, see Sejfudin Tokić, "Ethnische Ideologie und Eroberungskrieg," in Stefanov and Werz, eds., *Bosnien und Europa,* pp. 175–81.
110. Zdravko Grebo and Branislava Jojić, "Teze za model ustava Republike Bosne i Hercegovine," in Janjić and Shoup, eds., *Bosna i Hercegovina izmedju rata i mira,* pp. 147–66.
111. Nenad Kecmanović, "Fikret protiv Alije," *NIN,* October 9, 1992, p. 55.
112. Nenad Kecmanović, "Predsedništvo iznutra," *NIN,* October 2, 1992, p. 55.

Chapter 3: The Descent into War

1. *Danas,* March 17, 1992, as translated in Foreign Broadcast Information Service, *Daily Report: Eastern Europe* (henceforth: FBIS, *EEU*), March 24, 1992, p. 29.
2. These developments are ably summarized in Marie-Janine Calic, *Der Krieg in Bosnien-Hercegovina: Ursachen Konfliktstrukturen Internationale Lösungsversuche* (Frankfurt: Suhrkamp Verlag, 1995), chapter 3.
3. Xavier Bougarel, "Bosnia and Hercegovina: State and Communitarianism," in *Yugoslavia and After: A Study in Fragmentation, Despair and Rebirth,* David A. Dyker and Ivan Vejvoda, eds. (London: Longman, 1996), p. 96.
4. *Borba,* April 11–12, 1992, p. iv. See also Vladimir Goati, "Politički život Bosne i Hercegovine, 1989–1992," in *Bosna i Hercegovina izmedju rata i mira,* Dušan Janić and Paul Shoup, eds. (Belgrade-Sarajevo, [n.p. 1992), pp. 57–58.
5. For the example of Zvornik, see *Guardian,* April 13, 1992, p. 22.
6. *Borba,* November 6, 1991, pp. 4–5.
7. *Borba,* December 8, 1991, as translated in FBIS, *EEU,* December 30, 1991, p. 48.
8. Laura Silber and Allan Little, *Yugoslavia: Death of a Nation* (New York: TV Books, 1996), p. 294.
9. *Borba,* October 28, 1991, as translated in FBIS, *EEU,* November 22, 1991, p. 52.
10. Zagreb Radio, March 22, 1992, as translated in FBIS, *EEU,* March 23, 1992, p. 28.
11. *Borba,* April 2, 1992, p. 3. See also James Gow, "Military and Political Affiliation in the Yugoslav Conflict," *RFE/RL Research Report* 1, no. 20 (May 15, 1992), p. 25.
12. *Vreme,* April 13, 1992, pp. 8–9.
13. *Ibid.*
14. Yugoslav News Agency, May 12, 1992, as translated in British Broadcasting Corporation, *Summary of World Broadcasts* (henceforth: BBC, *SWB*), May 15, 1992, EE/1381/C1.
15. See Tom Gjelton, *Sarajevo Daily: A City and Its Newspaper* (New York: HarperCollins, 1995).
16. See *Hrvatski obzor,* May 22, 1995, as translated in FBIS, *EEU,* June 20, 1995, pp. 16–18.
17. Boban's role in the HDZ remains a matter of dispute. See Dražena Peranić, "Muke s Hercegovcima," *Nedeljna Borba,* January 15–16, 1994, pp. viii–ix. See also *Novi Danas,* August 24, 1992, as translated in FBIS, *EEU,* September 11, 1992, pp. 23–25.
18. See Peranić, "Muke s Hercegovcima."
19. On Kordić, see *Oslobodjenje* (European Edition), November 16–23, 1995, p. 7, and Silber and Little, *Yugoslavia: Death of a Nation,* p. 294.
20. Alija Izetbegović, *Odabrani govori, pisma, izjave, intervjui* (Zagreb: Prvo muslimansko Dioničko društvo, 1995), p. 82.

21. Alija Izetbegović, *The Islamic Declaration: A Programme for Islamization of Muslims and Muslim Peoples* (Sarajevo: Bosna, 1990), p. 5.

22. Silber and Little, *Yugoslavia: Death of a Nation*, p. 208.

23. *Financial Times*, March 7, 1992, p. 6.

24. Izetbegović, *Odabrani govori*, p. 102.

25. *Danas*, October 22, 1991, pp. 30–31.

26. *NIN*, December 27, 1991, as translated in FBIS, *EEU*, January 23, 1992, p. 58.

27. Miroslav Jancic, "Behind the Split," *War Report* 36 (September 1995), pp. 6–7.

28. Milovan Djilas, *Bošnjak Adil Zulfikarpašić*, 2nd edition (Zurich: Bošnjački Institut, 1994), p. 183.

29. Silber and Little, *Yugoslavia: Death of a Nation*, p. 292.

30. On the constitutional debates, see Steven L. Burg, "Political Structures," in *Yugoslavia: A Fractured Federalism*, Dennison Rusinow, ed. (Washington, DC: Wilson Center Press, 1988), pp. 9–22, and "Elite Conflict in Post-Tito Yugoslavia," *Soviet Studies* 38, no. 2 (April 1986), pp. 170–93.

31. Belgrade Domestic Service, October 30, 1990, as translated in FBIS, *EEU*, October 31, 1990, p. 73.

32. Tanjug, October 30, 1990, as translated in FBIS, *EEU*, October 31, 1990, p. 73.

33. See "Documents on the Future Regulation of Relations in Yugoslavia," *Yugoslav Survey* 1 (1991), pp. 3–24.

34. Tanjug, June 8, 1991, as translated in FBIS, *EEU*, June 10, 1991, p. 42.

35. Milovan Djilas and Nadežda Gaće, *Bošnjak Adil Zulfikarpašić*, 3rd edition (Zurich: Bošnjački Institut, 1995), p. 184.

36. Tanjug, October 1, 1991, as translated in FBIS, *EEU*, October 3, 1991, p. 43.

37. *Oslobodjenje*, January 31, 1991, as translated in FBIS, *EEU*, February 12, 1991, p. 60, and *Oslobodjenje*, May 18, 1991, as translated in FBIS, *EEU*, May 30, 1991, p. 29.

38. Susan L. Woodward, *Balkan Tragedy* (Washington, DC: Brookings Institution, 1995), p. 78.

39. For a different set of conclusions, see Silber and Little, *Yugoslavia: Death of a Nation*, p. 214.

40. Djilas, *Bošnjak Adil Zulfikarpašić*, 2nd edition, p. 212.

41. Adil Zulfikarpašić, *Adil Zulfikarpašić: Članci i intervjui* (Zurich: Bošnjački Institut, 1991), pp. 668–71. See *Borba*, July 31, 1991, p. 9, for a detailed review of the negotiations, which suggests that draft documents were completed July 24.

42. Interview with *NIN*, August 8, 1991 reprinted in *ibid.*, p. 554. See also *Danas*, August 13, 1991, pp. 28–29, and *Borba*, July 31, 1991, p. 9.

43. Djilas, *Bošnjak Adil Zulfikarpašić*, 2nd edition, p. 215.

44. Djilas, *Bošnjak Adil Zulfikarpašić*, 3rd edition, p. 187. For Kljujić's statement, see *Borba*, July 31, 1991, p. 9.

45. Emir Habul, "Geografije konflikta," *Oslobodjenje sedam dana*, April 5, 1992.

46. Milan Andrejevich, "Bosnia and Herzegovina Move Toward Independence," *Report on Eastern Europe* 2, 43 (October 25, 1991), p. 25. For a detailed account of the creation of the SAOs and HAOs, see Kasim I. Begić, *Bosna i Hercegovina od Vanceove misije do Daytonskog sporazuma (1991.-1996.)* (Sarajevo: Bosanska knjiga, 1997), pp. 56–60.

47. Tanjug, October 13, 1990, as translated in FBIS, *EEU*, October 15, 1990, p. 70.

48. *Danas*, November 26, 1991, as translated in FBIS, *EEU*, December 16, 1991, p. 56.

49. *Nedjelja*, November 17, 1991, p. 13.

50. *Süddeutsche Zeitung*, November 1–2, 1991. For a Bosnian account, see *Nedjelja*, November 17, 1991, pp. 12–13.

51. Sarajevo Radio, November 4, 1991, as translated in FBIS, *EEU*, November 5, 1991, p. 40.

52. Miloš Vasić, "A Dream Too Far," *War Report* 31 (February 1995), p. 23.

53. James Gow, "Military and Political Affiliations in the Yugoslav Conflict," *RFE/RL Research Report* 1, no. 20 (May 15, 1992), p. 25. Gow cites a figure of 45,000 armed HOS members, which seems to be an overestimate.

54. For Izetbegović's testimony, see Sarajevo TV, February 13, 1993, as translated in FBIS, *EEU,* February 16, 1993, p. 43. For the Patriotic League, see Šefer Halilović, *Lukava Strategija* (Sarajevo: Maršal, 1997), p. 166.

55. The International Criminal Tribunal for the Former Yugoslavia, *The Prosecutor of the Tribunal v. Dusko Tadic,* Case no. IT94–1–T, May 21, 1996, p. 62.

56. *Oslobodjenje,* January 19, 1993, p. 4.

57. *Borba,* October 28, 1991, as translated in FBIS, *EEU,* November 22, 1991, p. 52. See also *Nedjelja,* January 26, 1992, as translated in FBIS, *EEU,* February 13, 1992, pp. 32–33, and Sarajevo Radio, January 31, 1992, as translated in FBIS, *EEU,* February 3, 1992, p. 32.

58. *New York Times,* January 10, 1992, p. A2.

59. Begić, *Bosna i Hercegovina od Vanceove misije,* p. 48.

60. *Ustav Socijalističke Republike Bosne i Hercegovine s Ustavnim amandmanima I–IV i registrom pojmova* (Sarajevo: Službeni list SRBiH, 1978), p. 27.

61. See Article 3 of the constitution as revised and approved by the Presidency on February 24, 1993, in *Novi ustavi na tlu bivše Jugoslavije* (Belgrade: Medjunarodna politika, 1995), p. 160. For details of these amendments, see Robert M. Hayden, "Bosnia's Internal War and the International Criminal Tribunal," *Fletcher Forum of World Affairs* 22, no. 1 (Winter/Spring 1998), p. 54.

62. See Article 215 of the 1993 text of the constitution. *Novi ustavi,* pp. 227–28.

63. Texts in *Yugoslav Survey* 32, no. 3 (1991), pp. 62–64.

64. *Borba,* October 16, 1991, p. 1.

65. *Ljiljan,* July 6–13, 1994, p. 30.

66. *Ibid.*

67. Radio Sarajevo, October 14, 1991, as translated in FBIS, *EEU,* October 16, 1991, p. 44.

68. *Ibid.*

69. *Yugoslav Survey* 32, no. 3 (1991), p. 63.

70. *Ibid.,* pp. 63–64.

71. *Borba,* October 17, 1991, p. 3.

72. *Bulletin of the European Communities* (henceforth *Bull. EC*) 24 (5–1991), p. 63.

73. *U.S. Department of State Dispatch* 2, no. 22 (June 3, 1991), pp. 395–96 (emphasis added).

74. *New York Times,* June 6, 1991, p. A14.

75. Tanjug, January 24, 1991, as translated in FBIS, *EEU,* January 25, 1991, p. 70.

76. *Večernji List* (Zagreb), January 26, 1991, as translated in FBIS, *EEU,* January 31, 1991, pp. 53–54.

77. Tanjug, January 26, 1991, as translated in FBIS, *EEU,* January 28, 1991, p. 58.

78. Texts in Snežana Trifunovska, ed., *Yugoslavia Through Documents* (Dordrecht, Netherlands: Martinus Nijhoff, 1994), pp. 311–15.

79. Silber and Little, *Yugoslavia: Death of a Nation,* chapter 12.

80. For an account of the events involving Croatia, see Reneo Lukic and Allen Lynch, *Europe from the Balkans to the Urals: The Disintegration of Yugoslavia and the Soviet Union* (Oxford: Oxford University Press, 1996), chapter 9.

81. Paul S. Shoup, "The Future of Croatia's Border Regions," *Report on Eastern Europe* 2, no. 48 (November 29, 1991), pp. 26–33.

82. Silber and Little, *Yugoslavia: Death of a Nation,* p. 102.

83. *Ibid.,* pp. 171–73.

84. *Ibid.,* pp. 131–32.

85. Boris Raseta, "The Questions over Slavonija," *Balkan War Report* 33 (May 1995), pp. 3–8.

86. *Danas* (Belgrade), May 16–17, 1998, pp. 12–13.

87. *Ibid.,* May 23–24, 1998, p. 13.

88. *Slobodni Tjednik,* March 4, 1992, p. 22.

89. *New York Times,* September 26, 1991, p. A3; *Guardian,* September 26, 1991, p. 8; and *Borba,* September 26, 1991, p. 1, and September 28–29, 1991, p. 8.

90. Silber and Little, *Yugoslavia: Death of a Nation,* p. 182.

91. Tanjug, October 22, 1991, as translated in British Broadcasting Corporation, *Summary of World Broadcasts* (henceforth: BBC, *SWB*), October 24, 1991, EE/1211/B/1.

92. Silber and Little, *Yugoslavia: Death of a Nation,* p. 186. Veljko Kadijević, *Moje vidjenje raspada: Vojska bez državi* (Belgrade: Politika, 1993), p. 137.

93. Silber and Little, *Yugoslavia: Death of a Nation,* pp. 186–87.

94. *Ibid.,* p. 188.

95. Kadijević, *Moje vidjenje raspada,* p. 138.

96. Dragan Cicic, "A Means to an End: The UN and Rump Yugoslavia," *War Report* 37 (October 1995), pp. 38–39.

97. Kadijević, *Moje vidjenje raspada,* pp. 138–39 and 143.

98. *Vreme,* September 30, 1991, pp. 6–10, and October 21, 1991, pp. 8–11.

99. Tanjug, December 10, 1991, as translated in FBIS, *EEU,* December 11, 1991, p. 30.

100. Kadijević, *Moje vidjenje raspada,* p. 147. Sarajevo Radio claimed that 10,000 Bosnians were fighting in Croatia (December 9, 1991, as translated in FBIS, *EEU,* December 10, 1991, pp. 55–56).

101. David Owen, *Balkan Odyssey* (New York: Harcourt Brace, 1995), pp. 31–33.

102. *Bull. EC* 24 (7/8–1991), pp. 115–116, and *Bull. EC* 24 (9–1991), p. 63.

103. Jan Willem Honig, "The Netherlands and Military Intervention," in *Military Intervention in European Conflicts,* Lawrence Freedman, ed. (Oxford: Blackwell Publishers, 1994), p. 148. Cf. reports in *Times* (London), August 6, 1991, pp. 1, 8; August 7, 1991, p. 1; and August 8, 1991, p. 7.

104. James Steinberg, "Turning Points in Bosnia and the West," in *Lessons from Bosnia: Conference Proceedings,* Zalmay M. Khalilzad, ed., RAND Corporation no. CF-113–AF (1993), p. 7.

105. Jolyon Howarth, "The Debate in France Over Military Intervention in Europe," in Freedman, ed., *Military Intervention in European Conflicts,* p. 113.

106. *Washington Post,* September 17, 1991, p. A21; *New York Times,* September 17, 1991, p. A3, September 18, 1991, p. A7, and September 20, 1991, p. A6; *Times* (London), September 17, 1991, pp. 1A, 10A, 10D, and September 20, 1991, p. 1.

107. Trevor C. Salmon, "Testing Times for European Cooperation: The Gulf and Yugoslavia," *International Affairs* 68, no. 2 (1992), pp. 250–51.

108. *Guardian,* January 12, 1996, p. 10.

109. *New York Times,* September 24, 1991, p. A10.

110. *Bull. EC* 24 (10–1991), p. 86.

111. European Political Cooperation Press Release, "Declaration on Yugoslavia," no. 98/81 (n.d.).

112. The October 18 proposal can be found in Trifunovska, ed., *Yugoslavia Through Documents,* pp. 357–65.

113. The November 1 proposals can be found in *ibid.,* pp. 370–78. The October 23

draft can be found in *Borba*, October 25, 1991, p. 6. The November 4 version can be found in *Borba*, November 6, 1991, pp. 4–5.

114. For the text, see Trifunovska, ed., *Yugoslavia Through Documents*, pp. 365–68. The Milošević speech in response to the October 18 proposals can be found at pp. 363–64.

115. *Ibid.*, pp. 372–73.

116. *Ibid.*, pp. 360, 373.

117. For the statements of October 27 and 28, see *Bull. EC* 24 (10–1991), p. 89. The EC call for Security Council action was made on November 8 and can be found in *Bull. EC* 24 (11–1991), pp. 70–72, 91.

118. Borisav Jović, *Poslednji dani SFRJ* (Belgrade: Politika, 1995), p. 344.

119. Kadijević, *Moje vidjenje raspada*, p. 135.

120. *Ibid.*, p. 132.

121. Srdjan Radulović, *Sudbina krajina* (Belgrade: Dan graf, 1996), p. 42.

122. *Frankfurter Allgemeine Zeitung*, November 4, 1991, and *Süddeutsche Zeitung*, November 3, 1991.

123. Mensur Čamo, "Beogradska tajna večera," *Nedjelja*, November 10, 1991, p. 15.

124. Text in *Borba*, November 2–3, 1991, and Tanjug, November 1, 1991, as translated in FBIS, *EEU*, November 4, 1991, p. 29.

125. Belgrade Radio, November 5, 1991, as translated in FBIS, *EEU*, November 5, 1991, pp. 28–29.

126. For details, see Radulović, *Sudbina Krajina*, pp. 41–51.

127. Tanjug, January 8, 1992, as translated in BBC, *SWB*, January 10, 1992, EE/1274/C1. See also Radulović, *Sudbina Krajina*, p. 45.

128. Silber and Little, *Yugoslavia: Death of a Nation*, pp. 202–3.

129. *Nedjeljna Dalmacija*, January 16, 1992, pp. 14–15.

130. *Vreme*, November 18, 1992, pp. 5–8.

131. Slobodanka Kovačević and Putnik Dajić, *Hronologija Jugoslovenske krize (1942–1993. godina)* (Belgrade: Institut za evropske studije, 1994), p. 46, and Jović, *Poslednji dani SFRJ*, pp. 408–10.

132. UN Security Council documents S/23280 (December 11, 1991), and S/23592 (February 15, 1992).

133. UN Security Council document S/23592 (February 15, 1992). (See also document S/23592 Add. 1 [February 19, 1992].)

134. See Paul Diehl, *International Peacekeeping* (Baltimore: Johns Hopkins University Press, 1994), chapter 4.

135. Hans W. Maull, "Germany in the Yugoslav Crisis," *Survival* 37, no. 4 (Winter 1995–96), pp. 102–3. Woodward (*Balkan Tragedy*, p. 186) refers to the "relentless" pressure of Genscher for recognition of Croatia and Slovenia after July 1991.

136. Woodward, *Balkan Tragedy*, p. 178.

137. Beverly Crawford, "Explaining Defection from International Cooperation: Germany's Unilateral Recognition of Croatia," *World Politics* 48 (July 1996), pp. 482–521.

138. European Political Cooperation Press Release, "Declaration on Yugoslavia," Extraordinary EPC Ministerial Meeting, Rome (November 8, 1991).

139. For Opinion No. 1 of the Arbitration Commission of the Peace Conference on Yugoslavia (Badinter Commission) of November 29, 1991, see Trifunovska, ed., *Yugoslavia Through Documents*, pp. 415–17.

140. Hurst Hannum, "Self-determination, Yugoslavia and Europe: Old Wine in New Bottles?" *Transnational Law and Contemporary Problems* 3, no. 1 (Spring 1993), pp. 57–69.

141. John Newhouse, "The Diplomatic Round: Dodging the Problem," *New Yorker,* August 24, 1992, p. 65.

142. Silber and Little, *Yugoslavia: Death of a Nation,* pp. 199–200.

143. *New York Times,* December 7, 1991, p. 1. See also Carrington's remarks to ITV news November 11, 1991, as reported in FBIS, *EEU,* November 12, 1991, p. 35.

144. An excellent summary of these criticisms and the ensuing letters can be found in *New York Times,* December 14, 1991, p. 3. See also *Times* (London), December 17, 1991, p. 11. For mention of Vance's criticisms, see *New York Times,* December 19, 1991, p. A8.

145. *Europe Journée Politique,* no. 5626 (December 11, 1991), p. 3.

146. Genscher, *Erinnerungen* (Berlin: Siedler, 1995), p. 960.

147. *Europe Journée Politique,* no. 5631 (December 16–17, 1991), pp. 3–4.

148. Lori Fisler Damrosch, "Changing Conceptions of Intervention in International Law," in *Emerging Norms of Justified Intervention,* Laura W. Reed and Carl Kaysen, eds. (Cambridge, MA: Committee on International Security Studies, American Academy of Arts and Sciences, 1993), p. 99.

149. Complete text in *Bull. EC* 24 (12–1991), pp. 119–20. See also Trifunovska, ed., *Yugoslavia Through Documents,* pp. 430–31.

150. See Opinion No. 23 of the Arbitration Commission of the Peace Conference on Yugoslavia, in Trifunovska, ed., *Yugoslavia Through Documents,* pp. 474–75.

151. *Borba,* November 13, 1991, p. 6.

152. Tanjug, November 30, 1991, as translated in FBIS, *EEU,* December 3, 1991, p. 43, and Silber and Little, *Yugoslavia: Death of a Nation,* p. 216.

153. Warren Zimmerman, "The Last Ambassador," *Foreign Affairs* 74, no. 2 (March/April 1995), p. 16; Silber and Little, *Yugoslavia: Death of a Nation,* pp. 216–17; and Newhouse, "The Diplomatic Round," pp. 64–65. Genscher mentions this meeting, but fails to shed any light on what transpired (Genscher, *Erinnerungen,* p. 933). Woodward (*Balkan Tragedy,* p. 184) says that "President Izetbegović made an emotional appeal to Genscher in early December not to recognize Croatia prematurely, for it would mean war in his republic," but no source for this information is cited.

154. *Politika,* December 18, 1991, p. 2.

155. *Vjesnik,* December 25, 1991, p. 8.

156. Tanjug, December 21, 1991, as translated in FBIS, *EEU,* December 23, 1991, p. 54, and *Guardian,* December 23, 1991, p. 7.

157. *Vjesnik,* December 27, 1991.

158. Warren Zimmerman, *Origins of a Catastrophe* (New York: Random House, 1996), p. 178.

159. *Guardian,* December 31, 1991, p. 7.

160. *Ibid.,* January 24, 1992, p. 10. See also *Economist,* January 18, 1992, p. 49.

161. *New York Times,* January 10, 1992, p. A2.

162. *Politika,* December 30, 1991, p. 1.

163. Tanjug, January 21, 1992, as translated in FBIS, *EEU,* January 22, 1992, p. 38.

164. *Danas,* January 28, 1992, as translated in FBIS, *EEU,* February 16, 1992, p. 25.

165. Radio Belgrade, February 27, 1992, as translated in BBC, *SWB,* February 29, 1992, EE/1317/C1.

166. *Frankfurter Allgemeine Zeitung,* March 5, 1992, p. 3.

167. *Economist,* March 7, 1992, p. 49.

168. *Der Spiegel,* January 13, 1992, p. 124.

169. *Le Monde,* January 20, 1992, p. 3.

170. *Guardian,* January 24, 1992, p. 10.

171. *Ibid.,* January 24, 1992, p. 10.

172. *Vreme*, January 27, 1992, p. 6.

173. Jović, *Poslednji dani SFRJ*, p. 427.

174. Zimmerman, *Origins of a Catastrophe*, p. 191.

175. *Ibid.*, p. 192.

176. *Ibid.*

177. "U.S. in Declaration on the Yugoslav Republics," *U.S. Department of State Dispatch* 3, no. 11 (March 16, 1992), p. 210.

178. *Washington Post*, March 11, 1992, p. A11, and *New York Times*, March 12, 1992, p. A7.

179. Jović, *Poslednji dani SFRJ*, p. 420.

180. *Ibid.*, p. 421.

181. Silber and Little, *Yugoslavia: Death of a Nation*, p. 217.

182. Jovan Ilić, "Tri varijante," *Epoha*, vol. 1, no. 1 (October 22, 1991), pp. 15–20.

183. See especially Milošević's November 5 statement at the EC conference, cited above (note 125); his interview with *Vecernje Novosti* printed December 30, 1991, as translated in FBIS, *EEU*, January 30, 1992, pp. 68–71; and his speech to the Serbian National Assembly of February 27, 1992, cited earlier (note 165).

184. *Borba*, December 23, 1991, pp. 1–2.

185. *Ibid.*, February 6, 1992, p. 5.

186. *Times* (London), July 12, 1991, p. 10.

187. *Borba*, January 8, 1992, p. 6. Zagreb Radio, December 31, 1991 (as translated in FBIS, *EEU*, January 2, 1992, p. 39) gives the speech but omits the references to Bosnia.

188. *Borba*, January 16, 1992, p. 8. Koljević's interpretation of the talks is given in *Vjesnik*, January 27, 1992, as translated in FBIS, *EEU*, February 7, 1992, p. 30.

189. *Borba*, January 16, 1992, p. 8, and Belgrade Radio, January 14, 1992, as translated in FBIS, *EEU*, January 15, 1992, p. 44.

190. Karadžić, it should be noted, also spoke of cantonization at this time, declaring that he favored cantonization and confederalization of Bosnia, "so that it becomes a Balkan Switzerland" (Belgrade Radio, February 6, 1992, as translated in FBIS, *EEU*, February 7, 1992, p. 27).

191. This debate is also treated in Hayden, "Bosnia's Internal War," p. 59.

192. *Oslobodjenje*, January 26, 1992, p. 1.

193. *Danas*, January 27, 1992, as translated in FBIS, *EEU*, February 7, 1992, p. 31. Belgrade Radio reported on January 25 (as translated in FBIS, *EEU*, January 27, 1992, p. 38) that agreement was not close.

194. *Borba*, February 11, 1992, p. 5. For the negative reaction of the SDA to the Livno document see Belgrade Radio, February 12, 1992, as translated in FBIS, *EEU*, February 14, 1992, p. 35.

195. *Borba*, February 4, 1992, p. 9.

196. *Ibid.*, February 29–March 1, 1992, p. 3, and *Der Standard*, February 27, 1992, p. 1, as translated in FBIS, *EEU*, February 28, 1992, p. 25.

197. *Oslobodjenje* (European edition), March 9–16, 1995, p. 3.

198. Tanjug, February 25, 1992, as translated in FBIS, *EEU*, February 26, 1992, p. 31.

199. Lewis MacKenzie, "Tragic Errors," *MacLean's*, December 12, 1994, p. 35.

200. *Guardian*, February 24, 1992, p. 1.

201. *Süddeutsche Zeitung*, February 15, 1992. On the other hand, the situation in Bosnia received practically no coverage in the *Süddeutsche Zeitung* during January–February 1992. The American press largely ignored the crisis, with some notable exceptions by Chuck Sudetic of the *New York Times*.

202. Belgrade Radio, February 6, 1992, as translated in FBIS, *EEU*, February 7, 1992, p. 27.

203. The text of the agreement was published in *Vjesnik,* February 27, 1992, as translated in FBIS, *EEU,* March 11, 1992, p. 37.

204. For the SDA press conference see Tanjug, February 26, 1992, as translated in FBIS, *EEU,* March 2, 1992, p. 36.

205. Tanjug, February 25, 1992, as translated in BBC, *SWB,* February 27, 1992, EE/1315/C1.

206. Tanjug, March 11, 1992, as translated in BBC, *SWB,* March 13, 1992, EE/1328/C1.

207. *Ibid.*

208. *Borba,* March 10, 1992, p. 8.

209. *Ibid.,* March 9, 1992, p. 1.

210. *Vjesnik,* March 13, 1992, p. 7.

211. *Oslobodjenje* (European edition), March 19, 1992, p. 3, and *Politika* March 19, 1992, p. 5.

212. *Oslobodjenje* (European edition), March 19, 1992, p. 3.

213. *Ibid.*

214. The text of the agreement can be found in FBIS, *EEU,* March 19, 1992, pp. 21–22. Later information was secured from the EC Conference on Yugoslavia, *Background Documents Pack* (mimeo). For an excellent account of the March 18 Villa Konak meeting, see *Vreme,* March 23, 1992, pp. 7–8.

215. *International Herald Tribune,* August 15–16, 1992, p. 4.

216. March 18 statement of constitutional principles, point D.2, as translated in FBIS, *EEU,* March 19, 1992, p. 22.

217. For a good summary of the positions of the three parties, see *Borba,* March 27, 1992, as translated in FBIS, *EEU,* April 8, 1992, p. 24.

218. *Oslobodjenje,* March 19, 1992, p. 3.

219. *Ibid.*

220. *Borba,* March 27, 1992, p. 9, reported that the map was passed out to newsmen after the press conference by Cutileiro.

221. The EC, or "Cutileiro," map of March 18 was reproduced, among other places, in *Borba,* March 19, 1992, p. 2. *Politika,* March 19, 1992, p. 5, published three maps, which it claims were those submitted to Cutileiro by the SDA, SDS, and HDZ.

222. It has frequently been asserted that Izetbegović was the first to repudiate the agreement. See, for example, Woodward, *Balkan Tragedy,* p. 281. Cutileiro, in his letter cited earlier, claimed Izetbegović repudiated the agreement in June.

223. *Borba,* March 23, 1992, p. 7.

224. *Ibid.,* March 26, 1992, p. 2.

225. In an interview with *Oslobodjenje* and *Večerne novine,* reported by Tanjug, March 25, 1992, as translated in FBIS, *EEU,* March 25, 1992, pp. 45–46.

226. Sarajevo Radio, March 30, 1992, as translated in FBIS, *EEU,* March 31, 1992, p. 27.

227. Belgrade Radio, March 26, 1992, as translated in FBIS, *EEU,* March 27, 1992, p. 39.

228. *Borba,* March 27, 1992, p. 3.

229. *New York Times,* August 29, 1993, p. 10.

230. *Ibid.,* September 30, 1993, p. A24.

231. Zimmerman, *Origins of a Catastrophe,* p. 190.

232. *U.S. Department of State Dispatch* 3, no. 8 (February 24, 1992), p. 128.

233. *Medjunarodni Problemi,* no. 1–2 (1992), p. 195.

234. Zimmerman, *Origins of a Catastrophe,* p. 176.

235. *Ibid.,* p. 187.

236. *Danas,* January 27, 1992, as translated in FBIS, *EEU,* February 7, 1992, p. 32.

237. *Borba,* April 1, 1992, p. 7.
238. Begić, *Bosna i Hercegovina od Vanceove misije,* p. 102.
239. See U.S. Commission on Security and Cooperation in Europe, *The Referendum on Independence in Bosnia-Herzegovina* (Washington, DC: March 12, 1992); *Oslobodjenje* (European edition), March 9–16, 1995, p. 3; *Borba,* April 1, 1992, p. 9; and Begić, *Bosna i Hercegovina od Vanceove misije,* pp. 71–79. According to Begić (p. 78), local Serb authorities blocked the referendum in Bosansko Grahovo and Drvar.
240. Goati, "Politički život Bosne i Hercegovina," p. 61.
241. Silber and Little, *Yugoslavia: Death of a Nation,* p. 206.
242. Tanjug, March 6, 1992, as translated in FBIS, *EEU,* March 10, 1992, p. 36.
243. *Guardian,* March 3, 1992, p. 1.
244. *Politika,* March 6, 1992, p. 1.
245. *Borba,* March 6, 1992, p. 3.
246. *Guardian,* March 4, 1992, p. 18, and *Frankfurter Allgemeine Zeitung,* March 5, 1992, p. 3.
247. *Borba,* March 6, 1992, p. 4. For Bosanski Brod, see *Ljiljan* (Sarajevo), January 12–19, 1994, p. 18, and December 27–January 3, 1996, p. 3.
248. Tanjug, July 13, 1993, as translated in FBIS, *EEU,* July 13, 1993, p. 34. For more information on Sijekovac, see chapter 4, note 199.
249. Sarajevo Radio, March 13, 1992, as translated in FBIS, *EEU,* March 16, 1992, p. 18.
250. *Borba,* March 27, 1992, p. 1.
251. *Ibid.*
252. Sarajevo Radio, March 29, 1992, as translated in FBIS, *EEU,* March 30, 1992, p. 47.
253. *Borba,* March 24, 1992, p. 3, and Tanjug, March 21 and March 22, 1992, as translated in FBIS, *EEU,* March 23, 1992, p. 26.
254. Tanjug, March 29, 1992, as translated in FBIS, *EEU,* March 31, 1992, p. 32.
255. A list of the victims in Bijeljina is given in *Borba,* April 7, 1992, p. 1. They appear all to be Muslims.
256. See *Borba,* April 6, 1992. The headline reads: *"Teror, anarhija"* ("Terror, Anarchy").
257. *Borba,* April 6, 1992, p. 1.
258. Ljiljana Smajlović, "From the Heart of the Heart of the Former Yugoslavia," *Wilson Quarterly* (Summer 1995), p. 111. See also Halilović, *Lukava strategija,* p. 165.
259. The critics of the German policy are numerous. They include Henry Kissinger ("Bosnia: Only Just the Beginning," *Washington Post,* September 11, 1995, p. A21), General Colin Powell (see Abe Rosenthal, "A Gift from Powell," *New York Times,* September 19, 1995, p. A21), Zimmerman ("The Last Ambassador," p. 13), Misha Glenny (*International Herald Tribune,* July 30, 1993, p. 6), Woodward (*Balkan Tragedy,* pp. 187–89), Crawford ("Explaining Defection"), and Newhouse ("The Diplomatic Round: Dodging the Issue"). For treatment of the problem from the German perspective, see Maull ("Germany in the Yugoslav Crisis"), Calic (*Der Krieg in Bosnien-Hercegovina,* pp. 38–39), and Michael Libal ("Germany and Yugoslavia 1991–1992: The Issues," Center for International Affairs, Harvard University, n.d.; and "Germany and Yugoslavia, Myths and Realities," unpublished paper presented to the Center for International Affairs, Harvard University).
260. Zimmerman, "The Last Ambassador," p. 16.
261. For this argument, see Steinberg, "Turning Points in Bosnia and the West," p. 7.
262. Maull, "Germany in the Yugoslav Crisis," p. 104.
263. See Libal, "Germany and Yugoslavia, Myths and Realities," p. 10. Libal was head of the South-East European Desk in the German Foreign Ministry from 1991 to 1995.

264. Vasić, "A Dream Too Far," p. 24.

265. *Washington Post,* February 8, 1993, p. 1. Zimmerman (*Origins of a Catastrophe,* pp. 185 and 188) recounts the warnings he received from Generals Kadijević and Adžić in Belgrade in January 1992, as well as Karadžić's threat that "the independence of Bosnia would lead to catastrophe." Svetozar Stojanović reports that on March 20 he warned Ambassador Zimmerman that there would be serious consequences if Bosnia were recognized, and recommended that the Americans support cantonization as a solution to the crisis. According to Stojanović, Zimmerman was "convinced that the West with its 'authoritative recognition' of Bosnia-Herzegovina would deter the conflicting national communities from going to war." *Propast komunizma i razbijanje Jugoslavije* (Belgrade: Filip Višnjić, 1995), p. 108.

266. *Economist,* December 9, 1995, p. 6.

267. Belgrade Radio, February 27, 1992, as cited in FBIS, *EEU,* February 28, 1992, p. 33.

268. Zimmerman, *Origins of a Catastrophe,* p. 19.

269. *Vreme,* January 20, 1992, p. 24–25, as translated in FBIS, *EEU,* January 30, 1992, p. 68.

270. Sarajevo Radio, November 29, 1991, as translated in FBIS, *EEU,* December 3, 1991, p. 42.

Chapter 4: The War on the Ground, 1992–94

1. See Tom Gjelten, *Sarajevo Daily: A City and Its Newspaper Under Siege* (New York: HarperCollins, 1995), pp. 20–21, and Bratislava-Buba Morina, ed., *Stradanja Srba u Sarajevu: Knjiga dokumenata,* (Belgrade: Komesarijat za Izbeglice SR Srbije, 1995), p. 101.

2. *Oslobodjenje,* May 7, 1993, p. 6.

3. Nikola Heleta, *Goražde '92–'95: Stradanje Srba* (Belgrade: Prosveta, 1996), pp. 15–18.

4. Robert Donia and John V.A. Fine Jr., *Bosnia and Hercegovina: A Tradition Betrayed* (New York: Columbia University Press, 1994), p. 254.

5. For the demonstrations in Sarajevo, see Tanjug, April 6, 1992, as translated in Foreign Broadcast Information Service, *Daily Report: Eastern Europe* (henceforth: FBIS, *EEU*), April 13, 1992, p. 22. For Doboj, see *Danas,* June 2, 1992, as translated in FBIS, *EEU,* June 18, 1992, pp. 17–18. For Cazinska Krajina, see Tanjug, April 24, 1992, and Radio Sarajevo, April 25, 1992, as translated in FBIS, *EEU,* April 27, 1992, pp. 33, 34.

6. See Smail Čekić, *The Aggression on Bosnia and Genocide Against Bosniacs, 1991–1993* (Sarajevo: Ljiljan, 1994), and Smail Čekić, "Vojne pripreme za agresiju na republiku Bosnu i Herzegovinu," in *Agresija na Bosnu i Herzegovinu: Borba za njen Opstanak, 1992–1995 Godine,* Mustafa Imamović, ed. (Sarajevo: Pravni Fakultet Univerziteta u Sarajevu, 1997), pp. 79–96.

7. See the interview with Jusuf Pusina, then Bosnian minister of the interior, in *Večernji list* (Zagreb) September 16, 1992, as translated in FBIS, *EEU,* October 7, 1992, p. 2. Cf. Noel Malcolm, *Bosnia: A Short History* (New York: New York University Press, 1994), p. 230.

8. *Borba,* April 11–12, 1992, p. iv.

9. Sarajevo TV, February 13, 1993, as translated in FBIS, *EEU,* February 16, 1993, p. 43.

10. The International Criminal Tribunal for the Former Yugoslavia, *The Prosecutor of the Tribunal v Dusko Tadic,* Case no. IT94–1–T, May 21, 1996, p. 662.

11. *Borba,* April 10–11, 1993, p. 1.

12. Belgrade TV, April 26, 1992, and Zagreb Radio, April 26, 1992, as translated in FBIS, *EEU,* April 27, 1992, pp. 29–30.

13. For the statement by Gen. Kukanjac, see Tanjug, April 26, 1992, as translated in FBIS, *EEU,* April 27, 1992, p. 29. The fullest description of these events is to be found in Laura Silber and Allan Little, *The Death of Yugoslavia* (London: Penguin Books/BBC Books, 1995), pp. 255–68. For a participant's account, see Lewis MacKenzie, *Peacekeeper: The Road to Sarajevo* (Vancouver: Douglas & McIntyre, 1993), pp. 164–74. Gjelten describes heavy fighting on May 13 as part of a Serb attempt to break through to the Tito barracks, where the JNA was surrounded (*Sarajevo Daily,* p. 108).

14. Šefer Halilović, *Lukava Strategija* (Sarajevo: Maršal, 1997), pp. 62–63.

15. UN Security Council document S/24049 (May 30, 1992), p. 3.

16. *Washington Post,* June 20, 1992, p. A18.

17. *Ibid.,* June 27, 1992, p. 1.

18. See Dragan Todorović, "Grad oslobodjen od normalnog života," *Borba,* May 13, 1992, p. 3.

19. Chuck Sudetic, "Blood and Vengeance: One Family's Story of the Massacre at Srebrenica and the Unending War in Bosnia," *Rolling Stone,* December 28, 1995–January 11, 1996, p. 90. See also *Washington Post,* September 10, 1992, p. A18; *Oslobodjenje* (European edition), May 20–27, 1994, p. 20, and May 27–June 3, 1994, p. 24; and Ed Vulliamy, *Seasons in Hell: Understanding Bosnia's War* (New York: St. Martin's Press, 1994), pp. 177–78.

20. "Meeting in Sarajevo Between Co-Chairs and President Izetbegovic. . . ," Archive Document *Balkan Odyssey,* CD-ROM Academic Edition vol. 1.1 (London: The Electric Company, 1995).

21. *Oslobodjenje* (European edition), March 11–18, 1994, p. 11, and June 10–17, 1994, pp. 20–21.

22. *Independent,* April 9, 1994, p. 8.

23. UN Security Council document S/PRST/1994/6 (February 3, 1994).

24. *NIN,* March 11, 1994, as translated in FBIS, *EEU,* April 7, 1994, p. 37.

25. *New York Times,* May 13, 1994, p. A10. Cf. *Washington Post,* March 7, 1993, p. C3.

26. *Washington Post,* July 31, 1995, p. 1.

27. For the Serbs, see *ibid.,* July 11, 1994, p. A1, and November 3, 1994, p. A31. For the Muslims and the Croats, see Edgar O'Ballance, *Civil War in Bosnia 1992–1994* (New York: St. Martin's Press, 1995), p. 215.

28. *Eksklusiv* (Split), June 9, 1995, as translated in FBIS, *EEU,* June 21, 1995, p. 26. For an interview with Tirić, see *Ljiljan,* January 19–January 26, 1994, pp. 6–7.

29. *Guardian,* August 31, 1994, p. 9.

30. *New York Times,* June 12, 1994, p. 14.

31. Christopher Collinson, "Bosnian Army Tactics," *Jane's Intelligence Review* 6, no. 1 (January 1994), pp. 11–13.

32. *Vreme,* March 14, 1994, as translated in FBIS, *EEU,* April 14, 1994, pp. 48–49, and *New York Times,* October 28, 1994, p. 1.

33. See the remarks of Safet Oručević, mayor of Mostar, in *Oslobodjenje* (European edition), June 16–23, 1994, p. 20. See also *Washington Post,* September 1, 1993, p. A25, and *Borba,* November 16, 1993, p. 4.

34. Kasim I. Begić, *Bosna i Hercegovina od Vanceove misije do Daytonskog sporazuma (1991.-1996.)* (Sarajevo: Bosanska knjiga, 1997), pp. 134–35.

35. *Guardian,* March 18, 1996, p. 8.

36. Criminals involved in the defense of the city included Ramiz Delalić-Ćelo,

Mušan Topalović-Caco, and Juka-Jusuf Prazina. For Prazina, see *Borba,* May 12, 1992, p. 2; *Večernji List* (Zagreb), February 12, 1993, as translated in FBIS, *EEU,* February 19, 1993, p. 31; and *Politika* (Belgrade) August 6, 1993, p. 6. For Čelo and Caco, see "Final Report of the Commission of Experts," UN Security Council document S/1994/674 (December 28, 1994), vol. II, annex VI, part I, p. 10.

37. *Oslobodjenje* (European edition), January 5–12, 1995, p. 6.

38. *Ibid.,* January 12–19, 1995, p. 11.

39. See Miloš Vasić, "Začin u ekspres-loncu," *Vreme,* August 29, 1994, pp. 8–9.

40. "Ubijanje Sarajeva," *Borba,* May 11, 1992, p. 3.

41. "Final Report of the Commission of Experts," vol. II, annex VI, part 1, p. 10.

42. For more on Usora, a mixed Croat-Muslim town in the Tešanj (Doboj) area, and how the two communities held together, see *Oslobodjenje* (European edition), September 15–22, 1994, p. 27.

43. See *Borba,* January 18, 1993, p. 5; Jan Honig and Norbeert Both, *Srebrenica: Record of a War Crime* (New York: Penguin Books, 1997), pp. 78–79.

44. *Guardian,* March 15, 1993, p. 1.

45. Honig and Both, *Srebrenica,* pp. 83–91.

46. *New York Times,* April 13, 1993, p. 1.

47. *Washington Post,* April 14, 1993, p. A23.

48. *New York Times,* April 15, 1993, p. A12, and *Washington Post,* April 17, 1993, p. 1. For his earlier advocacy of air strikes, see "Interview with David Owen on the Balkans," *Foreign Affairs* 72, no. 2 (Spring 1993), p. 5.

49. *Washington Post,* April 19, 1993, p. A1, and April 21, 1993, p. A16.

50. Honig and Both, *Srebrenica,* p. 106; see also *New York Times,* April 27, 1993, p. A6, and June 5, 1993, p. 6.

51. *Ibid.,* July 10, 1993, p. 1.

52. *Ibid.,* July 14, 1993, p. A3. On the shelling of the water pump, see *Ibid.,* July 13, 1993, p. A10.

53. *Ibid.,* July 24, 1993, p. 1.

54. *Ibid.,* July 30, 1993, p. A6.

55. *Ibid.,* August 4, 1993, p. A8.

56. *Le Monde,* August 10, 1993, p. 3.

57. Agence France Presse (henceforth: AFP), August 5, 1993, and *New York Times,* August 6, 1993, p. 1. For Mladić concessions, see Tanjug dispatch, August 8, 1993, as translated in FBIS, *EEU,* August 9, 1993, p. 26.

58. AFP, August 6, 1993, and *New York Times,* August 7, 1993, p. 1.

59. Tanjug, August 9, 1993, as translated in FBIS, *EEU,* August 9, 1993, p. 26.

60. *Washington Post,* August 5, 1993, p. A20.

61. See Miloš Vasić, et al., "Masakr na Markalama," *Vreme,* February 14, 1994, pp. 10–14.

62. *Washington Post,* February 8, 1994, p. A15, and Slobodanka Kovačević and Putnik Daljić, *Hronologija Jugoslovenske krize 1994* (Belgrade: Institut za evropske studije, 1995), p. 45.

63. *Washington Post,* March 15, 1994, p. A14.

64. *Ibid.,* April 8, 1994, p. A26.

65. Yossef Bodansky and Vaughn S. Forrest, "The Truth About Goražde," U.S. House of Representatives, Task Force on Terrorism, May 4, 1994 (mimeo).

66. "Chronology of events, Gorazde, 10–16 April, 1994," Archive Document *Balkan Odyssey,* CD-ROM Academic Edition vol 1.1 (London: The Electric Company, 1995).

67. *New York Times,* April 17, 1994, p. 13, and *Washington Post,* April 17, 1994, p. A26.

68. London Press Association, April 20, 1994, as reported in FBIS, *EEU,* April 21, 1994, p. 32.

69. AFP, April 22, 1994, as translated in FBIS, *EEU,* April 22, 1994, p. 33.

70. *New York Times,* April 24, 1994, p. 1. The secretary-general later noted the presence of Bosnian military installations of strategic importance in several of the safe areas, in UN Security Council document S/1994/1389 (December 1, 1994), p. 9.

71. When the Serbs withdrew from Goražde, they were reported to have first blown up "a water treatment plant" (*New York Times,* April 25, 1994, p. A1).

72. *Washington Post,* April 24, 1994, p. 1. For the NATO Council decision, see *New York Times,* April 23, 1994, p. 1, and *Washington Post,* April 23, 1994, p. 6.

73. *New York Times,* April 23, 1994, p. 6.

74. *Washington Post,* April 24, 1994, p. 1.

75. *Ibid.,* April 25, 1994, p. A14. See also *New York Times,* April 23, 1994, p. 7.

76. *Washington Post,* April 25, 1994, p. A14.

77. *New York Times,* April 26, 1994, p. A8.

78. *Washington Post,* April 26, 1994, p. A8.

79. *New York Times,* April 30, 1994, p. 3.

80. For Kessler's statement see *Independent,* April 29, 1994, p. 12. See also *Times* (London), May 3, 1994, pp. 3, 12A. For Rose's statement see *Borba,* April 28, 1994, p. 3.

81. *Washington Post,* April 30, 1994, p. A18.

82. *Ibid.,* May 3, 1994, p. A17; May 6, 1994, p. A30; and May 10, 1994, p. A14.

83. Kovačević and Daljić, *Hronologija 1994,* p. 130.

84. Tanjug, September 19, 1994, as reported in *Yugoslav Daily Survey* 580 (September 20, 1994), p. 6.

85. *New York Times,* September 25, 1994, p. 14, and Hiraqi News Agency (Zagreb) September 25, 1994, as translated in British Broadcasting System, *Survey of World Broadcasts* (henceforth: BBC, *SWB*), September 27, 1994, EE/2111/C.

86. *Ibid.*

87. Prime Minister Haris Silajdžić in *Le Figaro,* June 6, 1994, as translated in FBIS, *EEU,* June 7, 1994, pp. 35–36.

88. *Oslobodjenje* (European edition), September 28–October 1, 1994, p. 8. Cf. *Delo,* June 30/July 1, 1994, as translated in FBIS, *EEU,* July 6, 1994, p. 46.

89. *New York Times,* September 25, 1994, p. 14.

90. *Guardian,* October 8, 1994, p. 14.

91. *Ibid.,* October 21, 1994, p. 13.

92. Christopher Collinson, "Bosnia This Winter," *Jane's Intelligence Review* 5, no. 2 (December 1993), pp. 63–67.

93. Info Radio Paris, March 13, 1994, as translated in BBC, *SWB,* March 15, 1994, EC/1946/C. See also *New York Times,* March 14, 1994, p. A8.

94. *Washington Post,* August 22, 1994, p. A12.

95. AFP, September 21, 1994. On the role of Mladić, see *Vreme,* August 22, 1994, pp. 11–13.

96. *Guardian,* December 5, 1994, p. 9, and *Washington Post,* December 5, 1994, p. A1.

97. *Ibid.,* November 25, 1994, p. 1.

98. *New York Times,* November 15, 1994, p. A1, and November 24, 1994, p. A8. It has been suggested to the authors that the UN preferred not to delineate safe area boundaries for fear they would become the focus of fighting.

99. UN Security Council document S/1994/1389 (December 1, 1994), p. 5.

100. *New York Times,* November 19, 1994, p. 6.

101. *Guardian,* November 18, 1994, p. 27.

102. *New York Times,* December 4, 1995, p. 1.

103. *Washington Post,* November 5, 1994, p. A17. UNPROFOR sources identify November 3 as the date the missiles were fired.

104. On the NATO air strikes, see *Washington Post,* November 24, 1994, p. A1. For a report of the additional Serb missile attacks, see *Guardian,* November 17, 1994, p. 12.

105. *Washington Post,* November 23, 1994, p. A15.

106. *New York Times,* November 24, 1994, p. A8.

107. *Washington Post,* November 24, 1994, p. A1, and November 30, 1994, p. A31; *New York Times,* November 25, 1994, p. 1, and November 28, 1994, p. A10.

108. An excellent example of such criticism can be found in an opinion essay by Ian Black, the diplomatic editor of the *Guardian,* November 24, 1994, p. 14. At the same time, the *Guardian's* editorial position opposed air strikes because they "never offered a coherent strategy which has a remote chance of success" (*Guardian,* November 23, 1994, p. 25).

109. *New York Times,* November 24, 1994, p. 1.

110. *Guardian,* November 24, 1994, p. 1.

111. *Washington Post,* November 23, 1994, p. A15.

112. *New York Times,* November 26, 1994, p. 1.

113. *Ibid.,* November 25, 1994, p. A16.

114. *Guardian,* January 29, 1996, p. 9.

115. *Washington Post,* November 27, 1994, p. A44.

116. The U.S. plan is described in *New York Times,* November 25, 1994, p. A1, and December 4, 1994, pp. 1 and 22.

117. *Ibid.,* December 4, 1994, p. 20.

118. *Ibid.,* November 25, 1994, p. 1.

119. *Ibid.,* November 17, 1994, p. A7.

120. *Washington Post,* November 26, 1994, p. A1.

121. UN Security Council document, S/PRST/1994/74 (November 29, 1994).

122. *New York Times,* December 14, 1994, p. A11.

123. *Ibid.,* December 6, 1994, p. A3.

124. *Guardian,* December 8, 1994, p. 11.

125. *New York Times,* November 27, 1992, p. 1.

126. *Ibid.,* June 15, 1997, p. 12.

127. For this charge, see Sejo Omeragić, "MacKenzie na spisku ratnih zločinaca," *Ljiljan,* March 30–April 6, 1994, p. 18.

128. Ben Cohen and George Stamkowski, eds., *With No Peace to Keep: United Nations Peacekeeping and the War in the Former Yugoslavia* (London: Grain Press, 1995).

129. Sudetic, "Blood and Vengeance," p. 97.

130. *Washington Post,* August 10, 1994, p. A13.

131. "The Lost American," *Frontline,* WGBH Television (Boston), October 4, 1997. See also "Third Periodic Report on the Situation of Human Rights for the Territory of the Former Yugoslavia," UN Economic and Social Council, Commission on Human Rights, document E/CN.4/1994/6 (August 26, 1994).

132. Charles G. Boyd, "Making Peace with the Guilty: The Truth About Bosnia," *Foreign Affairs* 74, no. 5 (September–October 1995), pp. 22–38. Compare John E. Sray, *Selling the Bosnian Myth to America: Buyer Beware* (Fort Leavenworth, KS: Foreign Military Studies Office, 1995 [mimeo]).

133. *Boston Globe,* August 15, 1992, p. 19.

134. Sylvia Poggioloi, "Scouts Without Compasses," *Nieman Reports* (Fall 1993), p. 16.

135. Nik Gowing, "Real-Time Television Coverage of Armed Conflicts and Diplomatic Crises: Does It Pressure or Distort Foreign Policy Decisions?" *Working Paper* No. 94–1, The Joan Shorenstein Barone Center on the Press, Politics and Public Policy, Harvard University (June 1994), p. 63.

136. Andrew Kohut and Robert C. Toth, "The People, the Press, and the Use of Force," Times Mirror Center for the People and the Press, Washington, DC (August 14–19, 1994), pp. 13–16. A similar review can be found in Richard Sobel, "U.S. and European Attitudes Toward Intervention in the Former Yugoslavia: Mourir pour la Bosnie?" in *The World and Yugoslavia's Wars*, Richard H. Ullman, ed. (New York: Council on Foreign Relations, 1996), pp. 146–51.

137. Times Mirror Center for the People and the Press, *America's Place in the World: An Investigation of the Attitudes of American Opinion Leaders and the American Public About International Affairs* (Washington, DC: November 1993), p. 92.

138. Andrew Kohut and Robert C. Toth, "Managing Conflict in the Post–Cold War World," Times Mirror Center for the People and the Press, Washington, DC (August 2–6, 1995), p. 6.

139. *Washington Post*, May 2, 1993, p. C1.

140. Gowing, "Real-Time Television Coverage," pp. 18, 41.

141. *New York Times*, November 11, 1994, p. A10.

142. According to these sources, the incident occurred at approximately 0900 hrs on the 24th. Two explosions were heard, with an impact point located at GR BP93715961. The incident was noted in the media, but not attributed to either side; see *New York Times*, December 25, 1994, p. 11, and *Washington Post*, December 25, 1994, p. 1.

143. *New York Times*, August 1, 1995, p. A6.

144. MacKenzie, *Peacekeeper*, p. 194.

145. Gjelten, *Sarajevo Daily*, p. 117.

146. Federal Government of Yugoslavia, *Report Submitted to the Commission of Experts Established Pursuant to Security Council Resolution 780 (1992)* (Belgrade: 1992), item I-070.

147. *Independent*, August 22, 1992, p. 1.

148. Miloš Vasić, "Ubijanje Sarajeva," *Vreme*, June 1, 1992, pp. 12–15.

149. Tom Gjelten, "Blaming the Victim," *The New Republic*, December 20, 1993, p. 14.

150. David Binder, "Anatomy of a Massacre," *Foreign Policy* 97 (Winter 1994–95), pp. 74–75.

151. Binder, "Anatomy of a Massacre," p. 75, and UNPROFOR, "UNPROFOR Investigation Report: Sarajevo Market Explosion of 5 February 1994," annex C (mimeo).

152. *New York Times*, February 8, 1994, p. 1.

153. "UNPROFOR Investigation Report," p. 3.

154. *Sunday Times* (London), October 1, 1995, p. 15, and David Binder, "Bosnia's Bombers," *The Nation*, October 2, 1995, pp. 336–37.

155. *Sunday Times* (London), October 1, 1995, p. 15.

156. Binder, "Bosnia's Bombers," p. 337.

157. *Washington Post*, August 30, 1995, p. A20.

158. *Ibid.*, November 15, 1995, p. A20.

159. Binder, "Bosnia's Bombers," p. 337.

160. See *Sunday Times* (London), October 1, 1995, p. 15. An account of the alleged contents of the document was published by *Borba*, October 5, 1992, p. 2.

161. Cited in Binder, "Anatomy of a Massacre," p. 72.

162. See U.S. Committee for Refugees, *World Refugee Survey 1994* (New York:

U.S. Committee for Refugees, 1995), p. 120; Anthony Borden and Richard Caplan, "The Former Yugoslavia: The War and the Peace Process," *SIPRI Yearbook* 1996 (Oxford: Oxford University Press, 1996), p. 203. The 200,000 figure appears to be derived from estimates published by the Bosnian government during the course of 1994. See *Nedeljna Borba,* April 9–10, 1994, p. vi, for data from the Sarajevo State Commission for Gathering Facts About War Crimes. The figure of 200,000 casualties was also used by the director of the Institute for Research on Atrocities Against Humanity and International Law, Smail Čekić, in an article in *Oslobodjenje,* March 9, 1993.

163. The data did not include victims of the Srebrenica-Žepa massacre. "Socijalno-zdravstvene posljedice agresije na republiku BiH," *Bilten Zavoda za zdravstevenu zaštitu R/F BiH* 182 (October 9, 1995), p. 1. See also Arif Smajkić, et al., "Study: Health Consequences of the Aggression Against the Republic B&H and the Possibilities of Restoration: Summary," University of Sarajevo, National Institute of Public Health with School of Public Health (July 1995), unpaginated.

164. Mustafa Imamović, "Agresija na Bosnu i Hercegovinu i njene neposredne posledice," in Imamović, ed., *Agresija na Bosnu i Hercegovinu,* p. 12.

165. "Humanitarian Costs of the Fighting in the Balkans," unclassified CIA memorandum (November 25, 1995). For alternative estimates, see *Preporod* (Sarajevo), June 15, 1998, p. 8.

166. George Kenney, "The Bosnian Calculation," *New York Times Magazine,* April 23, 1995, pp. 42–43.

167. *Ibid.,* p. 42.

168. *SIPRI Yearbook 1996,* p. 24.

169. "Strogo povjerljivi bilans," *AIM* (Banja Luka), May 26, 1997, as reported in *Siemvesti* (May 30, 1997) electronic mail edition (Siemvesti@morag.umsmed.edu).

170. For a brief account of how the issue came to the attention of the media, see Alexandra Stiglmayer, "The War in Former Yugoslavia," in *Mass Rape: The War Against Women in Bosnia-Herzegovina,* Alexandra Stiglmayer, ed. (Lincoln, NE: University of Nebraska Press, 1994), pp. 25–26.

171. Michele Mercier, *Crimes Without Punishment: Humanitarian Action in Former Yugoslavia* (London: Pluto Press, 1994), p. 118. For the figure 30,000, see Imamović, ed., *Agresija na Bosnu i Hercegovinu,* p. 13.

172. U.S. Congress, Select Committee on Intelligence of the United States Senate and Committee on Foreign Relations of the United States Senate, *War Crimes in the Balkans* (Washington: USGPO, 1996), p. 17. For a review of the data see Dorothy Q. Thomas and Regan E. Ralph, "Rape in War: Challenging the Tradition of Immunity," *SAIS Review* (Winter–Spring 1994), p. 93. See also Adriana Kovalovska, "Rape of Muslim Women in Wartime Bosnia," *ILSA Journal of International and Comparative Law* 3, no. 3 (Spring 1997), pp. 931–44.

173. "Situation of Human Rights in the Territory of Yugoslavia," UN Economic and Social Council document E/CN.4/1993/50 (February 10, 1993), Annex II, pp. 63–73.

174. Beverly Allen, *Rape Warfare: The Hidden Genocide in Bosnia-Herzegovina and Croatia* (London and Minneapolis: University of Minnesota Press, 1996), p. 42. See also Cherif Bassiouni, "Sexual Violence: An Invisible Weapon of War in the Former Yugoslavia," *Occasional Paper* no. 1, International Human Rights Law Institute, DePaul University College of Law (1996). For criticism of such charges, see Maja Korać, "Representation of Mass Rape in Ethnic-Conflicts [sic] in What Was Yugoslavia," *Sociologija* (Belgrade) 36, no. 4 (October–December 1994), pp. 495–514.

175. UN document A/50/329 (August 4, 1995), p. 17.

176. UN Security Council document S/23900 (May 12, 1992), p. 3.

177. "Humanitarian Costs of the Fighting in the Balkans," unclassified CIA memorandum (November 25, 1995).

178. For the latter figure, see *Washington Post,* November 16, 1994, p. A19; for the former, *New York Times,* April 24, 1995, p. 1.

179. Arif Smajkić, et al., *Zdravsteno-socijalne posljedice agresije na Bosnu i Hercegovinu* (Sarajevo: Zavod za zdravstvenu zasštitu, Republike i Federacije Bosne i Hercegovine, 1994), p. 3.

180. Imamović, "Agresija na Bosnu i Hercegovinu i njene neposredne posledice," p. 12, and Halilović, *Lukava Strategija,* p. 103.

181. Srdjan Bogosavljević, "Ethnic Recomposition in Former Yugoslavia," unpublished paper (February 1996).

182. *BH Opstinas population 96* (map) at http://www.oscebih.org.

183. See the following submissions by the Croatian government: "Extermination of Catholics in the Archdiocese of Vrhbosna-Sarajevo," UN Security Council document S/26378 (August 30, 1993), and "Report on War Crimes and Grave Breaches of Paramilitary Forces Against Croatian Civilian Population in Central Bosnia and Northern Herzegovina," UN Security Council document S/26454 (September 16, 1993).

184. For the results of a CIA study of ethnic cleansing in Bosnia, see *War Crimes in the Balkans,* p. 8. See also *New York Times,* March 9, 1995, p. 1, and *European,* March 31–April 6, 1995, p. 1.

185. David Rieff, *Slaughterhouse: Bosnia and the Failure of the West* (New York: Simon and Schuster, 1995), p. 113.

186. The International Criminal Tribunal for the Former Yugoslavia, *The Prosecutor of the Tribunal v. Dusko Tadic,* Case no. IT94–1–T, May 21, 1996, p. 652.

187. "Final Report of the Commission of Experts," vol. I, pp. 151–82. For background, see *Vreme,* August 17, 1992, as translated in FBIS, *EEU,* September 8, 1992, pp. 33–34.

188. "Bosnia-Hercegovina: 'Ethnic Cleansing' Continues in Northern Bosnia," *Human Rights Watch/Helsinki* 6, no. 16 (November 1994). See also Diane Paul, "No Escape: Minorities Under Threat in Serb-Held Areas of Bosnia," *Refugee Reports,* November 30, 1994, pp. 1–9.

189. See the testimony of Diana Paul in Commission on Security and Cooperation in Europe, *Banja Luka: Ethnic Cleansing Paradigm, or Counterpoint to a Radical Future?* (Washington, DC: USGPO, 1996), pp. 9–18. See also "Northwestern Bosnia: Human Rights Abuses During a Cease-Fire and Peace Negotiations," *Human Rights Watch/Helsinki* 8, no. 1 (February 1996), pp. 29–30.

190. Ejub Štitkovac and Jasmina Udovički, "Bosnia and Hercegovina: The Second War," in *Yugoslavia's Ethnic Nightmare: The Inside Story of Europe's Unfolding Ordeal,* Jasminka Udovički and James Ridgeway, eds. (New York: Lawrence Hill Books, 1995), p. 181. For the charge that Serb extremists had killed Serbs who tried to protect Muslims, see "Situation of Human Rights in the Territory of Yugoslavia," UN Economic and Social Council document E/CN.4/1993/50 (February 10, 1993), p. 7.

191. Such an effort is under way at the Humanitarian Law Center in Belgrade. For a detailed account of Serb atrocities in eastern Bosnia from a Bosnian point of view, see Nijaz Mašić, *Istina o Bratuncu: Agresija, Genocid, i Oslobodilačka Borba 1992.-1995.* (Tuzla: Opština Bratunac sa Privreminim Sjedištem u Tuzli, 1996).

192. *Guardian,* February 3, 1997, p. T8.

193. *Washington Post,* April 16, 1992, p. 16. On Zimmerman being lied to, see Warren Zimmerman, "The Last Ambassador: A Memoir of the Collapse of Yugoslavia," *Foreign Affairs* 74, no. 2 (March/April 1995), p. 19.

194. *Washington Post,* April 25, 1992, p. A33.

195. Gowing, "Real-Time Television Coverage," pp. 39–45. See also Roy Gutman, *A Witness to Genocide* (New York: Macmillan, 1993), pp. vii–xvi.

196. Mercier, *Crimes Without Punishment,* pp. 113–16.

197. "Human Rights Situation and Reports of the Special Rapporteurs and Representatives: Situation of Human Rights on the Territory of the Former Yugoslavia," UN General Assembly and Security Council document, A/47/666–S/24809 (November 17, 1992), p. 38.

198. See the Yugoslav government report to the UN, "Memorandum on War Crimes Committed Against the Serbian People. . . ," UN General Assembly and Security Council document A/48/229–S/26261 (August 6, 1993).

199. Serbs charged that atrocities were committed against the Serbs in the village of Sijekovac. See Drago Jovanović, ed., *Iskorenjivanje srba u Bosni i Hercegovini* (Belgrade: Rad, n.d.), pp. 63–76. What really happened, however, was in dispute at the time. For charges of rape against Serb women, see the Yugoslav government report "Memorandum on the Crimes of Rape of Children, Girls and Women of Serbian Nationality. . . ," UN General Assembly and Security Council document A/48/74–S/25216 (February 3, 1993).

200. *Politika,* May 22, 1992, p. 14.

201. Alexandra Stiglmayer, "The Rapes in Bosnia-Herzegovina," in Stiglmayer, ed., *Mass Rape,* p. 140.

202. See the Greek ecclesiastical journal *Synaxi* 44 (October–December 1992), pp. 47–51, and Anatasije Jevtić, "Testimony of Orthodox Bishop of Hercegovina Dr. Anatasije Jevtic, September 28, 1992," *Position of the Serbian Orthodox Church Regarding the War in the Former Yugoslavia* (September 1994). The most comprehensive account of events in Herzegovina (from a Serb point of view) can be found in Dušica Bojić, ed., *Stradanja srba u Mostaru i dolini Neretve: Knjiga dokumenata* (Belgrade: Komisarijat za Izbeglice Republike Srbije, 1996).

203. See the report of the Yugoslav government, "Report Submitted to the Commission of Experts. . . ," UN document YU/SC 780–92/DOC-1/E (Belgrade 1992).

204. "Situation of Human Rights in the Territory of Yugoslavia," UN Economic and Social Council document E/CN.4/1993/50 (February 10, 1993), p. 16. See also D.N. Griffiths (a member of the EC observation team in Herzegovina at the time), "Waging Peace in Bosnia," *Proceedings* no. 120, U.S. Naval Institute (January 1994), p. 33. For an overview of Yugoslav and Serbian government reports, see Pavle Jevremović, "An Examination of War Crimes Committed in the Former Yugoslavia," *Medjunarodni Problemi/International Problems* (Belgrade) 46, no. 1 (1994), pp. 39–73.

205. *Ethnic Cleansing of Croats in Bosnia and Herzegovina, 1991–1993* (Mostar: n.p., 1993).

206. See the following submission by the Croatian government: "Statements of Eyewitnesses to the Massacres at the Village of Doljani on 28 July 1993," UN Security Council document S/26617 (October 23, 1993).

207. UN Security Council document S/1994/154 (February 10, 1994).

208. "Final Report of the Commission of Experts," vol. VIII, p. 16, and "Human Rights Situation and Reports of the Special Rapporteurs and Representatives: Situation of Human Rights on the Territory of the Former Yugoslavia," UN General Assembly and Security Council document A/47666–S/24809 (November 17, 1992). For the John Burns report, see *New York Times,* July 29, 1993, p. 1.

209. Vasić, "Začin u ekpres-loncu," pp. 6–9.

210. Dušica Bojić, ed., *Stradanja srba u Sarajevu: Knjiga dokumenata/Suffering of the Serbs in Sarajevo: Document Book (Records)* (Belgrade: Komesarijat za Izbeglice Republike Srbije, n.d.), *passim.*

211. *New York Times,* November 12, 1997, p. 1, and *Svijet* (Sarajevo), November 16, 1997, pp. 8–14.

212. Gordana Igric, "Not Just the Victim," *War Report* 57 (December 1997–January 1998), pp. 9–10, and *Svijet* (Sarajevo), November 16, 1997, pp. 8–14.

213. *Ljiljan,* January 11, 1995, p. 11, and Halilović, *Lukava strategija,* p. 135.

214. Bojić, ed., *Stradanja srba u Sarajevu,* pp. 293–326.

215. *Ibid.,* pp. 327–33.

216. "Bosnia-Hercegovina: Sarajevo," *Human Rights Watch/Helsinki* 6, no. 15 (October 1994), p. 21.

217. *Ibid.,* p. 29.

218. *Ibid.,* p. 26.

219. Interviews by one of the authors with Serbs from Tuzla. On the events of May 15, see Mayor Beslagić's interview in *Washington Post,* March 25, 1993, p. A10. See also *New York Times,* March 29, 1993, p. A8.

220. *Christian Science Monitor,* October 28, 1994, p. 2.

221. "Sixth Periodic Report on the Situation of Human Rights in the Territory of the Former Yugoslavia," UN Security Council document S/1994/265 (March 7, 1994), p. 9.

222. On the impact of refugees, see Ivan Čolović, "Beograd-Tuzla, tamo i ovamo 4,040 km," *Republika* (Belgrade), November 16–30, 1994, pp. 19–20.

223. Médecins du Monde and Clair Boulanger, Bernard Jacquemart and Philippe Granjon, *L'Enfer Yougoslave: Les victimes de la guerre témoignent* (Paris: Belfond, 1994), pp. 232–34.

224. See "Bosnia-Hercegovina: Abuses by Bosnian Croat and Muslim Forces in Central and Southwestern Bosnia-Hercegovina," *Human Rights Watch/Helsinki* 5, no. 18 (September 1993).

225. *New York Times,* June 4, 1992, p. A3. See also Stražina Živak, *Logor Čelebići 1992.-1994.* (Pale: SRNA, 1997).

226. For an account of the campaigns in eastern Bosnia, see Honig and Both, *Srebrenica,* pp. 80–81. For an account told from the Muslim side, see the interviews with Muhamed Hadžimuratović-Cile in *Oslobodjenje* (European edition), May 20–27, 1994, p. 20, and May 27–June 3, 1994, p. 24.

227. *Washington Post,* August 31, 1992, p. A12, and *New York Times,* September 10, 1992, p. A10; see also *Politika,* September 7, 1992, and Tanjug, October 1, 1992, as translated in FBIS, *EEU,* October 2, 1992, p. 28.

228. The Committee for Collecting Data on Crimes Committed against Humanity and International Law, *War Crimes Against Serbs on the Territory of Goražde (1992–1994)* (Belgrade: n.p., n.d.). For a Western account, see Honig and Both, *Srebrenica,* p. 79. For a Serb account of events in Bratunac, see Milivoje Ivanišević, *Hronika našeg groblja: ili slovo o stradanju Srpskog naroda Bratunca, Milića, Skalona i Srebrenice* (Belgrade-Bratunac: Komitet za prikupljanje podataka o izvršnim zločinima protiv čovečnosti i medjunarodnog prava, 1994). See also *Borba,* August 3, 1992, p. 2, and October 6, 1995, p. 3.

229. See the following submission by the Yugoslav government: "Third Report Submitted to the Commission of Experts," UN Security Council document S/1994/548 (May 9, 1994), pp. 183–213, and *Borba,* January 18, 1993, p. 5.

230. Silber and Little, *Death of Yugoslavia,* p. 294.

231. *Washington Post,* October 1, 1993, p. A33, and February 16, 1994, p. A14.

232. *Ibid.,* April 22, 1993, p. 1. For a Muslim account, see Imamović, "Agresija na Bosnu i Hercegovinu i njene neposredne posledice," pp. 16–17.

233. UN Security Council document S/26454 (September 16, 1993), and "Bosnia Hercegovina: Abuses by Bosnian Croat and Muslim Forces. . . ." On the massacre at

Stupni Do, see UN Security Council document S/1994/154 (February 10, 1994). For British charges of ethnic cleansing by the Muslims against the Croats, see UN Security Council document S/26616 (October 22, 1993).

234. Vulliamy, *Seasons in Hell*, p. 119, and *Washington Post*, August 23, 1992, p. A19. For a different view, see *Vreme*, August 24, 1992, as translated in FBIS, *EEU*, September 4, 1992, p. 22. For the war crimes trial of Hazim Delić, Esad Landzo, and Zejnil Delalić, accused in the case, see *Guardian*, March 11, 1997, p. 12.

235. *Oslobodjenje* (European edition), January 6–13, 1994, p. 12, and April 29–May 6, 1994, p. 23.

236. *Neue Zuricher Zeitung*, March 22, 1994, p. 7. See also *Oslobodjenje* (European edition), November 26–December 3, 1993, p. 11, for the destruction of the town of Počitelj. On the ethnic cleansing of Mostar and detention of Muslims, see "Fourth Periodic Report . . . ," UN Economic and Social Council, Commission on Human Rights document E/CN.4/1994/8 (September 8, 1993).

237. The camps included Dretelj and Gabela. *Washington Post*, September 7, 1993, p. A18. For descriptions of the two camps, see "Final Report of the Commission of Experts," vol. IV, annex VIII, pp. 113–14.

238. Tanjug, August 16, 1992, as translated in FBIS, *EEU*, August 17, 1992, p. 30.

239. *Oslobodjenje* (European edition), January 12–19, 1995, p. 11.

240. Samuel Totten and William S. Parsons, "Introduction," in *Genocide in the Twentieth Century*, Samuel Totten, William S. Parsons, and Israel W. Charney, eds. (New York: Garland Publishing, 1995), pp. xi–lvi.

241. Patricia Viseur Sellers, "Gender, the Genocide Convention and the Tribunal on the Former Yugoslavia," *ISG Newsletter* 15 (Fall 1995): 1–3, and Helen Fein, *Genocide: Sociological Perspective* (London: Sage Publications, 1993), pp. 19–20.

242. "Discriminating Genocide from War Crimes: Vietnam and Afghanistan Reexamined," *Denver Journal of International Law and Policy* 22, no. 1 (Fall 1993): 29–62.

243. Mercier, *Crimes Without Punishment*, pp. 112–13.

244. Jean E. Manas, "The Impossible Trade-off: 'Peace' versus 'Justice' in Settling Yugoslavia's Wars," in *The World and Yugoslavia's Wars*, Richard H. Ullman, ed. (New York: Council on Foreign Relations, 1996), p. 50.

245. *Večerne novosti* (Belgrade), June 29, 1994, p. 2.

246. *NIN*, July 29, 1994, as translated in BBC, *SWB*, August 2, 1994, EE/2063/C.

Chapter 5: The Vance-Owen Plan

1. These issues are explored more fully in Steven L. Burg, *War or Peace? Nationalism, Democracy and American Foreign Policy in Post-Communist Europe* (New York: New York University Press, 1996).

2. Radio Zagreb, May 7, 1992 as translated in British Broadcasting Company, *Summary of World Broadcasts* (henceforth: BBC, *SWB*), May 9, 1992, EE/1376/C1/1.

3. *Oslobodjenje* (European edition), October 11, 1996, p. 3. The latter point is made repeatedly in Šefer Halilović, *Lukava strategija* (Sarajevo: Maršal, 1997).

4. *New York Times*, September 8, 1993, p. A3.

5. Alija Izetbegović, speech delivered in Mecca, May 1994, in *Odabrani govori, pisma izjavei intervjui* (Zagreb: Prvo muslimansko Dioničko društvo, 1995), p. 102.

6. For Grebo's views on nationalism, see Miloš Vasić, "Začin u ekspres-loncu," *Vreme*, August 29, 1994, pp. 8–9.

7. For Western reports, see *New York Times*, October 10, 1994, p. A3; *Washington Post*, November 16, 1994, p. A19; and *Guardian*, September 20, 1993, p. 10, and

October 15, 1994, p. 27. See also Yahya M. Sadowski, "Bosnia's Muslims: A Fundamentalist Threat?" *Brookings Review* 13, no. 1 (Winter 1995), pp. 10–15, and Vasić, "Začin u ekpres-loncu."

8. Vasić, "Začin u ekspres-loncu."

9. *New York Times,* October 30, 1992, p. 1.

10. Paul F. Diehl, *International Peacekeeping* (Baltimore: Johns Hopkins University Press, 1994), p. 195.

11. Robert L. Hutchings, *American Diplomacy and the End of the Cold War: 1989–1992* (Washington: Woodrow Wilson Center Press, 1997), p. 308. For a similar view, see David C. Gompert, "The United States and Yugoslavia's Wars," in *The World and Yugoslavia's Wars,* Richard H. Ullman, ed. (New York: Council on Foreign Relations, 1996), p. 129.

12. *Washington Post,* July 2, 1992, p. A1.

13. Gompert, "The United States and Yugoslavia's Wars," pp. 128–29.

14. Hutchings, *American Diplomacy,* p. 320.

15. Gompert, "The United States and Yugoslavia's Wars," p. 141.

16. James A. Baker III, *The Politics of Diplomacy* (New York: G.P. Putnam's Sons, 1995), pp. 636, 637. For a contemporary statement of this position, see *Washington Post,* May 13, 1992, p. A28.

17. Jacques Poos, in *Times* (London), June 29, 1991, p. 24. Cf. comments by Brent Scowcroft, President Bush's national security advisor, and by then Deputy Secretary of State Lawrence Eagleburger, reported in Michael Kelly, "Surrender and Blame," *New Yorker* (December 19, 1994), p. 45.

18. *New York Times,* June 19, 1992, p. A6.

19. David Gompert, "How to Defeat Serbia," *Foreign Affairs* 73, no. 4 (July–August 1994), p. 41. Cf. Gompert, "The United States and Yugoslavia's Wars," pp. 124–25, where the argument is presented somewhat differently as "a peaceful dissolution was infeasible."

20. *Washington Post,* May 16, 1992, p. A1.

21. Baker, *Politics of Diplomacy,* pp. 649–50.

22. *Washington Post,* May 13, 1992, p. A28.

23. Nik Gowing, "Real-Time Television Coverage of Armed Conflicts and Diplomatic Crises: Does It Pressure or Distort Foreign Policy Decisions?" *Working Paper* no. 94–1, The Joan Shorenstein Barone Center on the Press, Politics and Public Policy, Harvard University (June 1994), p. 41.

24. Baker, *Politics of Diplomacy,* pp. 643–44.

25. *Ibid.,* p. 645.

26. *New Europe* (September 17–23, 1995), p. 2.

27. *New York Times,* July 16, 1992, p. A8.

28. *Ibid.,* June 5, 1992, p. A8.

29. *Ibid.,* December 23, 1991, p. A1.

30. UN Security Council document, S/23900 (May 12, 1992), pp. 8–9.

31. *Guardian,* May 28, 1992, p. 6.

32. Marten van Heuven, "Rehabilitating Serbia," *Foreign Policy* 96 (Fall 1994), p. 38. See also Lawrence Freedman, "Why the West Failed," *Foreign Policy* 97 (Winter 1994–95), p. 62.

33. *Washington Post,* April 17, 1992, p. A25.

34. Reuters dispatch, May 24, 1992. For details of this incident, see Michele Mercier, *Crimes Without Punishment: Humanitarian Action in Former Yugoslavia* (London: Pluto Press, 1994), pp. 72–73.

35. Remarks made on May 24, 1992, as reported in *U.S. Department of State Dispatch* 3, no. 22 (June 1, 1992), p. 430.

36. *New York Times,* May 26, 1992, p. A6, and May 29, 1992, p. A1. Cf. *Times* (London), May 27, 1992.

37. *Washington Post,* May 29, 1992, p. A25.

38. *Los Angeles Times,* May 31, 1992, p. 1.

39. For the text of Resolution 757 see UN Security Council document S/RES/757 (May 30, 1992).

40. UN Security Council document S/24049 (May 30, 1992). See also document S/24000 (May 26, 1992).

41. See Susan L. Woodward, "Yugoslavia: Divide and Fall," *The Bulletin of Atomic Scientists* (November 1993), pp. 24–27, and Miroslav Prokopijević and Jovan Teokarić, *Ekonomske Sankeije UN: Uporedna analiza i slućaj Jugoslavije* (Belgrade: Institute za europske studije, 1998).

42. *Washington Post,* June 5, 1992, p. A44.

43. *New York Times,* June 24, 1992, p. A9.

44. *Washington Post,* June 27, 1992, p. A1, and *New York Times,* June 29, 1992, p. A1.

45. *Ibid.,* June 29, 1992, p. A1.

46. *Washington Post,* June 13, 1992, p. A16.

47. *Ibid.,* June 27, 1992, p. A13.

48. Pia Christina Wood, "France and the Post–Cold War Order: The Case of Yugoslavia," *European Security* 3, no. 1 (Spring 1994), pp. 139–40.

49. For evidence of these divisions, see *Current Digest of the Post-Soviet Press* (henceforth: *CDPSP*), 44, no. 22 (July 1, 1992), pp. 2–6.

50. *Washington Post,* July 1, 1992, p. A28.

51. *Guardian,* June 3, 1992, p. 8.

52. AFP, June 11, 1992.

53. Lewis MacKenzie, *Peacekeeper: The Road to Sarajevo* (Vancouver: Douglas & McIntyre, 1993), p. 301.

54. *New York Times,* July 18, 1992, p. 4.

55. *Washington Post,* August 11, 1992, p. 10.

56. *New York Times,* August 9, 1992, p. 1.

57. *Washington Post,* August 6, 1992, p. A1.

58. *New York Times,* August 6, 1992, p. A23.

59. *Washington Post,* August 10, 1992, p. A12.

60. *New York Times,* August 12, 1992, p. A8, and August 14, 1992, p. A6. *Washington Post,* August 12, 1992, p. A24. For the testimony itelf, see U.S. Congress, Senate Committee on Armed Services, *Situation in Bosnia and Appropriate U.S. and Western Responses,* Hearing Before the Committee on Armed Services, United States Senate, 102nd Cong., 2nd Sess. (August 11, 1992), pp. 39–40.

61. *New York Times,* August 10, 1992, p. A8.

62. The discussion below is based on the verbatim record, printed as International Conference on the Former Socialist Federal Republic of Yugoslavia, *The London Conference 26–27 August 1992.*

63. *Ibid.,* p. 48.

64. "Direct Governmental Involvement in the Search for a Negotiated Settlement. . . ," Archive Document *Balkan Odyssey,* CD-ROM Academic Edition v1.1 (London: The Electric Company, 1995).

65. UN Security Council document S/24333 (July 21 1992).

66. *Guardian,* September 3, 1992, p. 6.

67. Owen, *Balkan Odyssey,* p. 62.

68. The following is drawn from UN Security Council document S/24795 (November 11, 1992), pp. 13–14.

69. *Ibid.,* annex VII, part I (B.1), p. 45.

70. *Borba,* December 19–20, 1992, p. 3.

71. UN Security Council document S/25015 (December 24, 1992), pp. 6–8.

72. UN Security Council document S/24795 (November 11, 1992), p. 16.

73. *ICFY/6,* annex (mimeo). (Text of the proposed "Constitutional Structure for Bosnia and Herzegovina . . . as slightly modified to take into account the consultations with the parties on that proposal and to reflect some additional points advanced by the Co-Chairmen on 2 January 1993.")

74. Published as Annex VII of S/24795.

75. UN Security Council document S/24795 (November 11, 1992), p. 46.

76. UN Security Council document S/25015 (December 24, 1992), p. 8.

77. Owen, *Balkan Odyssey,* pp. 78–79.

78. UN Security Council document S/25015 (December 24, 1992), p. 8.

79. UN Security Council document S/25050 (January 6, 1993).

80. *ICFY/6,* section IV.A.2(a), pp. 6–7.

81. *Washington Post,* December 11, 1992, p. A52.

82. UN Security Council document S/25050 (January 6, 1993), p. 13.

83. Owen, *Balkan Odyssey,* p. 85.

84. Elizabeth Drew, *On the Edge: The Clinton Presidency* (New York: Simon and Schuster, 1994), p. 144.

85. *Oslobodjenje,* January 22, 1993, p. 4.

86. UN Security Council document S/25221 (February 2, 1993), p. 3.

87. Owen, *Balkan Odyssey,* p. 97.

88. UN Security Council document S/25100 (January 14, 1993), pp. 7, 8.

89. *New York Times,* January 23, 1993, p. 3; see also *New York Times,* January 20, 1993, p. A6, and January 21, 1993, p. A3.

90. UN Security Council document S/25221 (February 2, 1993), p. 3.

91. *Ibid.,* p. 4, and Annex II, pp. 13–15. (Cf. the version in S/25050, which specifies the map.)

92. The following is based on the account in *Danas,* April 2, 1993, as translated in Foreign Broadcast Information Service, *Daily Report: Eastern Europe* (henceforth: FBIS, *EEU*), April 22, 1993, pp. 28–30.

93. UN Security Council document S/25221 (February 2, 1993), p. 34.

94. *Ibid.,* p. 36.

95. *Ibid.,* p. 34.

96. *Ibid.,* annex V, pp. 34ff.

97. For advocacy of this approach, see Arend Lijphart, "The Power-Sharing Approach," in *Conflict and Peacemaking in Multiethnic Societies,* Joseph V. Montville, ed. (Lexington, MA: Lexington Books, 1990), pp. 491–509.

98. Owen, *Balkan Odyssey,* p. 91.

99. UN Security Council document S/25100 (January 14, 1993), pp. 4–5.

100. *New York Times,* January 7, 1993, p. A23, and January 8, 1993, p. A25.

101. Owen, *Balkan Odyssey,* pp. 93–94.

102. *New York Times,* September 28, 1992, p. A1.

103. *Ibid.,* December 17, 1992, p. A1.

104. *Ibid.,* January 22, 1993, p. A1.

105. *Ibid.,* January 28, 1993, p. A7.

106. Maynard Glitman, "US Policy in Bosnia: Rethinking a Flawed Approach," *Survival* 38, no. 4 (Winter 1996–97), p. 72.

107. *New York Times,* April 4, 1994, p. 1.

108. Owen, *Balkan Odyssey,* p. 108.

109. *Ibid.*, pp. 110–112.

110. U.S. Department of State, Office of the Assistant Secretary/Spokesman, *Statement by U.S. Secretary of State Warren Christopher*, February 10, 1993, p. 2.

111. Drew, *On the Edge*, p. 146.

112. *Statement by U.S. Secretary of State Warren Christopher*, February 10, 1993, p. 4.

113. Drew, *On the Edge*, p. 149.

114. "Direct Governmental Involvement in the Search for a Negotiated Settlement. . . ."

115. Owen, *Balkan Odyssey*, pp. 104–5.

116. UN Security Council document S/25248 (February 8, 1993), p. 2.

117. *Ibid.*, annex III (map), p. 9.

118. UN Security Council document S/25403 (March 12, 1993), p. 2.

119. Drew, *On the Edge*, pp. 146, 147.

120. "Direct Governmental Involvement in the Search for a Negotiated Settlement. . . ."

121. UN Security Council document S/25248 (February 8, 1993), annex 1, p. 8.

122. *Ibid.*, annex 1, p. 4.

123. UN Security Council document S/25403 (March 12, 1993), p. 7.

124. UN Security Council document S/25479 (March 26, 1993).

125. UN Security Council document S/25403 (March 12, 1993), p. 3.

126. UN Security Council document S/25479 (March 26, 1993), pp. 4–6.

127. UN Security Council document S/25403 (March 12, 1993), p. 5.

128. UN Security Council document S/25479 (March 26, 1993), p. 5.

129. UN Security Council document S/25248 (February 8, 1993), pp. 3–4.

130. UN Security Council document S/25479 (March 26, 1993), p. 10.

131. *Ibid.*, p. 5.

132. *Borba*, April 16, 1993, p. 13.

133. UN Security Council document S/25479 (March 26, 1993), p. 4.

134. *Ibid.*, p. 13.

135. For the withdrawal-of-forces provisions, see *ibid.*, p. 12. For additional details, see *Oslobodjenje* (Sarajevo), March 25, 1993, and March 26, 1993, as well as the report of Radio Zagreb of April 3, 1993, as translated in FBIS, *EEU*, April 6, 1993, p. 28.

136. *Danas*, April 2, 1993, as translated in FBIS, *EEU*, April 22, 1993, pp. 28–30.

137. UN Security Council document S/25479 (March 26, 1993), Annex V, pp. 42–43.

138. *Times* (London), March 26, 1993, p. 10.

139. "Note of Lord Owen's Reaction to UN Secretary General's Attitude. . . ," Archive Document *Balkan Odyssey* (CD-ROM), Academic Edition v1.1 (London: The Electric Company, 1995).

140. Former U.S. Ambassador to the UN Jeane Kirkpatrick and former CIA Director William Colby each called for unilateral intervention in testimony to the Senate in February (*New York Times*, February 19, 1993, p. A3). Former Secretary of State George Shultz had already done so in December 1992 (*New York Times*, December 9, 1992, p. A3).

141. For reports of such preparations, see *ibid.*, March 11, 1993, p. A1, and "ICFY Diplomacy from 1 February to 8 March, 1993," Archive Document *Balkan Odyssey* (CD-ROM), Academic Edition v1.1 (London: The Electric Company, 1995).

142. UN Security Council document S/25248 (February 8, 1993), p. 2.

143. Owen, *Balkan Odyssey*, pp. 132–33.

144. *Ibid.*, pp. 124–25.

145. *Washington Post*, April 17, 1993, p. 1.

146. *Borba*, April 16, 1993, p. 13.

147. *New York Times*, April 20, 1993, p. 10.

148. Owen, *Balkan Odyssey*, p. 151.

149. Laura Silber and Allan Little, *The Death of Yugoslavia* (London: Penguin Books and BBC Books, 1995), pp. 308–9.

150. "Details of ICFY diplomatic activity, 26 March–16 April 1993," Archive Document *Balkan Odyssey* (CD-ROM), Academic Edition v1.1 (London: The Electric Company, 1995).

151. "Details of ICFY diplomatic activities 20–24 April 1993," Archive Document *Balkan Odyssey* (CD-ROM), Academic Edition v1.1 (London: The Electric Company, 1995); Owen, *Balkan Odyssey*, p. 144; and *Borba,* April 26, 1993, p. 1.

152. Silber and Little, *Death of Yugoslavia,* p. 309.

153. *New York Times,* April 25, 1993, p. 20, and *Borba,* April 26, 1993, p. 1. Text of the agreement can be found in UN Security Council document S/25700 (April 30, 1993), pp. 17–19.

154. *Ibid.,* p. 19.

155. "Details of ICFY diplomatic activity, 26 March–16 April 1993."

156. *Ljiljan,* March 15, 1993, as translated in FBIS, *EEU,* April 23, 1993, pp. 36–42, but esp. pp. 40–41.

157. *New York Times,* March 11, 1993, p. A1.

158. "ICFY Diplomacy from 1 February to 8 March 1993."

159. *New York Times,* April 22, 1993, p. A25.

160. *Ibid.,* April 27, 1993, p. A7.

161. *Washington Post,* April 28, 1993, p. A1. Cf. Owen, *Balkan Odyssey,* p. 146.

162. *Washington Post,* April 17, 1993, p. 1.

163. *Politika,* April 27, 1993, p. 1.

164. *New York Times,* April 27, 1993, p. A7.

165. Silber and Little, *Death of Yugoslavia,* p. 313.

166. UN Security Council document S/25709 (May 3, 1993), pp. 4–11.

167. Silber and Little, *Death of Yugoslavia,* p. 316, and Owen, *Balkan Odyssey,* pp. 154–55.

168. *New York Times,* May 17, 1993, p. A1.

169. Karadžić on Radio Belgrade on April 24, 1993, as reported in *Borba,* April 26, 1993, p. 5.

170. *Washington Post,* May 15, 1992, p. 1, and *New York Times,* May 15, 1993, p. 1.

171. *Washington Post,* May 12, 1993, p. A24.

172. *New York Times,* May 23, 1993, p. 133.

173. *Borba,* December 25, 1992, p. 14.

174. *Washington Post,* March 25, 1993, A10.

175. *Ibid.,* March 19, 1993, p. A52.

176. Drew, *On the Edge,* p. 149.

177. *Ibid.,* pp. 151–52.

178. *New York Times,* April 27, 1993, p. A6.

179. *Washington Post,* April 28, 1993, p. A1, and April 29, 1993, p. A35, and *New York Times,* April 29, 1993, p. A1, and May 1, 1993, p. 5.

180. *Ibid.,* April 29, 1993, p. A1, and May 1, 1993, p. 5. Cf. Drew, *On the Edge,* p. 154.

181. See President Clinton's remarks to the press in *Washington Post,* April 24, 1993, p. A16, and the report in Drew, *On the Edge,* p. 155.

182. *Washington Post,* April 29, 1993, p. A35, and *New York Times,* April 29, 1993, p. A1.

183. *Ibid.,* May 1, 1993, p. 5.

184. Drew, *On the Edge,* p. 154. Note that Drew gives a different date (April 27) for this meeting, but offers a similar description of its substance.

185. *New York Times,* May 2, 1993, p. 1. Cf. *Washington Post,* May 2, 1993, p. 1.

186. *New York Times,* May 10, 1993, p. A9.

187. Drew, *On the Edge,* p. 155.

188. For criticism on this point, see *New York Times,* May 2, 1993, p. IV:19.

189. *Washington Post,* May 2, 1993, p. 1.

190. *New York Times,* May 2, 1993, p. 1.

191. *Ibid.,* May 4, 1993, p. A1.

192. *Washington Post,* May 4, 1993, p. A1, and *New York Times,* May 4, 1993, p. A1.

193. *Washington Post,* May 4, 1993, p. A18.

194. *New York Times,* May 4, 1993, p. A1.

195. *Washington Post,* May 5, 1993, p. 1.

196. Clinton finally laid out the rationale for "lift and strike" in an interview with the *Washington Post* (May 14, 1993, p. 1), after he had abandoned the idea in face of European resistance. He called the policy a "disciplined lifting of the arms embargo" to "level the playing field." Air strikes would be limited to cases in which artillery attacks by the Serbs continued, suggesting that the "strike" feature of the plan was closely related to the humanitarian issue, rather than part of a larger strategic plan.

197. Owen, *Balkan Odyssey,* p. 161.

198. Accounts of these discussions are provided in *New York Times,* May 7, 1993, pp. A1 and A12, and May 9, 1993, p. IV:4. For French resistance, see Wood, "France and Post Cold War Order," p. 146.

199. *New York Times,* May 24, 1993, p. A7.

200. *Ibid.,* May 25, 1993, p. A1.

201. *Ibid.,* January 23, 1993, p. 5, and February 3, 1993, p. A8.

202. UN Security Council document S/25248 (February 8, 1993), p. 2.

203. *New York Times,* March 11, 1993, p. A1.

204. *Washington Post,* April 28, 1993, p. A16, and May 6, 1993, p. A1.

Chapter 6: Negotiating Partition, 1993–94

1. *New York Times,* May 19, 1993, p. A10.

2. *Ibid.,* May 21, 1993, p. A1.

3. *Washington Post,* May 23, 1993, p. A1, and *New York Times,* May 23, 1993, pp. 1, 12. Cf. Owen, *Balkan Odyssey,* pp. 170–73.

4. *Le Monde,* May 29, 1993, as cited in Pia Christina Wood, "France and the Post Cold War Order: The Case of Yugoslavia," *European Security* 3, no. 1 (Spring 1994), p. 147.

5. *New York Times,* June 8, 1993, p. A3.

6. *Ibid.,* June 10, 1993, p. A8.

7. *Ibid.,* June 4, 1993, p. A12.

8. *Ibid.,* June 16, 1993, p. A13.

9. Draft resolution of June 29, 1993.

10. "Direct Governmental Involvement in the Search for a Negotiated Settlement. . . ," Archive Document *Balkan Odyssey* (CD-ROM), Academic Edition v1.1 (London: The Electric Company, 1995).

11. *New York Times,* May 23, 1993, p. 12.

12. *Borba,* June 24, 1993, p. 1.

13. *New York Times,* June 24, 1993, p. A12.

14. *Borba,* June 19–20, 1993, p. 5.

15. *Washington Post,* July 30, 1993, p. A14.

16. UN Security Council document S/26066 (July 8, 1993), p. 4.

17. "Discussion with Foreign Ministers before European Council, Copenhagen, 20 June 1993," Archive Document *Balkan Odyssey* (CD-ROM), Academic Edition v1.1 (London: The Electric Company, 1995).

18. *Boston Globe,* December 5, 1993, p. 1.

19. *Washington Post,* July 29, 1993, p. A16.

20. *Ibid.,* July 22, 1993, p. A1.

21. *Ibid.,* July 28, 1993, p. A1.

22. *New York Times,* July 26, 1993, p. A7. Cf. *Politika,* July 28, 1993, p. 7, and *Le Monde,* August 1–2, 1993, p. 3.

23. *Washington Post,* July 30, 1993, p. A1. Cf. *Ibid.,* July 31, 1993, p. A16.

24. Elizabeth Drew, *On the Edge: The Clinton Presidency* (New York: Simon and Schuster, 1994), pp. 274–75. Cf. *New York Times,* July 14, 1993, p. A3, and *Washington Post,* July 22, 1993, p. A1.

25. *Ibid.,* August 7, 1993, p. A1. For details of the decisionmaking process, see *ibid.,* August 19, 1993, p. A1.

26. *Ibid.,* August 1, 1993, p. A1.

27. *Ibid.,* August 2, 1993, p. A14.

28. *Ibid.,* August 3, 1993, p. A1.

29. *Ibid.,* August 4, 1993, p. A1.

30. For Briquemont's opposition, see *Le Monde,* August 10, 1993, p. 3. Gen. Powell's criticism can be found in *Washington Post,* August 4, 1993, p. A1. Owen's comments can be found in an Agence France Presse (henceforth: AFP) dispatch of August 4, 1993.

31. *New York Times,* August 11, 1993, p. A3.

32. *Ibid.,* August 16, 1993, p. A6.

33. *Washington Post,* August 6, 1993, p. A1.

34. *Ibid.,* July 27, 1993, p. A18.

35. "Direct Governmental Involvement in the Search for a Negotiated Settlement. . . ," Archive Document *Balkan Odyssey* (CD-ROM), Academic Edition v1.1 (London: The Electric Company, 1995).

36. Owen, *Balkan Odyssey,* pp. 194–95.

37. Sarajevo Radio, July 18, 1993, as translated in Foreign Broadcast Information Service, *Daily Report: Eastern Europe* (henceforth: FBIS, *EEU*), July 19, 1993, p. 41.

38. *Washington Post,* May 4, 1994, p. D1.

39. *Der Standard* (Vienna), July 29, 1993, as translated in FBIS, *EEU,* July 29, 1993, pp. 32–33.

40. *Die Woche* (Hamburg), July 29, 1993, as translated in FBIS, *EEU,* July 30, 1993, pp. 40–41. This is the same interview as that published in *Der Standard,* but includes several remarks by Ganić not given in the *Der Standard* dispatch.

41. *Ibid.*

42. Kurier (Vienna), August 25, 1993, as translated in FBIS, *EEU,* August 25, 1993, p. 35.

43. *Voice of Arabs* (Cairo), August 4, 1993, as translated in FBIS, *EEU,* August 4, 1993, pp. 35–36.

44. Sarajevo Radio, August 24, 1993, as translated in British Broadcasting Corporation, *Summary of World Broadcasts* (henceforth: BBC, *SWB*), August 26, 1993, EE/1777/C.

45. Sarajevo Radio, July 11, 1993, as translated in FBIS, *EEU,* July 12, 1993, p. 24.

46. Kasim I. Begić, *Bosna i Hercegovina od Vanceove misije do Daytonskog sporazuma (1991.-1996.)* (Sarajevo: Bosanska knjiga, 1997), pp. 140–42.

47. *Ibid.,* pp. 138, 141.

48. *Washington Post,* August 1, 1993, p. A27. The text of the constitutional agreement can be found in UN Security Council document S/26233 (August 3, 1993), appendix II, pp. 11–17, and *Borba,* August 2, 1993, p. 9.

49. *New York Times,* August 17, 1993, p. A6, and UN Security Council document S/26337/Add.1 (August 23, 1993), appendix II, part 2, pp. 22–23. For the map, see UN Security Council document S/26337 (August 20, 1993), p. 5. For Serb demands on how Sarajevo was to be partitioned, see *Washington Post,* December 20, 1993, p. A22.

50. *Borba,* June 18, 1993, p. 7.

51. *NIN,* July 9, 1993, pp. 30–31.

52. A discussion of the two maps can be found in *Borba,* August 14–15, 1993, p. 2.

53. UN Security Council documents S/26337 (August 20, 1993), S/26337/Add.1 (August 23, 1993), and S/26337/Add. 2 (August 23, 1993).

54. *Borba,* August 24, 1993, p. 12.

55. UN Security Council document S/26260 (August 6, 1993), appendix IV, pp. 30–32.

56. Based on a schematic diagram published in UN Security Council document S/26337 (August 20, 1993), p. 6.

57. Owen, *Balkan Odyssey,* pp. 211–12.

58. On the final percentages, and the five parts of the agreement, see Tanjug dispatch of August 21, 1993, as translated in BBC, *SWB,* August 23, 1993, EE/1774/C1.

59. *Washington Post,* August 23, 1993, p. 14.

60. *Ibid.,* August 27, 1993, p. A1.

61. *Ibid.,* May 4, 1993, p. A1.

62. *New York Times,* August 30, 1993, p. A7.

63. *Washington Post,* August 31, 1993, p. A16.

64. See *Borba,* August 28–29, 1993, p. 3 for objections from Bosnian Serbs. For objections from Bosnian Croats, see Croatian Radio (Zagreb), August 24, 1993, and Croatian TV Satellite Service (Zagreb), August 24, 1994, both as translated in BBC, *SWB,* August 26, 1993, EE/1777/C.

65. UN Security Council document S/26337/Add. 1 (August 23, 1993), p. 8 (appendix I).

66. *New York Times,* August 26, 1993, p. A13.

67. *Ibid.*

68. *Ibid.,* August 28, 1993, p. 4, and August 29, 1993, p. 10. *Borba,* August 30, 1993, p. 2.

69. *Ibid.*

70. Begić, *Bosna i Hercegovina od Vanceove misije,* p. 143 (note 13).

71. *Borba,* August 30, 1993, p. 2.

72. *Washington Post,* September 3, 1993, p. A1.

73. *Wall Street Journal,* September 3, 1993, p. A12.

74. *Washington Post,* September 8, 1993, p. A23. Cf. *New York Times,* September 8, 1993, p. A3.

75. *Ibid.* See also *New York Times,* September 10, 1993, p. A3.

76. *Washington Post,* September 9, 1993, p. A32.

77. *Ibid.,* September 11, 1993, p. A18.

78. *New York Times,* October 3, 1993, p. 10.

79. *Washington Post,* September 11, 1993, p. A18.

80. *Ibid.,* September 17, 1993, p. A34.

81. Sarajevo Radio, September 18, 1993, as translated in FBIS, *EEU,* September 20, 1993, p. 39.

82. *AFP,* September 18, 1993, and *New York Times,* September 20, 1993, p. A10.

83. Slobodanka Kovačević and Putnik Dajić, *Hronologija jugoslovenske krize (1942–1993 godina)* (Belgrade: Institut za evropske studije, 1994), p. 239.

84. UN Security Council document S/26486 (September 23, 1993).

85. Begić, *Bosna i Hercegovina od Vanceove misije*, p. 146.

86. *New York Times,* October 3, 1993, p. 10; September 22, 1993, p. A12; September 29, 1993, p. A3; and September 30, 1993, p. A1.

87. Owen, *Balkan Odyssey,* p. 220.

88. *Washington Post,* September 30, 1993, p. A20.

89. *Ibid.*

90. *New York Times,* September 30, 1993, p. A1.

91. *Ibid.,* October 6, 1993, p. A8. Cf. *Washington Post,* September 26, 1993, p. A42.

92. "Discussions with the parties 4–25 October 1993," Archive Document *Balkan Odyssey* (CD-ROM), Academic Edition v1.1 (London: The Electric Company, 1995).

93. Srdjan Radulović, *Sudbina krajina* (Belgrade: Dan graf, 1996), p. 70.

94. "Discussion between Foreign Ministers on the political agenda, Foreign Affairs Council, Luxembourg, 22 November," Archive Document *Balkan Odyssey* (CD-ROM), Academic Edition v1.1 (London: The Electric Company, 1995).

95. "Direct Governmental Involvement in the Search for a Negotiated Settlement. . . ."

96. *Guardian,* January 3, 1994, p. 8.

97. Owen, *Balkan Odyssey,* p. 233.

98. *New York Times,* January 6, 1994, p. A9; January 7, 1994, p. A1; and January 8, 1994, p. 6.

99. Owen, *Balkan Odyssey,* p. 240.

100. *New York Times,* December 1, 1993, p. A8.

101. Owen, *Balkan Odyssey,* p. 243.

102. *New York Times,* January 31, 1994, p. A9, and February 1, 1994, p. A8; *Boston Globe,* February 1, 1994, p. 8.

103. *New York Times,* February 14, 1994, p. A6.

104. "Direct Governmental Involvement in the Search for a Negotiated Settlement. . . ." See also *New York Times,* January 25, 1994, p. A1, and January 28, 1994, p. A6.

105. *Ibid.,* January 25, 1994, p. A1.

106. *Ibid.,* January 6, 1994, p. A8.

107. *Ibid.,* January 28, 1994, p. A6.

108. *Ibid.,* January 27, 1993, p. A8, and *Boston Globe,* February 1, 1993, p. 8.

109. *New York Times,* January 12, 1994, p. 1.

110. *Ibid.,* January 20, 1994, p. A8.

111. Nik Gowing, "Real-Time Television Coverage of Armed Conflicts and Diplomatic Crises: Does It Pressure or Distort Foreign Policy Decisions?" *Working Paper* no. 94–1, The Joan Shorenstein Barone Center on the Press, Politics and Public Policy, Harvard University (June 1994), pp. 69–76. See also *New York Times,* February 6, 1994, p. 13; February 7, 1994, p. A1; and February 8, 1994, p. A1. For an informative retrospective account of U.S. decisionmaking see *New York Times,* February 14, 1994, p. A6.

112. *New York Times,* February 14, 1994, p. A6.

113. *Ibid.,* January 12, 1994, p. A8.

114. Owen, *Balkan Odyssey,* p. 255.

115. *New York Times,* February 10, 1994, p. 1.

116. *Washington Post,* February 7, 1994, p. 1.

117. Slobodanka Kovačević and Putnik Dajić, *Hronologija jugoslovenske krize 1994* (Belgrade: Institut za evropske studije, 1995), pp. 47–48.

118. *Washington Post,* February 11, 1994, p. 1, and Kovačević and Dajić, *Hronologija jugoslovenske krize 1994,* pp. 46, 47.

119. *Washington* Post, February 14, 1994, p. A20, and February 17, 1994, p. A25.

120. Kovačević and Dajić, *Hronologija jugoslovenske krize 1994*, p. 51.

121. For details of the agreement as reported in the press, see *Washington Post,* February 20, 1994, p. A1.

122. *New York Times,* February 18, 1994, p. 1, and *Washington Post,* February 18, 1994, p. 1.

123. *Ibid.,* February 11, 1994, p. 1, and February 13, 1994, p. A27. See Kovačević and Dajić, *Hronologija jugoslovenske krize 1994,* p. 50, for General Mladić's statement of February 15 that Serb artillery would not be withdrawn because "[the Serb] people cannot be left to the mercy of the fanaticism of the Muslim units."

124. See *NIN,* March 11, 1994, as translated in FBIS, *EEU,* April 7, 1994, p. 38.

125. *New York Times,* February 8, 1994, p. A14.

126. For a sampling of negative Russian responses to the NATO ultimatum, see *Current Digest of the Post-Soviet Press* (henceforth: *CDPSP*) 46, no. 6 (March 9, 1994), pp. 6–8.

127. *New York Times,* September 23, 1994, p. A35.

128. *Washington Post,* February 20, 1994, p. A30.

129. *New York Times,* February 16, 1994, p. A7.

130. *Nezavisimaya gazeta,* February 19, 1994, as translated in *CDPSP* 46, 7 (March 16, 1994), pp. 3–4.

131. Owen, *Balkan Odyssey,* p. 268.

132. *New York Times,* February 18, 1994, p. A10.

133. *Ibid.,* April 26, 1994, p. A6, and April 30, 1994, p. 3.

134. *Ibid.,* February 20, 1994, p. 10.

135. *Ibid.,* February 11, 1994, p. A1.

136. *Ibid.,* February 11, 1994, p. A7.

137. UN Security Council document S/1994/173 (February 14, 1994), p. 5. See also *New York Times,* February 11, 1994, p. A6, and February 13, 1994, p. 12.

138. *Guardian,* February 12, 1994, p. 13.

139. *New York Times,* February 15, 1994, p. A12.

140. *Ibid.,* March 1, 1994, p. A1.

141. *Ibid.,* February 12, 1994, p. 5.

142. Testimony to the Senate Foreign Relations Committee, February 23, 1994, as reported in Federal Information Service, *Daily Digest of the Congressional Record,* 103rd Congress, 2nd session (electronic edition, document no. y4.F76/1:IR1).

143. AFP, February 11, 1993.

144. United Press International dispatch (henceforth: UPI), February 11, 1994.

145. *Washington Post,* February 21, 1994, p. A18. Note that the ambassador's name is presented here in the Westernized form in which it was used at the time. It appears elsewhere (e.g., Begić, *Bosna i Hercegovina od Vanceove misije,* p. 281 [note 1]) as "Šaćirbegović."

146. *Washington Post,* February 21, 1994, p. A18.

147. *Ibid.,* May 20, 1992, p. A24.

148. *Borba,* June 15, 1993, p. 5. See also *Washington Post,* May 19, 1993, p. A23.

149. *Borba,* June 15, 1993, p. 5.

150. *Oslobodjenje* (European edition), January 6–13, 1994, p. 3.

151. Radulović, *Sudbina krajina,* pp. 58–59. See also *New York Times,* January 21, 1994, p. 3.

152. *New York Times,* January 21, 1994, p. 3.

153. For an "insider's" account of the negotiations leading to federation, see George Rudman, "Backtracking to Reformulate: Establishing the Bosnian Federation," *International Negotiation* 1, no. 3 (1996), pp. 525–45.

154. *Oslobodjenje* (European edition), February 11–18, 1994, p. 10.

155. UPI, February 19, 1993, and February 21, 1993.

156. *New York Times,* February 24, 1994, p. A1, and *Guardian,* February 19, 1994, p. 11, and February 24, 1994, p. 26.

157. *Ibid.,* February 24, 1994, p. 14.

158. Croatian TV satellite service, February 24, 1994, as translated in BBC, *SWB,* February 28, 1994, EE/1933/C.

159. *Washington Post,* February 25, 1994, p. 26. Cf. Rudman, "Backtracking," pp. 536, 539.

160. Croatian TV satellite service, February 24, 1994, as translated in BBC, *SWB,* February 28, 1994, EE/1933/C.

161. *New York Times,* March 2, 1994, p. 1, and *Oslobodjenje,* March 11–18, 1994, pp. 4–5.

162. *Neue Zuricher Zeitung,* March 11, 1994, p. 3.

163. *Washington Post,* March 14, 1994, p. A13.

164. *Ibid.,* March 13, 1994, p. A26.

165. *Oslobodjenje* (European edition), April 8–15, 1994, p. 1, and *Washington Post,* April 8, 1994, p. A26.

166. Zagreb Radio, March 3, 1994, as translated in FBIS, *EEU,* March 4, 1994, pp. 36–37.

167. Rudman, "Backtracking," pp. 538–39.

168. For a detailed account of American views, see *New York Times,* March 13, 1994, p. 10.

169. *Ibid.,* April 8, 1994, p. A1.

170. Article 1 of the constitution read as follows: "Bosniacs and Croats, as constituent peoples (along with Others) and citizens of the Republic of Bosnia and Herzegovian, in the exercise of their sovereign rights, transform the internal structure of the territories with a majority of Bosniac and Croat population in the Republic of Bosnia into a Federation." Text as adopted in Washington, D.C., March 13, 1994 (mimeo).

171. *Oslobodjenje* (European edition), April 22–29, 1994, p. 32.

172. *Ibid.,* May 20–27, 1994, p. 4.

173. *Washington Post,* May 12, 1994, p. A22, and *Oslobodjenje* (European edition), May 13–20, 1994, p. 1, and May 20–27, 1994, p. 3. For the seven points of the Vienna agreement see *Ibid.,* p. 4.

174. *Ibid.,* p. 3.

175. Sarajevo Radio, May 30, 1994, as translated in FBIS, *EEU,* May 31, 1994, p. 41.

176. *Oslobodjenje* (European edition), May 13–20, 1994, p. 1.

177. *Ibid.,* June 3–10, 1994, p. 3.

178. *Ibid.,* December 15–22, 1994, p. 7.

179. *New York Times,* February 11, 1994, p. A6, and February 13, 1994, p. 12.

180. "Direct Governmental Involvement in the Search for a Negotiated Settlement. . . ," note 26.

181. Misha Glenny, remarks at a meeting of the American Association for the Advancement of Slavic Studies, Washington, D.C., October 28, 1995.

182. *New York Times,* April 6, 1994, p. A1.

183. *Washington Post,* April 22, 1994, p. 1.

184. *Ibid.,* April 24, 1994, p. C1.

185. *Ibid.,* May 11, 1994, p. A23.

186. *Ibid.,* May 12, 1994, p. A22.

187. *New York Times,* April 19, 1994, p. A10; April 20, 1994, p. A1; and April 21, 1994, p. A8.

188. *Guardian,* February 21, 1994, p. 8. See also *New York Times,* February 23, 1994, p. A8.

189. On the reduced role of the ICFY, see UN Security Council documents S/1994/811 (July 8, 1994), pp. 13–16, and S/1994/1454 (December 29, 1994).

190. "Direct Governmental Involvement in the Search for a Negotiated Settlement. . . ."

191. Sarajevo Radio, April 28, 1994, as translated in FBIS, *EEU,* April 29, 1994, p. 33.

192. Kovačević and Dajić, *Hronologija jugoslovenske krize 1994,* p. 104.

193. *Washington Post,* May 15, 1994, p. A30.

194. "Direct Governmental Involvement in the Search for a Negotiated Settlement. . . ."

195. "Contact Group negotiations 26 April 1994–14 May 1994 [as seen by Lord Owen]," Archive Document *Balkan Odyssey* (CD-ROM), Academic Edition v1.1 (London: The Electric Company, 1995).

196. Cf. the views reported in *New York Times,* April 12, 1994, p. A10; April 16, 1994, p. 4; and April 17, 1994, p. IV:4. See also the selection of views published in the Russian press, as translated in *CDPSP* 46, 15 (May 11, 1994), pp. 5–9.

197. *New York Times,* April 19, 1994, p. A10, and April 26, 1994, p. A7.

198. *Izvestia,* April 20, 1994, as translated in *CDPSP* 46, 16 (May 18, 1994), p. 1.

199. *Ibid.,* p. 5.

200. "Direct Governmental Involvement in the Search for a Negotiated Settlement. . . ."

201. *Ibid.*

202. *New York Times,* June 6, 1994, p. A3.

203. As we noted in chapter 4 (notes 87 and 88), the Bosnian government argued that the fighting in Bihać was an internal matter not subject to the cease-fire.

204. UN Security Council document S/1994/1081 (September 21, 1994).

205. *Washington Post,* August 3, 1994, p. A22.

206. *New York Times,* May 13, 1994, p. A10, and May 18, 1994, p. A7.

207. "Direct Governmental Involvement in the Search for a Negotiated Settlement. . . ."

208. *New York Times,* July 7, 1994, p. A1. Cf. *Washington Post,* July 8, 1994, p. A16.

209. Laura Silber and Allan Little, *The Death of Yugoslavia* (London: Penguin Books/BBC Books, 1995), p. 376.

210. Begić, *Bosna i Hercegovina od Vanceove misije,* pp. 211–13.

211. "Direct Governmental Involvement in the Search for a Negotiated Settlement. . . ."

212. *Ibid.* See also the report on French-American discussions in *New York Times,* June 9, 1994, p. A1. Cf. *Washington Post,* July 6, 1994, p. A21.

213. *New York Times,* June 10, 1994, p. A6, and July 2, 1994, p. 3. *Washington Post,* July 2, 1994, p. A8.

214. *Ibid.,* July 18, 1994, p. A1.

215. *Ibid.,* July 26, 1994, p. A12.

216. *New York Times,* July 22, 1994, p. A3. Cf. *Washington Post,* July 22, 1994, p. A20.

217. *Izvestia,* August 3, 1994, as translated in *CDPSP* 46, 31 (August 31, 1994), p. 21.

218. *New York Times,* July 6, 1994, p. A3, and *Washington Post,* July 6, 1994, p. A21. Compare the contrasting U.S. and Russian positions expressed at a joint news conference in Geneva, reported in *New York Times,* July 31, 1994, p. 12.

219. *Washington Post,* August 1, 1994, p. A17.

220. Silber and Little, *Death of Yugoslavia,* p. 378.

221. Tanjug, July 31, 1994, as translated in FBIS, *EEU,* August 1, 1994, p. 53.

222. *Washington Post,* July 31, 1994, p. A25, and August 1, 1994, p. A16.

223. Tanjug, July 31, 1994, as translated in FBIS, *EEU,* August 1, 1994, p. 54.

224. *Washington Post,* September 9, 1994, p. A11.

225. Silber and Little, *Death of Yugoslavia*, p. 379. Cf. *Washington Post*, July 27, 1994, p. A22, and July 28, 1994, p. A26.

226. *Ibid.*, July 29, 1994, p. A32.

227. *New York Times*, August 12, 1994, p. A3, and *Washington Post*, August 12, 1994, p. A33.

228. *Ibid.*, August 13, 1994, p. A14.

229. *Ibid.*, August 11, 1994, p. A19.

230. *New York Times*, September 4, 1994, p. 4, and September 9, 1994, p. A1.

231. *New York Times*, November 11, 1994, p. A1.

232. *Boston Globe*, May 12, 1996, p. 15.

233. *New York Times*, April 17, 1996, p. A1.

234. *Washington Post*, April 14, 1995, p. A1, and *New York Times*, April 15, 1995, p. 3.

235. *Ibid.*, April 26, 1996, p. A6.

236. *Ibid.*, September 27, 1994, p. A19, and September 28, 1994, p. A9.

237. *Ibid.*, April 17, 1996, p. A1.

238. *Ibid.*, April 26, 1996, p. A6.

239. *Ibid.*, November 26, 1994, p. 7.

240. *Ibid.*, February 21, 1995, p. A8, and March 1, 1995, p. A5.

241. *Washington Post*, July 28, 1995, p. A1.

242. *New York Times*, November 5, 1994, p. 1. See also the retrospective account of covert British involvement in *Guardian*, April 2, 1996, pp. 1, 11.

243. *Washington Post*, August 3, 1994, p. A22.

244. Tanjug, August 4, 1994, as translated in FBIS, *EEU*, August 4, 1994, p. 28.

245. *Washington Post*, August 5, 1994, p. A23, and Kovačević and Dajić, *Hronologija jugoslovenske krize 1994*, p. 135.

246. *Ibid.*

247. *Guardian*, August 5, 1994, p. 23.

248. *Boston Globe*, October 5, 1994, p. 77, and *New York Times*, October 5, 1994, p. A9, and October 6, 1994, p. A14.

249. "ICFY Mission in Belgrade," Archive Document *Balkan Odyssey* (CD-ROM), Academic Edition v1.1 (London: The Electric Company, 1995).

250. *Vreme*, August 22, 1994, pp. 11–13.

251. Kovačević and Dajić, *Hronologija jugoslovenske krize 1994*, p. 212.

252. *New York Times*, August 6, 1994, p. 4.

253. *Borba*, August 6–7 1994, p. 20.

254. *Guardian*, September 22, 1994, p. 12.

255. *Washington Post*, December 5, 1994, p. A1.

256. *New York Times*, November 25, 1994, p. A1.

257. UN Security Council document S/1994/1389 (December 1, 1994).

258. *New York Times*, November 25, 1994, p. 1.

259. *Ibid.*, December 4, 1994, p. 1.

260. *Ibid.*, November 29, 1994, p. A16.

261. *Ibid.*, November 30, 1994, p. A1.

262. *Ibid.*, November 28, 1994, p. A11, and November 29, 1994, p. A1.

263. *Ibid.*, December 2, 1994, p. A1.

264. *Ibid.*, December 6, 1994, p. A1.

265. *Ibid.*, December 8, 1994, p. A1.

266. "NATO's Role in Bringing Peace to the Former Yugoslavia," *NATO Basic Fact Sheet* no. 4 (March 1997), p. 7 @ http://www.nato.int/docu.

267. *Washington Post*, August 2, 1994, p. A19.

268. *New York Times,* December 8, 1994, p. A1.
269. *Ibid.,* December 9, 1994, p. A1.
270. *Guardian,* December 7, 1994, p. 22.
271. *Ibid.*
272. *New York Times,* February 12, 1994, p. 5, and March 13, 1994, p. 10.

Chapter 7: Imposing the Dayton Agreement

1. See, for example, the comments of unnamed administration officials cited in *New York Times,* March 13, 1994, p. 10.
2. See, for example, the essays by Warren Zimmerman in *Washington Post,* May 14, 1995, p. C7, and *New York Times,* June 23, 1995, p. A21; and by Marshall Harris and Stephen Walker in *ibid.,* August 23, 1995, p. A21.
3. For Gingrich's call, see *ibid.,* December 5, 1994, p. A1.
4. *Ibid.,* November 29, 1994, p. A16.
5. *Ibid.,* November 30, 1994, p. A1.
6. For a retrospective account of the internal debate in the Clinton administration, see *ibid.,* December 4, 1994, p. 1. Cf. Michael Kelley, "Surrender and Blame," *New Yorker,* December 19, 1994, pp. 49–51.
7. *New York Times,* December 6, 1994, p. A1.
8. *Ibid.,* December 18, 1994, p. 1.
9. *Ibid.,* January 21, 1995, p. 1.
10. *Ibid.,* January 23, 1995, p. A5, and *Washington Post,* January 28, 1995, p. A23.
11. *Contact Group Ministerial Communique,* Brussels, December 2, 1994, as cited in Fiona M. Watson and Tom Dodd, *Bosnia and Croatia: The Conflict Continues,* Research Paper 95/55 (London: International Affairs and Defence Section, House of Commons Library, May 1995), p. 11.
12. *New York Times,* December 5, 1994, p. A12.
13. *Ibid.,* December 6, 1994, p. A3, and December 9, 1994, p. A12; *Guardian,* December 8, 1994, p. 1.
14. Agence France Presse (henceforth: AFP), January 9, 1995. See also *New York Times,* January 10, 1995, p. A9.
15. AFP, January 30, 1995.
16. *Washington Post,* February 22, 1995, p. A19.
17. *New York Times,* January 21, 1995, p. 1.
18. *Washington Post,* January 24, 1995, p. A13.
19. AFP, February 13, 1995.
20. *Ibid.,* February 14, 1995.
21. *Washington Post,* February 15, 1995, p. A15.
22. *Ibid.,* March 7, 1995, p. A11.
23. *Ibid.,* February 25, 1995, p. A1.
24. *New York Times,* March 3, 1995, p. A3.
25. *Guardian,* April 17, 1995, p. 18.
26. *New York Times,* June 1, 1995, p. A10.
27. For the authorization, see *ibid.,* December 9, 1994, p. A1. For Holbrooke's argument, see Richard Holbrooke, *To End a War* (New York: Random House, 1998), pp. 66–68.
28. *New York Times,* June 5, 1995, p. A1.
29. *Ibid.,* June 1, 1995, p. A10, and June 4, 1995, pp. 1, 16.
30. *Ibid.,* June 8, 1995, p. A10.

31. *Ibid.*, June 3, 1995, p. 5.

32. *Guardian*, May 31, 1995, pp. 12, 13.

33. "NATO's Role in Bringing Peace to the Former Yugoslavia," *NATO Basic Fact Sheet* no. 4 (March 1997) @ http://www.nato.int/docu/, p. 7.

34. Watson and Dodd, *Bosnia and Croatia: The conflict continues*, pp. 21–22.

35. *Boston Globe*, May 25, 1995, p. 1.

36. *New York Times*, April 20, 1995, p. A3.

37. *Financial Times*, June 28, 1995, p. 12, as cited in Richard H. Ullman, "The Wars in Yugoslavia and the International System After the Cold War," in *The World and Yugoslavia's Wars*, Richard H. Ullman, ed. (New York: Council on Foreign Relations, 1996), p. 24.

38. *Washington Post*, June 12, 1995, p. 1.

39. For retrospective accounts and analyses of the events at Srebrenica, see *Boston Globe*, October 1, 1995, p. 1; *New York Times*, October 8, 1995, p. 1; *Washington Post*, October 26, 1995, p. 1, October 29, 1995, p. 1, and November 9, 1995, p. A22. See also the analyses in Jan Honig and Norbeert Both, *Srebrenica: Record of a War Crime* (New York: Penguin Books, 1997).

40. Michael Kelly, "The Negotiator," *New Yorker*, November 6, 1995, p. 85.

41. *New York Times*, July 20, 1995, p. A1.

42. *Ibid.*, July 23, 1995, p. 8.

43. *Washington Post*, March 3, 1996, p. C1. The timing of the decision appears to be corroborated by an account in *New York Times*, July 23, 1995, p. 8.

44. *Ibid.*, June 9, 1995, p. A10.

45. *Ibid.*, July 12, 1995, p. A6.

46. *Ibid.*, July 13, 1995, p. A6.

47. *Ibid.*, June 5, 1995, p. A1; July 12, 1995, p. A6; and July 14, 1995, p. A1.

48. *Ibid.*, July 14, 1995, p. A1.

49. *Ibid.*, July 23, 1995, p. 8.

50. *Ibid.*, August 21, 1996, p. A6.

51. *Ibid.*, August 13, 1995, p. 1, and August 19, 1995, p. 1.

52. *Ibid.*, October 28, 1995, p. 1.

53. *Guardian*, July 31, 1995, p. 7.

54. *Washington Post*, February 14, 1995, p. A11.

55. Milos Vasic, "The Decline and Fall of Western Slavonia," *War Report* 33 (May 1995), p. 5, and Boris Raseta, "The Questions over Slavonia," *War Report* 33 (May 1995), pp. 7–8.

56. Senad Pecanin, "Climb Any Mountain?" *War Report* 33 (May 1995), p. 12.

57. AFP, May 3, 1995.

58. *Ibid.*, May 4, 1995.

59. *Guardian*, May 20, 1995, p. 11.

60. AFP, May 8, 1995.

61. *New York Times*, May 27, 1995, p. A1.

62. Cf. *Ibid.*, June 3, 1995, p. 1, and June 4, 1995, p. 1.

63. *Ibid.*, August 12, 1995, p. 5.

64. *Ibid.*, June 11, 1995, p. 14.

65. AFP, May 23, 1995.

66. For (partial) accounts of these negotiations, see *Washington Post*, May 26, 1995, p. A37; *New York Times*, May 18, 1995, p. A6, May 24, 1995, p. A7, May 26, 1995, p. A7, and June 1, 1995, p. A12; AFP, May 18, 1995; and *Guardian*, May 20, 1995, p. 11.

67. AFP, May 24, 1995.

68. *New York Times*, June 8, 1995, p. A10.

69. On alleged divisions in the administration, see *Boston Globe,* June 8, 1995, p. 23, and *Borba,* August 22, 1995, p. 3. For Holbrooke's interpretation, see Holbrooke, *To End a War,* p. 63.

70. *New York Times,* September 3, 1995, p. IV:6.

71. *Guardian,* July 7, 1995, p. 15; James Gow, "Bosnia I: Stepping Up the Peace?" *World Today* 51, 7 (July 1995), p. 127.

72. *Washington Post,* August 8, 1995, p. A14.

73. *Ibid.,* August 10, 1995, p. 22.

74. AFP, August 1, 1995, and ITAR-TASS, August 1, 1995, as translated in BBC, *SWB,* August 2, 1995, SU/2371/B.

75. Philip Schwarm, "Divided We Stand," *War Report* 33 (May 1995), pp. 8–9.

76. *New York Times,* August 18, 1995, p. A4, and AFP, August 17, 1995.

77. *Ibid.,* August 26, 1995, p. 2.

78. *Ibid.,* August 28, 1995, p. A1.

79. *New Europe,* September 3–9, 1995, p. 3.

80. *Ibid.,* p. 25.

81. *Washington Post,* August 30, 1995, p. A20.

82. *New York Times,* August 28, 1995, p. A1.

83. *New Europe,* September 3–9, 1995, p. 25.

84. *Washington Post,* September 1, 1995, p. 1. Cf. *New Europe,* September 3–9, 1995, p. 3.

85. Kelly, "The Negotiator," p. 88.

86. Holbrooke, *To End a War,* p. 113.

87. *Ibid.,* pp. 130–31.

88. *Washington Post,* September 22, 1995, p. A1.

89. The formal agreement was signed November 12.

90. Maynard Glitman, a former deputy assistant secretary of defense for Europe and NATO, makes essentially the same argument in "US Policy in Bosnia: Rethinking a Flawed Approach," *Survival* 30, no. 4 (Winter 1996–97), p. 74.

91. *New York Times,* March 13, 1995, p. A9.

92. *Ibid.,* July 25, 1995, p. A6.

93. Patrick Moore, "An End Game in Croatia and Bosnia," *Transition* 1, 20 (November 3, 1995), p. 6.

94. *New York Times,* August 13, 1995, p. 1.

95. Kasim I. Begić, *Bosna i Hercegovina od Vanceove misije do Daytonskog sporazuma (1991.-1996.)* (Sarajevo: Bosanska knjiga, 1997), p. 266.

96. "NATO's Role in Bringing Peace," p. 7.

97. *New York Times,* November 26, 1994, p. 7.

98. *Ibid.,* February 21, 1995, p. A8, and March 1, 1995, p. A5; *Washington Post,* February 21, 1995, p. A1; and *Guardian,* February 25, 1995, p. 12.

99. *New York Times,* March 1, 1995, p. A5.

100. For an extensive review of the evidence, see *Washington Post,* July 28, 1995, p. A1.

101. *Washington Post,* April 14, 1995, p. A1. See also *New York Times,* April 15, 1995, p. 3. For an overview, see *Los Angeles Times,* April 5, 1996, p. 1.

102. *Washington Post,* July 28, 1995, p. A1.

103. *Ibid.,* February 2, 1996, p. 1. See also *ibid.,* May 12, 1996, p. A1, and September 22, 1996, p. A1.

104. *New York Times,* April 17, 1996, p. A1.

105. *Ibid.,* October 28, 1995, pp. 1, 5. See also *Washington Post,* August 11, 1995, p. 1.

106. *Ibid.,* July 28, 1995, p. A1.

107. *Ibid.,* July 28, 1995, p. A32.

108. *New York Times,* May 11, 1995, p. A3.

109. UN Security Council document S/1995/444 (May 30, 1995).

110. *New York Times,* June 1, 1995, p. A13.

111. *Ibid.,* May 26, 1995, p. A8, and July 16, 1995, p. 8.

112. AFP, May 24, 1995.

113. *Guardian,* May 29, 1995, p. 9.

114. *New York Times,* July 16, 1995, p. 8. For the national composition of UN-PROFOR troops, see UN Security Council document S/1995/222 (March 22, 1995), Annex I, pp. 27–30.

115. *New York Times,* May 30, 1995, p. A1.

116. *Ibid.,* June 4, 1995, p. 14.

117. *Ibid.,* May 31, 1995, p. A1.

118. *Guardian,* June 1, 1995, p. 7.

119. UN Security Council document S/1995/470 (June 9, 1995). Authorization to expand UNPROFOR to accommodate the rapid reaction force was granted in Resolution 998 (June 16, 1995).

120. UN Security Council document S/1995/470 (June 9, 1995), p. 5.

121. *New York Times,* July 15, 1995, p. 5.

122. *Ibid.,* July 20, 1995, p. A1.

123. *Ibid.,* July 12, 1995, p. A6; July 13, 1995, pp. A1, A6; and July 18, 1995, p. A1.

124. *Ibid.,* July 13, 1995, p. A1.

125. *Ibid.,* July 14, 1995, p. A1.

126. *Boston Globe,* July 14, 1995, p. 1.

127. *New York Times,* July 18, 1995, p. A7.

128. *Ibid.,* July 29, 1996, p. A1.

129. *Ibid.,* July 18, 1995, p. A1.

130. *Guardian,* July 13, 1995, p. 1.

131. *New York Times,* July 18, 1995, p. A1.

132. *Independent,* July 23, 1995, p. 19.

133. *Washington Post,* July 17, 1995, p. A15.

134. *Ibid.,* July 18, 1995, p. A17.

135. *Ibid.,* July 19, 1995, p. A17.

136. *Guardian,* July 18, 1995, p. 9.

137. *New York Times,* July 18, 1995, p. A1.

138. *Ibid.,* July 21, 1995, p. A1.

139. For the positions and statements of the participants, see the report in *ibid.,* July 22, 1995, p. 1. See also *Washington Post,* July 22, 1995, p. 1. For Holbrooke's view, see *To End a War,* p. 71.

140. *New York Times,* July 22, 1995, p. 1. See also *Washington Post,* July 22, 1995, p. 1.

141. *New York Times,* July 22, 1995, p. 4.

142. *Ibid.,* July 27, 1995, p. A1, and July 28, 1995, p. A4.

143. *Guardian,* July 24, 1995, p. 9.

144. AFP, July 21, 1995.

145. *New York Times,* July 22, 1995, p. 1.

146. *Independent,* July 23, 1995, p. 19. Cf. the brief report of British/American agreement in *New York Times,* July 21, 1995, p. A1.

147. Tanjug, July 21, 1995, as translated in BBC, *SWB,* July 24, 1995, EE/2363/C.

148. AFP, July 22, 1995.

149. *New York Times,* July 24, 1995, p. A7, and *Guardian,* July 25, 1995, p. 9.

150. *Washington Post,* July 25, 1995, p. A11.

151. *Ibid.,* July 24, 1995, p. 1; *New York Times,* July 24, 1995, p. A1; and *Guardian,* July 24, 1995, p. 1, and July 25, 1995, p. 1.

152. *Washington Post,* July 29, 1995, p. A16.

153. *Ibid.,* and *Guardian,* July 24, 1995, p. 1.

154. AFP, July 18, 1995.

155. *Ibid.,* July 15, 1995, and July 20, 1995. See also *ibid.,* August 23, 1995.

156. *Ibid.,* July 18, 1995, August 23, 1995, and August 26, 1995.

157. *New York Times,* August 17, 1995, p. A11, and Zagreb Radio, August 29, 1995, as translated in Foreign Broadcast Information Service, *Daily Report: Eastern Europe* (henceforth: FBIS, *EEU*), August 30, 1995, p. 25.

158. *Guardian,* July 24, 1995, pp. 1, 9.

159. *Ibid.,* August 29, 1995, p. 10.

160. *Washington Post,* July 29, 1995, p. A16.

161. *New York Times,* July 26, 1995, p. A1.

162. *Guardian,* July 26, 1995, p. 8.

163. *Washington Post,* July 30, 1995, p. A23.

164. *Guardian,* July 27, 1995, p. 9.

165. *New York Times,* August 2, 1995, p. A6, and *Guardian,* August 2, 1995, p. 9.

166. *Washington Post,* July 30, 1995, p. A23.

167. AFP, August 4, 1995.

168. *New York Times,* August 13, 1995, p. 1.

169. *Ibid.,* August 9, 1995, p. A7.

170. *Ibid.*

171. Holbrooke, *To End a War,* pp. 74–75, 86.

172. *Washington Post,* August 16, 1995, p. A26.

173. *New York Times,* August 9, 1995, p. A7, and August 10, 1995, p. A1; *Washington Post,* August 9, 1995, p. A16; *Independent,* August 11, 1995, p. 8; and *Guardian,* August 14, 1995, p. 9.

174. Richard Holbrooke, "The Road to Sarajevo," *New Yorker,* October 21 & 28, 1996, p. 99, and *To End a War,* p. 93.

175. *Guardian,* August 19, 1995, p. 1.

176. *New York Times,* August 2, 1995, p. A6.

177. *Washington Post,* August 16, 1995, p. A26.

178. *New York Times,* August 16, 1995, p. A8, and *Washington Post,* August 17, 1995, p. A24.

179. *New York Times,* August 19, 1995, p. 4.

180. *Ibid.,* August 11, 1995, p. A3. See also *Washington Post,* August 16, 1995, p. A26.

181. *Boston Globe,* September 8, 1995, p. 2.

182. AFP, September 8, 1995. See also Scott Parrish, "Twisting in the Wind: Russia and the Yugoslav Conflict," *Transition* 1, no. 20 (November 3, 1995), pp. 28–31, 70.

183. *Washington Post,* August 22, 1995, p. A14.

184. *Ibid.*

185. *New York Times,* August 16, 1995, p. A8, and August 18, 1995, p. A4.

186. *Ibid.,* August 26, 1995, p. 2, and August 28, 1995, p. 1, and *Washington Post,* August 26, 1995, p. A18.

187. Begić, *Bosna i Hercegovina od Vanceove misije,* p. 274 (note 2).

188. *New York Times,* August 29, 1995, p. A1.

189. *Ibid.,* August 29, 1995, p. A10, and August 30, 1995, p. 1.

190. *Guardian,* August 31, 1995, p. 14. Holbrooke mentions no such deal in his account of the meeting in *To End a War,* pp. 96–97.

191. *New Europe,* September 3–9, 1995, pp. 3, 25, and September 10–16, 1995, p. 27.

192. *Washington Post,* August 30, 1995, p. 1.

193. *Ibid.,* November 15, 1995, p. A20.

194. *Ibid.,* September 3, 1995, and Kelly, "The Negotiator," p. 85.

195. *Guardian,* September 12, 1995, p. 15.

196. *Washington Post,* November 15, 1995, p. A20.

197. Elaine Sciolino, "Madeleine Albright's Audition," *New York Times Magazine,* September 22, 1996, p. 67.

198. *Washington Post,* November 15, 1995, p. 1.

199. *New York Times,* September 5, 1995, p. A1. See also *Washington Post,* September 7, 1995, p. 1.

200. *Ibid.,* September 3, 1995, p. 1.

201. *New York Times,* September 6, 1995, p. 1.

202. *Guardian,* September 4, 1995, p. 8.

203. Holbrooke, *To End a War,* p. 143.

204. Kelly, "The Negotiator," pp. 85–86; Holbrooke, "The Road to Sarajevo," pp. 100–104; and Roger Cohen, "Taming the Bullies of Bosnia," *New York Times Magazine,* December 17, 1995, pp. 58–95. Holbrooke gives a more diplomatic account of the meeting in *To End a War,* pp. 148–52.

205. *New York Times,* September 19, 1995, p. A1.

206. *Independent,* September 16, 1995, p. 8.

207. *New York Times,* September 3, 1995, p. 8, and September 15, 1995, p. A1; and *Washington Post,* September 15, 1995, p. A1.

208. *Ibid.,* September 16, 1995, p. A23.

209. *Los Angeles Times,* September 14, 1995, p. A1.

210. *Washington Post,* November 16, 1995, p. 1.

211. *New York Times,* September 18, 1995, p. A1.

212. *Ibid.,* September 7, 1995, p. A1, and September 19, 1995, p. A1.

213. Cohen, "Taming the Bullies," p. 78. For Holbrooke's account, see *To End a War,* pp. 160, 164–65.

214. *New York Times,* September 22, 1995, p. A12, and September 29, 1995, p. A3.

215. Owen, *Balkan Odyssey,* p. 337.

216. *Washington Post,* September 10, 1995, p. A27.

217. *Ibid.,* September 13, 1995, p. 1.

218. *New York Times,* September 14, 1995, p. A1. Holbrooke reports that Pentagon leaders made the same argument to U.S. policymakers on September 11, in *To End a War,* p. 146.

219. *New York Times,* September 9, 1995, p. 1.

220. *Ibid.,* September 9, 1995, p. 4.

221. *Washington Post,* September 11, 1995, p. A26.

222. *Ibid.,* September 22, 1995, p. A1.

223. *Independent,* September 1, 1995, p. 10.

224. *Washington Post,* September 22, 1995, p. A1.

225. *Independent,* September 12, 1995, p. 8.

226. *New York Times,* September 13, 1995, p. A11.

227. *Guardian,* September 12, 1995, p. 3.

228. *Independent,* September 12, 1995, p. 8.

229. *Washington Post,* September 13, 1995, p. A1.

230. *New York Times,* September 15, 1995, p. A8.

231. *Ibid.,* September 20, 1995, p. A14.

232. *Washington Post,* September 26, 1995, p. A13.

233. Begić, *Bosna i Hercegovina od Vanceove misije,* p. 278 (note 9).

234. *New York Times,* September 26, 1995, p. A14.

235. *Ibid.,* October 9, 1995, p. A8.

236. *Ibid.,* September 27, 1995, p. A10 (emphasis added).

237. *AFP,* September 25, 1995.

238. Zlatan Cabaravdic, "An Escalating Power Struggle over Bosnia's Political Future," *Transition* 1, no. 20 (November 3, 1995), pp. 22–23.

239. *New York Times,* September 30, 1995, p. 5.

240. *Ibid.,* September 28, 1995, p. A12; September 29, 1995, p. A3; and October 9, 1995, p. A8.

241. *Guardian,* September 30, 1995, p. 2.

242. *Washington Post,* October 6, 1995, p. 1 and Holbrooke, *To End a War,* p. 195.

243. *New York Times,* October 6, 1995, p. A8.

244. *Ibid.,* October 12, 1995, p. A1.

245. *Washington Post,* October 8, 1995, p. C7.

246. *New York Times,* October 15, 1995, p. 10.

247. *Washington Post,* October 5, 1995, p. A34.

248. *New York Times,* October 14, 1995, pp. 1, 4, and *Boston Globe,* October 14, 1995, p. 2.

249. *New York Times,* October 18, 1995, p. A1.

250. *Ibid.,* October 31, 1995, p. A9.

251. Pauline Neville-Jones, "Dayton, IFOR and Alliance Relations in Bosnia," *Survival* 30, no. 4 (Winter 1996–97), p. 48.

252. The following account of the negotiations is based on Anthony Borden and Drago Hedl, "How the Bosnians Were Broken," *War Report* 39 (February–March, 1996), pp. 26–42; *New York Times,* November 23, 1995, pp. A1, A10; *Washington Post,* November 23, 1995, p. A1; and *Boston Globe,* December 7, 1995, p. 1.

253. Begić, *Bosna i Hercegovina od Vanceove misije,* p. 281 (note 1).

254. Proximity Peace Talks, Wright-Patterson Air Force Base, Dayton, Ohio (November 1–21, 1995), mimeo (unpaginated).

255. *Washington Post,* November 23, 1995, p. A1.

256. Borden and Hedl, "How the Bosnians Were Broken."

257. *Ibid.,* p. 35.

258. Borden and Hedl report Silajdžić's demand was to extend the enclave to the Drina. But this must be a misunderstanding, as the enclave already reached the Drina and to divide Republika Srpska territory in the manner opposed by Milošević would have required extending it to the border.

259. *New York Times,* December 24, 1995, p. 1.

260. Borden and Hedl, "How the Bosnians Were Broken," p. 39. See also Holbrooke, *To End a War,* pp. 295ff.

261. Borden and Hedl, "How the Bosnians Were Broken," p. 39, and *New York Times,* November 23, 1995, p. A1.

262. *New York Times,* November 23, 1995, p. A1.

263. Borden and Hedl, "How the Bosnians Were Broken," p. 40.

264. *Washington Post,* November 23, 1995, p. A1. For Holbrooke's account of the tense final negotiations over the map, see *To End a War,* pp. 299–309.

265. *New York Times,* November 23, 1995, p. A1.

266. *Ibid.*

267. *Boston Globe,* December 7, 1995, p. 1.

268. *New York Times,* November 22, 1995, p. A1.

269. Borden and Hedl, "How the Bosnians Were Broken," p. 41.

270. *Washington Post,* November 24, 1995, p. 1.

271. *New York Times,* November 25, 1995, p. 3.

272. Begić, *Bosna i Hercegovina od Vanceove misije,* pp. 282–83.

273. Neville-Jones, "Dayton, IFOR and Alliance Relations in Bosnia," p. 49.

274. Robert Hayden, "The Dayton Draft for a Bosnian Constitution: Constitutional Joke or Constitutional Fraud?" (mimeo)

275. Arend Lijphart, "The Power-Sharing Approach," in *Conflict and Peacemaking in Multiethnic Societies,* Joseph V. Montville, ed. (Lexington, MA: Lexington Books, 1990), pp. 491–501.

276. Croatian Satellite TV Service, February 5, 1995, as translated in BBC, *SWB,* February 7, 1995, p. EE/2221/C.

277. *Guardian,* March 28, 1994, p. 9, and September 14, 1994, p. 9.

278. *Oslobodjenje* (European edition), April 1–8, 1994, p. 11, and *New York Times,* October 21, 1994, p. A8.

279. *Ibid.,* October 9, 1995, p. A8.

280. Dayton Agreement on Implementing the Federation of Bosnia and Herzegovina of 9 November 1995 (electronic mail text).

281. *BosNews,* as transmitted electronically in *Bosnet Digest* 4, no. 499 (at http://bosnet@grad.applicoms.com).

282. *Vjesnik,* April 30, 1994, as translated in FBIS, *EEU,* May 6, 1994, p. 31.

283. Dayton Agreement on Implementing the Federation of Bosnia and Herzegovina of 9 November 1995, Annex, para. 9.

284. *New York Times,* September 20, 1997, p. 3.

285. Text contained in OSCE Press Release no. 6/96 (January 1996).

286. "The NATO-led Stabilization Force (SFOR) in Bosnia and Herzegovina," *NATO Basic Fact Sheet,* no. 11 (April 1997) at http://www.nato.int/docu.

287. *New York Times,* December 19, 1997, p. A20.

288. Neville-Jones, "Dayton, IFOR and Alliance Relations in Bosnia," p. 51.

289. Details of the program have been culled from a series of press releases and other public documents available on the U.S. State Department World Wide Web site dedicated to Bosnia (at www.state.gov/www/regions/eur/bosnia).

290. For a critical review of the "train and equip" program, see *Military Watch,* Balkan Institute vol. 2.11 (May 29, 1997) at http://www.balkaninstitute.org.

291. *Military Watch,* Balkan Institute, vol. 1.17 (October 31, 1996) at http://www.-balkaninstitute.org, p. 3.

292. *Ibid.,* vol 2.1 (January 9, 1997) at http://www.balkaninstitute.org, p. 2.

293. *Ibid.,* vol. 2.11 (May 29, 1997) at http://www.balkaninstitute.org, p. 6.

294. "Briefing on Train and Equip Program for the Bosnian Federation," U.S. State Department, Bureau of Public Affairs (July 25, 1996).

295. *Military Watch,* Balkan Institute, vol. 2.11 (May 29, 1997) at http://www.-balkaninstitute.org, p. 5.

296. *New York Times,* November 8, 1996, p. A1.

297. *Ibid.,* October 3, 1997, p. A1.

298. *Ibid.,* October 3, 1997, p. A8. For an analysis of the overall military situation, and of the train and equip program, see International Crisis Group, *A Peace, or Just a Cease-Fire? The Military Equation in Post-Dayton Bosnia,* ICG Bosnia Project (De-

cember 15, 1997), electronic edition (available at www.intl-crisis-group.org); and "Dayton Implementation: The Train and Equip Program," *Special Report* (Washington, DC: United States Institute of Peace, September 1997).

299. Charles G. Boyd, "Making Bosnia Work," *Foreign Affairs* 77, no. 1 (January–February 1998), p. 49.

300. *Washington Post,* November 22, 1995, p. A22.

301. *Times* (London), November 2, 1994, p. 19.

302. *The Fall of Yugoslavia,* 3rd edition (New York: Penguin Books, 1996), p. 272.

303. For public commentary to this effect, see *Washington Post,* September 8, 1995, p. A25.

304. *Ibid.,* November 23, 1995, p. A32.

305. The following account is based on Paul Shoup, "The Elections in Bosnia and Herzegovina: The End of an Illusion," *Problems of Post-Communism* 44, no. 1 (January–February 1997), pp. 3–15.

306. *Washington Post,* September 8, 1995, p. A27.

307. *Ibid.,* December 13, 1995, p. A29.

Chapter 8: Dilemmas of Intervention

1. Carnegie Commission on Preventing Deadly Conflict, *Preventing Deadly Conflict: Final Report* (Washington, DC: Carnegie Commission on Preventing Deadly Conflict, 1997).

2. See Steven L. Burg, *War or Peace? Nationalism, Democracy and American Foreign Policy in Post-Communist Europe* (New York: New York University Press, 1996), pp. 179ff.

3. UN Security Council document S/23900 (May 12, 1992), p. 6.

4. See Lt. Colonel Bob Stewart, *Broken Lives: A Personal View of the Bosnian Conflict* (London: HarperCollins, 1993). See also the account of "Britain's secret war in Bosnia," in *Guardian,* April 2, 1996, pp. 1, 11.

5. See, for example, calls by former British Prime Minister Margaret Thatcher (*New York Times,* August 6, 1992, p. A23); former U.S. Secretary of State George Shultz (*New York Times,* December 9, 1992, p. A3); former U.S. ambassador to the UN Jeane Kirkpatrick and former CIA director William Colby (*New York Times,* February 19, 1993, p. A3); and by 100 prominent former political leaders and others (*Wall Street Journal,* September 2, 1993, p. A12).

6. James Gow, *Triumph of the Lack of Will* (New York: Columbia University Press, 1997), p. 2.

7. *Ibid.,* p. 306.

8. *New York Times,* August 3, 1992, p. A19. Cf. *Ibid.,* September 28, 1992, p. A15 and December 7, 1992, p. A19. Lewis had several times earlier called for action, but largely on the grounds of interest; see, for example, *ibid.,* May 17, 1992, p. E17; June 14, 1992, p. E19; and August 7, 1992, p. A27.

9. *Ibid.,* December 13 1992, p. IV:17.

10. *Ibid.,* February 14, 1994, p. A4.

11. Philip Schwarm, "Divided We Stand," *War Report* 33 (May 1995), p. 8.

12. *New York Times,* July 11, 1993.

13. Fen Osler Hampson, *Nurturing Peace: Why Peace Settlements Succeed or Fail* (Washington, DC: United States Institute of Peace, 1996), pp. 208, 210.

14. *Ibid.,* p. 221.

15. John J. Mearsheimer and Robert A. Pape, "The Answer," *New Republic* (June 14, 1993), pp. 22–28.

16. James Goodby, "When War Won Out: Bosnian Peace Plans Before Dayton," *International Negotiation* 1, no. 3 (1996), pp. 516–17, and Saadia Touval, "Coercive Mediation on the Road to Dayton," *International Negotiation* 1, no. 3 (1996), pp. 547–70.

17. Rudman, "Backtracking to Reformulate: Establishing the Bosnian Federation," *International Negotiation* 1, no. 3 (1996), p. 543.

18. I. William Zartman, "The Unfinished Agenda: Negotiating Internal Conflicts," in *Stopping the Killing: How Civil Wars End,* Roy Licklider, ed. (New York: New York University Press, 1993), p. 24.

19. Hampson, *Nurturing Peace,* p. 230.

20. Elizabeth Drew, *On the Edge: The Clinton Presidency* (New York: Simon and Schuster, 1994), p. 144.

21. *New York Times,* April 23, 1993, p. A1.

22. Hampson, *Nurturing Peace,* p. 230.

23. For an argument along these lines, see the article by Henry Kissinger in *Washington Post,* December 10, 1995, p. C9.

24. Hampson, *Nurturing Peace,* p. 217.

25. Timothy W. Ryback, "Violence Therapy," *New York Times Magazine,* November 30, 1997, p. 123.

26. John Paul Lederach, *Building Peace: Sustainable Reconciliation in Divided Societies* (Washington, DC: United States Institute of Peace, 1997), p. 94.

27. For a similar argument, see Charles G. Boyd, "Making Bosnia Work," *Foreign Affairs* 77, no. 1 (January–February, 1998), pp. 52–53. For evidence of willingness at the grass roots to engage in cross-boundary economic activities, see the survey data reported in "Economy May Provide Common Ground for Bosnians," *Opinion Analysis,* Office of Research and Media Reaction, U.S. Information Agency (Washington, DC, September 5, 1997).

Bibliography of Works Cited

Newspapers, News Services, and Translations

Agence France Presse (AFP)
Borba
Boston Globe
Bulletin of the European Communities
Christian Science Monitor
Current Digest of the Post-Soviet Press
Daily Report: Eastern Europe (Foreign Broadcast Information Service)
Danas
Der Spiegel
Economist
Europe Journée Politique
European
Financial Times
Frankfurter Allgemeine Zeitung
Guardian
Independent
International Herald Tribune
Le Monde
Ljiljan
Los Angeles Times
Medjunarodni Problemi
Military Watch (Balkan Institute) at http://www.balkaninstitute.org
Nedjelja
Nedeljna Dalmacija
Neue Zuricher Zeitung
New Europe
New York Times
NIN
Nova Hrvatska

Oslobodjenje
Oslobodjenje (European edition)
Oslobodjenje sedam dana
Politika
Republika (Belgrade)
Slobodni Tjednik
Süddeutsche Zeitung
Summary of World Broadcasts (British Broadcasting Corporation)
Sunday Times (London)
Svijet
Times (London)
United Press International (UPI)
U.S. Department of State Dispatch
Vjesnik
Vreme
Wall Street Journal
Washington Post
Yugoslav Daily Survey
Yugoslav Survey

UN Security Council Documents

S/23280 (December 11, 1991)
S/23592 (February 15, 1992)
S/23592 Add. 1 (February 19, 1992)
S/23900 (May 12, 1992)
S/24000 (May 26, 1992)
S/24049 (May 30, 1992)
S/RES/757 (May 30, 1992)
S/24333 (July 21, 1992)
S/24795 (November 11, 1992)
S/25015 (December 24, 1992)
S/25050 (January 6, 1993)
S/25100 (January 14, 1993)
S/25221 (February 2, 1993)
S/25248 (February 8, 1993)
S/25403 (March 12, 1993)
S/25479 (March 26, 1993)
S/25700 (April 30, 1993)
S/25709 (May 3, 1993)
S/26066 (July 8, 1993)
S/26233 (August 3, 1993)
S/26260 (August 6, 1993)
S/26337 (August 20, 1993)
S/26337/Add.1 (August 23, 1993)
S/26337/Add. 2 (August 23, 1993)
S/26378 (August 30, 1993)
S/26454 (September 16, 1993)
S/26486 (September 23, 1993)
S/26616 (October 22, 1993)

S/26617 (October 23, 1993)
S/PRST/1994/6 (February 3, 1994)
S/1994/154 (February 10, 1994)
S/1994/173 (February 14, 1994)
S/1994/265 (March 7, 1994)
S/1994/548 (May 9, 1994)
S/1994/811 (July 8, 1994)
S/1994/1081 (September 21, 1994)
S/PRST/1994/74 (November 29, 1994)
S/1994/1389 (December 1, 1994)
S/1994/674 (December 28, 1994)
S/1994/1454 (December 29, 1994)
S/1995/222 (March 22, 1995)
S/1995/470 (June 9, 1995)

UN General Assembly and Security Council Documents

A/47/666–S/24809 (November 17, 1992)
A/48/74–S/25216 (February 3, 1993)
A/48/229–S/26261 (August 6, 1993)

UN Economic and Social Council Commission on Human Rights Documents

E/CN.4/1993/50 (February 10, 1993)
E/CN.4/1994/8 (September 8, 1993)
E/CN.4/1994/6 (August 26, 1994)

Statistical Materials

Central Intelligence Agency. "1990 Election Results in Sarajevo Opština by Ethnic Compositions of Political Parties." IMF 027 (R00480) 11/09/95.
Miljković, Dušan, ed. *Yugoslavia 1945–1985: Statistical Review*. Belgrade: Federal Statistical Office, 1986.
OSCE. "BH Opstinas population 96." (Map) at http://www.oscebih.org.
Savezni zavod za statistiku. *Demografska statistika 1981*. Belgrade: Savezni zavod za statistiku, 1986.
———. *Nacionalni sastav stanovništva SFR Jugoslavije*. Vol. 1. Belgrade: Savezni zavod za statistiku, 1991.
———. "Stanovništvo prema nacinalnom sastavu i tipu naselja." *Popis stanovništva 1981*. Vol. 1. Belgrade: Savezni zavod za statistiku, 1991.
———. *Statistički Bilten* no. 1295 (Nacionalni sastav stanovništva po opštinama). Belgrade: Savezni zavod za statistiku and Savremena administracija, 1991.
Shoup, Paul S. *The East European and Soviet Data Handbook: Political, Social, and Developmental Indicators, 1945–1975*. New York: Columbia University Press, 1981.

Other Materials

Allen, Beverly. *Rape Warfare: The Hidden Genocide in Bosnia-Herzegovina and Croatia*. London and Minneapolis: University of Minnesota Press, 1996.

Andrejevich, Milan. "Bosnia-Herzegovina: Yugoslavia's Linchpin." *Report on Eastern Europe* 1, no. 49 (December 7, 1990), pp. 20–26.

————. "Bosnia and Herzegovina Move Toward Independence." *Report on Eastern Europe* 2, no. 43 (October 25, 1991), pp. 22–26.

Arnautović, Suad. *Izbori u Bosni i Hercegovini '90.* Sarajevo: Promocult, 1996.

Azinović, Vlado. "Bosna i Hercegovina u državnoj zajednici jugoslavenskih naroda." In Dubravko Lovrenović, et al., *Istina o Bosni i Hercegovini.* Sarajevo: Altermedia, 1991. Pp. 61–79.

Baker, James A. III. *The Politics of Diplomacy.* New York: G.P. Putnam's Sons, 1995.

Banac, Ivo. "Bosnian Muslims: From Religious Community to Socialist Nationhood." In Mark Pinson, ed., *The Muslims of Bosnia-Herzegovina.* Cambridge: Harvard University Press, 1994. Pp. 129–53.

Bandžović, Safet. *Ratne tragedije Muslimana.* Novi Pazar: Udruženje pisaca Sandžaka, 1993.

Bassiouni, Cherif. "Sexual Violence: An Invisible Weapon of War in the Former Yugoslavia." *Occasional Paper* no. 1. International Human Rights Law Institute, DePaul University College of Law (1996).

Bataković, Dušan T. *Prelude to Sarajevo: The Serbian Question in Bosnia and Herzegovina, 1878–1914.* Belgrade: Serbian Academy of Sciences and Arts, 1996.

Bauer, Harry, and Thomas Kimmig. "Frieden um jeden Preis." In Stefanov and Werz, eds., *Bosnien und Europa.* Pp. 42–59.

Begić, Kasim I. *Bosna i Hercegovina od Vanceove misije do Daytonskog sporazuma (1991.-1996.).* Sarajevo: Bosanska knjiga, 1997.

Binder, David. "Anatomy of a Massacre." *Foreign Policy* 97 (Winter 1994–95), pp. 70–78.

————. "Bosnia's Bombers." *The Nation,* October 2, 1995, pp. 336–37.

Bodansky, Yossef and Vaughn S. Forrest. "The Truth About Goražde." U.S. House of Representatives, Task Force on Terrorism, May 4, 1994 (mimeo).

Bogosavljević, Srdjan. "Bosna i Hercegovina u ogledalu statistike." In Janjić and Shoup, eds., *Bosna i Hercegovina izmedju rata i mira,* pp. 24–40.

————. "Ethnic Recomposition in Former Yugoslavia." Unpublished paper (February 1996).

Bojić, Dušica, ed. *Stradanja srba u Sarajevu: Knjiga dokumenata/Suffering of the Serbs in Sarajevo: Document Book (Records).* Belgrade: Komesarijat za Izbeglice Republike Srbije, n.d.

————. *Stradanja Srba u Mostaru i dolini Neretve: Knjiga dokumenata.* Belgrade: Komisarijat za Izbeglice Republike Srbije, 1996.

Borden, Anthony, and Richard Caplan. "The Former Yugoslavia: The War and the Peace Process." *SIPRI Yearbook 1996.* Oxford: Oxford University Press, 1996. Pp. 203–50.

Borden, Anthony, and Drago Hedl. "How the Bosnians Were Broken." *War Report* 39 (February–March, 1996), pp. 26–42.

Bougarel, Xavier. *Bosnie: Anatomie d'un conflit.* Paris: La Découverte, 1996.

————. "Bosnia and Hercegovina: State and Communitarianism." In David A. Dyker and Ivan Vejvoda, eds., *Yugoslavia and After: A Study in Fragmentation, Despair and Rebirth.* London: Longman, 1996. Pp. 87–115.

Boyd, Charles G. "Making Peace with the Guilty: The Truth About Bosnia." *Foreign Affairs* 74, no. 5 (September–October 1995), pp. 22–38.

————. "Making Bosnia Work," *Foreign Affairs* 77, no. 1 (January–February 1998), pp. 42–55.

Bringa, Tone. *Being a Muslim the Bosnian Way: Identity and Community in a Central Bosnian Village.* Princeton: Princeton University Press, 1995.

Brown, Michael E., ed. *Ethnic Conflict and International Security*. Princeton: Princeton University Press, 1993.

Burg, Steven L. "Elite Conflict in Post-Tito Yugoslavia." *Soviet Studies* 38, 2 (April 1986), pp. 170–93.

———. "The Political Integration of Yugoslavia's Muslims: Determinants of Success and Failure." *The Carl Beck Papers in Russian and East European Studies* 203 (1983).

———. "Political Structures." In Dennison Rusinow, ed., *Yugoslavia: A Fractured Federalism*. Washington, DC: Wilson Center Press, 1988. Pp. 9–22.

———. "Research Note: New Data on the League of Communists." *Slavic Review* 46, 3–4 (Fall/Winter 1987), pp. 553–67.

———. *War or Peace? Nationalism, Democracy and American Foreign Policy in Post-Communist Europe*. New York: New York University Press, 1996.

Burg, Steven L., and Michael L. Bernbaum. "Community, Integration, and Stability in Multinational Yugoslavia." *American Political Science Review* 83, no. 2 (June 1989), pp. 535–54.

Cabaravdic, Zlatan. "An Escalating Power Struggle over Bosnia's Political Future." *Transition* 1, no. 20 (November 3, 1995), pp. 22–23.

Calic, Marie-Janine. *Der Krieg in Bosnien-Hercegovina: Ursachen, Konfliktstrukturen, Internationale Lösungsversuche*. Frankfurt: Suhrkamp Verlag, 1995.

Čamo, Mensur. "Beogradska tajna večera." *Nedelja,* November 10, 1991, p. 15.

Carnegie Commission on Preventing Deadly Conflict. *Preventing Deadly Conflict: Final Report.* Washington, DC: Carnegie Commission on Preventing Deadly Conflict, 1997.

Čekić, Smail. *Agresija na Bosnu: Genocid nad Bošnjacima 1991–1993*. Sarajevo: Ljiljan, 1994.

———. *The Aggression on Bosnia and Genocide Against Bosniacs, 1991–1993*. Sarajevo: Ljiljan, 1994.

———. "Vojne pripreme za agresiju na republiku Bosnu i Herzegovinu." In Imamović, ed., *Agresija na Bosnu i Herzegovinu: Borba za njen Opstanak,* pp. 79–96.

Ćerić, Salim. *Muslimani srpskohrvatskog jezika*. Sarajevo: Svjetlost, 1968.

———. *O jugoslovenstvu i bosanstvu*. Sarajevo: Oslobodjenje, n.d.

Cicic, Dragan. "A Means to an End: The UN and Rump Yugoslavia." *War Report* 37 (October 1995), pp. 38–39.

Ćimić, Esad. "Osobenosti nacionalnog formiranja muslimana." *Pregled* 4 (April 1974), pp. 389–408.

Cohen, Ben, and George Stamkowski, eds. *With No Peace to Keep: United Nations Peacekeeping and the War in the Former Yugoslavia*. London: Grain Press, 1995.

Cohen, Roger. "Taming the Bullies of Bosnia." *New York Times Magazine,* December 17, 1995, pp. 58–95.

Collinson, Christopher. "Bosnian Army Tactics." *Jane's Intelligence Review* 6, no. 1 (January 1994), pp. 11–13.

———. "Bosnia This Winter." *Jane's Intelligence Review* 5, no. 2 (December 1993), pp. 63–67.

Čolović, Ivan. "Beograd-Tuzla, tamo i ovamo 4,040 km." *Republika* (Belgrade), November 16–30, 1994, pp. 19–20.

Committee for Collecting Data on Crimes Committed against Humanity and International Law. *War Crimes Against Serbs on the Territory of Goražde (1992–1994)*. Belgrade: Committee for Collecting Data, n.d.

Cooper, Robert and Mats Berdal. "Outside Intervention in Ethnic Conflicts." In Michael E. Brown, ed., *Ethnic Conflict and International Security*. Princeton: Princeton University Press, 1993. Pp. 181–206.

Ćorović, Vladimir. *Političke prilike u Bosni i Hercegovini*. Belgrade: Politika, 1939.

Crawford, Beverly. "Explaining Defection from International Cooperation: Germany's Unilateral Recognition of Croatia." *World Politics* 48 (July 1996), pp. 482–521.

Damrosch, Lori Fisler. "Changing Conceptions of Intervention in International Law." In Laura W. Reed and Cal Kaysen, eds., *Emerging Norms of Justified Intervention.* Cambridge, MA: American Academy of Arts and Sciences, 1993. Pp. 91–110.

Dayton Agreement on Implementing the Federation of Bosnia and Herzegovina of 9 November 1995.

Dedijer, Vladimir, and Antun Miletić. *Genocid nad Muslimanima, 1941–1945: Sbornik dokumenata i svjedočenja.* Sarajevo: Svjetlost, 1990.

Diehl, Paul. *International Peacekeeping.* Baltimore: Johns Hopkins University Press, 1994.

Djilas, Milovan. *Bošnjak Adil Zulfikarpašić.* 2nd edition. Zurich: Bošnjački Institut, 1994.

Djilas, Milovan, and Nadežda Gaće. *Bošnjak Adil Zulfikarpašić.* 3rd edition. Zurich: Bošnjački Institut, 1995.

"Documents on the Future Regulation of Relations in Yugoslavia," *Yugoslav Survey* 1 (1991), pp. 3–24.

Donia, Robert J. *Islam Under the Double Eagle.* New York: Columbia University Press, 1981.

Donia, Robert J., and John V. A. Fine, Jr. *Bosnia and Hercegovina: A Tradition Betrayed.* New York: Columbia University Press, 1994.

Donia, Robert J., and William G. Lockwood. "The Bosnian Muslims: Class, Ethnicity, and Political Behavior in a European State." In Suad Joseph and Barbara L.K. Pillsbury, eds., *Muslim-Christian Conflicts: Economic, Political and Social Origins.* Boulder: Westview, 1978.

Drew, Elizabeth. *On the Edge: The Clinton Presidency.* New York: Simon and Schuster, 1994.

Ethnic Cleansing of Croats in Bosnia and Herzegovina, 1991–1993. Mostar: (n.p.) 1993.

European Community Conference on Yugoslavia. *Background Documents Pack* (mimeo).

European Political Cooperation Press Release. "Declaration on Yugoslavia." no. 98/81 (n.d.).

———. "Declaration on Yugoslavia." Extraordinary EPC Ministerial Meeting. Rome: November 8, 1991.

Federal Government of Yugoslavia. *Report Submitted to the Commission of Experts Established Pursuant to Security Council Resolution 780 (1992).* Belgrade: (n.p.) 1992.

Federal Information Service. *Daily Digest of the Congressional Record.* 103rd Congress, 2nd session. Testimony [of Warren Christopher] to the Senate Foreign Relations Committee. February 23, 1994. (Electronic edition, document no. Y4.F76/1:IR1.)

Fein, Helen. "Discriminating Genocide from War Crimes: Vietnam and Afghanistan Reexamined." *Denver Journal of International Law and Policy* 22, no. 1 (Fall 1993), pp. 29–62.

———. *Genocide: Sociological Perspective.* London: Sage Publications, 1993.

Freedman, Lawrence. "Why the West Failed." *Foreign Policy* 97 (Winter 1994–95), pp. 53–69.

———, ed. *Military Intervention in European Conflicts.* Oxford: Blackwell Publishers, 1994.

Genscher, Hans-Dietrich. *Erinnerungen.* Berlin: Siedler, 1995.

Gjelten, Tom. "Blaming the Victim." *The New Republic,* December 20, 1993, pp. 14–16.

————. *Sarajevo Daily: A City and Its Newspaper.* New York: HarperCollins, 1995.

Glenny, Misha. *The Fall of Yugoslavia: The Third Balkan War.* 3rd revised edition. New York: Penguin Books, 1996.

Glitman, Maynard. "US Policy in Bosnia: Rethinking a Flawed Approach." *Survival* 38, no. 4 (Winter, 1996–97), pp. 66–83.

Goati, Vladimir. "Politički život Bosne i Hercegovine." In Janjić and Shoup, eds., *Bosna i Herzegovina izmedju rata i mira,* pp. 41–52.

Golubic, Stjepko, Susan Campbell, and Thomas Golubic. "How Not to Divide the Indivisible." In Rabia Alia and Lawrence Lifschultz, eds., *Why Bosnia?* Stony Creek, CT: Pamphleteer's Press, 1993. Pp. 209–32.

Gompert, David C. "How to Defeat Serbia." *Foreign Affairs* 73, no. 4 (July/August 1994), pp. 30–47.

————. "The United States and Yugoslavia's Wars." In Richard Ullman, ed., *The World and Yugoslavia's Wars,* pp. 122–44.

Goodby, James. "When War Won Out: Bosnian Peace Plans Before Dayton." *International Negotiation* 1, no. 3 (1996), pp. 501–23.

Gow, James. "Military and Political Affiliations in the Yugoslav Conflict." *RFE/RL Research Report* 1, no. 20 (May 15, 1992), pp. 16–25.

————. "Bosnia I: Stepping Up the Peace?" *World Today* 51, 7 (July 1995), pp. 126–28.

————. *Triumph of the Lack of Will.* New York: Columbia University Press, 1997.

Gowing, Nik. "Real-Time Television Coverage of Armed Conflicts and Diplomatic Crises: Does It Pressure or Distort Foreign Policy Decisions?" *Working Paper* No. 94–1. The Joan Shorenstein Barone Center on the Press, Politics and Public Policy, Harvard University (June 1994).

Grebo, Zdravko, and Branislava Jojić. "Teze za model ustava Republike Bosne i Herzegovine." In Janjić and Shoup, eds., *Bosna i Herzegovina izmedju rata i mira,* pp. 147–66.

Griffiths, Lt. Cmdr. D.N. "Waging Peace in Bosnia." *Proceedings,* U.S. Naval Institute, no. 120 (January 1994).

Hadžijahić, Muhamed. *Od tradicije do identiteta: Geneza nacionlnog pitanja bosanskih Muslimana.* Sarajevo: Svjetlost, 1974.

————, Mahmud Trajlić, and Nijaz Sukrić. *Islam i muslimani u Bosni i Hercegovini.* Sarajevo: Starješinstvo Islamske zajednice, 1977.

Halilović, Šefer. *Lukava strategija.* Sarajevo: Maršal, 1997.

Hampson, Fen Osler. *Nurturing Peace: Why Peace Settlements Succeed or Fail.* Washington, DC: United States Institute of Peace, 1996.

Hannum, Hurst. "Self-determination, Yugoslavia and Europe: Old Wine in New Bottles?" *Transnational Law and Contemporary Problems* 3, no. 1 (Spring 1993), pp. 57–69.

Hayden, Robert M. "Recounting the Dead: The Rediscovery and Redefinition of Wartime Massacres in Late- and Post-Communist Yugoslavia." In Rubie S. Watson, ed., *Memory, History and Opposition Under State Communism.* Santa Fe, NM: School of American Research Press, 1994. Pp. 167–84.

————. "Bosnia's Internal War and the International Criminal Tribunal." *Fletcher Forum of World Affairs* 22, no. 1 (Winter/Spring 1998), pp. 45–64.

————. "The Dayton Draft for a Bosnian Constitution: Constitutional Joke or Constitutional Fraud?" (mimeo).

Heleta, Nikola. *Goražde '92–'95: Stradanje Srba.* Belgrade: Prosveta, 1996.

Heywood, Colin. "Bosnia Under Ottoman Rule, 1463–1800." In Pinson, ed., *The Muslims of Bosnia-Herzegovina,* pp. 22–53.

Holbrooke, Richard. "The Road to Sarajevo," *New Yorker,* October 21 and 28, 1996, pp. 88–104.

———. *To End a War.* New York: Random House, 1998.

Honig, Jan Willem. "The Netherlands and Military Intervention." In Freedman, ed., *Military Intervention in European Conflicts,* pp. 142–53.

———, and Norbeert Both. *Srebrenica: Record of a War Crime.* New York: Penguin Books, 1997.

Hópken, Wolfgang. "Yugoslavia's Communists and the Bosnian Muslims." In Kappeler, et al., eds., *Muslim Communities Reemerge,* pp. 214–47.

Horowitz, Donald L. *Ethnic Groups in Conflict.* Berkeley: University of California Press, 1985.

———. *A Democratic South Africa?* Berkeley: University of California Press, 1991.

Howarth, Jolyon. "The Debate in France Over Military Intervention in Europe." In Freedman, ed., *Military Intervention in European Conflicts,* pp. 106–24.

Human Rights Watch. "Northwestern Bosnia: Human Rights Abuses During a Cease-Fire and Peace Negotiations." *Human Rights Watch/Helsinki* 8, no. 1 (February 1996).

———. "Bosnia-Hercegovina: 'Ethnic Cleansing' Continues in Northern Bosnia." *Human Rights Watch/Helsinki* 6, no. 16 (November 1994).

———. "Bosnia-Hercegovina: Sarajevo." *Human Rights Watch/Helsinki* 6, no. 15 (October 1994).

———. "Bosnia-Hercegovina: Abuses by Bosnian Croat and Muslim Forces in Central and Southwestern Bosnia-Hercegovina." *Human Rights Watch/Helsinki* 5, no. 18 (September 1993).

"Humanitarian Costs of the Fighting in the Balkans." Unclassified CIA memorandum (November 25, 1995).

Hutchings, Robert L. *American Diplomacy and the End of the Cold War: 1989–1992.* Washington, DC: Woodrow Wilson Center Press, 1997.

ICFY/6, Annex (mimeo). [Text of the proposed "Constitutional Structure for Bosnia and Herzegovina . . . as slightly modified to take into account the consultations with the parties on that proposal and to reflect some additional points advanced by the Co-Chairmen on 2 January 1993."]

Igric, Gordana. "Not Just the Victim." *War Report* 57 (December 1997–January 1998), pp. 9–10.

Ilić, Jovan. "Tri varijante." *Epoha* 1, 1 (October 22, 1991). Pp. 15–20.

Imamović, Mustafa, ed. *Agresija na Bosnu i Hercegovinu: Borba za njen Opstanak, 1992–1995 Godine.* Sarajevo: Pravni Fakultet Univerziteta u Sarajevu, 1997.

———. "Agresija na Bosnu i Hercegovinu i njene neposredne posledice." In Imamović, ed., *Agresija na Bosnu i Hercegovinu: Borba za njen Opstanak,* pp. 9–22.

International Conference on the Former Socialist Federal Republic of Yugoslavia. *The London Conference, 26–27 August 1992.*

The International Criminal Tribunal for the Former Yugoslavia. *The Prosecutor of the Tribunal v. Dusko Tadic.* Case no. IT94–1–T. May 21, 1996.

International Crisis Group. *A Peace, or Just a Cease-Fire? The Military Equation in Post-Dayton Bosnia.* ICG Bosnia Project (December 15, 1997), electronic edition (available at www.intl-crisis-group.org).

"Interview with David Owen on the Balkans." *Foreign Affairs* 72, no. 2 (Spring 1993), pp. 1–9.

Irwin, Zachary T. "The Islamic Revival and the Muslims of Bosnia Hercegovina." *East European Quarterly* 17, no. 4 (January 1984), pp. 437–58.

Ivanisević, Milivoje. *Hronika našeg groblja: ili slovo o stradanju srpskog naroda*

Bratunca, Milića, Skalona, i Srebrenice. Belgrade-Bratunac: Komitet za prikupljanje podataka o izvršnim zločinima protiv čovečnosti i medjunarodnog prava, 1994.

Izetbegović, Alija. *Odabrani govori, pisma, izjave, intervjui.* Zagreb: Prvo muslimansko Dioničko društvo, 1995.

―――. *The Islamic Declaration: A Programme for Islamization of Muslims and Muslim Peoples.* Sarajevo: (n.p.) 1990.

Jancic, Miroslav. "Behind the Split." *War Report* 36 (September 1995), pp. 6–7.

Janjić, Dušan, and Paul Shoup, eds. *Bosna i Hercegovina izmedju rata i mira.* Belgrade: Dom Omladine, 1992.

Jelenik, Yeshayahu A. "Bosnia-Herzegovina at War: Relations Between Moslems and Non-Moslems." *Holocaust and Genocide Studies* 5, no. 3 (1990), pp. 275–92.

Jevremović, Pavle. "An Examination of War Crimes Committed in the Former Yugoslavia." *Medjunarodni Problemi/International Problems* (Belgrade) 46, no. 1 (1994), pp. 39–73.

Jevtić, Anatasije. "Testimony of Orthodox Bishop of Hercegovina Dr. Anatasije Jevtic September 28, 1992." *Position of the Serbian Orthodox Church Regarding the War in the Former Yugoslavia* (September 1994).

Jovanović, Drago, ed. *Iskorenjivanje srba u Bosni i Hercegovini.* Belgrade: Rad, n.d.

Jović, Borisav. *Poslednji dani SFRJ.* Belgrade: Politika, 1995.

Kadijević, Veljko. *Moje vidjenje raspada: Vojska bez državi.* Belgrade: Politika, 1993.

Kappeler, Andreas, Gerhard Simon, and Georg Brunner, eds. *Muslim Communities Reemerge.* Durham, NC: Duke University Press, 1994.

Karchmar, Lucien. *Draza Mihailovic and the Rise of the Chetnik Movement.* New York: Garland Publishing, 1987.

Kecmanović, Nenad. "Fikret protiv Alije." *NIN,* October 9, 1992, p. 55.

―――. "Predsedništvo iznutra." *NIN,* October 2, 1992, p. 55.

Kelly, Michael. "Surrender and Blame." *New Yorker,* December 19, 1994, pp. 44–51.

―――. "The Negotiator." *New Yorker,* November 6, 1995, pp. 81–92.

Kenney, George. "The Bosnian Calculation." *New York Times Magazine,* April 23, 1995, pp. 42–43.

Kočović, Bogoljub. *Žrtve drugog svetskog rata u Jugoslaviji.* London: Veritas Foundation Press, 1985.

Kohut, Andrew, and Robert C. Toth. "Managing Conflict in the Post–Cold War World." Washington, DC: Times Mirror Center for the People and the Press, August 2–6, 1995.

―――. "The People, the Press, and the Use of Force." Washington, DC: Times Mirror Center for the People and the Press, August 14–19, 1994.

Korać, Maja. "Representation of Mass Rape in Ethnic-Conflicts [sic] in What Was Yugoslavia." *Sociologija* (Belgrade) 36, no. 4 (October–December 1994), pp. 495–514.

Kovačević, Slobodanka, and Putnik Dajić. *Hronologija Jugoslovenske krize (1942–1993. godina).* Belgrade: Institut za evropske studije, 1994.

―――. *Hronologija Jugoslovenske Krize 1994.* Belgrade: Institut za evropske studije, 1995.

Kovalovska, Adriana. "Rape of Muslim Women in Wartime Bosnia." *ILSA Journal of International and Comparative Law* 3, no. 3 (Spring 1997), pp. 931–44.

Kržišnik-Bukić, Vera. *Cazinska buna 1950.* Sarajevo: Svjetlost, 1991.

Kurspahić, Kemal. "How Not to Save Bosnia," *East European Reporter* (November/December 1992), p. 63.

Lederach, John Paul. *Building Peace: Sustainable Reconciliation in Divided Societies.* Washington, DC: United States Institute of Peace, 1997.

Libal, Michael. "Germany and Yugoslavia, 1991–1992: The Issues." Center for International Affairs, Harvard University (n.d.).

————. "Germany and Yugoslavia, Myths and Realities." Unpublished paper presented to the Center for International Affairs, Harvard University (n.d.).

Lijphart, Arend. *Democracy in Plural Societies*. New Haven: Yale University Press, 1977.

————. "The Power-Sharing Approach." In Joseph V. Montville, ed., *Conflict and Peacemaking in Multiethnic Societies*. Lexington, MA: Lexington Books, 1990. Pp. 491–509.

Lockwood, William G. *European Muslims in Western Bosnia*. New York: Academic Press, 1975.

"The Lost American." *Frontline*. WGBH Television (Boston), October 4, 1997.

Lukic, Reneo and Allen Lynch. *Europe from the Balkans to the Urals: The Disintegration of Yugoslavia and the Soviet Union*. Oxford: Oxford University Press, 1996.

MacKenzie, Lewis. *Peacekeeper: The Road to Sarajevo*. Vancouver: Douglas & McIntyre, 1993.

————. "Tragic Errors." *MacLean's*, December 12, 1994, p. 35.

McRae, Kenneth, ed. *Consociational Democracy: Political Accommodation in Segmented Societies*. Toronto: McClelland and Stewart, 1974.

Malcolm, Noel. *Bosnia: A Short History*. New York: New York University Press, 1994.

Manas, Jean E. "The Impossible Trade-off: 'Peace' versus 'Justice' in Settling Yugoslavia's Wars." In Ullman, ed., *The World and Yugoslavia's Wars*, pp. 42–58.

Mašić, Nijaz. *Istina o Bratuncu: Agresija, Genocid i Oslobodilačka Borba, 1992.-1995.* Tuzla: Opština Bratunac sa Privremenim Sjedištem u Tuzli, 1996.

Maull, Hans W. "Germany in the Yugoslav Crisis." *Survival* 37, no. 4 (Winter 1995–96), pp. 99–130.

Mearsheimer, John J., and Robert A. Pape. "The Answer," *New Republic* (June 14, 1993), pp. 22–28.

Médecins du Monde et Clair Boulanger, Bernard Jacquemart and Philippe Granjon. *L'Enfer Yougoslave: Les victimes de la guerre témoignent*. Paris: Belfond, 1994.

Mercier, Michele. *Crimes without Punishment: Humanitarian Action in Former Yugoslavia*. London: Pluto Press, 1994.

Moore, Patrick. "A Return of the Serbian-Croatian Conflict?" *RFE/RL Research Report* 2, no. 42 (October 1993), pp. 16–20.

————. "An End Game in Croatia and Bosnia." *Transition* 1, 20 (November 3, 1995), pp. 6–10.

Morina, Bratislava-Buba, ed., *Stradanja Srba u Sarajevu: Knjiga dokumenata*. Vol. 1. Belgrade: Komesarijat za Izbeglice SR Srbije, 1995.

NATO Basic Fact Sheet, no. 4 (March 1997) at http://www.nato.int/docu.

"The NATO-led Stabilization Force (SFOR) in Bosnia and Herzegovina." *NATO Basic Fact Sheet*, no. 11 (April 1997) at http://www.nato.int/docu.

Neville-Jones, Pauline. "Dayton, IFOR and Alliance Relations in Bosnia." *Survival* 30, no. 4 (Winter 1996–97), pp. 45–65.

Newhouse, John. "The Diplomatic Round: Dodging the Problem." *New Yorker*, August 24, 1992, pp. 60–71.

Newman, Saul. *Ethnoregional Conflict in Democracies: Mostly Ballots, Rarely Bullets*. Westport, CT: Greenwood Press, 1996.

Novi ustavi na tlu bivše Jugoslavije. Belgrade: Medjunarodna politika, 1995.

O'Ballance, Edgar. *Civil War in Bosnia, 1992–1994*. New York: St. Martin's Press, 1995.

Omeragić, Sejo. "MacKenzie na spisku ratnih zločinaca." *Ljiljan*, March 30–April 6, 1994, p. 18.

OSCE Press Release, no. 6/96 (January 1996).

Owen, David. *Balkan Odyssey.* New York: Harcourt Brace & Co., 1995.
————. *Balkan Odyssey.* CD-ROM Academic Edition. vol 1.1. London: The Electric Company, 1995.
Paul, Diane. "No Escape: Minorities Under Threat in Serb-Held Areas of Bosnia." *Refugee Reports,* November 30, 1994, pp. 1–9.
Parrish, Scott. "Twisting in the Wind: Russia and the Yugoslav Conflict." *Transition* 1, no. 20 (November 3, 1995), pp. 28–31, 70.
Pecanin, Senad. "Climb Any Mountain?" *War Report* 33 (May 1995), p. 12.
Peranić, Dražena. "Muke s Hercegovcima." *Nedeljna Borba,* January 15–16, 1994, pp. viii-ix.
Pinson, Mark, ed. *The Muslims of Bosnia-Herzegovina.* Cambridge: Harvard University Press, 1994.
Poggioloi, Sylvia. "Scouts Without Compasses." *Nieman Reports* (Fall 1993), pp. 16–19.
Posen, Barry R. "The Security Dilemma and Ethnic Conflict." In Brown, ed., *Ethnic Conflict and International Security,* pp. 103–24.
Prokopijević, Miroslav, and Jovan Teokarić. *Ekonomske sankcije UN: Uporedna analiza i slučaj Jugoslavije.* Belgrade: Institut za Evropske Studije, 1998.
Promitzer, Christian. "Die Einebnung der Vielfalt: Nationen und Nationalismus in Bosnien-Herzegowina und im ehemaligen Jugoslawien." In Stefanov and Werz, eds., *Bosnien und Europa,* pp. 15–33
Proximity Peace Talks. Wright-Patterson Air Force Base, Dayton, Ohio (November 1–21, 1995), mimeo (unpaginated).
Purivatra, Atif. *Nacionalni i politički razvitak Muslimana.* Sarajevo: Svjetlost, 1972.
Radulović, Srdjan. *Sudbina krajina.* Belgrade: Dan graf, 1996.
Ramet, Sabrina. "Primordial Ethnicity or Modern Nationalism: The Case of Yugoslavia's Muslims, Reconsidered." In Kappeler, et al., eds., *Muslim Communities Reemerge,* pp. 111–38.
Raseta, Boris. "The Questions over Slavonija." *Balkan War Report* 33 (May 1995), pp. 3–8.
Redžić, Enver. *Muslimansko Autonomaštvo i 13. SS Divizija.* Sarajevo: Svjetlost, 1987.
————. *Nacionalni odnosi u Bosni i Hercegovini 1941–1945 u analizama jugoslavenske istoriografije.* Sarajevo: Akademija nauka i umjetnosti Bosne i Hercegovine, 1989.
————. *Tokovi i otpori.* Sarajevo: Svjetlost, 1970.
Reid, Scott. *Canada Remapped: How the Partition of Quebec Will Reshape the Nation.* Vancouver: Pulp Press, 1992.
Reuter-Hendrichs, Irena. "Jugoslawiens Muslime." *Südosteuropa Mitteilungen* 2 (1989), pp. 105–15.
Rieff, David. *Slaughterhouse: Bosnia and the Failure of the West.* New York: Simon and Schuster, 1995.
Rothschild, Joseph. *Ethnopolitics: A Conceptual Framework.* New York: Columbia University Press, 1981.
Rudman, George. "Backtracking to Reformulate: Establishing the Bosnian Federation." *International Negotiation* 1, no. 3 (1996), pp. 525–45.
Ryback, Timothy W. "Violence Therapy." *New York Times Magazine,* November 30, 1997, pp. 120–23.
Sadowski, Yahya M. "Bosnia's Muslims: A Fundamentalist Threat?" *Brookings Review* 13, no. 1 (Winter 1995), pp. 10–15.
Salmon, Trevor C. "Testing Times for European Cooperation: The Gulf and Yugoslavia." *International Affairs* 68, no. 2 (1992), pp. 233–53.

Schwarm, Philip. "Divided We Stand." *War Report* 33 (May 1995), pp. 8–9.

Sciolino, Elaine. "Madeleine Albright's Audition." *New York Times Magazine,* September 22, 1996, pp. 63–67, 86–87, 104–5.

Sekulic, Dusko, Garth Massey, and Randy Hodson. "Who Were the Yugoslavs? Failed Sources of a Common Identity in the Former Yugoslavia." *American Sociological Review* 59 (1994), pp. 83–97.

Sellers, Patricia Viseur. "Gender, the Genocide Convention and the Tribunal on the Former Yugoslavia." *The ISG Newsletter* 15 (Fall 1995), pp. 1–3.

Shoup, Paul S. *Communism and the Yugoslav National Question.* New York: Columbia University Press, 1968.

———. "The Future of Croatia's Border Regions." *Report on Eastern Europe* 2, no. 48 (November 29, 1991), pp. 26–33.

———. "The Elections in Bosnia and Herzegovina: The End of an Illusion." *Problems of Post-Communism* 44, no. 1 (January–February 1997), pp. 3–15.

Silber, Laura and Allan Little, *The Death of Yugoslavia.* London: Penguin Books/BBC Books, 1995.

———. *Yugoslavia: Death of a Nation.* New York: TV Books, 1996.

Sisk, Timothy D. *Power Sharing and International Mediation in Ethnic Conflicts.* Washington, DC: United States Institute of Peace Press, 1996.

Smajkić, Arif, et al. "Study: Health Consequences of the Aggression Against the Republic B&H and the Possibilities of Restoration: Summary." University of Sarajevo, National Institute of Public Health with School of Public Health (July 1995), unpaginated.

———, et al. *Zdravsteno-socijalne posljedice agresije na Bosnu i Hercegovinu.* Sarajevo: Zavod za zdravstvenu zaštitu, Republike i Federacije Bosne i Hercegovine, 1994.

Smajlović, Ljiljana. "From the Heart of the Heart of the Former Yugoslavia." *Wilson Quarterly* (Summer 1995), pp. 100–13.

Sobel, Richard. "U.S. and European Attitudes Toward Intervention in the Former Yugoslavia: Mourir pour la Bosnie?" In Ullman, ed., *The World and Yugoslavia's Wars,* pp. 146–81.

"Socijalno-zdravstvene posljedice agresije na republiku BiH." *Bilten Zavoda za zdravstevenu zasštitu R/F BiH* 182 (October 9, 1995).

Sray, John E. *Selling the Bosnian Myth to America: Buyer Beware.* Foreign Military Studies Office, Fort Leavenworth, Kansas, 1995 (mimeo).

Stefanov, Nenad, and Michael Werz, eds. *Bosnien und Europa: Die Ethnisierung der Gesellschaft.* Frankfurt: Fischer Taschenbuch Verlag, 1994.

Steinberg, James. "Turning Points in Bosnia and the West." In Zalmay M. Khalilzad, ed., *Lessons from Bosnia: Conference Proceedings.* RAND Corporation no. CF-113–AF (1993).

Stewart, Bob (Lt. Colonel). *Broken Lives: A Personal View of the Bosnian Conflict.* London: HarperCollins, 1993.

Stiglmayer, Alexandra. "The War in Former Yugoslavia." In Alexandra Stiglmayer, ed., *Mass Rape: The War Against Women in Bosnia-Herzegovina.* Lincoln, Neb: University of Nebraska Press, 1994. Pp. 1–34.

———. "The Rapes in Bosnia-Herzegovina." In Stiglmayer, ed., *Mass Rape,* pp. 82–169.

Štitkovac, Ejub, and Jasmina Udovički. "Bosnia and Hercegovina: The Second War." In Jasminka Udovički and James Ridgeway, eds., *Yugoslavia's Ethnic Nightmare: The Inside Story of Europe's Unfolding Ordeal.* New York: Lawrence Hill Books, 1995. Pp. 164–94.

Stojanović, Svetozar. *Propast komunizma i razbijanje Jugoslavije.* Belgrade: Filip Višnjić, 1995.

"Strogo povjerljivi bilans." *AIM* (Banja Luka), May 26, 1997, as reported in *Siemvesti* (May 30, 1997) electronic mail edition (Siemvesti@morag.umsmed.edu).

Sučeska, Avdo. "Osnovne osobenosti položaja Bosne u Osmansko-turskoj državi." In Dubravko Lovrenović, et al., *Istina o Bosni i Hercegovini.* Sarajevo: Altermedia, 1991. Pp. 29–41.

Sudetic, Chuck. "Blood and Vengeance: One Family's Story of the Massacre at Srebrenica and the Unending War in Bosnia." *Rolling Stone,* December 28, 1995–January 11, 1996, pp. 90–103, 147–50.

"Svedocenje Stipe Mesica pred Haskom sudom," as reported in *Siemvesti* (May 22, 1997) electronic mail edition (Siemvesti@morag.umsmed.edu).

Tepić, Ibrahim. "Položaj Bosne i Hercegovine u osmanskom carstvu." In Lovrenović, et al., *Istina o Bosni i Hercegovini,* pp. 43–60.

————. "Državnopravni i politički položaj BiH za vrijeme austrougarske vladavine 1878–1914." In Lovrenović, et al., *Istina o Bosni i Hercegovini,* pp. 51–60.

Thomas, Dorothy Q., and Regan E. Ralph. "Rape in War: Challenging the Tradition of Impunity." *SAIS Review* (Winter–Spring 1994), pp. 81–99.

Times Mirror Center for the People and the Press. *America's Place in the World: An Investigation of the Attitudes of American Opinion Leaders and the American Public About International Affairs.* Washington, DC: November 1993.

Todorović, Dragan. "Grad oslobodjen od normalnog života." *Borba,* May 13, 1992, p. 3.

Tokić, Sejfudin. "Ethnische Ideologie und Eroberungskrieg." In Stefanov and Werz, eds., *Bosnien und Europa,* pp. 175–81.

Tomasevich, Jozo. *War and Revolution in Yugoslavia, 1941–1945: The Chetniks.* Stanford: Stanford University Press, 1975.

Totten, Samuel, and William S. Parsons. "Introduction." In Samuel Totten, William S. Parsons, and Israel W. Charney, eds., *Genocide in the Twentieth Century.* New York: Garland Publishing, 1995. Pp. xi–lvi.

Touval, Saadia. "Coercive Mediation on the Road to Dayton." *International Negotiation* 1, no. 3 (1996), pp. 547–70.

Trifunovska, Snežana, ed. *Yugoslavia Through Documents.* Dordrecht, Netherlands: Martinus Nijhoff, 1994.

Ullman, Richard H., ed. *The World and Yugoslavia's Wars.* New York: Council on Foreign Relations, 1996.

————. "The Wars in Yugoslavia and the International System After the Cold War." In Ullman, ed., *The World and Yugoslavia's Wars,* pp. 9–41.

United States Institute of Peace. "Dayton Implementation: The Train and Equip Program." *Special Report.* Washington, DC: United States Institute of Peace, September 1997.

UNPROFOR. "UNPROFOR Investigation Report: Sarajevo Market Explosion of 5 February 1994." (mimeo).

U.S. Commission on Security and Cooperation in Europe. *The Referendum on Independence in Bosnia-Herzegovina.* Washington, DC: March 12, 1992.

————. *Banja Luka: Ethnic Cleansing Paradigm, or Counterpoint to a Radical Future?* Washington, DC: U.S. Government Printing Office, 1996.

U.S. Committee for Refugees. *World Refugee Survey, 1994.* New York: U.S. Committee for Refugees, 1995.

U.S. Congress. Senate Committee on Armed Services. *Situation in Bosnia and Appropriate U.S. and Western Responses.* Hearing Before the Committee on Armed Services, United States Senate, 102nd Cong. 2nd Sess. Washington, DC: U.S. Government Printing Office, August 11, 1992.

U.S. Congress. Select Committee on Intelligence of the United States Senate and Committee on Foreign Relations of the United States Senate. *War Crimes in the Balkans.* Washington, DC: U.S. Government Printing Office, 1996.

U.S. Information Agency. Office of Research and Media Reaction. "Economy May Provide Common Ground for Bosnians." *Opinion Analysis.* Washington, DC: September 5, 1997.

U.S. Department of State. Bureau of Public Affairs. "Briefing on Train and Equip Program for the Bosnian Federation" (July 25, 1996).

U.S. Department of State. Office of the Assistant Secretary/Spokesman. *Statement by U.S. Secretary of State Warren Christopher* (February 10, 1993).

Ustav Socijalističke Republike Bosne i Hercegovine s Ustavnim amandmanima I-IV i registrom pojmova. Sarajevo: Službeni list SRBiH, 1978.

van Heuven, Marten. "Rehabilitating Serbia." *Foreign Policy* 96 (Fall, 1994), pp. 38–48.

Vasic, Milos. "The Decline and Fall of Western Slavonia." *War Report* 33 (May 1995), p. 5.

———. "A Dream Too Far." *War Report,* 31 (February 1995), pp. 21–26.

Vasić, Miloš. "Začin u ekspres-loncu." *Vreme,* August 29, 1994, pp. 8–9.

Vasić, Miloš, et al. "Masakr na Markalama." *Vreme,* February 14, 1994, pp. 10–14.

Vucinich, Wayne S. "Yugoslavs of Muslim Faith." In Robert J. Kerner, ed., *Yugoslavia.* Berkeley: University of California Press, 1949.

Vulliamy, Ed. *Seasons in Hell: Understanding Bosnia's War.* New York: St. Martin's Press, 1994.

Watson, Fiona M., and Tom Dodd. *Bosnia and Croatia: The Conflict Continues.* Research Paper 95/55. London: International Affairs and Defence Section, House of Commons Library, May 1995.

West, Rebecca. *Black Lamb and Grey Falcon: A Journey Through Yugoslavia.* New York: Viking Press, 1968.

Wood, Pia Christina. "France and the Post Cold War Order: The Case of Yugoslavia." *European Security* 3, no. 1 (Spring 1994), pp. 129–52.

Woodward, Susan L. *Balkan Tragedy.* Washington, DC: The Brookings Institution, 1995.

———. "Yugoslavia: Divide and Fall." *The Bulletin of Atomic Scientists* (November 1993), pp. 24–27.

Zartman, I. William. "The Unfinished Agenda: Negotiating Internal Conflicts." In Roy Licklider, ed., *Stopping the Killing: How Civil Wars End.* New York: New York University Press, 1993. Pp. 20–34.

Zimmerman, Warren. "The Last Ambassador: A Memoir of the Collapse of Yugoslavia." *Foreign Affairs,* 74, no. 2 (March/April 1995), pp. 2–20.

———. *Origins of a Catastrophe.* New York: Random House, 1996.

Zulfikarpašić, Adil. *Članci i intervjui.* Sarajevo: Bošnjački institut, 1991.

Živak, Stražina. *Logor Čelebići 1992.-1994.* Pale: SRNA, 1997.

Index

A

Abdič, Fikret, 25, 44, 68, 131,
    154
  in 1990 elections, 51
  in 1996 elections, 385
Adžic, Blagoje
  on JNA withdrawal, 129–30
Agrokomerc affair, 44
air strikes, 243, 267
  in Bihać, 156–58
  blocked, 150
  on Goražde, 344–46
  NATO, 147, 150, 152, 286, 290,
    291, 336, 352–54, 355
  opposition to, 163, 253–54
  U.S. public opinion on, 251, 252
Ajanović, Irfan, 111
Akashi, Yasushi, 149, 152, 158, 302
  on air strikes, 150, 286
  U.S. criticism by, 290
Albania, 56, 96
Albright, Madeleine, 151, 322,
    349
  on air strikes, 340
  on responsibility for massacres,
    168–69

Albright, Madeleine (continued)
  threat to resign, 331
  on use of force, 223, 291, 323,
    353
Alexander, King of Yugoslavia, 20
Alipašino Polje market, 213–14
Alliance of Reform Forces of
    Yugoslavia, The (SRSJ), 48–49,
    57
  in 1990 elections, 50–51
All-National Parliament, 65
Ankara, 356
Annan, Kofi, 141
Argentina, 307
Arkan. See Raznjatović, Željko
arms embargo, 85
  Bosnian government exempt from,
    212
  issue in U.S. elections, 319–20
  lifting of, 250–51, 278, 304–305,
    307–308, 313, 314–15, 345
  U.S. violation of, 232, 338–39
Army of the Serb republic, 205
Arnautović, Suad, 47, 49, 57
Assembly of the Serb Nation of
    Bosnia-Herzegovina, 74
Austria, 19–20, 35–36

B

Babić, Milan, 89–90, 99
Badinter, Robert, 93
Badinter commission, 86, 93, 96
Bajina Bašta, 134
Bajramović-Ćelo, Ismet, 138, 139
Baker, James
  on Bosnian independence, 100–101,
    115
  on U.S. involvement, 201
  use of media by, 202
Banac, Ivo, 21
Banja Luka, 354–55
Bartholemew, Reginald, 236
Bay of Boka Kotorska, 21
Begić, Kasim, 138
Belgrade. *See* Bosnian Serbs;
    Karaždić, Radovan
Belgrade initiative, 71, 309
Beschloss, Michael, 164
Bihać, 133, 149
  cease-fire in, 129–30
  fighting in, 154–59
  on partitioning of Bosnia, 276
  See also Cazinska Krajina
Bijeljina, 55, 119, 129
Bildt, Carl, 345, 346
Biljana Plavšić, 64
Black Swans, 137
Boban, Mate, 66, 216, 245
  on Bosnian independence, 106, 107
  removed as President, 293
  on Vance-Owen Plan, 224, 227
Bogosavljević, Srdjan, 42, 171
bombing. *See* air strikes
Boras, Franjo, 51–52, 104
Borba, 46, 79, 151
Borovo Selo, 81–82
Bosanska Gradiška, 134
Bosanska Krajina, 23, 33, 97
  Croat takeover, 331
  ethnic cleansing in, 174, 177
Bosanska Krupa, 276

Bosanska Posavina, 23, 32
Bosanski Brod, 64, 119, 134, 198
Bosanski Petrovac, 129–30, 358
Bosansko Grahovo, 153, 348
Bosniacs, 195, 295; *See also* Muslims
Bosnia-Herzegovina
  after Dayton Agreements, 415–18
  change in territories, 331, 332 map,
    333 map
  contested issues in, 5–9
  in Dayton Agreement, 367–69
  ethnic composition of, 25–33, 172,
    224–25, 229–30
  on eve of war, 62–63, 117–20
  following 1990 elections, 58–61
  history, 16–17, 18–23, 34–37
  independence of, 47, 58, 70–73,
    102–105
    debate in parliament over, 105–108
    negotiations on, 75–79, 108–17
  interim government in, 228–29,
    236–37
  international recognition of, 96–98,
    99–101, 121–24
    Serb opposition to, 101–102
  national identity in, 18–23
  nationalist revolution in, 63–69
  partitioning of, 191–93, 263, 266
    in Dayton Agreement, 362–67
    Invincible proposal for, 280–81
    negotiations on, 268–71, 281–83,
      350–52, 356–58
  regions of, 23–24
    center and periphery, 33–34
  as republic status, 21
  and Serb nationalism, 44–45
  under Communist rule, 40–44
  See also Bosnian conflict; Bosnian
    Federation
Bosnian conflict
  casualties, 169–71, 439n.162
  efforts to end, 317–18, 322–27; *See
    also* Contact Group
  interpretations, 190–91

Bosnian conflict *(continued)*
  onset of, 129–31
  outside of Sarajevo, 133–39
  prevention of, 62–63, 120–27,
    389–93, 396–98
  result of, 185–87
  in Sarajevo, 142–44
  source of, 29, 63–69
  U.S. public opinion on, 163–64
  See also ethnic conflict; international
    community
Bosnian Croat army (HVO), 176,
  227
Bosnian Croats
  after Dayton Agreements, 386
  on Bosnian independence, 111
  on EU Action Plan, 282–83
  map proposed by, 219, 220 map
  on Muslim military control, 241–42
  offensive against Bosnian Serbs,
    354–55
  political interests of, 197–98, 256
  population of, 26, 27, 29
  U.S. support for, 337
  on Vance-Owen Plan, 216–17,
    236–37
Bosnian Federation, 293, 294–98, 304,
  319, 355–56
  after Dayton Agreements, 373–77
  maps proposed for, 296–97
  military equipment in, 379
Bosnian government
  after Bosnian conflict, 186–87
  attacks on Muslims by, 165–66
  and London agreements, 212–13
  map proposed by, 219, 221 map, 226
    map
  oppose Owen-Stoltenberg plan,
    277–78
  political interests of, 256
  on safe areas, 264
  on Vance-Owen Plan, 216, 217,
    224–25, 236, 242–43
  See also Izetbegović, Alija; Muslims

Bosnian Institute for Public Health of
  the Republic Committee for
  Health and Social Welfare, 169,
  171
Bosnian Muslims. *See* Muslims
Bosnian Serb Republic, 193, 355, 375
  in Dayton Agreement, 367
Bosnian Serbs, 12, 309
  accused of genocide, 183, 184
  after Bosnian conflict, 185–86
  air strikes on, 352–54
  on Bosnian independence, 103, 104,
    109
  concessions made to, 334, 335–36
  during World War II, 37, 38–39
  ethnic cleansing of, 176
  on EU Action Plan, 282–83
  on eve of war, 73–75
  favored in Vance-Owen Plan, 230–31
  on independence from Yugoslavia, 74
  map proposed by, 222 map, 236–39
  negotiations with Contact Group,
    304, 305–307
  negotiations with U.S., 319–21
  oppose Vance-Owen Plan, 247–50
  and partitioning of Bosnia, 274, 277,
    284, 285, 349
  political interests of, 191–94, 256
  population distribution of, 26, 27–33
  relationship with Russia, 301, 350–51
  status in Bosnian federation, 295, 297
  ultimatum given to, 287
  union with Serbia, 34–35
  United States support for, 315
  and Vance-Owen Plan, 217, 225–27,
    230–31, 234–36, 246, 247–50
  withdrawal of troops by, 240
  withdrawal of weapons by, 288–89,
    354
  See also Bosnian conflict; Bosnian
    Federation; Greater Serbia;
    Serbia; Serbs
Boutros-Ghali, Boutros, 132, 166
  on air strikes, 150, 286
  in London meeting, 214

Boutros-Ghali, Boutros *(continued)*
  on Markala massacre, 166
  on military withdrawal, 305, 312, 313
  on Sarajevo airport, 207
  on UN involvement, 91, 204, 210,
    242, 342
Boyd, Charles G., 162
Bošnjaks, 195–96
Bratunac, 179
breadline massacre, 165–66
Briquemont, Francis, 143, 268
Brkić, Milenko, 66, 112
Brunei, 307
Brussels, 117
Brzezinski, Zbigniew, 247
Brčko, 276, 362, 364, 365–66
Bugojno, 135, 224, 269, 276
Buha, Aleksa, 274
Bulatović, Momir, 86, 247, 280
Burns, John, 244
Bush, George, 132, 201, 209–10
Busovača, 135, 224
Butmir, 139

C

Canada, 268
cantonization, 59
Čapljina, 180
Carnegie Commission on Preventing
  Deadly Conflict, 389
Carrington, Lord Peter, 94, 98, 123,
  209
Carter, Jimmy, 317, 320
Catholic Church, 25, 36, 107
Cazinska Krajina, 18, 23, 25, 82
  arms trading in, 138
  cease-fire in, 129–30
  control over, 33
  fighting in, 134, 152, 154, 155–56
  uprising in, 35
  WWII massacres in, 38
cease-fire, 129–30, 135, 148, 288
  after Markala massacre, 145–46

cease-fire *(continued)*
  between Muslims and Croats, 146,
    245, 293
  in Croatian war, 82
  inability to negotiate, 359–60
  in Sarajevo, 142–43
  through Jimmy Carter, 317, 324
  violation of, 152–53
  without political settlement, 279
Čekić, Smail, 130
Čengić, Muhammed, 55
Central Intelligence Agency (CIA),
  142
Cheney, Richard, 207
Chirac, Jacques, 326, 342
Christopher, Warren, 232, 233, 278,
  286
  in Dayton Agreement, 364, 366
  on economic sanctions, 306
  on Markala massacre, 166
  on safe areas, 264
  on US involvement, 247, 252, 254,
    265, 299, 323
Churkin, Vitaly, 147, 288, 301
Claes, Willy, 353
Clinton, Bill, 210, 231, 307
  on arms smuggling, 308
  on military involvement, 278–79
  pressure placed on, 307
  radio address by, 289
  response to Serb shelling, 342
  on use of force, 210
  See also Clinton administration;
    United States
Clinton administration
  on air strikes, 142, 353
  on arms embargo, 305
  decision to use force, 300, 322–24,
    382
  on economic sanctions, 141
  See also Clinton, Bill; United States
Collinson, Christopher, 138
communism, 4, 21, 40–44
  political fragmentation under, 46

communism *(continued)*
  reformed, 48
  removal of, 63
Conference on Security and
  Cooperation in Europe (CSCE),
  85, 87
Contact Group, 263, 265, 408
  formation of, 263, 265, 300
  negotiations with Milošević, 328
  plan of, 301–304
    reaction to, 305–307
    revised, 321–22
Convention for a New Yugoslavia, 103
Čosić, Dorbrica, 225, 226, 227, 247,
  248, 250
Council for National Equality, 76, 105
criminal gangs, 177
Croat Defense Council (HVO), 133,
  135, 293
Croatia
  on Bosnian federation, 294
  Bosnia partitioned to, 20–21, 22 map
  German recognition of, 92–95
  leadership in, 65–66
  offensive action by, 328, 331
  political factions in, 65–66
  recognition of, 96, 121, 395–96
    and recognition of Bosnia, 122–24
  secession of, 69–70, 88
  vs. Serbs over Bosnia, 35–36
  U.S. support for, 337, 339, 349
  UN military in, 91
  See also Bosnian Croats; Croats;
    Tudjman, Franjo
Croatian Defense Forces (HOS), 74,
  137, 197–98
  ethnic cleansing by, 176
Croatian Democratic Union (HDZ),
  12, 51–52, 53, 81
  on Bosnian independence, 104–105,
    106–108
  factions of, 65–66
  map proposed by, 112, 114 map
  on Vance-Owen Plan, 216–17

Croatian Democratic Union of
  Bosnia-Herzegovina (HDZ), 48
Croatian Krajina, 328
Croatian National Union (HNZ),
  35–36
Croatian Ustashe, 37, 38, 39
Croatian War, 81–84, 98
  European involvement, 85–92
Croats
  displaced, 172
  during World War II, 38
  ethnic cleansing by, 176, 180
  ethnic cleansing of, 176–77, 178, 179
  on eve of war, 73, 74–75
  fighting with Muslims, 134–36, 138,
    146, 244, 245–46, 269–70,
    292–94
  See also Bosnian conflict; Bosnian
    Croats; Croatia
Cuny, Fred, 162
Cuskić, Fikret, 137
Cutileiro, Jose, 108, 110, 208
Cutileiro negotiations, 108–17

D

Damjanović, Sretko, 160
Damrosch, Lori Fisler, 95
Danas, 67, 99, 116
Dayton Agreement, 8, 318, 360–62
  constitution of, 367–73
  map from, 362–67
  military provisions in, 377–81
  United States role in, 412–15
de Charette, Hervé, 345
de Cuellar, Xavier Perez, 94, 95, 97
de Deus Pinheiro, Joao, 99
Delimustafić, Alija, 68, 131
Delić, Rasim, 138, 143, 153, 351
Demurenko, Andrei, 168
Der Kurier, 270
Derventa, 119
detention camps, 180
Diehl, Paul, 199–200

Die Woche, 270
Divjak, Jovan, 177
Djukić, Djorde, 138
Doboj, 133
Dobrinje, 139
Dole, Robert, 252, 319, 322
Donia, Robert, 129
Donji Vakuf, 224, 276, 354
Drew, Elizabeth, 252
Drina, 20
Dubrovnik, 83
Dudaković, Atif, 154
Duraković, Nijaz, 48, 51

E

Eagleburger, Lawrence, 100, 210,
    232
EC Conference on Yugoslavia, 84,
    86–87
economic sanctions, 132, 141,
    204–206, 282–83, 302
    in Contact Group negotiations,
        306
    lifting of, 249, 310, 330–31
    tightening of, 141, 243
Economist, 99
Efendić, Hadžo, 119
elections
    1990, 46–53, 54, 56–61, 391–92
    1992, 203
    1996, 319–20, 385–86
    1996 U.S., 319–20
enclaves. *See* Bihać; Goražde;
    refugees; Srebrenica; Žepa
Epoha, 102
ethnic cleansing, 12, 32, 65, 119,
    171–81
    of Muslims, 13, 65, 135, 136
ethnic conflict, 4–5, 17
    approaches to, 6–9
    in Bosnia, 5–6, 7–8
    international response to, 9–11
    issues leading to, 4–6

ethnic conflict *(continued)*
    moral issues on, 11–15
    See also Bosnian conflict; ethnic
        composition
ethnic composition, 25–33, 171–72,
    274–75
    in Dayton Agreement, 370–72
    in Vance-Owen plan, 224t
European Commission on Human
    Rights, 218
European Community (EC)
    Action Plan of, 282–83
    intervention strategies, 84–87,
        394–96
    negotiations sponsored by, 108–17
    recognition of Bosnia by, 96, 99,
        100–101
    disagreement on, 92–95
    effect of, 97–99
    role of, 79–80, 89–90
    See also ICFY; international
        community; Owen, Lord David
European Court of Human Rights, 218
European Union (EU). *See* European
    Community (EC)
exclusion zones, 148–49, 152,
    288–90; *See also* safe zones
Extraordinary EPC, 93

F

Federation of Bosnia-Herzegovina.
    See Bosnian Federation
Fein, Helen, 181–82
Financial Times, 163
Fine, John, 129
Fojnica, 129, 224
Foreign Affairs, 162
Foča, 38, 129
France, 85, 243, 347
    on air strikes, 267, 348
    concessions to Serbs by, 322
    on military withdrawal, 313, 329
    pressure on U.S. by, 285–86,
        299–300

France *(continued)*
role in Bosnian conflict, 128–29
on use of force, 207, 312, 326
See also Contact Group;
international community
Franjević, Mate, 415
Frasure, Robert, 328, 330

G

Galbraith, Peter, 337, 360
Galvin, John, 294
Ganić, Ejup, 52, 194, 294, 298
accommodation with Serbs by,
269–70
opposition to demilitarization by, 223
Gelb, Leslie, 401
genocide, 181–85, 325
prosecution for, 14
See also ethnic cleansing
Genscher, Hans Dietrich, 92, 94–95,
97
Germany, 85
during World War II, 38–39
recognition of Croatia and Slovenia,
92–94, 121, 122
See also Contact Group;
international community
Gingrich, Newt, 319
Gjelten, Tom, 166, 165
Glamoč, 153, 348
Glenny, Misha, 25
Gligorov, 96
Gompert, David, 200–201
Goražde, 129
air strikes on, 344–48
attack on, 146–52
in Dayton Agreement, 362, 364
ethnic divisions in, 63–64
and partitioning of Bosnia, 274, 275
WWII massacres in, 38
Gore, Al, 223, 322, 337
Gornji Vakuf, 135, 224
Goulding, Marrack, 203–204

Gow, James, 401
Gowing, Nik, 164, 175
Grachev, Pavel, 301, 306, 344–45
Gradačac, 133, 139
Granić, Mate, 292
Graz agreement, 108
Graz map, 192–93
Great Britain, 85, 343
on air strikes, 268, 346, 348
role in conflict, 128–29
on use of force, 207, 325–26, 345–46
on withdrawal of troops, 323–24
See also Contact Group;
international community
greater Serbia, 21, 37, 72, 84, 89,
102–103, 121–22, 198
Grebo, Zdravko, 12, 59, 139, 196
Green Berets, 74, 130, 131
Green Cadre, 38
Greve, Hanna, 173
Grude, 66
Guardian, 99, 311
Gulf War, 392–93

H

Hadžić, Ismet, 139
Halilović, Šefer, 74, 131, 138, 194, 245
Havel, Vaclav, 141
Hayden, Robert, 371
Helsinki Watch, 178
Herak, Borislav, 160
Herceg-Novi, 21
Herzegovina, 23, 25, 74
Croats, 66, 197, 374–75
ethnic cleansing in, 180
fighting in, 119
See also Bosnia-Herzegovina;
Croatia
Holbrooke, Richard, 308, 321, 334,
352
on air strikes, 353
in Dayton Agreement, 366
negotiations by, 335–36, 359

Hollingsworth, Larry, 140–41
Horowitz, Donald, 9
hostages, 147, 148, 159, 324, 329
Hrasnica, 272
Hubul Emir, 73
humanitarian relief, 142, 159, 160,
    199, 201, 398–400
Hungary, 307
Hunter, Robert, 158
Hurd, Douglas, 202, 209
Hutchings, Robert, 200

I

ICFY (International Conference on the
    Former Yugoslavia), 211–14
demise of, 281–82, 288–89
negotiations by, 236, 240–41
proposals by, 217–21, 223 map
report by, 309–10
role in Vance-Owen plan, 214–14,
    218, 228, 229, 248
Imamović, Mustafa, 171
Implementation Force (IFOR), 377–78
Independent, the 166
Independent State of Croatia (NDH),
    20, 39
International Committee of the Red
    Cross (ICRC), 204; See also Red
    Cross
international community, 256, 314
affected by media, 164, 202, 286–87
on Bihać crisis, 156–59
on Bosnian independence, 195
intervention by, 9–11, 79–81,
    128–29, 284
    diplomatic, 329–37, 404–407
    failed, 381–82, 393–98
    humanitarian, 204–05, 398–400
    military, 186–88, 208–111,
        400–404
on Muslim-Croat fighting, 292
negotiations within, 202–203
on partitioning of Bosnia, 281–84

international community (continued)
preventive efforts by, 120–27,
    392–93, 396–98
recognition of Bosnia by, 96–98,
    99–101, 195
response to Markala massacre, 145
role after Dayton Agreement, 416,
    417–18
role in greater Serbia, 103
safe areas protected by, 254–55
sanctions by, 205–206
takeover Sarajevo airport,
    207–208
See also Contact Group; France;
    Germany; Great Britain; ICFY;
    Russia, United States; United
    Nations
International Criminal Tribunal, 14,
    184–85
Invincible proposal, 280–81, 303
Iran, 307, 308, 339
Islam, 12, 42, 44, 46–47
influence of, 196–97
Islamic Declaration, 46, 67
Italy, 38–39
Ivenić, Mladen, 385
Izetbegović, Alija, 46, 65, 66–68
in 1990 elections, 51, 52–53
in 1996 elections, 385
bodyguards for, 137
on Bosnian Federation, 373
on Bosnian independence, 70, 71,
    77–78, 112, 113, 114
on Contact Group proposal, 303
in Dayton Agreement, 364
on EC recognition, 96
on eve of war, 62
on JNA withdrawal, 129–30
kidnapping of, 131
negotiations by, 73, 236, 241,
    292–93, 300–301, 336
oppose Owen-Stoltenberg plan,
    277–78
on partitioning of Bosnia, 194, 269,
    282, 351, 358

Izetbegović, Alija *(continued)*
  request for military involvement,
    278–79
  on role of Islam, 46–47
  on Vance-Owen Plan, 216, 227, 234,
    242

J

Jablanica, 24, 135, 224
Jajce, 134, 276, 348, 354, 358, 374
Janvier, Bernard, 353
Johnson, Richard, 402
Joseph, Franz, 36
Jović, Borisav, 87–88, 99–100, 103
Juppé, Alain 251, 264, 286, 299,
    299–300; *See also* France

K

Kadijević, Veljko, 82, 83, 84, 88,
    98
Kalaj, Benjamin, 35
Karadžić, Radovan, 47, 65, 70, 118,
    141, 142, 148
  in 1996 elections, 385
  on Bosnian independence, 70–71,
    77–78, 106, 108, 109, 112
  and ethnic cleansing, 65
  on EU Action Plan, 283
  on flight ban, 250
  negotiations by, 75
  on partitioning of Bosnia, 59
  relationship with Mladić, 310–11
  on Sarajevo airport, 208
  on Vance-Owen Plan, 225–27, 227,
    246, 248
  on weapon withdrawal, 288
  See also Serb Democratic Party
    (SDS); Bosnian Serbs
Kecmanović, Nenad, 49, 51, 59, 61
Kenney, George, 170
Kessler, Peter, 151
Kiseljak, 136

Klarin, Mirko, 245, 266
Kljujić, Stjepan, 51–52, 66, 73, 106,
    107, 216
Ključ, 28
Knin, 348
Kohl, Helmut, 99
Koljević, Nikola, 51, 64, 72, 104
Konjic, 24, 135, 224
Kordić, Dario, 66
Kosovo, 56, 284
Kostić, Branko, 98, 129–30
Kozarac, 131–32, 173
Kozyrev, Andrei, 147, 148, 311–12
Krajina, 81–82, 89, 327, 331–33,
    339
Krajina Serbs, 89–90, 92, 159
Krajišnik, Momčilo, 53, 71, 105, 385
Kučan, Milan, 80–81
Kulenović, Džafer, 37
Kulen-Vakuf, 38
Kupres, 29, 153
Kurspahić, Kemal, 59
Kuwait, 379

L

Lake, Anthony, 349
  on arms embargo, 295, 307
  on use of force, 223–24, 320, 353
Lasić, Miro, 108
League of Communists of Yugoslavia
    (LCY), 45, 48
League of Communists-Social
    Democratic Party (SK-SDP), 48,
    50, 57
Lederach, John Paul, 416
Legija Kempler, 38
Leotard, Francois, 267
Lewis, Anthony, 230–31, 401
Libal, Michael, 97
lift and strike, 251–254, 450n.196
  failure of, 264, 314
Little, Allan, 163
Livno Declaration, 107

London agreements, 211–14, 215; *See also* ICFY
London conference (July 1995), 344–46
Lucien Karchmar, 39
Lugar, Richard, 252

M

McCaffrey, Barry, 251
McCurry, Michael, 267
Macedonia, 96, 101, 284
MacKenzie, Lewis, 132, 160, 268
McLaughlin, Mary, 148
McPeak, Merrill A., 251
Maglaj, 135
Malaysia, 307
Manas, Jean, 184
Marić, Velimir, 138
Markala marketplace massacre, 145–46
  effect of, 286–87
  media coverage of, 164–65, 166–69
Marković, Ante, 48–49
Martić, Milan, 82, 158
massacres
  during World War II, 37–38, 39
  media coverage of, 164–69
  in Srebrenica, 180
  See also Markala marketplace massacre
Mazowiecki, Tadeusz, 175–76, 178
media
  attack on UN by, 160–62
  criticism of, 162–63
  on Dayton Agreement, 366
  effect on policymaking, 164, 202, 286–87
  on ethnic cleansing, 175–76, 177
  ethnic polarization of, 64–65
  on Goražde attack, 151
  on Markala massacre, 145
Meier, Viktor, 99, 119

Mercier, Michele, 182
Mesić, Stipe, 82, 108
migration, 42
Mikulić, Branko, 44
military
  after Dayton Agreements, 386–87
  after partitioning of Bosnia, 276
  amount needed, 210, 257
  in Bihać, 159
  Bosnian, 328–29
  in Cazinska Krajina, 155–56
  Croat/Bosnian, 134, 337, 346–47
  in Dayton Agreement, 377–81
  desertion in, 84
  European, 85
  joint Muslim-Croat, 295
  in Krajina, 332
  NATO, 253
  in Sarajevo, 130
  U.S., 146, 200, 206–207, 305, 313, 317–18, 338–40, 401–402
  under Vance-Owen Plan, 221–24, 227–28
  withdrawal of, 149, 221–24, 240
  See also United Nations Protection Force (UNPROFOR); Yugoslav People's Army (JNA)
Military Professional Resources, Inc. (MPRI), 339, 379
Miljković, Huska, 38
  ethnic cleansing directed by, 175
  negotiations with U.S. by, 330–31
  on Vance-Owen Plan, 243–45
Milošević, Slobodan, 44
  on Bosnian recognition, 101–102
  conciliatory efforts by, 98–99
  on Croatian War, 82
  and Dayton Agreement, 363–64
  on EU Action Plan, 282–83
  on greater Serbia, 102–103, 121–22, 198
  on Krajina Serbs, 89–90
  negotiations by, 73, 211, 212, 280, 306, 328, 336–37

Milošević, Slobodan *(continued)*
pressure on Bosnian Serbs by,
335–36, 354
relationship with Bosnian Serbs, 65,
309–10
role in peacemaking, 331–32,
333–34
on Sarajevo airport, 207–208
on secession, 80–81, 87–89
on Vance-Owen Plan, 225–27, 235,
247–50, 248
See also Serbia; Serbs
Mitterand, Francois, 132, 243
mixed marriages, 42, 423.68n
Miškin, Vaso, 205
Mladić, Ratko, 131, 143, 288
on military withdrawal, 353
negotiations by, 140, 334
relationship with Karaždic,
310–11
response to air strikes, 147
on Sarajevo airport, 208
on weapon withdrawal, 288
Montenegro, 20, 21
approves EC draft, 86
in new Yugoslavia, 86, 98
Morillon, Philippe, 85, 140
Mostar, 29, 64, 133, 269
after Dayton Agreements,
375–77
attacks on, 135
in Bosnian Federation, 296, 298,
373–74
Muslim representation in, 37
and partitioning of Bosnia, 193, 276,
292, 296
rally in, 118
Mrkonjić Grad, 358, 364, 374
Mrkšić, Mile, 332, 333
Mt. Bjelašnica, 142–44
Mt. Igman, 152, 268
France shelling on, 347
Serbian battle for, 142–44
Muslimani, 19, 36

Muslim Bosniak Organization (MBO),
68, 72
Muslim-Croat Federation. *See*
Bosnian Federation
Muslim nationality, 41–42
Muslim Party of Democratic Action
(SDA), 12
Muslim Patriotic League, 119
Muslims
and 1990 elections, 52
after Bosnian conflict, 186–87
and Dayton Agreements, 364–65,
366–67, 386–87
attacks against other Muslims,
165–66
on Bosnian independence, 21, 45,
117–18
cultural identity of, 19–20, 36–37
displaced, 171, 172
during Austrian occupation, 35
during World War II, 37–38
ethnic cleansing by, 178–80, 180
ethnic cleansing of, 13, 65, 135, 136,
173–76
on EU Action Plan, 282
fighting with Croats, 134–36, 138,
146, 177, 244, 245–46, 269–70,
292–94
genocide against, 182–83
media focus on, 162–63
military control by, 241–42
military support for, 379–80
offensive against Bosnian Serbs,
354–55
and *Invincible* proposal, 280–81
and partitioning of Bosnia, 266,
270–71, 272, 274, 277, 284
persecution by, 177–78
political interests of, 194–97
population of, 26, 27–33
reluctance to negotiate, 357–58,
359–60
self-reliance of, 283–84
U.S. support for, 168, 319
under Communist rule, 43–45

Muslims *(continued)*
  See also Bosnian conflict;
    Izetbegović, Alija; Party of
    Democratic Action (SDA)
Myint-U, Thant, 160

N

Naletelić,-Tuta, Mladen, 137
nationalism, 11, 35–36
  political parties of, 46–48, 53, 57,
    63–69
  elections of, 49–53, 54
  disputes among, 55–56
  Serb, 44–46, 56
NATO
  air strikes by, 147, 150, 152, 156–58,
    267–68, 286, 352–54, 355
  on covert arms shipments, 309
  deployment of troops, 377
  on Goražde attack, 149
  on massacres, 167–68
  motives for involvement, 290
  peacekeeping role, 305
  ultimatum by, 287
Netherlands, 85
Newhouse, John, 93–94
New York Times, the, 160, 252–53
Nikiforov, Alexei, 302
Niković, Spiro, 129–30
NIN, 136, 185
no-fly zone, 140, 146, 232
Novi Pazar, 41

O

oblasts, 73
Odžak, 176, 375
Olovo, 64
olympics, 42
Orašje, 133
Orić, Naser, 133, 179–80
Oručević, Safet, 138
Oslobodjenje, 65, 105, 106, 139

Osmanlija, 19
Ottoman rule, 19, 26
Owen, Lord David, 213
  on air strikes, 141, 152, 243
  criticism of U.S. by, 255
  on economic sanctions, 282
  negotiations by, 244–45
  See also Vance-Owen Plan
Owen-Stoltenberg Plan, 154, 255,
  275–81

P

Pakistan, 307
Pale, 309
Palić, Avdo, 133, 140
Panić, Milan, 211, 212
Panić, Života, 82, 225, 227
paramilitary groups, 137
  ethnic cleansing by, 173, 174, 175,
    177
  role in genocide, 183
  See also military
Pardew, James, 379–80
partition, 9
Partnership for Peace program, 293–94
Party of Democratic Action (SDA),
  46–47, 51, 57
  on Bosnian independence, 71, 76,
    77, 108
  division within, 68
  ethnic division by, 63–64
  map proposed by, 113 map
  political interests of, 194, 195–97
  See also Izetbegović, Alija
Patriotic League, 74
Pazarić, 179
peasant revolts, 35
Pejanović, Mirko, 270
Pejić, Nenad, 65
Peronić, Davor, 66
Perry, William, 290, 305, 323, 337
Petković, Milivoj, 245
Plavšić, Biljana, 51, 385

Ploče, 274, 276, 282, 347
Pobjeda, 148
Pomfret, John, 161–62
Portillo, Michael, 346
Posavina, 133
    Croat displacement in, 172
    ethnic cleansing in, 176
    in Dayton Accord, 375
Powell, Colin, 231, 250–51, 268, 343
power-sharing, 6–7
    in Dayton Accord, 368–71, 372
Prazina, Jusuf, 138, 139
Prevlaka peninsula, 198
Prijedor, 28, 302, 362
Prozor, 24, 136

Q

Quebec, 5

R

Radio Television Sarajevo, 65
Radulović, Srdjan, 88
railways, 21–22
rallies, 46, 118
rapes, 170–71
rapid reaction force, 341, 347–48, 353
Raseta, Boris, 82
Raznjatović, Željko, 119
rebellions, 34–35
recognition, 94–98, 121–24
Red Cross, 131, 169, 179, 204
Redmond, Charles, 291
    on Invincible Proposal, 280–81
    negotiations by, 296, 312, 320
Redžić, Enver, 33
refugees, 140, 171–72, 416
Republic of Serb Krajina (RSK), 81
Republika Srpska. See Bosnian Serb
    Republic
Resolution 713, 85, 90
Resolution 749, 204
Resolution 752, 204, 205

Resolution 757, 132, 205
Resolution 758, 206
Resolution 770, 210
Resolution 781, 140, 250
Resolution 816, 250
Resolution 820, 243
Resolution 824, 149
Resolution 836, 267
Resolution 913, 156
Rifkind, Malcolm, 325, 344
Rijeka, 276
Rolling Stone, 161
Rose, Michael, 151
    on Bihać air strikes, 157–58
    and cease-fire, 153, 288
Rudman, George, 408
Russia
    on arms embargo, 304–305, 307
    on economic sanctions, 282
    monitor cease-fire, 288–89
    on safe areas, 156
    support Bosnian Serbs, 306, 350–51
    on use of force, 207, 243, 301,
        343–44
    on weapon withdrawal, 288
    See also Contact Group
Russo-Turkish war of 1871–78, 34–35
Ryan, Michael E., 251, 353

S

Sacirbey, Muhamed, 279, 350
safe areas, 254–55
    attacks on, 324, 325
    opposition to, 264
    violation of, 155–56
Sandžak faction, 194
Sanski Most, 28, 302, 362
Sarajevo, 24, 33, 159, 302
    barricades in, 118
    in Bosnian Federation, 296
    criminal gangs in, 138–39
    Croats in, 36
    in Dayton Agreement, 363

Sarajevo *(continued)*
  demilitarization of, 221–24
  disorder in, 153–54
  exclusion zone around, 152
  military in, 130–31
  and partitioning of Bosnia, 271–73,
    277
  renaissance of, 42
  shelling of, 131–133, 140, 145–46,
    211, 213–143, 349–50
  strangulation of, 142–44
  under Muslim control, 177–78
Sarajevo airport, 132, 133, 200,
  207–208
Saudi Arabia, 307, 379
secession of Croatia, 88
  secession of Slovenia, 87–88
self-determination, 17, 190
Semberija, 23
Serb Autonomous Oblasts (SAOs), 56,
  73, 88
Serb Democratic Party (SDS), 12, 45,
  47, 63
  in 1990 elections, 53–54, 57
  in 1996 elections, 385
  on Bosnian independence, 70–73,
    103, 117
  map proposed by, 115 map
Serbia, 20
  nationalist movement in, 44–46, 56
  negotiations with EC, 86–88,
    89–90
  opposition to Bosnian recognition,
    101–102
  on Slovenian secession, 80–81
  on UN peacekeeping role, 91
  war with Turkey, 34–35
  See also Serbs
Serbian Cheniks, 38, 39
Serbian-Croatian proposal, 266, 268,
  271, 273
Serbian Democratic Party of Croatia,
  81
Serbian Guard, 119
Serbian Radical Party, 203

Serb National Council, 73
Serbs, 159
  accused of genocide, 181, 183
  alliance with Croats, 136, 138
  attack Bihać, 154–159
  attack Goražde, 146–52
  attack Srebrenica, 140–42
  attack UN, 159
  battle for Mt. Bjelašnica/Mt. Igman,
    142–44
  blame for massacres on, 166–68
  on Bosnian independence, 102–104,
    117, 118
  displaced, 171–172
  ethnic cleansing by, 12, 172–76,
    177
  ethnic cleansing of, 178–80
  rapes by, 170–71
  shelling by, 132, 145–46, 152, 211,
    213–14
  under Muslim control, 177–78
  on Vance-Owen Plan, 216
  war with Croatia, 81–84
  withdrawal of troops, 149, 240
  See also Bosnian Serbs; Milošević,
    Slobodan; Serbia
Šešelj, Vojislav, 203
Sewall, John, 339–40, 374
Shalikashvili, John, 323, 343
Sheehan, John, 251
Shultz, George, 247, 278
Silajdžić, Haris, 109
  in 1996 elections, 385
  on air strikes, 157
  on Bosnian Federation, 294, 373
  in Dayton Agreement, 362, 364,
    464n.258
  negotiations by, 292, 321–22
  on partitioning of Bosnia, 194, 270,
    358
  and use of media, 202
Silber, Laura, 163
Skenderija, 138
Slavonija, 82

Slocombe, Walter, 290
Slovenia
  international recognition of, 92–95,
    96, 121–24
  secession of, 69–70, 80–81, 87–88
  on Vance-Owen Plan, 246
Smajlović, Ljiljana, 57, 120
Smith, Rupert, 341
Socialist Party, 203
Socialist Republic of Bosnia
  Herzegovina (SRBH), 96
Sol, Koos, 159
Spaho, Mehmed, 37
Split, 356
Sporazum, 21, 37
Srebrenica, 133, 149, 179
  attack on, 135, 140–42, 324–25
  effect of, 246–47, 342, 382
  and partitioning of Bosnia, 274,
    275
Stabilization Force (SFOR), 378
Stanković, Milovan, 185
Štitkovac, Ejub, 174
Stockhom International Peace
  Research Institute, 170
Stolac, 180, 298
Stoltenberg, Thorvald, 265, 360
Sudetic, Chuck, 161
surface-to-air missiles (SAMs), 156,
  157, 159
Switzerland, 5

T

Tarnoff, Peter, 290, 308, 349
Tarćin, 179
Tešanj, 135
Thatcher, Margaret, 210, 278
Tirić, Hase, 137
Tito, 20, 21, 69; *See also* Communism
Topalović,-Caco, Mušan, 68, 138, 139
Travnik, 135, 224, 275, 324
Traynor, Ian, 98, 119
Trebinje, 134

Trnka, Kasim, 46
Trnovo, 135, 269
Tudjman, Franjo, 66, 203
  on Bosnian independence, 104, 107
  on Greater Croatia, 198
  negotiations by, 245, 280, 292–93
  on partitioning of Bosnia, 82, 294,
    358
Turkey, 36, 379
Turks, 18
Turkuši, 19
Tutwiler, Margaret, 202
Tuzla, 129, 149, 324
  ethnic cleansing in, 178
  shelling of, 329
  voting in, 57

U

Udbina airbase, 156–157
UN Commission of Experts, 170, 173
UN Human Right Commission,
  170–71
United Nations (UN)
  criticism of, 159–62
  in Goražde, 150
  humanitarian aid through, 399–400
  motives for involvement, 290
  on Mt. Igman, 143–44
  presence in Bosnia questioned,
    151–52
  role in Bosnian conflict, 90–92,
    128–29, 199–200, 302
  See also ICFY; United Nations
    Protection Force
    (UNPROFOR); Vance, Cyrus
United Nations Charter, 10
United Nations High Commission for
  Refugees (UNHCR), 199
United Nations Protected Areas
  (UNPAs), 189
United Nations Protection Force
  (UNPROFOR), 315
  in Bihać, 154, 155

United Nations Protection Force
(UNPROFOR) *(continued)*
in Croatian War, 91, 92, 108
investigation on massacres by, 166
media attack on, 160–161
role of, 340
in Sarajevo, 199
in Sarajevo airport, 132
Serb weapons under control of, 288
in Srebrenica, 141–42
withdrawal of, 323–24, 329, 342
United States
accommodate Bosnian Serbs, 321,
356
air strikes by, 267
on Bihać crisis, 157, 158
on Bosnian independence, 114–16
and covert arms shipments, 307–308,
309, 338–39
criticism of Vance-Owen Plan by,
230
on demilitarization of Sarajevo,
223–24
on economic sanctions, 282, 302, 330
intervention strategies, 317–18,
383–85, 409–12
involvement in Bosnian conflict,
79–81, 90, 128–29
diplomatic, 311–16, 330–31,
407–408
military, 146, 200–202, 231–32,
246, 250–53, 278–79, 305,
378, 379–80
motives for, 290
pressure placed on for, 285–86,
299–300
public opinion on, 163–64
and use of force, 246–47, 266–67,
276, 301, 322–27, 334–35,
340–45, 400–402
lack of involvement by, 200–202
on Muslim-Croat fighting, 292–93,
295, 298, 299
negotiations with Bosnian Serbs,
319–21, 354

United States *(continued)*
opposition to Vance-Owen Plan,
257–58
proposal on partitioning, 349
react to Goražde attack, 147, 148–49
recognition of Bosnia by, 99–100,
121, 123
role in Dayton Agreement, 412–15
on safe areas, 264–65
six point plan by, 233–34
See also Contact Group;
international community
Usora, 139
Ustashe government, 37, 38, 39
Uzelac, Nikola, 83

V

Vance, Cyrus, 90–91, 118, 175
on Bosnian recognition, 94
failed plan for Croatia by, 91–92
in ICFY, 215
resignation of, 265
on use of force, 204
Vance-Owen Plan, 215, 265, 405–406
deficits of, 256–62, 406–407
demilitarization in, 221–24, 227–28,
240–41
failure of, 243–44
interim government proposed in,
228–29, 236–37
international safeguards in, 218, 229
map proposed by, 223 map, 224–25,
229–30, 234–35, 238 map
Serb opposition to, 237–39
territorial demands by, 226
U.S. opposition to, 230–31, 233,
234, 257–58
van den Broek, Hans, 343
Vareš, 129, 177, 283
Vasić, Miloš, 139
Velika Kladuša, 129–130, 154
Villa Konak, 109, 111
Vitez, 135, 136

Višegrad, 129
Vlasenica, 38
Vogošća, 272
Vrbas, 20
Vreme, 166
Vucinich, Wayne, 37
Vukovar, 82, 83
Vučković, Dušan, 137

W

Wahlgren, Lars-Eric, 141, 250
war. *See* Bosnian conflict, Croatian war
War Crimes Tribunal, 65
War Report, 160
Washington Post, 161, 253
weapons, 74
  Dayton Agreement provisions on, 378–79
  selling, 138
  smuggled, 307–309, 338–39
  withdrawal of, 145, 149, 287, 288–89, 354
West, Rebecca, 35
Western European Union (WEU), 85
Woerner, Manfred, 149
World War I, 36; *See also* Croatian War
World War II, 21, 25
  ethnic cleansing during, 33
  Yugoslavia during, 37–40
  war losses, 38, 39

Y

Yellow Wasps, 137
Yeltsin, Boris, 350
Young Muslims, 67

Yugoslav Council for the Defense of the Constitution, 87
Yugoslavia
  breakup of, 17, 69–79
  during World War II, 37–40
  formation of, 36
  See also Bosnia-Herzegovina; Croatia; Serbia; Slovenia; Yugoslavs
Yugoslavia: Death of A Nation, 163
Yugoslav League of Communists, 390
Yugoslav Muslim Organization (JMO), 20, 37
Yugoslav People's Army (JNA), 62, 119
  after Bosnian recognition, 101
  arms through, 74
  attacks by, 120
  in Croatian War, 82–84
  in Sarajevo, 130–31, 132
  withdrawal of, 90
Yugoslavs, 29, 32, 42, 45, 52
  population, 30–32
Yutel, 65

Z

Zenica, 171
Žepa, 140, 149, 253, 325, 342
Zepenić, Vitomir, 75
Zimmerman, Warren, 65, 98, 125, 175
  on Bosnian independence, 100, 113, 114–16
  on use of force, 299
Zubak, Krešimir, 293, 373, 379
  in 1996 elections, 385
  and Bosnian Federation, 294
Zulfikarpašić, Adil, 47, 68, 72, 73
Zvornik, 129